The Quest for Cheap and the Death of Globalization

A BARGAIN

GORDON LAIRD

EMBLEM

McCLELLAND & STEWART

Cloth edition published 2009
Emblem edition published 2010

Emblem is an imprint of McClelland & Stewart Ltd.
Emblem and colophon are registered trademarks of McClelland & Stewart Ltd.

Library and Archives Canada Cataloguing in Publication

Laird, Gordon, 1967–
      The price of a bargain : the quest for cheap and the death of globalization / Gordon Laird.

Includes bibliographical references and index.
ISBN 978-0-7710-4607-0

1. Consumers' preferences. 2. Discount. 3. Consumption (Economics).
4. Globalization. 5. Economic history — 21st century. I. Title.

HF1379.L354 2010   339.4'7   C2010-901542-8

We acknowledge the financial support of the Government of Canada through the Book Publishing
Industry Development Program and that of the Government of Ontario through the Ontario
Media Development Corporation's Ontario Book Initiative. We further acknowledge the support
of the Canada Council for the Arts and the Ontario Arts Council for our publishing program.

Typeset in Minion by M&S, Toronto
Printed and bound in Canada

This book is printed on acid-free paper that is 100% recycled,
ancient-forest friendly (40% post-consumer recycled).

 ANCIENT FOREST
FRIENDLY

McClelland & Stewart Ltd.
75 Sherbourne Street
Toronto, Ontario
M5A 2P9
www.mcclelland.com

1   2   3   4   5   14   13   12   11   10

Praise for *The Price of a Bargain*

"More than just being thorough, informed and relevant, this quietly alarming book observes globalization across varied chapters devoted to oil, shipping, debt, water and migrant workers. Neither shrill nor self-absolving, Laird quietly questions where we've been and where we're headed."
— Halifax *Chronicle Herald*

"As an investigative journalist . . . Laird knows how a gripping anecdote can bring the average reader into an otherwise complex and impenetrable topic."
— *Edmonton Journal*

"Our demand for more of the cheapest stuff money can buy is driving our society and world to the brink, says award-winning [author] Laird. In *The Price of a Bargain*, he plots a direct line from our bargain-hungry hands to disasters such as Alberta's tar sands, human-rights abuses in China and our hollowed-out economy."
— *Canadian Geographic*

"Will high prices save us? Do we have the capacity for change? Yes or no, the journey is fascinating."
— *Green Living*

"Laird deserves props for taking on the Big Box bastards. . . . In grab-you-by-the-lapels stories, Laird tells you the real cost of your got-it-for-nothing storegasm."
— Greg Palast, *New York Times* bestselling author of *The Best Democracy Money Can Buy*

"Laird is a reporter of rare skill and extraordinary thoughtfulness, and he has fixed his keen eye on one of the most crucial questions of this young, tumultuous century: the true cost of things. . . . [A]n invaluable primer on how to do the math accurately."
— Chris Turner, author of *The Geography of Hope*

"[A] gritty and entertaining look at our modern love affair with global bargains and Las Vegas sleaze." — Andrew Nikiforuk, author of *Tar Sands*

THE PRICE OF

for Lisa, Addison, and Myles

"Whatever degenerations there are in the world,
The root of all these is ignorance."

In Praise of Dependent Origination,
Je Tsongkhapa (1357–1419), translated by Thupten Jinpa

CONTENTS

INTRODUCTION: BLACK FRIDAY, 2008

Wal-Mart shoppers charge security guards at the fatal Black Friday incident at Green Acres Mall, Long Island, November 2008.

They emerged from the darkness and gathered like pilgrims, lining up beneath floodlights in the parking lot. Well before midnight, the first shoppers had already settled into chairs and under blankets for the long, cold vigil that was being staged outside nearly every major discount outlet across America.

But only one mall would be remembered in the years to come. By 1:00 a.m., hundreds had gathered in front of the Wal-Mart at Long Island's Green Acres Mall. All were there with a singular purpose. They had come for $9 DVDs and $5 Hannah Montana dolls that Wal-Mart had advertised in local flyers; others wanted the $25 microwaves and, most of all, 42-inch LCD televisions that had been marked down to $598. Everyone had a game plan for the store's 5:00 a.m. opening, because when big-box stores open on the first Friday after American Thanksgiving, shopping becomes a competitive sport. Above the crowd of shoppers, in five-foot-high letters, was the promise emblazoned on nearly every Wal-Mart in the world: *Satisfaction*

THE PRICE OF A BARGAIN

Guaranteed. As in previous years, most retailers opened for only a brief period during the early morning and offered only limited supplies of aggressively discounted products, so shoppers had come to expect lineups.

This morning was different. As Nakea Augustine recounted, when she arrived at Green Acres Mall at 2:00 a.m., the line was already two thousand people long. Having studied Wal-Mart's flyer, she was keen on the Hot Wheels Barbie Jeep advertised at more than 50 percent off. As she and a friend discussed shopping strategy, there was a violent surge from behind. "It got scary out of nowhere," says Augustine. "The crowd in the back just pushed." Someone grabbed her pocketbook off her shoulder, ripping her coat open. Others were punched and pushed to the ground; scuffles broke out.

Above the growing melee, someone had posted a handwritten sign: *Blitz Line Starts Here.* As the rowdy crowd counted down to five o'clock, the fights and pushing continued. Some shoppers, already injured, left the scene. There were broken arms, bruises, and head injuries. Inside, the eight security guards assigned to the front door began to worry.

On that morning of November 28, 2008, bargain-hungry crowds were staring down guards and doormen across America. Gunshots were fired at a Toys "R" Us store in Palm Desert, California, and two people were killed. Reports of fighting, damaged property, and vandalism filtered through the news. "They're more aggressive," one seasoned Wal-Mart shopper told the *New York Times.* "I've never seen anybody fight like this. This is crazy."

Facing a deep recession, record numbers of shoppers turned out at ungodly early hours to save a few dollars on Christmas toys for their kids, stock up on necessities, or score a luxury television or stereo before things got worse. In the end, an estimated 172 million people – just over half of North America's total population – would go shopping that Black Friday weekend.

If people had any chance of maintaining their standard of living and enjoying the consumer riches they had become accustomed to in previous years, they would need bargains – and lots of them. Retailers did not disappoint. With offers of up to 70 percent off – virtually giving products away in a calculated effort to bring in traffic – Black Friday 2008 marked the very pinnacle of discounting, one of the greatest consumer payoffs of all time.

"Five, four, three, two, one!" Beneath the blue and white Wal-Mart sign at Green Acres, the entrance doors opened a crack. The crowd surged forward with a force that knocked one of the doors off its hinges. One security guard used it as a shield against the torrent of people that streamed into the store. The door crumpled, its glass smashed, and people and workers began to fall inside Wal-Mart's foyer as more than two thousand manic shoppers rushed in. There were screams and panic as people poured over several fallen shoppers, security guards, and broken glass.

Eyewitnesses in the crowd would later recall that security guard Jdimytai Damour, thirty-four, was one of the first ones trampled to the floor. The temp worker had been recruited for door duty on Black Friday, along with several other workers who were employed by a service contractor that Wal-Mart had outsourced. Damour had already been working at the store for about a week in maintenance; like most others on duty that morning, he had no training in security or crowd control. He was built like a linebacker – six-foot-five, 270 pounds – but when the doors opened, he was quickly overrun after attempting to push people back. He had been protecting a young woman, Leana Lockley, who had also fallen. "I was screaming that I was pregnant, I am sure he heard that. . . . He was trying to block the people from pushing me down to the ground and trampling me," the nursing student recounted. "Mr. Damour was to the right of me, he was on his knees. I could look at him eye to eye, and he was trying to push them back, and the crowd pushed him down, and he fell on top of me."

Lockley was pulled to safety by her husband. Damour did not get up as more shoppers streamed over him. Other witnesses reported that he was gasping for air as people stampeded forward. Incoming crowds stepped on and knocked against police as they attempted to perform CPR on an unresponsive Damour. By the time paramedics arrived on the scene, most of the first wave of shoppers had passed through the entrance and filled the store. Inside, shoppers guarded the televisions; others swarmed the toy section. Damour died on the concrete floor between two vending machines, just inside Wal-Mart's entrance and only a few feet from where the greeters usually stand. While a small crowd had gathered around the horrible scene, many continued to shop. The store itself did not close until well after the paramedics had given up their attempts to revive Damour and police had begun to investigate the circumstances of his death. Nassau Police later described it as "utter chaos" and estimated that Damour had been "literally stepped on by dozens, if not a hundred, people." Damour's co-workers stood and said a prayer for him.

A full two hours after the opening rush, and an hour after Damour had been declared dead, shoppers were told that there had been a fatality and that the store was closing. Many refused to leave. One witness told the New York *Daily News* that shoppers acted like "savages." "When they were saying they had to leave, that an employee got killed, people were yelling, 'I've been in line since Friday morning!'" said Kimberly Cribbs. "They kept shopping."

Four shoppers were also injured; Wal-Mart would later pay nearly $2 million in damages. "They took the doors off the hinges," said Wal-Mart worker Jimmy Overby, still in shock. "He was trampled and killed in front of me. . . . I didn't know if I was going to live through it. I literally had to fight people off my back."

For better and for worse, ours is the age of the bargaineers – the engineers of bargains – whose factories extend from rice paddies to suburban basements everywhere. Each year we are drawn to their doors by the millions. And if it's not Wal-Mart that reels us in, then it's its big-box brethren – Costco, Home Depot, Best Buy, IKEA, Tesco – or smaller fish like the local dollar store. There are never single, isolated bargains. Most of us stalk value on a serial basis, sometimes in full contravention of common sense. Row upon row, aisle upon aisle, this realm of affordability, selection, and discount is a dominant force in today's world.

When we buy at our local dollar store or big-box mall, we embrace revolution: the most advanced logistics, marketing, and manufacturing network ever invented. Nearly everything from clothing to electronics miraculously decreased in price between 1990 and 2010. At one time our most expensive commodities – oil, diamonds, metals – were the core business of the planet's largest and most powerful corporations. Now snack food, paper goods, and pet supplies are the world's best-selling products. And by 2008 Wal-Mart's $405 billion in annual revenue surpassed the gross domestic product of Saudi Arabia, underlining the degree to which affordable consumerism has come to dominate global trade.

It's all part of a global shopping marathon that helped turn the world's developed nations into consumer economies. By the time Wal-Mart became the world's largest company in 2002, consumer spending comprised roughly 70 percent of all employment and economic activity within developed nations. Economists call this the service economy, and it is anchored largely by economic activity in finance, technology, and retail and wholesale trade, as well as all the other non-manufacturing business in media, entertainment, airlines, hotels, and restaurants. Personal savings were all but eliminated in the process, and by 2006 the average American household spent more than it earned – the lowest savings rate in seventy-three years, equalled only during the Great Depression, when nearly one in four adults were unemployed. By 2009, America's personal savings rate had barely budged at 3.6 per cent, reflecting a deeply overspent economy that was having trouble sustaining recovery, while China's stayed high at 38 per cent, reflecting its status as an emerging world power.

Here's the dangerous truth. Western economies are now as dependent on consumer spending as they are reliant on crude oil. If either shoppers or crude oil suddenly stopped moving the economy along, the result would be the same: sudden crisis that would affect our ability to access affordable food, fuel, and consumer goods.

With uncertain futures for both global finance and everyday shoppers, some are now even predicting a third depression, a period of economic failure deeper and more troubling than anything anyone has seen since the 1930s. "Unemployment – especially long-term unemployment – remains at levels that would have been considered catastrophic not long ago, and shows no sign of coming down rapidly," wrote economist Paul Krugman in June 2010. And it has much to do with the reality of millions of troubled households, and major governments who have become massively over-spent and can no longer easily maintain the equilibrium of economies driven by consumption.

How did this happen? Unlike the Great Depression, the erosion of household fortunes and the massive accumulation of personal debt weren't merely a symptom of economic crisis but an integral part of growth itself. In this economy, one dominated by retailers, financial services, and offshore manufacture, the overextension of shoppers fuelled broad-based prosperity – not just in America but around the world. Leveraged on inflated housing prices and generous credit card limits, this unprecedented bonanza of consumer liquidity hit like a gusher of oil. As shipping traffic and trade deficits boomed, American retail spending increased 43 percent per capita between 1992 and 2005. Other Western nations followed suit with service-dominated economies that long ago eclipsed traditional industry and agriculture – including Canada, which saw a 50 percent increase in retail sales between 1994 and 2007. Americans haven't been the only ones spending their way to prosperity: during the early 2000s, countries such as Italy, Britain, Canada, and France actually outpaced the United States in growth of consumer debt.

The shift from production to consumption during the late twentieth century represents a transformation in consumerism, trade, and society not seen in several generations. Where Henry Ford changed history with the invention of the assembly line in 1913, the quest for cheap reworked everything from global commerce to local economies in order to squeeze out untapped resources and savings.

The global financial crisis of 2008 was the first large-scale acknowledgement that unsustainable consumer debt lies at the core of Western economies. And with empty malls and bankrupt retailers piling up at the end of the millennium's first decade, it's clear that, in an age of climate change and energy anxiety, consumers themselves are a diminishing resource. After they posted the weakest holiday sales in more than forty years, big-box stalwarts such as Linens 'n Things and Circuit City were brought down by bankruptcies in 2008, and double-digit sales declines and profit losses continued to erode businesses and governments worldwide. By the end of 2008, the wave of retail store closures across the United States had reached 6,100, according to the International Council of Shopping Centers (ICSC), with a fifth of all enclosed malls failing. By early 2009 Newsweek reported that an estimated 150,000 retail outlets were expected to close, and by 2010, mall vacancy rates were still averaging among the highest levels in thirty years, with no immediate signs of relief. Only Wal-Mart, and a few other discounters and dollar-store chains, managed consistent, improved growth.

The thronging crowds that return to Black Friday each year haven't saved the economy, not because too few returned to keep shopping – in fact, 2009's Black Friday saw an impressive 192 million browsing stores and websites, hungry for deals. But everyone is buying less, a trend reflected in continued store closures, home foreclosures, and sagging consumer confidence. As shoppers continued to demand deals from their favorite big-box stores, America's trade imbalance grew in 2010, suggesting that dependence on globalization was increasing, not decreasing. For example: outgoing empty

6

shipping containers at the Port of Los Angeles – the most literal representation of America's trade imbalance with China – increased an amazing 57 per cent between 2008 and 2009, with stable growth in empty outgoing containers into 2010. "In an economy like this one, every retailer wants to be a discounter," said Tracy Mullin of the National Retail Federation.

Discounting as a future model for progress poses serious long-term challenges. Nations that cannot create value within their own economies inevitably run into trouble. Global discounting as pioneered by Wal-Mart is a force of value destruction that has been eroding the solvency of the modern consumer economy; oil dependence and its many consequences is another source of value destruction; China's withering commitment to subsidizing our world with cheap labour is yet another. In fact, Wal-Mart itself doesn't see its own future in the West. It is looking abroad: in 2010, 60 per cent of all new square footage will be opened by Wal-Mart International, the company announced at its annual investor conference in October 2009, "particularly in growth markets such as China and Brazil."

It's more than just big-box anarchy on Black Friday, although that fateful day in 2008 marked a turning point. After the wild-eyed hordes had hauled off their Samsung TVs, after the garbage, blood, and glass were cleaned up, and after all the recrimination and blame for the senseless death of Jdimytai Damour had passed, certain facts remained.

First, the golden age of affordable consumerism was short and poignant in its brilliance. We will very likely never shop this hard again.

And second, our whole system of cheap, from shipping to consumer credit, is leveraged in ways we are only just beginning to understand – and broken in ways that may not be easily fixed.

The glorious thing about the previous decade was that we rarely had to think too hard about where our stuff came from. It just arrived, and stores became bigger, prices decreased, and the depth and selection of goods increased. Banks and credit card companies made it easy to buy more. Developing nations like China supplied abundant labour. Why question a good thing?

In hindsight, it appears that globalization itself has become entangled in growth cycles that could turn out to be too good to be true. Our bargain-addicted consumer economy is dangerously leveraged on a series of innovations and inventions not built to last. Specifically, the fundamentals of growth – cheap credit, offshore labour, affordable energy, and transport – will be depleted or become unavailable during the twenty-first century. This web of interdependence will not unravel itself gracefully: there is no going back to normal, no rewind or reboot on global trade. Lack of access to affordable petrochemicals and fossil fuels, for example, could progressively disable whole segments of our economy. Offshore labour, available credit, and affordable transport are massive productivity and income subsidies that most consumers unwittingly depend upon. Factors such as climate change and chronic poverty impose additional threats to our supply chains, since globalized trade requires stability, not hurricanes and food riots.

The global debt and financial crisis that closed the first decade of the new millennium is just one aspect of the new era. It's not just about markets anymore. To grasp what will shape economies, nations, and communities in the years to come, we must look beyond the analysis and assumptions of the financial leaders who failed to accurately predict or protect against the biggest and most damaging crisis of our time. We have to look at the world not as a growth and wealth machine governed by orderly business cycles, but as something that performs and responds more like a stressed ecosystem, something full of non-linear change that requires stewardship and attention.

Bargaineering multiplied prosperity, but our deep dependence on this system has also multiplied negative impacts, costs, and risk. It's easy to complain about Wal-Mart and its kin, but much harder to find anyone who doesn't depend on or benefit from global supply networks. The world's largest companies depend on cheap. You depend on cheap. Hundreds of millions of people around the world, rich and poor, are part of this web. And for now, goods trade still drives globalization: it has a global value of $13.6 trillion, more than four times larger than that of services such as finance, software, and travel.

The quest for cheap has already consumed much of our easiest and richest gains in energy, transport, and manufacturing. Instead of local, sustainable production, a surprising amount of our ingenuity and capital is still being reinvested in carbon-intensive transport networks and unconventional forms of crude oil extraction, as well as subsidizing market failure – including trillions in bailouts and damage control for failed financial institutions around the world. And from the tar sands of northern Alberta to the borderlands of Arizona to the factory zones of mainland China and beyond, there is unrest: in lieu of governments and business, citizens and non-profits are taking bold steps to confront neglected aspects of our social, economic, and environmental future. Navigating the future therefore won't be as easy as some might think.

For example: some economists advocate that the only way to avoid greater crisis is through further public spending to restart the economy in a Keynesian rescue gambit. The thing is, America's GDP-to-debt ratio is already nearly 100 per cent, making it a debtor nation on a massive scale. Having splurged on things like bank bailouts and wars over the last decade, America may be short on resources to address the jobless recovery that threatens a looming depression. America's estimated 1.1-trillion-dollar deficit in 2010 was deemed a "national security threat" by the Brookings Institute, yet America cannot afford to ignore unemployment further. This is the paradox: public and private insolvency, along with a national business model dependent on spending, constrain America's ability to engineer its own solutions. Yet it cannot avoid facing the unemployment that is pushing millions of people out of the economy and out of their homes. In no small way, this is how some nations, America especially, will likely lose their status and standard of living in the twenty-first century. That Canada is tied to the future of the United States through its continued and unapologetic dependence on energy and manufacturing exports (tar sands crude and automobiles) is a major liability that many Canadian leaders have chosen to ignore.

One thing is for sure: decades of easy growth are behind us. Instead, there will be fewer Wal-Marts opening in the West, and only a portion of manufacturing and service jobs previously lost to offshoring and outsourcing will return. If offshore labour costs continue to increase alongside energy prices, inflation will once again become chronic: over time, we will pay more for gasoline, shipping, food, and everything else that has a cost structure tied to energy and globalization. Conservation and efficiency will begin to drive politics and culture. Localization and thrift will become even more popular, as people are faced with inventing their own solutions in the face of lackluster policy and leadership.

Likewise, economies dependent on consumer spending will experience greater volatility, and many nations will turn protectionist as the plenitude created by global trade erodes. Even global security will be affected as trade ties falter, national agendas diverge, and *Pax Americana* fades into history. It could be the death of globalization as we know it, and its passing would deprive us of its many flawed benefits while bequeathing a global legacy of unresolved problems.

Until recently, the dominant vision of progress in today's world was rapid growth, cheap products, and shoppers flush with high credit limits – basically, the global economic bubble of the booming 2000s, except forever. In hindsight, domestic job losses and the destruction of local commerce – common complaints against the big-box revolution – may prove to be the least of our worries. Rapid deglobalization could result in failed states, growth in poverty, and the rise of far-right nativist movements, as well as decreased co-operation on reducing greenhouse gas emissions. A world that spends heavily on cheap – burning through resources and consumer credit in pursuit of illusory growth – has become unsustainable, yet globalization without an exit strategy could be even more problematic.

Most importantly, when cheap fails us, we will have to invent a new status quo, one that more accurately reflects the true cost of things. There will be unexpected progress and collapse, new kinds of risk and new kinds of reward. There will be new kinds of change.

LANDSCAPES

OF PLENTY

THE BARGAINEERS:
FEAR AND HOUSEWARES IN LAS VEGAS

1

All business: Las Vegas, site of North America's largest bargain trade show.

Dollar-Store Nation

There is a moment, right before dawn, when Las Vegas finally empties out and stands quiet.

All the tourists have disappeared, leaving only maintenance workers, security guards, and a few hard-core gamblers hunched over cards amid a sea of empty tables. Outside on Las Vegas Boulevard, a blast of neon shines down on advertising flyers scattered across the sidewalk, offering blackjack games and Barry Manilow tickets to nobody in particular.

There is little allure to Las Vegas at 6:00 a.m. It's clear of gawkers and tour buses; nobody rambles on about old Vegas with Dean and Sammy or boasts of winning roulette against impossible house odds. There is no excitement, no action. At this ungodly hour Vegas is stripped down and idle – just stucco, glass, and air conditioning, its lights and billboards reminiscent of a gaudy convenience store vacant between shifts.

It is, however, the beginning of a new day in the world's most unlikely economy. Las Vegas fills its year with identical days that repeat endlessly, a lucrative grind of shopping, gambling, and serving. It is a deceptively simple business model: a $33.7-billion industry that manufactures virtually nothing.

Because of this, Vegas is one of the purest expressions of the modern service economy ever devised. Alternatively deemed the knowledge economy or the new economy, the modern service economy promised plenitude, productivity, and growth driven by technology, finance, and retail-driven trade, simultaneously deindustrializing to the point where consumer activity became the dominant source of prosperity.

By seven o'clock, the taxicab drivers and street cleaners no longer have Vegas to themselves; the first conventioneers hit the sidewalks and coffee stands. Each year thousands of meetings, events, and industry shows are held in Las Vegas, and everyone from actuarial accountants to adult entertainers now conducts business here. While much of this town is gorging on buffet breakfasts or sleeping off last night's debauchery, professionals and entrepreneurs from around the world convene to meet, deal, and negotiate.

In the shadow of the posh Venetian Hotel and Casino, attendees of today's big event arrive outside the Sands Convention Center carrying boxes, bags, and display cases. Their name tags announce America: *Duluth, New Jersey, Pasadena, Dallas*. These are the first of nearly 100,000 people who will attend one of the world's largest merchandise shows, a sprawling marketplace of retailers, wholesalers, manufacturers, importers, and amateur hucksters trying to hustle a buck. It is the biggest collection of bargain merchandise on the continent, spilling over into two other convention halls located nearby.

It's little bits of our everyday lives laid out on tables and shelves, almost exclusively manufactured in China and Southeast Asia. There are generic kitchen items – spatulas, scrubber pads – common to hundreds of thousands of households. I see toys from my kids' playroom: plastic sharks, blocks, stuffed animals. Crowds gather, searching for the world's best bargains. Storeowners from Lima, Peru, browse bedsheets. Iowa wholesalers offer replica Tiffany lamps. Chain-store retailers and dollar-store managers barter over all things both essential and unlikely, from toothbrushes to neon Bob Marley sculptures, samurai swords, witchcraft kits, and miniature motorcycles. Brand-name toothpaste and neon Jesus dioramas; Shrek backpacks and baby shoes.

Nobody knows exactly how many items are here. And it would be a superhuman feat to visit all eight thousand booths. But if you have shopped at a discount store, grocery chain, or dollar store, bought consumer items on eBay, browsed your local mall, or visited just about any other retail establishment across North America, there's a good chance you've spotted items that first appeared here. Even multinationals like Wal-Mart lurk at the ASD/AMD merchandise show in Las Vegas – incognito – looking for new ideas and products to give them a competitive edge over the scores of smaller and mid-size operators that nip at their heels.

Although dollar stores have existed since the 1950s, extreme-value retailing was invented only recently, created out of the chaos of the Wal-Mart revolution. Mass discount pioneers like Wal-Mart literally destroyed many conventional business practices during the 1990s. And as major discounters expanded into new global opportunities, supply chains multiplied, manufacturers spread across greater Asia, and logistics technologies assisted faster, cheaper international trade. Assaulted from unlikely places such as Las Vegas, Bentonville (the birthplace of Wal-Mart), and Chinese factory towns like Shenzhen, the very notion of wholesale and retail trade – traditional divisions that once structured business – no longer fully exists.

Consequently, commerce in low-cost global merchandise has opened up to anyone with good credit and a business plan. "Many people are learning from what Wal-Mart has done in the past," explains Sam Bundy, president of the trade show's merchandise group. "More and more middlemen are being cut out of supply chains and therefore it's less difficult to source directly than it was five years ago. You don't need the sheer purchasing power of Wal-Mart anymore to find suppliers and go direct." And it's here in Las Vegas where the world's leading extreme-value retailers – a mishmash category of dollar stores, discounters, and anyone else buying or selling insanely cheap products – now come to do business.

Sam Bundy explains how this event is actually an enormous trading floor, a bazaar of global proportions. "It's not just a show – people are here mainly to make deals, find new opportunities, and build existing business relationships," he says as we sit at his command post, a low-walled cubicle next to the constant din of buyers and sellers. "They are trading product, signing contracts, making shipping arrangements as we speak." The products on display here are actually sales samples, with each single stuffed animal or small appliance representing several orders – or hundreds of orders, if it's popular. Twice a year, bartering, buying, and selling at the Vegas show launches hundreds of thousands of products. In turn they will fill thousands of steel containers bound for the ports of Los Angeles and Long Beach, where the greatest percentage of North America's container ships arrive to off-load.

Many of today's conventioneers are would-be bargaineers – people who have been downsized or who are currently underemployed and looking for opportunity. Discount entrepreneurship is the realm of the involuntarily part-time worker, a growth sector even in Canada, where part-time work has grown twice as fast as full-time employment since 2001. The number of Americans involuntarily working part-time increased by 40 percent in 2008 alone – 3.1 million people who were working less because they couldn't find full-time jobs.

"Many people find it an attractive and alluring 'American dream' to run their own business, whether they've been downsized or are looking for alternatives to the typical nine-to-five job," reports Sam Bundy. "More often than not, individuals who have been downsized from large retail operations or wholesale operations are more apt to venture into independent retail."

"It's the professional flea marketer, for example, people who make an income and livelihood selling new goods," he says. "Selling a packet of socks for a dollar. They need to find cheap sources of product. And you have kiosks, carts in shopping malls, predominantly imports, fashion items, sunglasses, low-end toys. It all opens up new retail opportunities, as there is a very low cost base, a small capital infusion required. Barriers of entry are low, especially compared to a regular storefront."

Others attending the trade show represent online discount and dollar stores, covering a vast array of websites from eBay spin-offs to mass liquidators such as overstock.com and Woot. EBayers, for example, sell new products sourced directly from importers and manufacturers represented here in Vegas. "Most eBay super-sellers aren't selling and trading collectibles; they're selling consumer goods online – at least $35,000 each month," says Bundy. And as eBay's traffic plunged, late in the first decade of the new millennium, other sites such as Amazon, online classifieds, and specialty liquidators came to the fore.

While Wal-Mart became the world's largest company by trading on cheap stuff in the twilight of the twentieth century, small-time bargaineers now represent the economic heft of a Fortune 500 company. By the mid-2000s an estimated 200,000 to 250,000 North American dollar stores and micro-discounters posted upwards of $60 billion in annual sales – far less than behemoth Wal-Mart's $374 billion in sales for 2007, but roughly equal to Costco and Target. When compared to traditional commerce, it's a stagger-ing admission: independent and mid-sized discounters – people who sell imported party hats, paper plates, and confetti – account for as much annual revenue as many long-standing corporate institutions such as Microsoft, Dow Chemical, BMW, Boeing, and Time Warner. According to *Chain Store Guide*, the number of dollar stores across America nearly quadrupled between 1996 and 2007. And by early 2009, in the midst of global recession, most dollar stores were doing better than ever: Dollar General, the biggest American chain, posted nearly 10 percent sales growth at a time when even Target reported a 41 percent decrease in profits.

"It's an underappreciated part of the economy," says Bundy. "Much of the news is focused on the alpha players – the Wal-Marts of the world," he adds. "At our show, maybe 5 percent of businesses service the bigger retail, but the rest of commerce is conducted with independent retail. But there are so many of them, if you were to consolidate all the little guys, they rep-resent a pretty significant impact."

There are no fancy receptions, hospitality suites, or gift bags at this con-vention. This is global commerce at its grassroots. And no one here expects to discover the next iPod or BlackBerry – a singular killer product that will redefine the marketplace. That kind of expectation and hype is for the next electronics conference that rolls through Vegas. What bargaineers care about is price, volume, and speed; everything else is ancillary, and the prod-ucts themselves are often quite generic.

Nearby, on the trade floor, someone buys a forty-foot shipping container of sunglasses; someone else sells a shipment of kitchen scrub pads. Bundy gives me a list of some of his long-time contacts, professional bargaineers who are right now bartering, selling, and signing contracts somewhere out there in an ocean of cheap stuff. Yet he admits that one of the most power-ful players isn't even here – the consumer. In the economy of bargains, shop-pers play the most ruthless role of all. The growing numbers of consumers who shop without scruples or loyalty and who expect the best prices on the face of the planet – these are the people whom bargaineers regard with high respect and no small amount of fear. "There is no question that with consumers there are expectations," says Bundy. "And there will be continued pressures driven by the consumer, founded in expectation that we should be able to access these kinds of goods at value prices."

The dark side of the bargain juggernaut is too much success. Despite new challenges and fierce competition, consumers still demand perpetual discounts. "That makes for unsustainable growth," warns Bundy. "There will be ups and downs. There will be consolidation."

Despite the near-insatiable consumer demand for bargains, a significant number of bargaineers here will fail. All it will take is a stalled deal, an extra five-cent loss on a unit, or a lost shipment. Like the consumers who need and desire bargains, the independent bargaineer is leveraged on credit cards or household equity. There's not a lot of room for failure.

But those who can meet consumer expectation, surpass the competition, and somehow keep product flowing around the world will win big, Vegas style. After all, it worked for Wal-Mart. Even though it's many months before the global financial crisis hits, everyone here already knows that the stakes are high: the memory of failed twentieth-century discounters from Woolworth's to Kmart haunts this global trading floor. And while Woolworth's five-and-dime counters wowed consumers during the late 1800s – and launched retailing into the modern age – today's merciless shopper expects Everyday Low Prices as standard.

That's what makes bargaineering dangerous. "Before, you got a bargain: 'Wow, what a great find,'" says Bundy. "Now people just expect to get it."

The Quest for Cheap

It's midday inside the Sands Convention Center. Another plastic spatula, another Barbie doll knock-off. Amid seemingly endless rows of kitchenwares, toys, small appliances, and novelties, it's hard to believe that this cluttered collection of generic goods is the vanguard of global trade. Yet during 2006 alone, more than 182,000 new consumer products were introduced, roughly three hundred a day, and growing at a rate double that of 2004 and 2005.

Carlos Soto runs his own import business out of a small office on the edge of south-central Los Angeles. Standing behind a cardboard display of batteries, film, and disposable cameras, the Mexican-American Angeleno explains how he imports brand-name products from Korea directly to Central America, Mexico, and southern California. Filling several forty-foot steel containers each year with "grey market" Kodak and Duracell products is cheaper than purchasing identical American-sourced products, even after shipping them across the Pacific. "It's opportunity for small importers like me," he says of the price differentials between national markets. "People don't mind Korean-language labels – they want prices."

Soto is a soft-spoken family man: not exactly an obvious choice for a Wal-Mart giant-killer. Yet he sells batteries more cheaply than almost anyone else in North America, and his products wind up in the dollar stores that compete with Wal-Mart supercentres. That's a problem for Wal-Mart, at least as long as Soto can keep filling containers from Korea.

Today's new breed of discounters are the daredevils of today's retail economy, risking all to bring you new value, and there are almost as many inventive business schemes at this show as there are products. Squeezing income out of the twists and gaps in the global economy, entrepreneurs like Soto find opportunity in obscure, unlikely places – and discover ways to deliver affordable batteries and film to East L.A. strip malls, Guatemalan family *tiendas*, and Mexican department stores.

Several late-century developments helped transform bargain retailers from bottom-feeders to global kingpins. First, the invention of advanced logistics and Web technologies enabled whole armies of shipping containers, distributors, and factory workers to be mobilized for the timely delivery of cheap products. Second, the developing world opened for business, led by the likes of China, Mexico, and Vietnam, which facilitated off-shore capital and opened their gates to maquiladoras and special economic zones. Finally, the emergence of post-industrial consumer economies – Western nations with GDPs dominated by retail/service activity – both accelerated bargains and reinforced dependence on cheap stuff at an unprecedented scale.

One can track postwar consumerism alongside the gradual rise of discounting. The Las Vegas bargain show itself began as an army surplus sell-off in 1961, capitalizing on an excess of Cold War hardware manufactured by America's military-industrial complex; it was a discount business opportunity founded upon government contracts and the geopolitical climate.

19

Discounting evolved and the Vegas trade show had become primarily general merchandise by the 1970s, following the growth of dollar-store chains and discounters within the general North American economy.

Bargaineering represents the future, an emerging experiment in globalization and consumerism, but it represents the past as well. Everything from Wal-Mart to family dollar stores embodies many of the core ideas of late-nineteenth-century business magnate Frank Woolworth, who built one of the world's first global retail empires on a few scrappy five-and-dime stores in upstate New York.

In 1878 fledgling retailer Woolworth posted a sign in his Watertown store that changed the course of business: *ANYTHING ON THIS COUNTER 5 CENTS*. This was post–Civil War America, fraught with inflation, poverty, and political instability – hard times for many families. With so many households displaced or economically troubled, and retail of the day bound up in mandatory counter service and fat merchant markups, the time was ripe for bargains.

After a few initial business failures, not unlike Sam Walton's early years, Woolworth eventually found incredible success with his stores, which featured competitive prices, self-service, convenience, and variety. "Patrons of the day could not believe that 'all this' could be had for a few coins a piece," writes historian Karen Plunkett-Powell. "Woolworth was carrying everything from egg whips to tree ornaments to Horatio Alger books. It was the heyday of retail bargains, and Americans were having a field day taking advantage of them."

It was a late-Victorian dollar store built upon ladies' hair ribbons and accessories, household and kitchen items – domestic essentials and novelties. Cheap surplus merchandise came from local wholesalers, but Woolworth later sourced his own, original supplies from North America and Europe. Typical store stock in 1879 consisted of "toy dustpans, tin pepper boxes, biscuit cutters, animal soap, pencil charms, lather brushes, police whistles, [and] candlesticks."

Woolworth was laying the foundations of modern retail: customers were no longer forced to haggle over inflated prices or wait in front of dusty counters. And like Sam Walton, Woolworth learned from his early failures. He developed a ruthless scientific approach to retailing that was exceeded only by Bentonville in the 1990s: strategic location, relentless competition, tight margins and cost controls, emphasis on retail display and signage – and, of course, aggressively low prices. As Woolworth told one reporter, "Everybody likes to make a good bargain. Let him. Small profits on an article will become big profits if you sell enough articles."

The parallels to Wal-Mart are uncanny. Woolworth brought food into discount stores in 1897, installed cutting-edge technology (cash registers) in 1900, had expanded to 120 stores by 1904, and then went public in 1912 with a value of $65 million, an unprecedented fortune. By 1912 Woolworth's had more than six hundred stores in the U.S. and Europe and boasted annual sales equivalent to $1.1 billion today. And by the early 1900s serious competition had emerged. The likes of Kress and Kresge (Kmart) duplicated Woolworth's business model, and retail discounters became standard fixtures not only in every North American town and city but also across the U.K., Europe, and Australia, with some five thousand stores in America alone.

The success and growth of Woolworth's coincided with the twentieth-century shift from agricultural to industrial society: across the Western hemisphere, people moved off farms into cities, often becoming more active consumers in the process. Five-and-dime chains became a major force in twentieth-century economies, effecting the same deflationary forces attributed to modern discounters. "According to the US Bureau of Census, in 1935 there were 127,482 chain stores operating in the US," reports economists Daniel Levy and Andrew Young. "It follows, therefore, that a non-trivial proportion of the retail trade was conducted at fixed, nickel and dime, prices for about 40 years or perhaps even more, from the mid 1880s, to the mid 1920s and early 1930s."

By 1961 Woolworth's had become the world's first retailer to report $1 billion in annual sales. But the famed skyscraper that Frank Woolworth built in Manhattan before his death in 1919 had long ago ceased to be a centre of power. After 117 years, a much weakened Woolworth's sold off the last of its four hundred stores in 1997 and folded its remaining assets into a holding corporation named Venator. What happened? Postwar society became more affluent and suburban and increasingly abandoned the old downtown discounters in favour of enclosed malls. "Woolworth had trouble adapting their cut-rate downtown model to the new suburban shopping centers that sprang up around the country," notes historian Joshua Zeitz.

Woolworth's slow decline had everything to do with the birth of new-generation discounters who could exploit the suburbs and small towns. Wal-Mart, Kmart, and Target all opened within four months of each other in 1962. "By 1970 [these] 'big-box' budget retailers, to be joined later by new discount franchises like Toys 'R' Us, Circuit City, T. J. Maxx, Office Depot, and Best Buy, outsold traditional department stores as well as five-and-tens," writes Zeitz. "And rang a final death knell for the downtown business districts that Woolworth had long dominated."

The modern age of the bargaineer began with the 1976 opening of Price Club in San Diego, a corporate precursor to today's Costco founded by Sam Price. Until then, most consumers couldn't guess at the true wholesale value of their goods. Warehouse clubs changed the commercial landscape by offering up just about everything at near-wholesale prices by the pallet load. And as club stores became the fastest-growing format during the 1980s, a whole new generation of customers began to expect and demand their goods at cost – which in turn helped accelerate the development of the logistics, offshore labour, and discount revolution that eventually turned Wal-Mart into the world's largest company. "By the late 1980s, the line between the discount industry and other retailers had blurred to the point that the very notion of discounting lost any distinctive meaning," note business sociologists Misha Petrovic and Gary Hamilton.

Back in the 1970s, Sweden-based IKEA pioneered its own irrepressible template for modern discounting, mixing good design, affordability, efficient supply chains, and lots of particle board. Now the world's largest furniture manufacturer, IKEA shares Wal-Mart's secretive approach to global retailing as well as a common talent for giving consumers more for less. Elsewhere in Europe the success of the hypermarket, a combination supermarket and general merchandise store, launched other global giants. France's Carrefour, the world's second-largest retailer, became the first foreign retailer in Asia in 1989; Britain's Tesco, the world's fourth-largest retailer, has managed to execute its own brand of global discounting so effectively that Wal-Mart has copied a number of its core strategies. Together, leading discounters from across Western nations helped break up price monopolies enjoyed by many manufacturers and traditional retailers, often at the cost of domestic manufacturing jobs and local commerce.

As discounters triumphed, the department store turned into an endangered species: store counts for American mass merchandisers – department stores, largely – shrunk by 44 percent between 1996 and 2007. Likewise in Canada, discounters began outselling department stores as early as 1994, while many traditional retailers and grocery stores suffered a slow decline, including the now-departed Eaton's, once Canada's largest retailer. "Of the forty-two department store chains operating in 1980," note Petrovic and Hamilton, "only 20 remained in business a decade later. Fully 80 per cent changed hands during that time."

Carlos Soto's import business owes much to the crushing success of multinational discounters like Wal-Mart who have eliminated so many traditional grocery and department stores. When the global standardization of bar codes took place in 2005, for example, it was largely invisible to shoppers. But it was an efficiency gain for many major retailers and a huge boon to independent discounters and retailers, as it allowed for direct and accurate commerce in goods. With access to a universal code for products, "small stores [can] eliminate third, fourth and fifth parties," one independent grocer told the *National Post*. "They won't need brokers; they will be able to deal directly with manufacturers all over the world."

In short, retail outsourced itself during the late twentieth century by making near-wholesale prices readily available to consumers. As a result, dollar stores and small chains gained momentum. Where big-box retailers – supercentres and warehouse-style stores – ruled the 1990s, dollar stores and micro-businesses now saturate consumer markets with their "small-box" strategy. As of March 2007, for example, there were nearly 50,000 more convenience stores in America than a decade earlier – totalling 145,119 – and most are independently owned and operated. "Aggressive store count growth among the leading dollar store retailers is certainly a big part of [their] success," notes Todd Hale, ACNielsen senior vice-president. "But there are other factors as well. The variety of products carried by dollar stores is growing. And, dollar stores are benefiting from what I call 'the curiosity factor.' People want to see what's available on deep discount."

Consequently, some of Wal-Mart's toughest competition in the new millennium comes from small-time discounters like Soto, who can now source their own low-priced products directly from the same increasingly sophisticated Chinese manufacturers, and arrange container shipping around the world with little more difficulty than requisitioning a FedEx delivery. By the mid-2000s Wal-Mart and other major retailers – Kroger, Save-a-Lot, and Target – had added dollar-only sections to existing stores or were directly competing with extreme-value pricing in an effort to win back thrift-obsessed consumers. "National chains are moving more aggressively in this direction," confirms Sam Bundy. "The dollar-store segment boomed on a massive growth curve, larger than alpha or mid-size retailers, and they are opening up into non-traditional markets." Wal-Mart's experiments with a dollar-only section underline a harsh reality that Sam Walton himself helped invent – it's all about price. By 2009, in the midst of a consumer spending collapse, major dollar chains such as Dollar General and Family Dollar were actually growing faster than Wal-Mart.

Big or small, today's bargain trader is essentially an arbitrageur: someone who strategically exploits price and cost differentials between markets, profiting on imbalances. Arbitrage has traditionally been the dominion of corporate players in mergers and commodity or bond trades; think Wall Street, not dollar store. But today's retail-driven economy is itself built upon a set of systemic imbalances, not the least being the wage/labour differential between China and the West.

The biggest trade deficit in human history was launched one container at a time. "We receive twelve containers every week from Guangzhou, Hong Kong," says Brian Bulley of Encore Sales, a mid-size North American distributor of toys, housewares, and novelties. "We deal with quite a number of factories as well as offshore trading companies – one single Guangzhou outfit supplies us with nine thousand different items." Like many companies at the Las Vegas show, Encore supplies design specifications and artwork to a floating cast of factories, some of which might have only eight or twelve workers. It's a system of proxy companies and subcontracts in which buyers effectively lease offshore manufacturing capacity and rush goods to market before the demand changes.

There is amazing speed within these production cycles – women's apparel can see as many as seventeen different "seasons" every year – and it is possible for a product to be discontinued even before it reaches the consumer. It's a seemingly infinite network of companies and contracts, one that links hundreds of millions of people. "You are going to buy our product," says Bulley, "whether you know it or not."

Nearby, a Hasidic trader from Union City ambles over to Soto's tables to browse Korean batteries. He has his own booth a few aisles away, proffering toiletries and other drugstore items. "I'm surprised more people don't stop by our booth," he says. "We have a nice booth." Here on the front lines of the bargain trade, if you don't have either the best prices or one-of-a-kind items, business will evaporate, even on the second day of a trade show. He knows that shaving even a few points off his profits – which is no small thing in this high-volume, low-margin business – could make for a much busier day tomorrow.

The Union City trader praises Soto's business scheme and they trade cards. Nobody bothers to read the fine print on Soto's Korean batteries: *Made in China*.

Better than Wal-Mart

Few have witnessed the bargain revolution as close up as Danny Kole. Back in 1982, the South Los Angeles native and his brother began selling car stereos, tools, and hardware at flea markets. After scouring California for better merchandise at lower prices, they decided to start importing it themselves, and quickly got out of retail and into imports. These days they operate one of the biggest independent dollar and discount import operations in America and are a major presence at the biannual Las Vegas trade event. You probably don't know their business, but you've likely seen products that have streamed through their Carson headquarters, not coincidentally located a fifteen-minute drive from North America's busiest container port.

Kole remembers the days when mention of cheap imports conjured up scorn and skepticism. Using a telex machine and long trips to distant factories in mainland China, the Koles helped pioneer the kind of direct sourcing and importing that has become the backbone of today's consumer economy. "As dollar stores sprang up around the country, we realized that it was more than a fad," he says. "Without the Asian market, it would have never happened. We used to have a thousand items in stock, tools and housewares, which increased 20 percent a year. Now we have four thousand items, diversified to stationery, gifts, toys, photo frames. No single item makes up 1 percent of our sales."

Kole admits that the incredible growth of his business – his family's jump from flea markets to multi-million-dollar sales – is partly the result of good timing. "We rode the tide of imports," he recalls. "Anything that was a bargain, from one dollar to twenty cents, we'd try. There was so much out there that the consumer had not seen. And as 99-cent-price stores took off fifteen years ago, we went with that. We focused on price point. With so much merchandise available, we found that we could create a huge line of items available for a dollar."

During the 1990s factories became more sophisticated, barriers to trade were eliminated, shipping costs decreased, and, most important, competition between all these elements lowered prices even further. Kole now needs simply to review courier packages full of factory samples that arrive every day. Many are unsolicited submissions from manufacturers who want his business. "We used to travel to Asia and scrounge for as many items as we could find. Now there's not a day that goes by that we don't have several boxes from Chinese suppliers with samples."

For every item you see in a store, bargaineers like Danny Kole edit out hundreds more, turning down thousands of products submitted by off-shore factories. He estimates that for every six hundred items they keep maybe ten. On that basis, Kole might see as many as 240,000 different items in the process of stocking his current stable of 4,000.

This kind of fierce competition to reach consumers in the West results in further price drops even before products leave the factory. "New vendors constantly approach us," says Kole. "There is pressure on price. And if suppliers raise price, we will drop the item." Unlike Wal-Mart's famous tactic of pressuring manufacturers to roll back prices every year, bargaineers like Kole can simply wait for the next discount to arrive.

The orderly nation-based commerce of previous generations has been forever changed by the global surge in consumer goods. "The gamut of merchandise available through the sophistication of [offshore] factories has 100 percent changed the landscape of retail," says Kole. "The growth of Wal-Mart and Target has largely been driven by the profitability of imports, not by growth of domestic markets. It's the dollar-store-ization of the economy."

New-generation importers such as Kole will now sell wholesale to anyone. With $100 as their minimum order – down from $250 a few years earlier – small-time bargaineers don't need to buy whole containers of product. Heck, for $100 local households can shop here wholesale once every few weeks. "Our customers are everyone from a person running an eBay business out of a garage to South Americans buying containers," Kole says. Many are flocking to the bargain trade simply because people can make quick money: Kole shows a self-packaged pallet of kitchen goods, a prepackaged display of 1,600 items that can be set down anywhere. "We charge $1,000 for the fully loaded display," he says. "But you're going to turn this into about $2,500."

These are insane bargains. Kole shows me some kitchen knives that would normally retail for $3.99 to $5.99. Kole's price? 55 cents. Pens that sell for $2.99 retail are selling for 39 cents. Indeed, some discounters excel at selling the liquidated stock of big-box retailers – and still manage to gain more revenue per item. Kole displays closeouts acquired from major retailers, an increasingly common source of product as retailers cast off seasonal or surplus items in the accelerated push for fresh items and fashions. In his Los Angeles showroom Kole has a display of kids' college-style backpacks that were recently bought from Wal-Mart; the Wal-Mart sales tags, still hanging from the backpacks, say $14.88. "We're selling these for $2.50," he says with some pride – a discount of nearly 600 percent off the original retail price.

Ultimately, Danny Kole's secret weapon is the universal appeal of discounting. The strong psychic pull of discovering deals probably stems all the way back to the prehistoric hunter-gatherer societies that defined human commerce for roughly two million years. People are simply drawn to deals, says Kole, even if they don't need them. Even before the economic collapse, scores of affluent shoppers could be found snooping about in bargain bins: in 2003, roughly 49 percent of all American households with incomes of more than $70,000 regularly shopped in dollar stores.

"We do sell a lot more merchandise to inner-city L.A. than Beverly Hills," Kole admits. "But everyone likes getting a deal. It's the treasure-hunt mentality: 'Wow, I bought this for a dollar.'"

One major trend is the triumph of generic or no-name brands. Also known as private labels, these products are often identical to manufacturers' brand-name products but are sourced and packaged by retail and wholesale bargaineers. Wal-Mart's "Great Value" groceries, for example, have made incredible gains, and the company predicted in 2009 that its hundred different private-label brands would gain 40 percent market share by 2012. Meanwhile, traditional retailers and manufacturers continue to invest vast sums in marketing and design to cultivate the perception of brand value in consumers, be it perceived status, thrift, style, familiarity, or some other subjective quality that retailers and manufacturers have long conspired to instill in their products. In 2004 U.S. manufacturers spent $18.45 billion on in-store marketing for brand-name products. Bargaineers single-handedly reject the advanced marketing and branding techniques developed over a century of modern commerce, by simply offering low prices without fanfare. Brand names are progressively becoming less relevant in the process.

Yet bargains themselves are getting smaller in the face of rising prices and fierce competition. For example, Kole explains how many of his products can quickly be scaled back to ensure the all-important one-dollar price point that bargaineers strive for. "Facing greater cost, the size or quantity of items is decreased, not price point." Kole gives an example of some generic barbecue brushes that were recently altered at the factory in China. "We offered them at three for one dollar – an outrageous price," he says. "But when prices went up, then we shipped to sell at two for a dollar. The customer won't likely see this as any less of a bargain."

Yet getting less for less is exactly what has been happening in most stores in recent years. In an effort to preserve the appearance of low prices, Dove soap has shrunk by half an ounce, Hellman's mayonnaise is two ounces (56 grams) smaller, and paper-towel rolls have lost sheets, in some brands as much as eleven feet per package (for their part, manufacturers claimed that the shorter paper-towel rolls were in fact "thicker, stronger and last longer").

Danny Kole's downsized barbecue brushes are a portent of things to come. The "incredible shrinking package" is here to stay, argues Meg Marco of *Consumerist*, because "companies are fearful. There's nothing that sends fear into their hearts as much as price increases, because it makes people think twice."

For now, nobody seems too bothered at the prospect of one less barbecue brush. Want a brand-name backpack from Wal-Mart cheaper than at Wal-Mart? Easy, just wait a few weeks and then talk to your local bargaineer or search the Internet.

Tomorrowland

In the basement of the Sands Convention Center you can still browse army surplus and hardware items, just as early bargaineers did during the 1960s, when Sinatra and the rest of the Rat Pack were making lounge-lizard history upstairs in the original Sands Hotel. There's a rough edge to these basement bargaineers: biker T-shirts, brass knuckles, urban assault and SWAT fatigues, bulletproof vests, security cameras, and infrared goggles – all discounted, of course. The most popular items in the basement are the live 150,000-volt stun guns on display. A gaggle of off-duty security officers are taking turns picking up the pocket-sized weapons, tethered by wire to the display counter, and discharging them with a loud *zap* that echoes throughout the convention hall.

There are full-sized stun batons and purse-sized zappers, as well as concealable stun pens with an amazing 800,000-volt charge, packing enough juice to knock anyone out with just momentary contact. The rent-a-cops wave them around, pretending to chase each other – *zap, ka-zing*. Unfazed, the vendor behind the counter reads a magazine. It turns out that if people are given the chance to play with electroshock weapons in Las Vegas, even the most mild-mannered conventioneer will pick up a baton.

That one of the world's largest bargain markets convenes twice annually in Las Vegas is not coincidence, since this is Tomorrowland for the twenty-first century. Las Vegas has always been an economic frontier zone where new kinds of commerce have emerged, everything from money laundering to the modern entertainment corporation. From the beginning this desert outpost harboured schemers, fringe players, and wise guys. By the turn of the millennium the Vegas system had nearly been perfected: millions of people were passing through this place and leaving behind billions in revenue. Most would return home with few winnings, and, if statistics are correct, many returned again under the pretense of business or pleasure – and for some, (wink, wink) both.

Shopping and gambling have undergone a long period of convergence. Well before Wal-Mart became the world's largest company, Las Vegas established new frontiers in retail, demonstrating the potential of a nascent service economy. Archetypes for North America's economic future were constructed here, from the likes of the Circus Circus big top in the 1960s to today's integrated entertainment resorts and a network of large satellite casinos that now extends all the way to Macau. Even though many retail developers largely rejected megamalls and have turned towards deconstructed malls – open-air big-box shopping complexes known as lifestyle centres and power centres – Vegas remains on the cutting edge of retail engineering. It deploys spatial and sensory cues to attract, stimulate, and disorient large numbers of people simultaneously, as well as technology that logs detailed customer activity, carries out high-resolution data analysis, and allows dynamic adjustments in business strategy to extract maximum revenue from every shopper or gambler. In fact, Las Vegas now generates three times more revenue from food, shopping, and accommodation than from gambling. Even in the world's self-proclaimed gambling and entertainment mecca, the core business is just another day at the mall.

The Vegas fusion of casino, hotel, and retail that emerged by the early 1970s became the universal template for the modern megamall. Take away the lights, pirate ships, pyramids, and roller coasters, and many Strip resorts would resemble the kind of integrated shopping, movie, accommodation, and office complexes that have dominated the North American landscape for nearly a generation.

Although the Sands Hotel, demolished in 1996, was famously funded and managed by mobsters during its dreamy Sinatra-era heyday, the enduring legacy of Vegas is not organized crime and showgirls, but rather Vegas as a pioneer of post-industrial America. "Vegas is often described as a city of dreams and fantasy, of tinselish make-believe," writes Marc Cooper in *The Last Honest Place in America*. "But this is getting it backward. Vegas is instead the American market ethic stripped bare, a mini-world totally free of the pretenses and protocols of modern consumer capitalism."

What laid the foundation was deindustrialization and the major redistribution of wealth and power that ensued. During the early 1970s America became the first nation "in which the service sector accounts for more than half of total employment and more than half of Gross National Product," wrote Daniel Bell in his prophetic 1973 book, *The Coming of Post-Industrial Society*. "It is the first service economy, the first nation, in which the major portion of the population is engaged in neither agrarian nor industrial pursuits."

As postwar economies matured, industry and manufacturing declined and the service sector grew to nearly 80 percent of America's GDP. As trade-based globalization grew, both products and competition intensified as well. "Like flightless birds on a predator-free island, American companies had no defenses when hungry and hard-eyed competitors finally came hunting from overseas," writes Charles Morris in *The Trillion Dollar Meltdown*. "It was a slaughter. By 1980, for all practical purposes, America no longer manufactured televisions or radios, the Germans and Japanese controlled the machine tool industry, and American steel and textile industries were a catastrophe. Even IBM's mainframe computers were being challenged powerfully by Amdahl and Fujitsu."

By 2005, retail and wholesale commerce accounted for 35 percent of America's total domestic economic production (GDP), totalling $4.4 trillion in sales and exceeding industrial, manufacturing, and agricultural production combined. It is as pure a service economy as likely ever invented in human history, with 1.4 million retail outlets employing one in five American workers. Elsewhere it was much of the same: retail was the third-largest employer in the U.K. in 2007 and accounted for one-quarter of all private-sector employment in Canada.

Led by the United States and followed by most Western nations, this change from production to consumption is the hallmark of post-industrial society. Consequently, Wal-Mart emerged as the greatest ever post-industrial company, one that had aggregated incredible power and savings without having to bother with owning factories, energy, or natural resources. "Thanks to the Arkansas company, retailing trumped the high tech industry as a contributor to the late 20th century productivity surge," writes business professor James Hoopes. Business consultants McKinsey and Company have found that Wal-Mart created 25 percent of productivity gains in the U.S. economy between 1995 and 1999.

An imbalance of income, profit, and growth grew over the decades, in plain view of policy experts and elected officials. That was no accident. Regulatory structures and social supports were dismantled in America and other OECD (Organisation for Economic Co-operation and Development) nations in the late twentieth century, and bargaineers, traders, and financial wizards expanded to fill the void. "Americans were told, we would have to submit to the discipline of the free market," recounted American critic Ellen Willis in 2006. "[Former president] Carter embraced the neoliberal order with its mantra of austerity; he presided (with the help of Ted

Kennedy) over decontrol of oil prices and deregulation of the airline, trucking, and banking industries. Clinton supported the pro-corporate program of the Democratic Leadership Council and abolished the entitlement to welfare." A similar political/economic transformation occurred in Canada, Britain, and New Zealand, among others, as well as in scores of developing-world nations.

It's been a core ideology here in Las Vegas, where, practically speaking, self-regulation has been the rule since the 1960s. Most of the four-mile stretch of the Las Vegas Strip isn't actually inside the city limits, existing quietly as an unincorporated part of Clark County, Nevada. Not including state and federal governments, one of America's richest commercial areas is presided over by a single elected official. And as if to clarify its neoliberal stance, in 2006 the City of Las Vegas was the first in America to make it illegal to feed homeless people on public property.

On a broad scale, the ideological justification for liberalizing trade and neglecting economic outcomes was simply that prosperity was an end unto itself, the function of free markets. It was, in fact, a hedge – a calculated gamble that there would be enough growth to benefit those who suffered as economic activity was displaced and eliminated. "The ordinary course of change has winners and losers," explained former Federal Reserve chair Alan Greenspan in September 2008, as the global financial crisis unfolded. "Let's recognize that this is a once-in-a-half-century, probably once-in-a-century type of event."

As thinker for a whole generation of economic leaders, Milton Friedman championed monetarism and capitalism as the innovation to end innovations, yet this crusade for plenty was, in fact, a policy of Maximum Vegas – a trade-off of economic growth for new kinds of risk. As economist Paul Krugman has since argued, this near-religious belief in unfettered markets demonstrated by Greenspan and other neoliberals was just a gambit – and not a very good one either, since it allowed and encouraged growth to become leveraged on growth, and commodified debt to be massively resold without oversight in a way that would come to resemble a global pyramid scheme. "As long as housing prices kept rising, everything looked fine and the Ponzi scheme kept rolling," wrote Krugman in *The Return of Depression Economics and the Crisis of 2008*. This in turn "opened up large-scale

funding of subprime lending" through the now-discredited financial innovation of collateralized debt obligation.

The coy insider adage that even the squarest tourist at the airport is
tempted to echo, "whatever happens in Vegas, stays in Vegas," is no longer
true. It probably never was true, for what has been happening in Las Vegas
has been on export for the better part of the past fifty years. What happens
in Vegas most definitely now happens everywhere.

And in the tradition of Las Vegas's shady past, there were insiders who
knew that the great financial gamble was fixed all along, and that their best
opportunity was to take a cut, get out, and leave the suckers behind at the
table. "Let's hope we are all wealthy and retired by the time this house of
cards falters," admitted one Standard & Poor's employee as the financial
collapse began to build in 2007. "[It] seems to me that we had blinders on
and never questioned the information we were given, . . . Combined, these
errors make us look either incompetent at credit analysis, or like we sold
our soul to the devil for revenue."

This propensity to game the system, even to the point of fraud, wasn't
isolated behaviour; it was systemic. As New York state attorneys investi-
gated the financial collapse in 2009, it came to light that failed investment
house Merrill Lynch "secretly and prematurely awarded approximately 3.6
billion dollars in bonuses" during the fall of 2008. This was as its losses
were mounting towards catastrophic proportions and its new owner, Bank
of America, had requested $20 billion in emergency capital from the gov-
ernment. While millions of people lost retirement savings, homes, and
education funds, "Merrill chose to make millionaires out of a select group
of 700 employees," said New York Attorney General Andrew Cuomo.

This is the Las Vegas lesson for our time: one way or another, the house
pretty much always wins. At its upper levels, much of the modern service
economy – finance, retail, and gambling – is an insider's game. But unlike
the financial sector, Wal-Mart and modern Las Vegas leave surprisingly little
to chance. Engineering outcomes is paramount, simply because ventures
like gambling and retail require volume transactions on finely calculated
margins. Wal-Mart famously turned modern commerce upside down by
firmly setting price targets and telling manufacturers to meet the Everyday
Low Price and accept future rollbacks, or go home. Not only did this reverse

traditional power relations between manufacturers and retailers, it began an incredible process of transferring the substantial risk of cheap prices, low wages, and exceedingly tight margins, if any profits remained, onto the backs of manufacturers, local governments, and even consumers.

Behind this, an even larger process of offloading took place: uncontrolled pollution was unloaded into factory zones and shipping lanes; distant regions were tapped for cheap labour and resources while leaving behind underdevelopment and political oppression; consumers and companies alike were given access to destabilizing levels of debt, despite obvious risks, because even government stood to gain from the resultant surge in prosperity. The phenomenal rise of Wal-Mart and other global discounters during the 1990s onward has everything to do with these kinds of externalized costs, risks, and impacts that were rarely reflected in the business of everyday low prices. Discounters took many risks in retail strategy and global business expansion, but the modern supply chain itself was built upon calculated advantage, technology, and jurisdictional shortfalls. Not having to pay anything extra for carbon emissions, global poverty, or unemployment was what helped make bargaineering the kind of sure bet that a casino executive would love.

Simply put, you are not supposed to win. Out on today's casino floor, experienced gamblers still complain about how today's generation of corporate owners – expunged of all known organized-crime influences – have systematically crashed players' odds on favourite games such as blackjack. The calculated introduction of multiple decks, continuous shuffle machines, and advanced surveillance technologies has helped identify and eject professional players and lucky rubes who win too much too often. One system, costing about $20,000 per blackjack table, uses tiny infrared scanners to detect and record how each player plays each hand, building large databases – "a literal gold mine of research in devising new house advantages and in revealing and disarming evolving player strategies," says Marc Cooper. These databases effectively mimic the massive "data warehouses" created by alpha retailers, which use scanned purchases and customer incentive programs to create strategic advantage in the marketplace.

Electronic gambling machines and dollar stores infused the landscape at the same time: in 1989 there were 185,000 gambling machines in America, and by 2005 the total had grown to 740,000. That's double the number of

ATM bank machines, which happens to be a near-perfect illustration of a post-industrial economy: there are twice as many machines available to take your money as there are available to access it. The price point is uncannily similar as well, as twenty-five cents or a dollar covers a game of video poker or a dollar-store grab bag of novelties.

Of course you aren't supposed to find any bargains actually on sale at the Sands Convention Center or the adjacent Venetian, or across the street at the huge $2.7-billion Wynn Las Vegas Resort, which features the world's only casino with a luxury car dealership – it costs $10 admission just to look at a Ferrari. Industry mavens admit that the new, improved, pricier Las Vegas invented during the late 1990s is only partially about gambling. It is, more accurately, a retail/entertainment construct born of extensive study and calculation. "There will be the person who decides to spend $300,000 on a new Ferrari," says Ron Kramer, president of Wynn Resorts. "But then there's the larger market who can afford a $16 T-shirt and gets to take his picture next to the car." It's an old trick of retail: display impossible luxury and people will inevitably purchase a more expensive version of something affordable.

In the years before the big crash of 2008, Las Vegas attempted to immunize itself against bargains: the cheap buffets and discount luxury rooms were mostly gone. Even cold sandwiches in the basement of the convention centre were nearly $10 apiece; you'd get better value at the MGM Grand down at the fancy end of the Strip, which was perhaps precisely the point.

By March 2009 Wynn's stock price had crashed 85 percent. Harrah's, MGM Grand, and others representing scores of hotels and gaming establishments were having serious debt problems. Conventions were down nearly 20 percent. The package deals, buffets, and cheap rooms are back again and Las Vegas is scrambling to reinvent itself. In a world predisposed towards risk, nobody escapes discounting.

Under the Casino

"Hypocrite!" "Motherfucker!" In a subterranean maze of meeting rooms beneath Bally's casino, the American labour movement is falling apart. It's March 2005, and as bargaineers hustle shipping-container-loads of cheap imports a few blocks north at the Sands Convention Center, the American Federation of Labor's executive council meeting is fighting it out. The reason? Unions today represent only 12.5 percent of America's 124 million

"Mr. Wal-Mart Smiley Face" and "Maiden Overseas" lead a wedding procession on the Las Vegas Strip, in street theatre organized by the UFCW, November 2005.

workers, down from a peak of 33.2 percent of all workers in 1955. And nobody can seem to agree on how to stop what has become, by most accounts, a slow death spiral for organized labour.

The AFL-CIO has been the largest federation of organized labour in America since its inception in 1955, and was once the largest labour body in the world. And in the big casino of global trade, they are the ones who are coming up short. If Fortune 500 retailers and mass bargaineering represent the upswing of post-industrial society, the many woes of organized labour represent its down side: nearly 800,000 American manufacturing jobs disappeared in 2008 alone, striking at the very heart of union power.

"Factory employment is at its lowest level in more than 50 years," reported the National Association of Manufacturers in 2006. "In fact, of the top 28 manufacturing countries in the world (which account for 90 percent of global manufacturing output), just 5 have seen increases in manufacturing employment over the last 5 years: Argentina, Brazil, Spain, Thailand, and Turkey."

What happens to America's largest labour federation here in Las Vegas matters just about everywhere else. The decline of manufacturing jobs across the western hemisphere reflects the other side of the bargain boom: outsourcing, productivity gains through technology, and a whole host of transnational business connections have eroded steady paid employment. So great is the global job suck that many nations are even outsourcing unemployment. For example, Canada's manufacturing sector shed 250,000 jobs between 2004 and 2007, largely because companies closed factories in Canada and shifted production into the United States, to exploit excess workers and infrastructure abandoned by earlier outsourcing. The dual impact of offshore manufacturing and vast increases in productivity has helped to shrink union membership worldwide – except in China, of course, where a government-backed union is mandatory for most businesses and manufacturers.

And then there is Wal-Mart itself, a pioneer of post-industrial enterprise. The retailer's uncanny ability to bully suppliers into submission – "negotiating" on behalf of consumers – is the same skill-set deployed to drive away unions and play hardball with employees. For decades Wal-Mart's old-school labour tactics have resulted in unprecedented conflicts, including the world's largest class-action employment discrimination case, *Dukes v. Wal-Mart*; the swift closure of stores that do manage to unionize, such as the 2005 shutdown of a newly unionized outlet in Jonquière, Quebec; and individual cases of disabled or low-income workers forced into dismissal or mandatory overtime or subjected to litigation.

Even within pre-Obama America, a land rife with some of the most lax labour laws in the developed world, Wal-Mart still found a way to embroil itself in massive lawsuits and nasty allegations of misconduct. Between 2000 and 2005 the American National Labor Relations Board (NLRB) official findings of illegal conduct against major retailers were levied mostly against Wal-Mart: fifteen decisions of unfair labour practices out of a total of nineteen, even though all other major retailers – including Target, Costco, Home Depot, and Albertsons – collectively share more employees than the world's largest company.

While Wal-Mart has liberally stolen from the 1920s' anti-union playbook of dirty tricks, the company's labour battles illustrate the underbelly of the service economy. Whatever happens at Wal-Mart does not stay at

Wal-Mart: like Las Vegas, its influence and impact are unprecedented. Launched in 2001, the *Dukes* case encompasses 1.6 million current and former female employees who allege they were wrongfully denied fair pay and promotions on the basis of gender. Their claim was valued at $11 billion as of 2009. And while this charge should not surprise anyone familiar with Sam Walton's good-ol'-boy management style, Wal-Mart represents a post-industrial vanguard that affects hundreds of millions of people. In fact, the outcome of a single Wal-Mart lawsuit is monumental: *Dukes v. Wal-Mart* will, as the U.S. Chamber of Commerce argued in a 2007 legal brief, "virtually guarantee that employers will be subjected to large-scale employment discrimination class actions with billions of dollars in potential damages." This prediction would to some degree hold true: in December 2008, Wal-Mart paid an estimated $640 million to settle sixty-three different class-action suits that claimed the company "cheated hourly workers and forced them to work through breaks."

In this context, all the cursing, frustration, and infighting on full display at the Las Vegas labour summit comes as little surprise. They can see the end of an age, one that increasingly excludes them. And as leaders attack each other in meeting rooms and staffers scuttle in the halls, media observers and guests can only wonder what else is being said in closed-door meetings, as evidenced by the dour, ashen faces that emerge with only terse policy statements.

"These are the darkest days I've seen for American workers across the United States," says federation president John Sweeney, flanked by supporters. "Everything the union has fought for is all under attack." In recent months Sweeney has blamed Chinese imports, Republican policy, and corporate greed for the decline, noting that nearly 1,200 American companies eliminated pension plans in 2003. Burly kingpins such as Leo Gerard (steel) and Gerry McEntee (public sector) look uncomfortable and play down the rancour, claiming that it's just another meeting. But tellingly, leaders from three of the four largest unions are nowhere near Sweeney's podium, having mixed it up with the president and his cadre of machinists and steelworkers only a few hours before.

Elsewhere, Andy Stern, dissident leader of the powerful Service Employees International Union (SEIU), is circulating an inflammatory resolution. "It is not just hostile employer environment that is undermining our movement's campaign for workers rights," he writes. "It is also the failure of the AFL-CIO." Making it even more antagonistic, Stern was once Sweeney's protégé within the SEIU; he ran Sweeney's campaign to become federation president in 1995 and soon after replaced him at the helm of what is now North America's largest trade union.

In all of this there's no small amount of fear. These leaders have to figure out a way to renew memberships and win a long list of political battles over worker rights and organizing law, as well as break the union-free lock of new-millennium powerhouses like Wal-Mart. Ultimately, they must succeed, or else most everyone at this meeting loses their jobs. On the surface the dispute appears ideological: grassroots versus old school, new labour versus big labour. Yet it is far more than that. It is, in fact, a potentially insurmountable conflict that goes to the core of twenty-first-century change. The unions are divided by a growing service economy that creates more winners and losers than Vegas could ever dream of.

For unions, the hard truth is that there are now more service industry workers in America, some 21 million, than there are union members. The first six years of the twenty-first century, says *New York* magazine, were "the first sustained period of economic growth since World War II that fails to offer a prolonged increase in real wages for most workers," most of whom are service-based. In the eyes of some service union organizers, this new concentration of service workers represents growth potential, even if it means attempting to unionize retail and technology corporations that consider themselves post-union. Nevertheless, service unions like SEIU and its cousin the United Food and Commercial Workers (UFCW) have had success with adding new members to replace losses, and the SEIU is actually the fastest-growing union in North America.

Unions that represent workers in rust-belt industries – and some shrinking government sectors – see things differently. In 1969, for example, the machinists' union claimed 1 million members, but by 2005 that had shrunk to 380,000; more than 100,000 members had been lost since 2000 alone. The technology, industry streamlining, and offshoring that killed those jobs aren't going away anytime soon, and therefore manufacturing-sector unions don't see vast potential; they are circling the wagons. Put another way, "Stern insists that given the growing clout of global corporations, unions have no choice but to bulk up and adopt a private-sector growth strategy [of maximizing membership] – a tangibly different take than McEntee's politics-and-public-sector approach," observed *Business Week*.

Chatting in between sessions, observers note that a similar dispute occurred in America during the 1930s, when old-style craft unions faltered in the face of twentieth-century industrialization, with leaders famously coming to blows at a 1935 meeting in Atlantic City. Back then the fight was about how to respond to industrialization in an age of mass production. The reigning trades and craft unions were losing power as mass industry took over and factories churned out automobiles, appliances, and airplanes. In contrast, today's conflicts are about deindustrialization and the fact that the retail sector – the largest part of North America's service economy – represents 5 percent of union membership yet claims one in five of all workers. While organized labour has certainly had its low points – such as co-financing parts of Las Vegas with organized crime – labour's slow decline has also meant that issues of broad public benefit, such as health-care reform and welfare, received less attention during the years that America was playing casino with itself.

"The stale and paralyzed political dialogue . . . is a direct result of the deterioration of industrial America, followed by the rise of the Wal-Mart economy," notes journalist Matt Bai in a 2006 *New York Times* story on American union woes. "Lacking any real solutions to the growing anxiety of working-class families, the two parties have instead become entrenched in a cynical battle over who or what is at fault. Republicans have made an art form of blaming the declining fortunes of the middle class on taxes and social programs; if government would simply get out of the way, they suggest, businesses would magically provide all the well-paying jobs we need. Democrats, meanwhile, cling to the mythology of the factory age . . . ; if only Washington would close a few tax loopholes, they seem to be saying, the American worker could again live happily in 1950."

These and other troubles are on full display below Bally's. Today's union woes are largely about globalization and deindustrialization, which in turn reflects broader conflict and confusion about the growing dominance of post-industrial society – rife with underemployment, income insecurity, and eroding domestic production. In other words, some of the greatest conflicts of our time stem not only from anxieties about terrorism and geopolitics but also from the transformation of Western nations into shopping economies.

One starts to wonder if labour's unhappy family might find better odds to win upstairs on the blackjack or baccarat tables. Things are that bad. As one senior staffer confides, "We may have a federation after this week, but I don't know about the week after that."

The Battle of Las Vegas

A few years earlier, Las Vegas had been the site of the first major battle between organized labour and Wal-Mart. This showdown, which ran from 2000 to 2004, was a street-level organizing campaign to unionize several Las Vegas Wal-Mart outlets. What happened during the failed Vegas campaign does much to explain the bad blood, long silences, and outright fear gripping unionists clustered in the basement of Bally's casino.

With much fanfare, UFCW field organizers rolled into Las Vegas at the request of the union's head office in the fall of 2000. The UFCW was already strong and well-represented in the city's many casinos, restaurants, and grocery stores. It was part of the history of Vegas itself, back when organized crime and the Teamsters helped finance some of the Strip's first modern resorts. Today's Las Vegas remains highly unionized, a fact lost on many tourists, but not on strategists, largely because union membership has grown substantially within the city's many hotel and gambling establishments, adding more than 20,000 members since the late 1980s. Many within the UFCW well understood that a David and Goliath–style battle between labour and Wal-Mart was overdue, and they needed somewhere that could serve as a fail-safe laboratory for in-store unionizing.

In fact, a street battle between labour and Wal-Mart could not be avoided. During the 1990s, unions like the UFCW sniped at Wal-Mart through public relations campaigns focused on big-box dirt such as child-labour abuses and development subsidies from local government. While this did indeed taunt Wal-Mart into some embarrassing responses, a publicity-based attack did little to slow the continued expansion of Wal-Mart and its kin, especially the retailer's death-star strategy of deploying integrated grocery and retail supercentres across the western hemisphere. Unions and local commerce were getting squashed. "The Super center taught the supermarket industry a lesson in brute capitalism," recounts business journalist Anthony Bianco in *Wal-Mart: The Bully of Bentonville*. "The typical chain supermarket could not slash its prices to match the Super center opening across the street and still turn a profit, largely because it was locked into UFCW contracts paying workers 25 percent to 30 percent more than Wal-Mart's non-union staffers made. The result was that every time a new Super center opened up in America, two big supermarkets went out of business, taking some 400 high-paying jobs with them."

Wal-Mart was doing precisely this in January 2001 when the retailer simultaneously opened four different centres in Las Vegas, more than 500,000 square feet of union-free shopping. It was the largest retail opening by a single company in the city's history – no small feat – yet only part of a national forty-six-store deployment across America over three days. It was shock-and-awe retail strategy, carpet-bombing whole urban zones with bargains in a gambit to secure market share.

Almost 1,400 new Wal-Mart jobs were created that month in Las Vegas. UFCW operatives had already been busily infiltrating Wal-Mart stores and staff in a concerted effort to live up to claims that their union would indeed break open Wal-Mart nation-wide. The two sides, having circled each other for years, were finally face to face for a major smackdown.

"There was a small group of organized Wal-Mart workers under the radar before we arrived," recalls former UFCW organizer Bill Meyer, who coordinated the Vegas campaign from 2000 to 2004. "But Wal-Mart sent a slew of folks in there, 'people teams' they were called. It got to the point where workers were scared to death – that they weren't voting on a union but whether to keep the store open." The cat-and-mouse game required organizers to slip into Wal-Mart stores and parking lots unnoticed and attempt to persuade a majority of store workers to sign union cards, which, if successful, would initiate a legal vote among workers on whole-store unionization. It was like a Cold War espionage novel, except operatives weren't battling over nuclear secrets but rather the loyalties of low-wage workers. Secret meetings, surveillance, and psych tactics were deployed – not the least, McCarthyite manuals such as Wal-Mart's infamous booklet "A Manager's Toolbox to Remaining Union-Free."

Organizers converged on Sam's Club No. 6382, due west of the Las Vegas Strip. Things got ugly pretty quickly. "Anti-union workers were promised raises and promotions at some unspecified future date," reports Anthony Bianco. "Meanwhile, labour relations operatives from Bentonville stepped up the frequency of their anti-union seminars, segregating committed union supporters in separate sessions to keep them from influencing the other workers. Three large glass cases filled with anti-union messages were installed in the break room, covering an entire twenty-foot section of wall."

Nevertheless, Bill Meyer and other organizers managed to convince a majority of the Las Vegas store workers at Sam's Club No. 6382 to sign union cards, and the National Labor Relations Board scheduled an election. The battle escalated: intimidation, firings, and stacking the employee pool with new, union-unfriendly workers became common, some of which would later be documented and found illegal by the NLRB. In 2007 Human Rights Watch studied all the NLRB decisions against Wal-Mart and found that not only had many originated in Las Vegas, there was a clear pattern of "unlawful tactics, forbidden under US as well as international law, that Wal-Mart has repeatedly used to prevent workers from exercising their internationally recognized right to freedom of association." Wal-Mart, for its part, maintains that it never broke any laws.

The battle of Las Vegas was making international headlines, and Wal-Mart's dirty laundry was being aired. In September 2002 a federal judge determined that managers at three Wal-Mart locations in Las Vegas had broken the law a dozen times by "interrogating workers, confiscating pro-union literature and denying a promotion to a woman because she supported a union." And in 2003 it was revealed that Wal-Mart was assisting workers to sign up for income and health assistance: Las Vegas Wal-Mart management was actually providing instructions for workers to help verify employment status and apply for government assistance from social service agencies while working. Former ten-year Wal-Mart manager Gretchen Adams told PBS in 2003 that managers kept "a list of the state agencies so that we could have some place to send these associates . . . for Medicaid, for well-baby care, for whatever it is that they need." After years of criticism, by 2009 Wal-Mart had expanded health coverage just in time for the recession: only "5.5 percent of its employees now lack health insurance, compared with a nationwide rate of 18 percent," reported the *Washington Post*.

While some Las Vegas workers spoke favourably about Wal-Mart and asserted that no union was necessary, this did little to deter the union's organizing efforts, which became increasingly assertive. "It got to the point where as soon as [union] organizers got out of their cars, the security guards would be in the parking lots telling them to leave," says former cashier Alan Peto. He had attempted his own unsuccessful petition against low wages at Wal-Mart and reported on-the-job harassment, later filed as yet another official labour relations complaint.

In the end Wal-Mart gained the upper hand, and in a last-ditch measure, union organizers filed a complaint to the NLRB in November 2001. They intentionally postponed the vote to ensure that Bentonville's management would not succeed at further crushing it. As Meyer admits, this strategy probably cost them a long-term chance at victory, since Las Vegas is an itinerant town with high resident turnover, and Wal-Mart is a retailer whose average staff turnover approached 50 percent during the early 2000s. It wasn't long before the Wal-Mart workers who signed union cards had moved on, were transferred, or were fired. The critical in-store majority was lost. "We had a solid core of people that were going to vote for it," argues Meyer. "But Wal-Mart sent a slew of people in there, destroying the laboratory conditions. We felt confident that if people had been left alone, we would have succeeded."

It was a historic battle that will have implications for decades to come. Yet the odd thing is, none of the union honchos at the AFL-CIO conference underneath Bally's wants to talk about Wal-Mart in Las Vegas – especially the UFCW, which appears to be pretending that its campaign never happened. In one public session a journalist asks leaders about union strategy on Wal-Mart and gets the freeze: "Why would we reveal our strategy?" asks one leader icily. On several occasions I corner Greg Denier, UFCW communications director, to ask for an interview and some names of UFCW contacts who participated in the Las Vegas campaign. Amazingly, he's got nothing, as if all the labour organizers and millions spent on attempting to unionize Wal-Mart in Vegas had left no trace whatsoever. It's the same thing over at the UFCW Local 711 office – "Sorry, no comment." It's as though the whole chapter has been written out of history, like some Soviet-era purge, complete with missing names and faces smudged out of photographs.

It wasn't long ago that union operatives like Greg Denier were attempting to fight Wal-Mart out in the open. "Americans can't live on a Wal-Mart paycheck," Denier told *Mother Jones* magazine in 2003. "Yet it's the dominant employer, and what they pay will be the future of working America."

Despite the official silence, the truth eventually comes out. Las Vegas is a sore point for big labour, not because they didn't win – they haven't officially lost yet – but because the UFCW itself pulled the plug on the operation. What really happened, explains Bill Meyer, who agrees to talk only after his retirement from the UFCW, was a leadership change. In July 2004 newly appointed UFCW organizing director Bill McDonough terminated the program. "Bill wanted a different course and rode off the path," says Meyer. "There were real battles on philosophy internally. So they set aside the past and moved on." Moreover, an expensive California supermarket strike in 2004 had drained the UFCW's war chest, and "a Web-based campaign was cheaper." Even in the labour movement, it seems, there's no escaping downsizing.

The union moved away from organizing Wal-Mart workers to a public relations and Internet campaign called Wake Up Wal-Mart. "I understand why they made their decision," says Meyer. "But I would have done both campaigns." There was, he maintains, visible progress after the unsuccessful 2001 vote drive. Las Vegas union organizers had continued to sign up new Wal-Mart workers, reinforcing union presence and creating confidence. They had launched an independent radio show in Las Vegas to publicize the UFCW and conduct guest interviews with local players – a tactic already employed by labour activists in Hong Kong to advocate for illegal independent unions across mainland China. But "after we changed philosophies, you didn't see workers as much," says Meyer.

Back at Bally's casino, any mention of Wal-Mart presents an embarrassing contradiction. The UFCW, having eliminated its highly public Las Vegas organizing campaign, is still pushing hard for the same worker-oriented organizing across America – which is a battle that could also raise millions of dollars in new union dues. This is how the campaign in Las Vegas was a wager for everyone, but when the losses ran high, the union abruptly left the game.

From unions battling Wal-Mart to cutting-edge industries, Las Vegas offers up a view of the future that is either bright or dismal, depending on one's location in the retail supply chain. For many workers it's more like the dark ages of the 1920s, argues Meyer. He cites landmark mass layoffs at failed American retailer Circuit City in 2007, when the company fired 3,400 senior workers and then offered to hire them back at lower wages. As Daniel Bell predicted in *The Coming of Post-Industrial Society* more than thirty years ago, in the transition from "a goods producing to a service economy, the professional and technical class emerges as the predominant occupational group." And despite the "historical strength of trade unionism, [there are] increasing difficulties within the straits of a service economy and foreign competition." In other words, the so-called knowledge economy that springs from post-industrial society does not favour workers; rather, it often discards them or demotes them to contract or part-time work as the result of what turned out to be unsustainable economic growth.

This is why we find both bargaineers and labour leaders – two players at opposite ends of the global economic casino – trying to better their odds amid showgirls, tourists, and card games. Globalization has, if anything, increased our exposure to diverse and often seemingly random outcomes. In the end it may well prove more accurate to refer to our twenty-first-century milieu as a casino economy. "We have, in effect, turned into a winner-take-all economy, substituting the gambling hall for the factory floor as our governing economic metaphor, an assembly of individual strangers whose fortunes depend overwhelmingly on random luck rather than collective hard work," argues *New York* magazine's Kurt Andersen. "And it's been unwitting synergy, not unrelated coincidence, that actual casino gambling has become ubiquitous in America at the same time."

None of this is any comfort to the embattled labour unions underneath Bally's casino. After all the acrimony, long silences, and fading hope, everyone leaves Las Vegas unhappy: three of the four largest unions in the federation quit a few months later. The Teamsters, the UFCW, and Stern's SEIU are all out before midsummer, and a spin-off coalition, Change to Win, is founded in September 2005. In total, seven unions, representing 6 million workers, abandoned the AFL-CIO in the wake of the Las Vegas meeting.

Any hope of a unified labour force that could take on Wal-Mart died that day under Bally's casino. What was once Wal-Mart's greatest threat became a series of scattered coalitions and websites. The SEIU continued to add new union members, but most other unions faced declining membership. Andy Stern would eventually go on to share the stage with Wal-Mart CEO Lee Scott in 2007, together launching the Better Health Care

Together coalition. This hotly contended and somewhat ambiguous effort to address "healthcare reform" launched a new chapter in labour strategy that reflects the shifting business–activist alliances seen in issues like climate change. As if to underline his controversial post-ideological approach, Stern also forged ties with China's official state-controlled union, the All China Federation of Trade Unions (ACFTU), despite the union's alleged collusion in limiting workers' freedoms and ignoring human rights abuses.

Wal-Mart eventually did allow some of its stores to unionize – but only in China. Complying with Chinese law, and after a four-year ACFTU campaign to shoehorn itself into the hundred-plus Wal-Mart outlets operating across mainland China, Wal-Mart adjusted its most fervent anti-union policies for the world's largest marketplace. ("Should associates request formation of a union," read the company's one-line official statement, "Wal-Mart China would respect their wishes.") In a final post-Vegas twist, the enigmatic Stern reportedly played a part in bringing China's government-controlled union into Wal-Mart's stores. "Our members and their members work for the same employers," Stern told *The Nation* in 2007, explaining the strange turn of events. "I just think workers' solidarity has a lot more possibilities when you're not dealing with ideology."

At the end of it all, Bill Meyer remains philosophical, despite being defeated partly by his own union. "What we learned is that all of this did not go for naught," he says. "We found that many workers actually did want a union. It was the workers themselves."

"[But] we also learned that our system of labour laws is deeply flawed," he adds, citing delays in the complaints process and employer-friendly labour regulations. "Getting a contract would have almost been impossible; it would have taken years and years. So we were ultimately hampered by labour laws and a company with endless resources." Only late in 2007 were the original Wal-Mart labour complaints from 2000 resolved; the NLRB determined that Wal-Mart had acted illegally, and it was ordered to pay a few thousand dollars in lost wages and "post notices in its three stores disclosing its federal labor law violations." But it didn't matter anymore. The workers who had originally filed the complaints had long ago quit their jobs and moved on.

And what happened to the workers left behind after the UFCW campaign was cancelled? "There were a lot of great people who stuck their necks out," admits Meyer, recalling that most everyone who signed union cards either quit, transferred, or was fired. "Ethics had to be put aside for practicality. I felt horrible to leave. It was a four-year undertaking and we spent millions of dollars. Many were understandably bitter about it."

But hey, this is Vegas. Losing graciously is part of the drill. Former Wal-Mart workers such as Alan Peto have surprisingly little to say about being caught up in a battle of titans. "We went from a high of 30 organizers to only one," Peto says via email, regarding Wal-Mart's victory and the UFCW's retreat. Peto has moved on and now works in local law enforcement, but he's not forgetting what happened either. "Basically, everything Wal-Mart said about the UFCW in the anti-union meetings came true," he says regretfully. "Especially with regards to how the UFCW would ultimately abandon the workers."

In May 2009, the UFCW announced it would once again attempt store-level organizing of Wal-Mart workers in the hopes that newly elected president Barack Obama might facilitate better labour laws. Targeting a hundred stores across America, the union invoked 2008 election promises on labour reform known as the Employee Free Choice Act that, by 2009, had withered under the economic pressure of recession; even the act's stalwart Democrat supporters had been scared off from supporting anything that resembled growth-stalling legislation. "They know it will fail," said labour historian Nelson Lichtenstein of the UFCW's second quest to unionize Wal-Mart. "It's designed to fail . . . [but] demonstrating that failure shows we need something new."

Perpetual Bargain Machine

On the final morning of the Las Vegas bargain show, the trading floor begins to rumble. It's only a few hours before it's time to pack up and clear the building, but there's last-minute action. After four days of bartering, shipping arrangements, and bad coffee, eight thousand vendors start selling off everything – sales samples, display stands, anything not bolted to the floor – to the first person willing to hand over cash. The Sands Convention Center has just turned into the world's largest dollar store. You want something? Make an offer.

All the strange stuff gets bought up first: electrified mini four-by-four Jeeps, faux antique lighting, imitation motorcycle leathers, giant stuffed

author photo

No one leaves empty-handed: sellers become bargain shoppers on the final day of bargain trading in the Sands Convention Centre, Las Vegas.

animals, singing Elvis dolls. People are buying more than they can carry, all at super-discount prices. This is a triumphant moment. This is how discounters claimed a growing portion of the economy, one bargain at a time.

Discounting is the heart of modern commerce, and not the sector that got rich writing software, management consulting, or trading derivatives. This is the real-time iteration that encompasses many of the advances of post-industrial society – technology, transportation, management, and affordable energy – and applies them with devastating effect to everyday life. From the early 1990s to the late 2000s, consumers and bargaineers of all shapes and sizes managed to live the new-economy dream, and well outside the elite circles of Silicon Valley and Wall Street: uninterrupted growth, savings, and possibility, all without having to manufacture a single thing themselves. And while this twenty-plus-year span of the bargaineer's ascent to power is hardly a blip in the course of human history, it marks the fullest expression of globalization and its impact on our everyday lives.

Bargains have power precisely because cheap stuff delivered a veritable jackpot of value. Some analysts estimate that approximately $100 billion in new consumer spending was created through the first wave of the bargain revolution; other estimates claim that imports from China alone have saved U.S. consumers roughly $600 billion.

Bargains offered an economic boon to regular folks who didn't acquire new wealth during the bull markets and housing bubbles of the last decade. In glitzy TV ads in 2008 and 2009, Wal-Mart trumpeted savings as a form of income. "Let's say you spent a hundred dollars a week at the grocery store on these kinds of items . . . If you bought these kinds of items at Wal-Mart you could save over $700 per year," says a woman comparing bags of groceries. These claims are impressive, but they come from Wal-Mart's own consultants, Global Insight, who in 2006 claimed that whole families of Wal-Mart shoppers were saving a total of $2,500 annually.

Although Wal-Mart has perpetually overstated its benefit to the economy, it is real. Mass bargains are like a small pay raise, contributing at least $115 to the average American household in 2007, according to International Monetary Fund statistics on global trade. Perhaps more important than the actual household benefit is that cheap stuff represents the psychological heart of consumerism – the distant possibility of relative affluence and price accessibility for all classes of people everywhere. And in our emerging casino economy, where winners and losers abound as wealth and poverty grow in equal measures, the great majority of consumers continue to cling to bargains in an attempt to beat the odds of an unfair world. It's evidence of a perpetual bargain machine: simply put, consumers gorge themselves on imported cheap stuff that inevitably erodes domestic employment, thereby sparking further demand for bargains.

The disintegration of the AFL-CIO likely represents, among other things, future waves of dollar-store customers – involuntary bargain shoppers – in addition to the many former union workers already employed as involuntary part-time labour within the service sector. The Vegas bargain show is a prime example of cheap stuff becoming axiomatic, since many bargaineers, especially micro-businesses, eBay sellers, and mall-cart operators are, as Sam Bundy noted, also exiles from the world of full-time employment.

Nearly twenty years after imports began to flow in volume, and less than a decade since bargains came to dominate trade, discounters like Danny Kole are bracing for hard times ahead. What concerns Kole directly is the eventual demise of the dollar store. Within another decade, relatively few items in his warehouse might be sold profitably for a dollar. In the end it won't be lead-tainted jewellery and toys that drive away consumers, it will be price inflation. "Plastics, anything petroleum-based, have gone up in cost," reports Kole. "Anyone dealing with a plastics factory now receives regular notices announcing regular increases in price. That's the reality of it with plastics: the same person filling up their tank is doing the same thing buying a laundry basket or a plastic lunch box. They're going to pay more for it next year."

This is a little hard to imagine in the midst of the Las Vegas trade floor, where the cheapness seems to run on forever. Yet Kole imagines a time when bargains will come to resemble natural resources, subject to scarcity and price flux. "Over the long term, bargains will be similar to gas prices, with fluctuations and peak seasons," he says. "So companies will try to adapt, buying when products are less expensive."

Between expected shortages of both resources and consumers, Kole sees the potential limits and imperfections of the current system – and knows he'll be one of the businesses caught in the disconnect between expectation and reality. When oil peaked near $150 in 2008, which increased Kole's costs on everything from plastic to transport, people still wanted their bargains. "As times get tougher and tougher, people are even more looking for a deal," he says. "Customers are more educated now and if they don't see a good deal, they won't come back." Already most dollar-store chains are stocking more expensive items, partly because income-challenged consumers are doing more one-stop grocery shopping at dollar stores (again following Wal-Mart's highly successful expansion into groceries), but also because of the slowly declining number of products that are still worth a dollar. In many ways dollar stores are fast becoming miniaturized department stores as downsized consumers flock to extreme-value discounters in order to save on food and essential household items.

The post-industrial economy is a double-edged sword: bargaineers have more customers than ever and more products available to sell, but conditions make it increasingly difficult to engineer bargains. "The biggest intangible has been price pressures on both ends – inflation – driven by fuel prices, food prices going up," confirms Bundy. "There's a squeeze on the supply side too – cost of raw materials, especially in China, where you have Chinese consumption as well as raw goods scarcity. Sourcing costs have gone up because of this."

This is the experiment at the core of a consumer-driven service economy: How far can we bargaineer past known limits? Are there limits? "A post-industrial transformation produces no 'answers,'" predicted Daniel Bell in 1976. "It only establishes new promises and new powers, new constraints and new questions – with the difference that these are now on a scale that had never been imagined in world history." Consequently, trade in bargains influences international relations, interest rates, and gross national product on several continents. And what it lacks in imagination, quality, and possibility, it delivers in quantity, low prices, and the ever-present promise of good value.

For now the Las Vegas bargain show is an oasis: everyone sets aside business in these last moments and scoops up whatever trinket or household gadget catches their fancy. Compared to the sterile environment of malls and big-box stores, it's an image of commerce as it appeared well before plastic was ever invented, as thousands of bargaineers barter, haggle, and trade amid half-deconstructed stalls and shipping crates.

For some, today's prize is an executive putting set; for others, it's biker goggles and fake tattoos. I'm laying down a few dollars for some stuffed Hulk and Spider-Man dolls for my kids, and I negotiate a great price on a toy bin that would never fit on the airplane home. Some folks appear to have a flatbed truck waiting outside on the strip as they shamelessly haul out everything from fake palm trees to enormous gold-framed baroque paintings and life-size statues of American jazz musicians. Poor Coltrane, strapped to the back of a golf cart. Nearby, a six-foot-tall knock-off of

Caravaggio's *Inspiration of Saint Matthew* leans up against a concrete pillar, surrounded by Marilyn Monroe handbags and crates of poker chips.

The ebb and flow of people and products is more entertaining than Las Vegas itself, like watching the global economy set to "shuffle." And it is the smiles, the genuinely warm glow of the successful shopper, that register as people exit the building, arms filled with loot. This is the kind of magic you don't usually see in Vegas. In this moment everyone's a winner, and they know it.

QUANTUM CHEAP:
PROGRESS IS PRICE DESTRUCTION

2

Wal-Mart CEO Mike Duke rallies shareholders at the company's 2008 annual general meeting in Fayetteville, Arkansas.

The Fall and Rise of Wal-Mart

Eduardo Castro-Wright has a problem. The CEO of Wal-Mart USA stands before an expectant audience at a posh Arizona golf resort and is attempting to explain how Wal-Mart plans to conquer the twenty-first century. Nearly anyone who matters in retail is here: Macy's, Sears, JCPenney, Target, Nordstrom, plus scores of blue-chip manufacturers, consultants, and logistics experts – it's the closest thing to having the brain trust of North America's service economy collected in a single room. The battle of Las Vegas is behind them; their main concern is how to maintain revenue and precipitous rates of growth in a world already full of retailers.

Wal-Mart fancies itself as the one that will unlock this mystery. Rapid expansion within saturated and consumer troubled markets is the retail equivalent of what breaking the sound barrier was for postwar America – a quantum threshold that shows what ingenuity and true grit are all about. "Few retailers have changed the marketplace as much as Sam Walton did," says Castro-Wright, reminding everyone of the incredible rags-to-riches story of the world's greatest retailer. "He began in 1962, and it has grown to nearly $300 billion in sales. You do not do that without changing and innovating."

The thing is, executives attending this conference aren't buying Castro-Wright's message. Wal-Mart is in trouble, and everybody knows it.

It's 2007, and Wal-Mart has posted its worst monthly sales results since 1979. Humankind's largest company actually reached its peak back in 1999, when it entered the new millennium with a 106 percent increase in stock price and a 9.3 percent same-store growth rate. This after incredible gains throughout the 1990s, when the retailer famously opened thousands of new stores around the world and logged record profits. But to the horror of Bentonville's head office, Wal-Mart's stock value dropped 38 percent between 2000 and 2007 – a clear sign that investors had lost faith. The company appeared to be in the throes of a mid-life crisis.

With great anticipation, people listen for clues in the CEO's speech, not unlike Kremlinologists of yore, in an attempt to parse the future. Because Wal-Mart is the dominant force in an economy that is in turn dominated by retail and wholesale trade, Castro-Wright could read the phone book and people would still hang on to his every word. "We were the first ones to start a distribution network in the 1970s," he continues with casual resolve. "And in the 1980s we brought in a satellite network. Today we are continuously driving for innovation." These are slim clues indeed for the audience of retailers, scholars, and analysts attending this elite strategy conference.

Investors smelled failure, despite tremendous profits. In the twenty-nine years that Wal-Mart reported same-store growth, its profit and store count increased dramatically, but actual sales performance declined from a peak of 13 percent same-store growth in 1987, dropping to an all-time low of 0.8 percent in 2007. But not so for other discounters: Wal-Mart's arch-rival, Costco, posted as much as 5 percent same-store growth in 2007, more than quadrupling that of the Arkansas giant. An estimated one in four American households now owns a Costco membership. Sam Walton is rolling in his grave.

"Sam was a great innovator," says Castro-Wright, undaunted. "Sam said, 'Everything is changing around you; you can't succeed if you keep doing what you are doing today. You stay in front of change.'" While Castro-Wright is clearly one of Wal-Mart's brightest stars, it's clear that he drank the Bentonville Kool-Aid some time ago. With eerie devotion he invokes Wal-Mart's founder on a first-name basis, even though new-generation executives like Castro-Wright never met the legendary retailer before his death in 1992. And, notably, most of Wal-Mart's incredible growth and innovation occurred after Chairman Sam had passed. "We stay on the forefront of everything we do and we remember his teachings. We bring value to customers and communities."

This is perhaps how Wal-Mart's top executives rationalize outrageous salaries and bonuses: they don't often take questions and they rarely wander off message. Today's message is about Wal-Mart's corporate facelift, part of a multi-year plan to get the retailer back on track and – most important to Bentonville – regain the trust of investors.

Born in Ecuador, Castro-Wright came from a retailing family. He joined Wal-Mart in 2001 after stints in manufacturing at Honeywell and Nabisco. He made great progress with Wal-Mart Mexico, achieving record growth in sales, and in 2005 Castro-Wright was made CEO of Wal-Mart USA, responsible for many of Sam's flagship stores. The idea was that he might be able to work the same kind of magic that had made WalMex one of Wal-Mart's most successful international divisions. He is the company's great hope for a turnaround in its critical home market – which, by virtue of Wal-Mart's influence, makes Castro-Wright someone who holds the fate of consumerism in his hands.

What everyone else with a stake in the world's largest company really wants to know is: where's the growth? This question concerns the 1.9 million people directly employed by the retailer. After three decades of perpetual expansion, Wal-Mart's growth stall is causing panic because its core business strategy has always been pre-emptive growth: breaking into and disrupting markets with low prices before anyone else. Sam Walton's brilliance was in finding untapped potential within the underdeveloped retail markets of rural America. Walton filled in the open spaces on the map, and his successors accelerated this trend globally through logistics technology, offshore production, and aggressive business tactics.

Castro-Wright knows the stakes are high. Wal-Mart famously cannibalized the top retailers of the twentieth century, just as every business from dollar stores to fellow big-box discounters now nips at the heels of

Bentonville's Goliath. "In less than forty years the economic landscape has changed so dramatically that nearly all of the ten largest retailers of the 1970s are no longer the ten largest retailers today," he reminds everyone. "That tells you a lot – retailing is a Darwinian business."

Accordingly, investors devalued Wal-Mart's share price not because the company lacks profits but because the retailer's past strategy and success appear to be nearly impossible to duplicate in the future. Retail became a brutal zero-sum game in the twenty-first century. The most obvious example of this is Wal-Mart's supercentring of America: in its efforts to triple and sometimes quadruple its market share in any given location, Wal-Mart strategically oversaturates its own markets, at least as much as can be supported by its own supply chain network.

The result was famously demonstrated in Oklahoma City, where from 1997 onward the retailer closed an estimated thirty competing super-markets and reduced food prices by 15 percent with an invasion of eighteen different supercentres and markets, creating terminal retail saturation. As Sam Walton once bragged, "We became our own competition."

Castro-Wright inherited this end game from Lee Scott, who became Wal-Mart's president in January 2000, just after the company's stock peaked. While presiding over Wal-Mart's massive devaluation, Scott told shareholders in 2005, "We estimate there is room for almost 4,000 more Supercenters," even though the company was already flagging at 2,300. By late 2007, under investor pressure to curtail operations, it downscaled its expansion plans by 30 percent. Until that point Wal-Mart had managed to open a new store somewhere in America roughly every twenty-six and a half hours.

"There is turmoil in Bentonville at levels I don't think we've ever seen before," said Mark Hunter, one of America's top retail consultants, as I interviewed him in Tucson in 2007. "For a long time they have been quietly saying, 'We're going to become the first trillion-dollar company.' They are not going to become a trillion-dollar company. This is a company that is having major problems."

The company had boxed itself in. Wal-Mart can rework its image all it wants, spruce up its stores, and spend millions on public relations to patch up old battles, but it cannot escape itself. Its corporate DNA is growth and low prices built upon mastery of cost, logistics, and scale. And it has reshaped the marketplace in its image. Despite this, it wants to pursue the customers and markets that purchase more than the cheapest household goods. As proof, the retailer has dabbled with designer fashions, branched out into high-value electronics, and, with greater success, invaded groceries. But really, how can Wal-Mart squeeze more value out of a low-value market? It's like Krispy Kreme trying to become Starbucks, or McDonald's aspiring to gourmet pizza.

"They are trying desperately to move from supply chain master to merchandising guru," explains Hunter. "They are having problems, a lot of problems. . . . I think it's one of the bigger reasons for their earnings and store sales problems. They can't quite figure it out – 'How do we get consumers to buy more than just the basics, underwear and tissues?'"

In response to his critics, Castro-Wright outlines the need for Wal-Mart to segment itself, to become more things to more people, expanding into financial services and health care. As part of its makeover, Wal-Mart adopted a new marketing strategy and slogan in 2007, the first slogan change in nineteen years: "Save Money, Live Better."

Some, like Hunter, wondered if Wal-Mart was losing its nerve. Sure, the company has gone environmental: it hired a former Sierra Club president, became the world's biggest purchaser of organic dairy and produce, and sold more compact fluorescent light bulbs than any retailer in history – "worth some $3 billion in saved power bills," Castro-Wright reminds us, "or one million cars' worth of greenhouse gases." The retailer even luxed up its dowdy stores with brand names and modern colour schemes, an effort to appeal to larger urban markets that disdained Mr. Sam's hillbilly warehouse aesthetic. Small, European-style stores are rumoured to be their next big move. "[We're] taking it to the next level," says Castro-Wright. "We don't deal with the blue-grey big box anymore."

But Sam Walton never agonized over what a customer was feeling – he let low prices do the talking. Some, like Hunter, predicted that this kind of touchy-feely turnaround – "Save Money, Live Better" – was Kremlin-esque code for the unmentionable: higher prices. "The move signals a trend they have been establishing in the past several years, of increasing their prices on select items," says Hunter. They are clearly moving to a strategy of being the low-price leader on key items and taking higher margins on other items."

This wouldn't be bad news. A world with fewer of Wal-Mart's aggressive rollbacks would appeal to many, not least the majority of manufacturers, who have frequently been squeezed to the brink of bankruptcy by Bentonville's pathologically cheap purchasing department. The unions, workers, and activists and anyone else beaten down by the smiley steamroller would surely claim victory.

Wal-Mart is banking on the fact that it has become a major institution, a third order of public life, whose economic power and retail inertia could somehow defy trends. "Eighty-nine percent of Americans visited a Wal-Mart store last year," Castro-Wright reminds his Arizona audience. "And our studies showed that many want to feel smart more than trendy; [they want] unbeatable prices for quality product."

But this is about more than Wal-Mart. Well before the 2008 crash, the hyper-competitive markets that sustained the discount boom of the 1990s had begun to stagnate. Consumer bankruptcies, rising business expenses, an ongoing credit crunch, and rising gasoline prices were afflicting many traditional retailers. And more than anyone, retailers understand what happens when, in an economy driven nearly 75 percent by consumption, consumers don't show up for shopping duty. "Our customers have been hurting," admitted Office Depot's CEO Steve Odland in October 2008. "The global economy is at stake here."

Wal-Mart saw a different opportunity. It saw blood in the water in an approaching wave of retail bankruptcies, and Bentonville's head office announced aggressive new discounts even as Wall Street collapsed in late 2008. The company's gambit included an ingenious and oddly reassuring early rollout of holiday season decorations and 10 to 50 percent discounts on toys, including Barbie dolls and Tonka trucks for $10. It was Keynesian retailing as the company spent millions in forgone profits on price rollbacks, during a recession, in order to keep customers. Knowing that more shoppers were living from paycheque to paycheque, Wal-Mart claimed that the company had put Christmas on "fast track" because customers would be stretching their budgets over months in order to afford the gift-giving season. "It's starting now," said spokeswoman Linda Blakely. "Our price rollbacks make the prices comparable to what they were 20 years ago."

When Black Friday 2008 arrived, just before U.S. jobless claims jumped towards 600,000 in a single month, Wal-Mart finally found its mission.

As the financial crisis took hold and the world plunged into a broad and potentially bottomless recession, Wal-Mart rolled out massive bargains, culminating in the deadly shopping riot at Green Acres Mall. Most major retailers conceded that there was no choice: like it or not, they were all competing with Wal-Mart and anyone else who could deliver radical deals.

Wal-Mart accomplished the near-impossible. By February 2009 it had increased same-store sales growth by 50 percent – adding $4.1 billion in additional revenues – compared to the same three-month holiday period a year earlier. Back when the economy was booming and shoppers were spending, Wal-Mart couldn't get respect from investors. However, facing the worst economic conditions since the Great Depression, it nearly doubled sales growth at a time when many retailers were falling fast. (Wal-Mart's same-store sales increased 5.1 percent during February 2009, compared with impressive declines of 26 percent for Saks, 30 percent for Abercrombie & Fitch, and 12 percent for Gap.)

Wal-Mart's epic but often derided quest for cheap suddenly had historic purpose. Wal-Mart's new motto – "Save Money, Live Better" – "has galvanized the entire organization around a common purpose," said Eduardo Castro-Wright, now vice-chairman of Wal-Mart, in 2009. The company pledged to feed and clothe its customers more affordably than anyone else on the planet. "Nowhere has price leadership been more important to our customers than in grocery," Mr. Castro-Wright continued, "[and] we continue to increase the price gaps between our competitors and Wal-Mart in food and consumables." At least for that moment, it was clear that discounting, not finance, technology, or any other industry, had become the consumer's last refuge.

Having finally found success, Wal-Mart proceeded to fire eight hundred people from its head office in Bentonville. "The business model that Sam Walton created is perfectly positioned for the environment we live in now," said Wal-Mart's new CEO, Michael T. Duke. "I do believe this is Wal-Mart's time."

The Tyranny of Price
Sam Walton once claimed that Wal-Mart could "restore manufacturing capacity, improve our national economy, and renew our pride in American craftsmanship." But times have obviously changed and the company's

vision today is a little different. Wal-Mart's post-2008 turnaround has much to do with the fact that so many others are failing.

One thing is for sure: the incredible wealth and growth that defined the booming 1990s is history. Amid the evidence of Wal-Mart's doldrums, there's plentiful concern among Castro-Wright's Arizona audience that the last significant wave of retail growth happened in the 1990s, as new mini-malls and big-box stores cluttered the landscape, leaving a large portion of the service economy vulnerable to increases in energy and housing prices and credit collapses. The scores of shoppers flooding Wal-Mart in the face of economic hardship make it clear: there is interdependence. We are Wal-Mart – and Wal-Mart is us.

Yet in a service economy clogged with retailers, there are few growth frontiers left except price, which underlines a fundamental problem with this economic model: in the end, many will not survive the race to the bottom. The twenty-first century poses serious challenges for all growth-dependent industries. Within service-dominated economies, market saturation creates hyper-competition. As demonstrated by Wal-Mart's revitalization, new profits or sales generated will likely be stolen from someone else's bottom line. In this kind of environment, a major retailer who cannot show growth likely cannot compete – not just for customers but also for everything from energy to logistics.

For example, Eastern Europe, Asia, and developing countries elsewhere offer the only remaining major growth markets and are being pursued by everyone from Wal-Mart to Home Depot, Germany's Metro, and France's Carrefour. But international expansion has been spotty for many retailers. Wal-Mart's failure in Germany, along with money-losing operations in Japan and elsewhere, cloud the retailer's claims that new growth abroad can solve its home-market woes. International sales accounted for 22 percent of its 2006 sales of $345 billion, most of which were in Canada, Britain, and Mexico – retail markets already facing saturation. Developing markets in Central America, Brazil, Argentina, and China hold the most potential, but few guarantees.

Wal-Mart remains addicted to growth in ways that boggle the mind. First and foremost, consumer-economy stalwarts like Wal-Mart require large economies of scale and competitive expansion to compensate for outrageously low profit margins. Perpetual deep discounting means that

Wal-Mart collects as little as half as much profit per sale as traditional retailers – only 3.24 cents for every dollar. This is a testament to the retailer's innovation and discipline, since no other company in history has managed to make so much money on such a small profit margin. But it also means that growth is almost mandatory for success, since Wal-Mart must compensate for rising expenses and the demand for deeper discounts with higher sales volumes. So when investors devalued Wal-Mart despite consistently huge profits, it was because they understood the nature of the service economy: if you aren't growing, you're dying.

Growth also matters because every business from dollar stores to international retailers is using the same logistics and manufacturing networks that Wal-Mart helped pioneer. The arrival of the U.K.'s Tesco in North America, for example, was heralded as a major challenge to Wal-Mart's dominance. Tesco, the world's fourth-largest retailer, planned to spend $2 billion between 2007 and 2012 to launch Fresh & Easy markets in Wal-Mart's homeland. By 2008 it was already surpassing most American stores in average sales per square foot and had announced another 150 locations. By tweaking the Wal-Mart model – strategically sized stores, better products, more convenience – new-school retailers such as Tesco and Costco were literally out-Wal-Marting the world's leading retailer, at least before the recession hit.

And it is within the United States, the world's leading consumer market, that new growth is least forthcoming. By 2009 American consumer confidence had reached a twenty-six-year low and major retail bankruptcies were nearly a monthly occurrence. "It's no longer reorganization or even liquidation for these companies," bankruptcy lawyer Sally Henry told the *New York Times*, noting the disappearance of retailers such as the Bombay Company, Linens 'n Things, Circuit City, and Sharper Image. "In many cases, it's evaporation." In the same market that helped create the world's largest retailer, consumerism was in contraction. The International Council of Shopping Centers, a leading retail trade organization, estimated that overall store closures increased 25 percent from 2007 to 2008.

"We have to find a way to help these companies because they're our lifeblood," says Mark Hunter. "If we can't find ways, we're going to be in big trouble pretty quickly."

John Fleming, Gallup's chief scientist, concurs. Wal-Mart's fate, to a surprising degree, is our fate too. "The retail economy *is* the economy; there is no such thing as a [separate] industrial economy and retail economy," he says. "Everything is interconnecting and one move changes all the dynamics for all the others. And the fact is that we're now connected to markets offshore, so what happens in China tomorrow directly affects us, from currency fluctuations to energy."

The sub-prime mortgage crisis that began in 2006 is a perfect example of the new risks posed by deeper, more global interdependence, says Fleming. Even though experts predicted the mortgage crisis years in advance, discount home financing reduced consumer equity, which in turn eroded consumer credit and spending. When complex derivatives were sold on that debt, the cumulative effect was crushing: 8 to 10 million American foreclosures by 2009 and 2 million negative-equity homeowners in Britain by 2010. It's chilling proof of how complex modern economies can fail quickly.

"I think our first big test arrived with trouble in the home finance business," says Fleming. "[It's] a perfect storm, where people just can't afford to keep the consumer economy going anywhere because it is fuelled by credit, not real assets." By 2009 at least $8 trillion had been lost as a result of the credit crisis, which caused an expected $60 billion reduction in overall consumer spending, a loss that the leading retailers take very personally.

Here in Arizona, the mood surrounding Castro-Wright's keynote presentation is sometimes bittersweet: not long after assuming the top position in the economies of the world, retailers also inherited a whole host of problems and issues that are much bigger, and well beyond their ability to control. Specialists like John Fleming are here to help merchants wring new value and customers out of declining markets. And the lessons of a humbled Wal-Mart have not gone unnoticed. "This is the engine of the whole economy," Fleming says. "Look at the auto industry and at housing and at all these sectors of our economy that are so critical to driving consumer spending. Those people are feeding money into the Wal-Marts and into all these other companies, our retail space. It is going to be interesting."

Outside the conference hall, golfers tee up in the hot Arizona sun. Because we're near Tucson, gateway city to the largest continual wave of illegal migration in the world, Central American migrants are often holed up in the rocky hills above the golf resort, having travelled north from

Mexico in search of better wages. With our oasis of air conditioning, concierge service, and ice water in the middle of their escape route, it's an unwitting convergence of today's service economy. Between Castro-Wright's $7.3 million annual compensation package and the average income for an Arizona farm labourer, it's a wage differential of about 3,470 percent within a few hundred metres.

Thousands of migrants pass this way every few weeks, navigating the deadly Sonoran Desert in the dark. Thousands more never make it across, deported by border patrols, succumbing to heat exhaustion, or killed by thieves who roam the desert. All have bypassed the low-wage maquiladoras at the Mexican border that make affordable textiles and electronics for many of the retailers represented by Castro-Wright and his audience. After surviving the Arizonan desert, many migrants wind up outside a Home Depot or Wal-Mart somewhere else in North America, watching shoppers come and go, waiting for cash labour jobs.

Wal-Mart's newest motto – "Save Money, Live Better" – explains a lot about why so many different people arrive at big-box malls every day with enough optimism to return again the following week. Shoppers aspire to save more, while migrants are here to live better, and vice-versa. It also underlines the scale of our gambit in the twenty-first century: *can* we save more and live better?

The Fall of the Mall

It used to be the world's largest shopping mall. Opened in 1981, the West Edmonton Mall was the ultimate in destination shopping, proffering an indoor roller coaster, an ice rink, and a water park, as well as more than eight hundred stores in a single enclosed space. Before big-box stores ruled the landscape, the enclosed mall was North America's retail mainstay, featuring large department stores surrounded by smaller outlets, food courts, and specialty shops. Over the course of major expansions during the 1980s and 1990s, the West Edmonton Mall, or WEM, aggregated the contents of several big-city regional malls and added a fantasy hotel, pirate ship, and mini-golf course.

More than anything, it was a statement of optimism – that somehow people might travel hundreds or even thousands of miles to the world's largest mall and the world's largest parking lot, set in a suburb of the

author photo

The very first Old Navy outlet still operates at 280 Metro, the world's first known big-box mall, in Colma, California.

snowy prairie city of Edmonton. Despite its cold, remote location, shoppers converged anyway, and for twenty-three years the WEM defended its world's-largest title against up-and-comers such as the Mall of America in Bloomington, Minnesota. It was during these last two decades of the twentieth century that jobs disappeared offshore, household debt boomed, and Western economies hedged their future on consumer-driven growth. Like Sam Walton's legendary ascent from small-time Arkansas discounter to global retail kingpin, the unlikely success of a massive retail theme park on the northern fringe of urban North America was testament to what seemed to be unlimited growth potential for the shopping economy.

Yet by the mid-2000s the West Edmonton Mall was already a shadow of its former self, its attractions faded and downsized, its original store count atrophied by 25 percent. The mall's illustrious submarine ride, replete with live dolphins, had been replaced by bumper boats; vacant spaces left by closed movie theatres were filled in by a skateboard park and a paintball gaming area. Large parts of the mall still retained its original 1980s motif of chintzy glass and mirrors, while others had devolved into a sort of Franken-mall, with cobbled-together plumbing fixes in the bathrooms, broken tiles on its foundations and floors, and a tired, neglected amusement park. Vacancies littered the various shopping areas, and there were less desirable additions: head shops, dollar stores, and adult erotica outlets.

As supercentres and big-box "power centres" emerged during the 1990s, traditional shopping centres declined, leaving behind a growing number of deserted regional malls. Under the pressure of Wal-Mart, the hard edge of consumerism emerged, as factors like global competition, distribution networks, and aggressive discounting trumped pirate ships, aquariums, and vacation shopping. Stores became leaner, highly dispersed, and retail itself became riskier and more chaotic.

Consequently, shopping and gambling converged in the twenty-first century, turning places like Las Vegas into shopping destinations and, more deeply, turning consumerism into an act of embodied risk. Indeed, one of the WEM's busiest areas is the Palace Casino, a modest two-storey slots-and-tables establishment with a stucco and neon front that looks out over the mall's vast parking lot. There's a payday-loan storefront inside the mall across from the casino, as well as a banking machine. Inside it's like any other casino: stoic players at tables and machines, joylessly handing over their hard-earned cash for a chance at a modest windfall. Among shoppers out in the mall, it's the same thing: a dutiful yet dour observance of shopping, dispassionate consumers wandering in a landscape of diminishing rewards.

This relentless churn of people, places, and products is endemic to service economies – and to retail in particular. Employees come and go. Malls are created and destroyed as a matter of commerce. While the WEM was built as a permanent attraction, its decline was precipitated by scores of big-box stores in the surrounding area, run by chains that regularly close their own stores and reopen down the street if they can capture extra sales or savings in the process. In 2009, for example, Wal-Mart announced that it was closing six Sam's Clubs in Canada while opening twenty-six new supercentres. Wal-Mart is famous for such a strategy, to the frustration of many business associations and municipal governments, which rightly charge that local economies suffer – especially when millions in development subsidies are granted. Really, what kind of business perpetually and systematically liquidates its own infrastructure?

Some say it all started in Colma, California. Colma is a strange little micro-city on the edge of San Francisco that boasts more dead residents than living – seventeen different cemeteries operate within its tiny 2.2-square-mile footprint. Here, just off Interstate 280 and sandwiched between the Woodlawn and Greenlawn cemeteries, is the root of modern retail: 280 Metro Center, a nondescript open-air mall launched in 1986 that eventually became known as the world's first power centre, or big-box mall.

Undeterred by the 1.5 million dead people that surround 280 Metro, a stream of shoppers moves in and out of cars, carrying bags, children, strollers. A single fast-food outlet, a drive-through McDonald's, appears to be favoured by both local police and teens. Contractors and handypeople haul drywall and lumber from the nearby Home Depot, while steady traffic at the Starbucks inside Barnes and Noble serves as the mall's social centre.

In other words, 280 Metro looks much like any other open-air shopping mall in North America: a ring of rectangular buildings around a huge parking lot. There's no commemorative plaque or museum here, unlike at Sam Walton's first variety store in Bentonville, Walton's Five and Dime, which was long ago converted into a shrine to Walton's humble beginnings, replete with the founder's pickup truck and other sacred memorabilia. The banal stuccoed façade of Colma's big-box mall is actually much more relevant: in spite of the zealous tributes to Chairman Sam, 280 Metro is the true face of bargaineering today, the front lines of our retail economy.

The power centre ushered in the retail surge of the 1990s by featuring "category-killer," stores such as Office Depot, PetSmart, and Best Buy, which ably destroyed local competition through superior prices and selection. In Colma's case, Home Depot, Bed & Bath, Nordstrom, and Old Navy collectively anchor the mall; by erecting a semicircle of these mini-warehouses, 280 Metro dominates all retail within a ten-mile radius. It is effective because it is convenient and reflects high consumer demand for bargains: over 70 percent of merchants here are category killers, all of whom offer some degree of discount.

Merritt Sher stumbled upon this simple but powerful formula in the mid-1980s. The veteran developer, who is credited with numerous revitalization projects across the United States, recalls the beginnings of 280 Metro as an experiment designed to bring together independent merchants, not to develop a powerful new retail weapon. "We had known Home Depot, Bed & Bath, Trader Joe's as independent retailers," he explains. "So we clustered a half-dozen stores and called it a promotional centre."

Back in the 1980s, 280 Metro was a strange experiment in a world that was defined by large indoor destination malls anchored by department stores such as Sears and JCPenney. "It seemed unthinkable to people back then that we could build an uncovered shopping centre at an interstate off-ramp," says Sher. "It began as specialty retail, but it evolved. It was just something ready to happen."

At the time, large regional malls were always attached to one or two major department or grocery stores, but as bargains began to drive the economy, shoppers increasingly grew frustrated with having to hike extra distances through enclosed malls to get at products. Sher's experiment with clustered independent retailers began to accelerate as those independents became national, then multinational. As companies like Wal-Mart, Costco, and Target grew, power centres became our dominant retail form in the early 1990s. By 1993, for example, sixteen new power centres opened in the U.S., compared to only four major new malls. By 2007 not a single enclosed mall was being developed, while an estimated sixty to seventy had opened each year during the 1980s.

Sher sees this kind of major change in retail as an evolution. "Thirty years ago, a store like Woolworth's had all these category-killer stores under one roof: it was called the department store," he says, explaining how retail deconstructed itself during the twentieth century. "Our original power centre didn't have discount stores; it was strictly independent and specialty. But after a while it became a combination of new things, and we define it now as having the discount component."

The big box proved to be an ideal meeting ground for consumers and the global supply chain. Consequently, Sher's experiment in independent retailing spelled the demise of the spacious covered mall that defined mid-century North America. Despite the modernist aspirations of traditional enclosed malls – with their fountains, food courts, and arching glass-covered gallerias – convenience and price-cutting ultimately prevailed, stripping retail down to its bare essentials. Ironically, as shopping became more important within both national and international economies, our retail landscapes became more nondescript: retail boxes with glass doors, a parking lot, and container-loads of product arriving around the back. Where Gruen's (and America's) first climate-controlled mall was heralded as a "pleasure dome with parking" by *Time* in 1956, Colma's 280 Metro saw no such fanfare upon its 1986 launch – although Sher joked at the time that Metro's adjacent cemeteries made it easy to "shop till you drop." By 2006 more than half of all purchases were being made in retail environments under 200,000 square feet – big-box stores, supercentres, neighbourhood malls – as opposed to large regional malls and megamalls.

At Colma one can witness the very apex of retail evolution and not even recognize it, because even now the format faces its own troubles. The mid-size retailers that populate these environments are the ones at greatest risk and will bear the brunt of economic hard times long before Wal-Mart passes into history. At 280 Metro, for example, home goods retailer Bed Bath & Beyond suffered share devaluation of as much as 40 percent in 2007, and double-digit losses. Anchor store Home Depot saw a 24 percent drop in profits in 2006–07, when $1.4 billion in sales simply disappeared; by January 2009 it had laid off seven thousand workers amid sinking revenues. Nearby, Starbucks has had its own well-publicized troubles, pronouncing the late 2000s the weakest run in the company's four-decade history: its share values depreciated by 50 percent, and 2008 saw layoffs of one thousand employees and store closures surpassing six hundred.

As for the bargain traders convening in Las Vegas who worry about the fate of globalization, stakes are high here in Colma. Poorly disguised warehouses like these convene a great bulk of consumer sales across the developed world. Like it or not, the big-box mall has become the main-street economy in many towns and cities – and what happens in Colma most definitely matters nearly everywhere else.

In the shadow of the San Bruno Mountains, you can occasionally detect crematory smoke from the adjacent cemeteries wafting above Colma's mall. But the rotten-egg smell isn't from the dead people. Across the road from 280 Metro stands a Home Depot that was built on one of San Francisco's largest dumps, the Junipero Serra Landfill. An enclosed gas flare burns off methane created by twenty-five years' worth of rotting garbage from deep beneath the store, reducing the possibility of an explosion or subterranean bubble. This means that on any given day, big-box shoppers are breathing trace amounts of either human ash or gasified garbage – yesteryear's consumers and products from across the San Francisco peninsula.

Graves, garbage, and shopping malls certainly haven't been bad for Colma. In 2006, for example, an acre of land here was worth $2 million and a $20-million casino had been proposed near the Serbian cemetery. Think of Colma as a pioneer city for the twenty-first century: relying on service-sector industries such as retail and burial, it has never manufactured anything of note, and its 1,200 living residents enjoy free cable TV, paid for by the never-ending tax revenue generated by the town's post-industrial business mix – as long as people keep shopping and dying, that is. Having a twenty-four-hour Home Depot around the corner, built on a mountain of garbage, is an added bonus.

"It's great to be alive in Colma!" is the town's unofficial motto.

More like, "Coming to a town near you."

Progress Is Price Destruction

It's another hot day in Tucson. Outside, golfers continue to tee up on an absurdly green fairway, surrounded by giant saguaro cactuses and sun-baked creosote bushes. Heat stroke is a common golf injury here. The yellow desert rolls away into the distance, all the way to the boundary with Mexico, where the U.S. military has recently been deployed in an attempt to stem the incessant human tide flooding the border. As golfers work on their handicaps and migrants try to outrun Blackhawk helicopters, the world's leading retailers reconvene indoors to agonize about their future.

It's survival of the fittest all the way around, and anyone looking for reassurance will be disappointed. "In a Wal-Mart world, you're either predator or prey," says Michael Bergdahl, point-blank. "It doesn't matter if you are a lion or a gazelle, you and your team had better be up and running every morning."

Bergdahl doesn't work for Wal-Mart anymore, but he served under Sam Walton as "Director of People" during the leader's final years, and has since carved out a career as a public intellectual for a company that often refuses to speak for itself. The kill-or-be-killed sentiments are classic Bentonville. For a corporation that's often been associated with Christian fundamentalism, one still pervaded by Sam Walton's Presbyterian notions of "servant leadership," there's a tremendous amount of evolutionary theory bandied about in its boardrooms. Wal-Mart's rise is usually attributed to this brutal Darwinian streak that redefined discounting and enabled retail's transformation into a major economic force. Wal-Mart, of course, sat atop this food chain. "Walton focused on how little he could get for every item as opposed to how much he could charge," says Bergdahl. "This was a major change in its day."

It's more than just survival of the fittest. Wal-Mart didn't become humankind's largest-ever company simply on hustle and competitive drive. If that were the case, shopkeepers and bazaar sellers from Korea to Pakistan would be running the economy. Contrary to popular belief, Sam Walton did not invent the new economy. We live in a world where if Wal-Mart didn't already exist, someone would have invented something similar.

History suggests that discounters inevitably rise and fall during times of societal transformation. Frank Woolworth, for example, built his empire on North America's first major wave of rural dispossession and urbanization; discounting heralded the great wave of industrialization that was ultimately consolidated during the twentieth century's world wars. For Woolworth's, the rise of the industrial economy provided not only hordes of new customers but also a degree of affordability, selection, and technological advancement. These ultimately turned Woolworth's five-and-dime stores into a global phenomenon, a Wal-Mart prototype before container ships and Internet communications. Pioneer mass merchants such as Woolworth's and Sears were an expression of the industrial age; in turn, early bargaineering helped accelerate industrialization and consumerism across North America and Europe. "Branded, standardized products came to represent and embody the new networks and systems of factory production and mass distribution," writes historian Susan Strasser. "Formerly *customers* – purchasing the objects of daily life from familiar craftspeople and storekeepers – Americans became *consumers*."

In other words, major social and economic shifts inspire discounting, and in turn, bargains expedite change. For example, supermarkets emerged out of the Great Depression of the 1930s as a strategic response to rising consumerism and a mass desire for discounts. "Entrepreneurs understood the new conditions of a consumer culture in crisis: a population accustomed to branded goods, increasingly equipped with automobiles and refrigerators, and looking for low prices as the Depression deepened," writes Strasser. And by the 1950s an estimated half of all American grocery purchases were in supermarkets.

Bargains suggest an alternative account of human progress: great historical watersheds are actually quantum economic shifts structured around vanquishing costs. Everything from energy supplies to consumerism to colonialism has revolved around price destruction and realizing new value through new processes, such as global sourcing and assemblage. For example, steam engine efficiencies increased fifty times between 1700 and 1930, unleashing tremendous wealth and savings potential. Bread-making became much more affordable with the advent of automated mills perfected in the early 1800s, which helped both household finances and family nutrition. Productivity gains and technological innovations have slashed prices and displaced jobs ever since, especially in today's world of low-cost technology, where DVD players and iPods have become affordable in ways that few ever predicted. "Wal-Mart is the logical end point and the future of the economy in a society whose pre-eminent value is getting the best deal," writes economist Robert Reich.

Progress is price destruction. Many have bemoaned our big-box world, blaming the likes of Sam Walton for causing the world's perils by selling cheap stuff en masse, outsourcing jobs, and squandering valuable resources. Yet today's bargain economy stands at the apex of an industrial–economic evolution that began in the nineteenth century with vulcanized rubber, early crude oil markets, and the combustion engine. Big-box stores, globalized production, and container ships are not an anomaly. In fact, bargains represent the pinnacle – if not the perfection – of twentieth-century capitalism, with all of its creative and destructive capacity.

In North America, business empires have traditionally been founded upon energy, transport, and technology. The five richest barons of industry (measured by wealth as a percentage of the economy) show a clear pattern. John D. Rockefeller created Standard Oil when he was thirty-one; he would eventually control as much as 90 percent of North America's oil markets. Cornelius Vanderbilt commanded steamships and railroads and eliminated competition by fiercely (and sometimes illegally) undercutting prices. John Jacob Astor, pioneer fur trader; Stephen Girard, shipping magnate; and Bill Gates, of course, round out the five richest-ever, with Gates's invention of MS-DOS helping to launch the global IT boom.

The retailers that rule today's service economy constitute a different order of business: Wal-Mart encompasses energy, transport, *and* technology. From the embodied energy within petrochemical plastics to the logistics technologies and steel containers that deliver the plastic to suburban stores, the modern discounter incorporates the twentieth century's leading industries with surprising effectiveness. As Michael Bergdahl frequently reminds clients and audiences around the world, retail and wholesale trade are too narrow a description for the modern mega-retailer. "Wal-Mart is not a merchandise-driven company," he says. "Wal-Mart is a logistics and retail-driven company that also has retail stores. Everything at Wal-Mart is a commodity."

Wal-Mart accomplished its rise to power by pushing prices *lower* than anyone ever before. Other barons of industry did precisely the opposite: oil companies conspired to fix prices and destroy public transit systems during the first half of the twentieth century; Microsoft famously pushed the limits of antitrust law and was fined 899 million euros by the European Commission in 2004; and railroads are still being accused of price-fixing.

Wal-Mart's pricing may be populist, almost egalitarian, but its business practices are ingeniously monolithic. Anything inside Wal-Mart's circle of influence, from chasing off union organizers in parking lots to launching stores in rural China, is subject to its monopoly-like grip. Suppliers, manufacturers, and transport companies have been trained and disciplined to serve the retailer's supply chain vision.

Manufacturers have faced hardship and sometimes bankruptcy in attempting to keep up with ongoing retailer and consumer demand for discounts. It's an unprecedented shift in business history – the lowly discounter now holds all the power, enjoying the kind of business leverage that rivals OPEC in the world of crude oil. Wholesale negotiations with suppliers are nothing short of ruthless; for example, Wal-Mart requires an annual drop in suppliers' prices or a quality upgrade, most of which is passed on to consumers. The discount squeeze means that vendors must be as relentless at managing their own costs. They need, in fact, to turn themselves into miniature versions of Wal-Mart if they hope to access the one-fifth of all retail sales that Wal-Mart controls.

Irrelevant to all but the most curious shoppers, this kind of deep re-engineering of commerce has created billions in productivity, savings, and new revenue. The ongoing adoption of RFID tagging – essentially a wireless bar-code system – will create, executives claim, an estimated $8.35 billion in annual savings for the company. And by using its supplier-integrated supply chain, Wal-Mart's efforts to reduce packaging between 2008 and

2013 will save $3.4 billion. Much of this kind of systemic change happens on the backs of suppliers and partners to whom Wal-Mart cheaply outsourced some of its greatest efficiency and productivity gains.

"Companies like Wal-Mart make money on money because it finds ways of carrying as little inventory as possible," explains Bergdahl. Wal-Mart looked at its expenses more than a decade ago and decided that it was warehousing too many products for too long, thereby creating long periods where its money was tied up in inventory. Instead it invented a continuously replenishing supply chain in which manufacturers technically own their products almost up to the point of sale. "Wal-Mart doesn't have warehouses anymore. They want as little inventory as possible to ensure sixty-day credit terms – it now pays big time to carry only as much inventory as they need in the store." It seems like a minor detail, but Wal-Mart makes millions by not actually paying many suppliers for in-store products until the customer makes a purchase. In this way, manufacturers and suppliers increasingly assume much of the risk and the costs associated with owning unsold product.

And while traditional corporate giants like General Motors and Dell increasingly became shell companies reliant on third-party contracts, Wal-Mart itself became bigger and bigger. It is a bastion of vertical integration in a world of dissolution. "For Wal-Mart, it is still cheaper to build than to buy, and to employ workers rather than subcontract them," notes labour historian Nelson Lichtenstein. "The same technologies and cost imperatives that have led to the decomposition and decentralization of so many other institutions, including government, health care, entertainment, and domestic manufacturing, have enabled Wal-Mart and other retail distribution companies to vastly enhance their own managerial span of control." Or as Bergdahl likes to note, "the thermostats in every single one of the Wal-Mart stores are controlled from Bentonville: the manager doesn't even control the temperature of his own store."

In some ways Wal-Mart's massive success is still a mystery, even to itself. In 2009, Wal-Mart's sales were still roughly quadruple those of all the top ten American department stores combined: Sears, JCPenney, Nordstrom, and Macy's, among others.

Wal-Mart as the world's largest company and world's largest employer really shouldn't be possible. In economics, the theory of the firm suggests that there are practical upper limits to the size of any corporation, mainly because of inefficiencies, costs, and/or managerial failures that inevitably limit growth. The firm simply grows too large to manage, and the humans inside it lack the information and controls to deal with the increased complexity. As General Motors outsourced and diversified, it became smaller, at least in terms of its managerial reach. Wal-Mart has defied these trends, and it has also become the focus of new economic theory, since its success still defies convention.

Wal-Mart is forcing us to question much of what we know about capitalism. Not since the beginnings of the age of commercialism in the seventeenth century – an age of monolithic companies such as the Dutch East India Company that enjoyed state-level powers – has a company so globally influential and powerful existed. "Wal-Mart is a living breathing behemoth of a top-down corporation despite the assertion, found in fashionable management theory, that such companies are dead dinosaurs," writes management professor James Hoopes. "Wal-Mart shows that high technology is fostering its own form of the huge, highly centralized corporation run with ruthless, hierarchical efficiency."

This is how discounting is reinventing capitalism: not by sheer force, a singular commodity, or a unique invention, but adaptively, with puritanical commitment to price. It's what Castro-Wright calls "disruptive innovation." This sea change is still occurring, a shift that recalls Henry Ford, the champion and innovator of North America's industrial golden age. Ford's factory line integrated process and efficiency to create high-value products that helped underwrite twentieth-century industrial progress. Ford's innovation in manufacturing, marketing, and distribution – a new system of commerce – changed our economy forever. And where crude oil, the assembly line, and the combustion engine were the tools of Ford's success, offshoring, consumer credit, and logistics are the raw materials of post-industrial powerhouses like Wal-Mart, which have used these resources to attain profits and scale that are rivalled only by global energy giants such as Exxon Mobil.

Like Henry Ford, bargaineers sometimes show a utopian streak. For all their Darwinist bluster, these merchant pioneers have frequently argued that consumerism can somehow be perfected, not unlike Mao Zedong's exhortations to perfect Chinese Communism. "If we work together, we'll lower the cost of living for everyone," Sam Walton famously claimed. "We'll give the world an opportunity to see what it's like to have a better life."

Unlike Ford and other manufacturers who created well-paying jobs for generations of Western consumers, Wal-Mart builds stores and sales, both of which have proven to be impermanent. Even its celebrated and reformed health-care coverage relies "heavily on the government and other employers to play a role," reported the *Washington Post* in 2009. "Despite revenue that is expected to exceed $400 billion for 2008, the company charges its low-wage workers a substantial portion of their income for medical coverage."

Post-industrial commerce is starting to look a lot like a frontier resource scramble. Are global discounters like Wal-Mart systematically mining our world for opportunity? As a resource, the spending power of Western consumers has largely been tapped, so harvesting customers displaced from failing and bankrupt competitors is the next frontier. In 2009, Deutsche Bank identified "$9.6 billion of sales up for grabs from stores that are closing and potentially $17.8 billion more from weak stores."

Wal-Mart found success through technology, company culture, and managerial excellence. But for the rest of us, the company's innovation invokes a previous century: dominance, extraction, and depletion. It's a commercial pattern that more than resembles a natural resource company. Check the growing tally of ghost malls and idle big-box stores around the world. The disconnect between local and global economic interests is resulting in empty malls and abandoned commercial zones. Likewise, once Exxon is finished with Nigerian oil, don't expect them to stick around and support community economic development projects; likewise Total in Burma and China's state oil companies in Angola and Sudan. The downside of globalization is that it made resource imperialism applicable to nearly everyone.

If you don't like Wal-Mart's oddly colonial style of business, then tough. If critics want to take the company on, "they need to bring their lunch, because we're not going to lay down," boasted former CEO Lee Scott in a 2005 interview, while under fire for exporting jobs and destroying local business. "We've got nothing to apologize for."

"After all, the economic change [that] Wal-Mart represents creates a handful of losers even as the vast majority of ordinary Americans gain," argued Scott. "But at the end of the day, when someone builds a better mousetrap, it's not the American way to deny average folks the chance to improve their lives. The horse and buggy industry wasn't permitted to crush the car."

New Kinds of Change

Why now? Wal-Mart achieved its quantum leap from national retailer to global kingpin during the second half of the 1990s, even though it had been operating for decades, and discounters have been with us since the late nineteenth century. The speed of this transformation is notable: it was only in 1995 that Wal-Mart became the world's largest retailer. That was the same year that the Fortune 500 included retailers in its listings for the first time, and by 2002 Wal-Mart was claiming the top spot as the world's largest company by revenue. In 2006 Americans spent $2.25 trillion at shopping centres, roughly equal to the gross domestic product of Germany, and 12.6 million shopping-centre employees represented nearly a tenth of America's urban work force.

The speed of Wal-Mart's consolidation suggests the kind of major change that many scholars ascribe to the Industrial Revolution, especially the second Industrial Revolution, a period of development during the late 1800s that, among other things, first introduced mass-produced consumer goods. And while the technology of today's bargain revolution is not entirely new, as in the Industrial Revolution, there has arguably been a delay in the impact of many twentieth-century inventions that deferred this transformation until the end of the century. Andrew Atkeson and Patrick Kehoe of the Federal Reserve Bank of Minneapolis described this as "a productivity paradox, a surprisingly long delay between the increase in the pace of technical change and the increase in the growth rate of measured productivity." Productivity in this case is not just machines and factories, but the accelerated output of a global system of production and consumption that defines Western service-sector economies.

In other words, the advent of electricity, the combustion engine, petroleum refining, petrochemicals, telephones, and indoor plumbing did not immediately change the world. Similarly, more recent innovations such as the container ship, the computer, the shopping mall, and the credit card – all established in the 1940s and 1950s – only began to deliver their full impact during the 1990s, concurrent with the arrival of Wal-Mart and other retailers as global forces. It did not happen overnight, but once it gained momentum, the influence of Everyday Low Prices became profound. The late-1990s spike in America's trade imbalance, consumer debt levels, and Wal-Mart's employee and revenue growth – all of which doubled or tripled between 1995 and 2005 – underlines the accelerated growth of retail and wholesale trade within most developed countries. Daniel Bell may have coined the term *post-industrial society* in 1973, but it was our late-century discounting boom, technology, and finance bubble that brought it to fruition.

When this sort of accelerated transition does occur, it creates imbalances and unpredictable outcomes, the "disruptive change" that today's discount retailer attempts to engineer through outrageously low prices. The nature of this kind of change is not well understood. It is not technology-driven, but technology-dependent; it is not cyclical, but far from linear; governments and large companies figure prominently, but are nevertheless interdependent with workers and consumers from rural China to northern Canada.

The modern analogue to this kind of sudden systemic change is not economic but environmental. For example, much of our understanding of climate change, and its ecological and economic impacts, has mistakenly focused on gradual change, with the ongoing buildup of greenhouse gases in the atmosphere leading to an incremental increase in global temperatures. "This line of thinking, however, fails to consider another potentially disruptive climate scenario," writes Robert Gagosian, president of the Woods Hole Oceanographic Institution. "It ignores recent and rapidly advancing evidence that Earth's climate repeatedly has shifted abruptly and dramatically in the past, and is capable of doing so in the future."

NASA's top scientist of climate change, James Hansen, has been studying ocean–atmospheric interactions for decades in the interests of better understanding the past and future of radical modal change. It turns out that, like our closely linked economies of production and consumption, the planetary balance of climatic energy is much more interdependent and potentially volatile than originally thought. "Our climate has the potential for large rapid fluctuations," he writes in a landmark 2007 report. "Indeed, the Earth, and the creatures struggling to exist on the planet, have been repeatedly whipsawed between climate states."

Change can build up in the depths and then burst forth, moving rapidly. "The ocean's slow response delays [climate change] effects," writes Hansen. "But there is the danger of setting in motion a warming of the deep ocean that will lock in disastrous impacts which will unfold for future generations."

Like ecosystems, economies seek out equilibrium. On a planetary basis we observe this most elemental dynamic in the ocean–atmosphere mechanisms that Hansen and others predict may one day collapse. On a slightly smaller scale is the human-made attempt to conjoin Asia's hungry pool of workers and bargain-hungry Western consumers. And where there is disequilibrium, there is failure: a global economic slowdown marked alternately by overproduction and underconsumption in an environment of critical resource scarcity. Indeed, it will be through the bargain economy – specifically its dependence on container shipping, fossil fuels, coastal ports, and geopolitical stability – that the economic impact of climate change is first observed.

Volatility dominated global food and resource markets during the 2000s. From 2000 to 2006, for example, the United Nations observed a 278 percent increase in the price of mineral commodities and a 50 percent overall increase in the real prices of non-fuel commodities. In 2008, in the face of global incidence of malnutrition and food-based unrest, the U.N. reported that world food prices had reached the highest levels in thirty years – an increase of 83 percent since 2005. Most notably, Thai medium-quality rice, a global benchmark, more than doubled in price between 2007 and 2008.

Gone is the time when Western shoppers were not affected by the price of rice, petrochemicals, or steel. The mass production of cheap stuff shaped globalization as a force of convergence, connection, and interdependence. These connections also amplify market failure. For example, logistics experts at the Port of Los Angeles reported in 2008 that the cost of building a new container ship had increased nearly 50 percent, owing largely to price increases in steel and crude oil – cost increases that have been driven by China's double-digit economic growth and Western economies' reliance on consumption. These days, Korean shipyards, American SUVs, and Chinese factories increasingly compete for the same resources. Eventually this cost reaches the consumer: American toy manufacturers estimated that between 2006 and 2007 the cost of plastic went up 25 percent because of higher energy prices – even before crude hit US$100 a barrel – resulting in a 10 percent increase in the retail price of many toys.

Likewise, the cost of everything from plastic to factory labour climbed and fell and climbed again during the first decade of the twenty-first century, accelerated by new demand from developing countries. The price of copper – crucial to electronics, appliances, and home renovations – increased 400 percent between 2004 and 2008. The persistent though erratic increase of crude oil prices in recent years has especially led to questioning the future viability of a bargain-based world, since affordable energy, transport, and petrochemicals are essential to globalization. Chinese logistics costs as a percentage of product price were "up to 50 percent higher than in North America or Europe," even before the fuel-price spike of the late 2000s.

In other words, globalization both creates volatility and suffers its consequences. This is especially notable during periods of acute scarcity of essentials such as oil and rice, because disruptive change wears down the resilience of households, countries, and businesses, compromising their ability to weather difficulty without failure. And patterns of disruptive change, both economic and environmental, pose a threat to the highly refined version of globalization that Wal-Mart and its kin helped invent.

While Wal-Mart is able to prosper in an environment of economic decline, it cannot indefinitely survive a broader disruption of its core resources: affordable energy, logistics, labour, and consumers. As we've learned since the 1990s, very little is decoupled or independent in our world anymore.

As Thomas Homer-Dixon argues, "synchronous failure" may already be evident in our planet's troubled climatic, social, and economic systems. "In coming years, our societies won't face one or two major challenges at once, as usually happened in the past," he writes. "Instead, they'll face an alarming variety of problems – likely including oil shortages, climate change, economic instability, and mega-terrorism – all at the same time. . . . [B]loody social revolutions occur only when many pressures simultaneously batter a society that has weak political, economic, and civic institutions."

As global economies and global climate fall in and out of equilibrium, we experience volatility, strained coping mechanisms, and new patterns of change. What climate change also teaches us is that appearances are deceiving. The size and inertia of planetary energy systems create delayed impacts, as well as the possibility for remedial action. Things may look normal, but there is ultimately no way of knowing when modal change might cause even greater upheaval. The speed and scope of economic collapse are what surprised many people when the American economy suddenly shed 4.4 million jobs within four months in 2008–09. Globally, "the current pace of decline is breathtaking," said Robert Barbera, chief economist for the Investment Technology Group, in 2009. "We are now falling at a near record rate in the postwar period and there's been no change in the violent downward trajectory."

James Hansen argues that as we continue to chart new frontiers, it's likely at our own peril. During the current century we will discover what happens when the Arctic ice cap melts completely for six months of the year. And – not unrelated – can we still fill a Wal-Mart store with bargains when shipping costs quadruple and crude oil commands $200 a barrel?

"Civilization developed, and constructed extensive infrastructure, during a period of unusual climate stability, the Holocene, now almost 12,000 years in duration," writes Hansen. "That period is about to end."

The Problem of Value

Even in a world full of change, Wal-Mart still views itself as a catalyst. "How do you bring innovation that is disruptive?" Eduardo Castro-Wright asks the audience near the end of his talk at the Tucson retail summit. There is a pause. Nobody answers.

Disruptive innovation was the hallmark of the 1990s Wal-Mart revolution, but as long-term growth frontiers diminish, innovation is in short supply. Here in Tucson, retail true believers like Michael Bergdahl invoke Wal-Mart's talent for survival and adaptation, if only because the company has frequently been underestimated, most notably before its 2009 comeback. "Wal-Mart will continuously reinvent itself: it's not going to be the same business we saw last year," says Bergdahl. "Wal-Mart is a very nimble company. You'd think they'd be like an aircraft carrier and have difficulty turning, but they're more like a PT boat and can change very rapidly. Because change is a way of life at Wal-Mart."

Others, like Gallup's John Fleming, foresee a much more divisive future for consumerism, full of winners and losers. "I think we're in for a big comeuppance," says Fleming, "which is why it makes it more imperative to focus on ways to drive organic growth with relatively low costs, because technology improvements have [already] happened," referring to the gains of the 1990s retail boom.

"We'll see some incremental improvements in the future, but nothing like what we've seen to drive increased productivity," he says. For global retailers and manufacturers, many obvious innovations have already been implemented. In other words, for discounters, much of the easy growth and profits is over. "Technology productivity has flattened," says Fleming. "The cost reductions through quality improvements and supply chain management are going to flatline. Where are we going to get the next frontier of incremental value? It has to be in generating a greater price from products that we offer and increasing the productivity in the people who work for us."

Paradoxically, in the service of bargains we are having trouble creating value. Even with Wal-Mart's claim to be creating immense value – an estimated 3 percent decline in American consumer prices between 1985 and 2006 – our economies are full of bankruptcy, poverty and worry. Why? One reason is that while bargains have proven themselves indispensable, they present a fundamental contradiction. Not only have bargains helped to turn many Western jurisdictions into shopping economics, but the bargains themselves are endangered by their own success. Where past business models found ways to create value out of manufacturing, marketing, or technological innovation, the core mission of the modern bargaineer is in fact value destruction: undercutting competition, shedding profit, paying suppliers less.

Wal-Mart collects only half as much in profit for every dollar of merchandise sold as the average American department store. In a world obsessed with price, Wal-Mart's competitive advantage is the profit it willingly gives up in order to sell more. Yet the difference between Wal-Mart's 3.2 cents profit per dollar sold and the 6.1 cents collected by general merchandise stores in 2005 is one kind of value destruction. Any business that wants to survive within markets dominated by this company must give up revenues just to stay competitive.

In many ways, Wal-Mart has merely been fulfilling its destiny, and discounting's pervasive race to the bottom is proof of its influence and success. "A successful discount strategy implies value destruction," argue business professors Michael Anderson and Flemming Poulfelt in their 2006 book,

Discount Business Strategy. Perhaps more important, they observe that "the potential value destruction stemming from the introduction of a discount strategy is unstoppable once the disruption commences." As examples they cite successful discounters Skype, IKEA, and Costco, all of which redefined their respective markets through radically disruptive pricing. "A disruptive strategy, once released into the business world, could have far-reaching consequences [such as] bankruptcy and [industries] falling prey to the disruptive nature of the discount strategy and the value destruction that followed in its wake." In other words, discounting is proving to be a grand, global-scale experiment in production and consumption, connectivity and interdependence.

The question of value is critical for the twenty-first century, not only in terms of market failure and resource crisis but also previously undervalued aspects such as carbon emissions and local economic security. "The problem of value must always hold the pivotal position," economist Joseph Schumpeter argued, "as the chief tool of analysis in any pure [economic] theory." It was back in 1942, during another period of social and economic upheaval, that Schumpeter published his now-famous thesis on creative destruction. He viewed capitalism not as a series of rational consumer choices but as an evolutionary firestorm. This "perennial gale of creative destruction," he wrote, is frequently misunderstood: "the problem that is usually being visualized is how capitalism administers existing structures, whereas the relevant problem is how it creates and destroys them."

Perhaps not coincidentally, Schumpeter paid close attention to retail industries and the greater service sector, which by mid-century had already begun to resemble their modern-day incarnations. With eerie precision he describes Wal-Mart's organizational, logistics, and productive assault on traditional commerce. What "keeps the capitalist engine in motion [is] new consumer goods, . . . new methods of production, or transportation, [and] new forms of industrial organization that capitalist enterprise creates," he writes in *Capitalism, Socialism and Democracy.* "In the case of retail trade the competition that matters arises not from additional shops of the same type, but from the department store, the chain store, the mail-order house and the super market, which are bound to destroy those pyramids sooner or later."

Or as Bergdahl succinctly puts it, "There's no intrinsic value at Wal-Mart to any particular product; the value is about the lowest possible prices." With this simple aim the retailer disrupted its market to great advantage and exploited the ensuing destruction of its competition, yet the impact of discounting has continued.

Today the result is not only low prices but a marketplace that cycles through products at an accelerated rate. One 2007 study examined an average of 650,000 UPCs (universal product codes) annually over nearly a decade; more than 80 percent of the products available in 2003 did not exist in 1994, representing an enormous volume of discrete items that were, in Schumpeterian fashion, created and destroyed as a matter of commerce. Of those 650,000 product codes, which represent roughly 40 percent of America's consumer price index, between 1999 and 2003 more than 60 percent had been discounted to the seller's minimum reservation price. In other words, the majority of the products were sold at the very lowest price that retailers and manufacturers could tolerate.

This is how your local outlet store and discount fashion boutique and online liquidators like Woot.com manage to move so much product so cheaply: the global supply chain is perpetually jettisoning surplus goods. Even with this waste and churn, many global supply chains are operating on dangerously low margins, some just one bad deal away from collapse – as evidenced by the epidemic of retail bankruptcies from 2008 onward.

"One of the major trends of retailing is this relentless cycle which turns stuff into commodities," explains Eric Arnold, distinguished professor at the Terry J. Lundgren Center for Retailing. "And when things turn into commodities, of course you get into a price race, which is always a price race to the bottom. And so hard discounting, as it infiltrates and prolifer-ates and expands, drives more things into a commodity space – that drives down everybody's origins or reduces margins. That is a problem."

Wal-Mart has been rightly commended for some of its efforts to reduce pollution, waste, and greenhouse gas emissions. It has expanded its social and health policies. Yet the company is still as dedicated as ever to creating massive change and maximum sales. Its mission remains to sell more cheap stuff than anyone else, even if it does so using less energy per sale. "No other instrument is perceived with such acuity by the customer as the price," David Bosshart writes in *Cheap*. "And no other instrument is more exciting when it is wielded as a weapon."

And if Wal-Mart and other global discounters continue to control market leadership in the twenty-first century, what does that mean for everyone else?

Retail Economy, Survivor Edition

Whoever would have thought that a stay at a $400-a-night golf resort could be so gruelling? In this air-conditioned vacuum, time stands still as top executives drone on under artificial lights amid stale coffee. The most barren strip mall begins to hold appeal as the world's leading retailers grind out presentations about their accomplishments and future strategies.

And this is the future, or at least one version of it. Some, such as retail icon Terry Lundgren of Macy's, obfuscate weak sales figures by talking about "the relentless pursuit of newness" and boast of spending as much as $1 million per store on fitting rooms. "Great leaders are talent multipliers," says the photogenic Lundgren, smiling for the cameras. Investors were not impressed: Macy's stock dropped nearly 40 percent between 2007 and 2008. By the time real trouble hit, late in 2008, Macy's was offering aggressive copycat discounts, much to the detriment of is profits, which had sunk by 59 percent in early 2009. ("Macy's is in huge trouble," warned J.P. Morgan analyst Charles Grom in 2008. "The only way Macy's will make it is for someone to take it private and spend a few billion dollars re-merchandising the store.")

Others, such as Robert Eckert, CEO of Mattel, outline calculated plans for children's "lifestyle products" that sell "consistent emotional connections and turn shoppers into diehard fans." Not many months later, Mattel would recall more than 20 million lead-tainted toys, many sourced from China, which produces about 65 percent of the company's products; the company had closed its last American factory in 2002. "We love Christmas Day at Mattel," jokes the CEO, displaying his new diversified Barbie collection. In 2007 Eckert would claim a 68 percent pay increase, totalling $12.2 million, despite Mattel's financial losses and damaged reputation. By 2009 Mattel's profits had dropped nearly 50 percent.

One of the few retail honchos willing to talk is Peter Abbott, a Wal-Mart manager whom I manage to collar just before Castro-Wright's presentation. He admits that his industry faces major challenges. "You can't please everybody," he says, "but we can make 80 percent of the people happy by [trying] to do what we do right."

True to form, Wal-Mart is hoping to engineer its way through the great environmental, social, and economic challenges of the twenty-first century. "We're looking seriously at sustainability – reducing plastic, cardboard packaging – because that's also going to give us the possibility of shipping twenty more cases for the price of one," says Abbott. "We're going to have to understand what makes each store tick, because every time we turn our inventory one full time in a store, we get seven-tenths profit. So we have to keep those turns going, keep that inventory moving."

But Abbott doesn't sugar-coat the obvious and immediate facts: slipping consumer fortunes and an oversaturated market. "It's a tough situation [for people] with rent going up, utilities, gas prices," he says. "You've got to bring your A game to work every day. You can't have any misses."

A world dependent on shipping and shopping has created new opportunities, new connections – and new problems. The dark side of discounting scares even Wal-Mart. When Eduardo Castro-Wright invokes "innovation that is disruptive," he's not wishing for his own firm's success to be hijacked by dollar stores, unsustainable price competition, and consumer failure. Yet as Schumpeter predicted, the forces unleashed by innovation frequently end in destruction. What many of his more famous free-market acolytes (such as housing-bubble champion and former U.S. Federal Reserve chair Alan Greenspan) failed to foresee is that not all market-driven destruction is creative or productive, especially as we enter a difficult period of deglobalization.

Bargains are not forever. Our access to cheap consumer credit, cheap shipping, cheap energy, and cheap offshore labour is ultimately tied to the fate of globalization during the twenty-first century. Accelerated by generational issues such as climate change, growing competition for natural resources, and chronic underdevelopment, the end of cheap is not merely about price. As a highly distributed and interdependent economic mode, a troubled bargain economy threatens to undo many of the gains of globalization, especially the broad affordability of material goods that most national economies have become dependent upon.

It doesn't take much to sabotage this system. By late 2008, for example, the long-term possibility of a global cost/price spiral – multifactor inflation that threatens to gradually disable supply chains – had become clear: "Since 2002 the [U.S.] dollar has plunged by 30 percent against major world currencies," reported *Business Week*. "Wages in China are rising. [And] the cost of sending a 40-foot container from Shanghai to San Diego has soared by 150 per cent, to $5,500, since 2000. If oil hits $200 a barrel, that could reach $10,000." Inflation abated during the global financial crisis, but by mid-2009, essentials like food and fuel were already on the rise again.

On one hand, our system of cheap manufacture is a multiplier of value and affordability, one that uses critical innovations – rich labour markets, cheap logistics, bountiful energy, and easy consumer debt – to create plenitude and accessibility that, though far from perfect, is unprecedented in the history of humankind. Even in the developing world a new middle class has emerged from the manufacturing zones of Asia and Eastern Europe, and an estimated 500 million people were at least temporarily lifted out of poverty, mostly in China, India, and Southeast Asia, partly through the wealth redistribution effected by our singular drive to make more stuff cheaper.

But despite its many gifts, discounting is also a destabilizing force – the greenhouse gas of a consumer-driven economy – that is already helping to undo the past decade's gains. Westerners have focused on security concerns in recent years, and not without justification, but it is the humble bargain that is associated with some of the greatest long-term social, economic, and environmental issues of our time.

Yet ours is a world still highly dependent on cheap oil, container shipping, and endless plastic. In a Schumpeterian twist, the tough times of 2008 onward began to float the fortunes of the world's largest discounters. Consumers abandoned their Vegas dreams and lined up for rationed rice and generic prescription drugs at their local supercentre. Pioneer discounter IKEA reported record revenues in 2009, cutting 5,000 jobs in the process. With new profits and a rebounding share price, Wal-Mart enjoyed a sales bump as the consumer crisis began to crescendo. "Tough times are actually a good time for Wal-Mart," says Thomas M. Schoewe, Wal-Mart's chief financial officer.

Even as consumers flock to discount retailers during hard times, bargains push us further towards a profound correction in the distribution and price of some of our most valuable resources. Channelled by Wal-Mart, Home Depot, Carrefour, and untold millions of factory workers, our systems of production and consumption will change, sometimes violently.

Like the petroleum that greases our economy, affordable consumerism is proving to be unsustainable, a twentieth-century boon that, in the face of trade imbalances, consumer failure, and climate crisis, will eventually be depleted. This isn't some market-based correction, the kind of sudden crash that affects overvalued stocks and commodities. This could be a corrective on growth itself: the end of cheap production.

"How do I stay in front and derive value for consumers?" Castro-Wright asks his audience while searching around for his next flow chart. Again, nobody answers.

OUT OF THE

BARGAIN BASEMENT

CHINA CRISIS: THE END OF CHEAP LABOUR

A migrant worker falls asleep on the side of a road in rural Henan province, China.

Homecoming

North from Hong Kong's central Kowloon station, the train to mainland China snakes through the rolling hills of the New Territories, passing an array of factories, farms, and massive apartment blocks. The northern edge of Hong Kong is surprisingly lush and green, despite the urban density of its waterfront; small mountain parks, Confucian shrines, and hidden gardens all rush past as the express train hurtles towards the border. Despite Hong Kong's 1997 reunification with China, its northern frontier remains a tightly controlled zone. The playgrounds, markets, and apartment complexes of the New Territories give way to military bunkers, barbed wire, and army guard towers. This is the gateway to Shenzhen, Guangzhou's fastest-growing city, and it looks remarkably like a prison.

More than 160,000 people cross the Luohu district point of entry daily, a tide of businessmen, students, and workers funnelling through the armed checkpoint. Shenzhen connects tens of millions of Western consumers with an archipelago of southern China factories that produce the majority of our cheap merchandise. It is the epicentre of bargaineering in today's world. My pants, shirt, backpack, socks, and hat were all made in Guangzhou province, so arriving here isn't a journey so much as a homecoming.

The scale of activity in Shenzhen is one of the world's modern industrial wonders: each day, tonnes of raw materials arrive by boat and 109,000 steel containers of finished product are removed for export. That's about one twenty-foot container every second, a veritable river of toys moving atop cargo ships that float down the Pearl River Delta towards the open water of the South China Sea. As of 2001, an estimated 95 percent of Wal-Mart's Chinese purchases were made here in this sprawling concrete-tower and factory zone. With the help of big-box retailers, China has captured over 70 percent of the world's market for toys, furniture, and DVDs, as well as more than half of world production of bicycles, cameras, telephones, and shoes. To sustain this output, China has also become the world's largest producer of coal, steel, and cement.

This was possible because of hundreds of millions of migrant workers stranded inside Shenzhen's foreboding gates. Great numbers of these migrants have left behind family and children to work in special economic zones along the coastline. Most rarely return to their home villages more than once or twice a year, but they religiously send money, which has become the largest source of income in many rural areas. In distant factory cities they collectively produce nearly 80 percent of the world's toys, among many other things, for about $165 a month in wages.

It's a career path that many Western consumers would never consider. From Mongolia to India, fleeing the countryside in the hope of finding a factory job and sending money home has defined hundreds of millions of people from the 1980s onward. In China, the total number of farmers-turned-migrant-workers doubled between 1996 and 2008, increasing from 72 million to 130 to 200 million, based on government estimates. Generations of rural peasants had quietly suffered through Mao's unsuccessful attempts to modernize China – including famine, widespread violence, and isolated bouts of cannibalism – only to become a massive stranded labour pool.

The train from Hong Kong stops and passengers disembark into a drab immigration building. Documents are checked. Everywhere, ads and brochures advertise Shenzhen's modest enticements: a Hard Rock Cafe, four-star hotels, gourmet restaurants, several theme parks. After crossing a short bridge that spans the no man's land between the old British colony and the new China, one descends into the chaos of the train station. Scores of beggars and hucksters ply the street outside, while kiosks in the station offer free tours of upscale apartment buildings and housing developments. These were some of mainland China's first gated communities, developments not unlike the posh high-security residential complexes of North America.

By the early 2000s China had become the Saudi Arabia of cheap. By combining logistics, technology, and hundreds of millions of dispossessed farmers, China reduced costs 40 to 50 percent on many consumer and industrial products. It was a Schumpeterian price event – non-linear, disruptive, singular – offering a quantum leap in profit, growth, and affordability that helped float the post-industrial economies of the developed world. It became a fast-moving feudal state powered by technology and capitalism, with megamalls for some and mud huts for others.

Yet as products flowed and new factories sprang up during the early 2000s, Shenzhen was increasingly marred by battles between militant migrant workers and hired gangs of thugs; worker advocates were brutally attacked, and the streets outside the factory walls were sometimes unsafe. Much to the dismay of government and many factory owners, migrants and workers organized increasingly sophisticated legal challenges, inciting workplace sabotage, and pushing back the restrictions on mobility and residency that had made China's captive labour market critical to globalization.

Shenzhen has since become a window into the uncertain fortunes of the Western consumer. Facing the fastest-rising prices in more than a generation – food costs jumped by more than 23 percent in 2008 – China's government raised minimum wages and tightened labour and environmental regulations in order to quell unrest and protest. This affected retail prices halfway around the world: after uninterrupted savings since the 1980s, the average price of goods from China began to increase in 2007, peaking in 2008 at an average 9 percent price increase.

Caught between rising costs at home and low prices demanded abroad, a wave of factories closed down. The Asian Footwear Association estimates that in 2007 alone, nearly a thousand shoemaking factories out of eight thousand closed or moved out of the region. "There are about 70,000 factories in the Pearl River Delta today. Many of them are talking about reducing their workforce or even shutting down," said Stanley Lau, deputy chairman of the Federation of Hong Kong Industries, to the *New York Times* in 2008. "We expect more than 10 percent of these factories will be closed in a year or two." In early 2009 Lau predicted that another 5 to 10 percent would close because of global recession.

This is highly relevant to the rest of the world because contemporary China operates on a growth pact: either there is 8 percent annual economic growth or there is trouble. China's ruling class is walking a tightrope in its chosen model of accelerated development, one that includes not only its 1.3 billion citizens but also nations who rely on China for everything from cheap stuff to debt financing. Where Wal-Mart is hooked on growth as a matter of profit, China is addicted to growth as a matter of survival. The world's most populous country faces a very thin margin of error. Too little development, and poverty and hunger dangerously afflict 300 million of China's poorest – and the ensuing chaos wreaks havoc with global supply chains. But too much development has already created widespread inflation, pollution, and inequity.

The global economic crisis that began in late 2008 forced the question of China's precarious balance, since it was unlikely, if not impossible, that the nation would continue unscathed. By the time Prime Minister Wen Jiabao addressed the National People's Congress in March 2009, it was clear that the ruling Communist Party of China (CPC) was sparing little expense in its efforts to hold the country together, from launching one of the world's largest stimulus plans ($585 billion) to increasing what Wen described as China's "social safety net programs" by nearly 18 percent.

It's hardly the first time that China's government has poured resources into saving itself; it has systematically pumped billions into places that it perceives as vulnerable, from the rebellious central Asian frontier of Xinjiang to the feudal heartland of rural China. Social instability, according to the CPC, has long been the single greatest threat to modern China. In fact, the last time China encountered this kind of economic and social strife was probably in the years before the failed democratic uprising of spring 1989 and the tragic Tiananmen Square massacre that ensued.

Thanks to China, more than just about any other nation, we do not often pay the true cost of things. Its productive role within global commerce has meant that it, like other developing nations, has often internalized and obscured extra costs – child labour, pollution, national debt. In doing so, it has cushioned the global disconnect between high-impact prosperity and lower costs. Not having to pay for things such as higher wages, greenhouse gas credits, and worker safety is what has helped deliver such incredible value to both consumers and corporations since the 1980s.

Yet China may need us less in the future. Indeed, it has ample reasons to seek out a gradual decoupling from the very nations that helped fund its rise to power, not least the United States. Decades of bargain-fuelled trade and foreign direct investment literally financed China's transition from a needy developing nation to an emerging global power with growing autonomy. In the meantime, everything from blood oil in Africa to the buying power of Chinese consumers is now part of China's growing sphere of influence.

The financial crash of 2008 mostly sidestepped Chinese households, which carry high savings and don't generally hold stocks and bonds. But millions are still suffering the impacts. What began as a financial crisis of debt and irresponsible risk turned into a force of deglobalization, one that underlined China's chronic struggles with poverty, underdevelopment, and total dependence. By the end of 2008 an estimated 63,000 Chinese factories had closed; exports had dropped 25 percent by early 2009. Some economists were betting that China would be lucky to sustain 5 percent growth as the global economic crisis deepened, which would veer into the country's danger zone of destabilized growth. Meanwhile, an estimated 20 million unemployed workers from China's factory zones journeyed back to their home villages and towns. That's a lot of people not making DVD players, not getting paid, not distributing their earnings, and not showing up again the next day to do the very same thing all over again.

Trade with unstable Western economies is becoming a liability in China's quest for superpower status, and Pacific Rim nations are searching for alternatives. As concerned Chinese prime minister Wen Jiabao said in March 2009, "We have lent a huge amount of money to the U.S. Of course we are concerned about the safety of our assets. To be honest, I am definitely a little worried."

China can't abandon its export-dependent model of growth, not yet. China needs its U.S. currency assets to stay healthy in the short run, as well as to keep bargain-based globalization alive long enough to remedy its own domestic troubles. And yet the bargain revolution may one day be remembered not only in terms of prosperity and peak globalization but also in terms of geopolitics and the power transfer from West to East. If China, Taiwan, Korea, and other emerging economies can successfully decouple from the insolvent markets of the West, access to impoverished labour markets will decline as well. Already China has sought out ways to increase wages and improve labour laws in order to keep value at home instead of subsidizing consumers. This is one way that regional and national forces are already undermining globalization in the twenty-first century. It is also why Western consumers should care more about dirt-poor farmers and migrant labourers in China and beyond: the cheap, available labour that long filled our big-box stores with bargains is gradually becoming a threatened resource, one for which there is yet no ready alternative.

Into the Bargain Machine

If political revolutions during the twentieth century had succeeded in emancipating more than a billion rural peasants from Mexico to China, Wal-Mart might still be just a curious retail phenomenon. Surprisingly, the greatest productive force of our time was launched by a communist, not Sam Walton: the late Deng Xiaoping – Mao's successor, the architect of modern China, and leader of the bloody crackdown against China's democracy movement in Tiananmen Square.

Back in 1979, when Shenzhen was still knee-high in mud and rice paddies, Deng pronounced the area China's first Special Economic Zone, or SEZ. At the time, Wal-Mart was a regional merchant spread across eleven states and had just earned its first $1 billion in sales. Deng's then-radical design for capitalist development within the confines of China's one-party state emphasized foreign investment and export – a pragmatic strategy to kickstart and refinance China's pallid economy by catering to the West's hunger for cheap, plentiful housewares, clothing, toys, and electronics. It would be a mutually beneficial wealth transfer. Thousands of factories sprouted across China, creating millions of jobs and an avalanche of products.

And as dirt-poor farmers became assembly-line workers, communist ideology eroded and China doubled its share of the world economy between 1990 and 2000. This was an unprecedented growth rate – six times that of any other nation. It became, as *Business Week* aptly described it, an "exporting colossus, powering growth of nearly 10 percent a year for the past three decades."

Most of that growth was initially launched from Shenzhen, Guangzhou, and other centres along the dense Pearl River Delta, north of Hong Kong. By 1990 Shenzhen had already captured half of all China's incoming foreign investment. Fuelled by the decade-plus consumer bonanza in the West, it continues to capture a sizable portion of the estimated $1 trillion in total foreign investment that has entered China since 1979. According to Hong Kong consultants Enright, Scott & Associates, Shenzhen's economy expanded an incredible 28 percent annually between 1980 and 2004.

This is how filling big-box stores full of affordable appliances, electronics, and textiles sometimes benefits the world: the remittances of factory workers to home villages has kept China's vast hinterland out of deeper poverty and crisis. In countless small payments throughout China's most impoverished provinces, the average $2,000 annual salary of a Chinese factory worker has helped to stay the downward spiral of depopulation, economic depression, and poverty where Mao Zedong failed. Indeed, some have even argued that cheap stuff has become an agent of global peace, if past history is any indication, since nations that share a big-box store chain have yet to go to war with each other.

Yet never before has the Middle Kingdom so closely resembled the kind of capitalist dystopia that Chairman Mao used to rail against. Until the 1970s, Shenzhen village was a pre-industrial remnant that had remained largely unchanged for nearly two millennia. This former coastal village was named Bao'an County in 331 A.D., during the Eastern Jin Dynasty; it was renamed Shenzhen in 1410, during the Ming Dynasty. A few years after Deng's launch of the Shenzhen Special Economic Zone in 1980, the old fishing village was surrounded by 100,000 new residents. By 2008 an estimated 11 million people had converged on a city that never stops building factories, glass office towers, and cheap apartment blocks. Shenzhen, roughly translated, means "deep drain."

Shenzhen now boasts China's highest per capita ownership of credit cards – several per permanent resident, on average. Hong Kong businessmen have fathered thousands of children here with Shenzhen girlfriends, many of whom will never travel past Shenzhen's southern gates. There are also more brothels than anywhere else in China, not to mention the country's highest concentration of migrant labour – about three-quarters of the city's residents are without a permanent address.

Out on the street, vendors sell a mind-boggling variety of counterfeit consumer goods, everything from huge stuffed Mickey Mouse dolls to Prada and Hugo Boss knock-offs. Pirated DVDs, prostitutes, fake Rolex watches are proffered. Hastily erected steel and glass buildings clutter the skyline, and concrete walkways carry people over dusty, congested avenues. Within minutes, street children swarm visitors. One eight-year-old desperately clings to my leg and refuses to let go; he's either crying or pretending to cry. Locals later explain that Shenzhen gangsters run the kids. Western executives are occasionally kidnapped here, so it's no coincidence that all the major tourist attractions are safely located near the edge of the city. Most of the city's 20,000 foreign expats actually live about an hour's bus ride from the city's crime-ridden centre, at scenic Shekou Harbour.

People don't come here for the scenery. This is one of the first urban areas in the world created purely for export manufacture, and it features enormous walled factory complexes, corporate-sponsored streets, and a constant influx of workers and entrepreneurs. It is a site of enormous hardship, ingenuity, and hope. It encompasses tiny workshops and modern mega-factories. Here workers toil at everything from sorting electronic waste contaminated with heavy metals for menial pay to operating high-tech assembly machines for wages that rival those of China's middle class. And everyone suffers from China's famous air pollution: an unpublished 2002 study by researchers with the Chinese Medical Association noted that of 11,348 schoolchildren tested in Shenzhen, 65 percent had unsafe levels of lead in their blood according to World Health Organization (WHO) guidelines – a figure that rises to 80 percent in nearby Guiyu, where families recycle computers, cellphones, and other e-waste.

Wal-Mart has bravely launched nine supercentres in the Shenzhen area. Built to the company formula – everything is red, white, and blue – they carry local specialties, items common to a typical Chinese grocery store: dried squid snacks, shrimp chips, spicy green peas, and rice cookers. With 40,000 employees working in 100-plus stores across China, the hope is that the burgeoning consumer classes will train themselves to scavenge for bargains in big-box stores just like North Americans and Europeans. It's the worst-kept secret of global commerce: the only viable opportunity for quantum growth in sales and profits is to transform Asian workers into consumers. As Joe Hatfield, then president of Wal-Mart China, told the *Los Angeles Times* in 2003, the Middle Kingdom is a source of great optimism. "What this place is going to look like 10 to 20 years from now – and what the consumer will be ready to buy – is hard to even think about," Hatfield said. "There are 800 million farmers out there who've probably never even tasted a Coke."

For a growing number of Chinese, this represents both betrayal and danger. In a Hong Kong office tower a short train ride from Shenzhen, exiled labour activist Han Dongfang is putting the final touches on his weekly Radio Free Asia program, which broadcasts news and interviews to millions of listeners across China's mainland. All is not well in the factory lands that fill our big-box stores; protests, industrial accidents, food riots, and violent attacks against workers and organizers – Han Dongfang hears it all. "Yesterday someone called in to report two thousand people at a protest in front of one factory," he says, estimating that he fields about eighty news calls a month, all of which are conveyed to listeners in Mandarin. People share information on corruption, human rights abuses, layoffs, and unpaid wages. China's government tries – unsuccessfully – to jam the signal.

"Sometimes people call me from in front of a demonstration of a thousand people, or when an accident happens, or just to discuss a situation," he says. "And after every incident reported, I do the same thing: I call factories, union leaders, local government officials to prove the story and ask their opinion. Often they say the same general things: 'It's a period of adjustment,' or 'We need to push reform.'" Han often attempts to mediate disputes with factory managers and party officials in an effort to find solutions without violence, arrests, or job loss.

But protests and unrest have increased. Based on government sources, "the number of mass protests, demonstrations, sit-ins and strikes in China soared from around 10,000 in 1993 to 60,000 in 2003, with the total number of participants [totalling] 3.07 million," notes a 2008 report by Han's China Labor Bulletin and the Montreal-based Rights and Democracy. (The report, titled *No Way Out*, was compiled over five years of research; it says that "there is currently at least one strike involving over 1,000 workers every day in the Pearl River Delta alone.") As the vice-president of Shenzhen's Federation of Trade Unions put it in 2008, strikes had become "as common as arguments between a husband and wife."

Back in May 1989, Han, a former electrician and People's Liberation Army soldier, found himself in Tiananmen Square in Beijing by accident. He founded China's first independent labour union just a few days before the tanks rolled into the square and began shooting. Ever since then he's invoked the Chinese vision of democracy – min zhu, "the people are the master" – that spread across the nation in the spring of 1989 and was soon driven underground after democracy protests in Beijing and most other major Chinese cities were crushed.

Ever since Tiananmen, explains Han, there have been successive years of double-digit economic growth. China became the world's largest trading nation after Germany, exporting and importing roughly $1.5 trillion worth of goods and services annually. Unlike Germany, which became a leading trading nation through high-value exports – luxury cars, engineering, precision machinery – China's exports run the gamut from super-cheap to affordable luxury items and high-tech. An estimated 80 million jobs are now tied directly to China's booming export sector. Even though many rural poor have seen improvements, these gains have not kept pace with the rest of China, and the number of Chinese unofficially estimated to be living on less than a dollar a day in 2007 was still 300 million.

The reality of failed revolution is that China spent decades nearly frozen in time, delaying development, education, and income for most citizens while the rest of the world marched forward. The paradox of uneven development is, of course, that it makes offshore manufacturing highly attractive. This is a country full of both high-tech logistics and dirt-poor migrants. China's greatest problem is the very thing that has made it such an effective instrument of mass production: it can exploit its workers and economy in the short term, but the poverty, social dispossession, and underdevelopment that created the surplus labour pool still exist.

China's social, environmental, and economic limits are being tested as a result of our insatiable appetite for cheap stuff. And the leading pillars of the Western economy – the likes of Wal-Mart, Dell, Tesco, and Carrefour – are betting heavily that there are no limits, despite growing evidence to the contrary. Consequently, "strikes and work stoppages are part of daily life in the Pearl River Delta," says Han. "This is in spite of the fact that, under the current constitution of the People's Republic of China, workers do not have the right to strike."

Between the limited freedoms and the corruption that reach to the highest levels of business and government, "young workers are without a future," Han says of the millions who toil in Shenzhen and beyond. "Hundreds of thousands of factories are in the same situation: no money, no jobs, no unemployment fund, no retirement fund. Factories are often just a channel for money, which is why many fail: corrupt managers have several houses instead and don't pay their workers." Consequently, the biggest threat to social and economic stability in China is not students with democracy banners or Islamic terrorists from central Asia, but hundreds of millions of scruffy migrant workers who have been cheated out of wages, abused, and have few prospects.

With his unique window on China's hidden struggles, Han's fear is that it is advancing not towards stability and market-driven democracy – as many Western politicians once claimed – but towards an uneasy hybrid of diminished freedoms, strife, and unstable development. He argues that no amount of growth or investment alone can fix China, since part of today's emerging crisis began in 1989, when patriotic young Chinese chanted "*min zhu*" in their unsuccessful call for accountability and good government. "Democracy is more and more out of people's lives," says Han sadly. "It has become a thinker's activity, not connected with the people."

Yet because of this, Han is probably the most popular pirate radio broadcaster in the world. He shakes his head in disbelief. That China has drifted from communism is no secret. But what is it becoming? He doesn't hesitate: "An explosion."

Joint Ventures

Back in the 1960s, Communist cadres ordered Shenzhen farmers and fishermen to sing revolutionary songs on their way to work, with the hope that Hong Kong residents just over the wall would be impressed by China's revolution. At the time, Hong Kong was Asia's leading global trade and finance hub, a bastion of free-market capitalism, low taxation, and industrialization.

But after Deng Xiaoping's market-based economic reforms began in Shenzhen in 1980, Hong Kong was among the first to outsource. By 1989 most of Hong Kong's manufacturers had been lured across the border. As international investment poured into Shenzhen, the city became the richest jurisdiction in all of China. Its workers still sing songs – at least, the ones who work for Wal-Mart. "My heart is filled with pride . . . I long to tell you how deep my love for Wal-Mart is . . ."

It didn't happen by accident. The country's ruling class spent the past quarter-century building and cultivating everything that a global retailer like Wal-Mart or Home Depot might require, including the enforced stability of a massive one-party state that spends billions on transport networks, its military, and domestic surveillance technologies. "There might be places in other parts of the world where you can buy cheaper, but can you get [the product] on the ship?" Wal-Mart's Shenzhen manager told the *Washington Post* in 2004. "If we have to look at a country that's not politically stable, you might not get your order on time. If you deal in a country where the currency fluctuates, everyday there is a lot of risk. China happens to have the right mix."

In 2002 Wal-Mart opened its global procurement office in Shenzhen, arguably the company's first major management relocation outside Bentonville. During the early 2000s the company's internal sourcing and purchasing agency employed approximately 1,500 people in Shenzhen and two dozen international satellite offices. It was the natural site for Wal-Mart's offshoring efforts: of the fifty-five countries that Wal-Mart imported goods from in 2001, China accounted for two-thirds of all purchases in terms of value. Wal-Mart doesn't share its procurement data, but American consultants Booz Allen Hamilton estimate that it sourced $2 billion worth of products from China in 1998, more than $18 billion in 2004, and $30 billion in 2008. That's a fifteen-fold increase within a decade.

With the patronage of majors such as Wal-Mart, Shenzhen has become an economic trailblazer for continental Asia. Thousands of other towns and cities across the developing world have studied the Shenzhen model in the hope that they might transform their own economic backwaters. "Shenzhen will become the most beautiful city in the nation, able to compete with the garden state of Singapore," predicted local Communist Party secretary Zhang Gaoli in 1999.

Joint ventures began in China as a precondition for foreign investment and manufacture, since Deng and other leaders knew that they needed Western wealth to kick-start China's economy. Known for frequent failures and scant legal protections, the joint venture became China's chosen means for controlling and shaping incoming foreign investment. While mandatory joint-venture requirements for corporations were eliminated by the early 2000s, a much grander, more global joint venture had already been formed. In 2001 foreign retailers bought $30 billion worth of goods from China, equivalent to 11.3 percent of the country's total exports; by 2002 the total was estimated to have reached $35 to $40 billion. And by 2007 Europe and the United States accounted for 41 percent of China's total exports.

In order to maintain their competitive edge, major retailers such as Wal-Mart continued to integrate themselves deep into the economy of China to gain new savings and efficiencies. By the early 2000s, with more than 80 percent of the six thousand foreign factories that supply Wal-Mart already located in China, this exceedingly American corporation (and others that have settled here) had essentially become part Chinese. Between 2001 and 2006 "Wal-Mart was responsible for . . . 11 percent of the growth of the total U.S. trade deficit with China," reports the Economic Policy Institute in Washington, D.C.

It's an unexpected evolution of Sam Walton's quest, but it's all consistent with his original cost-cutting credo. "For the benefit of the consumer, we should buy merchandise where we get the best value," explained Andrew Tsuei, managing director of Wal-Mart's Shenzhen headquarters. Following suit, Home Depot and other major retailers set up their own procurement centres on the mainland.

Despite its many detractors, China succeeds because it now does capitalism better than most anyone else, often beating formerly imperialist nations at their own game, dirty tricks and all: currency manipulation, subtle protectionism, economic threats. China's nation-crushing competitive advantage is founded on the very capacity for "disruptive innovation" that Wal-Mart USA's Castro-Wright advocates. In much the same way that Wal-Mart revolutionized retailing by bringing together marginal consumer markets and logistics technology, China has reinvented production itself, merging global demand and low-income workers.

The significant retail markup that low Chinese prices allowed was a central factor in the stratospheric rise of retail during the 1990s, resulting in the likes of Wal-Mart, Carrefour, and Tesco becoming some of the world's largest and most profitable companies. A plastic toy that retails for $4.50 at Wal-Mart comprised only 45 cents in labour costs at some of its cheapest rates during the late 1990s, which underlines the degree to which offshore labour subsidizes companies and consumers. Value is added, as economists often say, along the supply chain, which somehow ends with the consumer paying a retail price that is ten times the actual labour cost.

To meet demand, China's transportation infrastructure saw massive investment, largely geared to manufacture and trade, in its attempt to move goods and materials faster than any First World nation. In 2003 Shenzhen became the fourth-busiest container port in the world, thanks to US$4.3 billion invested in its facilities since 1979. By 2008 China had become a logistics superpower, claiming three out of the five busiest container ports in the world: Hong Kong, Shanghai, and Shenzhen.

In addition, China adds an estimated 3,000 new kilometres of domestic highway every year. Its national network of 30,000 kilometres is second only to America's national highway system. Based on China's impressive web of land and sea links, the United States Department of Commerce estimates that by 2010, 35 percent of the world's shipping traffic will originate from China.

The image of a primitive 1970s-era factory powered by coal furnaces and peasant labour is no longer applicable in major centres such as Shenzhen. Higher-value businesses like Dell, Apple, Hewlett Packard, and others have adopted China-based production precisely because of the advanced technology, information management, and automation now available. Indeed, sometimes the very same factories churn out brand-name and discount no-name versions of the same product. As James Fallows reported in 2007, no less than three competing brands of low-cost laptops emerge from the same Shenzhen factory, and an estimated 90 percent of all laptops are now manufactured by one of five Chinese companies: Inventec, Compal, Quanta, Wistron, and Asustek.

Foxconn, the Taiwanese company that is a prime manufacturer for technology titans like Nokia, Dell, and Apple, is the most dominant producer in Shenzhen; its walled city-factory, Longhua Science and Technology Park, claims 270,000 workers. Foxconn is China's biggest single exporter of goods, and a prime example of how special economic zones have diversified into the sort of high-value products once manufactured much closer to consumers. Nearly 90 percent of all USB flash drives are manufactured here.

Think of Shenzhen every time Apple rolls out another iPod or iPhone – an estimated 10 million iPhones were distributed globally in 2008 alone. There is no other place on the planet that can reliably manufacture and broadcast millions of high-value products and still manage to pass along a healthy profit to Western companies. By taking a mere $25 profit per phone, Apple launched the miracle of the $199 iPhone in 2008 – an item that originally retailed for as much as $599. This not only helped demolish pricing for many high-end personal devices but also refuelled the fading consumer dream with proof that cheaper, better, and more plentiful might still be possible.

China's diversification from manufacturing cheap novelties during the 1980s to high-value technologies by the 2000s is one of the most dramatic expressions of how that country has come to anchor Western consumerism. And it does this through a factory system that could never exist in a Western democracy. China's strategic approach to everything from infrastructure development to macroeconomic policy – as well as its ability to defer the consequences of severe underdevelopment, protest, and poverty – likely wouldn't be possible in a country with meaningful elections. In fact, the fierce efficiency of its growth-without-democracy approach is precisely why China maintains an economic lead over other major developing-world players such as India, even though India's legal system, democratic government, high rates of education, and respect for intellectual property make it an obvious choice for global business.

The reality is that China's one-party state allows for large, radical reconfigurations of work and society in the service of cheap that have yet to be reproduced anywhere else. Teeming with migrant labourers, for example, Foxconn's city-within-a-city serves 150,000 lunches daily, the production lines operate around the clock, and the starting wage is 60 cents an hour. Foxconn founder Terry Gou is worth an estimated $10 billion alone. His clients Nintendo (Wii), Apple (iPhone), Motorola (cellphones), Sony (PlayStation), and Dell (computers) represent billions more in domestic sales created through supply chains that no longer represent any clear nationality.

Can't live with it, can't live without it – failed revolution is synonymous with cheap stuff in our world. More often than not, globalization has taken root in developing countries that have suffered through colonialism and failed revolution: India, China, Vietnam, parts of Southeast Asia, Mexico, Central America, and much of Eastern Europe. As these enclaves opened up for business, the global labour supply increased fourfold between 1980 and 2007, according to the International Monetary Fund. In 2008 the World Bank claimed 500 million people were lifted out of poverty, mostly in China, India, and Southeast Asia – partially through the wealth redistribution effected by our singular drive to make more stuff more cheaply.

On the ground, though, these aggregate income gains are not always evident. With one of China's worst records for violence and workplace injury in a police state full of industrial accidents, Shenzhen sometimes seems more like a scene out of Karl Marx's nineteenth-century England than a high-tech centre of growing importance. This economic frontier is sometimes brutal. Not long before I arrived in Shenzhen on one visit, a fire ravaged a Taiwanese joint-venture electronics factory, killing twenty-four women and youths; management had blocked half the fire exits in order to thwart people stealing products. In keeping with the local business culture, the company's official name is Vast Profit Limited.

Sometimes workers don't even come here by choice, as evidenced by the 2008 discovery of a child-labour ring north of Shenzhen that resulted in the rescue of more than a hundred children by Chinese authorities. Lured and captured from the distant poverty-stricken rural province of Sichuan, the children, aged thirteen to fifteen, were forced to work as much as three hundred hours a month for little or no pay. The reported incidence of forced labour has increased, evidence of better policing and vigilance on the issue, but also reflective of desperate economic realities. Faced with a plethora of new costs, some Chinese manufacturers still resort to withholding wages, illegal working conditions, and child labour to meet the low-cost demands of export markets. Subsequent reports from Chinese media suggested that as many as a thousand children were working in factories in Dongguan, directly north of Shenzhen. "[This] case is quite typical," Hu Xingdou, of the Beijing Institute of Technology, told the *International Herald Tribune*. "China's economy is developing at a fascinating speed, but often at the expense of laws, human rights and environmental protection."

Evidence of slavery also surfaced in 2007, when officials in Shanxi and Henan provinces rescued hundreds of adults and children who had been captured and forced to work in rural brick kilns.

Pressure to keep costs contained has also resulted in periodic waves of faulty products and toxic materials. It's all about Everyday Low Prices. Facing fierce competition in retail markets, for example, global bargaineers like Wal-Mart used their clout to refuse cost increases on labour or materials. This in turn downloads cost pressures onto Chinese factories, many of which cannot deliver low prices and also live up to labour and environmental standards, let alone provide fair wages and safe working conditions.

It's the same value destruction that discounting effected in the retail environments of the West. But its consequences here in the developing world are potentially more serious and threaten to undo some of the income and development gains of past decades. "People have always said foreign investment is the hope of China. This is our bridge to the world," says Han Dongfang. "But what comes across the bridge are twelve-hour shifts, seven-day workweeks and only two trips to the bathroom a day. What comes across are factory fires that kill hundreds of workers who are locked in because their bosses are afraid they will steal the products. The Chinese government has put an invisible net across the bridge that allows money to come in but not the freedoms of a civil society, not the rule of law and not free trade unions." One result is enough random violence to count as a low-level civil war, something that has frequently gone unreported. Readily available explosives from China's countless construction sites, for example, make domestic terrorism a too-common occurrence.

It is possible that China may come out ahead of everyone else – if it can survive itself, that is. Even after the crash, ongoing trade deficits continue to speak to China's central role within globalization, and of its surprising resilience. In particular, the nation carries special clout as an owner of the developed world's national debt, most notably a $1.4 trillion surplus of American debt. With its trade surplus, the Chinese government has long been purchasing U.S. treasury notes, which are debt-financing instruments issued by the American government. In other words, the largest trade imbalance in human history – one that inevitably affects all nations – is being collectively underwritten by those toiling in fields and factories. "On average, each Chinese peasant owns $1,000 in US Treasury bonds," notes

David Dollar, director of the World Bank's Beijing office. "He may not have a tractor and his kids may not have schools, but he has that bond."

In many ways, Wal-Mart and its kin are just middlemen. The real joint venture is the fragile interdependence that exists among Western consumers, the Chinese government, and migrant labour. We need cheap goods; they need income. It's a relationship that has become more complicated in the twenty-first century. And without this compact, there is scant reason to hustle millions of steel containers across the face of the planet.

Mao's Unlucky Heartland

At first glance, rural China is a postcard vision. Oxen, pigs, and ancestral homes dot a countryside blanketed by lush rice paddies that stretch to the horizon. Locals drive ancient tractors and dredge irrigation canals, usually knee-deep in mud. Framed in endless hues of green and brown, Shaoshan village is nearly hidden in the rolling hills of central Hunan province. It is a picture of living history, a place where people tend fields that have been farmed continuously for the past 5,800 years.

What isn't apparent is that pesticides and fertilizers have killed off most marine life in the water. Whatever else grows here will surely be damaged by coal-fuelled acid rain that now falls like vinegar throughout parts of central China. And whatever crops aren't damaged by acid rain may be washed away by Hunan's annual floods that kill as many as three thousand people annually, destroying millions of homes, and threaten famine by submerging crops. If it's not floods, then it's drought: millions can lose access to drinking water during semi-annual heat waves. Incredibly, tornadoes and cholera outbreaks also afflict this region, the very centre of China's rural heartland, during particularly unlucky years.

As one emerges from Shaoshan's crumbling train station, the air is humid and heavy; it's a dour, languorous place where locals still stare at foreigners. And it's strangely quiet, more than a little empty, not least because many locals have abandoned the countryside. More than 80 million rural Chinese gave up farming between 1996 and 2006. Those who remain face frequent hunger and persistent hardship. Local income remains well below a dollar a day.

At the centre of it all is a faded tourist attraction. Within a cluster of Soviet-era hotels, semi-vacant souvenir stands, and weathered statues is a

Justin Guariglia/www.guariglia-chen.com

Mao Zedong's portrait hangs over Shaoshan train station, Hunan province, China.

mud-walled farmhouse with a pigpen, dirt floors, and a kitchen. It was here that young Mao Zedong once fed chickens and planted rice. Shaoshan is where Mao first began to dream of revolution, setting into play a series of events that would change world history.

Although large by peasant standards – its thirteen small rooms and mud courtyard made it a monster home in prewar China – Mao's birthplace isn't much to look at. It is dank and dark inside, and while his old wooden bed still stands in his room, there are few signs that a family actually lived here. Yet Mao's modest farmhouse drew as many as 3 million annual visitors at the height of the Cultural Revolution in the late 1960s. Nearby hotels, exhibits, and restaurants are still adorned with socialist banners, grandiose Mao dioramas, and busts of Marx and Lenin. Outdoor loudspeakers blast revolutionary songs from the 1960s most hours of the day, as if that might lessen the boredom of the guards and custodians who tend this empty place.

Official signs and plaques, riddled with spelling errors, proclaim mundane aspects of young Mao's life – here he went swimming; there he worked in the rice paddy – but Shaoshan offers little insight into what eventually drove Mao Zedong to the ideological folly that would result in mass persecution and starvation during the darkest hours of his rule. Indeed, infant mortality still runs high, corrupt officials steal land and money, and an ongoing epidemic of suicides – over half the world's daily total, largely among young rural women – speaks to the hardship that has driven millions of rural Chinese to abandon their villages and seek out employment in distant factories.

Many peasants wind up destitute and unemployed in China's regional cities, such as Changsha, the provincial capital of Hunan, which sits on the Xiang River a short train ride from Shaoshan. It is here that Mao completed part of his education and founded the Hunan branch of the Chinese Communist Party. Even at 6:00 a.m., all along Wuyi Donglu, Changsha's central avenue, lines of beggars and migrant workers silently wait, many holding signs offering their skills for pay or begging for money with tales of hardship.

Around the corner, on Shaoshan Lu, a new Wal-Mart supercentre waits for customers. It serves a small but growing urban middle class. Including Changsha, Hunan province holds 68 million people – nearly twice the population of Canada – but boasts only three Wal-Mart outlets. Wal-Mart's central Changsha location, despite being located in one of China's most depressed provinces, still manages to clear more than its $60,000 target in daily sales while paying its workers $84 to $96 a month, well below most of Shenzhen's lowest wages.

Former backwaters like Changsha boomed during the 2000s as they become new bargain zones for export and domestic production, adding chemical factories and heavy machinery and consumer goods production, and expanded at rates that outpace first-generation special economic zones like Shenzhen. Changsha's GDP increased 14 percent annually between 2001 and 2006, compared with China's national average of 9 percent. And like Shenzhen, Changsha's boom relies heavily on direct foreign investment to accelerate development; by 2006 investment was pouring in at five times China's national average, mostly from Hong Kong, Singapore, and Japan. It has been a boom economy within the world's leading boom economy.

Why? Since the early 2000s, depressed provinces such as Changsha have been selling cost advantage to a world nervous about prices. Production capacity is moving inland, following the trail of cheap land and labour. In

2005, minimum wages in regional capitals like Changsha and Chengdu were little more than half of Shenzhen's minimum wage. Out on the coast, factory owners were getting crushed by rising costs and unsympathetic customers. One Shenzhen shoe-factory owner interviewed by the *Asia Times* reported that the cost of steel for buttons had tripled between 2004 and 2008; sewing machine oil and labour costs had increased 20 percent. Already weakened by years of cost-cutting on behalf of Western retailers, manufacturers pushed their operations deeper into the Chinese hinterlands. As the Asian Footwear Association reported in 2007, of the thousand shoemaking factories that closed or moved out of the Pearl River Delta region, 25 percent relocated to Southeast Asia; 50 percent moved inland to places like Hunan; and the rest were simply mothballed until further notice.

The list of products available from Hunan's cinder-block factories reads like a manifest from the Las Vegas bargain show. Your recordable CDs and DVDs may have come from Hunan's Forescape; Hunan Palette Garment offers "deluxe business suits, group uniforms, and shirts"; Shaodong Chenwang hardware specializes in pliers and pincers; non-stick frying pans come from Hunan Wujo Light Industry and Chemicals, bamboo flooring from Hunan XiangZhu, and paint rollers and drywall tools from Hunan General Industrial.

Amazingly, a new factory can be built in Hunan's capital region in as little as forty-five days. It is brute economic development, accelerating a largely pre-industrial agricultural region into the twenty-first century. Hunan is now one of China's ten most paved regions, boasting 1,800 kilometres of expressways. Changsha's new port on the Xiangjiang River, a tributary of the Yangtze, can transport full containers of product all the way to Shanghai within a few days.

It is through rural development that China's central government hopes to curb income disparities and improve living standards. Launched in 2004, the government's strategic plan guiding this second wave of development – fittingly titled "The Rise of Central China" – seeks to nearly double the transport and production capacity of its central provinces by 2012. For a while it was working too: "In the first three quarters of 2007, six central provinces, including Anhui, Henan, Hubei, Hunan, Jiangxi and Shanxi attracted $11.5 billion in foreign investment, a 46.2 percent increase," reported the *China Daily* in 2008.

It is true that the spread of factories, technology hubs, and rapid urbanization across the commercial zones of China and Southeast Asia has resulted in gradual decreases in infant mortality, improved health care, and a net increase in life expectancy, not to mention colour televisions. Yet many rural Chinese are still second-class citizens.

Of the millions of peasants who are officially migrant, most are subject to laws and regulations that limit their movement, settlement, and rights. China's emergence as a manufacturing superpower has everything to do with its long-standing system of rural/urban apartheid, which created the world's largest captive labour pool. It was a Mao-era policy that established a rigid permit-based separation between city and country residents, known as *hukou* (household registration system). Following the introduction of special economic zones and post-Deng market liberalization, migrants began to roam in search of work in the cities and factory zones, estranged from the very countryside that Mao once saw as the core of the revolution. Without official resident status, migrants are subject to exploitation and can be denied health care, education, and housing. They are, however, welcome in factory enclaves like Shenzhen. It is, as Amnesty International summarized in 2007, "a regulatory and administrative foundation for discrimination against internal migrant workers."

Consequently, a considerable number of people remain on the losing side of China's two-caste system. Wandering Changsha's gritty streets, one can see unemployed soldiers sleeping on traffic dividers between expressways, homeless peasants pushing their belongings past shopping malls, and, as elsewhere in China, the sick, the disfigured, and the disabled – many claim from workplace accidents – begging for money. Hundreds of millions of Chinese have fallen through the cracks of the former "iron rice bowl" of Chinese socialism. This matters globally because China's rural/urban disparity is increasing, despite official efforts: over half of China's 1.3 billion residents are rural – 736 million, more than double America's population.

Market liberalization and globalization were touted as poverty solutions, yet the income of urban residents in 2006 was 3.28 times that of rural Chinese, a disparity that has been growing since the late 1990s. Along with corruption and factory closures, income disparity is the root of China's domestic security crisis. When three thousand workers from two major

Changsha factories staged a sit-in protest over low wages and labour rights in 2007, it was because many workers saw no other choice. "This is a problem caused by the state owned enterprise reform," said one worker. "There are very few factories in Changsha now. Factories here used to make a lot of profit but [during the economic reform] corrupted officials came in and left workers with little money. Most people get several hundred Yuan retirement pension and some have even less. . . . We can't take it anymore."

The Fine Balance

It's not as though country folk are reckless. Indeed, they've been an accepting and tolerant bunch for the past hundred years. But the reality is that they have few political options when corrupt state officials steal money, increase prices, or impose unfair taxes. "Legitimate complaints that are repeatedly ignored by the government are the basis of the most incendiary cases [of rural conflict]," explains David Zweig of Hong Kong's University of Science and Technology, a few weeks before I travel to Hunan. "They are very, very prepared to use civil disobedience to push their point because they recognize that the legal channels are not going to work."

And even though legal challenges have become more common, the causes of unrest are persistent. Many Chinese can't make ends meet; public and private corruption results in unpaid workers and squandered education and health funds; and working conditions are often illegal or unsafe. Conflict is always close to the surface. Not long before I arrived in Hunan, for example, police clashed with five thousand farmers in a village outside Changsha, killing at least one person and injuring a hundred. The farmers had assembled to protest corruption and overtaxation. Several days later a bomb detonated on a public bus in downtown Changsha, seriously maiming several passengers – an event that police linked to earlier protests. Ten days later another bomb went off in a village south of Changsha, killing ten people. Several months later, a man armed with explosives hijacked a city bus and demanded to be taken to the municipal government offices; police sharpshooters killed him within three hours.

Civil order stands in a fine balance in China's depressed regions, and the smallest incident can result in riots, factory closures, and widespread disobedience. In recent years economic and political unrest have given way to something that Mao Zedong would never have imagined: environmental protest. According to China's Ministry of Public Security, pollution is one of the top five threats to China's peace and stability. *Mother Jones* magazine reported that an estimated one thousand pollution-triggered "public disturbances" occurred weekly in 2005, including riots against proposed chemical plants, lead poisoning, and urban development.

Hunan's affordable labour, wide-open tracts of land, and hunger for business have everything to do with its incredible, lung-wrenching air pollution. At one time many locals were willing to endure pollution for the sake of development. In 2003 Changsha was already China's seventh most polluted city. By 2006 an estimated 19 percent of the agricultural land in Hunan and other southern provinces had been damaged by acid rain. One has to experience this kind of pollution to fully appreciate how it has come to sabotage economic growth: large diesel and coal particulates, random chemical fumes, ozone that grows thick as fog as it bakes in the sunlight, and enough sulphur emissions to make Changsha itself a major cause of acid rain. Asthma and respiratory illnesses are commonplace; within a few days of arriving, I caught a nasty non-specific throat infection that lasted for weeks.

There's a regional smokestack effect. Changsha and eight smaller cities within an hour's drive account for 70 percent of Hunan's economic output and create a similar share of its pollution. No wonder, since China now leads the world in overall production of airborne particulates. In fact, NASA estimates that between 2002 and 2005, the amount of Chinese pollution arriving in North America was "equivalent to about 15 percent of local emissions of the U.S. and Canada."

Even outside Changsha, the air quality along country roads is surprisingly bad: ancient tractors and scooters belch out clouds of black smoke across incredibly beautiful scenes. In the factory lands on the fringe of greater Changsha, mercury and cadmium from smelters and chemical plants pollute the Xiangjiang River, which supplies drinking water for much of central Hunan. Mercury, a highly concentrated neurotoxin, was released in large quantities from thermometers, barometers, vapour lamps, and batteries as well as in the preparation of chemical pesticides. But cadmium levels peaked by as much as eighty times the national standard after one 2006 industrial accident, endangering the water for 6.5 million people. "About 10 million residents in the [Changsha] cluster have been threatened by industrial discharge[s] which flow into the river," Hunan's head of the provincial environmental department, Jiang Yimin, admitted to the *People's Daily* in 2006.

Even "taxi drivers are not willing to drive passengers to the industrial zone in [Changsha's] northern part, where a cluster of more than 200 paper-making, glass-production, smelting and even pesticide factories exist," reported the *People's Daily*. Headlines continue to come out: in 2008, sul-phuric acid leaked into the water supply from a chemical factory in Chenxi county, poisoning at least twenty-six villagers; a 2006 study found that chil-dren living in China's industrial areas, on average, show lead blood levels eleven times the WHO standard. And in 2008 China's State Environmental Protection Administration reported that about a quarter of all the water in China's seven main river systems is too toxic for human contact.

Consequently, new regulations have been created. "In recent years, growing pollution concerns have prompted Beijing to pass stricter envi-ronmental legislation, including a 2003 law that requires factories to gain approval for onetime 'environmental impact assessment' reports," wrote journalist Christina Larson in 2008. "China's officials face what may appear to them to be an uneasy choice: allow citizens to use these laws to their fullest extent, or risk a precipitous rise in protests."

For decades Hunan was known for revolution, not pollution – Mao Zedong's utopian China of lush rice paddies, rosy-faced workers, and shiny new tractors. But here in China's rough-and-tumble economic frontier, environmental crisis is another threat to twenty-first-century economic growth. It's a strange throwback to imperial times, when natural disasters such as killer floods or drought could inspire peasants to rise up against the prevailing dynasty. China's ruling government knows this history of environmental protest well, fears it, and has taken some action to lessen its risk. But with the dual effect of climate change and regional despoilment raging across China – desertification, drought, deadly floods, pollution-related disease – the environment is proving to be a profound limiting factor for the country, and for the goods-driven globalization that it helped create.

Hunan was a place where many companies hoped to escape the labour, environmental, and social constraints that had begun to sabotage China's price advantage elsewhere. But this was an illusion, as it was only a matter of years before this advantage was consumed – globalization dissolves its frontiers. As Alexandra Harney reported in 2008, Changsha manufacturers were already seeing the same kind of accelerating costs during 2007 and 2008 that had driven producers out of Shenzhen in the first place. "Labor, which once accounted for 5 per cent of costs, had risen to 15 per cent," she writes in *The China Price*. "Wages are going up, prices are coming down," said one Changsha factory manager. "Our profits are smaller."

Places like Hunan province are where our system of overdue externalities, growth-obsessed development, and dependence on non-renewable resources is breaking down. "I think a lot of the prices we've been paying from China don't reflect the full cost, such as environmental compliance and social compliance," says Harney. "But as China has started to tighten up some of its labour laws, and greater environmental enforcement, we're starting to see prices rising. It's about what costs have been neglected in the past as much as what's changing now on the ground."

In Mao's hometown, Hunan's most famous village, authorities did what many other governments have done in the face of crisis and economic hardship – they built a theme park. In 1994, around the time when Wal-Mart was becoming the world's largest company, China attempted to reinvent Mao's hometown of Shaoshan by building an $8-million collection of revolutionary vignettes and 3-D dioramas across the road from his original farmhouse. At Mao Zedong Memorial Park visitors can explore highlights of the brutal Long March to Mao's Yan'an cave headquarters, the launch pad for the final 1949 campaign for Beijing. As a sign declares outside, visitors are encouraged to live China's revolution for themselves "and excitedly read an interesting and vivid no-word history book."

This is retro socialism at its finest. To many, Shaoshan is still hallowed ground, a world pilgrimage site that, at its peak in 1966, saw as many as 2.9 million visitors annually. By 1980, the inaugural year of the Shenzhen SEZ, visitors had fallen off to 230,000. Lately numbers have been picking up as "red tourism" and nostalgia for the stability and isolation of Mao-era China have taken off among growing numbers of disaffected and increasingly nationalistic Chinese. The government claimed an estimated 3.2 million visitors in 2008, many of whom attended annual birthday celebrations for the chairman that featured music and fireworks performances, patriotic tributes, and "longevity noodles."

The original attractions remain popular, a nostalgic throwback to the Cultural Revolution of the 1960s, back when China was strong, proud, and somewhat insane. The farmhouse is adjoined by a Museum of Comrade Mao, where painstakingly preserved personal effects – swim trunks, school books, eyeglasses – and gushing cult-of-personality tributes give it an uncanny resemblance to Bentonville's Sam Walton museum.

Besides the Mao tourism, the main growth industry in Shaoshan appears to be prostitution. In the former barber shop of my hotel, a gaggle of young Chinese women lounge and make phone calls, occasionally leaving to go upstairs to service single men from the cities who arrive at Shaoshan's largest, slightly decrepit, and very Soviet-style hotel by train and automobile. Some of the women are clearly underage. They keep ringing up to my room, offering services, and I have to decline politely, then less politely as the evening wears on – *Buyao! Buyao!* (Don't want! Don't want!) One can hear the hotel's ancient phone system ringing randomly throughout the hotel. Hotel management put on dull, unknowing stares when I raise the issue the next day. Only a stone's throw from Mao's hallowed ancestral home, teen prostitutes prove that, despite improvements, fifty years of failed revolution have done surprisingly little to deliver Mao's kinfolk from hardship.

Shaoshan's prostitutes are likely earning far more than they would make dressed in blue, restocking shelves and giving the Sam Walton cheer daily at Changsha's Wal-Mart. For doubtless legitimate reasons, Shaoshan's working girls have also chosen not to venture into the troubled factory lands of Shenzhen to live within walled compounds, to eat, sleep, and assemble DVD players until their hands are too damaged to work, or they are assaulted, or they can no longer afford urban living expenses, and return home not much wealthier than before.

By 2009 many were returning home as waves of factories closed across China. Ironically, China's old system of household registration is gradually being dismantled just as many returning migrants are realizing that they have nowhere else to go. This sudden exodus has not been seen in China since Mao Zedong's Cultural Revolution forced urban youth out of China's cities to farms and prison camps during the late 1960s. It's a foreboding set of social and economic circumstances, possibly greater than Mao himself ever had to face. And would the chairman ever have escaped Shaoshan if he were a grade-school student today? Would he have wound up assembling toys for Disney, or would his family have been lucky enough to afford the luxury of secondary schooling that eventually propelled him towards leadership?

After assuming power in 1949, Mao seldom visited Shaoshan, favouring luxury resorts such as Lushan, an old European-built hideaway in the mountains of Jiangxi. Between 1959 and his death in 1976, he returned home only twice.

How KFC Helped Save the Revolution

It was another busy afternoon in a city that never sleeps. Late in 2007, labour rights activist Huang Qingnan was chatting with his friend Mr. Zhu in front of an apartment block in Shenzhen's Longgang district. There was a lot to talk about: China's government was getting ready to implement its new Labour Contract Law, which would provide new rights and greater job security to hundreds of millions of migrant workers. Things such as severance pay, overtime, and employment contracts – familiar to developed-world workers – were on the horizon in a rare set of concessions designed to help reduce growing unrest and poverty among the large populations of migrant workers that overflowed nearly every major Chinese city. Home to global technology giant and notoriously predatory employer Huawei Technologies, the Longgang district is a rough-and-tumble factory suburb where an estimated 80 percent of its million residents are unregistered migrants. As co-founder of Shenzhen's Dagongzhe Centre for Migrant Workers, Huang Qingnan was in the neighbourhood to enquire about a worker who had reportedly been beaten by a local factory boss over unpaid wages.

Dressed in dark clothing, two figures emerged out of the nearby crowd and approached Huang from behind. Without warning, they each drew a sixteen-inch blade out of a newspaper and began hacking at the labour activist's legs and back. He tried to lunge towards one attacker but soon collapsed on the sidewalk, convulsing in a pool of blood. His friend Zhu hurled rocks and chairs until the assailants escaped on a motorcycle. Huang's left leg was slashed to the bone, and his torso was covered in deep cuts. By the time he reached Longgang Central Hospital he had almost died from blood loss. Doctors were able to save his left leg but necrosis has left him crippled, despite multiple operations for skin grafts and nerve and blood vessel repair. Five men were arrested several months later for the crime.

The surprise attack made headlines across China, but its cause was no mystery. "Violence has been continuously getting more and more severe [and] the reason I was attacked can only be because they fear the influence of the centre," said Huang as he recovered in hospital. "And they hope that violent means will prevent the centre from operating."

Before the attack, Huang Qingnan and his colleagues had been busy at the Dagongzhe Centre, a storefront office in a rundown section of Shenzhen that educates workers and provides free legal advice. Piles of books and brochures clutter the desks inside the agency; some dusty safety helmets decorate the front window. A poster above the door reads *Be Independent, Be Self-strong, Be United, and Help Each Other*. As the registered manager of the non-profit agency, Huang was becoming known as someone who could help workers calculate wages to ensure fair payment and advise on legal rights, as well as help workers launch private lawsuits, the main tool for settling serious grievances with Chinese employers. "Production-line workers perhaps do not understand the new law. What we did was just popularize the law," explains Dagongzhe staffer Luo Chunli. "Honestly speaking, companies want to stop us from promoting the law. They are afraid that more workers will fight for their legal rights."

In helping migrants assert their new legal powers, Huang Qingnan and fellow advocates had hit upon a huge growth industry. Research in 2007 by China's *Jinan Daily* estimated that 80 percent of all migrant workers "did not know what a labour contract was." The activists had inadvertently tapped into the fact that migrants are the backbone of the economy, comprising 70 percent of construction workers, 68 percent of manufacturing employees, and 80 percent of coal miners. (In 2007 Amnesty International reported that approximately 90 percent of workers suffering from workplace-related diseases were migrants, as were 80 percent of those who died in mining, construction, and chemical factories.)

Many predicted that China's new labour reforms, which came into full effect in mid-2008, would be a disaster for business. In a full-page ad in the *Hong Kong Economic Journal*, a group of local business leaders claimed that the law was making workers "uncooperative" and that activists were exploiting its terms to disrupt production. Another group claimed the new law would be responsible for the closure of 10,000 businesses across Guangdong province alone.

Business had good reason to fear the reforms, because an avalanche of legal activism and lawsuits had already begun. As local media reported, the Dagongzhe worker centre had "successfully helped workers file a large number of severance pay claims. It now seems that targeted attacks on legal activists like Huang – as distinct from the use of hired thugs to break up wildcat strikes – may constitute a new stage of retaliation. Local observers speculate on possible collusion between employers and police, government officers or organized crime syndicates in these attacks."

In the end, China's government increased the minimum wage in central Shenzhen by 17.6 percent, despite several previous years of wage inflation. This is how a dusty little storefront offering legal advice became dangerous. The attack on Huang, for example, was not an isolated incident. A month earlier, hired thugs with steel pipes had twice smashed windows and desks at the Dagongzhe Centre. Without explanation the first time, they tore through the tiny storefront, thankfully sparing the centre's sole computer. On the second visit there was a message: "I'm telling you not to open the centre!" shouted one of the gang members. At about the same time, Li Jinxin, an assistant with a Shenzhen law firm, was kidnapped and beaten with steel pipes. "[Employers] wish we did not exist," explained Li, who suffered a broken leg and other injuries. According to a 2008 United Nations Human Rights Council report, "there were three policemen on patrol outside the offices at the time of the attack who looked on without taking any action against the attackers."

Street violence and criminal activity are not the only issue. What vexes China isn't insufficient security – after all, it's not hard to find security forces in a police state – but social and political decay. The main worry for activists like Han Dongfang isn't the dictatorship of the big-box stores that so many North Americans have decried, but the collapse of China's central government – and an emerging set of political and economic warlords. Corrupt local officials, well-connected industrialists, savvy party operatives are well positioned to exploit any sort of failure in China's monolithic party structure.

"The Communist Party is a huge monster, and once it loses control, it will be controlled by local interests," says Han. Even China's well-funded army, the former soldier suggests, cannot be trusted. "What will the army do?" he asks, worried about the future. "The central Communist Party will lose credibility when enough people can't eat. And who will be the new rulers? The corrupted people. Even worse, they will use democracy to campaign for themselves. After the Communist Party, the country will be ruled by a mafia."

This is a difficult admission, considering that Han spent several hard years in prison for his role as a democracy advocate and labour organizer in 1989. After being tortured, nearly succumbing to drug-resistant tuberculosis, and losing a lung in prison, he has lived in partial exile in Hong Kong since 1997, restricted by authorities from crossing over to the Chinese mainland into Shenzhen and beyond. He recalls that poverty, epic corruption, and poor working conditions troubled China in the days before students and citizens challenged the government at Tiananmen: during the summer of 1989, some 10 million Chinese were unemployed. "The explosion may eventually come," Han says, looking back on his decade-long crusade for rights and accountability. "People hate their local officials and the local officials hate the central government, which is trying to protect itself. That is why there is so much fighting."

China's Communist Party has been systematically crushing all possible domestic opposition ever since Mao arrived in Beijing. It is therefore very difficult to make change happen, even reforms that could help the Party save itself. Within China, activists, intellectuals, and lawyers still face severe constraints; fines, prison time, and persecution await anyone who steps outside an unclear set of official boundaries – someone like Han Dongfang, for example, who formed China's first outlaw independent union at Tiananmen Square in 1989.

Here's the curious part: it was the Chinese government that authored the 2008 labour reforms in the first place. China's government controls the country's only authorized union that represents workers. Even the legal right to strike was floated as a possibility by the Shantou chapter of the union in 2008.

China's labour reforms had much to do with the fact that migrants aren't just a necessary source of value, profit, and growth in China, they're a political party-in-waiting. Migrants comprise an estimated one-third of the population of China's capital city, Beijing, and nearly half of Shenzhen's estimated 8 million. Faced with challenging domestic circumstances, China chose to raise wages at the expense of consumers worldwide.

Labour reforms and legal accountability are the very things that may well save China from itself – at no small cost to corporations and consumers who depend on cheap exports. In July 2008, for example, Wal-Mart quietly announced its first-ever collective agreement with a Chinese union, in the northeastern town of Shenyang. Not only is the world's largest company the begrudging host to Chinese unions, it has also conceded significant wage increases to China's government-controlled union: 8 percent annually until 2009, well beyond anything conceded to most workers in North America and Europe.

Officially representing nearly 200 million people, the All-China Federation of Trade Unions (ACFTU) has previously been a "communist party apparatus," writes Karl Schoenberger in *Levi's Children*. ("Having the ACFTU represent the workforce brings party surveillance and the vestiges of a semi–totalitarian state into your factory: pregnancies can be monitored, for example, in the enforcement of the government's one-child policy," says Schoenberger. "Often, however, there's no union in sight.")

Yet major export manufacturers such as Foxconn, Shenzhen's largest foreign-owned enterprise, have been targeted by union organizers. Government-approved unionists approached the electronics giant early in 2007, launching a street-level campaign outside the Longhua Street compounds where many of Foxconn's 200,000 workers live. In a strange echo of the battle of Las Vegas, Chinese unionists canvassed in front of Hui Long Supermarket, imploring Foxconn workers to become union members. "Union cards were issued on the spot," reported the *Beijing News*. "And by midday, the creation of the Foxconn [union] branch was announced."

And after KFC, McDonald's, and Pizza Hut were discovered to be paying illegally low wages in 2007, it was the ACFTU that struck an agreement to unionize all outlets across China. As with Wal-Mart's new wage concessions, the relationship is no longer docile and subservient. ("We are not setting up this union just to have a union," said one KFC worker. "The key issue for us is to form an effective union.") In KFC's Hubei province outlets, vestiges of independent local union organizing emerged, precisely the kind of freedom of expression and political activism that has been met with jailings, torture, or persecution ever since Mao took power in 1949. "Its significance was extraordinary," reported *China Youth Daily* in 2008. "Unions at all levels, and the Party and government administration in all localities all unequivocally agree that the interests and dignity of our workers and our national legal system cannot be sacrificed in exchange for foreign investment."

"The pressure of workers' actions is changing the legislative landscape in China," confirmed Han Dongfang as he spoke to a U.S. congressional hearing in 2008. "Laws are being amended to better serve workers' interests."

The process tipping the balance against "foreign investment" and in favour of Chinese workers actually began at a Wal-Mart outlet in Fujian province in 2006. Much like the failed attempt to organize unions in Las Vegas, this effort was a grassroots assault on Wal-Mart's anti-union defences. And it was orchestrated with uncharacteristic effectiveness by China's state union. "To force Wal-Mart to establish a trade union, the ACFTU went to the grassroots and covertly organized a small group of workers to apply to set up a union in one of Wal-Mart's stores in Quanzhou City," reports *China Labor Translations*. "This was the first time that the ACFTU had started the process of union-building from the bottom-up."

The process was so successful that China's state union decided to unionize all Wal-Mart stores in the same manner, encompassing 50,000 Wal-Mart China employees. Faced with defeat, Wal-Mart "chose to formally co-operate with the ACFTU in establishing workplace unions in every Wal-Mart store in China." Consequently, the "Five-Point Memorandum" drafted by Wal-Mart's China head office and union representatives in August 2006 formed the basis for "an open and fair election process" for every local store union committee, a grassroots process that ensured national collective agreements and unprecedented wage hikes from 2008 onward. If Wal-Mart China wants to close stores, lay off workers, or change many aspects of its operation, it will now have to consult the world's largest union.

The view on the ground is a little more complicated. Li Qiang regularly travels to China to inspect factories and interview workers. As director of New York–based China Labor Watch, he continues to marvel at this strange mix of authoritarian rule, free-market capitalism, and re-emergent socialism. Rights and freedoms granted as an economic tool can just as easily be cancelled if foreign investment needs new incentives or global retailers become more useful to China's domestic goals. "It's not that workers don't have any rights," he says. "It's that we still ultimately have no way to influence government." China's non-governmental agencies and civil society advocates are still either closely watched or outlawed completely. "The law improves labour conditions but does not provide workers with more power."

And reforms can be used to hide abuses. At one Wal-Mart shoe factory that Li inspected in 2008 – Shenzhen's Hantai Shoe Production Ltd. – the union chair is actually a Taiwanese manager and workers are routinely required to work unpaid segments of overtime. "There is no workers' committee [and] workers' representatives are not elected by workers," he says. "The union's establishment is merely a decoration to pass the clients' audits." Most of the five thousand workers at the suburban factory are required to pay 32 percent of their base monthly wages for food and dormitory lodging, many workers are not permitted food or bathroom use during shifts, and poor ventilation and blocked emergency exits underline ongoing safety issues.

Even years after Wal-Mart and other multinationals pledged to improve conditions and create ethical sourcing networks, sweatshop-like conditions still prevail. As Li reports, even though an official Wal-Mart audit of Hantai occurred a few months prior to his inspection, "no conditions were improved," although factory management did post a list of official Wal-Mart regulations.

"Some foreign companies in China haven't behaved well in dealing with their workers' interests and rights," admitted ACFTU's Wang Ying to the *New York Times* in 2008. "As the economy and society develops, China needs to improve workers' legal rights and interests, which is a demand of a civilized society."

But here is the strange truth: KFC, Wal-Mart, and McDonald's helped save the revolution – and China's failing status quo – by doing precisely what they've often refused to do at home: instituting better wages, workplace democracy, and greater accountability. By late 2008 the ACFTU had launched a national campaign that proposed to unionize an estimated 80 percent of the largest foreign companies operating in China, with the goal of having all non-state-owned companies unionized by 2010. Nonconforming companies will be blacklisted by the Party and subject to audits, tax investigations, and possible prosecution, making any resistance to unionization within China essentially illegal.

Whether these reforms and wage increases will survive a global economic collapse doesn't change the fact that China needs to keep more money at home. Having made itself the world mecca of bargains, it has begun to nationalize its price advantage through labour, environmental, and social reforms, as well as an ever-changing web of tariffs and currency adjustments. The value that was once passed along to consumers is increasingly being retained within China's economy, a process that is designed to increase the collective wealth of China at the expense of foreign operators and distant consumers.

Why many foreign corporations persist and endure is simply because they badly need China. They need China not just as a source of product but also, more importantly, for the future, as an emerging consumer market that could replace the overspent mature consumer markets of their home countries. The average Chinese citizen still spends only half as much as he or she saves, as opposed to many Western consumers, who are barely above zero net worth. That 50 percent savings of 800 million working Chinese is capitalism's Holy Grail in the twenty-first century. And if accessing that pool of consumer capital meant hosting communist unions, swearing an oath to Mao Zedong's memory, or even blood sacrifice, there's a pretty good chance that the world's leading service-sector corporations would agree.

For its part, Wal-Mart was among the first major Western corporations to accede to China's demands for in-store unionization, which had extended through nearly all of its Chinese stores by the end of 2008. After fighting vehement battles against worker organizing and activism everywhere else, Wal-Mart was remarkably understated about opening its doors to the world's largest union. "We have a good relationship working with the union," said Jonathan Dong of Wal-Mart China. "The union provides a complement to what we do."

The Beginning of the End of Cheap

In a coastal town near Shanghai, an old friend of mine recalls his days working in a Shenzhen toy factory. It was during the mid-1990s and he had just graduated from university with a degree that wasn't particularly valuable. So he rode a hard-seat train for two days, arrived in Shenzhen, and

This is what democracy looked like several days before the crackdown at Tiananmen Square, Beijing, June 1989.

found work immediately. "It was a job, not very fun," he says. We first met soon after I arrived at his provincial university to study Mandarin as a foreign exchange student in 1989. Like many Chinese of his generation, he's not jumping up and down ranting about labour abuses or lamenting globalization. It was a job, nothing special, and his recollection sounds a lot like those of North American kids who worked in a warehouse or washed dishes for summer pay. "Long hours, boring, bad food."

Most Westerners would not last the marathon train ride on a Chinese hard seat, let alone suffer Shenzhen's factory complexes. My friend's understatement belies the discomfort and long hours that many mainlanders manage without complaint, all in aid of a better life for themselves and their children. Thanks to a mildly profitable stay in Shenzhen, he's about to buy his first house and perhaps one day marry his girlfriend. His career prospects are solid. For him a sojourn in Shenzhen was a transition – the world that Sam Walton and Deng Xiaoping helped build hasn't been without benefit.

But factory labour might have been a permanent prospect if he'd been any more active in the failed democracy movement of May and June 1989.

That's when we became friends, as we swarmed the streets along with thousands of other students in one of a hundred mini-uprisings across China inspired by the students in Tiananmen Square. It was the spring of a lifetime as we cut classes, drank tea, and translated slogans. Our university town, while a thousand miles from Tiananmen, still topped 10,000 in the city square before the army massacred thousands in the capital – then everyone scattered.

I returned years later to see what was left behind. "Many of my classmates who were ringleaders still have trouble with the government," my friend says. "They cannot advance in their jobs and must work for others if they want to succeed. I can talk about this now because we are old and do not have connection with these things anymore." Tiananmen, like Shenzhen, is behind him. Like others of his generation – the generation that now manages and owns factories as well as works in them – he is getting on with his life.

We sit together in a chic Taoist teahouse in the same coastal city, catching up on old times only a train ride away from the incredible glass towers and high-priced designer malls of Shanghai. We're no longer students in a would-be revolution, echoing cries of "*min zhu*" amid a crowd of thousands. He has a cellphone, a house, and, I'm guessing, a much larger TV than mine. In this nation of peasants, his arrival into the middle class from Tiananmen via Shenzhen is China's version of the American Dream.

Just like my old schoolmate, China doesn't really want to build cheap stuff anymore; it wants your job as consumer. In 2007, for the first time, domestic consumption contributed more to China's economic growth than foreign exports: it was 37 percent of China's GDP, while foreign demand/net exports were 21.4 percent. Although China is still a long way from the 70-plus percent consumption GDP of Western nations, this nevertheless represents one of several strategic movements away from bargain manufacturing as a pillar of China's economy. In other words, the very thing that kick-started China's emergence out of the dark days of the 1970s – foreign capital and export manufacture – is slowly being eclipsed by the emergence of other priorities, not the least a Western-style consumer economy. "This is a healthy development trend," argues Shi Jianhuai, of Peking University's School of Economics. "We cannot depend on foreign demand (for economic growth) in such a big economy as China."

It's an important juncture. China's national interests are now diverging from those of its major trading partners. And they are diverging not just in trade but also energy supplies, currency reserves, and international development. Many Chinese have assumed this from the beginning, knowing that they would not forever be manufacturing Malibu Barbie or Tickle Me Elmo. Westerners, caught up in a wave of consumer rapture that has since turned to panic, have been slow to recognize this.

"The government's intention is to decrease the volume of exports and to provide workers with a fair wage," explains Li Qiang. "First, the government wants to encourage economic development away from coastal areas and toward the countryside," he says, noting inland movement away from special economic zones like Shenzhen. "And second, because workers' wages are so low, they can't be consumers. The government needs more responsive consumers to stimulate the market and decrease long-term social instability."

"The Chinese government is attempting to decrease the gap between rich and poor in China by using rights and legislation as a tool for economic policy," says the former Sichuan province resident. "Chinese goods will become more expensive, but the transition from manufacturing to consumerism is an essential path in the view of government."

China's apparent trajectory is deglobalization. One way or another, it wants to remove its rich subsidies from the global marketplace, and in so doing, become the superpower that many predicted it would become. China cannot reach its goals by continuing to improve the living standards of its trading partners. And as crises emerge in the twenty-first century, the nation's ruling class may be forced to diverge or decouple more quickly than Western nations expected.

The end of cheap will not be sudden, but it has already begun. China's move to higher-value products is one aspect of an effort to export less value. Its often-neglected social and environmental problems now create additional drag on Western bargains, as China can no longer fully internalize these costs. And predictably, it has taken a tougher stand on trade and the management of its currency, which trading partners have long alleged has been undervalued and has thereby given China an unfair trade advantage.

China was already putting the screws to foreign investment and exporters even as labour costs increased during the mid-2000s. In 2007 Beijing selectively cut export subsidies, "eliminating rebates . . . for more than 500 types of high-polluting goods such as fertilizer and leather," reported *Business Week*, "while further whittling down rates for some 2,800 other low-tech products."

And in 2008 China opposed all the developed nations in the World Trade Organization on agricultural free trade, effectively collapsing seven years of talks. Eager to join the WTO since the 1990s for the benefits of greater trade liberalization, China (along with India) eventually chose instead to protect its farmers against agricultural imports, claiming "a food-security policy of relying on domestic supply" in the face of global rice shortages and depressed rural income. After an estimated 20 million Chinese farmers were evicted between 1992 and 2005 because of land development, the government has begun to protect its 750 million rural residents even at the expense of international trade. Chinese farmers now directly benefit from additional protections such as limits on industrial development and conversion of farmland to factories, as well as the promise of greater environmental protection that will ensure improved conditions for Chinese citizens but create new challenges for manufacturers. (In the past, the United States, the European Union, Canada, and Japan dominated trade talks. China emerged as an advocate of Third World economies, demanding and largely receiving the dual rights of food protectionism and continued free trade in goods, much to the dismay of Western nations. "It is a massive blow to confidence in the global economy," claimed Peter Power of the European Commission. "The confidence shot in the arm that we needed badly will not now happen.")

The other, potentially huge consideration is that China, like many other nation-investors, was badly burned by its American investments in the early days of the global economic crisis. Will it continue to purchase American debt as an investment? The future of globalization appears to hang on this one question alone. China's ongoing purchase of U.S. treasury notes has not only allowed Americans to finance large government deficits – spending on the Iraq war, stimulus programs, and bank bailouts – but has also enabled the continuation of large trade imbalances generally, by creating the illusion of stability. "Like so many imbalances in economics, this one can't go on indefinitely, and therefore won't," writes James Fallows. "But the way it ends – suddenly versus gradually, for predictable reasons versus during a panic – will make an enormous difference to the U.S. and Chinese economies over the next few years, to say nothing of bystanders in Europe and elsewhere."

This is how the economic DNA of nations was rewritten as one side of the Earth increasingly produced a growing range of goods and the other side consumed them. In the United States, household consumption expenditure nearly doubled between 1990 and 2001, while at the same time the American trade deficit increased almost fivefold. (In particular, America's trade deficit with China soared to $177.47 billion in 2006 from $102 billion in 2005; it had advanced to $183 billion by 2008.)

It has been assumed that this severe confluence of economies – or "Chimerica," as economist Niall Ferguson describes it – is the trade equivalent of mutually assured destruction. It won't fail, because no one can afford failure. Because about 30 percent of America's trade imbalance comes from Chinese imports, the Middle Kingdom knows well that it would be unwise to sabotage the U.S. consumer economy. Moreover, U.S. dollars account for an estimated 70 percent of China's holdings, the largest foreign reserves in the world, and any major move against America could massively devalue China's incredible nest egg. Much depends on how these countries manage their currencies and how much additional debt they create. But tough times have caused strains as well as unprecedented new public and private debt – and America isn't as great an investment as it used to be. The U.S. "should make the Chinese feel confident that the value of [its American] assets at least will not be eroded in a significant way," said Yu Yongding, former adviser to China's central bank, in 2009, who scolded America for "reckless policies."

In many ways the trade imbalance is no longer about trade. It is about power and wealth transfer. Networked commerce has resulted in the creation of soft empires, zones of influence and connection that overlap among nations, governments, and companies. The American government, the Chinese government, and major retailers such as Wal-Mart all have power and influence well beyond their respective jurisdictions, yet none enjoys full independence. "The integration of the four fifths of the world that is poor with the one fifth that is wealthy has the potential to be one of the two or three most important economic developments of the past millennium, along with the Renaissance and the Industrial Revolution," predicted Harvard economist Lawrence Summers in 2006.

Yet for all its strength as the world's largest country holding the world's largest pile of money, China's position is surprisingly tentative. China gained strength in the world precisely because it managed to mitigate, defer, and obscure the consequences of unsustainable growth. For over three decades East and West alike enjoyed a free ride on pollution, social strife, violence, and poverty. The impacts have most dramatically accrued in China, and its government has used up considerable capital, resilience, and goodwill in an impressive attempt to manage the unmanageable.

China is leveraged, but not in the same way as its cash-poor trading partners: it is dangerously top-heavy, since the labour, resource, and environmental capital at the bottom of its economy have eroded. And China has depended on growth and the trickle-down effect of new wealth to smooth over the cracks and cleavages that still erode its foundations.

In hindsight, this growth strategy was a gambit on a scale that may not be witnessed for another generation. For years China was the turnaround story in market-based poverty-reduction development. ("China alone accounted for over 75 percent of poverty reduction in the developing world over the last 20 years," claimed the World Bank in a 2005 brief.) But as economies slowed and became more expensive, these market-based gains eroded as well – not just in China, but everywhere, including among the estimated 400 million poor in India and the price-shocked population of Vietnam, who suffered through Asia's worst inflation: 27 percent in 2008.

And now that much of globalization's easy growth is behind us, China's underclass still persists, better off than when Mao came to power in 1950 but not improved enough to guarantee stability in the twenty-first century. It turns out that the number of chronically poor may have been vastly underestimated all along – three times that of mid-2000 estimates – suggesting that the long-term benefits of globalization and growth may not be as large or as permanent as expected. "The number of people in China living below the World Bank's dollar-a-day poverty line is 300 million," argued Albert Keidel, of the Carnegie Endowment for International Peace, in 2007. "This more accurate picture of China clarifies why Beijing concentrates so heavily on domestic priorities such as growth, public investment, pollution control and poverty reduction." Keidel recalls that back in the 1980s and 1990s, China's dollar-a-day poverty count was likely more than 500 million people. "China has made enormous strides in lifting its population out of poverty," he concludes. "But the task was perhaps more gargantuan than most people thought and progress has been overstated."

China's addiction to economic growth to stave off poverty is its defining national liability, in the same way that America and other nations are saddled with consumer insolvency and energy inefficiency. And it all started with the lowly bargains in a fishing village near Hong Kong.

For these and other reasons, the late 1990s probably represented the peak of China's capacity to deliver to Western consumers profit and savings. These days, nations might be wise to place a risk premium on China. China's problematic and highly asymmetrical power structure still threatens a modal shift similar to those studied in climate-change science. If it fails, it will likely fail big. But instead of melting polar ice caps leading to a catastrophic sea rise or rapid temperature gains, China threatens a different sort of change, and not a nice one, either: abrupt, disruptive, and likely violent. This of course would cause economic crisis elsewhere, especially given China's part ownership of the American economy and integration with Europe, Canada, and the rest of Asia. Even its energy partners in Africa would suffer greatly. In other words, growth without accountability is ultimately problematic, and a random shift within China's simmering internal crisis could sabotage Western economies well before environmental impacts, energy costs, and trade deficits stem the flow of bargains.

Sudden, disruptive change is hardly a rarity in Chinese history. The day before the 1989 massacre in Tiananmen Square that claimed between eight hundred and three thousand lives, my Chinese friend decided to show me his family home. As student protests raged on the streets outside and across China, we wandered into a maze of old *hutongs* (alleys) to where brick-and-mud apartments surrounded a tiny courtyard. Inside, where his grandmother once lived (previous generations had toiled in the countryside), we sat at a tiny square table and drank tea. Then he unveiled his prize possession, a 26-inch colour television, something that in 1989 had probably cost him dearly. There was no electricity, but we sat there and stared at it anyway.

That was the end of something. A day later, China's ruling class turned away from reform and police and army forces marched to violently quell protests across the country. As time passed, former protesters became shoppers and workers. Televisions became larger, cheaper, and more plentiful. Wal-Mart, McDonald's, and Carrefour came calling, and students studied business and got jobs and largely forgot dreamy, dangerous notions of a democratic China.

After the tanks rolled in Beijing, I remember wandering the streets near Shanghai. Buses were overturned, barricades had been erected – students had temporarily locked down the city in protest of the killing at Tiananmen. Mostly the streets were empty; some of the protesters were already in hiding. It felt as if the whole country had been wiped clean.

However, it is the bargain that heralds the end of an intense but surprisingly short chapter in the history of human development. We rewired global trade and employment to leverage a vast labour resource that is no longer stable. In the process, China and other cheap producers helped insulate consumers from the consequences of growth and scarcity. Trouble is, China has now made it clear that it no longer wants that role – a risky proposition for everyone involved.

author photo

CONTAINER TRADE:
CARGO CULTS OF THE TWENTY-FIRST CENTURY

4

-The "Ever Dynamic" container ship, owned by Taiwan's Ever-green Line, docks at the Port of Los Angeles.

An Economy on the Docks

As I look out over the Pacific Ocean, a giant container ship approaches, gliding carefully into the inner harbour of North America's busiest port. It's hardly a ship; more like a motorized island, OOCL *Tianjin* is over 1,000 feet long, 140 feet wide, and more than ten storeys high from sea level to bridge tower. Guided by GPS satellites, thousands of on-board sensors, and remote video cameras, the ship's pilots carefully steer the vessel into dock at Pier F. *Tianjin* has circled the Pacific Rim, north from Hong Kong, up past Japan towards the Aleutian Islands south of Alaska, then back south to here, the combined ports of Los Angeles and Long Beach.

As it settles into dock, *Tianjin*'s massive hull eclipses the horizon. A vessel of this class, one too large to fit inside the Panama Canal, sails around the world seven or eight times each year, arriving full from Asia and returning east nearly empty. Onshore, a ragtag fleet of semi-trailer trucks buzzes about the port and Greater Los Angeles, delivering containers to countless warehouses, rail yards, and long-haul trucking depots.

In less than eight hours *Tianjin* will unload nearly eight thousand steel containers, each twenty to forty feet long, all filled with consumer goods that will be loaded onto rail cars and trucks and hauled inland to distribution centres and retail outlets as far away as New York, Toronto, and Chicago.

Less than one hundred years ago, this port was 800 acres of mud flats at the mouth of the Los Angeles River. Now it's 43 miles of modern harbour encompassing a total of 15,100 acres of wharves, cargo terminals, cruise ship docks, roadways, rail yards, and shipping channels that collectively move 11 million containers annually. Past civilizations built pyramids and temples as a testament to their ingenuity and affluence. Instead, we move shipping containers on a monumental scale, something that will surely amaze and impress future generations.

Our world is defined by transport. From the 1980s onward, booming trade with Pacific Rim nations turned major port cities such as Los Angeles into transport thoroughfares clogged with gigantic container ships, endless trains of intermodal containers, and vast truck fleets that roamed the interstates the way that bison once ruled the prairie. Amazingly, nearly half of all American container trade – roughly 9 million steel boxes – manages to travel through Los Angeles, the continent's most congested and traffic-dysfunctional megalopolis. And many people, locals included, would be surprised to learn that goods movement – not tourism or movies – has been one of California's biggest sources of new employment in recent decades.

Consequently, transport just isn't transport in today's world: it is a force that has unlocked new profit, speed, and a cornucopic flood of affordable products that launched globalization into overdrive. In today's global shopping economy, advances such as offshore labour, petrochemicals, and credit cards are rendered meaningful only by modern logistics networks, constellations of technology and hardware that made the Earth appear nearly flat. Firms able to harness the power of transport and logistics management have proven to be some of the most successful – and in the case of Wal-Mart, the most resilient – corporations of our day.

Yet in making the world smaller and flatter, the logistics solutions of the twentieth century are creating new problems. Here in Los Angeles, the persistent soot and haze created by the non-stop transport of goods are directly responsible for an estimated 2,400 California deaths each year and contribute to one-third of the region's air pollution. Even during prosperous economic times, L.A.'s transport-dominated economy was battered by everything from local environmental protest to cutthroat global competition for the cheapest shipping rates. When consumer demand began to collapse in 2008, containers, cars, and recycling began to pile up in and around the dockyards. The delicate balance of L.A.'s high-volume, low-margin economy came undone, in no small way contributing to California's struggles with insolvency. Facing over 10 percent unemployment in 2009, California's economy – once touted as a beacon of innovation – was crashing like a played-out resource economy from the previous century, not unlike the frontier oil booms that once defined L.A.'s waterfront.

Moreover, the shape of global commerce itself is proving to be less than flat. *Wired* magazine famously named the shipping container the "20-ton packet," but the globalization-as-flat-network metaphor was easier to sustain during the 1990s, when resources and fuel were cheaper. The paradoxical reality is that our web of trade and transport is dynamic but often fiercely exclusionary and dependent on past-century luxuries like cheap oil and cheap steel.

On the docks of L.A.'s harbour, things still look pretty routine. Two-ton containers briskly travel off ships, load onto trucks or trains, and then disappear. Empty ships float off into the distance and new ones, laden low with anonymous cargo, arrive to unload again. And so it continues, even in the wake of a global economic crisis, partly because there is yet no other plan for the future. You'd never guess that toys covered in lead paint and toothpaste laced with antifreeze chemicals rolled through here not long ago. Or that America's Homeland Security can't reliably monitor for dirty nuclear bombs inside containers that could detonate anywhere between here and Duluth.

City of Containers

In the very middle of the harbour front, the looming 5,000-foot span of the Gerald Desmond Bridge connects the port facilities on Terminal Island with downtown Long Beach and one of America's busiest trucking routes, the northbound Interstate 710. Even with 200 feet of vertical clearance, the space beneath the bridge is still too small for many large ships. Some actually wait for low tide to edge underneath with a few feet of safe clearance.

Above, up on the road, container trucks haul past, inching up the incline of the bridge deck and racing down the other side. Departing trucks sprint towards the 1-710, which links the port with warehouses and rail yards across greater L.A. and destinations beyond.

The bridge's huge span isn't enough: port advocates say L.A. needs a new bridge system to keep truck traffic moving, one that runs four lanes, not two. More urgent perhaps is that this "official welcoming monument" of L.A. is slowly falling apart. The bridge has been crumbling for years, and blocks of concrete occasionally crash into the ocean below. At last report, replacing the bridge will cost $800 million. In the meantime, engineers have hung netting beneath it in an effort to catch the larger chunks.

Getting out of L.A.'s port itself is just the beginning. Anyone who drives northbound Interstate 710 knows that the traffic is often insane. Drivers can easily get lost in the flow of trailer-bound containers trying to escape the harbour, like a guppy among whales. The rumbling stampede of semis, which are blamed for everything from increased pollution-related deaths to road accidents, is actually part of a highly orchestrated flow of rail and road traffic that exits the harbour twenty-four hours a day.

Miles inland, one is still surrounded by containers. Intermodal yards are large staging grounds where trucks transfer containers from ships to trains. Across the inland empire and beyond are countless warehouses and trans-shipment docks where containers are unloaded, repacked with goods, and launched directly to retail stores or even larger regional distribution centres. Inland ports – distant staging grounds connected by rail – have been proposed at Antelope Valley, on the edge of the Mojave Desert, more than seventy miles from the harbour. "There is no land to expand the port facilities," argued one government planner in 2007. "You need at least 500 acres for a decent inland port facility, and that kind of land is not available in the urban core."

And when this not-so-graceful ballet of rigs, ships, and trains jams up, the results can be devastating. The ports of Los Angeles and Long Beach have experienced repeated major delays, including a 2004 record overflow of a hundred ships backed up out of the harbour or diverted. The gridlock froze one-third of all American imports at the time, costing as much as $4 billion in the process, thanks to congestion, labour troubles, and record-setting trade volumes. "[In 2004] the Port of Long Beach compared the scene to the World War II invasion of Normandy," reported one industry magazine. In a world of lean inventories, just-in-time production, and high demand, slowdowns cause considerable trouble.

Los Angeles has suffered in the past because of congestion. Some ships, following Wal-Mart's lead, now circumnavigate Central America, crossing through the Panama Canal to Atlantic-side ports in the Gulf of Mexico and on the eastern seaboard to gain nominal time savings. In the upside-down world of logistics, many bargains now travel farther to arrive sooner, resulting in an ever-growing fleet of ships sailing ever more unlikely routes to gain small advantages.

Anthony Otto, vice-president of the Long Beach terminal of Hong Kong–based Orient Overseas Container Link (OOCL), looks down from an office three storeys above the pier and marvels at how much has changed since he first entered the business some twenty-three years ago. As late as the 1970s, many ships still loaded and unloaded bulk goods and individual boxes, barrels, and pallets – the equivalent of the Dark Ages in logistics. "At the time everyone knew that containerization was growing, but it was not anywhere near the magnitude that it is today," says Otto. "Since then, it has quadrupled in size." As facilities continue to grow, new piers are built and the port continues to expand closer and closer to the open ocean that lies beyond the breakwater of the harbour.

Everything gets bigger, including a trend toward the gargantuan in ships and infrastructure that began with containerization. "You've got ships that continue to get bigger and bigger and more forty- and forty-five-foot-long containers," says Otto. "Terminals – big terminals – were built quickly; anyone who wanted to sign up for one, anyone who felt they could fill it with international freight, containerized cargo – a terminal was relatively easy to come by."

During the three-decade growth spurt that closed the twentieth century, L.A.'s Bay of San Pedro was gradually filled by larger and larger piers, warehouses, cranes, and fuel facilities. Quantum savings were created through what became known as containerization – goods, materials, and parts packed into twenty- and forty-foot-long steel containers.

This is where the new economy emerged out of the old economy. The pre-container "break-bulk" system of loading cargo in ship holds dated back to the days of the Phoenicians. Commercial containerization was proven by American Malcolm McLean in 1956, with the first successful voyage of the *Ideal-X* container ship from Newark to Houston. Before that it was not unusual for a shipment to incur as much as 50 percent of its costs for a few kilometres of travel portside at either end of its journey: piece-by-piece freight handling is time consuming and labour intensive. The steel box revolutionized the shipping industry. Now, with increasingly automated cranes, cars, and GPS tracking, it is possible to load or unload a single container every one to four minutes while a ship is docked. According to Matson Navigation, containerization increased the productivity of the shipping industry 6,752 percent between 1959 and 1976 (measured in tons of goods moved per working hour). It eliminated jobs, accelerated cargo, and saved massive amounts of money. Average port time shrunk from three weeks to eighteen hours.

"Consider the economics," writes historian Marc Levinson, author of *The Box*, a popular history of containerization. "Loading loose cargo [was] a back-breaking, laborious business." In 1956, the average medium-sized ship would cost $5.83 per ton of cargo, but on McLean's *Ideal-X*, the world's very first container ship, the cost was already less than 16 cents a ton. "All of a sudden, the cost of shipping products to another destination was no longer prohibitively expensive," says Levinson.

By 1979 the Port of Long Beach had changed over most of its facilities to move containers and automobiles. That same year, Hanjin Container Lines launched regular shipping between Asia and the L.A. harbour. Within two years, China Ocean Shipping (COSCO), which is wholly owned by the Chinese government, had made Long Beach its very first port of call; it would become one of the world's largest shipping companies. The local transport industry grew to include air freight, as evidenced by the growth of nearby LAX, now the world's fourth-busiest airport, which carried more than 2 million tons of air cargo shipments in 2003. Commerce accelerated as advanced logistics networks evolved, in step with containerization, to enable all manner of just-in-time manufacturing and retailing. And as discounting gradually consumed retailing, the L.A. harbour became bigger and bigger, a place where post-"Panamax" vessels are commonplace – ships too huge to fit inside the 110-foot-wide Panama Canal.

Even though an incredible amount of commerce passes through Greater L.A., what happens here is just the tip of the iceberg. Global logistics expenditure in 2002 was estimated by Michigan State University to be approximately $6.7 trillion, up from $5 trillion in 1997. This figure suggests that nearly 14 percent of the world economy (by GDP) is given over to fleets of trucks, airplanes, and container ships.

In this new world, transport of consumer goods has itself become a major industry, on par with the world's largest national economies. Greenhouse gas emissions from international shipping now exceed the total emissions of most nations listed in the Kyoto Protocol. Moreover, with massive clouds of air pollution floating over the Pacific Ocean from Asia's factories and power plants, changing hemispheric weather patterns and raining emissions down on North American shoppers, it's clear that our world has become connected in ways that defy categorization.

Between 1990 and 2001, the American trade deficit increased fivefold. Other Western nations followed suit with smaller but still significant imbalances. By the mid-2000s, Asian trade accounted for as much as 90 percent of shipments coming into L.A.'s ports. And as of 2003, the top twelve importers of containers at Los Angeles/Long Beach were all major retailers, and mostly discounters: Wal-Mart, Home Depot, Target, Lowe's, Kmart, IKEA, Payless Shoes, Pier 1, Big Lots, Toys "R" Us, Limited Brands, and Michaels. In other words, a significant part of southern California's economy is now dedicated to unloading ships from China, Vietnam, and Japan that in turn fill big-box stores across North America. Los Angeles delivers an amazing amount of international trade: Chicago receives 60 percent of its imported goods through L.A., for example.

Everything from medical supplies to consumer electronics, kitchen utensils, designer clothing, power tools, and automotive parts are inside the countless steel boxes. On any given day, Anthony Otto and everyone else working on the docks could glance up and see their next microwave or set of golf clubs floating by, buried deep inside a hundred-foot stack of containers. "The [trade] imbalance is huge," says Otto, eyeing the harbour, "and not a whole lot of finished product is going back that way."

Despite L.A.'s investment in port facilities, about 40 percent of the containers moving through here are still empty – most are returning to the Far East. The containers that return with contents, says OOCL service director Paul Conolly, are often filled with low-value goods or recycling. "The majority of the [return] cargo is waste paper, scrap metal, a lot of hay, chemicals," he says. "Basically, it's raw materials." Some 11.6 million tons of recovered paper and cardboard were sent from America to China in 2008. Port authorities there confirm that the main imports are petroleum, electronics, plastics, furniture, and clothing; top exports include petroleum products, waste paper and scrap metal, chemicals, and plastic.

It does seem strange that some of the world's most advanced transport systems, along with the largest container ships in the world, are used to deliver recycling to China. Chronic trade imbalances mean that as much as 40 percent of Pacific Rim shipping business often involves cargo that isn't worth the value of the steel box it's shipped in. "Everything that is brought over from Asia is in a [cardboard] box," explains Conolly. "And often those boxes are just thrown away – or they can be taken back, recycled in the paper plants in China, and reused to make more boxes to repackage." There is a steady but small flow of trade in certain higher-value goods and parts, such as ball bearings and specialty chemicals, but if any finished product is actually shipped to Asia, it is likely be a faulty one being returned to the original factory or supplier.

It's estimated that the global shipping industry spends $11 billion annually managing and moving empty containers around the world. Representing one-twentieth of all global trade, Los Angeles could be spending as much as $550 million annually just to manage its empties. Many containers aren't returned, however, and they pile up like multicoloured Lego blocks all around the Los Angeles Basin. As cargo volumes boomed, the City of Angels gradually became the City of Containers. By 2009, with the collapse in demand for American exports, the number of empty containers handled at the Port of Los Angeles was increasing – a unique situation, since all other container counts at the port complex were decreasing in the face of the global economic meltdown.

But people still need underwear and toothpaste. At the deep end of Long Beach's harbour, a steady parade of rumbling trains and trailer trucks glides a few metres above the ocean, along narrow fingers of landfill where salt water once washed against warships, sloops, and canoes. Everyone remembers, earlier in the 2000s, during the boom economy, when massive container ships like *Tianjin* were occasionally backed up in L.A.'s harbour out into the open ocean, piled high with flat-screen TVs and gaming consoles, like a lineup of anxious shoppers on Black Friday. Recent years have been less memorable. Business is bad. The docks are still busy – surprisingly so, with only 10 percent fewer shipments in March 2009 than the previous year. But there are also growing piles of near-worthless recycling that China doesn't want anymore, more empty containers than ever, and a glut of Japanese cars that too few people want to purchase. There is no happy medium, it seems.

The Global Pipeline

Eliminating piece-by-piece freight handling at both ends of the voyage was an economic master stroke, akin to the advent of commercial jet travel and Internet commerce. Modern shipping redefined global trade in much the same way as railways once revolutionized the landscape of late-nineteenth-century North America: railways made fortunes, built empires, and set the pattern for the kind of settlement and sprawl that eventually provided an ideal habitat for big-box stores. Today, all that is cheap owes something to the incredible speed and volume at which hundreds of thousands of nearly identical steel containers hurtle around the world.

Despite trumpeting of the knowledge economy within the developed world, the vast majority of global trade is still in goods, not services. Materials and goods are worth $13.6 trillion, more than four times international trade in services. This differential is profound, given that many domestic economies are dominated by consumption and service-related activities, yet the actual business of global trade is still highly material, as it has been since the beginning.

The goods-movement industry on display in L.A.'s harbour is only part of a vast and growing system of manufacturers, shippers, contractors, merchants, and retailers. The current stage of globalization was possible because of the late-twentieth-century emergence of supply chain management, which realized the full potential of transportation networks by borrowing from advances in military logistics. Complex contractual and logistical arrangements, supported by a cast of thousands, have now created an assembly line so huge that buyers and manufacturers often never know each other's identities, let alone communicate directly.

Although offshore manufacture and containerization had existed for years, hyper-efficient trade emerged as communications technology flourished, companies collaborated and shared information, and sophisticated analytical and tracking tools emerged. The IT surge of the 1990s created the necessary Web-based software and real-time communication links to accelerate trade worldwide. Along with thousands of shipping containers criss-crossing the globe, a new science emerged to investigate concepts such as continuous replenishment (low inventory, rapid manufacture and delivery of products) and disintermediation (eliminating wholesalers and middlemen). This is how Wal-Mart worked behind the scenes during the 1990s to hobble its competition. GPS-based tracking, bar-code links, and Web-based management systems completed the replacement of paper-based logistics that began with Japanese just-in-time production for automobiles and now incorporates current space and military technology. By 2000, U.S. industry had spent an estimated $950 billion on logistics alone, the core aspect of supply chain management.

This new phase of global commerce helped Wal-Mart and Carrefour to become bigger than ever, but it also resulted in the outsourcing of whole companies. Dell Computers, for example, built its success on being a computer company that doesn't actually make computers, but is instead an aggregate of far-flung production networks. Companies created alliances with suppliers, sharing information to make ordering, inventory, and accounting more automatic. Wal-Mart was among the first to share sales data with major suppliers. "Every time a box of Tide is rung up at the cash register," according to the company, "Wal-Mart's data warehouse takes note and knows when it is time to alert P&G to replenish a particular store. As a result, Wal-Mart stores rarely run out of stock of popular items."

Moreover, the nature of goods trade is itself highly distributed: more parts, components, and materials are shipped than finished goods. In 2003, 54 percent of global manufacturing imports were actually "intermediate goods" – parts, packaging, materials, all sourced for particular products – en route to assembly before heading to market, which in turn has increased the number of overall trips. Your LCD television indeed took one long journey across the ocean, but its parts may have travelled even farther.

This is Fordism on a planetary basis, a disjointed but highly coordinated process in which manufacturers, traders, and retailers often appear to function as a single company. As trade pioneer Victor Fung describes it, the "borderless manufacturing" of the modern supply chain changed production-consumption around the world. The modern supply chain was invented by people like Fung, whose venerable Hong Kong–based family firm, Li & Fung, was the very first Chinese-owned export company. From the success of developing a new kind of firecracker in 1907 to managing the supply chain for fashion, toy, and appliance buyers – Gap, Levi Strauss, Marks and Spencer, Gymboree – companies such as Fung's are creating "a new kind of multinational," as he told the *Harvard Business Review* in 2000.

As befits a global giant, Li & Fung is now incorporated in Bermuda but operates mainly from Hong Kong's Kowloon Peninsula. It is one of the world's largest trading companies, with $5.5 billion in sales and six thousand employees worldwide. And it stays well removed from actual production. "We are a smokeless factory. We do design. We buy and inspect the raw materials," explained Fung. "But we don't manage the workers and we don't own the factories. . . . We work with about 7500 suppliers in more than 26 countries . . . more than a million workers engaged on behalf of our customers."

One result is increased intra-Asia trade, the kind of regionally zoned commerce that could one day replace globalization. "Today Asia consists of multiple networks of dispersed manufacturing – high-cost hubs that do sophisticated planning for regional manufacturing," says Fung of the new production networks. "Bangkok works with the Indochinese peninsula, Taiwan with the Philippines, Seoul with Northern China."

While the European Union offers some regional protection from de-globalization, major Western economies like Germany and the United States are still hard-wired for global trade. By 2007 American business was spending $1.4 trillion on logistics, amounting to 10.1 percent of the nation's GDP. It was the age of FedEx, Amazon, eBay, and a booming retail trade increased demand for transport. For its part, America not only created a hungry consumer base but also championed global trade liberalization. The United States played a formative role in shaping and controlling postwar trade agreements such as the 1947 GATT, whose primary function was to liberalize global commerce. This resulted in an increase in overall world trade from $365 billion in 1950 to $6.4 trillion in 2000.

Ensuring access to ocean transport has, until recently, been how nations and companies established political and economic clout. Europe dominated the shipping industry during the 1980s, when Maersk of Denmark seized opportunity from the 1970s collapse of the industry – when shipbuilding costs soared 400 percent between 1970 and 1975, thanks largely to high oil prices – and bought ships and shipping companies at bargain prices. Like retail, shipping is highly competitive; its history is littered with bankrupt companies and failed endeavours. Maersk discounted shipping rates and accumulated container ships as companies from the steamship era slowly died off and America lost dominance as a merchant marine fleet; in 1999 it purchased container pioneer Malcolm McLean's company, Sea-Land Service. By 2005 Maersk had accumulated more than five hundred container ships and cornered one-sixth of the global shipping market, becoming the largest container-ship operator in the world.

Indeed, Maersk became the Wal-Mart of the logistics world, and the scale and ferocious efficiency with which it operated, pioneering ever-larger container ships and ever-faster port facilities, ultimately helped consolidate the modern supply chain. "Where it sees leverage then expect a list of demands typically involving a reduction in price," wrote *PortStrategy* magazine in a September 2008 editorial. "There is a ruthless determination afoot in Maersk Line to improve business performance with this described as focused on four key elements: filling ships with profitable cargo; product reliability; faster more responsive service; and reduced complexity and cost."

But, like trade, transportation has never been neutral. When the United States completed its network of interstate highways in the 1950s, it was with a mind to national security: ground transportation for mobile missiles in a nuclear world was seen as strategic. Likewise, trade agreements and international systems of currency that were developed during the twentieth century have tipped the balance of power towards those who already own supply chains and transport networks. As Joseph Stiglitz explained in *Making Globalization Work*, an estimated $500 billion flowed from poor countries to rich countries in 2006 simply through the regular functioning of the global reserve system – the system by which countries accumulate foreign currency through trade, mostly in American dollars. The back-and-forth of trade, represented by resources and container units, creates currency structures and transactions that fund American public debt while eroding the wealth of developing nations. "We can think of this as a round-robin, with money flowing from the developing countries to the United States, and then flowing back again," writes Stiglitz. "There is something peculiar – one might say wrong – with the system, especially since the interest rate they receive . . . is so much lower than the interest rate they pay when they borrow the money back again."

This sort of bad deal has been perpetuated by China in its methodical creation of the world's largest foreign reserves – again, mostly in the form of American dollars that support U.S. debt. China gets poor returns from its American holdings, but it gains better leverage on other things, such as its own currency, inflation, and possibly geopolitical economic status. By tolerating low returns from American bonds and keeping its own currency undervalued, China's government has lowered material standards for its citizens while gaining tremendous international clout.

Ironically, many poorer countries hang on to currency as a form of "self-insurance," writes José Antonio Ocampo in a 2007 United Nations study: currency from a rich country such as the United States has been assumed to be assured and stable. But Ocampo warns of the "fallacy of composition," whereby if everyone accumulates large resources of the same currency as insurance, profound instability is created. It is very hard to bail out this system when it collapses, as evidenced in 2009, when it became clear that there was too much unevenly distributed globally funded debt, including $1 trillion in U.S. debt held by China alone.

The money system behind global trade, it turns out, threatens both rich and poor. It poses another level of risk created through leveraging of growth, trade, and currency exchange, a pattern of escalation not unlike the unregulated transactions that precipitated the 2008 financial collapse. "Self-insurance is not only a costly form of insurance for individual countries but also a source of instability to the global economy," concludes Ocampo. There are "many similarities with the instability that a national banking system faced in the past in the absence of a lender of last resort."

On the ground, globalization is also governed by transport networks that can additionally exclude and disable economies. Regional manufacturing clusters in Chinese cities purposefully dominate whole categories of product: there is growing protectionism; there are pressures on shippers to skip smaller countries and ports in order to save money; global banking and aid agencies require growth-intensive and open trade development. This isn't the flat world of open networks that was optimistically proclaimed during the mid-2000s. Globalization at the end of the age of bargains is a series of product pipelines. This reality reflects the natural-resource intensity of major economies, the centralization of ownership of non-renewable resources such as oil and gas, and the vast network of actual pipelines required to affordably deliver energy resources to keep ships, factories, and trucks operating.

The ruthless competition for cheap within the shipping sector has directly created inequity around the world. "Container shipping, it is clear, has helped some cities and countries become part of the new supply chains, while leaving others to the side," writes Marc Levinson. "It has assisted the rapid economic growth of Korea while offering precious little to Paraguay." Poorer countries, whose ports are less busy or less well managed, lose out. Either a country invests billions or it is excluded, it seems. This does much to explain the vast difference between Asia and other developing areas in overall trade growth from the late 1980s onward. The World Bank has estimated that if Peru were as effective at port management as Australia, its foreign trade would have increased 25 percent.

Functionally, globalization is heavily networked but does not perform like a network; it is selectively connective, and surprisingly arbitrary. "The massive ports constructed in China, Malaysia, and Thailand during the 1990s were investments in globalization," says Levinson. "Factories whose goods use those ports will have the lowest rates and the lowest costs in lost time. A country cursed with outmoded or badly run ports is a country that faces great obstacles. . . . The big containerships that link national economies in the global supply chain, carrying nothing but stacks of metal boxes, will pass it by."

The Heart of Los Angeles

Los Angeles didn't want to be passed by. Los Angeles bet its future on global transport for the same reason that hordes of people walk into Wal-Mart looking for part-time jobs: it needed cash. Before the shipping boom, L.A. was suffering from broad-based unemployment. Between 1987 and 1994, the city's military manufacturing base eliminated nearly 200,000 jobs as the Cold War finally drew to a close. It was part of a larger unemployment free fall in which many high-value jobs disappeared during a long period of deindustrialization that deeply eroded the black and Latino working class. Whatever new jobs emerged, such as those within the growing warehousing and transport industry, were temporary or for reduced wages, or both. "LA is the hole in the national bucket," wrote Berkeley's Stephen Cohen at the time. "Twenty-seven per cent of [America's] entire 1990–92 job loss took place in Greater Los Angeles."

Things got worse. Amid growing unemployment, riots exploded in 1992, resulting in fifty-five deaths and $1 billion in damage. Along with several earthquakes and fires, the L.A. riots marked a breaking point, a foreboding glimpse of the post-apocalyptic city depicted in action movies. It was, as historian Mike Davis notes, "possibly the first multi-ethnic rioting in modern American history . . . economically desperate Latinos in some of the city's poorest neighbourhoods, Mexican immigrants from South Central LA, and Salvadorian immigrants in the Park District in Hollywood joined in the looting."

Faced with a grim future, Los Angeles hedged on its growing port complex, along with rail-yard expansions, highways, and warehouses that shaped its urban landscape into something that might be able to process the massive crush of incoming goods from Asia. As port owners, the cities of Los Angeles and Long Beach dredged the harbour deep enough and built piers long enough to accommodate ships larger than anyone had ever seen before.

But it wasn't cheap. For decades, ports around the world have competed for shipping traffic, building bigger and bigger facilities on spec in an effort to lure ever-growing volumes of trade. Southern California didn't share the fate of Peru, Paraguay, or Baltimore largely because "Los Angeles and Long Beach feverishly made massive investments in container facilities in order to capture larger market shares of the burgeoning trans-Pacific containerized-cargo trade," notes Stephen Erie in *Globalizing LA*. Greater Los Angeles had entered a phase of globalization megaprojects. The cities invested $2 billion each on their respective port facilities during the 1990s as well as undertaking the $2.4 billion Alameda rail corridor project – a dedicated freight line launched in 2002 that runs mostly in a trench from downtown L.A. to the ports.

By 2007 the ports claimed one in eight of all jobs in the L.A. region, to help ferry electronics, fashion, and auto parts – an estimated 8.4 million container units annually – from Asia's borderlands to the doorsteps of Hollywood and Vine.

The rebirth of Greater Los Angeles as a global transport hub is synchronous with the rise of Wal-Mart as the world's largest company. In 1994, just as Wal-Mart set its first $1-billion-a-week sales record, Los Angeles surpassed New York as America's busiest customs district. By 2005 Wal-Mart alone had imported 695,000 container units through the region's ports, much of it consisting of the company's annual $30 billion worth of Chinese imports. Together, these 695,000 containers would completely fill the world's largest container ship, the massive 1,300-foot-long *Emma Maersk*, sixty-three times.

Like Asian manufacturing economies and Western retailers, the business model of shipping is highly growth-dependent; to realize economies of scale and to beat growing costs, bigger is better. Shipping is where the giganticism of global trade comes into full view: ever-growing container ships and ever-growing dock facilities, automation, and technology. And with it comes a new growth imperative, because the industry requires new efficiencies and speed to fight against increased congestion, declining revenues, and increased costs.

Los Angeles has found that there are limits, however, not only because this capital-intensive industry hasn't always delivered expected economic benefits, but also because surrounding communities are now protesting, advocating, and successfully blocking port expansion in a last-ditch effort to avoid becoming overrun with pollution. "If the port expands, we're going to reach a point where we are not going to build roads fast enough," says Tom Politeo, a resident of the South L.A. harbourside community San Pedro.

Politeo's family has lived alongside L.A.'s harbour since the 1940s. He recalls a childhood with clean air, clean water, and towns largely free of congestion and disease. He remembers days when his family would set out in boats to bring fish in from San Pedro Bay. "There was a time when goods movement did not make up such a large percentage of our economy, and when fishing was the biggest industry."

Population and economic growth are expected to add millions of cars to L.A.'s roads and highways, and Los Angeles is already America's capital of traffic congestion. Billions more could be spent on upgrading and expanding transport infrastructure and highways. L.A.'s two main port freeways, for example, the Harbor 110 and the Long Beach I-710, were both built by government in the 1960s and need serious fixing. As America debated its economic stimulus plan in 2009, the sticker prices for trade infrastructure emerged: $6 billion for a truck tollway between Los Angeles and Long Beach, as well as replacement of another major harbour bridge, the Schuyler Heim, worth $1 billion.

As with other partially or fully deregulated industries, such as Enron, and America's sub-prime housing crisis, the costs borne by taxpayers can be considerable. New challenges and failures are generated within privately owned transport networks, yet they often become public expenses. "We laid the groundwork to move goods very cheaply," says Politeo. "The public picks up the expense, not only of the infrastructure, but of pollution as well. So include the social costs of living in a country devoted to transport. There are many costs associated with moving goods and moving people. We don't pay for all this up front. We have a subsidy for mobility."

Some of the greatest costs haven't even been counted yet. In Los Angeles, port-related pollution caused an estimated 29 premature deaths, 750 asthma attacks, and 6,600 lost work days in 2007. And while the low-grade diesel fuel burned by container ships saves money, the Pacific Institute has estimated that freight transport will cost California residents $200 billion in health impacts by the early 2020s.

Global connectivity isn't all that it's cracked up to be. After several decades of trade expansion, Greater Los Angeles is reaching its limits. Its highways are nearly full; its air is thick with diesel particulates. In response, the port is attempting to spread itself across the entire geographic area of the L.A. Basin and beyond. What began as shipping and a harbour is now generally known as the "goods movement industry," since this broad network of transport is no longer bound to the waterfront. "Southern California is America's gateway to the global economy and plays a central role in sustaining the nation's prosperity," said L.A. mayor Antonio Villaraigosa in 2007. "As container traffic continues to grow, we must invest more in our goods movement infrastructure while addressing the environmental and health impacts of ever-expanding international trade."

Just as Los Angeles was attempting to address congestion woes, several other issues reached critical mass: fuel prices, climate-change regulation, and unprecedented global competition for ships and steel. It was a perfect storm of problems. Los Angeles and Long Beach port authorities had already proposed spending more than $13 billion in expansion projects and upgrades up to 2020. New facilities would build vertically, stacking containers like high-rise buildings, creating greater densification and diminishing congestion. In addition, ongoing efforts would be made to optimize L.A.'s rail corridor and decrease container dwell-times on the docks. Port-side density would double – as would estimated capital costs – running up to 10,000 container units an acre.

Meanwhile, the logistics industry was facing its own difficulty. During a series of commodity and energy price spikes in the mid-2000s, it became evident that the years of easy growth were gone and that supply chains were vulnerable. The Council of Supply Chain Management Professionals estimated that total logistics costs to American business had increased 52 percent between 2003 and 2008. "We will not see a return to prosperity for some time," warned the council's Rosalyn Wilson. "I think logistics costs will claim an even higher percentage of GDP in [the future]." Trucking costs alone increased $36 billion in the United States in 2007, leading to the closure of more than two thousand trucking companies in the same period. In essence, a one-year rise in the price of crude oil had nearly eliminated the systemic savings of twenty years of supply chain engineering, yet sub-$100 oil in 2009 did not proportionately undo past cost increases.

"The cost of shipping a standard 40-foot container from East Asia to the US eastern seaboard . . . tripled since 2000 and will double again as oil prices head towards $200 per barrel," predicted economist Jeff Rubin in a 2008 brief. "Unless that container is chock full of diamonds, shipping costs have suddenly inflated the cost of whatever is inside. And those inflated costs get passed on to the Consumer Price Index when you buy that good at your local retailer." Shipping rates crashed after the financial collapse of 2008, but the lesson was clear: the affordability of goods movement is governed largely by the future price of non-renewable energy. "This is not just about steel, but also maple syrup and avocados and blueberries at the grocery store," said Rubin. "Avocado salad in Minneapolis in January is just not going to work in this new world, because flying it in is going to make it cost as much as a rib eye."

The embodied energy cost of modern transport hits shipping lines hard. "A container ship over the last, say, five to six years has probably gone up 40 to 50 percent in price," says Paul Conolly. "On the steamship side, steel has been a major factor, and the cost of building one of these container ships now has risen exponentially."

Even Maersk, the world's largest shipping line, was losing money on container operations during the early 2000s. It was forced to cut back on the number of delivery locations, thereby limiting access to trade and the company's five hundred container ships and 1.9 million containers. ("Maersk is undertaking the biggest cost-reduction plan in its 103-year history by cutting about 15 percent of the labor force at the container unit," reported Bloomberg in 2008 – as many as 10,000 people lost their jobs. Ironically, Maersk's oil and gas division, which operates drill platforms from Qatar to the North Sea, posted a 58 percent increase in profits for the same period, resulting in total profits of $4 billion for the company.) Like other shipping companies, Maersk began to pass along increased material and operational costs to customers and thus managed to regain profitability by late 2008. By 2009, shippers had the opposite problem: the growing expense of fuelling and maintaining idle ships.

"Either way, fuel drives everything," says Anthony Otto. "Not only the ships but every piece of equipment that we run is on fuel – that consumes a lot of fuel. Everything gets moved around, so our fuel costs have gone up tremendously." That transport is so closely tied to energy prices in a world facing long-term scarcity is a problem for Los Angeles, Rotterdam, Singapore, and anywhere else that depends on fast, affordable trade. Geopolitics, congestion, climatic instability, and the cost of sustaining far-flung manufacturing empires pose a deep threat to a consumer universe dependent on closely controlled costs.

The thing is, Los Angeles is a long way from becoming locally self-sufficient. It needs globalization badly, even if globalization itself isn't looking so good. As late as 2008, Los Angeles port authorities still optimistically predicted that trade volumes would triple or even quadruple between 2000 and 2020. Yet L.A. would never be able to fit in all this cargo unless it invested billions in new port infrastructure – and unless the entire Los Angeles region continued to shape itself around goods movement. Yet there is disruption and trouble if there is too much trade (congestion, pollution) or too little (unemployment, economic dependence). This is precisely the kind of paradox that dims the once-bright future of globalization. Los Angeles appears committed to the cost of sustaining a global transport hub in the future, but potential deglobalization, environment, and energy costs in the twenty-first century make transport a risky gambit.

Shipping demonstrates the new vulnerabilities of growth-dependent, globalized industries. Port security – scouting for dirty nuclear bombs hidden in an annual flow of three thousand incoming container ships – and the disruptive impact of climate change are serious new cost threats. "They are real costs that the shipping industry has to bear at this time," admits Conolly. "The terminals, the steamship lines, the trucking industries – all the various components of the supply chain are subjected to those two really important factors now. And they are not going to go away; they are real issues that are facing us."

Gridlock

Wilmington is one of those in-between places that you usually never hear about. This harbourside community was annexed by the City of Los Angeles in 1909 and has dutifully served as the backbone of the city's expansion ever since. Wilmington was the site of the region's first wharf and part of the 1784 Spanish land grant of Rancho San Pedro. It is a working-class community set amid old refineries, warehouses, ports, and highways, its greatest claim to fame its role as a post-industrial location for Hollywood movies. You've already seen it in movies – *Terminator 2*, *Fight Club*, *Crash*, *Gone in 60 Seconds*, among others.

But this is where L.A.'s transport economy was born. It was here that Los Angeles pioneer Phineas Banning dredged a ten-foot-deep harbour channel through the mud flats in 1871 and moved some 50,000 tons of cargo within a year. Banning had a notion of the importance of networks: he connected the harbour's muddy berths with a stagecoach line that went north to Salt Lake City, Utah, and east to Yuma, Arizona. By 1868 Banning had built one of L.A.'s first railroads, connecting San Pedro Bay with the inland settlement of Los Angeles. Once the area was annexed by L.A., industrial development gradually built up around Wilmington, encompassing oil refineries, freeways, and military installations as well as America's largest port complex.

By the 1990s the Latino community found itself hemmed in by industry. Wilmington sits in the middle of a constellation of eight major refining facilities within ten miles, six of which are in the community itself. Some refineries date back to the 1930s, when L.A. was growing around what is still one of America's largest-ever oil finds: the 3 billion barrels in the

author photo

Container trucks race north on the Long Beach Freeway towards downtown Los Angeles.

Wilmington field, which lies beneath the harbour, the community, and part of neighbouring Long Beach. By the 1940s L.A. and Long Beach had sucked so much oil out from under the harbour that the east side of Terminal Island began to sink below sea level; massive amounts of seawater had to be injected back into the shallow formation. The refineries remain critical to L.A.'s transport, manufacturing, and sprawl-defined economy: much of the region's diesel, jet fuel, gasoline, and feedstocks for chemicals and plastics is refined locally from imported crude. With California oil nearly depleted, the refineries import more than 50 percent of their crude from the Middle East and Latin America, adding to the strategic importance – and congestion – of L.A.'s port facilities. By 2021 more than 90 percent of southern California's crude oil will be imported through its ports, peaking at an estimated 1.3 million barrels per day by 2040, half of which will be delivered by aptly named "very large crude carriers" (VLCCs) from the Middle East.

Even though much of America's retail inventory travels around or through Wilmington, the community itself has no big-box malls or major retail. There is no Starbucks, Wal-Mart, or Home Depot here, just family-owned corner stores, car washes, some fast-food chains, and L.A.'s first Der Wienerschnitzel hot dog restaurant. The reason? Wilmington doesn't have enough people or enough money to attract major retailers. Although invisible to retail America, Wilmington remains critical to goods movement, since a great many harbour workers live here and the community's land base has hosted port expansions and secondary industries since the beginning.

"Almost every family I know has someone suffering from asthma, respiratory health problems, lung disease, or cancer," says Jesse Marquez, founder of Wilmington's Coalition for a Safe Environment. "People die prematurely [in L.A.] so that Wal-Mart, Nike, Kmart, and others can make billions in profits."

From 2002 onward, he says, citing port studies, the harbour was single-handedly generating more than 20 percent of all particulate emissions – considered the most deadly form of air pollution – across southern California. And despite new laws, countless air-quality meetings, and a $2 billion promise to slash harbour emissions by 50 percent between 2006 and 2012, the port-side neighbourhoods of San Pedro, West Long Beach, and Wilmington are still pushing back hard on development, increasingly galvanized by the deadly air from the harbour's ceaseless operation of trucks, ships, and trains.

Because of California's relatively progressive environmental legislation, and the fact that ports and government can no longer afford to exclude harbourside communities, the locals have new clout. "Do they really want to be dealing with us as part of their growth factor?" asks Marquez, who has lived in Wilmington his whole life. "We were totally ignored before. Now they deal with us." Some were surprised that a community with a median household income of $35,000 could tackle a multi-billion-dollar industry, but it's a battle that has been brewing for years. Wilmington and San Pedro, to the southwest, have previously launched secession movements, environmental coalitions, and countless challenges to what some have described as pollution-based discrimination. Wilmington and West Long Beach stand closest to all the refineries, docks, and rail yards, and they are nearly 90 percent Latino.

Southern California has a long and not particularly nice tradition of loading low-income black and Latino communities with pollution from the region's industrial development, from oil jacks in residential Long Beach neighbourhoods to "Asthma Town" in Huntington Park and the high rates of birth defects and cancer discovered in Bell Gardens during the 1980s. In the latter case, high levels of hexavalent chromium from nearby chrome-plating facilities were measured; the plants were adjacent to Suva Elementary School, and the neighbourhood became infamous for birth defects and miscarriages. In all of L.A.'s incarnations – early oil patch, mecca of automobiles and development sprawl, home of the military-industrial complex, globalized transport hub – there have always been communities that take the brunt of the city's drive for new growth.

Some studies indicate that environmental injustice in southern California persists because of the city's dependence on transport. "Asians, African Americans, and Latinos have the highest population cancer risk estimates, with risks nearly 50% higher [from airborne toxins] than that for Anglos," noted a 2002 study by investigators from San Francisco State University and the University of California. And while land value, or lack thereof, has long been associated with pollution exposure, what has changed in Los Angeles is the kind of pollution: from toxic sites across low-income zip codes to diesel-sourced pollution affecting poorer neighbourhoods near freeways and goods movement sites. Particulate counts near rail yards, trucking corridors, distribution centres, and port terminals are generally 1.5 to 4 times greater than the California average. While the region has fought smog levels since the 1970s with some success and had reduced overall particulate levels by the mid-2000s, in 2008 it remained America's most polluted city on the basis of year-round particulates. If anything, the ports have proven the hardest to reform. Port-side communities such as Long Beach, San Pedro, and Wilmington still sustain some of the highest levels of air pollution in the country, even as California becomes one of the continent's most progressive jurisdictions for climate and air-quality legislation.

Decades-old diesel trucks crowd the port area, belching out some of the worst particulate contamination and leading to the common local observation "This is where old trucks come to die." Many container ships still burn bunker fuel within the harbour – the lowest-grade diesel fuel available, so coarse and dense that it is mostly solid at room temperature and needs to be heated in order to combust. If it were coming from a single smokestack – such as those sported by the enormous prewar coal-fired power plants – this kind of low-grade, inefficient, highly polluting combustion would never be tolerated in California in the twenty-first century. But because marine vessels themselves have been scarcely governed by international regulations on emissions and pollution, and because L.A.'s truck-dependent port system is populated by independent low-income drivers, some of the most primitive, polluting engines outside the developing world have amassed at San Pedro Bay to unload the newest technology from Apple, Dell, and Hewlett Packard.

What this means in real terms is that a local school has some of the worst air quality in all of North America. Hudson Elementary School is on the border between Wilmington and Long Beach, right alongside the Terminal Island Freeway, where parents counted 590 container trucks passing per hour, one of the largest reported truck volumes in the port area. A daycare centre stands on the same block as Hudson School and the truck-congested freeway. Within a few miles' radius are major rail yards, railway corridors, and several large oil refineries. When the refineries flare off waste gases, Hudson School often locks its kids indoors, but the school doesn't always have notice, as in the case of "unplanned" flarings only reported later in the news.

Hudson School itself looks perfectly normal – just another one-storey brick school, well-kept, with the Hudson Hawks team logo painted on the outside; adjacent is a public park with ball diamonds and trees and a playground. But a child who hangs out here long enough has double the risk of asthma compared to national averages. "When our team came out here and did air monitoring in the classroom," says Elina Green, project manager for the non-profit coalition Long Beach Alliance for Children with Asthma, "particulate counts were 8,000. But out here in the park, it was 40,000. And as different trucks and trains went by, you'd see spikes." In other words, all day, Hudson School kids breathe air similar to what other schoolkids breathe only while in the middle of L.A. traffic en route to school, according to a 2003 study prepared for the California Air Resources Board.

Asthma is the leading cause of missed school days in the area, reports Green. It is also the most prevalent admission diagnosis in local pediatric intensive care units. Longer-term effects are highly likely: teens growing up in southern California's most congested areas show a fivefold risk of reduced lung function. As local emergency room doctor John Miller told PBS in 2006, "You realize from looking at the numbers, looking at the science that we're living in a diesel death zone."

It's a health crisis, says Green, looking out across the baseball diamonds to the line of trucks driving north on the Terminal Island Freeway. "The thing about particulates is that they are so small they can bypass front-line body systems and go deep into parts of the body."

Scientific understandings of air pollution hazards changed significantly during the period when goods movement became a significant global industry. Beginning in the early 1990s, fine particulate matter – microscopic soot produced by incomplete combustion, particularly from sulphur-rich diesel sources – caught the attention of cancer and air-quality specialists. Other pollutants such as ozone irritate the respiratory tract, inducing asthma attacks, chest pain, and chronic respiratory irritation; particulates, on the other hand, penetrate deeply into the body, sidestepping many of its natural defences. Particulates of 2.5 microns or less can find their way throughout the body – into the brain, the inner organs, and deep inside the lungs. Particulates are far more dangerous than previously believed, not only because of their deep incursion but also because they are acidic and can deliver trace amounts of chemicals and heavy metals – benzene compounds, lead, cadmium, and nickel.

It turns out that the most affordable transport fuels – diesel and bunker fuel – are also the dirtiest and most dangerous. This dependence on cheap fuel has been the defining factor in making L.A.'s ports an environmental justice hotspot. "Mobile sourced emissions are the primary driver of health risk, accounting for about 70% of the estimated excess cancer incidence, the majority of this from diesel particulate pollution," reported the Pat Brown Institute, an L.A.-based think-tank, in 2007. "Although much of the Los Angeles region is bathed in a cloud of air pollution, the cancer risk is associated with our transportation network." Consequently, California's Air Resources Board doubled its estimate of pollution-caused deaths in 2008, based on revised risk assessment of diesel-related fine particulates smaller than 2.5 microns. Fine particulates, in other words, had suddenly become 70 percent more dangerous than previously thought, in the eyes of California's state air-quality authority. "We're talking about people losing at least 10 years of their life," said Linda Smith of the Air Resources Board.

Asthma in children is the front-line effect of chronic air pollution, but more disturbing links may become clearer in coming decades. A 2003 study by the California Department of Health Services suggested an association between increased childhood leukemia rates and high exposure to hazardous air pollution in California, based on data collected between 1988 and 1994. Researchers found "a significant trend with increasing exposure level for childhood leukemia in tracts ranked highest for exposure" – as much as 32 percent above normal.

Green explains how land at the ports could be better utilized to remove truck traffic in favour of dedicated rail lines, but this kind of upgrade, although common in European ports, is deemed financially impossible. "They have land, but it's about political will. They want that land for other uses, such as new shipping berths. We've been opposing that. We could modernize and clean up around here."

Gridlock in L.A. encompasses far more than ships, containers, and traffic. The entire urban basin is at odds with itself: having lost several generations of manufacturing jobs, the region needs all the transport-related jobs it can scrounge; inner-city communities are fighting hard in the face of increased port traffic and the dire consequences of diesel pollution; and profit margins are drying up for shipping companies and trucking contractors, leading to new pressure for cost-cutting and expansion. By 2008, sixteen major expansion projects were already planned for the ports. Many of these, including proposed rail-yard expansions across from Hudson School, were blocked or stalled by community opposition.

Tom Politeo suggests that L.A.'s dependence on trucks – and publicly subsidized highways and facilities – was an ideological choice that reflects the brutal side of the region's legacy of frontier commerce. "What we have is an economy not based on free trade but [on] privilege," he says. "And that is part of the reason we are so dependent on trucks, for example. We've painted ourselves into a corner, as the system is connected to truck access, not rail access. Trucking was deregulated in the 1970s, for much reduced cost and much reduced responsibility." Port-related sprawl happened because it was cheap; truck-based connections to rail yards persist because they utilize free public road connections to private rail facilities.

In 2008 California introduced land-use laws that constituted America's most comprehensive effort to reduce sprawl, a major cause of transport-based air pollution. But the crux of the ports remained: crumbling bridges, highways and stacked-up containers everywhere. Green says that upgrading infrastructure in high-congestion areas can still result in greater congestion. "The common argument is that to improve emissions, you make freight move faster. So you expand the freeway to improve emissions. We know that if trucks drive between forty and seventy miles an hour, we can reduce pollution. But we also know that if they expand a freeway, then growth is expected to triple. In ten years we could find ourselves back where we are right now."

Full-Cost Progress

Responding to years of protest and impasse, L.A.'s $2-billion green plan, launched in 2006, was the most ambitious of its kind in North America. Within this, the greening of L.A.'s sometimes ancient fleet of deregulated and independently owned hauling trucks is no small undertaking. Nor are efforts to persuade marine operators, whose ships do not fall under the jurisdiction of local or state agencies, to burn cleaner fuel while near the coast. Elsewhere, goods-transport pollution remains a serious problem. Voluntary guidelines in New York have not been successful; Houston's port is still polluted. ("Unfortunately, little of the enthusiasm for environmental protection engendered by [New York's] Green Port Program has produced concrete air pollution reductions," says researcher James Cannon.)

In southern California, few disagree about the reality of traffic congestion, air pollution, and the public health crisis. But it remains difficult to decide who will pay to clean up this legacy. Who can reform globalization in South Los Angeles? It turns out that the higher cost of cleaner fuel and lower emissions is, like $150 oil, a mortal threat to industries and politicians that have built their livelihoods on cheap. Several months after diesel was named the top port pollutant in 2008, California air regulators approved new guidelines to reduce ocean-going ship emissions. A program promoting low-sulphur fuels was launched in 2009, with stringent international rules on shipping fuels taking full effect in 2015. Some shipping companies volunteered immediate fuel upgrades, but the Pacific Merchant Shipping Association complained about jurisdiction. Indeed, shippers had already blocked a 2006 state regulation to impose cleaner fuel usage.

"Cleaner fuel" is no understatement. Typical bunker fuel contains up to 45,000 parts per million (ppm) of sulphur; by comparison, California diesel trucks can burn diesel that contains no more than 15 ppm of sulphur.

Shipping's pollution impact is huge, and the cost is not insignificant: ships entering California waters will spend an extra $30,000 per trip simply to burn cleaner fuel within 24 nautical miles of the coast.

By mid-2009, the U.S. Environmental Protection Agency had announced plans with Canadian regulators to designate the entire North American coastal region an "emission control area." Extending nearly 400 kilometres from the coastline, the zone would require shippers to burn cleaner fuel in order to reduce sulphur emissions by 96 percent by 2015. The new standard will prevent an estimated 8,300 deaths annually, a small but significant portion of the 60,000 deaths worldwide attributed to shipping emissions. The total cost of the new North American fuel standard will be $3.2 billion, or $18 per container.

Likewise, there is no cheap way to clean up trucks. In 2008 the ports launched a $1.6-billion clean truck replacement effort, offering subsidies to replace the aging fleet of about 16,800 rundown rigs: truckers could purchase a new $100,000 diesel rig with the latest in emissions technology for a mere $30,000. The American Trucking Association filed a federal suit to block the effort, claiming "intrusive regulatory systems."

It is a war over pennies per product, but the total sums are huge. A 2007 study by the Pacific Institute estimated that the total cost of using cleaner technology in the Los Angeles ports alone will be $6 billion to $10 billion by 2020, while the California Clean Air Resources Board reports this would save $3 billion to $8 billion in total health impacts.

Like a bad day on the I-710, the gridlock seems endless. In July 2008 California state senator Alan Lowenthal succeeded in passing a bill to impose a fee on cargo containers that would levy millions to help clean up the ports and reduce community impacts. The $30 fee per twenty-foot container unit, or TEU, would add about half a cent per laptop or five cents per big-screen television. California's Chamber of Commerce derided the legislation, which it claimed "increases the cost of shipping goods and makes California less competitive by imposing an illegal per-container tax."

When a coalition of environmental groups launched a lawsuit over government laxity on air pollution in 2008, Jack Kyser, chief economist with Los Angeles County Economic Development, threatened disaster. Lawsuits and reforms, he said, "could choke off a lot of international trade" and result in cost increases for all imported goods. "Sometimes, people don't understand the ultimate consequences of what they do. Start stocking up on your tennis shoes and other necessities."

In a cost-critical environment there are fewer win-win solutions, and the political landscape really does look like a parking lot. L.A. mayor Antonio Villaraigosa pledged to transform his city into "the greenest big city in America" but has reportedly refused to limit port growth. "When we met him last year," Jesse Marquez recounts, "he could not accept one thing: no port growth. Port growth was where his head was at." For many, port growth is the key to replenishing high-quality manufacturing jobs that disappeared.

It is true that the economy itself now operates on a just-in-time basis, with surprisingly little slack, especially when politicians are confronted with new costs and potential job loss. California's Board of Equalization estimated in 2008 that each new percentage rise in overall tax could eliminate as many as 58,000 jobs.

Jesse Marquez wants his community to be known for more than dirty ports and that fantastic helicopter chase scene from 1991's *Terminator 2*. Shot on the Terminal Island Freeway, it was a pop culture moment watched by a generation. Arnold Schwarzenegger, the present California governor and then-Terminator, roared past local oil refineries, pursued by an unstoppable assassin from the future. Hudson School was down there, somewhere outside the frame, as Schwarzenegger blasted his way towards the port facilities at Terminal Island, where he began his film career with the 1977 cult classic *Pumping Iron*.

Now, as governor riding herd over the world's tenth-largest economy in an age of job losses, pollution controls, and uncertain economies, Schwarzenegger had vetoed several earlier attempts to impose an environmental per container fee on port traffic. Combined fees for clean fuel, trucks, and greener port infrastructure could surpass $100 on some containers, posing a significant cost and job-loss threat in a regional industry that needs to move 11 million containers to stay solvent. Everyone is in favour of the environment these days, no question, but economic cost pressures and political failures, like the Terminator, always come back.

Marquez makes no apologies for helping to block port development, even if that means holding hostage the estimated $250 billion worth of annual trade that flows through these two ports. As founder of L.A.'s Coalition for a Safe Environment and co-chair of the Sierra Club's Harbor

Vision Task Force, he reports that community opposition has helped stop seven different proposed terminal projects since the mid-2000s. "They had nearly zero port growth in 2007 and 2008. Some of that is the economy, but some of that is the growth factor. That's good news. Before, development was based on their needs and didn't take the community into account."

With the help of the Natural Resource Defense Council, Marquez and others gained a $57-million community-based trust fund in 2008 for cleaner technologies, renewable power, and air cleaners for medically vulnerable residents, as well as to fund impact and advocacy studies. "We went way beyond anything we accomplished in the past," he says. "Every single mitigation measure we have identified over the last seven years, we finally achieved. This is about full-cost accounting."

Into the year 2010 and beyond, Wilmington will also see construction of a $57-million parkland buffer, six thousand new trees, and a $212-million waterfront project, as well as a green technology centre. "Wilmington will not be forgotten," said Mayor Villaraigosa in 2009. "We've got a lot of work left to do."

Marquez has just returned from Europe, where he toured the ports of Rotterdam and Hamburg, marvelling at the electric trains and windmills, the automated cranes and dedicated on-dock rail – not a diesel rig in sight. The self-described "Wilmington homeboy" says he's seen the future, and it looks a lot different from the industrial waterfront that lies at the end of many local streets. Clean, efficient cargo transportation technologies such as magnetic transport and electric trains, he says, would make an enormous difference, yet North Americans have trouble investing in long-term gain.

"Before, investments were based on corporate need, and they didn't take into effect the environment, they didn't take into effect any of the public health concerns or other socio-economic impacts." But, says Marquez, it's still a lot better than China. "This is America," says the lifelong resident. "They can't just push projects through and then put us in jail."

As shippers and other port industries suffer losses and insolvency, there may be fewer resources to address greenhouse gas emissions from the worldwide fleet of 47,000 commercial shipping vessels – whose collective emissions output is estimated to be as much as twice that created by global air travel.

Engineering and technology can make our world greener, but ingenuity can no longer guarantee the savings that made supply chains synonymous with globalization. Across the harbour, people such as Anthony Otto and Paul Conolly at OOCL are now responsible for responding to vast external changes that are affecting their business, as well as to growing volatility in prices, global trade, labour, and environmental issues. It's harder to make money, harder to keep everyone happy, harder to plan for the future. The law of diminishing returns applies to a system attempting to optimize its last few percentiles of capacity. "It is actually, on a per unit basis, about a break-even," says Otto. "You are able to squeeze that much more through, [but] you consider what your lease agreement is with the port. While the labour and certain costs associated with the operation go up incrementally, I still think you are much better off the denser you go." Industry doesn't have much of a choice. Bigger ships, higher trade volumes, and expensive technologies – some of which are already in operation in China and Europe – are necessary to address congestion and air pollution, but this kind of built-up expansion is far more capital intensive than past port expansions, which simply spread horizontally over a greater surface area.

It is the Schumpeterian curse: innovation expedites an economic model towards its limits. Solutions such as containerization and massive ships provided new productivity, affordability, and speed to consumers and global business. However, as the cost structure of transport and manufacture changes during the twenty-first century, they will require increasing amounts of capital, natural resources, and management, as well as public sacrifice and environmental impact, to sustain. Inputs increase (energy, capital investment, technology expenditure) and returns are static or decreasing. In the terms of modern economic theory, one emerging view is that the "scale/effects property" of mature systems is broken: increased investment in technology and research, for example, does not yield increased results. ("Evidence shows that resources devoted to R&D have been increasing exponentially, but the growth rates . . . remain roughly constant over time," note Elias Dinopoulos and Fuat Şener.)

The impasse at L.A.'s ports is a lesson about how past solutions don't often work anymore, yet the drive to recapture yesterday's prosperity and affordability is still strong. This is why ports like Los Angeles, along with manufacturers, retailers, and consumers, will likely spend extra billions for incremental gains while at the same time remaining fundamentally challenged by the same problems. In other words, containerization helped liberate trade during the twentieth century, but as we move deeper into the new millennium, we are clearly still stuck inside the box. Indeed, by 2009, L.A.'s port authority was offering a 10 percent discount on container traffic as an incentive to keep business moving, but by June 2009, container traffic had dropped 19 percent.

Major clients such as Wal-Mart keep pushing for discounts, according to other harbour professionals, even though it is clear that the shipping industry is undergoing a long-term crisis. "They will sit down there and say, 'Look, this is what we are going to pay. Take it or leave it. And if you do not do it, you are going to lose these 29,000 containers a month,'" explains Manny Aschemeyer of California's Marine Exchange. This is especially relevant for the ports, given that upwards of 20 percent of all business here is related to top retailers such as Target, Home Depot, and Wal-Mart.

When the going gets tough, everyone still wants a deal. "Oh yeah, everybody wants their stuff," says Otto. "And quicker and cheaper."

The Hill and the Harbour

Envisioned as the city of the future in movies, books, and television – as both promised land and dystopia – Los Angeles strains to reconcile the contradictory currents of a much larger transport-dependent global economy. Yet it is in L.A.'s past as the site of one of the world's first great oil booms that transport's destiny comes into focus. Modern logistics is, more than anything else, upgraded energy: steel, diesel, and bunker fuel. The quantum savings rendered by modern container shipping were created through what could be our last societal binge of affordable crude oil.

There's a spot in Long Beach, not far from the Memorial Medical Center, where hulking steel pumpjacks still dot the hillside. This is Signal Hill, a mini-city enclave less than two and a half miles square peppered with wells that tap into the Long Beach oil field, the very first of the major oil discoveries of the 1920s. The Signal Hill discovery launched America's first great oil boom, which, along with discoveries in the harbour and elsewhere, made southern California the world's biggest oil producer, responsible for roughly one-quarter of the world oil supply by 1923. At that time, Signal Hill was the biggest oil field of all. With nearly three hundred wells

author photo

A now-defunct Circuit City and working oil jack in Signal Hill, California.

squeezed within its tiny, hastily incorporated municipal footprint, the city-within-a-city resembled a cluttered forest of drilling derricks and primitive storage facilities.

These days the oil doesn't run quite as plentifully, so the thinning collection of oil jacks, robotically lurching up and down as they plunge into the earth's crust for hydrocarbon, has been surrounded by malls, hospitals, and houses. Whole city blocks of reddish earth are still dotted by occasional oil jacks, dilapidated machinery, and pipeline connections; nothing grows in these shadows that signify former oil tanks, toxic waste pits, and well sites.

Near the edge of the Signal Hill West oil field is a lone pumpjack encircled by a newly built wooden fence, and around that, like a large black moat, is a parking lot. Surrounding the two-storey jack is a 24-acre big-box mall anchored by Home Depot, built in 2005, which nestles up to the San Diego Freeway to the north. Unlike Colma's pioneering Home Depot that was built on a mountain of garbage, this one sits atop a declining oil field. The so-called brownfield site has, since the 1920s, along with other Signal Hill rigs, pulled nearly 1 billion barrels of oil out of the ground; 614 million barrels had already been extracted by 1938. You'd never guess that this suburban big-box mall was part of the historic setting of Upton Sinclair's famous novel *Oil!* and inspiration for P.T. Anderson's 2007 film, *There Will Be Blood*.

Yet this was the birthplace of industrial California, and of the oil riches that helped build Hollywood, new highways, huge real estate developments, and glamorous family dynasties. "Southern California was the Kuwait of the Jazz Age," journalist Eric Schlosser told the *New York Times* in 2008. "An enormous amount of money was quickly made there and spent in all kinds of extravagant ways. . . . This was a whole new society in the making, and it was being fueled by oil money the likes of which no other city had ever seen before."

Looking south from the Home Depot parking lot, you can see Long Beach unfold towards the harbour; massive gantry cranes, grazing at the water's edge, unload container ships, some twenty-five storeys high. Directly across the street from Home Depot, just the other side of East Spring Street, are at least twenty square blocks of dusty moonscape in the middle of the city – the remains of Signal Hill's oil boom. The Environmental Protection Agency (EPA) estimates that 60 percent of the land within this tiny municipal enclave has contamination issues. Kitty-corner to the Home Depot mall is a 56-acre jumble of rusting tanks, pumpjacks, metal scrap, and large expanses of dark soil and gravel dotted by shrubs and ratty-looking palm trees. Here seepage from more than eighty years of petroleum development runs as deep as ten to fifteen feet underground, laced with aromatic hydrocarbons, heavy metals, and methane. A broken network of old oil pipelines traverses the site, some buried just beneath the surface, some exposed above. This land has been slated for multiple developments – most recently as a sports park – but remains idle, in part because of the potentially large cost of removing the contaminated topsoil.

Signal Hill's transition from oil field to big-box mall demonstrates two sides of an economy built on extraction. The large pumpjack that stands in front of Home Depot is sucking increasingly valuable crude out of the ground and passing it along to local refineries for upgrading. Modern retail operations follow a different business model but a similar trajectory: supply chains extract cheap resources and labour, pipeline it through ports like Los Angeles and other logistics channels, and create profit margins on large volumes of sales, with further inputs from cheap labour and cheap, sprawl-fuelled land – in no small way floated by the pool of liquid cash created through discount mortgages, credit cards, and other forms of leveraged consumer spending devised by the financial prospectors of the late twentieth century.

The resource play that has become the global supply chain begins and ends here. Nearby are Target and Costco. Wal-Marts are to both north and south. There's a Circuit City, now defunct, across the parking lot. The big-box stores are filled with many familiar products unloaded from L.A.'s container ships. The petrochemicals that were used to manufacture the CD cases, plungers, power-tool casings, weatherstripping, and electronics came mostly from the other side of the ocean, probably south China and its large refineries, which in turn are stoked with crude oil and feedstocks from the Middle East. The modern supply chain was meant to achieve efficiency and competition, speed and precision. But much of our bargaineered world is still embodied hydrocarbon – crude oil, petrochemicals, plastics – and steel. Add to this the trucking and rail transport on both ends of the journey, plus the final drive home from the big-box store with the customer.

Besides the new North American shipping fuel standard for 2015, governments beyond L.A. continue to push for reduced emissions and more stringent fuel requirements, and shipbuilders are creating larger, more energy-efficient vessels. Wal-Mart has made much of its own cost-saving, energy-saving logistics efforts: cutting total packaging by 5 percent by 2013 will, it claims, save 1,358 barrels of oil, 5,190 trees, and 727 shipping containers annually. Moreover, the company has pledged to improve the energy efficiency of its suppliers as well, using its command/control mastery of the supply chain to institute emissions savings.

Unlike other transportation challenges, there are few transitional technologies for modern bulk, tanker, and container ships – no Prius, no hybrid solution for the shipping world. The International Bunker Industry Association has argued that if ships did burn higher-quality fuel – as opposed to the cheap sludge from refinery waste streams – "refineries would need to process roughly 12 million additional barrels of crude oil daily, more than the entire output of Saudi Arabia." While some experiment with sail technologies to capture wind, and hull coatings to reduce barnacles and friction, the vast majority of our trade still sails under combustion, just as it did a generation ago. Although Wal-Mart, Office Depot, and other big-box chains have added solar panels to stores and gained upwards of 25 percent immediate energy savings, some argue that global population increases and growth-driven development alone will cancel out efficiency gains.

"A conceit of the New Economy is that it promises freedom from the smokestacks and sweatshops of the past two centuries," writes journalist Wade Graham. "In some swaths of formerly industrial North America, factories have been replaced by Wal-Marts and FedEx vans. But this is only a local illusion, a magic trick of trade and geography, obscuring the underlying fact that the New Economy not only rests on the grimy, polluting old one but propagates, multiplies, and feeds it, spreading it around the world. . . . We click off our wishes on Web sites, setting in motion diesel engines by the tens of thousands: trucks, loaders, cranes, and locomotives, armadas of little smokestacks toiling to deliver us the goods."

When our systems are stressed and pressed towards their limits, not only do savings diminish and costs increase, but the broad interconnectedness of these systems itself becomes a liability: air pollution, congestion, climate change, affordability, and public health problems crop up simultaneously. Even terrorism is a factor here, since a single hit to the ports could disable America's largest regional economy.

The fate of Los Angeles is a global story, one that is revealing a complex future. In many ways we played globalization like an oil or gold boom, extracting as much as possible as quickly as possible, but things aren't what they used to be.

In a *Terminator*-style twist, California is returning to its past to help save the future. Late in 2008 it was revealed that the old Wilmington oil field beneath the harbour might still hold $1 billion worth of revenue by 2018. It's an unexpected cash windfall for the cities of Los Angeles and Long Beach, which have begun to strain under growth and cost pressures at their respective ports, as well as for the state of California and Occidental Petroleum, which would deploy new injection technology to squeeze hidden hydrocarbons out of the recesses of the muddy harbour.

Long Beach mayor Bob Foster touted the plan to protract the life of the aging oil field as a "win-win for everyone." The ports themselves could gain $150 million, and some valued relief from their current entrapment within billions in new environment-related expenses, increased operating costs, and the continued threat of decreased growth in container traffic. New money from oil could offer some latitude to address the environment/ community gridlock that threatens the ports.

Yet new exploration and new drilling give rise to the spectre of fiascos like the 1969 spill from a platform in Santa Monica Bay that leaked 200,000 gallons of crude into an 800-mile oil slick that fouled local beaches. In September 2008, U.S. congressional Democrats reversed a decades-old policy against offshore drilling, potentially opening up vast stretches of ocean from Florida to California. (In a not unrelated move, oil companies contributed $90 million to California political campaigns in 2006.) Onshore, depleted oil fields across the L.A. Basin are being drilled again, from Beverly Hills to the harbour and beyond.

Perhaps with the new scramble to secure oil, southern California is rediscovering its 1920s self: its formative boom years before the global bust of the 1930s, a speculative torrent of land, oil, and incoming investment to spur growth ever forward. But then, as now, L.A.'s "homegrown wealth and commerce were insufficient to support the region's lavish super-structures of consumption," writes historian Mike Davis. "As Upton Sinclair noted, Los Angeles was fundamentally 'parasitic' on prosperity produced in other regions – a kind of 'cloud society,' levitated by the influx of wealthy migrants."

Unlike Sinclair's 1920s microcosm of frontier industry, today's players in Wilmington and Long Beach are also the world's largest corporations, rep-resenting the vanguard of the global economy: Wal-Mart, Chevron, ConocoPhillips. Los Angeles launched the modern oil industry, pioneered automobile culture and urban sprawl, and helped deliver the world into container-ship consumerism. And despite California's strong environ-mental track record, on many fronts it is still attempting to revive old solu-tions – drilling deeper, shipping faster – as future challenges bear down, based on an irrepressible optimism about the limits of our material world.

Upton Sinclair made Signal Hill famous, but his tales of desperation, corruption, and conflict seem nearly quaint in hindsight. Sadly, in our time, the squandered fortunes, depleted economies, and polluted zones are no longer limited to a dusty little 2.5-square-mile patch of land.

ALL IS PLASTIC:
THE SMALL WORLD OF HYDROCARBONS

5

Above the tar sands: Suncor's
Millennium mine.

The Wal-Mart of Oil

Flying a few hundred feet above the forest, the
helicopter sways into a turn. Below are count-
less trees – pine, spruce, and larch – along with tracts of rich green muskeg
and lakes. This is the boreal forest, or taiga, a dense and huge swath of
biome that circles the Subarctic from Alaska to northern Europe to eastern
Siberia. It is the biggest terrestrial ecosystem in the world.

There are small green lakes amid the trees, and great swaths of open
muskeg that look like verdant meadows from above. The muskeg is what
makes the boreal region unique; a biomass-rich sponge of sphagnum moss,
water, dead plants, and small shrubs and trees, it can reach as deep as thirty
metres underground. As you glide over this Amazon of the north, the trees
and muskeg give way to cutlines, which turn into sandy berms dotted with
black puddles. It's not a desert but the outer edge of a huge tailings pond,
part of a series of oily lakes and contaminated sand flats created by the
mass production of synthetic crude.

This is the most visible manifestation of an estimated $218 billion worth of oil-mining projects proposed for northern Canada, covering an area the size of Florida or Great Britain. Bitumen – essentially heavy oil laced with soil and water – occurs naturally in Alberta's Athabasca region and beyond. Other forms of unconventional crude can be found around the world, from the light heavy oil of Venezuela to the bitumen-like gravel of American oil shale. It is called unconventional simply because it is too remote, too dirty, and too expensive to extract.

All that has changed. Unconventional crude has become a strategic energy source in the twenty-first century. The tar sands of northern Alberta are the largest of many global unconventional-energy plays that will run for at least the next fifty to a hundred years; other heavy oil, shale, or bitumen deposits of commercial magnitude are already in production in Russia, Venezuela, Iran, and China. All are energy intensive and therefore create a much larger greenhouse gas impact than conventional oil and gas extraction. In North America alone there is an estimated 1.1 trillion barrels of recoverable unconventional crude. Canada's tar sands represent the largest portion of this virtual reserve, marshalling new investment and capacity that already provides one-fifth of all American oil imports, but there is also an estimated total of 100 billion barrels of heavy oil in California, Alaska, and Utah, as well as Alabama, Kentucky, Missouri, and Texas.

It's all part of a global trend of progressively unaffordable energy. As the International Energy Agency (IEA) reported in 2007, "$22 trillion of investment in energy supply infrastructure is needed to meet projected global demand [because] the world's primary energy needs are projected to grow by 55% between 2005 and 2030."

The helicopter banks again and reveals the Syncrude tailings pond in the distance. At about 540,000 cubic metres in volume, this pond and its huge earthen berm are rated as the world's second-largest dam after China's Three Gorges. Other tailings ponds – large lakes really – litter the landscape below. The massive ponds tell their own story: each day, Canada exports 1 million barrels of oil to the United States and dumps 90 percent of the 3 million barrels of water used in daily production into the tailings ponds. It's as much water as might be used by a city of 2 million people, and it's toxic enough to kill any fish within a few days.

The ground changes from dirty gold sand to black as we pass over the edge of the outflow to the pits. Here in the dark expanse of Suncor's strip mine, dug fifty or even seventy-five metres deep into the boreal forest, the world's largest trucks rumble to and from even larger electric-powered excavators unloading house-sized chunks of oily earth into the trucks' payload areas. Many are mighty Caterpillar 797Bs, roughly fifteen metres long and three storeys high – and designed specially for bitumen mining. Worth about $5 million each, there are 185 of them working the pits, plus countless smaller trucks and support vehicles buzzing about. Only the month before my visit, a contractor from the Caterpillar dealership was crushed by one of his own trucks; a few months prior, a Suncor employee was run over while driving his small pickup truck past a 797B hauler. In the latter case, as with other, similar accidents over the years, the Cat driver simply didn't see the regular-sized truck before it was too late. Despite safety precautions, driving the world's largest trucks is much like manoeuvring an apartment building on giant pontoon tires while hauling four hundred tonnes of muskeg at fifty kilometres an hour.

Extracting oily dirt and turning it into gasoline or diesel is no small thing. Based on technologies developed during the 1940s and 1950s, tar sands mining is an extremely physical, resource-intensive process that turned into a full-fledged oil rush during the early 2000s, when high oil prices and depleting global reserves of conventional crude made bitumen economically attractive to energy multinationals. During the 1970s, two companies toiled along the banks of the Athabasca River, methodically digging open-pit mines to expose the bitumen underneath the muskeg. There are now eighty-seven major projects underway, representing nearly all of the world's major oil companies.

This is the future of oil: a high-impact ground war on scarcity waged by giant machines and even bigger corporations. As an aggregate, it is the largest industrial project on the planet, with an estimated 173 billion barrels of recoverable crude, advertised by government reports as the second-largest proven reserves after Saudi Arabia. And it's just getting going too, since only about 3 percent of the available bitumen has been recovered. Once the tar sands reach full production later this century, it is expected that Canada will become the second-biggest oil producer in the world.

From the air, the mining process resembles a gigantic rally race as trucks accelerate away from excavators in sequence, rumble around twists and turns inside the mine, and race towards the hopper bins closer to the centre of the facility, where extraction and refining take place. Loads are dumped and crushed by enormous rotating steel teeth at the bottom of the hoppers, then sent by conveyor belt to the long, cone-shaped extractor cells that will begin to wash the bitumen out of the soil. The bitumen is later transported, pulverized, washed, steamed, diluted with solvents, and finally refined in a process that resembles the industrial scale and factory infrastructure of several major steel mills or aluminum foundries. Meanwhile, the trucks turn around and race back to the excavator, governed by a central dispatch unit that plots and monitors their progress with GPS.

As viewed from above, this spectacle of the world's largest trucks racing to fill the tanks of North American SUVs is purposeful and precise. Each scoop of the excavator is timed and is designed to fill the truck's payload bin in four scoops. The 797Bs burn 105 litres of fuel each hour (that's less than one mile per gallon) and must be operated nearly continuously for maximum operating returns. There is a microwave in each of the large excavator-shovellers that enables workers to stay inside their machines without cafeteria visits – a micromanaged, Wal-Mart–style productivity gain that will earn $700 million in additional revenue during the lifetime of Suncor's mine operations.

This is what an oil boom would look like if Bentonville ran things: advanced logistics, communications technology, and disciplined management, all to deliver an affordable product across great distances. Unlike conventional energy developments, where billions are spent just to locate hydrocarbon deposits, exploration costs here are minimal, since everyone already knows where the resource is located, more or less. In other words, the tar sands are really about manufacturing process and logistics.

Wal-Mart, as the market shaper of the twenty-first-century economy, has been described as a global logistics and management company that also happens to run retail stores. Here in the tar sands, an operation like Suncor's is the Wal-Mart of the energy world: it requires scale, abundant input, merciless engineering, profit-oriented efficiency, and plentiful public subsidies such as tax allowances and royalty holidays, as well as no limits to emissions and expansion. The modern tar sands operator is both a fully integrated manufacturing operation and a third order of government that also happens to sell energy.

The helicopter finally reaches the edge of the Athabasca River, having traversed kilometres of black pits and racing trucks. Across the river lies Suncor's city of steel: a Disney World–sized extraction and refining site that is the pride of the industry. This is where bitumen mining became profitable, through a modern alchemical process of wringing black gold from dirt.

For decades few investors bothered with the tar sands, simply because it was too costly. This pricey collection of megaprojects is a cutting-edge experiment in creating new energy, which forms the foundation of our ability to enjoy cheap products and essentials. Yet there is no guarantee that unconventional crude will keep energy affordable, if only because the business itself is expensive. During late 1970s, industry per-barrel operating costs in the tar sands were roughly on par with the price of conventional crude; profits were often consumed by the cost of making the oil. Thanks to technological advances, Suncor's per-barrel costs dropped as low as $8.30 during the late 1990s and early 2000s – a significant cost reduction on par with Wal-Mart's supply chain miracle of the 1990s. And, like Wal-Mart, Suncor and other companies improved their cost advantage on an operational scale – getting bigger, always – as well as from regulatory laxity that minimized or deferred environmental and climatic responsibilities, allowing for lower-cost self-regulation and voluntary measures. (To its credit, Suncor and other producers pay much better than Wal-Mart, with many skilled operators in the mines earning well over $100,000 annually, which to most is ample repayment for having every working hour clocked and tracked by the company.)

"We're the single largest player in the world's biggest oil basin," Suncor CEO Rick George told *Forbes* magazine in 2003. "And we're next to the world's biggest market." At the time, George disclosed that his ultimate goal, besides adding another 140,000 barrels a day, was to decrease per-barrel costs to $6, making Suncor North America's cheapest and likely most profitable producer of oil on the continent. But in 2008 costs boomed – $30 dollars per barrel, quotes a company rep when I tour the ground site later – and this steep rise had everything to do with increased costs of labour, steel, and energy. By the time energy prices peaked in 2008, operators such as Suncor had incurred a 55 percent operating-cost increase compared to 2005. In late 2008, companies with projects still in development stated that they would need oil to be at minimum $100 a barrel in order to break even. And when oil prices crashed as the financial crisis hit, waves of project cancellations and delays were announced, shelving $39 billion worth of projects as of February 2009.

This is mainly because the tar sands manufacture high-quality energy by using mainly other forms of high-quality energy, materials, and resources. New hydrocarbon is being pulled from the earth, true, but for every barrel of synthetic crude it takes two tonnes of soil, as much as four barrels of water, and, on average, between four and six times as much energy as conventional oil extraction. "The entire process is fueled by natural gas, and the energy consumed is awesome," writes journalist Andrew Nikiforuk in *The Tar Sands*. "Every 24 hours the industry burns enough natural gas to heat four million American homes in order to produce one million barrels of oil."

Behind the scenes there have been improvements. Early on, for example, it required almost as much energy to produce a barrel of oil as was embodied by the oil itself. By 2008 the average natural gas requirement was about one-sixth the energy value of a finished barrel. But the process still creates as much as three times the greenhouse gas emissions of conventional oil production. In late 2008, tar sands production was still being predicted to nearly double by 2015 – and its greenhouse gas emissions are likewise predicted to increase from approximately 40 million tonnes of carbon to 67 million tonnes during the same period. For most of the 2000s, uncontrolled greenhouse gas emissions were one of the great competitive advantages of the tar sands, since provincial goals for carbon reduction have been largely intensity-based (that is, a percentage reduction per barrel). As of 2009, no companies have been subjected to absolute limits or cap-and-trade reductions – essentially a greenwashed emissions regime that has helped keep manufactured crude as cheap as possible.

Unlike discount retail, energy more directly – and ominously – controls our long-term fate. If all the estimated 1.1 trillion barrels of unconventional oil in North America are eventually exploited, the climatic impact could be catastrophic. A 2008 report by the World Wildlife Fund (WWF) and Co-operative Financial Services estimated that this maximum-extraction scenario could result in atmospheric carbon dioxide increases of between 49 and 65 parts per million, pushing past existing climate-stabilization targets and potentially forcing the global mean temperature to increase two degrees – to far greater climatic volatility, disease, and famine. "The human race is going to extreme lengths to 'recarbonise' its activities, at a time when rapid decarbonisation is needed," charged the WWF.

The helicopter returns with its cargo of passengers, all stunned by the scale of the devastation levied upon the boreal forest: toxic sand flats, acidic lakes full of hydrocarbon effluent, and open pit mines that go on for miles. But the billions of dollars behind the tar sands is the true wonder, since this is about the persistence of hydrocarbons, our deep dependence on plastics and combustion, and the impetus to make unconventional fuels more affordable.

The revolution of cheap that made Wal-Mart king – and made life more affordable for millions of cash-strapped people – was actually part of the world's last great resource boom. When oil nearly hit $150 in 2008, the modern supply chain began to falter under higher prices, proving that all the transport, plastic, and urban sprawl associated with discounting is ultimately a story about energy. And while our first hundred years were about the discovery of energy supplies, our next hundred years will be defined by energy scarcity and a global scramble to control some of the dirtiest and most costly hydrocarbon deposits in the face of climate insecurity.

Modern consumerism has never been without reliable supplies of affordable energy. The tar sands exploitation in northern Alberta and its expensive oil-manufacturing operations are a well-financed gamble in favour of chronically expensive crude oil. Does the quest for cheap end here?

The Race for Crude

When journalists arrive in Fort McMurray to visit the tar sands, obligatory scenes are reported from a town bursting at the seams: the Tim Hortons coffee drive-through that is lined up even at 4:00 a.m.; scores of workers living in campgrounds and converted garages and sleeping in trucks; incredulous locals amazed that their town could explode from 25,000 people twenty years ago to an expected population of 250,000 in another two decades. Between construction projects for bitumen mining and extraction facilities and the ramped-up pace of existing operations, the tar sands have created a seemingly endless fountain of high-paying jobs. During peak periods this is a place where a high school dropout can make

THE PRICE OF A BARGAIN

$100,000 in the first year, drug abusers get rehired at the next company down the road, and people come from thousands of miles away to work for a year or two, then stay for ten.

New jobs and new fortunes are being created out of global anxiety over the end of affordable energy. The social impact of a $218-billion oil rush is considerable. "Look at the parking lots around here," says union organizer Leroy Nippard. "They're full: multiple families living in a two-bedroom apartment. You need a $200,000 salary to get by." The rush of capital into the tar sands has resulted in a rush of people – thousands upon thousands of workers who live in work camps near project sites and around Fort McMurray. It's likely the only place on the continent where people can sell a mobile home for $500,000, or where companies are sometimes so desperate for skilled workers they offer complimentary flights, rent support, and generous cash incentives. It's also the only place on the continent, if not in the world, where unions are booming: Nippard's union of operating engineers has nearly doubled its membership in the past two years, and only half of the tar sands construction sites are unionized. "Basically we're just getting in there and taking it out as fast as possible," says Nippard.

Yet the activity here is still surprising, considering the relatively small amounts of oil involved. By the 2020s, for example, the Athabasca mines will deliver more than 3 million barrels a day into a world that, as of 2005, was already consuming 83 million barrels. The unconventional crude of Canada's tar sands is a mere drop in the oceanic daily consumption of oil.

But those extra few million barrels are critical, not only because global demand continues to grow but also because bitumen deposits represent a significant portion of new oil reserves not controlled by OPEC, China, or Russia. Moreover, our pool of conventional energy resources is shrinking as state-owned oil companies – represented by OPEC, China, Russia, Mexico, and South America – have come to control the vast majority of proven oil reserves. In 1978, major oil corporations controlled approximately 70 percent of all oil and gas reserves; by the late 2000s they controlled 20 percent. Put another way, of the world's largest oil-and-gas-producing companies in 2005, the top five were all state-owned: by Saudi Arabia, Russia, Iran, Mexico, and China.

This makes large new sources of unconventional energy such as the tar sands far more strategic and valuable than previously thought. "The international oil companies cannot dictate the tempo any more," said analyst Fadel Gheit of Oppenheimer & Co. in 2008. "They can try projects that didn't work two years ago, but it's not a question of money. They don't have access to resources."

Indeed, the billions invested in the tar sands are proof that the world's largest non-state companies believe in the inevitable rise of crude prices – and a long-term supply crisis. "Normally, high prices would mean higher supply," said Fadhil Chalabi, former Iraqi oil ministry undersecretary, in 2008. "What is happening is something different. The international companies are denied access to areas of abundant oil within OPEC, and it's getting costlier in other areas."

At the 2008 World Petroleum Congress, it was announced that the reach of state-owned companies had increased, with about 90 percent of world reserves within countries that limit foreign investment in energy. The ability of the remaining 10 percent to support North America, much of Europe, and the developing world is in doubt, says the International Energy Agency, with a non-OPEC supply forecast that one analyst described as "paltry." Looking ahead, the IEA predicted some demand caused by high prices, but that production and available oil supply will decrease at an even faster rate. "We are clearly in the third oil shock," said the agency's executive director, Nobuo Tanaka. Even as oil prices crashed during the global financial crisis, the IEA continued to predict the return of $100-a-barrel oil, doubling to $200 by 2030. ("It is becoming increasingly apparent that the era of cheap oil is over," noted the IEA's *World Energy Outlook* in November 2008.)

The International Energy Agency predicted that Canada will lead all non-OPEC nations in new production, adding an expected 1.2 million barrels daily by 2013, followed by Brazil, which in 2008 boasted the world's largest single new oil discovery in nearly a decade, in an ultra-deep offshore basin – seven kilometres down – off the country's Atlantic coast. As previously strong exporters such as Mexico and Iran begin weakening, they may become chronically dependent importers of oil much like the United States, a one-time world leader in crude exports (back when Los Angeles was known for its oil wells, not movies and container ships).

With the rise of unconventional crude, it would be wrong to suggest that the oil age is ending. In fact, there is much evidence to suggest that we are only just now entering the last oil age – a potentially very expensive and destructive one. This scenario is potentially more destructive than peak oil – the near-term decline of hydrocarbon that has been widely and often fervently predicted – because it represents a revival in marginal forms of non-renewable energy that threatens our long-term environmental and economic security. Within the context of unresolved global carbon standards, the next hundred years could be spent paying ever more for fossil fuels, investing valuable resources into developing these fuels, and creating untold new greenhouse gas emissions, all the while undermining efforts to create renewable power and conserve carbon.

Peak oil at the very least offered the promise of scarcity-induced change. As we explore the limits of globalization – from the erosion of cheap labour and shipping to overspent consumer economies – our hydrocarbon chain has already begun to cannibalize itself. Based on 2008 projections, much of the natural gas from yet-to-be-constructed Arctic pipelines from Alaska and Canada's Mackenzie Delta could easily be consumed by the burgeoning energy needs of tar sands producers. In other words, clean-burning natural gas, which has only recently become one of our most strategic energy sources, is being turned into an energy source to make synthetic crude for a continent whose auto fleet is nearly as inefficient as it was in the 1970s.

This is part of a broader shift in power that will see globalization eroded by competition for energy. Countries and corporations are competing not just for new energy supplies but for whole energy supply chains: pipelines, petrochemicals, refining, and low-cost regulatory zones with lax emission controls. Not coincidentally, it is debtor nations – both developing-world countries and overspent Western powers – that are losing out in this contest. As America's Energy Information Agency noted in its 2008 forecast, non-OECD nations, rich with population and resources, will nearly double the average economic growth of high-income economies in the West between 2005 and 2030. The crusade for the world's last affordable hydrocarbons has already begun, and this contest has everything to do with the growing interest in Alberta's bitumen as well as the exploiting of blood oil in Sudan and Angola.

At different points during the twentieth century, America led the world in oil exports, then in manufacturing, and more recently in spending and imports. In terms of global economic dominance, it's a pattern of decline.

Western nations still hold most of the clout – diplomatic, military, engineering, consumer, cultural – but this is not the same as controlling or better conserving what Thomas Homer-Dixon has described as "society's critical master resource." Energy is essential for maintaining stability and prosperity. "When it's scarce and costly, everything we try to do, including growing our food, obtaining other resources like fresh water, transmitting and processing information, and defending ourselves, becomes harder," writes Homer-Dixon in *The Upside of Down*. "And, as the system gets larger and larger and more complex, more and more energy is needed to keep it operating."

The main response to this challenge has been to attempt to increase supplies – the energy paradigm of the previous century – despite grand inefficiencies and neglect of renewable energy development. As evidenced by the tar sands, some of the world's largest energy corporations are adding new oil reserves by paradoxically burning up valuable resource inputs – natural gas, water, air, as well as imported machinery, trucks, and workers – to manufacture oil out of dirt. Consequently, a growing portion of the oil that supports our consumer world is getting ever more expensive and dirtier, and its development, production, and consumption are causing a broad range of unexpected consequences.

Plastic Is Power

The world's largest ethylene facility stands tall in the middle of the Canadian prairies. If you live in North America and have recently used a foam cup, a plastic bag, or a plastic outdoor children's toy, there's a good chance its molecules were born here. Set amid farmers' fields in central Alberta, the shining towers and stacks of Nova's Joffre plant are built on top of the expansive natural gas reserves of the Western Canada Sedimentary Basin, a rich geological formation of hydrocarbons that also encompasses the tar sands a long half-day's drive to the northeast. This basin has served as the anchor for nearly all of Canada's oil and gas production since 1947. It turned Canada into the world's second-largest exporter of natural gas and, along with world-class crude resources such as the tar sands, helped transform this Canadian province into the Saudi Arabia of North America.

The sprawling complex at Joffre is as big as a small town, but it's mostly empty – much is automated, and most of the visible fumes from its stacks are actually water vapour. Three different plants here churn out 6 billion pounds of ethylene annually, plus more than 2 billion pounds of poly-ethylene, "the workhorse of plastics." Turning liquid gas into intermediate plastics is surprisingly straightforward: ethane is heated, then cooled to extreme temperatures, altering the molecular structure into ethylene, which is a gas at room temperature. Ethylene is either piped or trucked for intermediate or end-use manufacturing or further processed on site into polyethylene by polymerizing the gas into long-chain plastics, which results in tiny white pellets by the ton. Fifteen percent of the pellets are bagged and sent to Asia, and others are put on boxcars and rolled out across North America to make plastic packaging, bags, milk containers, garbage bags, kayaks, toys, garden sheds, and piping. Co-products include nylon rope, various kinds of synthetic rubber, and building materials. "Ethane is a primary building block," says Al Poole, the site director. "Everything from auto parts to textiles, food services, and pharmaceuticals."

It was for the rich deposits of natural gas that the Joffre facility was built here. It grows out of farmland, towering over verdant plains that first drew settlers in the late 1800s. Launched in 1979 as part of a comprehensive energy strategy for Alberta that grew out of the 1970s energy crisis, the Joffre site is sixty-one hectares of orderly, efficient manufacturing capacity.

Our voracious appetite for plastic is now the stuff of everyday life. Americans alone now consume roughly 100 billion plastic bags annually, requiring approximately 12 million barrels of crude. It all started during the late nineteenth century, when oil, gas, and aromatic hydrocarbons became the focus of experimentation and industrial process. In 1899, for example, Germany's Hans von Pechmann accidentally discovered poly-ethylene, which has since become one of the most common materials of our time.

As the most diverse set of substances ever manufactured by humans, mass-produced hydrocarbons bless dollar stores with plastic, make fertil-izer for food production, and fill hospitals with drugs. They help make everything from herbicides to DVD players both essential and affordable. The products of the world's industrial carbon chain – polymers, styrene, methane, nitrogen, paraffins – are the lifeblood of the twenty-first century. Global category-killers like Wal-Mart, Exxon, Dow, and Monsanto have built themselves upon extracting value from the hydrocarbon chain – and making this value available to consumers in the form of plastic, gas, and a plethora of low-cost end-use products.

There's a strong historic correlation between the world GDP and petro-chemical development: our prosperity is plastic, and vice versa. Ethylene in particular is closely associated with the wealth of nations. "Just look at the historic correlation between the world GDP and ethylene demand," argued Dr. Rajesh Ramachandran in 2005, when he was president of Dow Canada. "In the history of business as we know it, I'm not sure you can find another such strong long-term correlation in existence."

It's a compelling theory. World ethylene production has almost tripled since 1980, more or less in step with the rapid growth of globalization. Ethylene is derived from ethane, a natural gas liquid that is also refined from crude. Most consumers don't know that this double-bonded hydro-carbon is the most prolifically produced organic chemical in the world. It dates back to 1795, when several Dutch chemists synthesized it in their efforts to create "Dutch oil," or ethylene dichloride, a handy paint remover and modern-day component of the global environmental hazard polyvinyl chloride, or PVC.

Ever since, plastics and chemicals have helped serve as the backbone of rapid industrial growth. These materials were instrumental in the postwar automotive and consumer revolution pioneered by the United States. Earlier still, chemical dyes were crucial to the textile industries of the Industrial Revolution. More recently, efficient advanced applications of plastics have literally stretched valuable hydrocarbon molecules and extended the role of plastic into building materials, transport, and auto-motives, often replacing wood, paper, and steel. Everything from LCD screens to artificial limbs became cheaper, partly because of engineering and manufacturing advances in the petrochemicals field.

As petrochemical demand has grown in recent decades, land and ocean pollution by waste plastic has also grown considerably – notably the North Pacific "island" of waste plastic reported since the 1990s. Closer to home, phthalates and other plastic additives have become pervasive within our own bodies, leading to an outcry over endocrine disruption and the haz-ardous use of petrochemicals within daily life. It's hard to be energy effi-cient without plastic. One of the great ironies of modern life is that we have to burn up hydrocarbons in order to save even more hydrocarbons, as in the Tyvek plastic house wrap and closed-cell foam insulation common to most residential builds. Tyvek requires 35 litres of fuel to create, but once installed, it can save 1,250 litres of heating fuel annually.

At Nova's nearby research facility, research director Eric Kelusky shows how long-chain polymers are engineered to create new kinds of plastic and to create more product out of the same mass of polyethylene pellets. Fewer hydrocarbons can be used to create the same product because longer-chain polymers can be made stronger, without losing their supple, rip-resistant qualities. Since the 1970s the average plastic bag requires 200 to 300 percent less material to manufacture. "Yet the number of things getting packaged has grown even more," says Kelusky. "Thirty years ago, people didn't eat yoghurt. And a lot of things that were made of metal, glass, or even wood are now made of plastic. It's usually cheaper to use plastic."

Kelusky shows off Nova's laboratory where they manufacture short runs of various products using factory equipment. Unlike plastics with reactive and noxious additives – such as bisphenol A in polycarbonates or chlorine in PVC – basic polyethylene is upgraded mineral oil. On one machine is a new variety of film being air-blown into thin sheets, like bubble gum expanding. Polyethylene chips are heated and fed into a large blower – a 2.5-metre-wide steel doughnut – that sends a shimmering circular curtain of thin molten plastic three metres into the air, where it is collected, air-cooled, and rolled onto three-metre-wide spools. This is plastic wrap, and it is mesmerizing. "It's quite an art to engineer these," Kelusky says. "It's all about melting, pumping, and pressure – getting flow of air on each side of the polymer."

One positive development from the new plastics was radical reduction of food waste, within both the developed and developing worlds, with the advent of packaging films, especially in India, where refrigeration is minimal – less spoilage, improved shelf life, and better access to fresh food. Back home, the ordinary milk bag was invented and then improved. "We manipulated the length and composition of the molecule chains so that milk bags had a special set of properties," says Kelusky. "They now seal better, last longer, and do not break easily."

When Nova's Joffre site ships pellets to China, some of that same plastic is later shipped right back to us as packaging or product. But China soon won't need North American plastic: the new world map of petrochemicals shows that productive capacity – and power – is relocating to the East and the Middle East. Approximately ten times the polyethylene output of Joffre will be produced in the Middle East by 2013, with five to six times the number of Joffre's world-class crackers going online in East Asia. Although per capita demand for polyethylene is still 800 percent greater in developed countries, it is expected that non-Western nations will create nearly all new demand for plastics during the twenty-first century.

The global dispersion of petrochemicals has become a map of world power. Since the mid-twentieth century, countries with plentiful crude oil but no added-value industries are usually oil oligopolies or military juntas that funnel resources to richer, more powerful nations through global energy trades – Angola, Nigeria, Iran, Iraq, Russia. But look at the leading OPEC nations, rapidly industrializing Asian nations, and the common denominator is geopolitical might fuelled by flourishing refineries and petrochemical complexes, not democracy. Consequently, finance, influence, and access to resources will be increasingly controlled out of Dubai, Shanghai, Beijing, and Singapore. It has something to do with the higher concentration of education and technology required to sustain advanced hydrocarbon industries – nearly 30 percent of chemical industry workers have university degrees – plus the industry's ten-times-input value multiplier that can, in turn, multiply the nation's own wealth and power.

Despite this, many developed economies are deindustrializing – losing valuable petrochemical capacity in particular – simply because they can no longer compete on a global basis. Refinery and petrochemical complexes across North America and Europe have been closing since the mid-2000s. Even within the formerly prosperous petrochemical zone south of the tar sands boom in Alberta, several major sites have closed since 2005. They include one of Alberta's original refineries, at Devon, which opened in 1950 next to what was once one of the world's largest oil fields, Leduc Number One, as well as Edmonton's Celanese plant. In August 2006, Dow Chemical announced that it was closing three petrochemical plants in Alberta and Ontario, adding to the estimated fifty manufacturing facilities that the world's second-largest chemical company has shuttered worldwide since 2003. As one local observed, many large companies just don't see any future except for bitumen. "It's pretty much dried up around here and they're all going up north. It's in the oil sands now," says Tony

McCormick, who started working at the pioneering Devon plant during the 1960s.

The trend is global. In 2008, Dow Chemical announced that it would idle 40 percent of its European styrene capacity (polystyrene plastic and foam are commonly used for electronics, containers, and packaging) and 30 percent of its North American acrylic acid production (essential for other plastics and paints). Five thousand jobs and twenty facilities were eliminated. At the same time Dow also announced worldwide price increases – as much as 25 percent – in order to offset the rising cost of production, citing everything from the slowdown in American auto sales to the steep rise in global energy prices. "Our feedstock and energy costs are up more than 40 percent compared with the same six months of last year," explained Dow's CEO, Andrew N. Liveris, in 2008.

Global price differentials for natural gas, the common fuel required for petrochemical feedstocks and value-added industrial processes, tell the whole story: in May 2008 Saudi Arabian natural gas prices were 700 to 1,000 percent cheaper than those of North America, the U.K., and Europe. In a world where economic dominance is increasingly tied to energy costs and the ability to get more out of every hydrocarbon molecule, new facilities in the Middle East and Asia carry a profound cost advantage.

By its own estimates, Dow Chemical's global operations consume the equivalent of a Middle Eastern country's daily gas production. The company claimed that its bill for hydrocarbon feedstocks – natural gas liquids and crude by-products that are the building blocks of plastic and chemical production – plus the energy required to manufacture and refine had increased 400 percent, from $8 billion in 2002 to more than $32 billion in 2007. Dow continued to increase prices for its petrochemicals into 2009, even as the global economy was stalling and crude oil fell to less than $40 a barrel ("Raw material prices are once again on the rise, despite the impact of the global economic downturn," said Mark Bassett, Dow's global business director, in March 2009).

Some companies are transitioning out of hydrocarbons altogether. The DuPont corporation began to move away from decades of plastics and chemical development during the early 2000s and into agribusiness and biotech. "We believe we are in a resource-constrained world and it will continue," said Chad Holliday, who was chairman in 2007. After selling off 20 percent of its business – including oil interests in Conoco, textiles, and pharmaceuticals – DuPont is chasing the commercial development of second-generation biofuels, specifically cellulosic ethanol: automotive fuels derived from wood chips and corncob waste. Critics chided that DuPont, still a major producer of plastics and chemicals, might be using ethanol production – which is not economical without subsidies – to sell more corn seed, pesticides, and other agribusiness products. (American ethanol produced during the subsidized boom of the mid-2000s frequently required more energy to produce than it created, a feat of inefficiency not even managed by the tar sands.)

Because petrochemicals are a twentieth-century business – encompassing manufacturing, employees with good salaries, high-value products, and dependence on affordable energy and pliant environmental standards – the departure of these industrial giants is a telling sign. "Globally [North America] is the highest-cost location from an energy standpoint," admits Rajesh Ramachandran. "Add to that an ethane disadvantage that is even more significant compared to the rest of the world, you've got an almost perfect storm brewing. It's the worst disadvantage, if you will, for the petchem industry. And in the petchem industry about 80 percent of our cost is associated with raw materials and energy."

Soon the Joffre site will no longer be the world's largest. With cost advantages all but eliminated in mature Western markets, Dow Chemical is moving investment to the Middle East and Asia, helping to build the world's largest and newest petrochemical complexes on top of the cheapest natural gas in the world. In 2008, a week after Dow announced production declines and price increases for North America and Europe, it announced a $26-billion joint venture with state-owned Saudi Aramco to build in Saudi Arabia what may become the world's largest petrochemical complex. Middle Eastern petrochemical output will nearly double between 2000 and 2010.

In other words, Dow closed its plants not for lack of demand for plastic but because the energy markets of the West are facing long-term crisis. "It's definitely a very challenging time. We cannot even know the gravity of the challenge that is ahead of us," Ramachandran says. "If we look at it globally, Dow itself has announced the building of two or three crackers in the Middle East in the next three to five years – over twenty crackers [are] being built in the Middle East. Not a single one is being built here."

Inefficiencies created by the generally wasteful economies of many Western nations haven't helped either. In most world markets, natural gas is usually priced much cheaper than crude oil and reaches price parity with crude only on rare occasions. In other words, natural gas offers as much as a 50 percent discount when compared to the energy value embodied by crude oil. Exploiting the price differential between lower-cost natural gas inputs and higher-price synthetic crude is currently what makes the tar sands economical. "We currently use a significant portion of Alberta's gas to extract oil [from the tar sands]," says Dow's Ramachandran. "This is akin to using hundred-dollar bills to light the candles at the dinner table. Mandating the use of natural gas for [tar sands] power is costly and inefficient." In other words, inefficient economies are subject to a second deindustrialization in the twenty-first century. As high-value production moves elsewhere, petrochemicals are just the tip of the iceberg.

People who live near long-standing petrochemical complexes – in such polluted communities as Sarnia, Niagara Falls, Lake Charles, Houston, and Los Angeles – may rightfully applaud a downturn in petrochemical manufacturing. But what has become clear is that plastic is still an indicator of wealth and influence, not unlike the sailing fleets of former imperial nations, or gold reserves during the twentieth century. Those who have it tend to prevail, for the very reason that nearly everything we touch has some sort of petrochemical basis.

The erosion of the plastic and chemical industries would be far less worrisome, and might even be considered an environmental triumph, if not for two very relevant realities. First, we are years, if not decades, away from transitioning from plastics and petrochemicals as building blocks of modern civilization. The volatile erosion of an industry responsible for everything from fertilizer to Aspirin threatens profound destabilization of all but the most self-sufficient economies – including food shortages and compromised health – similar to that which sudden polar melting threatens within larger climatic systems. It's not just about plastic bags.

Second, aspects of petrochemical manufacturing will play an important role in the production of sustainable solutions, such as the high-purity silicon wafers required for solar power and computers. High-performance chemicals and materials are necessary to a green economy. The unmanaged erosion within major world economies of this capital-intensive, skills-intensive technological capacity – and the gradual but persistent movement of this capacity to the Middle East, in particular – is a substantial concern. Second-generation affordable thin-film solar cells; conductive polymers (which received the 2000 Nobel Prize) that have been formed into organic LED lighting and solar cells; and infrared solar cells printed on plastic sheets all hold promise for mass-produced renewable power in the future. Chemicals, advanced materials, and manufacturing will be strategically important resources that could radically reduce our greenhouse gas impacts. So, with the production of solar cells increasing rapidly, who will control the essential manufacturing inputs and raw materials?

Probably not those nations whose bloated service economies ignored the perils of deindustrialization and neglect of energy policies, green technology, and conservation. The fate of First World debtor nations is becoming more clear: in March 2009 it was announced that Nova Chemicals – and its prized Joffre ethane complex – was being sold to the Middle Eastern giant International Petroleum Investment Corporation for the bargain sum of $2.3 billion. Nova was overly leveraged before the global collapse of 2008, and its stock plunged 66 percent almost overnight. When the former provincial corporation went public in 1998, its stock price was $30; by February 2009 it was $1.28. Many felt that the sale of the homegrown asset to Abu Dhabi represented a colossal failure, indicative of an undergoverned deregulated industry that had passed its prime.

Nova's collapse is evidence of synchronous market failure on an astounding number of levels. But it's also quite simple. While Alberta mined itself for natural resources, others came to mine Alberta. "There were no rules," explains Don MacNeil, an Alberta union president and long-time energy industry observer. "We get left with the debt, the greenhouse gases, and the tailings." Alberta's cheap natural gas resources may run out long before the last bitumen is mined. It's possible that major new pipelines and liquid natural gas terminals for offshore deliveries can't or won't be built fast enough. And with Arctic gas so distant and industrial demand continuing to increase, MacNeil wonders, "What are we going to heat our homes with in 2014?"

Eric Kelusky has a suggestion: burn plastic for its energy value. Most finished plastics actually have richer energy density – stored energy by mass – than crude oil.

Plastic is one of the most difficult areas of material recycling. "I looked at recycling for much of my career," says Kelusky. "The tough thing is the potential mix of materials. Pesticides can get mixed into food-grade plastics." Halogenated plastics such as PVC contain chlorine or fluorine, for example. In fact, one of the ongoing controversies about plastic recycling is that, despite best intentions, consumer plastics can often only be down-cycled into secondary plastics that can't be recycled again, such as park benches or plastic lumber.

Our daily plastics have been engineered for specific applications: microwavability, vapour permeability, flexibility, rigidity. Plastic films are engineered to heat and cool at different rates, which is why some prepared-food containers don't burn the skin when heated. Even the plastic membrane on most single-use yoghurt containers is specially created to be cheap, strong, yet very flexible in order to resist pressure; grocers worldwide had reported mass spoilage because many kids and certain adults couldn't help but puncture the drum-like tops. Plastic drink bottles make good polar fleece jackets, but to date plastic recycling has had a limited effect and has yet to stem the consumption of new, "virgin" hydrocarbons.

It is precisely because there are so many different kinds of plastics – each with a different molecular composition and physical characteristics – that a household bag of assorted recycling can't easily be turned into a cheap source of food-grade or manufacturing-grade plastic. So the best option is simply to use less plastic.

When Wal-Mart announced a major plastic conservation program in 2008, in partnership with the Environmental Defense Fund, it was both an environmental and a cost-saving advance, expected to eliminate 135 million pounds of plastic waste globally. It would give customers an opportunity to continue recycling shopping bags, which in the eyes of some materials experts is still more about optics than efficient hydrocarbon usage. And it doesn't quite address the mountains of polyester, nylon, polyethylene, and polystyrene that Wal-Mart and other retailers sell on a daily basis, materials that form the core of their business. That's a lot of oil and gas and carbon emissions.

"Polyethylene seemed a great boon, not least to the food industry, when it was first invented," said Professor Tim Lang of England's Sustainable Development Commission on the anniversary of the plastic's discovery in

2008. "But it is now increasingly being seen as a mixed blessing. It has helped improve food hygiene at the cost of environmental degradation. It is a classic example of a short-term fix now unravelling."

Nations who are short on household savings and energy alternatives can't be too choosy in the twenty-first century. Kelusky advocates that we think practically about our situation. Collectively, Western consumers have a Saudi-sized pool of oil-equivalent plastic in their basements, garages, and backyards – especially after the crash of 2008, when recycling prices fell 50 percent and some Chinese recyclers began to refuse shipments. "The larger opportunity is to turn it back into fuel," says Kelusky, noting that northern Europe leads research and development on power generation. "The plastic is a rental." The molecules don't lie: per litre, polyethylene is 15 percent more energy-rich than crude oil. "There would be no landfill, and we're short on power. It would be intrinsically better than coal," he says. "If you wanted, you could take your blue box to the power station."

Alternatively, to make plastic recycling truly work, we would need to pay more for plastics with fewer additives; PVC and other plastics exist because poisonous additives like phthalates and bisphenol A were what made them cheaper. "A class of polymer that is a step better and doesn't require as much additive: simpler, but better," says Kelusky. "Better for recycling or fuel value because it is almost all hydrocarbon. But not everyone will pay for this. No one wants to pay extra. Over time this will be a problem."

Across the Desert
On the south side of the Taklimakan Desert stands a Central Asian oasis, the edge of a dusty city that was once the centre of a great Buddhist kingdom. As early as the second century A.D., Yarkant (Suoju, Shache, or So-ch'e in Chinese) was responsible for ideas and texts that changed the Chinese empire. These days Yarkant is a market town for low-income Uighurs, Islamic farmers and herders who have lived here for more than a millennium, and a strategic base for China's domestic security forces. With some of the lowest annual incomes in China, these ethnic-minority farmers and herders scratch out a living based on the trickle of moisture that flows from the Kunlun mountain range to the near south. Yarkant is literally wedged in between the outer edge of the Himalayas and a vast desert filled with hidden energy treasure. Along with nearby Kashgar

A police unit marches through the streets of Urumqi, Xinjiang, China.

(Kashi), it's also right next to Pakistan, Afghanistan, and the former Russian republics to the west.

Riding a public bus through the desert towards Yarkant, locals jump on and off in towns built of bricks and mud; many carry goods that they'll sell at market – goats, chickens, bundles of bread. The bus swerves past slow-moving tractors. On one side of the road are sand and scrub, the larger dunes of the desert beyond obscured by haze; on the other side sheep and a few yaks graze amid dried-up pastures. Mini-cyclones blow in from the desert and kick up dust storms that obscure the road. The bus stops suddenly in the middle of a long deserted stretch, more cyclones pass by, and a teenage boy wearing a Uighur *doppa* (traditional cap) steps up into the bus. He has appeared from nowhere and appears to be carrying nothing. Finding a seat while the other riders ignore him, he sits down, cradling in his palm a single white egg.

The bus pulls back onto the road and speeds east towards Yarkant. Outside, the scenery changes from yellow desert to scrubby trees and farms.

Despite dust storms, freezing nights, and persistent drought, the oases of the southern edge of Central Asia's great desert are surprisingly lush. They are watered by centuries-old irrigation channels and tunnels filled by mountain runoff, and the locals grow cotton, apricots, pomegranates, corn, and walnuts. With climate change, drought has affected the local economy: according to one government report, temperatures in the Xinjiang region have increased 1.6°C since the 1980s, well above most averages, and the glaciers that have long sustained agriculture and supplied the oases with water have begun to recede. Between the dwindling water supply and China's expansion into towns and cities all through the Taklimakan, Uighur society is threatened.

The centre of Yarkant has been largely paved over by Chinese development. Government offices, a modern bus station, and a police detachment dominate the broad main street lined with concrete planters and benches. It matches the template of China's urban colonial form – white tile, blue glass, and concrete – that can be found on the edges of its empire from here to Tibet to Inner Mongolia. Blaring karaoke emanates from the Yarkant Hotel, a Soviet-era establishment that was once the local HQ for Communist Party cadres. Inside, the archetypical padded armchairs with white doilies stand in a semicircle, waiting for old-school functionaries in Mao suits to lounge, smoking and drinking tea, and issue edicts. In the restaurant, Chinese entrepreneurs serve up delicacies in air-conditioned splendour while Uighur vendors peddle kebabs and naan flatbread from carts out on the street. The café, which serves up noodles and lamb, is the liveliest spot in town besides the Sunday market; its outer wall is a double-life-sized mural of John Rambo, from the 1980s classic film – except that this roughly painted Rambo, clothed in camouflage and madly firing off an AK-47, looks like an ethnic Uighur.

The mural is just another sign of the slow-burning battle between Chinese newcomers and Xinjiang's former Islamic majority. Here the police carry automatic weapons. Locals don't want to talk, politely pointing at police and shaking their heads. Nearby, a mostly deserted bowling alley stands next to a local café. Several blocks away is the Altun mosque from the tenth century, its prayer hall still open but empty. At the bus station travellers have to juggle schedules based on both Central Asian and Beijing time, since much of the region can hardly agree on a time zone, let alone mend fences in a struggle that's been simmering since the first century A.D.

All along the edge of the Taklimakan, within a few days' drive of the Pakistani and Afghani borders, are desert towns – Kashgar, Yarkant, and Hotan – that show signs of both rapid development and battle. In Kashgar, photos of bloodshed, captured guns, and murdered police are posted on buildings in an attempt to persuade locals to support police crackdowns against mosques and outspoken locals. Everywhere large banners urge Uighurs to follow China's strict family-control policy, something that has provoked the assassination of several Chinese enforcement officers. Partially used pharmaceuticals can be purchased in local bazaars – a reminder that annual income in the Uighur heartland remains even lower than in much of the rest of China.

Xinjiang is the site of one of Asia's longest-running intranational conflicts, a two-thousand-year battle over a desert kingdom. For some this is still East Turkestan, not the Middle Kingdom. Invaded by China in 1937 and consolidated by Mao Zedong in 1950, Xinjiang rarely captures international headlines, but open warfare, summary executions, and assassinations are commonplace. It was in Kashgar and nearby towns that several fatal incidents took place during the Beijing Olympics: twenty Chinese police officers and, reportedly, thirty-three civilians were killed in clashes and attacks during the month of August 2008. Consequently the region is a major concern for international human rights groups, like Amnesty International, that decry "gross and systematic" abuses, including continuing summary executions.

For now the Chinese appear to have largely won this war. And their conquest has much to do with long-term scarcity of cheap, accessible fossil-based power around the world, something that's begun to affect the economic powerhouse that constitutes China's southerly provinces and eastern coastline. This Central Asian frontier has become crucial to China's economic survival plans, especially given the nation's more recent efforts to transition from a low-cost manufacturing economy to a higher-value independent economy. In order to become stable and stave off protest and instability in its heartland, China needs high-quality energy, lots of it. Xinjiang has an estimated 10 trillion cubic metres of recoverable natural gas buried deep beneath the sands of the Taklimakan Desert, plus the largest single source of crude oil in China, roughly one-third of the country's reserves. Uighur nationalism – and its energy-rich homeland – stands in the way of the planet's fastest-growing consumers of power in the twenty-first century.

Elsewhere, corporations are tripping over each other to develop oil not controlled by state-owned companies. Here in western China it is a brutal and methodical consolidation of a new fossil empire. For years China relied upon imports. A net exporter during the 1980s, China is now the world's third-largest net importer of oil; it accounted for nearly 40 percent of new oil demand during the mid-2000s. And while it led world investment in renewable power in 2006, "China has poured billions of dollars of investment in[to] building power plants – at a rate of one large power plant (1000 MW) per week," wrote Jiang Lin in *Energy Policy*. "China in 2004 added the entire generating capacity of California or Spain in a single year."

For the world's engine of cheap, energy is the single biggest factor behind China's continued ability to sustain growth without imploding. China needs energy to continue its incredible output of domestic and export manufacture, especially high-value, high-margin items such as iPhones, laptops, and IT infrastructure. "More than 80% of crude oil in China is used in oil processing, chemical fiber manufacturing and chemical raw material production [for plastics and textiles]," notes the *China Chemical Reporter*. "Sufficient oil supply is the basis for the sustained development of these sectors."

China's campaign for energy extends well beyond Xinjiang. In the early 2000s China launched an ambitious campaign of energy acquisitions, partly funded by rich dollar reserves created through the bargain trade with Western nations. It now imports more oil from troubled petro state Angola than any other nation, and has profited greatly by aggressively pursuing supplies in Sudan, where China is the country's largest foreign investor. The country is spending billions on unconditional loans and grants across sub-Saharan Africa, essentially purchasing access to resources, including in U.S.-dominated Nigeria, where Americans thought they had a lock on offshore reserves until China signed a $2.27-billion oil deal in 2007. Likewise, China announced a $3-billion deal with Iraq in 2008, the first major foreign oil deal that country has made since 2003. By 2008 China had extended development and infrastructure loans to Angola for as much as $11 billion, even though NGOs (non-governmental organizations) estimate that $4 billion in oil revenues went missing from Angola's treasury between 1997 and 2002. Consequently, it is possible that your trendy made-in-China iPhone or laptop was made from blood-oil petrochemicals (China also has deep investment in Burma).

While America and its coalition of the willing have been fighting energy-tainted wars in the Middle East, China has been diligently poaching access to many of the world's last great conventional oil reserves. "Oil-related Chinese diplomacy has led to the bizarre accusation from Washington that Beijing is trying to 'secure oil at the sources,'" reported the *Asia Times* in 2007, "[which is] something Washington foreign policy has itself been preoccupied with for at least a century."

There is something very Cold War about China's more recent efforts to secure direct supplies at elevated prices, known as "off-take" or bilateral deals, in which the energy is bought up by private sale and taken completely off the market. "They didn't care about the price. All they cared about was locking up the supply," one anonymous oil executive told the *Globe and Mail* in 2008 about the Chinese offers. "China's goal is to get direct control of the barrels." This is how China, through multi-billion-dollar deals with African countries, is literally reserving its imported oil by owning it before it can ever be offered on the open market. Bidding wars and pre-emptive buying for other resources are also more than likely. "Commodities, including liquefied natural gas, rice, wheat, fertilizer and water, may be the next lock-up targets," writes the *Globe*'s Eric Reguly. "Sovereign wealth funds from China and the Arab world may wade into the game. Inevitably, more and more commodities will be taken off the global markets. At some point, the Americans and the Europeans will realize that paying market prices alone is not enough to secure supplies."

Energy is shaping up to be the arms race of the twenty-first century, something that will undermine trade, social justice, and security. Global fear of terminal scarcity is precisely what pushed $218 billion worth of investment into Canada's Athabasca Basin. Unprecedented energy competition between trading nations is a singular factor in what will make the IEA's predictions of $150 oil eventually hold true.

Globalization may be in peril, but the quest for cheap energy continues. As world oil prices rose during the 2000s, China also turned its sights towards its lower-cost domestic frontiers. Within the Tarim Basin, a geological formation that encompasses much of the Taklimakan Desert, are plentiful heavy crude, natural gas, and petrochemical feedstocks. Connecting it all is pipelines. In 2004 China completed its $6-billion pipeline to export Xinjiang's hydrocarbon riches. The massive West-East Gas Pipeline runs 4,000 kilometres from Xinjiang's capital, Urumqi, to Shanghai to supply natural gas for the polluted epicentre of the Yangtze economic boom. Construction of an even larger, 6,500-kilometre pipeline began in 2008; it's worth $10 billion and will run from Xinjiang to the southern manufacturing centre of Guangzhou. When they reach full operational status, the two pipelines will carry as much as 50 billion cubic metres of natural gas a year. Only the Three Gorges Dam project, which cost China's government about $25 billion, is larger in economic scale.

Tightly controlled by the Chinese government, Xinjiang is usually off limits to foreign journalists – I'm here on a tourist visa – but not to major multinational oil companies such as BP and Shell, which fly their flags up and down Beijing Avenue in Urumqi. And while tremendous wealth is being taken from the ground beneath these old Silk Road outposts of the Taklimakan Desert – a region formerly valued for its cotton and strategic proximity to Russia – little affluence has reached the Islamic population. Most Uighurs, Kazakhs, and other indigenous Central Asians still subsist on less than $200 a year.

China has pledged to modernize Xinjiang for its own good – a multi-billion-dollar plan that involves importing vast numbers of bureaucrats, soldiers, gas pipelines, and workers. "It's a top down approach to development, where the state decides what are the important projects like building railroads, roads, developing the oil exploitation of Xinjiang," Nicholas Becquelin of Human Rights in China told the BBC in 2003. "These are all major infrastructural programs that directly benefit the urban Chinese segment of the population. And there is nothing done seriously on poverty alleviation, rural development or minority empowerment in this program."

The local Chinese have been, predictably, the first to enjoy Xinjiang's boom, something that only fuels the long-standing feud. "The Chinese get all the favours and preferential treatment," complains my Urumqi guide, Rebiya. "There are few jobs for we Uighur." For emphasis, she points her finger like a gun and fires at a Chinese couple strolling by.

I've arrived in Urumqi – or Urumchi – only a few months after the last major clash between police and Uighur nationalists. As Rebiya and I stroll along, Urumqi presents itself as two cities: a hastily built Chinese city of concrete, glass, and brick, and a Uighur stronghold full of ancient mosques and markets. We walk towards the Sanxihangzi Market in the centre of town, passing the famous White Mosque, a two-hundred-year-old institution that Rebiya says is a frequent haunt of the secret police. Although Sanxihangzi is the oldest market in Urumqi, Guangdong developers recently gained permission to tear down its northern corner for a gleaming highrise. Fourteen storeys high, its footprint pushed aside fruit vendors and bread peddlers, much to the indignation of the locals, who consider the market a treasure of Uighur culture.

On the surface, the market is chaos: Pakistani traders wave bolts of imported silk; cartloads of naan bread, salted and savoury, are pushed through the crowd. As we walk through the narrow maze of stalls, Rebiya picks out from a cart piled high the choicest dried apricots as a gift, along with some sweet melons, fresh from the countryside. This is a place that considers firewood a cutting-edge fuel: the earthen ovens that cook the naan bread don't really work with anything else.

In the midst of an energy boom, the Uighurs have become a minority in their own land. The flood of Han settlers, businesses, industrial development, and police into Urumqi has in turn fuelled an anti-Chinese campaign that has given Beijing serious cause for concern with its political bombings, assassinations, and weapons smuggling. Xinjiang often exceeds Tibet in summary executions, a fact that China's affluent trading partners have chosen to ignore: the country was taken off the United Nations censure list in 2002 because member nations – and trading partners – elected not to question ongoing human rights violations.

Consequently, Xinjiang's economic divide and sustained political crackdown have pushed the traditionally moderate local population towards fundamentalism, a development actively exploited by radicals in Pakistan, Afghanistan, and the former soviet republics of Central Asia. Between thirty and three hundred Uighur Taliban fighters were reported captured by American forces during the Afghanistan war: Xinjiang's porous border ensures that radical elements, as well as guns and ammunition, continue to trade. China has continued to up the ante. In 2009, it announced plans to raze 85 percent of Kashgar's Old City, a move that would destroy one of the best-preserved Islamic cities in all of Asia. Kashgar's beautiful maze of lanes and mud-brick buildings is a treasure of Uighur identity, and is home to at least part of the region's small separatist movement.

The attacks of September 11, 2001, presented a tremendous political opportunity for Beijing to clamp down and push ahead in its energy plans. China has frequently accused protestors and cultural advocates of being part of the East Turkestan Islamic Movement (ETIM), which terrorism experts estimate has forty core members, based mostly in Pakistan. For its part, Beijing alleges that the ETIM is a "major component of the terrorist network headed by Osama bin Laden." Others speculate that part of the violence isn't political but stems from revenge or crime.

Official sources claimed that Xinjiang separatists committed more than two hundred acts of terrorism in China between 1990 and 2003, killing 162 people and injuring more than 440; Xinjiang police claim there were eight hundred "separatist incidents" in the first eight months of 2001 alone. In 2002 China's foreign ministry reported that U.S. president George W. Bush and Chinese president Jiang Zemin had agreed that "Chechnya terrorist forces and East Turkestan terrorist forces are part of the international terrorist forces, which must be firmly stopped and rebuffed."

The real threat of terrorism in Xinjiang remains indeterminate. Expatriate political networks have been subdued, trans-border traffic in dissidents has been slowed, clerics have been forced into political re-education, birth control is heavily enforced, and even the Uighur language, a distant relative of Turkish, has been banned from universities and schools for Communist cadres. In short, today's Xinjiang bears a harsh resemblance to Mao Zedong's Cultural Revolution; it's a zone of enforced progress and cultural oppression that in many ways appears to be moving backwards in time.

China's quest for cheap energy is surely manufacturing new instability. Some observers predict that anger against China will be increasingly redirected towards the United States and its allies. "There's real disillusionment and growing anger, not so much against China, but against the United States. Mosques are now raising warriors to go and fight," said Dru C. Gladney, a Xinjiang expert at the University of Hawaii. Speaking to a Beijing audience in 2003, Gladney reported that American policy in the Middle East is radicalizing the political underground in Xinjiang, which in turn may disable China's long-term ability to export cheap consumer items to the West. "There is no love or sympathy for Saddam Hussein [in Xinjiang] but there's certainly a lot more awareness of international politics and they're certainly in touch with Muslims around the world."

While China's manufacturing and oil production industries amplify Central Asian terrorism, Western corporations have also moved in. Even though China's state oil company competes with Shell in Nigeria, Shell remains one of the largest foreign investors in China. Its investments include a share in the $4.2-billion Nanhai petrochemicals plant in Guangdong, China's largest single refinery, completed in 2005. As one Shell executive explained in 2005, China will likely become the second-largest chemical market in the world by 2020. He added that the fact that China's per capita consumption of plastics was only twenty-two kilograms annually – compared to Japan's eighty-seven kilos per capita and a hundred kilos in America – was a measure of vast sales-growth potential. By 2010 Shell intends to have more than a third of its petrochemical production in Asia and the Middle East.

Beijing has dubbed Xinjiang its "sea of hope" because of the region's rich energy deposits, but for many foreign multinationals it is simply a foothold in the fastest-growing energy market in the world. As analysts have noted, Shell's aggressive entry into China is at least partly about cultivating relationships with the Chinese government, while gaining a strategic position at the confluence of Russia, China, and Central Asia. During the early 2000s Shell was a full partner in the first Xinjiang pipeline project. A huge trans-Asian pipeline network, one as complete as those in Europe and North America, was to begin in Xinjiang. "The West-East pipeline is a pathfinder for future pipelines and gas from farther afield," explained Shell Exploration (China) managing director Martin Bradshaw back in 2002. "[The pipeline] will be in line with international standards and . . . will benefit all ethnic groups." But not long afterwards, China's national oil company dumped its foreign partners and built the pipeline by itself.

With its strategy for Central Asia now solidly in place, China has begun to express the kind of explicit energy nationalism long predicted for the twenty-first century. "On the street and in the boardroom, there is a growing sense in China that we are now strong enough to do it all alone, which I think is wrong," said European Union trade commissioner Peter

Mandelson in 2008. He was speaking of both ongoing trade obstacles and "an unspoken economic nationalism that implies that foreign investment is no longer wanted or needed."

The inevitable consequence of building a modern-day manufacturing empire is a deep hunger for resources. And in the case of Xinjiang, the old geopolitics of Maoism – the manifest destiny of an ideological state – have been replaced by a one-party state deeply in need of large quantities of secure power. If China cannot feed its factories, refineries, and booming cities, then its growth stalls and the delicate political balance of its post-communist system is potentially outpaced by rural poverty, regional upheaval, and the debilitating cost of imported crude and natural gas. In the West, imported crude oil is still accepted as a necessary evil, even if it indirectly funds terrorism; in China, the prospect of escalating energy costs and excessive imports is seen as the end of China's miracle boom – and the onset of chaos and collapse.

The one thing everyone can agree upon is that the world still needs natural gas right now, lots of gas. What this means is that major pipelines – and the people who control them – are on par with the railway barons of the nineteenth century: energy suppliers hold the key to our economy, and those with transport and product will prosper. And a world that is starving for lack of natural gas cannot, practically speaking, effectively combat climate change or air pollution.

This is perhaps the ultimate measure of our deep and problematic connection to global networks of resource exploration and consumption. On one hand, China's often violent rule over regions like Xinjiang and Tibet might be cause for trade sanctions were it any other country not so vitally connected with the global supply chain. On the other hand, the more natural gas China burns, the less coal it needs to burn to make the same power. The environmental benefit of the natural gas pipeline will likely be reduced demand for other fossil fuels, and even a small offset in China will amount to a massive reduction in greenhouse gas emissions.

But as China amasses greater wealth and clout, and even begins to green its darkest corners, the nation continues to be challenged by its pre-revolutionary past: deep poverty that enables disease and conflict. Down the road from Yarkant, for example, is the equally ancient city of Hotan, where a mere 14 percent of the area's 1.4 million residents are Chinese.

Outside the Chinese core of the city, near a large market, is a women's health centre and micro-financing project, one of many foreign-funded development projects that is attempting, in partnership with local and regional government, to raise local incomes above the $1.25-a-day global poverty line – this despite billions in loans and grant support from the World Bank and other agencies for development in China's west. The women's clinic is clean, has windows, and has some medicine. "Eighty-five percent of women in the program require some kind of immediate medical attention," says the co-coordinator. "We have twenty-one-year-olds with cervical cancer, mysterious ailments, and diseases long ago eliminated elsewhere, such as typhoid, meningitis, and cholera. Many are prematurely aged, visibly disabled, fighting long-term infections." Yet some of these women are also successful entrepreneurs in the micro-lending program, selling naan bread, produce, and textiles, and have become the breadwinner in their family. It's a testament to how development can be highly selective: billions in energy projects attempt to create affordable fossil power and sustain China's growth miracle (and the West's shopping dependency), but so much has bypassed the people who literally live on top of the resource.

It's also testament to the long-standing and moderate vision of Islam here that women can earn the family's income and speak as freely as men, something that is being eroded by violence and oppression, as well as the incursion of terrorist operatives from abroad who seek to exploit Xinjiang's untapped strife. It is not the Taliban and other covert radicals whom locals fear here; it is reprisals from police that keep everyone looking over their shoulder, checking appearances, conversations, and friendships for signs of potentially incriminating anti-patriotic behaviour.

Hospitality and strength are on full display back in Rebiya's Urumqi home as she serves up a traditional welcoming feast of rice pilau, tomato and cucumber salad, mint tea, and savoury noodles. We sit around the low table in the living room and sample the feast, trading words for *apricot*, *plum*, *peach*, and *melon*. As the desert winds blow through Urumqi, Rebiya's cousin pulls out her *dutar*, a long, two-stringed guitar. After an old Turkic folk song she plays a Ricky Martin tune that blazed across China during the country's first fully televised soccer World Cup in 1999. Over the drone of the dutar they sing, "*allez, allez, allez.*" For all we know, Ricky Martin and the dutar may be the only things holding this place together.

Chief Alan Adam traces the growing patchwork of bitumen and uranium leases that have been sold on aboriginal lands in Fort Chipewyan, Alberta.

The River Runs North

The Athabasca River runs north. It snakes through the middle of one of the world's largest continuous bands of boreal forest, up to join other rivers and exit into the Arctic Ocean. That this river runs north, not south, is not only an impressive piece of geography but also an important geopolitical fact, says Athabasca Chipewyan chief Allan Adam. Because if North America's population to the south had to live along this 1,200-kilometre river, he argues, one of the world's largest energy developments would have been shut down long ago. The chief tells of rare cancers afflicting residents of the small downriver hamlet of Fort Chipewyan, toxins found in plants and animals, and air pollution that migrates north from the tar sands sites near Fort McMurray.

This is where the battle for cheap energy inevitably leads us: past our cities and malls, down our largest rivers, through our biggest ecosystems, and into places that are marked by countless shades of green and blue. These places are global biomass assets, but they are also a growing repository for fugitive effluent and toxins: poisons that have escaped not only tar sands developments but also millions of consumers and businesses in the south that contribute pollution to our great rivers.

"We have to slow down," Chief Adam told a Keepers of the Water conference that the community hosted a month earlier. "If we continue to let industry and government behave the way they've been behaving the last 40 years, there will be no turn[ing] back because it will be the total destruction of the land. . . . we'll be refugees in our own land."

Adam is chief of one of the two major First Nations and linguistic groups that share the Athabasca River watershed and delta. Two weeks later he's meeting with staff inside Fort Chip's municipal building. There's a map on the wall: bitumen leases have been sold solidly halfway along the Athabasca from Fort McMurray. That's industrial projects covering nearly a 140-kilometre radius, all stemming from Fort McMurray. Not only that, potentially rich oil and uranium deposits encircle the immediate community, the mineral rights to which have also already been sold off.

"There's uranium, gold – everything. We are leased out right around the border of the boundaries of our reserves – everything, all of it," says Adam, circling his hand around the topographic satellite map of the region. "Everybody's attention is on oil sands. The bigger picture is that if these plans were to let go and to keep on going the way they are going, there is no certainty for our people in the future. Nothing at all. And that's why, if people were to just stop and think that it has nothing to do with oil sands, it has a bigger picture. This is the whole area that we have to take a look at. And they are drilling here on the lake, not the land – they are drilling in the lakes all along here."

Uranium prices averaged $90 a pound in 2007, while a decade earlier it sold for $12. As the largest uranium producer in the world, Canada is hosting the equivalent of a twenty-first-century gold rush within a day's boat ride of the community: no fewer than fifty-nine junior uranium companies are currently active in the Athabasca Basin.

"There's huge development plans for this area," says Adam. "In fifty years we would be forced to leave this community. We would be refugees in our own homeland. They think I do not know that. I am fully aware. I am fully engaged in all talks from all over the place. I take my position very seriously; that is why I am very serious about what I am doing. People think I was playing a game. I am not playing no game. This is a serious, serious matter."

Fort Chip has been in turmoil since 2006, when the community's former physician, Dr. John O'Connor, went public with his concerns about an unusually high incidence of rare cancers in the community of 1,200 pre-dominantly aboriginal people. They included not just colon, prostate, and lung cancer, but also five cases of cholangiocarcinoma, a rare bile-duct cancer that O'Connor, in an interview with the Canadian Broadcasting Corporation, said he would expect to see in those numbers only in a large city. "Our people are dying like flies," says elder Alec Bruno over lunch at the nearby guest lodge. "I thought about maybe we should move the whole family away from here, away from this lake and the river, but then I thought 'Why should we move?' Our roots are here, our beliefs; our culture comes from here. This is our home. Why should we move? If anybody is to move, why cannot they move? It is just the way of our people."

Water and food contamination is a serious issue, since many people here still hunt and fish and, to various degrees, still depend on the land as a major food source. Many couldn't afford to buy all their food from the local store. "We live in isolation here," explains Alec Bruno. "We have no roof, and our way of life was a simple life until the grabbing of our land. We [still] depend on the land for our life."

One of the biggest concerns is seepage from the enormous tailings ponds adjacent to the mines and upgraders to the south. All water that moves past the tar sands winds up in the Athabasca Delta to the north, where Fort Chipewyan is located. The largest and oldest of these ponds are either near or directly alongside the river. Environmental organizations, governments, industry, and First Nations have been struggling over this for years. Data is lacking on the degree of seepage and contamination, but many maintain that's because government and regulatory standards don't mandate enough environmental and health monitoring, so naturally the data is insufficient.

And even with proof, Alberta's record on enforcement in the Athabasca region is spotty at best. Between 2006 and 2007 Alberta fined one company under provincial legislation; federal authorities, responsible for rivers and aquatic environments, laid no charges in the region under the Fisheries Act from 1988 to 2005. It turns out that Alberta's two largest cities collected more in library fines than two higher levels of government levied against polluters in 2006–07. "This is an industry that's spewing 1.8 billion litres of toxic waste in[to] tailings ponds every day, so looking at this and realizing the scale of it, it was really quite alarming," said Gillian McEachern, the senior campaigner at ForestEthics who wrote the study. "Alberta seems to be doing a good job at protecting its library books, [but] it's not doing a very good job at protecting the environment."

Chief Adam doesn't need convincing. He points to the map where Suncor's Pond One, the industry's first tailings pond, was built next to the Athabasca back in the 1960s. "Do you see Pond One right here? Now you start seeing this film line right here, where the water starts turning colour. Now you can only assume that something is going on within this area here, that something is going through here. Look at the colouration of it." It's just one of a 2008 total of sixty square kilometres of tailings ponds, many of which are within at least 1,600 metres of the Athabasca River. The existing extraction process includes injecting solvents and other ingredients, so the outflow is not merely bitumen froth and water. Natural Resources Canada notes that tailings include phenols, benzene, cyanide, heavy metals, and other known or suspected carcinogens. Fish cannot last four days in these waters. And there is collectively enough new sludge produced every day to fill 720 Olympic pools. Total waste solids and liquids contain persistent aromatic hydrocarbons (PAHs) equal to the contents of about three thousand *Exxon Valdez* tankers.

A 2007 report produced for Suncor reported seepage from Pond One through the bottom of the dyke at the rate of 1 million gallons (3.8 million litres) per day. "The ponds leak so routinely, in fact, that they are surrounded by medieval-looking moats equipped with pumping stations to return the seepage to the ponds," writes Andrew Nikiforuk in 2008's *Tar Sands*, the first exhaustive account of bitumen mining in Canada. The first major tailings pond was supposed to be temporary. "Engineers not only miscalculated how long they would need the pond (the initial projection was a few years) but underestimated the fluidity and instability of the tailings. A dam originally designed to be 40 feet high now towers over the river at 325 feet and stretches for two miles."

Inside Suncor's gates, visitors are kept on a very short leash, unable to view the mine sites directly or even leave vehicles to view the ponds next to the main access road. It's a cordial but tense situation, especially since two recent worker drownings in Suncor's ponds, as well as global headlines about 1,600 migratory birds that perished in the spring of 2008 when they landed on a nearby tailings pond at Syncrude. Between the dead ducks, new international scrutiny, and the spectre of more stringent emissions caps, there are easier places to practise public relations and environmental management than the tar sands.

On a site tour at Suncor, Mark Shaw, the company's director of sustainable development, reports that Pond One is due to be reclaimed by 2010. Parts are "mud mixed with water," some 103 hectares in total, and all are listed, like other ponds, as a company liability in regulatory filings. Shaw is responsible for turning several ponds into "viable landscapes" over the next few years, thereby making Suncor the first company to reclaim a tailings pond.

Shaw and his co-workers would much rather talk about technological innovation, such as the development of "dry tailings" – effluent processed with less water – as well as other environment-related engineering feats that cannot be demonstrated because they do not yet commercially exist. From $2 billion in funding for underground carbon storage, promised by Alberta's government in 2008, to proposed technologies that would use less natural gas and water (such as experimental "toe-to-heel" subsurface extraction, in which companies literally ignite underground bitumen deposits to loosen up and extract the lighter hydrocarbons), there is much that the industry and government have promised. But the truth is there's very little to show. Carbon capture will not be legally required in Alberta until 2018. Essentially the same industrial process developed in the 1960s still forms the core of operations, and even though several decades of engineering have produced significant efficiency and cost gains, it's the same surface-mining model. That steam-injection process was actually pioneered in southern California during the 1950s and 1960s, near Bakersfield, as part of enhanced extraction efforts to recover shallow reservoirs of heavy oil.

The reality is that the extraction technology at the core of these massive plants is the same process first invented in the 1920s and refined to become commercially viable in the 1970s. Among industries such as forestry, agriculture, and pharmaceuticals, Canada's energy sector has among the lowest spending on research and development as a percentage of revenue. And the expected cost of mitigating tar sands emissions isn't cheap: one 2008 estimate from the Alberta Research Council pegged it at $16 billion to sequester twenty megatonnes by 2020. Even then there are serious scientific questions about whether tar sands emissions can be meaningfully sequestered. ("Only a small percentage of emitted CO_2 is 'capturable' since most emissions aren't pure enough," said one government briefing note leaked in 2008. "Only limited near-term opportunities exist in the oil sands and they largely relate to the upgrader facilities.")

There's a strong engineering culture at work here, which is not unexpected given that these pits, ponds, and cities of steel have sprung from the minds of some of the world's leading technicians and scientists. Somehow visitors, taxpayers, and the rest of the world are being asked to trust engineers with managing the consequences of runaway growth. It's a version of the quaint techno-utopianism of the 1950s, except that, instead of flying cars and space homes, we're being asked to believe that industry-led innovation, with some publicly funded subsidies and research, can turn dirty oil clean again.

While business leaders have made great advances in policy and attitude – even supporting carbon taxes, as Nexen's CEO Charlie Fisher did in 2007 – tangible on-the-ground innovations are still scarce. Less than a year earlier, Alberta granted its first certification for reclaimed land at Syncrude, which represented less than 1 percent of its disturbed land from more than thirty years of operation. And even then the reclaimed land did not reestablish boreal forest with the massive biomass and carbon banking of real muskeg. The 104-hectare site, a park called Gateway Hill, is a former soil dump that now hosts transplanted trees, some interpretive trails, and a few artificial wetlands. It is a theme-park version of the boreal forest. As a Syncrude spokesperson put it at the launch, "If people aren't looking closely, it blends into the natural landscape."

The Kingdom

Of the many wonders of the tar sands, my attention was particularly caught by Mark Shaw's answer to my question about seepage from Suncor's ponds – a major source of concern regarding cancer at Fort Chipewyan as well as broader contamination of a watershed larger than most European countries.

How much do these ponds actually leak? "There is no leakage from this pond," says Suncor's director of sustainable development. "This dyke is largely sand [filled] with process-affected waters. What we know for sure is that the pond has no leakage. It's completely impermeable, or for those who are hydrogeologists, it's ten to the minus ten – it's not zero but some incredibly small number, because nothing is ever watertight."

Shaw argues that fine clay sediment and bitumen within the tailings settle out and help form this impermeable barrier, keeping contaminated water out of what is understood to be a fairly dynamic hydrological environment of muskeg, river, and underground streams. But Suncor obviously has a hard official position on the matter, which is not surprising given current investigations by several government agencies and more recent talk of legal action by the First Nations of Fort Chip. "There's really no leakage from the pond," Shaw repeats. "The process-affected water that was part of the dyke – rainfall will flush down some [traces]. But no fluid gets from the pond to the river."

It was the kind of cordial but firm denial one might hear from a Saudi prince or a Communist Party functionary. Welcome to the Kingdom: the bitumen projects of the Athabasca have become a semi-autonomous jurisdiction not subject to the same regulatory, environmental, and political accountability as the rest of the continent. The army of trucks, the massive tailings ponds, and the non-stop capital expansion of the tar sands are the result of companies' gaining government-scale powers to self-regulate, self-monitor, and even influence energy and climate policy. When Suncor says there is no leakage from its tailings ponds, despite substantive evidence that suggests otherwise, the real government has been unwilling to challenge the company's assertions. (In May 2008 Alberta's environment minister, Rob Renner, claimed that with any leakage, "the amount of water that would be outside of the pond itself would be diluted by a factor of about 40 million to one.")

That is one way in which the tar sands have become their own country. On many fronts, from environment to policing, these companies literally operate as government but still receive preferential tax and royalty treatment. The Canadian environmental non-profit KAIROS published a 2008 study finding that Canada spent $8 billion in cumulative tax subsidies to oil and gas between 1996 and 2002, and will spend another $1.5 billion on bitumen mining before the controversial tax breaks are phased out – amounting to a late-2000s subsidy of about $1 million per day. Although the primary regulator, Alberta's Energy Resources Conservation Board (ERCB), examines each individual project (with the input of Alberta Environment), it has yet to delay or stop any projects on environmental grounds.

The Cumulative Effects Management Association (CEMA), the task force that's grappling with the region's environmental and social concerns, lost its last credible members from the community and non-profits in 2008, after eight years of reports, negotiations, and a general inability to come to some agreement on environmental and health-based limits to development. "The Alberta Government has taken a 'talk and drill' approach to developing the oil sands," said Chris Severson-Baker of the Pembina Institute, a founding member of the group, on announcing its withdrawal from CEMA. "It has squandered an opportunity to get effective environmental management in place ahead of serious on-the-ground cumulative impacts. Now it must play catch up."

Everyone from Wal-Mart to China's Communist Party depends on affordable energy to maintain the bountiful supply chains that have increasingly driven our economies. China's interest in Canada's oil sands is widely known; in 2007 Sinopec bought 40 percent of the Northern Lights project, which is expected to deliver 1.3 billion barrels of synthetic crude over its lifetime. Canada also sells to and shares heavy oil technology with China – both nations share a distaste for the Kyoto climate-change protocol. Since 2009, growing opposition to dirty oil from American environmentalists has created a tar sands industry movement to bond more closely with Asian markets, where most governments do not yet have threatening climate controls or low-carbon fuel standards. The offshoring of Canada's climate and environmental responsibilities to the developing world – via multiple pipelines to the Pacific Ocean – has become a lucrative possibility for Canada's tar sands producers. It's a process "where we can get the highest net price to market," according to one Husky Energy spokesperson.

As echoed in the troubled politics of energy-rich nations around the world – Russia, Nigeria, Saudi Arabia, and here in Alberta – energy has often been closely associated with political underdevelopment and democratic decline. The top global crude reserves by country in 2007 tell part of the story: there is Saudi Arabia, Canada, Iran, Iraq, Kuwait – and only two other countries in the top ten, Venezuela and Russia, have democratic elections, and they are questionable ones at that. As Mikisew Cree representatives reported, there is little chance of escaping the reach of the industry; those who dissent are sometimes blacklisted, which exerts considerable pressure in a region dominated by a single industry. "We have no choice but to seek work [in the tar sands] because our way of life has been destroyed," said band official Steve Courtoreille. "Because we've been very outspoken in our belief in trying to protect the environment, we're not treated fairly," he added, regarding his band's regional business interests in aviation, construction, and energy services, which contribute important income to the community. "We do get threats in terms of losing our contracts. We're not going to get intimidated by anybody who comes and threatens our contracts."

Further evidence of the Kingdom is the historically close relationship between government and industry. In 2007 Suncor vice-president Heather Kennedy was appointed as a temporary senior bureaucrat to operate Alberta's Oil Sands Sustainable Development Secretariat and advise government on policy. Speaking behind closed doors to a delegation of environmental funders in Fort McMurray in 2008, Kennedy assures the group that, yes, government and industry can be trusted with management of the region. "When you are sitting on the world's largest resource, it does make some sense to look at how you extract it," she says. "It's important to switch from the idea that research or planning is a cost; we're going to invest in understanding thresholds, and we're going to invest in getting the right kind of data. And then you're going to get a nice tidy return on your investment, whatever that is, for your communities. . . . The oil sands are a whole series of lovely communities, social and visible communities. This is about people and people in those communities."

Sitting in the audience, Chief George Poitras of the Mikisew Cree not only questions Kennedy's vision of good government as a series of "tidy returns" on investment but takes advantage of the rare opportunity to ask why, after a decade of intensive growth in the tar sands, government and companies have no fixed limits or protective thresholds to development – and why there has been so little available information and studies carried out on tangible impacts on human communities such as Fort Chip. "Many times questions are raised about the pace of development, water quality, greenhouse gas emissions. What is often missed is the human life impact. Everybody wants to avoid that question, including the government of Alberta. Whenever we raise issues, they are swept under the carpet. Our doctor raised issues about the disproportionate number of health conditions that are showing up in Fort Chipewyan. But what happens? Your government and the federal government launched complaints, as opposed to heeding his advice and [addressing] health conditions and early death from cancers. . . . Do you think the people of Fort Chipewyan are delusional? Do you think we raise trouble just for the sake of it?"

There's a slight pause. "It's clear that the cancer concerns in that community are real. The illness is real. I don't think there's any doubt about that," Kennedy replies. "I think it's important to take a broad look at the potential causes, including the oil sands industry as a possibility, including other things." Studies are ongoing, she offers in conclusion.

The question still stands: have the Athabasca River and Delta become an economic sacrifice zone? The ethical and environmental lag in the world's largest energy play has everything to do with the fact that the engineering and managerial resources are being poured into cost management, the gargantuan effort to make cheap energy out of marginal hydrocarbons using high-value natural gas, steel, and labour. The fundamental conflict here is very twenty-first century: it's not oil wars between two competing countries, nor is it an outright scramble for resources like the Klondike gold rush or an early California oil field. This contest is about creating new supply as cheaply as possible, and the most efficient way to do this is to minimize regulation and policy that might inhibit growth. Suncor and other companies cannot control the price of steel, the supply of natural gas, or even labour supply. But they can influence government. Both companies and government have shown great skill in breaking down accountability mechanisms while companies gain government-style autonomy to conduct operations with minimal interference. The tailings ponds were built next to the Athabasca not because the industry had malicious intent, but because it was the cheapest, most convenient spot for their operations; they needed vast water supplies and the river was an efficient solution.

In a different yet profoundly similar way, Wal-Mart has also taken great liberties and gained new powers in its global efforts to achieve maximum savings and efficiency. It has bent and broken labour laws on an epic scale. It has gained easements and tax breaks for its own kingdom of supercentres, distribution centres, and markets. It has bullied suppliers, shippers, and anyone else who threatens to obstruct its mission. And as titans such as General Motors have declined and decentralized, Wal-Mart and its kin have grown larger and more powerful.

As James Hoopes wrote in the 2006 anthology *Wal-Mart*, the incredible success of the modern vertically integrated corporation forces us to reconsider what D.H. Robertson once described as "islands of conscious power" that arise in an "ocean of unconscious co-operation like lumps of butter." This was the old notion of the firm, and of how essentially undemocratic but managerially powerful competitive companies co-exist with free markets and elected governments. The size of the firm was optimized and often curtailed by its own limits and inefficiencies. (The vision also informs more recent arguments that defend globalization as a great equalizer, creating a "flat world" of many players.) But waves of successive technology and communication innovations since the Industrial Revolution have shown that "technological change clearly favoured managerial power over the free market," writes Hoopes. "The telegraph, railroads, and heavy machinery increased optimal firm size in many industries by enabling managers to lower corporations' internal costs for communication, distribution and production. . . . Therefore, the economic advantage of the new technology went to large management-intensive firms."

We have seen the dawn of the new corporate giant during the late twentieth century with the rise of the modern service/knowledge economy – retailers, technology giants, and financial services – and all have used technology to manage, aggregate, and monetarize resources in ways and combinations not previously seen.

In the case of the tar sands, the kingdom status of large companies exists through a fundamental conflict of public interest. It is estimated that government revenue from the tar sands will total $123 billion between 2000 and 2020; for Alberta it is hoped that this will replace the one-third of its revenue that it once collected from conventional oil and gas. Governments are also responsible for public health and the environment and are banking on these royalties. Moreover, these same governments are charged with various treaty and legal duties to First Nations, even though they directly benefit from the growth and success of companies operating in traditional territories. It goes a long way towards explaining why there are no stated limits for development based on cumulative impact assessments for the region's environment, nor is tar sands development itself yet limited by international commitments to reduce greenhouse gases.

The only relationship that isn't potentially compromised is the one between energy companies and their shareholders. Operations such as Suncor and Syncrude, and other major developments that have broken ground en route to collectively producing 3 million barrels a day, are legally bound to create returns for shareholders. This fiduciary duty does not necessarily extend to "external" market concerns such as aboriginal rights, climate change, and environmental and health impacts. In fact, companies that offer too much and voluntarily adjust operations to respect environmental limits and climate concerns could be sued for neglecting their duty to produce reasonable returns. This is one of many reasons why tacit self-regulation has largely been a failure not only within the tar sands but also regarding climate change globally and failed efforts to voluntarily reduce emissions. In both cases it is a well-documented failure, replete with mountains of reports, meetings, consultations, and applications. Nevertheless, millions have been spent to document the piecemeal process by which overdevelopment has taken place. It is greenwashing by bureaucratic means, and a regulatory and legal tangle that few can either comprehend or afford to challenge.

What if, by moving into final fossil fuels such as unconventional crude, the energy company is evolving into something potentially more influential than even Wal-Mart? The world's most profitable company in 2009 was not Wal-Mart but ExxonMobil, which owns a controlling interest in the $8-billion Kearl oil sands project, launching in 2010, as well as major shares in Syncrude. Ten years hence, when plastic is so valuable that people might want to burn it rather than buy more of it, when shipping costs could cull our avalanche of bargains to a meagre flow of semi-essential goods, and when consumers themselves discover that liquidity and credit cannot support an economy, who will hold more power: a discounter that once sold more diapers than anyone else, or the integrated energy company that can, for a price, alchemize dirt into oil?

ExxonMobil's advertising campaigns promise "more energy, fewer emissions [and] with technology, we can do both." But that's not what is happening on the ground. By 2009 Alberta's government had admitted that cancer rates in the community were, in fact, elevated. ("The overall findings show no cause for alarm," argued a provincial health official. "But they do, however, point to the need for some more investigation.") This wasn't the win-win future that some had been promised. Instead, our epic pursuit of cheap energy has resulted in conflicts, fossil fuel dependence, and diminishing supplies.

Alec Bruno worked at Suncor when the dyke for Pond One was being built, and knew, as did the province, that the ponds were leaking. "They don't want to know," he says, looking out over the lake, "yet they are concerned."

WE, THE RESOURCE:
JOURNEYS TO THE END OF CHEAP

6

Borderlands

It's 4:00 p.m. and another load has arrived. People file off what looks like a large tour bus and march forward in a rough line. Some are dressed in golf shirts and khakis, others in T-shirts and jeans. Most have knapsacks, the kind college kids haul around. Some people don't have anything.

As they walk along a tall chain-link fence and pass through a bright yellow gate, it looks like a shift change at a factory, or a bunch of tourists returning from a packaged day tour. Someone is selling snacks at the gate while a uniformed guard ensures that everyone passes through smoothly. This is just one of several busloads of illegal immigrants that have been caught by the U.S. Border Patrol somewhere in the Arizona desert – and they have just now been unceremoniously returned to Mexico at the Mariposa crossing at Nogales. On average, 1,500 of these returned un-documented travellers walk through this gate every day.

Most migrants visit the aid station a few hundred feet from the gate; it sits on a concrete island amid idling semi-trailers that form a circle around the border crossing. Here they receive food, water, advice on transport, discounted bus tickets home, medical assistance, and, for those planning an immediate return trip across the border, cautionary information on the perils of the Sonoran Desert. These are the lucky ones: since America's Immigration and Customs Enforcement (ICE) ended its "catch and release" policy in 2006, many non-Mexican migrants are detained without trial and not returned across the border – all part of what has become a government-sponsored $1-billion annual business chasing undocumented workers throughout America. The buses unloading returned migrants are actually run by Wackenhut, a multi-national security firm under contract to the American government.

Off in the distance, U.S. border guards patrol the American side with rifles and dogs. There were an estimated 18,000 U.S. border agents in 2009, twice the number a decade ago, plus a large floating pool of military, ICE agents, and others deployed by Homeland Security. Here on the Mexico side there's a single uniformed, unarmed guard at the yellow gate who looks as if he would be comfortable working shopping mall security; others are holed up in buildings and watchtowers nearby. We're in the geographic centre of what has become the world's busiest illegal border crossing; the number of undocumented migrants grew during the 1990s and peaked during the 2000s, with more than 300,000 people apprehended annually in Arizona by the mid-2000s. Yet everything here seems incredibly routine.

Inside the aid station, a large white tent, migrants arrive and linger, some just to gather themselves before the next stage of their journey, while others sit here because they have nowhere else to go. Some have been injured during the crossing or capture and are attended to by medics. The Sonoran Desert that straddles the Arizona-Mexico border is mostly fenceless, unlike in California, where the bulk of America's 580 miles of border wall has already been installed. The security buildup on the western edge of the Mexican-American border has pushed migrants east into Arizona, where thousands attempt to cross the desert each week.

"We were walking for three days and were caught," says one farmer from the Mexican state of Michoacán, who is travelling with several cousins. "Migration caught us and deported us. . . . We're really not sure where we were when they caught us. Maybe we were halfway there." Each paid as much as $3,000 to smugglers so that they might cross, disappear into Arizona, and resurface in California, Georgia, or even Canada with steady employment – construction, cleaning, landscaping – and send home money to family members. Workers can make more than five times the wages they might make at home – $60 weekly back in Michoacán, says another, versus $400 to $500 in the U.S. – and, like others, they have left behind children and parents whom they planned to support with remittance payments.

I ask the obvious question: will they try to cross again? "We are coming back with some minor injuries, and without any money, and they assaulted us in the desert, so . . ." His voice trails off. Who's "they"?

"There are people with guns that wander around in the middle of the desert and they do not really leave there," he says of the bandits who attacked his party. "They are just out there. Plus the route is pretty dangerous, pretty difficult." He's still undecided about his next move, as are many of the others who've just gotten off the Wackenhut bus. It's a long trip back to Michoacán, but whatever he's seen in the desert has him thinking hard about the wisdom of another attempt.

It's a deadly dilemma that U.S. authorities helped create, mostly under former president George W. Bush, whose administration authorized millions in infrastructure, technology, and personnel, including additional fencing worth as much as $7 million per mile along parts of the border. The militarization of the border peaked between 2006 and 2008, during Operation Jump Start, when six thousand armed National Guard members were stationed along the border to increase security, reduce drug traffic, and deter immigration. "The goal was to drive migrant traffic away from cities like San Diego and El Paso and into the remote desert on the assumption it would act as a deterrent," explained journalist Randal Archibold in 2007. "But while there is no way of knowing its overall effect, the strategy is serving at least in part as a funnel for untold numbers of migrants. [They] cross with little or no knowledge of the desert, whose heat, insects, wildlife and rugged terrain make it some of the most inhospitable terrain on the planet."

Nearby, at the Nogales headquarters of Grupo Beta, the Mexican state agency responsible for migrants, José Mon Martinez shows me just how bad it can get. In a backroom there are file photos of rescued and deceased migrants. One man lost a leg falling off a train, caught beneath the wheels.

A woman from Chiapas attempted to cross with seven children, not once but five times. Another man jumped from a border wall and fractured both ankles, others sliced their necks open on barbed wire, or mangled their feet walking five or six days while lost. The unluckiest ones become delirious with the heat and try to bury themselves in the dirt or take off all their clothes under the midday sun. Their bodies are often found shrivelled up, partially baked and decomposed by the intense heat. Those who are badly dehydrated might just go to sleep and never wake up.

Drugs are part of the violent mix, and the relative lawlessness of the Sonoran Desert attracts smugglers. Whole pack trains of mules and horses carrying millions of dollars worth of drugs are sometimes apprehended. Migrants who cross paths with professional criminals in the desert are sometimes executed, says Martinez – just a few more bodies to add to the more than five thousand drug-related killings that plagued Mexico in 2008.

Martinez informs migrants of all these risks; some listen and return home, but many don't. "Even if they increase the number of Border Patrol agents, the migration is never going to finish," he says. "It is not going to be stopped."

While the number of workers in Mexico's borderland maquiladora factories peaked in 2001, mostly because of Asian outsourcing, the migration of people and products across the Mexican-American border has continued. Everything from fresh produce to electronics crosses the border and infuses the North American economy with affordability, yet Mexico's dominant export is people – not just Mexicans but also vast numbers of poor farmers from across Central America who have travelled incredibly long distances to gamble their lives in the perilous trek. As Sheldon Zhang reported in his 2007 book, *Smuggling and Trafficking in Human Beings*, as many as 3,500 people have died crossing Arizona's southwestern frontier since 1995. When more than 500 died in the Sonoran Desert during 2005 alone, the Arizona border town of Pima had to rent a refrigerated truck to store all the extra bodies awaiting identification and cause-of-death determination by the county coroner.

Back in Tucson, a short drive north of the border, there's constant debate. Some locals spend their weekends driving water trucks into the desert and leaving behind maps for incoming migrants. Others, such as the Minutemen, spend months camped out along the border in a long defence line, waiting for migrants to emerge so they can detain "illegals," notify authorities, and have the migrants deported or jailed. "Half of North American migration occurs in Arizona," says Rev. Robin Hoover, an activist pastor and president of Humane Borders, an award-winning humanitarian group that maintains a prominent network of blue water barrels on the American side of the desert. "We have more apprehensions, we have more deaths, we have more agents, we have more boys, more toys, more this, more that. Nobody is happy with this migration. Landowners aren't happy; law enforcement is not happy; health-care folks aren't happy. I cannot name anybody that is happy. The human rights folks are not happy and the faith communities aren't happy. Civil society is pissed off."

So why does it happen? In short, we're deeply attached to cheap stuff, and we have come to depend on the affordability of Latin American labour on both sides of the border. "What we have here is a human artifice called the border that enables us to love Mexican tomatoes more than we love Mexicans," says Hoover. "That's the problem. Half of the tomatoes that are consumed in the United States are produced just south of here."

Many migrants plan to leave the U.S. and return home within a year or two, but most stay longer. In 2000 only about one in ten migrants returned within a year, according to the Public Policy Institute of California. Those who come north from Mexico and Central America stay in the United States because it has become too difficult to recross the border. "In its effort to lock people out," writes journalist Maggie Jones, "the U.S. government has instead locked them in."

By 2009 it was clear to nearly everyone, including the new Obama administration, that the strategy had failed. Mexican drug violence was at an all-time high, migrants continued to die in the desert, and America's immigration system had created a two-tier model of citizenship. The result was a massive pool of cheap labour stranded within the United States that had begun to mirror China's pool of displaced farmers, many of whom were still underemployed, had limited rights, and were vulnerable to labour abuses, homelessness, and substandard health care.

Transnational migration has created a nation within a nation. According to one 2009 Pew Hispanic Center report, a record 12.7 million Mexican immigrants were living in the United States in 2008 – the single largest immigrant population in the world. And an estimated 55 percent of these people are undocumented, subject to summary arrest and incarceration. Amazingly, 11 percent of all people born in Mexico currently reside in the United States, representing a massive human subsidy to a service economy addicted to cheap labour.

Globalization has succeeded mainly through the existence and management of imbalances, the opportunities presented by price differentials in wages, resources, and technological and managerial efficiencies. And, more broadly, borderlands and frontiers are integral to major economic transformations. Many of the great economic zones of our time are also highly militarized and managed: Singapore, the Mexican-American border, and south China, all of which became wealth and savings multipliers that helped raise standards of living around the world.

Indeed, the 1990s and 2000s will likely be seen as a dark time in the history of immigration. As trade flourished, Bush-era America "lavished scarce resources solely on hunting down and punishing illegal immigrants," said the *New York Times* in a 2008 editorial. "Its campaign of raids, detentions and border fencing was a moral failure. Among other things, it terrorized and broke apart families and led to some gruesome deaths in shoddy prisons. . . . But it also was a strategic failure because it did little or nothing to stem the illegal tide while creating the very conditions under which the off-the-books economy can thrive. And without a path to legalization and under the threat of a relentless enforcement-only regime, they cannot assert their rights."

Around the world an estimated 200 million legal and illegal migrants live outside their country of origin, according to the World Bank. This major reallocation of humanity is also helping to redefine society and politics in the U.K., Europe, Canada, and Southeast Asia. It represents a major subsidy to most economies, and a deep dependence on vast quantities of second-class citizens for landscaping, meat-cutting, and day labour. These people are Filipino nannies in Canada, Pakistani ditchdiggers in Dubai, Thai construction workers in Singapore, Dominican cab drivers in New York.

While internal migrants in India and China still outnumber transnational migrants – there are as many as 200 million internal migrants in China alone – the economic value of displaced foreign workers to developing nations is significant. One 2007 study by Ernst & Young found that curtailment of high levels of migration in Britain would surely decrease the country's economic growth; conversely, continued immigration would boost Britain's growth by as much as 20 percent. "Without a million and a half foreign workers since 1997, the UK economy would have suffered slower GDP growth, higher inflation and interest rates," the study concluded. And even though many of these European immigrants were as skilled as their U.K. counterparts, they earned only 60 percent of the average U.K. wage. When the European Union added eight Eastern European countries to its membership in 2004, it was estimated that 50,000 immigrants would arrive by 2008. Instead, more than 1 million Eastern Europeans legally entered Britain, infusing its economy with cheap skilled workers; this was hailed by many as a success story in decriminalizing global labour.

As with China, remittance monies sent home by migrants worldwide prop up poor households and local economies in ways that conventional forms of globalized trade have failed to accomplish. This redistribution of global wealth, worker by worker, has helped to stabilize globalization by forestalling deeper poverty within many developing-world countries. Egypt, for example, receives more in remittances than it collects from the Suez Canal, and incoming payments represent 54 percent of Tajikistan's entire economy. The World Bank's Dilip Ratha estimates that 200 million immigrants made $305 billion in remittance payments in 2008, a conservative figure that does not include informal and unrecorded payments. These payments to family and community increased globally by 73 percent between 2001 and 2005, and were distributed across an estimated tenth of the world's population.

Remittance is also an indirect measure of the significant savings created by foreign workers within their host economies, since they are paid a fraction of average wages. In other words, if foreign workers and migrants are on average making half what a regular worker would earn, then their remittances suggest that, roughly speaking, at least $305 billion was retained by host countries, representing a significant labour subsidy (not including the economic activity created by migrants living abroad). This infusion of labour savings globally is nearly identical to Wal-Mart's record-setting sales revenue for 2008, and nearly three times the world expenditure on foreign aid in 2003.

Migrant workers are essential to booming developing economies such as China, and they helped underwrite the rich standard of living enjoyed by most Western nations. Like affordable crude oil, migrants have anchored our world of cheap for several decades. But times have changed: many migrants have become tired of the risk, hardship, and criminalization, and more are staying on their farms and in their ghettoes. Many are returning home. With the global economy collapsing late in 2008, the World Bank noted that, for the first time in nearly a decade, remittance payments to Latin America and the Caribbean did not increase, and estimated that overall remittances would decrease as much as 5 percent in 2009. This even though experts predicted that low-wage migrant employment would stay relatively secure in America, partly because many are stuck, economically and legally, and because many resident Americans, even unemployed ones, are slow to take these jobs.

On a bench outside the Grupo Beta building, several migrants wait for a truck ride out of Nogales, away from the border. They've had enough. "I had this idea of going to the United States to look for work in a restaurant because supposedly you can earn more there," says Jolanda, who most recently cooked in a kitchen in Mexico City. She had been travelling with her brother and some other relatives in the company of a smuggler. "But the experience that I had in the desert was, well, very sad. It is a really sad reality because you come with this kind of vision or illusion of being able to help your family, and all that changes when you enter into the desert."

Travelling at night in the Sonoran wilds is cold and dangerous, full of sharp cactuses and uneven terrain. Jolanda says she is lucky to have come back with only a few bruises, not to have been assaulted or raped. "They take you through the desert where there is danger. And the people that are guiding you, they are going through very quickly. And I swear, if it were not for my brother, I would have [been left behind] there."

"I am not going to try again," she says. "The truth is that I actually handed myself in. You really come to value what it is that you've left behind in your hometown. You value your family and you value everything that you left behind and, just in a few words, you say, 'I am not returning.'"

This is one face of deglobalization in the twenty-first century. Jolanda no longer has any expectation of a better life in America, and she's certainly not willing to gamble everything so that Americans can live more cheaply. "You really have to fight for your life [out there]. I am going to return to my children and never leave them again."

The Great Consumer Collapse

There's another good reason for migrants like Jolanda to stay close to home. Even though the global income gap between rich and poor has increased over the past twenty years – when the rich became richer in three-quarters of all OECD nations – migrants and nearly everyone else now have a lot more in common. After the great crash of 2008 eliminated $11.1 trillion in household wealth in America and beyond, the kind of insecurity, under-employment, and economic worry suffered by migrant peoples for decades became acutely familiar to working households across the developed world.

If you're betting everything on the modern service economy, think again. All-access consumerism is likely finished – and with it the easy economic growth of the twentieth century, valuable opportunities for emerging nations, and the augmented buying power and affordability enjoyed by households around the world. "Suddenly consumers are focused on buying what they have to have as opposed to buying what they want to have," Howard Davidowitz, a financial consultant, told the *Wall Street Journal* in June 2008. "This is a permanent change for Americans, who will face a declining standard of living over the next 20 years."

It wasn't supposed to end up this way. For many, the global consumer revolution was about owning a bigger house, a nicer television, and laptops for the whole family. For others it meant the promise of affordable household supplies, school supplies, and children's clothing purchased at the local discounter or dollar store. Those who were poor were able to purchase more of what they needed, and those who were already somewhat comfortable acquired better clothes, video games, and furniture. Few households failed to enjoy the consumer credit and product bonanza that began during the 1990s.

But just as global migrant workers became economically integrated with Western nations, consumers themselves became a primary resource. Consumer debt, equity, and spending not only filled our postwar, post-industrial economies with growth and purpose but also filled the likes of Wal-Mart, Carrefour, Home Depot, and Target with money. And like any other resource, consumer debt was prospected, exploited, bought and sold, resulting in the risky practice of massive unregulated trade in debt derivatives.

In the nice middle-class suburb where I live, there are no abandoned homes or mass foreclosures. It's an older suburban neighbourhood, much like any other in North America. Lawns are mowed attentively, cars are washed, and kids play on the sidewalk. The houses themselves are mostly postwar bungalows set alongside newly built executive mini-mansions. There's relatively little crime, the air is clean, and the local public school is great.

But looking closer, there are signs of slippage. My neighbours across the alleyway, long-time renters, are now picking up the bottles and cans that we usually leave for homeless bottle collectors. And the homeless guys that are losing out on garbage picking occasionally sleep in our local playground, even though we're miles away from the nearest emergency shelter, where nearly half the residents already have part- or full-time jobs. These days the homeless are often already employed – and the employed are increasingly underhoused. In my city, average housing costs nearly 45 percent of average income, so you can bet that I'll be at Home Depot whenever I need to fix a toilet or a fencepost, trying to save a few dollars.

"The bottom line is that there has been basically no wealth creation at all since the turn of the millennium: the net worth of the average American household, adjusted for inflation, is lower now than it was in 2001," wrote Nobel laureate economist Paul Krugman in 2009. "The surge in asset values had been an illusion – but the surge in debt had been all too real. So now we're in trouble – deeper trouble, I think, than most people realize even now." And the paradox is that our rich consumer universe, even when it cuts prices on an ongoing basis, is failing us. As we complete the first decade of the millennium, a huge number of goods remain affordable, but our most essential requirements – food, housing, energy, health care, and education – have become progressively more expensive relative to average household income.

One's home is no longer just a castle – it's a bankroll. Besides borrowing against one's equity, payday loans and credit cards have become common ways to make ends meet. By 2003 the average Canadian household already held more debt than its annual income, and by 2008, U.S. household debt had grown to 100 percent of the GDP. Britain's uSwitch financial service diagnosed a "spendemic" in that country in 2008, with one in ten adults spending more than they earned on a monthly basis, doubling the number of credit cards over the course of a decade. "Britain is suffering from a bad case of affluenza," said consumer policy director Ann Robinson. "It's clear that our salaries can't keep up with our 'Hello' lifestyles."

Employment insecurity has had everything to do with household fragility: involuntary part-time labour – people who can't access full employment – has accounted for most part-time employment growth since 1969 in the United States, and it follows a similar pattern in OECD nations such as Canada and Great Britain. Overall, the employment growth rate actually peaked back in the 1970s, reports the U.S. Department of Labor, and "the growth rate of the labor force has been decreasing with the passage of each decade and is expected to continue to do so in the future."

Of course, many middle- and lower-income households had already been suffering for years. And this is one major reason why discounters, large and small, moved from the margins of economic life to the very centre: people needed savings in the face of insecure income and persistent cost increases for essential goods and services. While luxury products, natural resources, and high-value industries are still important – ExxonMobil and Dow Chemical are unlikely to disappear from the Fortune 500 anytime soon – the realities of today's world heavily favour those who can deliver bargains.

In 2005 Wal-Mart's former CEO Lee Scott famously claimed that the retailer saves consumers up to $100 billion annually through the "negotiating power" of millions of Wal-Mart shoppers. "We touch so many lives," said Scott. "There is almost [nothing] that does not have an interest in what we as a company are doing."

It is true that Wal-Mart and other bargaineers improved the fortunes of many. Because of incredible advances in keeping labour costs low and wholesale costs even lower, the world's leading bargaineers effect a deflationary pull in economies where they have dominance, through both increased profit per store and ongoing price rollbacks that lean heavily on suppliers to produce more for less. For example, furniture prices fell 4.1 percent between 2000 and 2004, according to a 2004 study by Washington's Institute for International Economics, largely because production shifted from North Carolina, the former centre of U.S. furniture production, to China. Even as manufacturing jobs disappeared in most service economies, global trade in bargains cushioned the impact of job losses and the decline of local economies with lower prices. The deflationary effect of bargains created a new kind of consumer dividend.

Despite persistent price drops in everything from female apparel to furniture, the average cost of housing, food, and transportation increased 25 percent between 1998 and 2008 in the United States, the world nexus of discounting. And in the homeland of Tesco, the world's fourth-largest retailer, Britain saw grocery prices increase 6.6 percent over the same period, followed by 4.8 percent in Europe. Even during the height of the crash, consumer prices continued to rise: 0.4 percent in February 2009, with the bulk of the increase due to food and fuel costs.

The broader benefits of bargains may have been tremendously oversold. Despite Wal-Mart's claims that it negotiates on behalf of consumers for better prices, things didn't get better. As the International Monetary Fund found in its 2007 *World Economic Outlook*, among eighteen developed nations from 1982 to 2002, lower prices and higher productivity resulting from the globalization of trade boosted average real pay by only 0.24 percent annually – $115 for the average American household. That's a significant shortfall from Wal-Mart's claimed 2007 benefit of $1,122 in increased purchasing power per household.

We enjoyed the fruits of a synchronous world, a globe woven tightly together by information technology, logistics, porous national economies, and a seemingly infinite thirst for products. But what we have left is a consumer economy that is surprisingly hollowed out, spent, mined. Consumer debt in the United States leads the world and grew from $2.1 trillion in 2003 to $2.5 trillion in 2008, a service economy producing less with greater productivity, fuelled by spending and leveraged against, it turns out, a surprising amount of nothing.

Retailing, and more specifically discounting, gave consumers more reasons to spend, and the combination of bargaineer ingenuity and the virtual wealth of credit-rich populations on several continents turned grocers and discounters into some of the world's largest multinationals. Nearly everyone played this convergence like an oil discovery, reaping tremendous early gains, extracting consumer surplus as hard and fast as possible.

Of course it wasn't a resource play but a reconfiguration. At the very same time that energy companies were bearing down on unconventional crude, turning old-fashioned oil drilling into an advanced manufacturing process, our leading service-sector companies were busily drilling for consumer value with the gusto of a Signal Hill oilman. Energy became more managerial, more process and supply-chain driven, while finance and retail focused on extraction – gushers of cash created through derivatives and a steady flow of sales pipelined through big-box power centres.

On the ground, many communities that host major big-box developments have reported essentially the same thing. Part of their economy gets sucked away and their main streets wind up looking like a ghost town. As the Institute for Local Self-Reliance (ILSR) has documented at length, local losses aren't merely in consumer dollars, but in lost public and civic resources as well. Full-cost accounting suggests that through new infrastructure and lost tax revenue, plus whatever incentives have been negotiated, "retail development can end up being a net drain on city finances." Some case studies suggest that "not only did main street retail produce lower service costs, it also generated more property tax revenue per square foot, because those retailers occupied higher-value, often historic, buildings."

If losses of high-value local and presumably more sustainable economic assets are the casualties of global retailing, then what happens when low-value, high-volume, carbon-intensive consumer systems begin to fail? The growing landscape of destitute regional malls, decommissioned big-box stores, and gaps in strip mall frontage is not reassuring. In July 2008, before the worst, Home Depot had already closed fifteen stores in the United States. "We are seeing significant pressure on the cost side as the price of basic commodities goes up," said CEO Frank Blake. "There isn't a well-worn path guiding us on what all these pressures will do to our business . . . but there is more risk than opportunities."

The golden age of modern consumerism was surprisingly brief, spanning from the mid-1990s (with breaks for stock market bubbles such as 2001's dot-com crash) to the late 2000s – arguably, just over a decade long. Of course it was more than just cheap. During this time there were tremendous advances in everything from consumer technologies to culinary sophistication and affordable luxury goods. There were also tremendous advances in overconsumption and materialism as entertainment, the kind of no-boundaries indulgence that would have floored Victorian puritans. In 1877's *Thrift*, Scottish reformer Samuel Smiles wrote: "It is the wastefulness of individuals that occasions the impoverishment of states. So it is that every thrifty person may be regarded as a public benefactor, and every thriftless person as a public enemy."

While consumers were enjoying the peak of globalization and others made millions trading on nothingness, the floodwaters gathered: housing asset inflation, underemployment, and predatory and irresponsible credit practices, which in turn helped fuel foreclosures and homelessness, as well as longer-term instability. Much of this prosperity was built not only on credit and finance but also on the assumption that opportune conditions for commerce, production, and consumption would persist indefinitely. That too was a gamble.

Maximum Vegas

Things don't look so good in the land of the high rollers. Las Vegas and the rest of Nevada were hit so hard by America's housing crash that hundreds of abandoned backyard pools had to be patrolled and drained to protect against mosquito-borne West Nile virus. Residents simply walked away from their houses, leaving little ghost-town patches of McMansions with abandoned dogs and cats turning feral in the desert heat. "Almost half of all mortgage holders in Nevada now owe more than their house is worth," reported *Time* magazine's Barbara Kiviat in 2008. "Mindboggling to think about. Basically what that means is if you want to sell your house, you've got to write a check to the bank on the day you close."

The global housing bubble was founded upon a great many contradictions, conflicts, and double standards, but the big gamble is now clear: while governments and business did much to restrain and moderate commodity inflation within economies during the 1990s and 2000s, asset inflation – the value of homes and property – was allowed to boom. Getting rich never seemed so easy. What we discovered is that in the end, asset inflation was a significant risk multiplier, and its delayed effects were ultimately far greater than many market-boosters would have imagined. It was economic growth based on pure speculation – on nothingness.

The housing boom of the 1990s onward was nearly perfectly post-industrial: new wealth and poverty were created in great swaths of disruptive change. The outcome of asset inflation was that a lot of people became rich with little or no effort: on paper they gained worth as markets grew. Simply by owning property in the right market, double-digit returns were very nearly guaranteed. But not only did this create a housing bubble, it also accelerated the income gap between rich and poor within most economies. Moreover, many governments did little to stem the erosion of full-time employment and income security or to address affordability concerns that were eroding middle and lower-wage incomes. A great many, from the European Union to Canada to Hong Kong, collectively managed to let runaway asset inflation – namely, housing price bubbles – leave behind many people who couldn't afford the price of admission. In the United States, sub-prime mortgages and other higher-risk house financing schemes were introduced to exploit lower-income, minority, and immigrant communities that, likely for the right reasons, wanted their own assets to provide for retirement, university education for their children, and all-round greater security. As housing scholar Duncan Maclennan argues, "global conditions had created both greater opportunity and greater inequality, mediated by national finance and policy systems."

In other words, housing has become a determinant of both consumerism and economic status: those who have housing assets are likely to spend more and therefore influence the economy through housing-backed debt, or "equity withdrawal." "Changing house prices affects household net worth, ability to borrow and spend and can have important implications for wider economic activity. The effect of rising housing prices on owner consumption and equity withdrawal is no longer doubted," writes Maclennan. "Equally falling home values reduce consumption, and these behaviours both reinforce the amplitude of economic cycles and make economic management via interest rates more difficult."

The sad truth is that many people will now never own their own home, let alone have the choice and affordability in rental accommodation enjoyed by previous generations. Post-2008, the lack of access to reasonable credit alone is tantamount to a huge housing price hike: even after the crash, when affordability returned to many markets, access to home ownership for many is blocked by now risk-adverse financial institutions that are limiting access to credit.

For a while it looked like the new millennium might be lucky for everyone. During the boom in retail, financial industries, tourism, education, media, and technology, analysts and pundits decided that this was in fact a "new economy," one that had attained a state of near-permanent, stable growth on the basis of an unprecedented mix of productivity (through new technology and communications), low unemployment (new service-sector jobs), low inflation (partially driven by a mass influx of bargains), and new wealth (stock market booms and increased profits).

"Just as the eighteenth and nineteenth centuries marked a change from agricultural to an industrial economy, and the first three quarters of the twentieth century marked a movement from a manufacturing to a service economy, the end of the twentieth century marked a movement to the weightless economy, the knowledge economy," writes economist Joseph Stiglitz in *The Roaring Nineties*. "[Yet] for all the talk of the New Economy ending the business cycle, the changes of the Roaring Nineties actually may have increased our economic vulnerability, by making the economy more sensitive, more responsive to shocks . . . We not only exposed the economy to more risk, we also undermined our ability to manage that risk." In other words, personal and household success increasingly hinge on one's ability to manage risk, calculate odds, and gamble on everything from household purchases to employment. What became painfully clear in the late 2000s is how risk-dependent we had become – and how much this had infused everything from finance to social policy.

There was plenty of warning. Even as Wal-Mart came to the fore, the dream of the new economy had begun to sour: welfare cuts and corporate scandals contrasted with dizzying financial gains and productivity leaps. Our first decade of cheap stuff was also the decade of Enron, under-employment, and welfare cutbacks. The new millennium presents a more advanced, and possibly more dangerous, set of circumstances. This is Las Vegas globalized. Or, as Nobel laureate Stiglitz argues, modern economies are about "making risk a way of life."

Consumerism was supposed to be about enjoyment, value, and security – an upgrade from the hunter-gatherer society – and not something intrinsically tied into a web of instability. One of the ways that Las Vegas crossed over into corporate and public governance is through the global preponderance of credit and credit mechanisms. Banks lent to banks to make money. Debt became a major financial product and a surrogate source of household income. It boosted productivity, and the massive liquidity created by societal debt surely enabled innovation, growth, and all-round good times.

The capacity for gambling already built into the financial system, in America as well as among the many European lenders who took risky positions, is still mind-boggling. In 2008, for example, there were about $1 trillion worth of sub-prime mortgages in the United States, all representing real assets of some kind, albeit discounted or damaged. By contrast, the derivatives on these amounted to $62 trillion. That's $62 trillion in wagers that required payouts and losses far beyond what any sensible casino would allow. This Vegas-extreme business model entailed a liquidity-to-debt ratio that should have been 12:1 but was running at 30:1 pre-collapse. (Incredibly, Securities and Exchange Commission chairman Christopher Cox said earlier in 2008, before the crash: "We have a good deal of comfort about the capital cushions at these firms at the moment.")

As Charles Morris explained in *The Trillion Dollar Meltdown*, the creation of deep risk was systemic. "Not long ago, the sum of all financial assets – stocks, bonds, loans, mortgages, and the like, which are claims on real things – were about equal to global GDP," he writes. "Now they are approaching four times global GDP. Financial derivatives, a form of claim upon assets, now have notational values of more than ten times global GDP."

The creation of new wagering opportunities bigger than anything else in the world was pure Vegas: side bets on the main action. As David Evans and Richard Schmalensee recount in their 1999 study *Paying with Plastic*, a pioneering industry trend during the 1990s was the increase in securities backed by consumer credit-card receivables – essentially a bond on debt. "Issuers have used securitization of existing card portfolios to fund future growth. These card-backed bonds are typically structured like corporate bonds, with no principal being repaid until bonds reach maturity." In 1990, 1 percent of total card balances was securitized in this way; by 1997 it was 50 percent.

The global expansion of credit, both consumer credit and as a derivative financial product, was an innovation that likely exceeds the impact of the shipping container. Beginning with the first Diner's Club cards in 1950, the credit card became a true economic force. Our world glides on the back of its magnetic stripe, which holds our names, account numbers, expiry dates, personal ID numbers, security info, and who knows what else. It's a logistics system of credit, with third-party transaction systems, debt ratings, and debt marketing.

Credit industry "islands" were created by some American states during the 1970s and 1980s in order to create usury-based development based on high credit-card interest rates. A famous example is Citibank's relocation of credit operations from New York, which capped rates at 12 percent, to South Dakota, which allowed companies to charge customers as much as 19.8 percent. Thresholds were lowered on credit cards during the 1990s, and the issuing companies assumed greater risk for the reward of having at-risk consumers carry greater balances from month to month, essentially pioneering the dynamic of sub-prime mortgages. New York state senator Alphonse D'Amato attempted reform in 1991 with a proposed amendment that would have capped credit cards at four points above the IRS overdue-tax rate, which was 10 percent at the time. As the amendment went before the U.S. Senate, the Dow dropped 120 points and MasterCard lost nearly 16 percent of its share value. The amendment was dropped.

Credit became a cultural force. In 2001 America's Citibank launched its "Live Richly" ad campaign. It was an impressionistic series of lifestyle ads, very unlike anything the financial services sector had ever devised. Images of kids playing, women dancing, happiness and contentment were accompanied by millennial axioms such as "There's more to life than money"; "Play as you go"; "The best moments in life are completely untaxable." To many it was a joke at the time, but it conveyed the popular weakness for the idea that debt isn't so much about obligation as empowerment. Somewhere along the way, debt and credit were not only normalized but fetishized, along with the big houses, SUVs, and designer lifestyles. When American personal savings dropped to a seventy-three-year low in 2006, the business of housing-backed debt – reverse mortgages, second mortgages, and lines of credit – created $900 billion in new consumer spending capacity in a single year.

Debt has had many cheerleaders, with some proponents arguing that debt is tantamount to civilization and has been an important part of family financial planning since the 1700s. "Although consumer debt has consistently risen in recent times, the default rate has remained remarkably stable," argued James Twitchell in *Two Cheers for Materialism*. "In fact, the increased availability of credit to a growing share of the population, particularly to lower-income individuals and families, has allowed many have-nots to enter the economic mainstream." Others have argued that the levels of debt in Western nations are perfectly fine and normal.

The debt proponents had good intentions. "Through the 1990s and until the last few months, the banner of universal homeownership was flown high by Democrats and Republicans," wrote Jim Dwyer in 2008. "Behind this virtuous cause was a jungle of counterintuitive arrangements, like loans with no down payment or income verification. These practices make sense only under a system in which the most valuable aspect of the loan papers themselves is that they can be bundled together and sold without any scrutiny of their actual worth. The result was a system of agreed-upon hallucinations."

The danger lies in Homer-Dixon's "synchronous failure" – not just a Wall Street bust, but a series of concurrent fundamental shakedowns: income failure, housing insecurity, economic decline. It's an example of how complex solutions such as credit derivatives can lead to even more complex problems. Even America's $700-billion bailout and rescue plan of 2008 was needlessly complicated, and some of the real fixes required were nowhere in the vicinity of Wall Street. "Down the road . . . we're going to really have to address the economy's real needs," economist Joseph Stiglitz told CNBC. "This is based on trickle-down economics: you throw enough money at Wall Street and some of it goes down . . . to help the economy." But, Stiglitz went on to say, the bailout plan was not doing enough of what needed to be done, such as recapitalizing the banking system, stemming the flood of foreclosures, and tackling growing unemployment.

Looking forward to the second decade of the millennium, it seems that a huge cultural change is imminent. Thrift, deep suspicion of debt, and other attitudes that defined people who lived through the 1930s Depression – and a 30 percent drop in all economic activity – will become mainstream again and shape our economies. Many of us will, in practice, become our grandparents.

Hitting Bottom

Whiz, as he calls himself, drags a Home Depot shopping cart out of the bush near the commuter-train station where he lives in Surrey, a suburban city near Vancouver. It is dusk as we leave his makeshift campsite, a torn pup tent amid scattered clothing and garbage, and set out across an abandoned lot, passing a small wooden cross that remembers a murdered prostitute named Dottie. We are looking for food.

Whiz has been on and off the streets for the past decade. What strikes him now is the growing number of people sleeping rough in the playgrounds

author photo

Tracking the suburban homeless: Whiz makes camp in the bushes of Surrey, British Columbia.

and parks of this residential neighbourhood. "It's busier, for sure," he says. "You look in the trees and bush, you'll find them. Out here you got to be careful not to trip on someone."

Whiz, net worth zero, is trying to find a way to better his situation. He may live in a tent but he's not so different from countless foreclosed Americans who in quiet desperation may be pushing their own orange Home Depot cart at their local big-box mall. On paper they are all the same: broke.

Homelessness is what a housing crisis looks like without bankers. Even before the crash of 2008, a great many households had already been primed for failure. "After all our economic achievements, the gap between rich and poor [in America] has only widened, with a median net worth of $833,600 among the top ten per cent and just $7,900 for the bottom 20 per cent," writes David Shipler in *The Working Poor*.

We roll past pawnshops and convenience stores towards the nearest homeless shelter – one of the few that serve this metropolitan area of 2.1 million. As we approach the building, others with backpacks and shopping carts emerge from the darkness in time to line up for the evening meal, which is prepared and served by a local church. To the amazement of many, the annual count showed that the number of people living outdoors or in shelters in this Canadian suburb nearly doubled during the early 2000s. They include addicts and former university students, young families and washed-up street hustlers. There are plenty of people who used to live in decent homes. Nearby cities and towns have the same problem, and they have taken to busing homeless people around one of Canada's largest urban regions in an attempt to find them shelter, medical care, and social assistance. As American, Canadian, and European studies have indicated, many of the new homeless are working people who already have low-income jobs. They are the new migrants within the developed-world economies.

It's a scene that is repeated every day in every major global city. Homelessness is now most commonly caused by poverty, which in turn is related to increased living costs, the rise of part-time labour, and government policies that ignored these developments while upper-income populations enjoyed unprecedented income gains during the 1990s and early 2000s. Median household income has actually decreased in Western nations since the 1990s. In America, for example, the average household is earning less than it did in 1999, marking the first time since records began that an economic expansion – in this case the booming 1990s – did not result in an aggregate advance in household income. As of January 2009, reports Steven A. Camarota of the Center for Immigration Studies, "24 million adult native-born Americans who have no education beyond high school . . . are either unemployed or not in the labor force, which means they are not even looking for work." That's equal to two-thirds of the entire Canadian population.

Globalization benefited consumers, to be sure – witness the under-$500 laptop – but it is also synonymous with stagnant income and unemployment. Ever since the 1990s, debates have raged about how much domestic unemployment and poverty can be directly blamed on the offshoring of manufacturing and services. In 2004, for example, *The Economist* claimed that job losses due to offshoring were less than 1 percent of the total, arguing that "the jobs lost are mainly a cyclical affair, not a structural one." Conversely, the National Association of Manufacturers, an industry lobby group, estimated in 2006 that roughly half of all manufacturing job losses were actually due to productivity gains, not outsourcing. In 2007 Washington's Economic Policy Institute determined that America's unprecedented trade deficit with China was a major cause of job loss, with a significant contribution from bargaineers large and small. "Between 2001 and 2006, [the] growing deficit eliminated 1.8 million U.S. jobs," argued the institute's Robert Scott. "Wal-Mart's trade deficit with China alone eliminated nearly 200,000 U.S. jobs in this period."

As economist Susan Houseman determined in 2007, the degree to which offshoring is integral to Western economies is underestimated because, "while any cost savings from outsourcing and offshoring are often counted as productivity gains, outsourcing and offshoring simultaneously place downward pressure on manufacturing workers' wages." That so much high-tech manufacture moved to China, Mexico, and Southeast Asia in the 1990s has as least as much to do with the incredible increases in labour productivity – "961 percent in semiconductors and . . . an astounding 1,495 percent in computers" – as with technological advances.

Productivity is key to the trend of "jobless growth" that has afflicted all nations dominated by service economies. Among other things, increased productivity means that the profit effect of lost jobs is truly amazing: between 2000 and 2006, for example, a 3.6 percent increase in the Fortune 500 workforce managed to generate 80 percent more profit. Companies burned by the tech meltdown and the 2001 recession "kept payrolls amazingly lean," explained *Fortune* magazine's Shawn Tully in 2007. "Of course, it was easier to do so with large pools of skilled workers available and union power at a nadir. By 2006 companies were barely paying any more for a unit of production than they did in 2000."

The stagnancy of incomes in Western nations means that even if housing affordability recovers, homelessness will continue to grow in many urban centres. The homeless are not outliers; they are a central consequence of a hollowed-out economy, since many of today's homeless were driven out by lack of income. The continuum of underhousing is profound and speaks to the shortage of real, broadly distributed savings and wealth within many Western economies; affordable rental accommodation remains tight and economic obstacles for the housing-poor are considerable. As many as 700,000 people are homeless in Los Angeles alone, representing a deep core of dispossession characterized by addiction, violence, and disease. This is profound market failure: housing markets have simply not provided secure or affordable housing in sufficient quantity. The United Nations estimates that up to 100 million people are homeless worldwide, many of them women and children. Underhousing statistics are worse, with an estimated 600 million living in shelter that is unfit, dangerous, or unhealthy.

It is oddly fitting that even on the issue of homelessness, a whole social universe away from the world of high finance, the emergent solutions are based upon taking risks. Philip Mangano, the American "homeless czar" and much-lauded executive director of the United States Interagency Council on Homelessness, is betting he can engineer double-digit reductions in the number of street people. Appointed by George W. Bush in March 2002, Mangano has worked with more than 220 municipalities and 320 local jurisdictions across the United States to develop and implement ten-year plans to end chronic homelessness. Depending on whom you ask, he's either the last great hope for solving homelessness in North America or the harbinger of collapse. "We found that long-term homelessness was often complicated with things like disability, addictions, mental health, or HIV," says Mangano. "[Consequently,] long-term chronic homeless people comprise 20 percent of the homeless population but use 50 percent of the resources. This is expensive. That's why we did cost-benefit analysis." Mangano has stirred up controversy as a major proponent of a strategy that focuses on the minority of chronic, long-term homeless people. It's business logic, as he readily admits, concerned mainly with reducing suffering, lost potential, and expenditure for the vast majority of people whose experience with homelessness is unnecessary.

Conceived in 1988 by the Los Angeles–based agency Beyond Shelter as part of an effort to rapidly house increasing numbers of homeless families, Housing First represents the first major change in national strategy in North America since governments began funding and building homeless shelters and emergency response systems. It's about saving money and saving people at the same time, a model of efficiency and logistics not normally seen in the social services. There are obvious cost savings in rescuing people from perpetual crisis. Mangano often cites the story of "Million-Dollar Murray," made famous by Malcolm Gladwell's coverage in the *New Yorker* in February 2006. As the story goes, two frustrated police officers tracked the costs of three chronically homeless individuals living in Reno, Nevada: two accounted for $120,000 and $200,000 in hospital expenses, respectively, during a year. Amazingly, the third – Million-Dollar Murray – tallied more than $1 million in annual expenses for hospitalization, incarceration, detox treatments, and ambulance rides. As Reno officer Patrick O'Bryan quipped, "We spent $1 million not to do anything about him."

Mangano's gamble is that homelessness can be successfully addressed by investing resources in housing the hardest to house, the most visible, the long-term homeless that people see on the streets every day. The thing is, most homelessness is not actually street homelessness and is neither visible nor chronic. Underhousing often begins with couch surfing and short-term accommodations. Moreover, "hidden homelessness" is growing fast in previously unlikely places: suburbs, small towns, even settlements in the Arctic. Broad swaths of the population now have housing-security problems and are at risk for homelessness. Furthermore, some accuse Mangano of attempting to download homelessness onto local authorities while political bosses decrease social investments. "While Mangano has been piling up frequent flier points visiting every part of the U.S. to convince state and local governments that they need to take up the responsibility for a 'housing first' policy for the homeless, his political boss – President Bush – has been gutting the U.S. federal government's funding for housing," writes the Wellesley Institute's Michael Shapcott.

While much of Europe is nearly a decade ahead of the United States in addressing homelessness as a threat to social and economic stability, other nations such as Canada have accumulated large homeless populations in spite of sustained economic growth. In 2006 the U.N. Committee on Economic, Social and Cultural Rights (UNCESCR) delivered a harsh rebuke of Canada's record on poverty and homelessness. The committee urged Canadian governments to "address homelessness and inadequate housing as a national emergency," and made particular note of long waiting lists for subsidized housing, inadequate minimum wages, social assistance rates that raised income to only 50 percent of poverty levels, high incidence of homelessness and hunger, and unfair treatment of the unemployed. The U.N. committee was surprised by the paradox of Canada's strong economic performance – as top G7 nation in overall economic performance in 2005 and 2006 – and its substantial underclass. "Despite Canada's economic prosperity, . . . 11.2 per cent of its population still lived in poverty in 2004," it noted. "[And] poverty rates remain very high among disadvantaged and marginalized individuals and groups."

When the Bush administration finally tallied up its figures in 2008, the number of chronically homeless people living in America's streets and shelters had dropped 30 percent between 2005 and 2008. While the United States has not yet achieved the kind of success reported by England, which began concerted efforts to reduce deep poverty and homelessness as early as 1997, thirty jurisdictions had already reported declines in their homeless populations in 2006, including the 28 percent dip recorded in San Francisco a year earlier and a 4 percent drop reported in Denver.

The U.S. National Coalition for the Homeless is skeptical that homelessness overall is actually declining. "The 10-year plans are an excellent step forward, but at the same time we need to remember the existing needs of everyone, to not cannibalize other funding while we do this thing for the chronics," said Zach Krochina, the coalition's economic justice policy coordinator, in 2006. The "chronics" are a minority. Of the 744,000 estimated homeless people in that country in 2005, the National Alliance to End Homelessness found that only a quarter were chronically homeless and about 41 percent were families. "Focusing on the more hard-core people is neglecting the plight of [working] homeless families," reported the *San Francisco Chronicle* in 2006. "In some communities, families constitute at least half of the homeless population. In San Francisco, they constitute up to 20 percent."

While the elimination of 50,000 street homeless in a few years is a significant achievement, urban centres still have growing homeless populations. New York, for example, reduced the number of chronically homeless people by more than 2,200, but the overall number of people counted as homeless – including the "hidden homeless" living in motels or sleeping in cars and other improvised shelters – actually increased by 2,200 people between 2005 and 2007, from 48,154 to 50,372. And those who survived homelessness would go on to face Medicare cutbacks by the same government that had tried to help them escape the streets. The good news is that a great many working households can be stabilized with income and health-care supports. Economic security is a grand new policy frontier in the twenty-first century.

In the meantime, some people win and some people lose. It's Las Vegas on an epic scale. While Mangano saved some money and some lives, at least for the lucky ones, the housing crisis was brewing in the background. High prices pushed people further towards homelessness, owners and speculators accumulated asset value, and housing became an even greater part of the problem.

Dangerous Goods

Russ Howard has taken a hostage. Surrounded by FBI agents, military contractors, and private security consultants of all kinds, the retired brigadier general stands behind a spectator, points a finger at his head, and says, "You've got thirty seconds to decide before you lose advantage to the shooter – what do you do?"

Given that most people in the room likely know how to clean, maintain, and fire automatic weapons, there's a surprising pause. Likely Howard intimidates them. As founding director of the Combating Terrorism Center at West Point and former commander of the Special Warfare Training Group at Fort Bragg, Howard knows something about risk and conflict in the twenty-first century. "Well, what is it?" he asks. "You're almost done."

Someone in the back proffers up, "Negotiate?" Another, "Stay calm?" "All wrong – you fight!" says Howard emphatically, and releases his hostage to applause. There was a time, he explains, when terrorists would negotiate, and many were engaged in some kind of determinate political process. Back in the 1970s and 1980s, "We taught people not to resist a hostage event, because people survived."

"But now there's no more taking hostages," says Howard. "Now they want a lot of people watching and a lot of people dying."

It's a fine spring day with no security threats or crises on the horizon, at least nothing that would bring extra business to the attendees of this logistics security workshop. Memories of September 11, 2001, are still fresh, though. History doesn't work in predictable ways, reminds Howard. And, as never before, our technologies can be used against us. If drugs, refugees, bad products, and diseases are often shipped by container, then why not a dirty nuclear bomb?

Our supply chains not only transport goods, they also amplify benefits and threats. The value multiplier created by the world's bargaineers is also a risk multiplier, encompassing long-term threats from carbon-intensive consumption to more direct and horrific concerns about our global logistics infrastructure being hijacked with potentially less planning and effort than it took to fly planes into New York's World Trade Center. The quest for cheap has not only failed to enrich average households, it exposes us to new threats and dangers. Not only are we, the consumers, a post-industrial resource, we've also become vulnerable in ways that few predicted.

"Picture this: a nuclear device goes off at Port of Long Beach," Howard says. "Al Qaeda takes responsibility. Who would we nuke? . . . This notion of transnational as opposed to state actors is different. You can't take the same measures." In addition to the fact that terrorists are better financed and better trained, they and nearly anyone else also have access to our supply chain. There are approximately 24,000 deep-water cargo ships operating worldwide, for example. This means that somewhere in the world a container ship makes a port call every ten minutes. For a terrorist, says Howard, that is an incredible opportunity. All anyone has to do is gather explosives, some radioactive material, detonating technology, and a legitimate-looking reason to load and ship a container.

A sophisticated nuclear bomb isn't what many experts worry about. The far simpler and accessible dirty bomb could broadcast contaminant over a much smaller area but cause major disruption. It isn't a weapon of mass destruction, but of mass disruption. Targeting any major aspect of our supply chain – rail cars, warehouses, transport convergence points – a dirty-bomb attack could amplify its impact tremendously by using a very small detonating package containing any of the nine commonly used radiological isotopes that are lost, stolen, or misplaced on a daily basis in many countries. And you don't need to travel to a former Soviet republic to easily obtain it. The International Atomic Energy Agency estimates that no fewer than 110 countries lack adequate controls over radioactive materials that could be used in a dirty bomb. "I'm very surprised that a radiological device hasn't gone off," says Matthew Bunn of Harvard's Belfer Center for Science and International Affairs. "There is a bigger puzzle – why no Al Qaeda attacks since Sept. 11 in the U.S.?"

One computer simulation by the Federation of American Scientists determined that detonating a device with 1.75 ounces of cesium could broadcast radioactive fallout over sixty square blocks. "Immediate casualties would be limited to people hurt by the blast," reported the *Los Angeles Times* in 2004, "but the simulation suggested that there would be cases of radiation sickness and that relocation and cleanup costs would reach tens of billions of dollars." And while radioactive material can be sourced from hospitals, construction sites, and research labs, it can still be hard to detect, even with the portable nuclear "sniffers" that are stationed around major ports. "You are always going to have difficulty detecting nuclear material," says Howard. "Whether it is a device or enriched uranium, you are always going to have a problem detecting it because . . . you've got to be so close – it is not something that you can monitor from the air."

What complicates the threat further is that the number of possible targets is immense. While major international ports do have security and monitoring programs, there are easier and more effective targets. "If I were a terrorist, I would not hit the ports," says Howard. In America there are a handful of major bridges that are essential to goods movement, such as the crumbling Gerald Desmond Bridge that connects the port facilities on Terminal Island with downtown Long Beach. "If you really want to cripple economically, you take those out. Pretty easy. It does not have to be a nuclear device; it could be just traditional explosives [laced] with biological [contaminant]. It is the effect of the port but not in the port."

Less threatening but far more pervasive is the spread of toxic, dangerous, and faulty products. In outsourcing nearly everything but themselves, today's discounters – and many retailers in general – often have absolutely no idea who actually produced their products or what they might contain. Goods and parts made offshore are often produced by subcontractors who use a fluid system of negotiations and bidding, creating a complex supply chain that even some of the world's largest corporations cannot untangle. And if one 2007 survey is even remotely accurate, a significant percentage of those products are hazardous to human life.

That bin of shiny costume jewellery, that Diego backpack, those sunglasses, countless painted wooden toys – everything is suspect. In recent years, rings and trinkets have been routinely discovered to contain more than 50 percent lead (legal limits in most countries are well under 1 percent). Children in particular are susceptible to lead poisoning, which can permanently damage physical and mental development. The effects of low-level lead exposure can be subtle and hard to trace, but enough concentrated lead finds its way into children to result in several reported deaths or critical poisonings each year. Lead can leach out into food, and surfaces can chip and create ingestible dust. Tragically, even small mistakes with a lead-tainted product can result in critical illness. A gumball-sized piece of toy jewellery ingested by a child in 2004 resulted in body lead concentrations twelve times the acceptable limit. A four-year-old in Minneapolis swallowed a single bracelet charm manufactured for Reebok in 2006; the preschooler died within days, and investigators later discovered that the item was nearly 100 percent lead.

Products contaminated by heavy metals first made headlines in the late 1980s, just as international trade in consumer goods began to accelerate. In 1990 the American government launched lawsuits against several toy companies responsible for toxic or dangerously designed toys, charging that federal safety rules had been violated about seventy times since 1986; consequently, spot testing was introduced. By 2004 a record-setting 150 million pieces of toy jewellery had been recalled, setting off repeated waves of consumer worry followed by government and business reassurances.

In any given year the product recall list reads like a sales brochure for the Las Vegas bargain show: holiday ornaments, pillow covers, paintbrushes, children's sunglasses, fashion bracelets, Halloween pails, race cars, key chains, mood rings. And where were many of these sold? Look no further. The world's three largest dollar-store chains accounted for more than 1.5 million lead-contaminated products of the total 17 million recalled from American retail in 2007, including Dollar General, which recalled more than 1 million items alone.

While governments scramble to add safety inspectors and new regulations, it remains nearly impossible to regulate the largest flow of products in the history of trade. As for self-regulation, the extra time and expense don't exactly gibe with the reality of discount business. Hand-held spectrometers that can accurately detect lead in plastics, paints, and textiles are worth about $29,000 each – equivalent to the monthly living expenses of about six hundred Chinese factory workers.

"There will be further product recalls," confirms industry expert Sam Bundy. "There will be a falling-out period with some stress on wholesale prices, but given the huge dependency on Chinese manufacturing, especially for small to mid-size retailers, I expect that this is a short-term problem. And in the long run it will force Asian manufacturers to raise quality standards." For those shoppers who have legitimate concerns about toxins, poisons, and other potentially harmful defects in cheap products, there are yet no guarantees, save for one small consolation: many different labels, from detergent to pet food, are manufactured by the same factory or corporation – therefore, whatever is dangerous at the dollar store may be equally so at Wal-Mart or one's local grocery store, brand name or not.

Despite all the bad press, toxic toys and household goods often have surprisingly little negative impact on retail sales. Dollar General, for example, increased its 2007 net sales by $325 million; Family Dollar Stores, which recalled 342,000 lead-tainted products in 2007, increased its revenues by $440 million. And sometimes toxic products travel to the impressively far-flung reaches of the modern supply chain and fall outside weak government inspection and monitoring. When toothpaste tainted with a poisonous antifreeze additive was found in Panama, for example, authorities initially assumed it was a local issue. It wasn't – and thirty-four countries later, tainted toothpaste had been found in Vietnam, Kenya, Tonga, Australia, and Dubai. In 2006 and 2007 more than 900,000 tubes were distributed across the United States and Canada, not only in dollar stores but also in prisons, hospitals, and hotels. Japan alone discovered 20 million tubes. The global flow of bargains into dollar stores and discount chains has delocalized health and safety hazards.

Not only do trade networks effectively distribute hazardous products, there is often surprisingly little regulation and monitoring. When the toothpaste scandal first broke in 2006, the Chinese government initially defended "legitimate" companies that used diethylene glycol as a cheap alternative to glycerin. However, Canada found levels of toxin in the toothpaste at twice the percentage discovered in deadly cough syrup that killed nearly 140 people in Panama. "It was inconceivable to me that a known toxic substance that killed all these people could be openly on sale and that people would go on about their business calmly, selling and buying this stuff," said Eduardo Arias, the Panama City resident who – unlike all the importers, governments, and retailers involved – actually read the ingredients label on the toothpaste and complained to authorities when he discovered diethylene glycol.

Assurances were made at the time by trade authorities and governments, but nothing prevented China's baby-formula crisis in 2008, when melamine-contaminated formula sickened 53,000 infants, hospitalized 13,000, and killed four. Melamine is an industrial chemical usually used in plastics and fertilizers; it is illegally used to boost protein counts and causes kidney failure or kidney stones. It has also been found in candy in several Connecticut stores, pretzels in Toronto, and instant coffee in British Columbia – the coffee had melamine levels three times those of China's contaminated formula. In mainland China the contamination was widespread. Testing revealed melamine at thirty-six different Chinese dairy companies, and it also turned up in products such as yoghurt. It was later discovered that some officials knew of the contamination as far back as 2007, and that a public health advisory had been delayed in order to avoid embarrassment at Beijing's 2008 summer Olympics. Several brands of baby formula from south China had been exported to elsewhere in Asia and Africa, setting off more searching for contaminated product.

As Chinese dairy farmers in Hebei explained to the *New York Times*, global dairy companies such as Sanlu, which is 43 percent owned by New Zealand interests, allegedly took advantage of regulatory loopholes, bribery, and corruption, and that the melamine was added at company-owned milk stations. It was a cost crunch behind the crisis that Sanlu and other major dairy companies were trying to manage within China's government price controls, which were an attempt to control already troubling inflation on essential goods. The controlled-price milk created intense internal pressures in a country where the cost of soymeal feed had increased 60 percent in 2007 and 2008, said the farmers. The virtual monopoly that major milk companies have on the $18-billion Chinese dairy market has meant that many farmers have been forced out of business by low price-fixing and simultaneously blamed for the contamination. ("I was one of the drafters of the China Dairy Products Quality Inspection report," said Professor Zhang Guonong of Jiangsu. "I found adulteration is extremely widespread: urea, soap powder, starch are very popular additives.") Several suspects in the dairy scandal would later be charged, and in 2009 dairy businessmen Zhang Yujun and Geng Jinpin were sentenced to death; three others received life sentences in prison, yet the government officials responsible for safety and regulation remained unscathed.

The millions of toys recalled throughout the 2000s had already shaken consumer confidence. Roughly half of the recalls originated from unsafe materials utilized in Chinese manufacture, and half stemmed from company-side faulty design and execution. The Toy Hazard Recalls website of the U.S. Consumer Product Safety Commission is an epic list of lead paint, fire hazards, and choking hazards. One 2007 recall, for Aqua Dots, led to a Hong Kong company that had manufactured millions of poisonous toy beads; fourteen children became sick after ingesting them, because an inexpensive glue additive mimicked the potent chemical depressant GHB, a "date rape" drug. The Hong Kong company, JSSY, had copied the beads from an identical Japanese product, but it had used the widely known and cheaper glue additive, which is tightly regulated in the United States. What became clear was the lack of regulation and monitoring in both China and import countries, even after previous waves of recalls and promises of reform. The *Beijing News* reported in May 2007 that China's General Administration of Quality Supervision's own results showed that 20 percent of toys and baby clothes failed safety tests. Plush toys were stuffed with low-quality fill and even garbage; other toys easily came apart or broke. The report also mentioned baby milk powder containing unspecified chemicals that could pose health risks.

A few months later, both Wal-Mart and Carrefour claimed that 99 percent of all Chinese-made toys were safe. "We have been purchasing from China for nearly 26 years," said Wal-Mart China's spokesperson in 2007. "Chinese products are economic in price and guaranteed in quality." While some advances have been made in the realm of ethical sourcing – such as Wal-Mart's 2008 departure from the Central Asian republic of Uzbekistan over child labour – a great many things get lost along the twisted supply chain.

Mattel's struggles with toy safety are a lesson in how supply chains continue to multiply risk. When the world's largest toy company announced 7.3 million of its own recalls in 2007, it was clear that supply chain failure wasn't limited to knock-offs and no-name toys for dollar stores. It was familiar household names: various Barbie, Elmo, Big Bird, and Dora toys produced between 2003 and 2006 were recalled. The crisis is endemic to the cheap manufacturing, and, it seemed, nearly impossible to eliminate, given previous failed promises to improve quality and screen for dangers. It continues to be small children who are most at risk, subject to potential lacerations, choking, and other injury caused by poor design. Mattel's CEO, Bob Eckert, insisted that the company had "rigorous standards" while apologizing for the recalls. He later fingered a Chinese subcontractor who had "utilized paint from a non-authorized third-party supplier."

There are an estimated 30,000 different toy products on sale at any given moment in the world. Mattel somehow managed to bring world attention to just a few – as well as to anger the world's largest country – even though the majority of its recalls were due to bad design, not bad materials. A month later, Mattel's executive vice-president for worldwide operations, Thomas Debrowski, met with Chinese officials to apologize. "Mattel takes full responsibility for these recalls and apologizes personally to you, the Chinese people, and all of our customers who received the toys," he said in a meeting with China's top safety official in Beijing. The "vast majority of those products that were recalled were the result of a design flaw in Mattel's design, not through a manufacturing flaw in China's manufacturers." China, of course, produces 65 percent of Mattel's toys and an estimated 80 percent of the world's toys in total.

By 2009, the Obama presidency had increased its consumer safety expenditure by 71 percent from 2007 levels. China's influence and emerging power in the realm of trade concern many. Mattel was probably wise to lose face and mend relations with the world's largest country – not just because China manufactures so much product, but also because there is no other place in the world as capable and cost-effective. It is still the world's supply chain superpower, even during an economic crisis. And as Mattel learned, you can't insult China anymore and expect the toys to keep flowing.

Newly deported migrants line up at an emergency aid station at Mariposa crossing, Nogales, Mexico.

No Returns

On a long detour from Nogales, Mexico, back to Tucson, I stop by the desert compound of Arizona's Minuteman Civil Defense Corps. Located north of the Sasabe border crossing in the Altar Valley, it is one of the more desolate and challenging stretches of the Sonoran Desert. Here the self-proclaimed civilian defenders have held a floating guard line against migrants on a part-time basis since 2006. The Minutemen are camping on the grounds of the historic King's Anvil Ranch, an hour's drive north of the border; the owners invited the would-be paramilitary force to set up operations here and scare off trespassers.

Gene Caferolla, the Minutemen's state director for Arizona, sits down underneath a large camouflage tent and welcomes me to Operation Stand Your Ground. Caferolla and two other defenders chat about life on the border; they're keen to make clear that they aren't anti-Mexican, at least in the way that explicitly racist immigration opponents make headlines. They give out water and food to those who want it, at least while they're waiting for the ICE or Border Patrol to arrive. Like other strident nationalists, they just want to roll back the clock to a time before free trade, back when nation-states were nation-states and people and products weren't as mobile as the weather.

Paradoxically, the Minutemen demand tighter border controls and immigration rules in order to protect freedom. This call to repel invaders, both economic and military, reflects deep currents in American culture regarding race and economic change. The result is an idealized past, a nativist paradise of intact pioneer cultures and national economies, even if that never truly existed in the first place. "My forefathers, they blazed the wilderness trail, fought wars to further this idea, and it has just been taken away from us. And that is why we are here," says Caferolla. "This is the end of America as we know it."

Their suggestion is that a true border, one that kept everyone inside their respective countries, would keep people employed in maquiladoras. It would also, Caferolla argues, be better than having them die out here in the desert. "It needs to be fair trade. Not free trade, but fair trade, and it is not," he says. "That's the biggest problem right there . . . and until we have that, we are all just going to have a lot of problems in the country."

Oddly, there are businessmen south of the border who would like to turn back the clock as well, to before 2001, when the Mexican maquiladora factory complexes were still growing. As economies contract globally, many have wondered why production hasn't yet returned to either Mexico or America.

The random dangers of the modern supply chain – poisoned toothpaste, toxic toys – are one reason to promote deglobalization. And certainly, in the face of global recession, there is new pressure to regionalize trade. The modern supply chain is vulnerable to cost and environmental constraints. And it is hard to imagine lowering global greenhouse gas emissions with so much of global GDP dependent on shipping product around the planet. Cutting down the traffic on our oceans could be a win-win for both environment and economy. Transport costs from Mexico are exponentially cheaper, just as Eastern European manufacturing continues to service the European Union. In 2004, for example, the cost of shipping from China was $2,500 per container, and for a $12 industrial item its containerized transport expense was $1.10; from Mexico, the same item would cost only 30 cents to deliver.

Yet there is no Restore button that returns resources, community economies, and jobs back to their original location. Globalization pursued cheap labour, but some of the productive capacity appears to be stranded. Whole supply chains are literally stuck in place. This suggests that many of our goods could stay fairly globalized even as globalization itself begins to wane. It's not unlike the reality of bottomed-out consumer spending that threatens the health of service economies: globalization without cheap inputs, cheap energy, and large-scale efficiencies will not deliver the same degree of affordability and plenitude. Nor will this complex system of production simply move itself closer to consumers when transport becomes chronically expensive. And if globalization cannot scale itself, not only will consumers suffer in a world of disappearing bargains, but transitions to more localized, sustainable trade networks may become more difficult as well.

It's an effect of market inefficiency and existing capital investment. Many of the foundries, factories, and skilled workers that competed for trade but lost out to China and other countries, are no longer operational or simply no longer exist. While multinationals like Mattel do have factories in lower-cost Indonesia and Thailand, the toy giant and many other businesses remain surprisingly captive inside China. It's what toy industry expert Eric Johnson of Dartmouth University has described as concentrated manufacturing, a reflection of the fact that globalization was built around clusters and pipelines, not open networks and wealth clouds, in order to achieve maximum cheap. "There are some very large companies in the back end of the supply chain that supply everybody," Johnson explained to *Foreign Policy* in 2007. "China is like the Silicon Valley of toys: There are literally thousands of very good toy suppliers there. There are manufacturers who just focus on plush toys and then there are people who just focus on injection-molded plastic and people who die cast, like Hot Wheels and Matchbox cars. So, for companies that don't do any of their own production, they really don't have anywhere to go but China. Thailand has a toy industry with some big players like Mattel, but it's nothing like China. And it's difficult to shift those capabilities."

China stands alone in certain categories: telecommunications, electronic machinery, and office machines. It has also shown a decided transition away from lower-value exports such as apparel, textiles, and footwear. Accordingly, the overall skill level dedicated to trade increased significantly between 1992 and 2005. The country enjoys the advantage of semi-captive production, especially in the capital-intensive, technologically advanced factories of Shenzhen. Moreover, China's surprisingly activist labour laws have sent a clear signal to non-state corporations operating there or that depend on its exports: be ready to pay more for less.

"The bulk of goods made in China – clothing, toys, small appliances, and the like – probably won't be coming back, because they require abundant cheap labor," predicted *Business Week*'s Pete Engardio in 2008. "If anything, their manufacture will go to other low-wage nations in Asia or Latin America." Some foreign factory owners and large corporations in China have been scheming to move away, to chase the frontiers of cheap labour as far as logistics networks will allow. Yet no clear "elsewhere" exists, because the size of the labour pool and the infrastructure found in China cannot easily be matched.

Nowhere else can offer the massive labour force and highly orchestrated political-logistics-economic convergence that are likely feasible only in a one-party state. China's bargain-industry complex is particularly irreplaceable in the realm of high-tech, capital-intensive consumer products. Losing a few jobs to Southeast Asia will not change China's dominance, especially for products such as iPhones and laptops, which comprised 64 percent of China's export growth for much of 2007. Indeed, high-tech merchandise comprised 29 percent of China's total exports in 2007, up from 15 percent in 2000.

While Vietnam is surely an Asian tiger in terms of rapid growth, its overall population, 84 million, is still smaller than that of Guangdong province, and less than 6 percent of China's 1.3 billion population. As a 2008 research report by the Royal Bank of Scotland (RBS) argued, Vietnam "lacks the same scale advantages. Its impact on global trade and inflation will also be marginal." The same is true of more remote locales within China, such as Gansu, Xinjiang, and even Tibet, that lack accessibility and sheer scale of population. For its part, high-value manufacturer Japan reported wholesale inflation that reached a twenty-seven-year record in 2008, reflecting similar trends in Korea and Taiwan, stemming from increased commodity prices for wheat, copper, oil, and coal. As Japan, the world's second-largest economy, prepared for recession, wholesale inflation attacked the profitability of its exports, which remain the main engine of growth for the country. The list of available manufacturing countries that can serve as global alternatives is actually quite small.

Mexico, for example, encompasses only 8 percent of China's total population, and persistent concerns about inadequate transportation networks and infrastructure, corruption, and social instability indicate that it is not a ready replacement for the Middle Kingdom. As North America's largest auto-producing nation, Mexico's trade impact is significant, but replicating China's 1990s mix of authoritarian efficiency, deep labour resources, and openness to global capitalism is perhaps impossible. Deglobalization is surely bringing more trade to both Mexico and other nations, but it will not result in the highly bargaineered, optimized supply chains that gave us $25 DVD players and nearly a decade of other price rollbacks.

If China's heartland can't engineer bargains, likely nobody can – and globalization will decline over the long-term partially on this basis. "Relocating labour-intensive production to Vietnam from China will have little impact on global consumer goods inflation," reports the RBS in *Vietnam: Not Another China.* "Hong Kong, Japan, Korea, Taiwan, and the United States accounted for the large share of foreign investment in China during the past decade [because] the labour-cost saving of moving to China was large. . . . The labour-cost saving of moving to Vietnam from China is far smaller."

Hong Kong's business community, which almost single-handedly devised the global supply chain decades ago, would have few qualms about moving its factories to Siberia if there was a clear advantage. They know globalization because they helped invent it. Yet a majority of Hong Kong factory owners surveyed in 2008 still see their future inside China: 14 percent were considering a move to Vietnam while 29 percent planned to move inland, where land and labour costs were still cheaper.

As Hong Kong's business leadership also knows, another reason for staying put is China's emerging middle classes, an attractive new market for at-home production of goods. Compared to the average debt-ridden Western consumer with credit problems, China's new shoppers come from households with high savings rates and growing incomes. In other words, the business case to stay in China includes not only its receding price advantage in a world rocked by inflation, but also the fact that its consumer class is becoming an attractive long-term gamble compared to troubled Western economies. Indeed, the case for remaining in China is no longer about simply saving money; it's about simultaneously attempting to sell to the world's fastest-growing consumer class.

This is the beginning of a strange and likely riskier new chapter in globalization. Spending backed by cheap credit is the fast-depleting domestic resource of service economies, just as value created through spending and outsourcing became the cash crop that enabled global retailers like Wal-Mart to profit on par with global energy companies like Exxon.

Much like the complex, resource-intensive risk multiplier of synthetic crude oil production from Alberta's tar sands, the modern supply chain – our primary hookup for cheap stuff – has reached its own mature phase, and the emerging solutions are not necessarily simple or elegant. It's nothing compared to a dirty nuclear bomb, but the potential consequences are hardly insignificant: global production stranded as national economies face simultaneous other failures could lead to sudden decreases in the affordability and accessibility of common products. If true, this kind of modal shift, which mimics a stressed climatic system, could be an unmanaged and damaging transition – not to a sustainable future either, but an avenue to increasingly desperate efforts to reinstate globalization in all its year 2000 glory.

Some industries are indeed mobile and will adapt. For example, we've seen the return of some furniture manufacturing to North America, including IKEA's first major North American factory, in Danville, Virginia, in 2008. The domestic employment benefit, however, is small. The factory added a mere three hundred new jobs paying the average regional wage of $29,000 – part of six thousand new jobs the area has accumulated since 2004. Previously the region had lost 30,000 jobs to the first wave of offshoring, and it conceded about $7 million in incentives to IKEA – about $23,000 per job. The return of manufacturing is tempered by the fact that the new factories are highly automated and job-efficient. The so-called "neighbourhood effect" of relocalized production has not occurred to the degree or with the speed that many predicted. Danville represents just 2.5 percent of the world's largest furniture manufacturer's overall workforce – not exactly an avalanche of jobs returning from overseas. "I don't see a surge of employment coming back to the manufacturing sector in the United States," predicted economist Jeffrey Sachs in 2008, on the opening of the $85-million IKEA factory. "That's what some people may be looking for when they hear that globalization will be impeded by rising energy prices. I would say don't hold your breath for that."

A few months later IKEA announced another major furniture factory partnership: in Thailand, worth about US$441 million over five years. The progressive but highly secretive Swedish multinational plans to open twenty more stores across Asia as part of its pursuit of the world's strongest growth market in fibreboard furniture, a popular segment that has grown 10 percent annually worldwide. "As part of the company's survival during the global economic slowdown, our expansion in Asia will help offset the plummeting sales in the US," said John Carlsson, IKEA's Asia business manager. "We are only slightly affected by the global economic recession although customers have less purchasing power. We have seen a bigger market share from our competitors who shy away from expensive furniture products."

There's one last reason for not returning production to Western consumers: we've run out of cheap resources. After Home Depot, IKEA is one of the largest single consumers of lumber and because of this it leans heavily on Russian forests and Chinese factories. Keeping its centre of production closer to strategic inputs and emerging markets makes business sense, even at the neglect of Western economies. "IKEA now buys more products from suppliers in China than any other country and according to industry analysts this percentage will increase as IKEA relentlessly lowers costs," noted Forests Monitor in a 2006 report.

Deglobalization will happen and is happening, but former consumer superpowers in the West are hardly protected. In the future, supply chains will likely be shaped more by resources and growth potential than by past history: it's possible that some G8 nations will just get cut out of tomorrow's supply chain, not unlike unlucky emerging nations that found themselves cut out of shipping networks during the 1980s onward. "There is a lot of discussion about pulling manufacturing back to Europe from China and India because container costs and fuel costs are favoring local production," said Roy Lenders, logistics consultant for Paris-based Capgemini, in 2008. "That trend is evident with a number of companies who are now setting up factories in Eastern Europe to move at least part of their manufacturing back [from China]. Wal-Mart buys most of its plastic products from China. Those products are made with oil, and manufacturers are experiencing huge increases in material costs. . . . Eighty percent of the raw material costs are related to oil, so production might even go to the Middle East to be close to oil production."

Indeed, supply chains may well attach themselves to nations still able to sustain lavish twentieth-century consumer spending patterns, including the small minority of energy-rich nations that are expected to benefit from persistent global demand for crude oil. "All of the logistics service providers I know of are operating in Dubai," noted Lenders in an interview with *Site Selection*. "It's a two-part strategy to reach companies in the Middle East and to mitigate the rising cost of oil. You can operate an intercontinental hub for both Asia and Europe."

For anxious, underemployed Western consumers, it is true that major relocalization does happen – just not always at home.

COST OPPORTUNITY

SHOCK THERAPY: CAN HIGH PRICES SAVE US?

New kinds of change: building-sized blocks of ice collapse into Neko Bay, Antarctica, 2008.

Last Discounts, Final Offer

There is no doubt that most everyone loves a bargain. Bargains represent the core work of Western civilization for the past two hundred years: more, cheaper, better. Accelerated by information technology, enriched by cheap offshore labour, and sustained by the biggest consumer binge in human history, retail discounters elevated the lowly bargain into something ubiquitous and profound. Led by some of the world's largest and most powerful companies, the planet has become economically interlinked in the service of bargains, from the Saudi oil that furnishes south China refineries and factories with petrochemicals to the sprawling network of transport and technology that brings plastic to the West.

By the mid-2000s our consumer system had reached its pinnacle – an avalanche of plasma televisions, iPhones, and discount fashion amid a global asset and securities bubble. Western shoppers expended vast quantities of cheap credit on products of unprecedented affordability and selection.

Prices in many sales categories decreased – arguably lowering real-time inflation by several points – while countless product innovations delivered more for less.

But while Western consumers concerned themselves with the front end of the global economy – the shiny retail part – a much bigger story was playing out in the background. As discount retailing moved from the periphery to the centre of economic life, the very DNA of our material world changed. We invented new sources of growth, productivity, and profit. Petrochemical advances created whole new generations of useful plastics, as well as deeper dependence on hydrocarbons. And the stranded labour markets of Asia, fraught with the complications of failed revolutions and chronic poverty, finally came online during the 1980s, creating the single largest productive force in human history. In 2007, for the first time, China surpassed Canada as the United States' leading supplier, meaning that the value of steel containers stuffed full of affordable merchandise and parts actually exceeded the continuous flow of Canada's massive energy exports, including a growing supply of tar sands crude that will eventually exceed U.S. imports from Saudi Arabia.

While some households accumulated great wealth during the 1990s and 2000s boom in financial markets, deals on everything from luxury electronics to household goods became the dividend for everyone else, an economic model that delivered prosperity on the giddy promise of shopping, shipping, and spending. The new economy had finally begun to pay off. And if that meant that our dividend came in the form of flat-screen televisions rather than household savings or job security, surprisingly few people seemed to care. Altogether it was a surreal accomplishment: twenty-first-century technologies – advanced IT, warehousing, GPS, management – operating full bore on the economic and environmental assumptions of the 1950s.

It is possible that we have reached the peak-oil equivalent of consumerism well before the proven arrival of peak oil itself. While total credit card debt increased by 50 percent in America between 2000 and 2008, consumer spending as a share of GDP began to drop in 2008. Our consumer universe has contracted with surprising speed: by mid-2009, reported the *Globe and Mail*, many retailers were suffering, with the consumer discretionary sector (non-essentials, including automobiles) losing profits by as much as 97 percent, and the only strong business growth coming from dollar-store chains, Wal-Mart, online retailers, and other discounters.

An estimated 38.8 million square feet of retail space became empty in 2009, driven by bankruptcies and closures of Circuit City, Linens 'n Things, and others. That's equivalent to more than a hundred Colma-sized power centres standing empty. Vacancies in big-box locations have led to interesting reuses, from gymnastics clubs to churches, charter schools, museums, and libraries. But it could be difficult to fill the urban, social, and economic hole left by the slow implosion of retail and wholesale trade within major Western economies. By 2009 America's second-largest mall operator, General Properties, had declared bankruptcy, buried by $25 billion in unmanageable debt. With commercial real estate worth $6.5 trillion half financed by debt, Foresight Analytics estimated in 2009 that a continued slump could create $250 billion in commercial real estate losses and drag down more than seven hundred banks. Even before 2008, the over-saturation of malls and retail in general had already begun to create decline, not the least Wal-Mart's own dismal performance between 2000 and 2007, when its stock value dropped 38 percent. "There was really no relationship between development and the increase in consumer spending," said Stacy Mitchell of the Institute for Local Self-Reliance to the *New York Times* in 2009, noting that retail space per capita had doubled between 1990 and 2005.

The decline of the modern shopping mall is one version of consumerism's troubled future, illustrative of the way in which Western consumers are being stripped of their VIP status. Until recently, globalization found new opportunity in borderlands: grey zones of untapped consumer equity, big boxes on the edge of town, unregulated finance, unconventional crude oil, and complex trade agreements that privileged growth over development. In particular, imbalances of income, environment, trade, and spending are something that all major trading powers continue to manage and address as a requirement of continued growth – with decreasing success. From the Mexican border to transcontinental pollution, the illusion was that there could be deep economic integration but that we could still control outcomes. The assumption was that imbalances would hold and the fences would work, and that growth would continue, even if it was founded on things like depleting resources, asset bubbles, and unsustainable household debt.

The good news is that deglobalization will return balance after years of inequitable growth; the bad news is that it won't be fair. Low-income households around the world will suffer from the lack of economic activity and the erosion of affordability as our universe of cheap contracts. One possible long-term scenario for the future simply follows current trends in natural resource consumption. As everything from copper to oil to water gradually increases in price because of a combination of scarcity and increased demand, it will become increasingly uneconomical to operate the global supply chains that once offered consumers great value.

In the process we are rediscovering the second law of thermodynamics, which governs the degradation of mature energy systems. "As a system's energy degrades, physicists say its 'entropy' – often described as its disorder or randomness – increases," writes Thomas Homer-Dixon in *The Upside of Down*. "Cities, ecosystems, and human bodies must have a constant input of high quality energy to maintain their complexity and order – their position far from thermodynamic equilibrium – in the face of nature's relentless tendency toward degradation and disorder . . . And, as the system gets larger and larger and more complex, more and more energy is needed to keep it operating."

In this view, the first stage of globalization created value and wealth multipliers, disruptive change, and innovation – as well as deep imbalances and deeper dependence on non-renewable resources. The second stage, which arguably began with the emergence of Wal-Mart as the world's largest company early in the new millennium, is a stage of managed imbalance and resource depletion that threatens not merely deglobalization – the contraction of integrated trade – but also erodes the foundations of security and prosperity that were constructed during the twentieth century.

Unlike previous crashes and bubbles, today's challenges aren't merely the result of market speculation, cyclical inflation, or political manipulation. This time, long-term trends figure prominently: depletion of consumer economies, erosion of Western trade dominance, population growth, energy nationalism, food scarcity, climate change. After enjoying decades of fierce price competition, shoppers are no longer fully insulated from the pitfalls of a world hooked on bargains.

The paradox is that a great many countries remain dependent on low-cost consumerism at the very moment when consumerism is faltering.

Indeed, the truth is that many countries can't easily afford a slowdown in consumption-based growth. An ongoing global recession could eliminate as much as 20 percent of the world's wealth, according to Nicholas Stern, a former World Bank chief economist, a crash that would disproportionately affect lower-income shoppers, minority communities, and developing nations around the world.

Before the crash, some argued that the boom in trade and consumerism posed a win-win set of outcomes for the middle class, the developing world, and titans such as Wal-Mart. Shaped by insourcing, outsourcing, and offshoring, the "flat world" had sometimes been heralded as the completion stage of globalization, a state of material grace and deliverance into prosperity that inspired early globalizers like Christopher Columbus. (And our world certainly seemed flat, at least on the basis of growth in international trade: world merchandise has increased in volume twenty-seven times since 1950, as compared to an eightfold increase in world GDP. Industrial tariffs in developed countries decreased from 40 percent in 1950 to less than 4 percent in 2008.)

But as our world becomes round again, much of our prosperity is still dangerously dependent upon unsustainable labour, transport, energy, and consumer debt. As we test the material limits of our world one deal at a time, our quest for cheap has become a source of crisis in the twenty-first century. From Asia's factory borderlands to rural Mexico, from Las Vegas to the Arctic Circle, we are still attempting to reckon the promise and consequences of Everyday Low Prices. One question emerges ahead of the others: can we survive the bargain?

Meet the New Boss

It's another anniversary of the Tiananmen Square massacre. Soldiers and plainclothes police prowl the streets of Beijing. Scraps of paper are inspected; no curious detail is left unexamined. They're after leaflets, posters, banners – anything that might remind locals of the tragic crackdown that, according to the government, never really happened. As I traverse Tiananmen, the main part of the square is walled off: a huge barricade shelters reconstruction of the world's largest public square, which is running conveniently behind schedule. As soldiers march in formation outside the temporary wall, workers are busily removing tank-tread scars from Tiananmen marble.

What happened here barely two decades ago is largely unknown to many young Chinese entering the workforce. As Geremie Barmé describes it, China after Tiananmen is the story of "how comrades have become consumers without necessarily also developing into citizens."

The night before, a lone protester walked in front of Mao's portrait here at Tiananmen's Gate of Heavenly Peace and managed to pass out a few anti-government leaflets before he was abducted by police and packed into a waiting van. "Long live Chairman Mao! Long live socialism!" proclaimed his manifesto. Protest and nationalism are very nearly synonymous: rife corruption and high taxes have inspired more Chinese to argue that the country suffers from too little revolution, not too much. But for the most part, Beijing stays silent, not because older people don't remember but because it's simply not worth ten years in jail.

The following morning a fleet of sport utility vehicles is parked strategically around Tiananmen. Behind tinted windows, public security officers watch for signs of trouble. In Tiananmen and beyond new fixtures of global architecture – the opera house and the Olympic bird's-nest stadium – testify to the aspirations of the Middle Kingdom: a superpower not just in population and production but in culture, politics, and global influence as well.

Anyone here waiting for a sign – some other glimmer of the vibrant democracy movement of 1989 – will have to settle for the glorious shopping malls of Beijing. While the People's Liberation Army tromps around the square, networks of gleaming multi-tiered malls proffer radical consumerism as China's post-democratic alternative. Prada, Gucci, and Nike all feature prominently, at prices that sometimes exceed New York's. Back home the mall is denigrated, but here in Beijing it offers genuine escape and relief in the midst of an aggressive police state.

This is how developing nations such as China may dominate the future: dedication to growth, dedication to ensuring efficient use of resources required for growth, and more new consumers than anyone has ever seen before. Unfortunately, democracy may have little or nothing to do with it. Bargains don't discriminate.

What Mao Zedong could not accomplish, the world's bargaineers now deliver, albeit with toxic toys, environmental devastation, and unprecedented job losses. The factory borderlands of China, Mexico, Central

America, Europe, and the rest of Asia have collectively hosted the largest migrations of people, products, and cultures in human history, and have also witnessed profound human and labour rights abuses. But, like the bargain itself, any easy gains in development through consumer-driven economic growth are likely behind us. China and other rapidly industrializing countries have come late to the party, and their efforts to forge a new version of the developed world's consumer dreams – appliances, cars, big-screen TVs – will have consequences.

As malls decline in Western markets, the newest and grandest mega-malls are now being built by the world's emerging nations. When the West Edmonton Mall lost its "world's largest mall" designation in 2004, it was Beijing's Golden Resources Mall – or "Great Mall of China" – that claimed the prize. Nearly 50 percent larger than anything found in Europe or North America, China's mall was not built for Western tourists – indeed, it is obscurely located past Beijing's third ring road – but designed by China's leadership to connect the nation's emerging middle class with made-in-China products. (China moved one step closer to its goal of becoming the world's leading consumer nation in the twenty-first century. Some five hundred malls were built across China's mainland between 2005 and 2008. Yet But here too the perils of consumerism are clear: in 2009 the South China Mall was all but deserted, its 1,500 store spaces largely vacant, as it awaited the millions of middle-class shoppers who don't yet exist.)

It's part of what appears to be a historic transfer of global economic and political power. As pioneering consumer economies in North America and Europe struggle with insolvency, emerging nations with little debt, plenty of consumer savings, and access to rich productive capacity and valuable resources are taking the lead.

Very likely the title of world's largest mall will stay where it is now – Dubai, in the United Arab Emirates – for quite some time. As financial markets were collapsing worldwide in October 2008, the Dubai Mall opened and immediately set new standards for opulence and conspicuous consumption, including the region's largest collection of haute couture, gourmet foods, and the world's largest indoor gold and jewellery market. The mall channels Las Vegas flash, Los Angeles boutiques, and Mall of America populism within 6 million square feet, creating a refugium of shopping that could probably withstand a few climate catastrophes. Dubai is also home to the nearby world's tallest free-standing building and world's largest indoor ski slope. Its status as a global financial and energy centre for the new century means that, as economies face troubling times, the voracious consumerism of the late twentieth century probably has a better chance of survival on the edge of the Persian Gulf than anywhere else. As long as oil reserves hold up, OPEC nations may be nearly unique in their continued ability to sustain the kind of giddy shopping binges and consumer bling that the rest of us now only dream of.

Want to take it one step further? Take this economic template and paste it onto the world's developing countries, where the emerging middle classes of China and India form the final growth frontier for global retailers and manufacturers in search of new alternatives to the turgid, troubled consumer markets of North America and Europe. Even if the growing population of the developing world embraces only a fraction of the high-impact consumerism of the West, it will remain a world-changing event. Having grown from a global population of 1.6 billion in 1900 to 6.8 billion in 2009, our planet will hold 9 billion people by 2050, according to the United Nations. Sometime in the next generation, more than 2 billion people will appear on our planet, and they'll want cellphones, pants, and groceries.

Wal-Mart, Carrefour, and other giant companies are already out on retail's frontiers, attempting to be first in line to sell large volumes, discount style, to the modest-income households of emerging economies. In 2009, for example, Mattel announced its intention to "aggressively" pursue expansion in China and abroad after a crushing 46 percent profit decrease during the disastrous 2008 holiday quarter. "We are betting on China's future," said Richard Dickson, Mattel's senior vice-president, on launching a bright pink six-storey Barbie store in Shanghai. "We are betting our brand will resonate in China and we are investing heavily."

In 2009, Procter & Gamble launched what it called "the most ambitious expansion plan in company history," to double annual sales – from $80 billion to $175 billion – within fifteen years through expansion into the developing world. The company announced plans for twenty new manufacturing plants in Asia, Africa, and Eastern Europe. "P&G's center of gravity will shift toward developing markets," said chief operating officer Robert McDonald, noting that the bulk of the world's population don't yet buy detergent, shampoo, and razors in the same massive volumes as Western consumers. With 90 percent of the planet's new babies born in countries without disposable diapers, the world's largest consumer goods manufacturer estimated that by pricing its products for lower-income households, it could more than double its sales of diapers to $20 billion by 2020.

From this viewpoint, affordable consumerism is actually a doomsday machine. Take the consumer out of the picture and Wal-Mart and its kin present as highly efficient mechanisms to accelerate the depletion of our last reserves of household equity and affordable natural resources. Even with the self-greening of Wal-Mart and other leading retailers and manufacturers, the growth model remains expansive. Like the tar sands of northern Alberta and other unconventional energy developments, it seeks to reduce the carbon impact of each sales unit while still aggressively pursuing growth.

The supply chain has brought us many gifts, but it also magnifies our individual planetary impact by creating consumer savings through energy-intensive transport and manufacturing; it creates new energy demand both at home and abroad. China's "plans for building nearly 100 new coal-fired power stations each year until 2012" have led to expectations that it will surpass the United States in greenhouse gas emissions by 2009. "The expansion of China's power plants alone could nullify the cuts required under the Kyoto Protocol from industrialized countries," writes Juli Kim of the Woodrow Wilson Center.

A significant portion of the environmental impact of bargaineering has been hidden – in the backwaters of rural Asia, on distant energy frontiers, and in the unregulated emissions of shipping fleets in international waters. In 2008, for example, researchers at Carnegie Mellon University determined that export production was responsible for 33 percent of all China's greenhouse gas emissions in 2005, up from 12 percent in 1987. Globally, this suggests an economic footprint of considerable size: the 1.7 billion megatons of CO_2 created by the production of Chinese exports in 2005 exceeded all of America's industrial emissions for the same year; it was larger than or comparable to levels of national emissions from Japan, Canada, the Russian Federation, and the Middle East.

True to its role as a leading nation in the twenty-first century, China has already launched large-scale energy efficiency programs and environmental protections – if only because the ruling government well understands that energy insecurity and environmental protest are some of its greatest weaknesses. Asian economies, and China's in particular, have persistently been underestimated in their tenacity and resilience. Ongoing trade and currency deficits in favour of China are now causing growing anxiety over the future of Western consumer dominance and the fate of globalization.

It's a question that came up during the 2008 U.S. presidential race, expressed as concerns about China's profound ownership of debt and tacit control over the U.S. economy. "The first step that has to be taken is obviously we have to stop mortgaging our economy to China . . . and asking them to finance our debt," campaigned John McCain in the midst of the 2008 economic collapse. Most analysts at the time disagreed, and countered that McCain and others were simply politicking, bashing China when in actuality most American politicians would be loath to lead the changes and sacrifices required. "If we really did want to change that, we would need to make fundamental changes on the economy and stop generating a trade deficit. There is no simple solution for that," scolded Ward McCarthy of Stone & McCarthy Research Associates.

There may not be much choice, since most leading consumer nations are also debtor nations. One in ten American households – a total of 15 million – held zero or negative equity in 2009. By 2010, America's nineteen largest banks face as much as $186 billion in credit card losses, reflecting an unsustainable average of $8,600 in outstanding credit card debt per household. In response, major card issuers planned to reduce available consumer credit by 57 percent between 2007 and 2010, a trend that will not only limit consumer spending power but force a long-term contraction within the service economy itself.

It's not even clear if Keynesian-style spending and investing can help a society so deeply in debt. "In the last eight years, Americans have spent an extraordinary amount of money and borrowed a lot to make that spending possible," wrote Harvard economist Edward L. Glaeser in 2009, noting that America's national debt had nearly doubled since 2000, increasing from $5.7 trillion to $10.8 trillion. Despite this, says Glaeser, "many macroeconomists tell us that all that spending is needed to undo the effects of all that spending."

This could be where Western dominance, and globalization dominated by consumer goods trade, fails in the new millennium. We could simply go broke as nations with less debt and more discipline take over. With the disappearance of ravenous consumer demand in the West, trade will become much more regionalized, with intra-Asian, European Union, and Middle Eastern trade zones consolidating.

As America sinks deeper in debt, and as corporations move further abroad in search of new growth, China will likely redefine the future of capitalism. "China will replace the U.S. as the motor of the world economy," billionaire investor George Soros predicted in May 2009. "The American economy is still bigger than the Chinese. However, China will begin to contribute more and more to global economic growth. Therefore, political power will shift from America to China."

Globalization reached its apex engineering bargains for Western democracies, but it is ending with an authoritarian consumer superpower and a small collection of hyper-solvent corporations, including Wal-Mart and ExxonMobil. Certainly, if the Western consumer shops less and saves more – as was evident by 2009 – it's good news for the planet. Yet even a slightly more deglobalized world will amplify this post-democratic trend: from Wal-Mart to OPEC, everything from electronics to energy to ownership of national debt will be increasingly subject to the growing influence of companies and countries that sometimes have little direct accountability to anyone besides shareholders and unelected governments.

Aside from India, whose democracy and localized commerce showed strength in the wake of the 2008 financial collapse, there are relatively few nations in ascendancy who might counter this autocratic trend in world affairs. With China's fierce competition for global resources, lack of reform on human rights, and unrest within its own hinterlands, the trajectory of its ruling party is uncertain; it could democratize suddenly, as Mongolia did in 1990, but most observers would not bet on this prospect. With a shrinking portion of its GDP dependent on exports (currently about 30 percent, which is less than for Germany), it is possible that China will eventually seek to extinguish its American currency reserves and ownership of American government debt in favour of higher-yield investments. In the end, America's diplomatic, military, and cultural supremacy may matter very little.

This is a change from traditional notions of progress. In postwar Europe, for example, Germany became the world's leading export nation through cultivating its engineering expertise and high-value manufacturing. Its products and brands, from Adidas to Volkswagen, are synonymous with modern efficiency and quality. It doesn't do bargains per se, but sells machines, petrochemicals, components, and services to consumer and producer nations alike. German firms designed part of China's Three Gorges Dam and supplied some of the massive digging machines and turbines required to accomplish what became the world's single largest public works project. As the third-largest producer of automobiles and the third-largest book market in the world, Germany exemplifies what post-Obama America might aspire towards: a country that makes real things – valuable things – and champions renewable energy. But with over 40 percent of its economic output dependent on exports, Germany's major problem is still globalization, and that there are far fewer people on the planet at the end of the millennium's first decade keen to pay retail prices for luxury autos. The German model still requires global growth and rich trading partners. In terms of true-cost pricing for carbon and essential resources, high prices can save us, certainly, but this doesn't mean that high-value trading nations are going to come out ahead.

In the West, people have been slow to realize the depth of this change. That's probably because the reality seems too ridiculous to admit. "The days when foreigners were willing to finance our deficits for free are gone forever," concludes Charles Morris. "The United States, the 'hyperpower,' the global leader in the efficiency of its markets and the productivity of its businesses and workers, hopelessly in hock to some of the world's most unsavory regimes."

Deglobalization

André Alexander points towards the sky. Above him looms a cinder-block shopping mall three storeys high. It is possibly the ugliest building in all of Lhasa. "That was it," he exclaims. "When this went up, we decided that something had to be done." Alexander says that the shopping mall – a grey glass-and-brick monster that looks like a fortress – was plopped down in 1993 on the Barkhor *kora*, one of Tibet's most sacred pilgrim routes. At the time the Chinese government was demolishing Lhasa's inner city to make way for commercial hotels and merchants. Thousand-year-old Tibetan mansions were pulled down and replaced with Chinese-style block housing at a rate of thirty-five buildings per year during the 1990s.

Justin Guariglia/www.guariglia-chen.com

Reaching globalization's limits: "Be a civilized citizen and build a civilized city" on a billboard outside of Lhasa, Tibet.

The Barkhor itself is a broad laneway that circles through the heart of Lhasa's 1,300-year-old inner city: crooked roads, alleyways, and passages wind outwards from the broad cobblestone street. Ancient crumbling stone buildings loom over the near-constant orbit of pilgrims. While famous temples and landmarks are being rebuilt across Tibet, Lhasa's historic inner city is gradually disappearing.

It was the mall that inspired Alexander to organize the Tibet Heritage Fund (TIIF), a joint Tibetan-European effort that between 1996 and 2000 restored heritage structures within Lhasa's inner city, one of the world's most historic neighbourhoods. André sees it as simply levelling the playing field, but it's hard not to forget that we're standing in the middle of an economic and cultural struggle that's been happening ever since the first century. Proud Tibetans point towards the ancient Zhol pillar standing neglected at the edge of the Chinese-built Potala Square. Erected in 764 A.D., the pillar records how Tibetan armies once occupied the Chinese capital of Xian. Conversely, Chinese visitors point towards the peaked rooftops found on many temples and correctly identify Han architectural influences.

We pass a corner of the Barkhor where more than seventy demonstrators, including monks and nuns, were reportedly shot and killed during riots in 1988, an incident echoed again in 2008. From a nearby stand Alexander picks up a *bangdian* apron, the traditional striped sash worn by Tibetan women, that was made in Chengdu, a Chinese province that lies at the eastern foot of the Tibetan plateau. "Most everything here is imported – Tibetans have so little power in their lives." The local economy has taken a beating since China opened up Tibet for business in the 1990s. A peek inside the shopping mall reveals a bevy of low-budget Chinese trinket stands and electronics merchants plying cheap goods from Sichuan and Guangzhou. "Tibetan people aren't as competitive as the Chinese," André explains, darting through a throng of pilgrims. "Lhasa's culture is cosmopolitan, but isolated: they didn't always have 1 billion people to compete with."

It makes Wal-Mart's urban invasion across the West look genteel. Indeed, Lhasa itself is a place where Tibetans are no longer the majority. It is a city that is actually several cities, principally the old inner city of pre-1959 Tibet and the large, ugly modern Chinese metropolis that has sprung up around it. If you count its suburbs, a prostitute encampment, and several large prison camps, Lhasa is a sprawling mess that resembles nothing that Tibet has ever seen before.

Globalization has been happening for a long time. As historians Ronald Findlay and Kevin O'Rourke note in *Power and Plenty*, its first significant wave was the great Mongol kingdom that encompassed Korea, China, Tibet, eastern Russia, and Central Asia between 1000 and 1350 A.D., peaking with the proclamation of Genghis Khan as universal ruler in 1206, which was followed by the capture of Beijing in 1215 and Kiev in 1240. *Pax Mongolia* was a multi-ethnic horseback army dominated by fierce Buddhists. The military empire encouraged east/west trade across multiple civilizations, resulting in a "non-hegemonic or horizontally linked 'world system'" that indirectly linked Britain with Japan. Uighurs and Tibetans worked within this system, influencing it through their administrative expertise and Buddhist teachings, respectively. Lhasa became an esteemed centre as successive khans assumed Tibetan Buddhism as their religion. There were early bargains too: one 1987 study determined that Chinese silk sold in

Italian markets during the Mongol Empire was priced at no more than three times its original purchase price in China.

Modern globalization achieved a different kind of triumph in bargaineering: ours was a revolution in production, consumption, and resource utilization, not geography, culture, and military reach. *Pax Mongolia* eventually faltered not because it ran out of resources – horses and grasslands remained plentiful – but because it could not overcome the entropy of managing 22 percent of the earth's land area in the face of China's Ming Dynasty. Even while Ming armies sacked strategic Mongolian cities and settlements, most communities and cities remained intact and the Mongols claimed global consciousness as their legacy.

Today's globalization is proving much less resilient, and while global consciousness remains strong – marked by healthy transnational communities and NGOs of all kinds – the material and environmental legacy is one of deeply embedded risk. After only a few decades of intensive bargaineering, our material systems are losing their capacity to absorb costs and impacts – and are becoming risk multipliers.

On one hand, we've discovered that bargaineering does not ensure affordability or create lasting wealth. The reality is that a growing portion of our economy is increasingly vulnerable to small increases in the prices of petroleum, plastic, labour, and other resources. This in turn causes disruption that affects the viability of trade. Even the most incremental rise in the cost of plastic threatens to derail the packaged prosperity enjoyed by Western consumers, Indo-Asian manufacturers, and almost everyone else in between. In the years before the 2008 crash, Chinese production became more costly because of shortages of workers, food, and resources, as well as new labour laws that increased wages. China's inflation surged to an eleven-year high in 2008 and food prices jumped by more than 23 percent, which in turn forced an estimated 20 percent increase in factory wages.

Deglobalization could have serious consequences. "I think there's a real danger that globalization could unravel," economist Niall Ferguson told the *Globe and Mail* in 2009. "There will be blood, in the sense that a crisis of this magnitude is bound to increase political as well as economic [conflict]. It is bound to destabilize some countries. It will cause civil wars to break out that have been dormant. It will topple governments that were moderate and bring in governments that are extreme."

Protectionism has returned. In 2009, for example, Mexico announced a series of tariff increases of between 10 and 45 percent, affecting $2.4 billion worth of American goods entering Mexico. Everything from cabbage, toilet paper, and deodorant to pencils, pork rinds, and Christmas trees was affected. "Clearly, this was designed to bring about some specific pain," said David Gantz, a professor of law at the University of Arizona.

As we move into the challenge phase of globalization, a period when old solutions will fail and new solutions may not come fast enough, there are echoes of previous rough transformations. Indeed, we based globalization on the extractive economies of Western nations during the nineteenth century. Driven by the post-industrial service economies of developed nations, we virtually mined cheapness from the farthest reaches of the planet, encompassing all the commercial and technological inventions from the Industrial Revolution onwards – petrochemicals and plastics, shipping, liberalized trade and the rise of the multinational, consumer credit, the combustion engine.

For many of us, deglobalization should offer some benefit: economies less tied to unsustainable growth, markets less expectant of unrealistic returns, and consumers less governed by objects of their desire. There is liberation in accounting for environmental and climate impacts, practising economic non-violence, and realizing that despite attempts to prosper with decoupled forms of commerce, we are still ultimately governed by interdependence. It's a lesson in cause and effect not only taught by a globalization now in its twilight years, but also as part of the teachings of more than a millennium here in Lhasa, even longer in China, and longer still in India, where the Buddha himself once instructed monks: "From the arising of this comes the arising of that. . . . From the cessation of this comes the cessation of that."

Ultimately there is no "Wal-Mart" that exists independent of everything else, only an aggregate of causes and conditions that weaves together the livelihoods of millions. There will be no Wal-Mart in one hundred years, just as only a shell of America's domestic auto industry now remains. Part of the ingenuity and technology of the modern mega-firm is to influence affairs, sway consumers, and channel resources as though a singular, monolithic power was actually at work. Yet communities that have fought and won against unwanted big-box stores, as well as governments that have refused to subsidize global commerce, have sometimes found that the reality is more porous, that change is possible, and that common sense can sway the balance of things.

Because of deep interdependence, we can't let globalization fail too quickly or without purpose. To be sure, in terms of climate, environment, and economy, the case for intensified local production and consumption is compelling. But rapid deglobalization could backfire too. Indeed, without NGOs and the cooperative global networks that economist Jeffrey Sachs advocates as essential to security and justice, former global powers such as Mongolia would likely have imploded late in the twentieth century, so deep was the poverty and lack of development that resulted when Russia pulled out after seventy-plus years of occupation in 1990. "The paradox of a unified global economy and divided global society poses the single greatest threat to the planet because it makes impossible the cooperation needed to address [our] remaining challenges," writes Sachs in his 2008 book, *Common Wealth*. "We've actually been there before. The first great wave of globalization in the nineteenth century ended up in the blood-drenched trenches of Europe in World War One."

The lesson from previous periods of deglobalization, such as the dark years surrounding the Great Depression and leading up to the Second World War, is that bad politics, fear, and strife can cause more damage than economic losses. Nativist movements, anti-immigration rallies, and nationalist fervor are already part of many countries, and it would be unwise to rule out destructive and emotional responses to many consumers' losing their reach and buying power. Buddhism teaches that loss of identity is something people fear as much as death. And given that many people in the developed world have known little else but two decades of consumer empowerment and reward, there will be inevitable dissent and fear about a future that guarantees less.

Along the outer edge of Tibet's medieval city, pilgrims follow an ancient circumambulation route, the Lingkor, that was here long before modern development covered it up. They swing prayer wheels and chant "*Om mani padme hum*" as they follow the ancient path now obscured by a freshly built four-lane highway. Pilgrims stop in their tracks to worship invisible temples and *chortens*, torn down in the mad swath of Chinese construction that's transforming the city. Blessed with several video surveillance cameras, the Lingkor links many of the new elements of the global economy: the route passes ancient stone carvings, an electronic stock exchange (Tibet's first), a go-kart track behind the Potala Palace, nondescript brothels, and stations of ever-watchful armed soldiers.

Returning from the Lingkor, I spot a gleaming item at a souvenir stand next to Lhasa's central temple. While very few of the statues and religious trinkets sold along the Barkhor are actually made in Tibet – most are imported from Nepal and India – several vendors sell real Tibetan heirlooms, many stolen from temples. It is possible to barter and bargain for things that are literally priceless. I recognize one artifact immediately: it is the hand of a golden Buddha, sawed off at the wrist, frozen in the flat-palmed gesture of generosity.

The Thermodynamics of Cheap

While one part of our economy wages a war on scarcity by burning up high-value resources, another part is rediscovering the "negawatt." The negawatt is what Amory Lovins once described as the cheapest energy of all: energy saved by efficiency and demand management, the energy never created because it wasn't required.

Energy efficiency is still the final frontier. During the first real energy crisis of the twentieth century – the OPEC embargo that followed the Yom Kippur War of 1973 – green energy took root: how-to books on solar power, passive heating, and wind power flourished. Tiny companies started up, building high-efficiency wood stoves and solar panels; books and magazines promoted a back-to-the-land ethos that championed smart energy alternatives. But the movement faltered: governments took to building nuclear power stations and, as global oil supplies revived, consumers enjoyed cheap energy prices again, enough to maintain the cars, homes, and appliances of the high-energy society built up during the 1950s and 1960s. Nevertheless, more than 150 nuclear power plants were built across North America, all of them commissioned before 1974. Finally, Syncrude started up in 1978 with government support, consolidating Canada's tar sands as an industry; the company had grown out of the panic of the 1970s energy crisis – and the rush to create large new sources of power through expensive megaprojects – and would become the largest producer of unconventional crude oil in the world.

But publicly subsidized megaprojects, luckily, aren't everyone's vision. About seven hundred kilometres north of the tar sands is the small First Nations community of Whatì, with about 485 residents. The Dogrib people here have fished and trapped in the north Slave Lake region for as long as anyone can remember. For decades the rustic log homes that overlook rugged Lac La Martre were powered by diesel generators that were never quiet and required expensive fuel brought in by tanker trucks via a 145-kilometre ice road from Yellowknife each winter.

During an energy audit in 2002, the community discovered that it had been collectively spending more than a million dollars annually on fuel for heating and transport. At just over $2,000 per resident, the annual energy expense was double or even quadruple that of most North Americans. And not only was the cost of imported fuel hobbling their local economy, air pollution created by non-stop diesel operation had been slowly poisoning the residents. The same diesel particulates that have been linked to cancer and asthma in Los Angeles were being broadcast in a poisonous halo around this community on the very northern fringe of the boreal forest. "Anyone living here is affected by the gas emissions. Adults, children, even if the doors are shut," said elder Jonas Nitsiza in 2002. "If they're sick [or] not feeling well, we know that the power plant is the main reason. The diseases originate from the power plant."

Nitsiza and others traced the change back to 1958, when the first diesel power plant was installed. "We tried to remove the power plant but could not find solutions. Many worked on this," said Nitsiza. "The children and the eighty-year-olds were young and energetic, with no sign of sickness, until the power plant was built in 1958." The 2002 report confirmed that diesel generation was the source of forty toxic chemicals and eight toxic gases found in the community. It's hard to separate the impact of diesel generation from other changes, such as the health effects of a less traditional, more sedentary lifestyle or climate change. But like aboriginal elders elsewhere in the north, many are reading the signs around them with greater certainty. "So much has changed. Trees changed before like world changed in one day. Now it varies – lake would freeze but not entirely. Even the colour of the trees changed."

The economic and social effects of climate change loom over northerners more than most people, but it was clear that the most immediate threat to Whatì's future was fossil-fuel dependence. Something had to be done. Beginning in 2002, Whatì embarked on an ambitious plan to achieve greater energy efficiency, seek out green sources of power, and somehow reconcile their energy requirements with the social, health, and economic development of their community. To reach the goal of "prosperous self-sufficiency," elders, youth, and adults worked with consultants and government to reduce greenhouse gas emissions by 50 percent within three years. Communities that get involved in renewable power are usually among the most efficient, so education and community consultation were used to encourage ownership and responsibility on the issue, to move people from being mere energy consumers to grasping their inherent stakeholder status.

Progress was made, and by 2008 plans and financing were being arranged for a $16-million micro-hydro installation. Local hydroelectricity using the abundant water resources of the region could replace much of the diesel generation, as well as contribute additional space heating. Solar hot-water heaters will add additional capacity. By 2009 Whatì was on its way to becoming a genuinely self-sustaining community.

One of the main reasons why Whatì and other communities suffered extra expense and disease for so many years, even after these effects became obvious, was that the internal combustion engine creates a very high-quality, dependable source of energy. If you live in the north especially, it's a great improvement to quality of life to have heat and electricity. And as millions of others have found, it's hard to let go of hydrocarbons, even if they're slowly killing us or draining our collective savings. To its credit, the community of Whatì correctly perceived its dilemma and sought to change its energy paradigm before too much damage was done. It's a lesson for the rest of us who are still highly dependent on fossil fuels.

History does not favour societies that fail to manage resource crises. "Societies that don't have enough access to high quality energy are likely to disintegrate," argues Thomas Homer-Dixon in *The Upside of Down*. Between the entropy of our material systems and the destabilization of natural systems, the threat of massive Schumpeterian change is real. "This would be destructive – not creative – catastrophe," he continues. "It would affect large regions and even sweep around the globe, in the process deeply damaging the human prospect. Recovery and renewal would be slow, perhaps impossible."

In our quest for cheap, this means that yesterday's solutions often turn out to be problems. For example, the Bush administration promised to fast-track America into alternative fuels by replacing 20 percent of U.S. gasoline consumption with renewable fuels by 2017. The result was a rediscovery of the first law of thermodynamics, which states that the energy in an isolated system remains constant and can be neither lost nor created. When American producers siphoned off one-third of U.S. corn production for ethanol refining during the mid-2000s, the net energy gain was often negative (factoring in energy inputs such as farming fuels, fertilizer, transport, etc.). As well, the dramatic government-sponsored reallocation of resources – for what was essentially energy upgrading with corn – inevitably resulted in food inflation internationally; tortilla prices in Mexico, for example, assumed crisis proportions.

The creation of "new" energy from unconventional sources is subject to similar thermodynamic constraints: bitumen-energy upgrading, hydrogen-energy manufacturing, and the more extreme high-cost frontier extraction (deep-water drilling, arctic drilling, subsea hydrates) all involve much steeper production costs than previously imagined, both to the consumer and to the planet in general. The actual amount of new energy harvested from this growing pool of marginal resources decreases with each passing decade, especially relative to population growth and the often inefficient energy demands of both emerging and established economies.

Moreover, we have become highly efficient in some ways but not in others, resulting in asymmetrical outcomes. We are optimized for bargains but not for energy usage. Wal-Mart can squeeze pennies out of manufacturers, reduce packaging, and push overhead and labour costs down, then put the product on a container ship burning bunker fuel and distribute it via diesel truck to big-box stores, where, more often than not, everyone shows up in a low-efficiency vehicle.

The global supply chain was founded on the operating assumptions of open energy systems, of cheap shipping, of big-box stores accessible by automobile, and of the embodied-energy materials themselves – such as plastics and fertilizer – not being subject to serious constraints or consequences.

The amount of energy required to sustain order in globalization's complex systems is immense: increased energy demand from China and India and consumption-fuelled growth in Western nations, all complicated by untimely chronic scarcity of our most valuable fossil fuels. Consequently, Wal-Mart's commitment to increase its transport efficiency by 50 percent by 2015 is minimized by the fact that it still seeks to champion and grow from a fundamental business model defined by embodied energy.

Record prices fetched for crude oil during the 2000s led business analysts to question the future viability of a bargain-based world, since everything from the cost of manufacturing to mass container transport depends on affordable energy. As the *Financial Times* of London speculated in 2008, "$100-plus [per barrel of oil] sustained for a year or more would do much more damage to the world economy than anything we have seen so far. The break point may well turn out to be pretty close to where we are now." But as both economies and environments falter, we are moving away from the illusion of open energy systems – boundless horizons of cheap energy, frontiers of plentiful resources rich with gigajoules of power – to the long-term reality of a closed, planet-based system subject to the complications of interconnected economies, population growth, and climate change. The closed energy system of the twenty-first century is twofold: the planet itself, plus a highly globalized economy that, in surpassing its operational limits, has begun to perform like a stressed climatic system.

Investment allocation tells us a story about a divergent future based on energy. "The next ten years will be crucial for all countries, including China and India, because of the rapid expansion of energy-supply infrastructure," said Nobuo Tanaka of the International Energy Agency in 2007. "We need to act now to bring about a radical shift in investment in favour of cleaner, more efficient and more secure energy technologies."

The United Nations Environmental Programme (UNEP) reported that worldwide investment in sustainable energy broke records in 2007, with $148.4 billion in new money raised. "[I]nvestment between now and 2030 is expected to reach $450 billion a year by 2012, rising to more than $600 billion a year from 2020." It was a 60 percent increase from the previous year, and very positive news.

But global spending on non-renewable energy exploration and production in 2008 was $418 billion – nearly triple the announced renewable investment in 2007 – up from $349 billion in 2007. This represents the growing expense of securing new oil and gas more than anything else. As Bloomberg reported in 2008, for non-state companies such as Exxon, Shell, and ConocoPhillips, "costs more than quadrupled since 2000 as explorers targeted more challenging reservoirs and demand rose for labor and material." Conventional oil used to cost $4 per barrel in 2000, but by 2007 extraction and production costs had increased it to $18, reflecting the same triple-digit cost increases as found in the tar sands.

Potential gains from energy efficiency are far more impressive than the declining returns of crude oil exploration – and cheaper too. "Global industry will need to invest an additional US$360 billion in energy efficient technology," reported the United Nations Foundation (UNF) in a landmark 2007 report, "Realizing the Potential of Energy Efficiency." "[But] the lifetime resulting savings in energy costs are estimated to be more than US$900 billion."

If the G8 nations alone – the richest nations of the northern hemisphere – doubled their rate of efficiency between 2012 and 2030, world carbon concentrations could be stabilized at 550 ppm (admittedly at the high end for climate stabilization). They would also be able to avoid spending $3 trillion on new power generation, save consumers $500 billion by 2030, and return the planet to 2004 energy consumption levels. "World governments should exploit energy efficiency as their energy resource of first choice because it is the least expensive and most readily scalable option to support sustainable economic growth, enhance national security, and reduce further damage to the climate system," argued the UNF.

These kinds of epic savings – essentially energy bargaineering – are not limited to affluent countries. The IEA argued that China alone could realistically cut its fuel use by 15 percent by 2030, and that energy efficiency could account for as much as 60 percent of that gain. By 2009 many countries had included renewable power and energy efficiency in their economic crisis stimulus packages. Britain, for example, announced that it would commit to making 24 million U.K. homes reach near-zero carbon emissions by 2030.

To answer efficiency and renewable power skeptics, it must be noted that the early decades of oil and gas were marked by slow returns. Surprisingly few people knew what to do with the stuff, aside from burning kerosene in lamps and greasing the axles of their horse-drawn carriages. Several more decades could make alternatives similarly essential and valuable, especially as renewable power becomes more affordable. The cost of solar photovoltaic cells, for example, has already decreased by 95 percent since the 1970s. There are quantum savings to be achieved in the twenty-first century, just not necessarily at the mall. And not with cheap energy.

The True Cost of Things

Early in 2001, I ventured up into Canada's High Arctic on a magazine assignment to write about climate change. Guided by a local hunter from Resolute Bay (Qausuittuq), we travelled out onto the pack ice. Here at Canada's second most northerly civilian settlement, local elders were reporting that the ice was breaking up weeks and even months earlier and behaving erratically. The plane ride into Resolute gave me a glimpse of a large crack in the ocean ice, even though it was still February, with daytime lows of minus 40° Celsius. Outside, it was too cold to talk – the wind chill was minus 70° or more. All we could do was gaze off into the distance, across the frozen ocean and islands of the Arctic towards a horizon lit by winter twilight. Except for the wind it was silent, but beneath us everything was in motion.

We were travelling the route of the legendary Northwest Passage, the world's last great unconquered ocean passage and the legendary direct route coveted by explorers since the reign of Queen Elizabeth I. To the local Inuit this largely icebound channel is a thoroughfare for polar bears, seal, walrus, hunters, wayward explorers, and pack ice. Later, skidding across the ice on the back of a snowmobile, I recalled the troubling stories of local hunters, who told of everything from freak floods and unusual bouts of open water and surges to disappearing wildlife – phenomena that run counter to generations of Inuit oral history and, more often than not, are reflected in the predictions of those who study climate change.

Not only are Inuit hunters losing their bearings while travelling on strange ice floes and resorting to GPS units for navigation, southerners have been travelling north to take their bearings and trace their own routes. In August 2007 the Northwest Passage was open to marine travel for the first time since records began, making it the world's most northerly navigational route. As ice coverage doggedly disappears across the summertime waters of the Arctic, shipping companies and trading nations are

author photo

Hans Aronsen of Resolute Bay tends sled dogs on the Northwest Passage, which had begun to show cracks even in February 2001.

jockeying to run some of the world's biggest container ships and tankers on regular routes through the Northwest Passage, well before 2040, the estimated date when all summer sea ice in the Arctic will have disappeared. This major new shipping route is worth billions: what once took twenty-nine days to sail between Rotterdam and Yokohama would take just fifteen across the Northwest Passage and the Arctic Ocean. For the Inuit, environmentalists, and many locals, it's a scenario that presents hazards nearly as concerning as the regional effects of climate change, including oil spills, lost shipping containers, oil drilling, and economic development – basically relocating southern industrial development to the edge of some of our most northerly habitable communities.

"Within a generation the Arctic Ocean will be opened up to general cargo shipping," said Inuit leader Sheila Watt-Cloutier in 2004. "This means wholesale social, economic, and cultural change in the circumpolar world, and will bring to the fore long-standing questions of national sovereignty and disputed boundaries. I don't think any of us are ready for these very big issues."

While eroding sea ice is of great concern to many hunters, it is the heavy metals and PAHs (polycyclic aromatic hydrocarbons) from the south that

THE PRICE OF A BARGAIN

worry so many others, the long-distance by-products of our cheap-energy addiction to coal-fired power, and the added load from cement plants and garbage incineration. Mercury accumulates in the Arctic: the persistent cold for much of the year literally freezes it out of the water vapour in the air so that it ends up on the ground. Caribou eat the lichens; polar bears and hunters – and their children – eat the caribou. "We are eager to manufacture metal, to forge steel and burn coal. Like in the south, all around the Great Lakes," says one Inuk. "For the average farmer in the south, there is quality control. But for caribou meat, all we can hope for is that it is the same as a hundred years ago."

Due to pervasive contaminants and the high cost of gas and equipment, more and more hunters have to shop for food. Iqaluit's Northmart, one of a handful of high-latitude supermarkets in the world, demonstrates a different, and more telling, economy: tomatoes and green peppers at $4 a pound, milk for $3 to $4 a litre. It may be howling cold outside, with blizzards blowing in off Frobisher Bay, but inside you can troll the aisles with your parka off, filling your cart with fresh (albeit expensive) dairy, bread, and produce. In addition to groceries, Northmart offers housewares, clothing, and equipment in several aisles, much like a Wal-Mart Supercentre, but smaller, more expensive, and with fewer white people.

This is one view of the future: a world without bargains. A litre of apple juice costs $5.89; hot dog buns are $4.99 – and that's after $18 million in annual transport subsidies from the government. Junk food and sweetened juices aren't subsidized, so a gallon jug of cranberry cocktail retails for $41.69. It's hard to hide the actual cost of things up here. Transport costs for green peppers and tomatoes are 20 percent of the retail price, whereas transport costs as a percentage of sales in the south were less than 2 percent in 2004. Gasoline here was $1.50 a litre by mid-2008 ($5.67 a gallon), even after $230 million in fuel subsidies; the real cost is likely closer to $11.00 a gallon.

While wrestling with food inflation, climate change, homelessness, unemployment, and other chronic issues, Nunavut's government had to raise an extra $100 million to cover energy price increases in 2008, or else let retail gasoline prices jump 50 percent. If consumer gasoline prices doubled, homelessness would likely double as well, given the large population of at-risk residents of Iqaluit who depend on gasoline and fuel oils for power. The local homeless shelter is nearly full already and the winters are deadly. A 2006 government report documented thirteen-year-old girls trading sex for shelter and single mothers with their babies sleeping inside banking-machine lobbies. Several local homeless men wander the Northmart on any given day as part of their ongoing effort to stay warm. "I've got to find that $100 million," said Nunavut energy minister Ed Picco. "Do I take it out of education? Do I take it out of health?"

Iqaluit is on the cutting edge of many of our most important twenty-first-century challenges. This is a land that is beyond cheap, a place that Wal-Mart and all other major retailers have forsaken – a place where people are too often forced to pay the true price of things.

The government has certainly done its part to reduce carbon intensity, to future-proof, and generally attempts to cope with the multitude of new pressures it faces. But when it comes down to it – when cheap is eliminated – people are often forced to choose between maintaining their material systems and infrastructure and sustaining "non-economic" assets such as health, education, and the environment. This choice, in fact, happens all the time, but we don't notice it because the consequences are deferred or delayed, or we're simply not paying attention.

What buys Nunavut time is the curious and much larger phenomenon of our societal capacity to absorb and tolerate high economic costs, particularly energy costs, without collapse. This is one of our hidden strengths: to demand bargains but demonstrate surprising adaptability when costs accumulate. Our markets, retailers, suppliers, and nearly everyone else are collectively disciplined and conditioned to deliver cheapness and suffer under price dictatorship (excepting the military-industrial complex, real dictators, and luxury goods manufacturers). Crude oil prices increased 60.1 percent in 2007 and 2008, but the newsworthy collapse was the failure of Wall Street's unregulated credit derivatives based on a housing bubble, not the energy and commodity inflation of the same period.

This may suggest hidden strength and resilience of some kind. Or it may be a lesson about how systems change in non-linear fashion. For example, if you travel straight out of Iqaluit across Frobisher Bay, south and east, you'll be in open water in the upper reaches of the Labrador Sea, an extremely deep stretch of ocean bordered by Greenland and Labrador. This is the site of the North Atlantic Deep Water, one of the great engines of oceanic currents in the northern hemisphere and responsible for anchoring planetary energy balances. Here water moves in deep channels, mixing with older waters as it moves towards the southern hemisphere. Some deep waters travel for 1,600 years before passing by Antarctica, turning north into the South Pacific, and finally upwelling in the North Pacific.

As Wallace S. Broecker first noted in 1987, and as other climatologists have concurred since, the great ocean conveyor belt is characterized by massive thermal inertia. Climate change happens as an echo: today's emissions don't immediately affect the earth's thermal cycles because of the planet's oceanic mass. And not only is change gradual – and very unlikely to reflect rapid loads and stresses – the true delayed response may be a climatic flip that would occur once certain thresholds of water salinity and temperature are reached. At that point, as has been debated, discussed, and fearfully speculated on at length, our climate may destabilize and begin to perform in erratic ways, such as cooling in northern Europe or accelerating sea level increases.

For people who are also concerned about the price of big-screen televisions, the take-away lesson is simple: as our material world and our economy under late globalization begin to perform more like a climatic system, we are incurring stresses and strains that will likely have critical, delayed consequences. Much like the problem of toxic debt with dangerously flawed financial products, the costs and dangers in the modern supply chain are not evident, nor are they passed along to consumers as the true price of things. This goes a long way to explaining how a crowded global economy managed to squeeze out persistent growth and productivity despite price increases, volatility, and other challenges. That Wal-Mart can still comfortably fill a supercentre at $150 oil-price spikes is an accomplishment to be sure. But three more years of $150 oil without reprieve would seriously constrain Wal-Mart's survival tools: its ability to hedge and purchase quantities of services, materials, and energy when prices are low; the continued inability of suppliers in the same situation to absorb costs; and the decreasing likelihood that customers themselves would continue to consume at past rates. On the whole, the real story of much of the 2000s is how modest overall price increases actually were, given the impressive price increases for food, oil, and commodities. "One of the surprises," said Patrick Jackman, a senior economist in the consumer price division of the U.S. Bureau of Labor Statistics, "is that the oil price surges of the 1970s passed through fairly quickly into consumer prices, and this time that is not happening."

The truth is that the world's biggest corporations have been internalizing costs in an effort to stay competitive – essentially creating consumer welfare. During the oil-price spike of 2008, Europe's leading discount airline, Ryanair, reported that 50 percent of its costs were fuel-related, and even Exxon claimed that it had sacrificed its refining margins in an effort to reduce retail gas increases to consumers.

Multinationals can't carry us forever, though. In the future, will there be any savings to pass along to consumers after we finish transporting bargains across the planet? Removing subsidies to consumers and business from the global economy would be a lot like removing automobiles from our cities: it is possible, and even desirable on many levels, but represents the kind of radical change that people rarely undertake voluntarily. And it is very difficult to convince developing nations to remove fuel and food subsidies. The 48 percent increase in global food prices between 2006 and 2008 had its most destructive impact on the developing world: approximately 100 million people across Africa, Asia, and the Americas are at critical risk as increases erode previous gains made against poverty.

But someone has to make sacrifices and take new kinds of risk. The cracks in the February ice in the Northwest Passage I witnessed in 2001 weren't an isolated event. In March 2008 the British Meteorological Office found that the coldest winter days in Canada and Russia had become four degrees milder since the 1950s. In global terms a four-degree overall increase – not just in far northern latitudes – would be a profound event, potentially causing water shortages, flooding in coastal cities, and the profligate spread of tropical disease.

High prices might well save us. In fact, as the Canadian Energy Research Institute (CERI) found in May 2009, if crude oil is too cheap – less than $90 a barrel – then energy producers will not make investments in efficiency and carbon capture. Low-priced fossil fuels pose fierce competition to more sustainable energy alternatives, not only in terms of direct competition for investment capital and government subsidy but also for regulatory and policy dominance. An economy that has no price or tax on carbon rewards massive investment in unconventional crude and discriminates against sustainable alternatives. "Every serious study of climate change done in Canada and abroad makes the same point," reported the *Globe and Mail*'s Jeffrey Simpson in 2009. "Unless governments put a price on carbon, there cannot be a serious attempt to reduce emissions." Moreover, if the carbon price per tonne is too low within any emissions trading system, such as it is in Alberta at $15 a tonne, the low cost is inadequate to stimulate alternatives; it is cheaper for companies to simply pay to pollute.

We cannot afford a cheap energy status quo. The cost of mitigating the worst effects of climate change could be roughly 2 percent of the world GDP, according to Britain's influential 2006 Stern Review, while the cost of inaction would be at least 5 percent, and possibly 20 percent. To achieve the radical reductions in greenhouse gas emissions that would assuredly stabilize the planet, our status quo will be challenged. Yet in 2009, Lord Stern, former chief economist of the World Bank, estimated that a green plan to save the future – one that addressed both the financial and environmental crises – might cost as little as just 0.8 percent of world GDP, or $400 billion. That's less than a single year's revenue for all the dollar stores, chain discounters, and global bargaineers combined.

Like the unseen effects of ocean currents and pack ice on global climate, there is a hidden world inside our economies and global systems of interdependence that is surprisingly forgiving and open. Many obstacles to change are either cognitive or cultural, and the problems are not always as concrete as one might think. Sometimes things happen just because of deep inertia, not because change isn't possible. We are habituated to patterns: grocery shopping, foraging for deals, aspiring to better gadgets. There is nothing to suggest that we can't change this in favour of competitive conservation or extreme local commerce. Like energy efficiency, it's hard to imagine why we haven't done it sooner.

Many people are forsaking malls and searching for value within their own communities. New kinds of co-ops, buying clubs, and barter economies are seen not merely as lifestyle choices, as proffered by "simplicity" gurus and glossy magazines, but as real-time alternatives to the challenges of twenty-first-century living. Millions are now experimenting with commerce by different means, often without credit cards, money, or retail outlets. Indeed, relief from the global economy is already available at the local level: an economic underground – a constellation of local currencies and community economic development initiatives – that presents a series of immediate alternatives, sometimes as a direct challenge to the growing clout of big-box retailers. As America's Institute for Local Self-Reliance has long argued, there are clear payoffs and gains to be achieved through local commerce. One 2007 study in San Francisco found that local bookstores create nearly double the economic activity in the area, and local toy stores create 2.2 jobs per $1 million in sales, versus 1.3 jobs created by toy chains.

Specifically, several policy fronts offer new opportunity and require innovation. First, our world is rife with subsidy, not just obvious subsidy such as public investment in logistics and transport infrastructure or tax breaks for unconventional crude development, but broader freebies such as cheap water, carbon, and clean air. The global interest in carbon taxes is one sign of the future – and preferably flat taxes implemented alongside cap-and-trade systems, because emissions credit systems have been vulnerable to cheating and manipulation. On a smaller scale, charging for things like plastic bags has been enormously successful: in 2009 British retailer Marks & Spencer reported an 80 percent reduction in plastic bag usage in a single year after implementing a small fee for single-use bags.

Second, government can and should set outcomes. Policy leadership is paramount in the twenty-first century, and there should be no further hesitation in forming policy objectives on everything from financial regulation to energy efficiency. Deregulation and market-set policy have clearly failed within multiple sectors; laxity in regulation on auto fuel efficiency standards has long created needless health, environmental, and economic damage. The extravagant stimulus spending of the late 2000s, however, is not a long-term option for Western debtor nations like the United States, and governments will have to conserve spending resources. Yet targeted consumer incentives for future essentials such as renewable energy – and not dubious alternative fuels like ethanol – are clearly needed on a broader scale.

Third, trade should no longer be decoupled from public safety, human rights, the environment, and national policy. Market-based engagement on rights in China – the argument that commerce leads to democracy and rule of law – has been overwhelmingly disproven. Did Western trading nations willfully neglect Tibet, Xinjiang, and other sites of human rights abuses just to keep bargains flowing across the ocean? It's hard to conclude otherwise. By contrast, when American leaders and NGOs promoted low-carbon fuel standards – and likely penalization of high-carbon "dirty" oil imports such as from Canada's tar sands – the impact was immediate, and it forced new progress on Canada's lagging environmental policy.

Fourth, income security will be a greater challenge in a deglobalized world. With homelessness peaking even before the crash of 2008, and globalized trade failing to enrich many developing nations, there is much to be done on making local economies and households more resilient. The World Bank estimated in 2009 that weaker economic growth could push as many as 46 million people into poverty. For many, education, health, and housing became more expensive as electronics and furniture became cheaper. We need to somehow reverse this trend. Localized solutions that have succeeded in developing countries, such as micro-lending and financial literacy training, have growing relevance and application in the developed world.

And finally, we may be forced to save globalization from itself. We need continued growth of global civil society, with NGOs, advocacy groups, and diplomatic efforts working with developing nations and emerging economic powers, as well as continued international cooperation on climate change, reform of trade and currency systems, undocumented migrants, and shipping emissions. America's dwindling superpower status will provide new opportunities but will also leave a vacuum in influence and leadership that must not default to opportunistic and anti-democratic interests.

Until we price in the true cost of things, we're faced with an economic tautology: bargaineering creates the need for further bargains. People may decry the local Wal-Mart and even deny the developing world the chance to enjoy the same pleasures, but they'll still buy cheap stuff. Consumerism has become, one way or another, one massive conflict of interest.

Those who experienced the "jobless recovery" of the 1990s may one day live to see the growthless economy. Nations built upon spending, shopping, and shipping will eventually consume – and potentially destroy – more than they contribute. Our revolution in affordable consumerism created prosperity, but also low wages, urban blight, environmental damage, labour abuses, and a cookie-cutter model of progress. Add climate change, financial collapse, and competition for global resources, and the modern bargain economy embodies many of the greatest challenges of the new millennium. Despite innovations and gains, ours is the generation during which the plentiful will become scarce – and cheap stuff will prove to be truly expensive. But setting the price of a bargain is still up to us.

SOURCES

As a reporter, one learns that the best and most revealing material is usually found through primary interviews – one-on-one investigations and discussions, ideally in the field. Within the bounds of time and budget, I attempted to carry out as much reporting as possible to ensure that key interviews from various locations were mostly my own. Over the course of ten years, and mostly since 2005, primary fieldwork and reporting were completed in Las Vegas, Tucson, Colma, Hong Kong, Shenzhen, Changsha, Beijing, Shanghai, Los Angeles, Calgary, Fort McMurray, Joffre, Xinjiang, Nogales, Vancouver, Lhasa, Inuvik, and Resolute Bay. Thanks to all who took the time to meet with me and share their knowledge.

In a few instances, such as the 2008 Black Friday shopping fatality at Long Island's Green Acres Mall and the early 2000s unionization campaign in Las Vegas, scene reporting was compiled from secondary sources and cross-referenced with select after-the-fact interviews with participants.

Behind the primary interviews and fieldwork lies a small mountain of secondary materials. This book builds upon the work of others, from journalists who documented the rise of global discounting during the 1990s to scholars who have plumbed the mysteries of rural China, Schumpeterian theory, petrochemicals, and the post-2008 financial crisis. Listed below are the books, reports, and magazine and newspaper stories that provided figures, context, and quotations. Apologies to anyone not duly credited for their work.

Introduction: Black Friday, 2008
Alpert, Lukas I., Carolyn Salazar, and Christina Carrega. "Victim's Life a Struggle." *New York Post,* November 29, 2008. http://www.nypost.com/seven/11292008/news/regionalnews/victims_life_a_struggle_141388.htm.

Associated Press. "Personal Savings Drop to a 73-Year Low." MSNBC, February 1, 2007. http://www.msnbc.msn.com/id/16922582/.

Burritt, Chris. "Wal-Mart Profit Beats Estimates as Shoppers Are Lured by Discounts." *Washington Post,* February 18, 2009. http://www.washingtonpost.com/wp-dyn/content/article/2009/02/17/AR2009021703165.html.

Crowley, Kieran. "Worker Killed in Wal-Mart Stampede." *New York Post,* November 28, 2008. http://www.nypost.com/seven/11282008/news/regionalnews/man_killed_woman_miscarries_in_wal_mart_141313.htm.

Dokoupil, Tony. "Is the Mall Dead?" *Newsweek,* November 12, 2008. http://www.newsweek.com/id/168753.

Hayasaki, Erika. "A Very Dark Black Friday." *Los Angeles Times,* December 6, 2008. http://articles.latimes.com/2008/dec/06/nation/na-trample6.

Hughes, C. J. "Foreclosures on Island Outpace Most of State." *New York Times,* February 13, 2009. http://www.nytimes.com/2009/02/15/nyregion/long-island/15forecloseli.html.

International Council of Shopping Centers. "U.S. Retailers See Encouraging Black Friday Numbers." *Shopping Centers Today,* December 2, 2008. http://www.icsc.org/srch/apps/newsdsp.php?storyid=2469&region=main.

Kamer, Pearl M. "Moving a Moving Long Island Economy." *Newsday,* January 4, 2009. http://www.newsday.com/news/opinion/ny-opfocus5985846jan04,0,4503627.story.

Misonzhnik, Elaine. "Store Closings Could Double in 2009." *Retail Traffic,* November 5, 2008. http://retailtrafficmag.com/news/retail_store_closings_2009/.

Organisation for Economic Co-operation and Development (OECD). "The Service Economy." Science Technology Industry (STI) Business and Industry Policy Forum Series. Paris: OECD, 2000. http://www.oecd.org/dataoecd/10/33/2090561.pdf.

Palmer, Kimberly. "The End of Credit Card Consumerism." *U.S. News & World Report,* August 8, 2008. http://www.usnews.com/articles/business/economy/2008/08/08/the-end-of-credit-card-consumerism.html.

Rosenbloom, Stephanie. "All Eyes on Holiday Shopping Turnout in Bleak Economy." *New York Times,* November 28, 2008. http://www.nytimes.com/2008/11/29/business/29black.html?_r=1.

Winzelberg, David. "Foreclosures Up on Long Island." *Spaced Out,* February 18, 2009. http://libn.com/spacedout/2009/02/18/foreclosures-up-on-long-island/.

Wölfl, Anita. "The Service Economy in OECD Countries." STI Working Paper 2005/3: Statistical Analysis of Science, Technology and Industry. Paris: Organisation for Economic Co-Operation and Development, 2005. http://www.olis.oecd.org/olis/2005doc.nsf/LinkTo/NT00000B62/$FILE/JT00178454.PDF.

World Trade Organization. "WTO: Developing, Transition Economies Cushion Trade Slowdown." Chart 3: Real Merchandise Trade Growth by Region, 2007. Press release, April 17, 2008. http://www.wto.org/english/news_e/pres08_e/pr520_e.htm#chart3.

Chapter 1: The Bargaineers
ABC News. "Greenspan to Stephanopoulos: This Is 'By Far' the Worst Economic Crisis He's Seen in His Career." Political Radar blog, September 14, 2008. http://blogs.abcnews.com/politicalradar/2008/09/greenspan-to-st.html.

SOURCES

Andersen, Kurt. "American Roulette." *New York Magazine,* January 1, 2007.
http://nymag.com/news/imperialcity/26014/.

Archibold, Randal C. "Las Vegas Makes It Illegal to Feed Homeless in Parks." *New York Times,* July 28, 2006. http://www.nytimes.com/2006/07/28/us/28homeless.html?partner=rssnyt&emc=rss.

Associated Free Press. "Merrill Bonuses Made 696 Millionaires: Probe." Google News, February 11, 2009. http://www.google.com/hostednews/afp/article/ALeqM5gsvuGTjGstoLsG9sl2Xl25mGS_0w.

Bai, Matt. "The New Boss." *New York Times Magazine,* January 30, 2005.
www.nytimes.com/2005/01/30/magazine/30STERN.html.

Bell, Daniel. *The Coming of Post-Industrial Society.* New York: Basic Books, 1976.

Beltrame, Julian. "Canadian Manufacturers Urged to Adapt to New Strong Dollar Reality, or Risk Dying." Sympatico MSN Finance, September 17, 2007. http://finance.sympatico.msn.ca/investing/news/businessnews/article.aspx?cp-documentid=5444721.

Bianco, Anthony. *Wal-Mart: Bully of Bentonville.* New York: Doubleday, 2006.

Bianco, Anthony, and Wendy Zellner. "Is Wal-Mart Too Powerful?" *BusinessWeek,* October 6, 2003. www.businessweek.com/magazine/content/03_40/b3852001_mz001.htm

Blodget, Henry. "Amazon Peak-Day Unit Orders Up Encouraging 17% Year-over-Year." *Business Insider,* December 26, 2008. http://www.businessinsider.com/2008/12/amazon-peak-day-unit-orders-up-an-encouraging-17-year-over-year-amzn.

Connolly, Ceci. "At Wal-Mart, a Health-Care Turnaround." *Washington Post,* February 13, 2009. http://www.washingtonpost.com/wp-dyn/content/story/2009/02/13/ST2009021300507.html.

Cooper, Marc. *The Last Honest Place in America.* New York: Nation Books, 2004.

Cutler, Jonathan, and Thaddeus Russell. "Workers of the World . . . Disunite!" *Christian Science Monitor,* July 6, 2005. http://www.csmonitor.com/2005/0706/p09s02-coop.html.

Dicker, John. "Union Blues at Wal-Mart," *The Nation,* June 20, 2002.
www.thenation.com/doc/20020708/dicker.

eBay Inc. "New Study Reveals 724,000 Americans Rely on eBay Sales for Income." Press release, July 21, 2005. http://investor.ebay.com/releasedetail.cfm?ReleaseID=170073.

Featherstone, Liza. "Andy Stern: Savior or Sellout?" *The Nation,* June 27, 2007.
http://www.thenation.com/doc/20070716/featherstone.

Flowers, Lana F. "Consumers Turn to Private Labels in Down Economy." *The Morning News: Local News for Northwest Arkansas,* February 20, 2009.
http://www.nwaonline.net/articles/2009/02/20/business/022209bizwmtprivate.txt.

Friess, Steve. "Las Vegas Sags as Conventions Cancel." *New York Times,* February 14, 2009. http://www.nytimes.com/2009/02/15/us/15vegas.html.

Gogoi, Pallavi. "Wal-Mart's China Card." *BusinessWeek,* July 26, 2005. www.businessweek.com/bwdaily/dnflash/jul2005/nf20050726_3613_db016.htm.

Greenhouse, Steven. "Trying to Overcome Embarrassment, Labor Opens a Drive to Organize Wal-Mart." *New York Times,* November 8, 2002. http://www .nytimes.com/2002/11/08/us/trying-to-overcome-embarrassment-labor-opens-a-drive-to-organize-wal-mart.html?sec=&spon=&pagewanted =all.

Gullo, Karen, and Margaret Cronin Fisk. "Wal-Mart Wins Request in Bias Case." *Washington Post,* February 14, 2009. http://www.washingtonpost.com/ wp-dyn/content/article/2009/02/14/AR2009021400071.html.

Hoopes, James. "Growth Through Knowledge." In *Wal-Mart: The Face of 21st Century Capitalism,* edited by Nelson Lichtenstein. New York: New Press, 2006.

Human Rights in China. "The All-China Federation of Trade Unions (ACFTU)." Human Rights in China, October 25, 2004. http://www.hrichina.org/public/ contents/article?revision%5fid=18142&item%5fid=18141.

International Council of Shopping Centers. "U.K. Communities Need Retail Development to Boost Economy, Report Says." *Shopping Centers Today,* January 16, 2009. http://www.icsc.org/srch/apps/newsdsp.php?storyid=2476 &region=main.

Kole Imports, Inc. "The Greatest Business?" *Dollar Store Newsletter,* 2005. http://www.koleimports.com/Newsletter/DollarStoreNews1.htm.

Krafft, Manfred, and Murali Mantrala, eds. *Retailing in the 21st Century: Current and Future Trends.* Berlin: Springer, 2006.

Leamy, Elisabeth, and Vanessa Weber. "Manufacturers Shrink Products, but Not Price." *ABC News,* March 24, 2008. http://www.abcnews.go.com/GMA/ story?id=4512700&page=1.

Lee, Christina. "Hot Topic: The Dollar Store's Rising Value." goWholesale, February 11, 2009. http://www.gowholesale.com/content/2009/02/11/hot-topic-the-dollar-stores-rising-value/.

Levisohn, Ben. "Las Vegas Suffers a Recession Hangover." *BusinessWeek,* March 4, 2009. http://www.businessweek.com/bwdaily/dnflash/content/mar2009/ db2009034_117651.htm.

Levy, Daniel, and Andrew T. Young. "'The Real Thing': Nominal Price Rigidity of the Nickel Coke, 1886–1959." *Journal of Money, Credit and Banking* 36, no. 4 (August 2004). http://129.3.20.41/eps/mac/papers/0402/0402013.pdf.

Meyerson, Harold. "Wal-Mart Loves Unions (in China)." *Washington Post,* December 1, 2004. http://www.washingtonpost.com/wp-dyn/articles/A23725-2004Nov30.html.

Parloff, Roger. "The War over Unconscious Bias." *Fortune,* October 1, 2007. http://money.cnn.com/magazines/fortune/fortune_archive/2007/10/15/100537 276/index.htm.

Petrovic, Misha, and Gary Hamilton. "Making Global Markets: Wal-Mart and Its Suppliers." In *Wal-Mart: The Face of 21st Century Capitalism,* edited by Nelson Lichtenstein. New York: New Press, 2006.

Pier, Carol. "Freedom of Association at Wal-Mart: Anti-union Tactics Running Afoul of US Law." *Human Rights Watch* 19, no. 2 (May 2007). http://www.hrw.org/reports/2007/us0507/9.htm.

Plunkett-Powell, Karen. *Remembering Woolworth's.* New York: St. Martin's Press, 1999.

Public Broadcasting Service (PBS). *NOW with Bill Moyers,* December 19, 2003. Transcript. http://www.pbs.org/now/transcript/transcript247_full.html.

Rosenberg, Arthur. "A Look into the Future of Dollar Store Retailing." *Chain Store Guide,* August 2007. www.csgis.com.

Spethmann, Betsy. "Tuning in at the Shelf." *Promo,* April 1, 2005. http://promo-magazine.com/retail/marketing_tuning_shelf/.

U.S. Bureau of Labor Statistics. "Employment Situation Summary." News release, March 6, 2009. http://www.bls.gov/news.release/empsit.nr0.htm.

Vance, Sandra, and Roy Scott. *Wal-Mart: A History of Sam Walton's Retail Phenomenon.* New York: Twayne Publishers, 1997.

Willis, Ellen. "Escape from Freedom: What's The Matter with Tom Frank (and the Lefties Who Love Him)?" Arthur L. Carter Journalism Institute, New York University. http://journalism.nyu.edu/faculty/files/willis-tomfrank.pdf.

Woellert, Lorraine, and Dawn Kopecki. "Moody's, S&P Employees Doubted Ratings, E-Mails Say." Bloomberg.com, October 22, 2008. http://www.bloomberg.com/apps/news?pid=20601087&sid=a2EMlP5s7iMo&refer=worldwide.

Working Life. "Showdown in Vegas: Is It Over?" Blog, March 1, 2005. http://workinglife.typepad.com/daily_blog/2005/03/showdown_in_veg_2.html.

Yee, Amy. "Las Vegas Bets Its Chips on Intimacy." MSNBC, May 2, 2005. http://www.msnbc.msn.com/id/7712207/.

Zeitz, Joshua. "Why Woolworth Had to Die." *American Heritage,* July 17, 2007. http://www.americanheritage.com/events/articles/web/20070717-woolworth-business-retail-five-and-ten-urbanization-suburbanization-walmart.shtml.

Chapter 2: Quantum Cheap

Andersen, Michael, and Flemming Poulfelt. *Discount Business Strategy.* Hoboken, NJ: Wiley, 2006.

Associated Press. "Profit at Mattel Is Reduced by Half." *New York Times,* February 3, 2009. http://www.nytimes.com/2009/02/03/business/03toy.html.

Atkeson, Andrew, and Patrick J. Kehoe. "Modeling the Transition to a New Economy: Lessons from Two Technological Revolutions." Federal Reserve Bank of Minneapolis Research Department Staff Report 296 (May 2006). http://www.minneapolisfed.org/research/SR/SR296.pdf.

Barbaro, Michael. "Big Retailers Scaling Back Expansion Plans and Shutting
Stores." *New York Times,* May 2, 2008. http://www.nytimes.com/2008/05/02/
business/02shop.html?_r=1&oref=slogin&ref=business&pagewanted=print.
———. "Retailing Chains Caught in a Wave of Bankruptcies." *New York Times,*
April 15, 2008. http://www.nytimes.com/2008/04/15/business/15retail.html
?_r=2&ei=5088&en=7937f306da360689&ex=1365998400&oref=slogin
&partner=rssnyt&emc=rss&pagewanted=print&oref=slogin.

Bianco, Anthony. *Wal-Mart: Bully of Bentonville.* New York: Doubleday, 2006.

Broda, Christian, and David E. Weinstein. "Product Creation and Destruction:
Evidence and Price Implications." University of Chicago Booth School of
Business, April 2007. http://faculty.chicagobooth.edu/christian.broda/
website/research/unrestricted/BrodaWeinstein_CreativeDestruction.pdf.

Chen, Shaohua, and Martin Ravallion. "The Developing World Is Poorer Than
We Thought, But No Less Successful in the Fight Against Poverty." World
Bank Policy Research Working Paper 4703 (August 2008).
http://www-wds.worldbank.org/servlet/WDSContentServer/WDSP/IB/
2008/08/26/000158349_20080826113239/Rendered/PDF/WPS4703.pdf.

Connolly, Ceci. "At Wal-Mart, a Health-Care Turnaround." *Washington Post,*
February 13, 2009. http://www.washingtonpost.com/wp-dyn/content/
story/2009/02/13/ST2009021300507.html.

"Consumers Choosing to Tough It Out with Wal-Mart." RetailWire, February 22,
2008. http://www.retailwire.com/Discussions/Sngl_Discussion.cfm/12773.

de Vries, Lloyd. "Wal-Mart Starts Holiday Toys Price War." *CBS News,* October 19,
2006. http://www.cbsnews.com/stories/2006/10/19/business/main2104968
.shtml.

D'Innocenzio, Anne, and Mae Anderson. "Store Closings May Send Customers
to Survivors." Yahoo! Canada Finance, March 3, 2003. http://ca.us.biz.yahoo
.com/ap/090303/dead_market_share.html?.v=2.

Engardio, Pete. "Can the U.S. Bring Jobs Back from China?" *BusinessWeek,* June
19, 2008. http://www.businessweek.com/print/magazine/content/08_26/
b4090038429655.htm.

Fishman, Charles. *The Wal-Mart Effect.* New York: Penguin, 2007.

Flowers, Lana F. "Wal-Mart Completes Headquarters Layoffs." *The Morning
News: Local News for Northwest Arkansas,* February 20, 2009.
http://www.nwaonline.net/articles/2009/02/21/business/
022109bizwmtlayoffs.txt.

Gagosian, Robert B. "Abrupt Climate Change: Should We Be Worried?" Woods
Hole Oceanographic Institution, January 27, 2003. http://www.whoi.edu/
page.do?pid=12455&tid=282&cid=9986.

Gogoi, Pallavi. "Wal-Mart's New Growth Opportunities." *BusinessWeek,* October
9, 2007. http://www.businessweek.com/bwdaily/dnflash/content/oct2007/
db2007108_116420.htm.

Goodman, Peter S., and Jack Healy. "Job Losses Hint at Vast Remaking of Economy." *New York Times*, March 7, 2009. http://www.nytimes.com/2009/03/07/business/economy/07jobs.html?_r=1&partner=rss&emc=rss.

Gunnison, Liz. "Macy's Magic Act." *Portfolio*, May 14, 2008. http://www.portfolio.com/news-markets/top-5/2008/05/14/Macys-Solid-Results.

Hansen, James, Makiko Sato, Pushker Kharecha, Gary Russell, David W. Lea, and Mark Siddall. "Climate Change and Trace Gases." *Philosophical Transactions of the Royal Society A* 365 (2007), 1925–54. http://pubs.giss.nasa.gov/docs/2007/2007_Hansen_etal_2.pdf (May 18, 2007).

"Heavy Discounting Hits Sears Profit, Raising Doubts about Revival Effort." *Wall Street Journal*, February 27, 2009. http://online.wsj.com/article/SB123564718748081221.html?mod=todays_us_marketplace.

"Home Depot Sales and Profit Fall in 2007." *Atlanta Business Chronicle*, February 26, 2008. http://www.bizjournals.com/atlanta/stories/2008/02/25/daily8.html?ana=from_rss.

Homer-Dixon, Thomas. *The Upside of Down*. Toronto: Random House, 2006.

Hoopes, James. "Growth Through Knowledge." In *Wal-Mart: The Face of 21st Century Capitalism*, edited by Nelson Lichtenstein. New York: New Press, 2006.

Hunter, Mark. "Emerging Retail Trend: Wal-Mart, the Blue Retailer," Emerging Trends at Retail blog, December 4, 2006. http://emergingtrendsatretail.blogspot.com/2006/12/emerging-retail-trend-wal-mart-blue.html.

Norman, Al. "Hey, We Cut Wal-Mart in Half!" *Huffington Post*, October 25, 2007. http://www.huffingtonpost.com/al-norman/hey-we-cut-walmart-in-h_b_69834.html.

Rosenbloom, Stephanie. "Retail Sales Slide Further, Except at Wal-Mart." *New York Times*, March 6, 2009. http://www.nytimes.com/2009/03/06/business/economy/06retail.html.

———. "Wal-Mart Outpaces a Weak Economy." *New York Times*, February 18, 2009. www.nytimes.com/2009/02/18/business/18shop.html?partner=rss&emc=rss&pagewanted=print.

Schumpeter, Joseph A. *Capitalism, Socialism and Democracy*. New York: Routledge, 1976.

Spector, Robert. *Category Killers: The Retail Revolution and Its Impact on Consumer Culture*. Boston: Harvard Business School Press, 2005.

Stelter, Brian. "Pressed by the Economy, Starbucks Lowers Its Forecast." *New York Times*, April 24, 2008. http://www.nytimes.com/2008/04/24/business/24sbux.html?scp=3&sq=starbucks&st=nyt.

Stempel, Jonathan. "One in Five U.S. Homeowners with Mortgages in Negative Equity." Yahoo! UK & Ireland Finance, October 31, 2008. http://uk.biz.yahoo.com/31102008/325/five-u-s-homeowners-mortgages-negative-equity.html.

Strasser, Susan. "Woolworth's to Wal-Mart." In *Wal-Mart: The Face of 21st Century Capitalism,* edited by Nelson Lichtenstein. New York: New Press, 2006.

Stribling, Dees. "Onward and Upward: Research Reveals Surprising Stats about the U.S. Shopping Center Industry." *Shopping Centers Today,* October 2007. http://www.icsc.org/srch/sct/sct1007/onward_upward.php.

Tubridy, Michael. "Defining Trends in Shopping Center History." International Council of Shopping Centers, May 2006. www.icsc.org/srch/about/impactofshoppingcenters/12_DefiningTrends.pdf

Watts, Robert, and Jonathan Oliver. "Britain Faces Crisis as Negative Equity to Reach 2 Million." *Sunday Times,* October 19, 2008. http://www.timesonline.co.uk/tol/money/property_and_mortgages/article4969314.ece.

Chapter 3: China Crisis

Amnesty International. "People's Republic of China – Internal Migrants: Discrimination and Abuse – The Human Cost of an Economic 'Miracle.'" Amnesty International, March 2007. http://www.amnesty.org/en/library/asset/ASA17/008/2007/en/dom-ASA170082007en.pdf.

Arrington, Michael. "Foxconn Building 800,000 iPhones a Week." TechCrunch, August 4, 2008. http://www.techcrunch.com/2008/08/04/foxconn-building-800000-iphones-a-week/.

Associated Free Press. "Wal-Mart Signs Pay Deals with Official Chinese Unions." Yahoo! Asia News, July 25, 2008. http://asia.news.yahoo.com/080725/afp/080725133252business.html.

Barboza, David. "Child Labor Cases Uncovered in China." *International Herald Tribune,* April 30, 2008. http://www.iht.com/articles/2008/04/30/asia/01china.php.

———. "China Says Abusive Child Labor Ring Is Exposed." *New York Times,* May 1, 2008. http://www.nytimes.com/2008/05/01/world/asia/01china.html.

———. "China Tells Businesses to Unionize." *New York Times,* September 12, 2008. http://www.nytimes.com/2008/09/12/business/worldbusiness/12yuan.html.

———. "Once Sizzling, China's Economy Shows Rapid Signs of Fizzling." *New York Times,* November 7, 2008. http://www.nytimes.com/2008/11/07/business/worldbusiness/07yuan.html.

Bradsher, Keith. "Exports Down Sharply for 2nd Month in China." *New York Times,* March 12, 2009. http://www.nytimes.com/2009/03/12/business/worldbusiness/12yuan.html?_r=1&partner=rss&emc=rss.

Buckley, Chris. "Update 1: Wal-Mart Sees China Productivity Beating Inflation." Reuters, February 25, 2008. http://www.reuters.com/article/rbssConsumerGoodsAndRetailNews/idUSPEK6745120080225?sp=true.

Cao, Belinda, and Judy Chen. "China Needs U.S. Guarantees for Treasuries, Yu Says." Bloomberg.com, February 11, 2009. http://www.bloomberg.com/apps/news?pid=20601080&sid=aG_eSDsmh7rw&refer=asia.

Castle, Stephen, and Keith Bradsher. "China's Shift on Food Was Key to Trade Impasse." New York Times, July 31, 2008. http://www.nytimes.com/2008/07/31/business/worldbusiness/31trade.html.

Castle, Stephen, and Mark Landler. "After 7 Years, Talks Collapse on World Trade." New York Times, July 30, 2008. http://www.nytimes.com/2008/07/30/business/worldbusiness/30trade.html.

Chan, John. "Rising Costs Throw Chinese Manufacturing into Crisis." World Socialist Web Site, March 17, 2008. http://www.wsws.org/articles/2008/mar2008/chin-m17.shtml.

Chen, Shaohua, and Martin Ravallion. "The Developing World Is Poorer Than We Thought, But No Less Successful in the Fight against Poverty." World Bank Policy Research Working Paper 4703 (August 2008). http://www-wds.worldbank.org/servlet/WDSContentServer/WDSP/IB/2008/08/26/000158349_20080826113239/Rendered/PDF/WPS4703.pdf.

"China Rushes Upmarket." BusinessWeek, September 17, 2007. http://www.businessweek.com/magazine/content/07_38/b4050055.htm?chan=search.

"China Strives to Narrow Urban-Rural Income Gap." ChinaDaily.com, October 14, 2007. http://www.chinadaily.com.cn/china/2007-10/14/content_6172555.htm.

Dai Xiangde and Wu Jinyong. "'Labour's Breakthrough at Wal-Mart." Business Watch Magazine, September 4, 2006. http://www.clntranslations.org/file_download/3.

Dean, Jason. "The Forbidden City of Terry Gou." Wall Street Journal, August 11, 2007. http://online.wsj.com/article/SB118677584137994489.html?mod=home_we_banner_left.

Ding Qingfen. "Moving Inland." ChinaDaily.com, February 25, 2008. http://www.chinadaily.com.cn/bw/2008 02/25/content_6480234.htm.

Engardio, Pete. "Can the U.S. Bring Jobs Back from China?" BusinessWeek, June 19, 2008. http://www.businessweek.com/print/magazine/content/08_26/b4090038429655.htm.

Fallows, James. "China Makes, the World Takes." Atlantic Monthly, July 2007. www.theatlantic.com/doc/200707/shenzhen
———. "The $1.4 Trillion Question." The Atlantic, January/February 2008. http://www.theatlantic.com/doc/200801/fallows-chinese-dollars.

Fu He. "Who Did Dagongzhe Offend?" Southern Metropolitan Daily, November 28, 2007. www.clntranslations.org/article/26/shenzhen-labor-activist-attacked.

Gan Lihua. "A Tough Context: Establishing the First KFC Trade Union Branch." China Youth Daily, July 15, 2007. http://www.clntranslations.org/file_download/17.

Gittings, John. "China's City of Dreams – and Extremes." *The Guardian,* May 5, 1999. www.guardian.co.uk/world/1999/may/05/johngittings1.

Gluckman, Ron. "Han Dong Fan: The Man Who Beat Beijing." *Asiaweek,* July 1997. http://www.gluckman.com/HanDongFang.html.

Goddard Space Flight Center. "Satellite Measures Pollution from East Asia to North America." PhysOrg, March 17, 2008. http://www.physorg.com/news124991552.html.

Goldstein, Carl. "Wal-Mart in China." *The Nation,* November 20, 2003. http://www.thenation.com/doc/20031208/goldstein.

Goodman, Peter S., and Philip P. Pan. "Chinese Workers Pay for Wal-Mart's Low Prices." *Washington Post,* February 8, 2004. http://www.washingtonpost.com/ac2/wp-dyn/A22507-2004Feb7?language=printer.

"Guangdong Cracks Down on Child Labor in Factories." ChinaDaily.com, May 3, 2008. http://www.chinadaily.com.cn/china/2008-05/03/content_6658027.htm.

Haddock, Ronald, and Paul Ngai. "China Sourcing: Balancing Global and Local Requirements." Booz Allen Hamilton, n.d. http://www.boozallen.com/media/file/150753.pdf.

"Half of China's Migrant Workers Unhappy with Social Status." ChinaDaily.com, January 13, 2008. http://www.chinadaily.com.cn/china/2008-01/13/content_6389912.htm.

Han Dongfang. "The Prospects for Legal Enforcement of Labor Rights in China Today: A Glass Half Full." *China Labour Bulletin,* May 1, 2008. www.clb.org.hk/en/files/File/HDF%20testimony%20for%20CECC%20hearing%20June%202008(1).pdf.

———. "A Turning Point for China's Trade Unions." *China Labour Bulletin,* August 20, 2008. www.clb.org.hk/en/node/100293.

Harney, Alexandra. *The China Price: The True Cost of Chinese Competitive Advantage.* New York: Penguin Press, 2008.

———. "Migrants Are China's 'Factories Without Smoke.'" CNN.com, February 3, 2008. http://edition.cnn.com/2008/WORLD/asiapcf/02/01/china.migrants/index.html#cnnSTCText.

Hong, Chen. "Employers Boost Wages in Bid to Attract Workers." ChinaDaily.com, February 19, 2008. http://www.chinadaily.com.cn/china/2008-02/19/content_6464947.htm.

Keidel, Albert. "China Regional Disparities: The Causes and Impact of Regional Inequalities in Income and Well-Being." Carnegie Endowment for International Peace, December 2007. http://www.carnegieendowment.org/publications/index.cfm?fa=view&id=19685&prog=zch.

———. "The Limits of a Smaller, Poorer China." *Financial Times,* November 14, 2007. http://www.carnegieendowment.org/publications/index.cfm?fa=print&id=19709.

Kim, Juli S. "Transboundary Air Pollution: Will China Choke on Its Success?" Woodrow Wilson International Center for Scholars China Environment Forum, February 2, 2007. http://www.wilsoncenter.org/index.cfm ?topic_id=1421&fuseaction=topics.item&news_id=218780.

KPMG Huazhen. "Changsha Investment Environment Study 2007." KPMG China, n.d. http://www.kpmg.com.cn/en/virtual_library/ Financial_advisory_services/Changsha_investment07.pdf.

Larson, Christina. "China's Pollution Revolution." AlterNet, January 8, 2008. http://www.alternet.org/environment/72995/?page=entire.

Leslie, Jacques. "The Last Empire: China's Pollution Problem Goes Global." Mother Jones, December 10, 2007. http://www.motherjones.com/environment/ 2007/12/last-empire-chinas-pollution-problem-goes-global.

Li Qiang. "Hantai Shoe Production Ltd." China Labor Watch, July 15, 2008. www.chinalaborwatch.org/20080715Wal.htm.

———. "New Labor Law's Effect on Chinese Workers' Rights." Unpublished paper, 2008.

Matus, Kira J. "Health Impacts from Urban Air Pollution in China: The Burden to the Economy and the Benefits of Policy." Master's thesis, Massachusetts Institute of Technology, 2005. http://dspace.mit.edu/handle/1721.1/32282.

MemoTrek Technologies Ltd. "Flash Price: Chinese Factories under Pressure." USB Flash Drives blog, March 2, 2008. http://www.memotrek.com/blog/usb-flash-drives/nand-flash-prices-chinese-factories-under-pressure.html.

Mutikani, Lucia. "McCain's China-Free Debt Plan Seen Unrealistic." Reuters, October 3, 2008. http://www.reuters.com/article/vcCandidateFeed2/ idUSTRE49281F20081003?sp=true.

Mydans, Seth. "In Vietnam, Even Ghosts Feel Inflation's Pinch." International Herald Tribune, August 19, 2008. http://www.iht.com/articles/2008/08/19/ business/dong.php.

Navarro, Peter. "China Price Project." PeterNavarro.com, n.d. http://www.peternavarro.com/chinaprice.html.

"Newly Industrialized Cities Battle Pollution." People's Daily, January 14, 2006. http://english.peopledaily.com.cn/200601/14/eng20060114_235469.html.

News Guangdong. http://www.newsgd.com/.

Nobrega, William. "Why India Will Beat China." BusinessWeek, July 22, 2008. http://www.businessweek.com/globalbiz/content/jul2008/gb20080722_942925 .htm.

"Official Union Must Back New Migrant Worker Legislators." China Labour Bulletin, March 4, 2008. http://www.china-labour.org.hk/en/node/100215.

Plafker, Ted. "Stable Growth an Elusive Target for China." International Herald Tribune, May 4, 2008. http://www.iht.com/articles/2008/05/01/business/ rasiachin.php?page=1.

Public Broadcasting Service (PBS). "Is Wal-Mart Good for America?" *Frontline,* November 16, 2004. http://www.pbs.org/wgbh/pages/frontline/shows/walmart/.

Rights & Democracy and *China Labour Bulletin.* "No Way Out: Worker Activism in China's State-Owned Enterprise Reforms." Montreal and Hong Kong: International Centre for Human Rights and Democratic Development and *China Labour Bulletin,* 2008. http://www.clb.org.hk/en/files/File/research_reports/no_way_out.pdf.

Schuman, Michael. "The Birth and Rebirth of Shenzhen." *Time,* August 14, 2006. http://www.time.com/time/nation/article/0,8599,1226199,00.html.

Scott, Robert E. "The Wal-Mart Effect: Its Chinese Imports Have Displaced Nearly 200,000 U.S. Jobs." Economic Policy Institute, June 26, 2007. http://www.epi.org/issuebriefs/235/ib235.pdf.

"Shenzhen Labor Activist Attacked." China Labor News Translations, December 6, 2007. http://www.clntranslations.org/article/26/shenzhen-labor-activist-attacked#sidebar.

"Shenzhen Minimum Wage Reaches 1,000 Yuan per Month." *China Labour Bulletin,* June 5, 2008. http://www.clb.org.hk/en/node/100258.

Shen Zhen Port. http://www.sztb.gov.cn:8080/szport/eng/Info/index.htm.

"Trade Unions at Wal-Mart and Foxconn." China Labor News Translations, March 21, 2007. http://www.clntranslations.org/article/4/wal-mart.

"Trade Unions in China: Membership Required." *The Economist,* July 31, 2008. http://www.economist.com/business/displaystory.cfm?story_id=11848496&fsrc=RSS.

Troy, Mike. "In-sourcing the Role of the Middleman." *DSN Retailing Today,* December 13, 2004. http://findarticles.com/p/articles/mi_m0FNP/is_23_43/ai_n8577533.

U.S. Department of Commerce. "Transportation." Commercial Service China, n.d. http://www.buyusa.gov/china/en/transportation.html.

Wang, Shunqin, and Jinliang Zhang. "Review: Blood Lead Levels in Children, China." *Environmental Research* 101 (2006), 412–18. http://www.wilsoncenter.org/topics/docs/lead_table_1.pdf.

Wines, Michael. "China Outlines Ambitious Plan for Stimulus." *New York Times,* March 5, 2009. http://www.nytimes.com/2009/03/05/world/asia/05china.html.

Wines, Michael, Keith Bradsher, and Mark Landler. "China's Leader Says He Is 'Worried' over U.S. Treasuries." *New York Times,* March 14, 2009. http://www.nytimes.com/2009/03/14/world/asia/14china.html.

World Economic Forum. "The Big Debate: Setting the Business Agenda." World Economic Forum Annual Meeting, January 25, 2006. http://www.weforum.org/en/knowledge/KN_SESS_SUMM_15840?url=/en/knowledge/KN_SESS_SUMM_15840.

Xin Zhiming. "NBS: Consumer Spending a Big GDP Factor." ChinaDaily.com,

December 11, 2007. http://www.chinadaily.com.cn/bizchina/2007-12/11/
content_6312714.htm.

Yoon, Eunice. "China's Inflation Highest in 11 Years." CNN.com, February 19,
2008. http://www.cnn.com/2008/BUSINESS/02/19/china.inflation/
#cnnSTCText.

Young, Nick. "How Much Inequality Can China Stand?" China Development
Brief, February 2007. www.chinadevelopmentbrief.com/node/1001.

Zhen, Wen. "3000 Teachers' Protest in South China Suppressed." Status of
Chinese People, December 17, 2008. http://chinaview.wordpress.com/
category/china/south-china/hunan/.

Chapter 4: Container Trade

American Lung Association. "Pittsburgh and Los Angeles the Most Polluted US
Cities." City Mayors, May 4, 2008. http://www.citymayors.com/environment/
polluted_uscities.html.

Bonacich, Edna, and Juan David De Lara. "Economic Crisis and the Logistics
Industry: Financial Insecurity for Warehouse Workers in the Inland Empire."
Institute for Research on Labor and Employment Working Paper 13, February
18, 2009. http://repositories.cdlib.org/cgi/viewcontent.cgi?article=1014
&context=uclairle.

Brekke, Erika. "Cleaning the Ports of L.A." On Earth, August 28, 2008.
http://www.onearth.org/article/cleaning-the-ports-of-la.

Chu, Hanna. "Signal Hill: From Oil to Million-Dollar Views." *Press-Telegram*,
August 12, 2007. http://www.presstelegram.com/wwl/ci_6606520.

Court, Jamie, and Judy Dugan. "Big Oil Buys Sacramento." *Los Angeles Times*,
May 14, 2007. http://www.latimes.com/news/opinion/la-oe-
court14may14,0,991123.story.

Davis, Mike. *City of Quartz: Excavating the Future in Los Angeles.* New York:
Verso, 1990.

Dinopoulos, Elias, and Fuat Şener. "New Directions in Schumpeterian Growth
Theory." In *The Elgar Companion to Neo-Schumpeterian Economics,* edited by
Horst Hanusch and Andreas Pyka. Cheltenham: Edward Elgar, 2007.

"Economic Impact Study Finds Trade Moving Through Ports of Los Angeles,
Long Beach and the Alameda Corridor Significantly Impact California's
Economy." Business Wire, March 22, 2007. http://www.businesswire.com/
portal/site/google/?ndmViewId=news_view&newsId=20070322005938&news
Lang=en.

Erie, Steven. *Globalizing L.A.: Trade, Infrastructure and Regional Development.*
Stanford, CA: Stanford University Press, 2004.

Fitz, Dennis R. "Characterizing the Range of Children's Pollutant Exposure
During School Bus Commutes." Report prepared for the California Air

Resources Board, October 10, 2003. http://www.arb.ca.gov/research/
schoolbus/execsum.pdf.

Fortson, Danny. "Shipping Surge Prompts CO_2 Concerns." *BusinessWeek*,
December 11, 2007. http://www.businessweek.com/print/globalbiz/content/
dec2007/gb20071211_579202.htm.

Fung, Victor, and Joan Magretta. "Fast, Global and Entrepreneurial: An
Interview with Victor Fung." *Harvard Business Review*, September 1, 1998.

Fung, Victor, William Fung, and Yoram (Jerry) Wind. *Competing in a Flat World*.
Upper Saddle River, NJ: Wharton School Publishing, 2008.

Graham, Wade. "Dark Side of the New Economy." On Earth, March 1, 2007.
http://www.onearth.org/article/dark-side-of-the-new-economy.

Hanson, Kristopher. "Port Is an Engine for Growth." *Press-Telegram*, February 23,
2007. http://www.presstelegram.com/outlook/ci_5290731.

Howard, John. "Job Loss, Business Impacts Seen in Proposed Sales Tax Hike."
Capitol Weekly, August 5, 2008. http://capitolweekly.net/article.php
?issueId=xas7u1nejid2da&xid=xb9i5bec3g9fea.

Janofsky, Michael, and Samantha Zee. "Oil Exploration Companies Look to
Beverly Hills." *Seattle Times*, July 2, 2008. http://seattletimes.nwsource.com
/html/businesstechnology/2008028848_beverlyhillsoil02.html.

Johnson, Keith. "Big (Green) Box: Retailers Get the Energy-Efficiency Gospel."
Wall Street Journal Environmental Capital blog, June 23, 2008.
http://blogs.wsj.com/environmentalcapital/2008/06/23/big-green-box-retailers-
get-the-energy-efficiency-gospel/?mod=relevancy.

Levin, Dan. "China's Big Recycling Market Is Sagging." *New York Times*, March
12, 2009. http://www.nytimes.com/2009/03/12/business/worldbusiness/
12recycle.html.

Levinson, Marc. *The Box: How the Shipping Container Made the World Smaller
and the World Economy Bigger*. Princeton, NJ: Princeton University Press, 2006.

Lifsher, Marc. "Long Beach Aims to Boost Output from Wilmington Oil Field."
Los Angeles Times, September 9, 2008. http://www.latimes.com/business/la-fi-
lboil9-2008sep09,1,4418419.story.

Lin, Rong-gong, II. "County Offers 'Inland Port' Plan." *Los Angeles Times*, July 12,
2007. http://articles.latimes.com/2007/jul/12/local/me-inlandport12.

Long Beach Alliance for Children with Asthma. "Reenvisioning the Landscape of
Children's Health." PediatricAsthma.org, n.d. http://www.pediatricasthma
.org/community_coalitions/long_beach_ca.

Lustgarten, Jeff, Theresa Adams Lopez, and Art Wong. "Economic Impact Study
Finds Trade Moving Through Ports of Los Angeles, Long Beach and the
Alameda Corridor Significantly Impact California's Economy." Alameda
Corridor Transportation Authority, Port of Los Angeles, and Port of Long
Beach press release, March 22, 2007. http://www.acta.org/newsroom/
Releases/018_REL_ACTA-Port_California_Press_Release.pdf.

———. "Updated Economic Impact Study Shows That Ports of Los Angeles, Long Beach and Alameda Corridor Remain Vital to U.S. Economy and International Trade." Alameda Corridor Transportation Authority, Port of Los Angeles, and Port of Long Beach press release, March 22, 2007. www.acta .org/newsroom/Releases/019_ACTA-Port_National_Press_Release.pdf.

"Maersk Machine Grinds on Mercilessly." Port Strategy, September 3, 2008. http://www.portstrategy.com/archive101/2008/september/insight__and__ opinion/the_strategist.

Morello-Frosch, Rachel, Manuel Pastor Jr., Carlos Porras, and James Sadd. "Environmental Justice and Regional Inequality in Southern California: Implications for Future Research." Environmental Health Perspectives, April 2002. http://www.ehponline.org/members/2002/suppl-2/149-154morello-frosch/ morello-frosch-full.html.

Ocampo, Jose Antonio. "The Instability and Inequities of the Global Reserve System." United Nations Department of Economic and Social Affairs, November 2007. http://www.un.org/esa/desa/papers/2007/wp59_2007.pdf.

"'Oil!' and the History of Southern California." New York Times, February 22, 2008. http://www.nytimes.com/2008/02/22/timestopics/topics_uptonsinclair_oil.html.

Organisation for Economic Co-operation and Development. "Moving up the Value Chain: Staying Competitive in the Global Economy." Paris: OECD, 2007. http://www.oecd.org/dataoecd/24/35/38558080.pdf.

———. "Structure and Trends in International Trade in Services." Organisation for Economic Co-operation and Development, n.d. http://www.oecd.org/ documentprint/0,3455,en_2649_34243_2510108_1_1_1_1,00.html.

Pacific L.A. Marine Terminal LLC. "L.A. Basin Crude Oil Supply Outlook." Pacific L.A. Marine Terminal, 2008. http://www.pacificenergypier400.com/ index2.php?id=62.

Palaniappan, Meena, Swati Prakash, and Diane Bailey. "Paying with Our Health: The Real Cost of Freight Transport in California." Pacific Institute, November 2006. http://www.pacinst.org/reports/freight_transport/ PayingWithOurHealth_Web.pdf.

Paleontological Research Institution. "The Story of Oil in California." n.d. http://www.priweb.org/ed-/pgws/history/signal_hill/signal_hill2.html.

Port of Long Beach. "Facts at a Glance." Port of Long Beach, n.d. http://www.polb.com/about/facts.asp.

Raine, George. "Containerization Changed Shipping Industry Forever." San Francisco Chronicle, February 10, 2006. http://www.seattlepi.com/business/ 259042_containerships10.html.

Reynolds, Angela, and Greg Holmes. Correspondence regarding the Draft Environmental Impact Report for the Long Beach Sports Park Project from the California Department of Toxic Substances Control, February 14, 2005. http://www.longbeach.gov/civica/filebank/blobdload.asp?BlobID=9087.

Reynolds, Peggy, Julie Von Behren, Robert B. Gunier, Debbie E. Goldberg, Andrew Hertz, and Daniel F. Smith. "Childhood Cancer Incidence Rates and Hazardous Air Pollutants in California: An Exploratory Analysis." *Environmental Health Perspectives,* April 2003. http://www.ehponline.org/docs/2003/5986/abstract.html.

Rodrigues, Alexandre M., Donald J. Bowersox, and Roger J. Calantone. "Estimation of Global and National Logistics Expenditures: 2002 Data Update." Working paper, Michigan State University, 2005. https://www.msu.edu/~rodri205/CV/Documents/ISL2005%20Article.pdf.

Rohter, Larry. "Shipping Costs Start to Crimp Globalization." *New York Times,* August 3, 2008. http://www.nytimes.com/2008/08/03/business/worldbusiness/03global.html.

Russo, Frank D. "PBS Show Shines Light on Los Angeles and Long Beach Port Air Pollution and Its Devastating Health Effects." *California Progress Report,* October 21, 2006. http://www.californiaprogressreport.com/2006/10/pbs_show_shines.html.

Sahagun, Louis. "Environmental Groups Threaten to Sue Port of Long Beach over Air Pollution." *Los Angeles Times,* February 7, 2008. http://www.latimes.com/news/local/la-me-port7feb07,0,2821444.story.

———. "Long Beach OKs Fee on Cargo to Fund Green Efforts." *Los Angeles Times,* December 18, 2007. http://www.latimes.com/features/lifestyle/green/la-me-port18dec18,0,2835624.story.

———. "Wilmington Looks to a Greener Future." *Los Angeles Times,* March 2, 2009. http://www.latimes.com/news/local/la-me-wilmington3-2009mar03,0,7927648.story?track=rss.

Schulz, John D. "Logisticians 'Survive the Slump,' but Costs Hit 10.1 Percent of GDP." *Logistics Management,* June 19, 2008. http://www.logisticsmgmt.com/index.asp?layout=articlePrint&articleID=CA6571518&article_prefix=CA&article_id=6571518.

"Ships Draw Fire for Rising Role in Air Pollution." *Wall Street Journal,* November 27, 2007. http://online.wsj.com/article/SB119611182359704284.html.

"A Shipshape Ports Bill." *Los Angeles Times,* July 21, 2008. http://www.latimes.com/news/opinion/la-ed-ports21-2008jul21,0,5370497.story.

Signal Hill Petroleum, Inc. "Real Estate." Signal Hill Petroleum, n.d. http://www.shpi.net/realestate.htm.

Stiglitz, Joseph. *Making Globalization Work.* New York: W.W. Norton, 2007.

Thompson, Don. "California Unemployment Rate Jumps to 10.1 Percent." *Forbes,* February 27, 2009. http://www.forbes.com/feeds/ap/2009/02/27/ap6108682.html.

United Nations Conference on Trade and Development. "Productivity of the World Fleet and Supply and Demand in World Shipping." *Review of Maritime Transport,* 2006. http://www.unctad.org/en/docs/rmt2006_en.pdf.

U.S. Environmental Protection Agency. "Brownfields Assessment Pilot Fact Sheet." Environmental Protection Agency, April 4, 2008. http://www.epa.gov/brownfields/html-doc/asignalh.htm.

White, Ronald D. "High-and-Dry Areas Vie for 'Inland Ports.'" *Los Angeles Times*, May 8, 2005. http://articles.latimes.com/2005/may/08/business/fi-cargo8.

White, Ronald D., and Louis Sahagun. "2 Big Haulers Sign on to L.A. Port's Clean-Truck Plan." *Los Angeles Times*, August 22, 2008. http://articles.latimes.com/2008/aug/22/business/fi-ports22.

Wienberg, Christian, and Alaric Nightingale. "Maersk Profit Advances 40% on Oil; Shipper Buys Rival." Bloomberg.com, August 27, 2008. http://www.bloomberg.com/apps/news?pid=20601085&sid=apot_AgiKjSc&refer=europe.

World Trade Organization. "WTO: Developing, Transition Economies Cushion Trade Slowdown." World Trade Organization, April 17, 2008. http://www.wto.org/english/news_e/pres08_e/pr520_e.htm.

Wright, Robert. "Buoyant Maersk Refloats Profit." *Financial Times*, August 27, 2008. http://www.ft.com/cms/s/0/a163eb9a-743f-11dd-bc91-0000779fd18c,dwp_uuid=e8477cc4-c820-11db-b0dc-000b5df10621.html.

Young, Samantha. "New Rules Cut Ship Pollution." *Press-Telegram*, July 24, 2008. http://www.presstelegram.com/ports/ci_9991063.

Chapter 5: All Is Plastic

Adams, Gary. "Petrochemicals . . . Positioning Latin America in a Changing Global Market." Paper presented at the 27th Latin American Petrochemical Annual Meeting, Buenos Aires, Argentina, November 17–20, 2007. http://www.cmaiglobal.com/Marketing/News/APLA07_Adams_WebPDF.pdf.

Alberta Department of Energy. "Alberta's Oil Sands 2006." Alberta Department of Energy, December 2007. http://www.energy.gov.ab.ca/OilSands/pdfs/osgenbrf.pdf.

Anglo Coal Australia. *Our News* 4 (December 2007). http://www.anglocoal.com.au/wps/wcm/resources/file/eb45854383345be/Final%20Draft%20-%20December%202007%20Newsletter.pdf.

A to Z of Materials. "Shell Eyes Big Opportunities in China." A to Z of Materials and AZojomo, September 22, 2005. http://www.azom.com/News.asp?NewsID=4002.

Banholzer, William F. "Changes in the Energy Market and Their Impact on the Chemical Industry." Dow Chemical Company, May 2008. http://news.dow.com/dow_news/speeches/20080502_banholzer.pdf.

Bi Mingxin. "World Bank's Loans to China Total $1.5 Bln in 2008 Fiscal Year." *China View*, June 25, 2008. http://news.xinhuanet.com/english/2008-06/25/content_8436378.htm.

Blas, Javier, and Carola Hoyos. "IEA Predicts Oil Price to Rebound to $100." *Financial Times*, November 5, 2008. http://www.ft.com/cms/s/0/ca2b5254-ab6a-11dd-b9e1-000077b07658.html?nclick_check=1.

Bloomberg.com. "China Spending on Energy Output Jumps as Demand Gains." Shanghai Zoom Intelligence Co., Ltd., October 19, 2006. http://www.zoomchina.com.cn/new/content/view/16387/81/.

Boyle, Edward. "Scoring the Scorecard." Paper, Film & Foil Converter, September 1, 2007. http://pffc-online.com/mag/paper_scoring_scorecard/.

Calgary Herald. "Alberta Promises Study in Wake of Toxic Oilsands Leak." Canada.com, May 27, 2008. http://www.canada.com/topics/news/story.html ?id=e2a21fcb-453f-49b3-ad10-23e50a2d0160.

"Canada Slips on Oil's Slide." Wall Street Journal, February 19, 2009. http://online.wsj.com/article/SB123500580587718267.html?mod=googlenews_ wsj.

Canadian Broadcasting Corporation. "'Comprehensive' Review of Fort Chipewyan Cancer Rates Announced." CBC News, May 22, 2008. http://www.cbc.ca/canada/edmonton/story/2008/05/22/edm-fort-chip.html.

————. "Fort Chip Doctor Rails Against Government Inaction." CBC News, November 16, 2006. http://www.cbc.ca/canada/north/story/2006/11/15/doctor-disgust.html.

————. "Oilsands-Area Hamlet Supports Whistleblower MD." CBC News, March 5, 2007. http://www.cbc.ca/canada/story/2007/03/05/alberta-doctor-070305.html.

————. "Plant Closure Marks End of an Era in Devon, Alta." CBC News, August 1, 2006. http://www.cbc.ca/canada/edmonton/story/2006/08/01/leduc-end .html.

————. "Secret Advice to Politicians: Oilsands Emissions Hard to Scrub." CBC News, November 24, 2008. http://www.cbc.ca/canada/story/2008/11/24/sands-trap.html.

ChemEurope. "Dow Acrylates Announces Global Price Increase." ChemEurope, March 18, 2009. http://www.chemeurope.com/news/e/98477/.

Chin, Josh, and Zachary Slobig. "Xinjiang's Melting Glaciers." Chinadialogue, March 20, 2008. http://www.chinadialogue.net/article/show/single/en/1820-Xinjiang-s-melting-glaciers.

China Chemical Reporter. "Petrochemical Industry Faced with Challenges." China Institute, University of Alberta, September 16, 2006. http://www.uofaweb.ualberta.ca/chinainstitute/nav03.cfm?nav03=50494&nav 02=49950&nav01=43092.

Condon, Bernard. "Wizard of Ooze." Forbes, March 3, 2003. http://www.forbes .com/forbes/2003/0303/060.html.

De Souza, Mike. "Calgary Herald: Fines Rare for Oilsands Players." ForestEthics, July 2, 2008. http://www.forestethics.org/article.php?id=2181.

Dyer, Geoff. "EU Hits Out at China's Economic Nationalism." Financial Times, September 25, 2008. http://www.ft.com/cms/s/0/acf09624-8b2e-11dd-b634-0000779fd18c.html.

Dyer, Simon. "Ducks Just Tip of Toxic Tailings Iceberg." Oil Sands Watch, February 17, 2009. http://www.oilsandswatch.org/op-ed/1784.

———. "Oil Sands Industry Blocks New Wetland Protection Rules." Pembina Institute, September 16, 2008. http://www.pembina.org/media-release/1697.

Edmonton Journal. "Alberta Oilsands Man Killed by Giant Truck." Canada.com, July 9, 2008. http://www.canada.com/topics/news/national/story.html?id=be60742c-b5fe-4ea3-8a7e-e2bf39923895.

Engdahl, F. William. "Darfur: Forget Genocide, There's Oil." *Asia Times,* May 25, 2007. http://www.atimes.com/atimes/China_Business/IE25Cb04.html.

Frigon, Mathieu. "Fertilizers, Ethanol and the Peaking of Natural Gas Production in Alberta." Library of Parliament Parliamentary Information and Research Service, October 10, 2007. http://www.parl.gc.ca/information/library/PRBpubs/prb0749-e.htm#fn9.

Goode, Erica, and Riyadh Mohammed. "Iraq Signs Oil Deal with China Worth up to $3 Billion." *New York Times,* August 29, 2008. http://www.nytimes.com/2008/08/29/world/middleeast/29iraq.html.

Haggett, Scott. "High Cancer Rate Near Oil Sands Confirmed." *Globe and Mail,* February 6, 2009. http://www.theglobeandmail.com/servlet/story/RTGAM.20090206.wcancer07/BNStory/National/.

Hannon, David. "Energy Prices Accelerate the Move to the Middle East." *Purchasing,* August 14, 2008. http://www.purchasing.com/article/CA6584559.html?q=energy+prices+accelerate+move+to+the+middle%2C.

Henton, Darcy. "Aboriginals Declare War on Oil Sands." *Edmonton Journal,* August 18, 2008.

Houser, Trevor. "The Roots of Chinese Oil Investment Abroad." *Asia Policy,* January 2008. http://www.nbr.org/publications/asia_policy/AP5/AP5_Houser.pdf.

Huntley, Chris. "Dow Announces Further Price Increases, Freight Surcharges and Idling of Plants." Reuters, June 24, 2008. http://www.reuters.com/article/pressRelease/idUS112199+24-Jun-2008+PRN20080624.

International Energy Agency. "World Energy Outlook 2007." Fact sheet, n.d. www.iea.org//textbase/papers/2007/fs_oil.pdf.

Jackson-Han, Sarah. "China's 'Other Tibetans,' the Uyghurs, Stage Protests." Radio Free Asia RFA Unplugged blog, April 2, 2008. http://rfaunplugged.wordpress.com/2008/04/02/chinas-other-tibetans-the-uyghurs-stage-protests/.

Junaid, Adiat, and Albert Koehl. "KAIROS Study Reveals Billions in Canadian Tax Subsidies to Big Oil Come at the Expense of Conservation and Climate." Ecojustice, April 15, 2008. http://www.ecojustice.ca/media-centre/press-releases/kairos-study-reveals-billions-in-canadian-tax-subsidies-to-big-oil-come-at-the-expense-of-conservation-and-climate/.

Leaton, James. *Unconventional Oil: Scraping the Bottom of the Barrel?* London: WWF-UK and The Co-operative Group, n.d. http://www.wwf.org.uk/filelibrary/pdf/scraping_barrell.pdf.

Lim, Louisa. "China's Uighurs Lose Out to Development." *BBC News,* December 19, 2003. http://news.bbc.co.uk/2/hi/asia-pacific/3330803.stm.

Lin, Jiang. "Energy Conservation Investments: A Comparison Between China and the US." ScienceDirect, March 23, 2006. http://www.sciencedirect.com/science?_ob=ArticleURL&_udi=B6V2W-4JJ84F9-1&_user=10&_rdoc=1&_fmt=&_orig=search&_sort=d&view=c&_version=1&_urlVersion=0&_userid=10&md5=f2f41e8ae6911da92cb1676dacfd40ef.

Nikiforuk, Andrew. *Tar Sands: Dirty Oil and the Future of a Continent.* Vancouver: Greystone, 2008.

Pett, David. "Failed Oilsands Projects Could Bring Runaway Costs in Line." *Financial Post,* September 22, 2008. http://network.nationalpost.com/np/blogs/tradingdesk/archive/2008/09/22/failed-oilsands-projects-could-bring-runaway-costs-in-line.aspx.

Polczer, Shaun. "Oil Sands Will Play Crucial Role in Future: Energy Giants." *Financial Post,* July 1, 2008. http://www.financialpost.com/reports/oil-watch/story.html?id=625335.

Ramachandran, Ramesh. "North American Petrochemicals: Walking a Tight Rope." Paper presented at the CERI 2005 North American Natural Gas Conference & Calgary Energy Show, Calgary, AB. Dow Chemical Canada Inc., March 7, 2005. http://news.dow.com/speeches/20050307a.htm.

Reguly, Eric. "Supply on Demand: Buyers Like China Are Bypassing Commodities Markets Altogether and Going Right to the Source." *Report on Business,* June 27, 2008. http://business.theglobeandmail.com/servlet/story/RTGAM.20080618.rmreguly0618/BNStory/specialROBmagazine/home.

Severson-Baker, Chris, and Simon Dyer. "Environmental Groups Pull Out of Multi-stakeholder Oil Sands Process." Pembina Institute, August 18, 2008. http://www.pembina.org/media-release/1678.

Sharp, Rob. "Polythene's Story: The Accidental Birth of Plastic Bags." *The Independent,* March 26, 2008. http://www.independent.co.uk/news/science/polythenes-story-the-accidental-birth-of-plastic-bags-800602.html.

Shell Global. "KPI: Energy intensity." Shell.com, n.d. http://www.shell.com/home/content/responsible_energy/performance/environmental/energy_intensity/energy_intensity_27032008.html.

Smith, Grant, and Jim Kennett "Not Enough Oil Is Lament of BP, Exxon on Spending." Bloomberg.com, May 19, 2008. www.bloomberg.com/apps/news?pid=20601087&sid=ajkOo5voC8xU&refer=home.

Stanislaw, Joseph A. "Power Play: Resource Nationalism, the Global Scramble for Energy, and the Need for Mutual Interdependence." Deloitte Development

LLC, 2008. http://www.deloitte.com/dtt/cda/doc/content/us_er
%20JAS_PowerPlay_FINAL.pdf.

"Two-Mouth Fish Fuels Oil-Sands Fears." *Toronto Star,* August 20, 2008.
http://www.thestar.com/News/Canada/article/481840.

U.S. Department of Energy. "International Energy Outlook 2008." Energy
Information Administration, June 2008. http://www.eia.doe.gov/oiaf/ieo/
highlights.html.

Vidal, John. "Canadians Ponder Cost of Rush for Dirty Oil." *The Guardian,* July
11, 2008. http://www.guardian.co.uk/environment/2008/jul/11/fossilfuels
.pollution.

"Wal-Mart to Cut Bag Usage." *Twice,* September 25, 2008. http://www.twice.com/
article/CA6599559.html.

Weber, Bob. "Piece of Oil Sands First to Be Certified as Reclaimed." *Globe and
Mail,* March 19, 2008. http://www.theglobeandmail.com/servlet/story/
RTGAM.20080319.oilsands20/BNStory/National/?page=rss&id=RTGAM
.20080319.oilsands20.

Wong, Edward. "Attack in West China Kills 3 Security Officers." *New York Times,*
August 13, 2008. http://www.nytimes.com/2008/08/13/sports/olympics/
13china.html.

Chapter 6: We, the Resource

Amiti, Mary, and Caroline Freund. "China's Export Boom." *Finance and
Development,* September 2007. http://www.imf.org/external/pubs/ft/fandd/
2007/09/amiti.htm.

Archibold, Randal C. "At the U.S. Border, the Desert Takes a Rising Toll." *New
York Times,* September 15, 2007. http://www.nytimes.com/2007/09/15/us/
15border.html.

———. "U.S. Plans Border 'Surge' Against Any Drug Wars." *New York Times,*
January 8, 2009. http://www.nytimes.com/2009/01/08/us/08chertoff.html.

Associated Free Press. "Gap Between Rich, Poor Growing, OECD Finds." Google
News, October 21, 2008. http://afp.google.com/article/
ALeqM5ibqxRYnbFgCrCxgLG_i57Bx4PXqA.

Associated Press. "Japan: Wholesale Inflation at 27-Year High." *New York Times,*
August 13, 2008. http://www.nytimes.com/2008/08/13/business/
worldbusiness/13fobriefs-WHOLESALEINF_BRF.html.

———. "Personal Savings Drop to a 73-Year Low." MSNBC, February 1, 2007.
http://www.msnbc.msn.com/id/16922582.

———. "35 Percent of Toys Contain Lead, Report Says." MSNBC, December 5,
2007. http://www.msnbc.msn.com/id/22103641/.

Bacon, David. "Trading on Migrant Labor." *The American Prospect,* June 11, 2007.
www.prospect.org/cs/articles?article=trading_on_migrant_labor.

Barboza, David. "China's Dairy Farmers Say They Are Victims." *New York Times,* October 4, 2008. http://www.nytimes.com/2008/10/04/world/asia/04milk.html.

Barboza, David, and Louise Story. "Mattel Issues New Recall of Toys Made in China." *New York Times,* August 14, 2007. http://www.nytimes.com/2007/08/14/business/15toys-web.html.

Berg, K.K., H.F. Hull, E.W. Zabel, and P.K. Staley. "Death of a Child after Ingestion of a Metallic Charm." *Morbidity and Mortality Weekly Report,* March 23, 2006. http://www.cdc.gov/mmwr/preview/mmwrhtml/mm55d323a1.htm.

Bogdanich, Walt. "The Everyman Who Exposed Tainted Toothpaste." *New York Times,* October 1, 2007. www.nytimes.com/2007/10/01/world/americas/01panama.html?scp=1&sq=The%20Everyman%20Who%20Exposed%20Tainted%20Toothpaste&st=cse.

British Broadcasting Corporation. "Millions 'Spend More Than Income.'" *BBC News,* January 22, 2008. http://news.bbc.co.uk/2/hi/business/7202121.stm.

Capps, Randolph, Michael E. Fix, Jeffrey S. Passel, Jason Ost, and Dan Perez-Lopez. "A Profile of the Low-Wage Immigrant Workforce." Urban Institute, October 27, 2003. http://www.urban.org/publications/310880.html.

Canadian Broadcasting Corporation. "20% of Chinese Toys, Baby Clothes Fail Safety Inspections." *CBC News,* May 28, 2007. http://www.cbc.ca/consumer/story/2007/05/28/china-product.html.

CNBC. "Nobel Laureate Solution." CNBC Video, October 1, 2008. http://www.cnbc.com/id/15840232?video=874100965&play=1.

"China Rushes Upmarket." *BusinessWeek,* September 17, 2007. http://www.businessweek.com/magazine/content/07_38/b4050055.htm?chan=search.

"The Competition for Low-Wage Jobs." *New York Times* Room for Debate blog, March 18, 2009. http://roomfordebate.blogs.nytimes.com/2009/03/18/the-competition-for-low-wage-jobs/?scp=3&sq=migrant%20benefit%20economy&st=cse.

"Competition from China: Two McKinsey Surveys." *McKinsey Quarterly,* May 2008. http://www.mckinseyquarterly.com/Strategy/Globalization/Competition_from_China_Two_McKinsey_Surveys_2147.

DeParle, Jason. "World Banker and His Cash Return Home." *New York Times,* March 17, 2008. http://www.nytimes.com/2008/03/17/world/asia/17remit.html.

Dwyer, Jim. "In a Sea of Foreclosures, an Island of Calm." *New York Times,* September 27, 2008. http://www.nytimes.com/2008/09/27/nyregion/27about.html.

Ebner, David. "A Nation of Debtors." *Report on Business,* September 26, 2008. http://www.reportonbusiness.com/servlet/story/RTGAM.20080926.wrcover27/BNStory/Business/home.

Elliott, Larry. "Migrant Workers Curb Wages and Keep Interest Rates Low to Boost Economic Growth." *The Guardian,* December 18, 2007. http://www.guardian.co.uk/business/2007/dec/18/economics.eu.

Engardio, Pete. "Can the U.S. Bring Jobs Back from China?" *BusinessWeek,* June 19, 2008. http://www.businessweek.com/print/magazine/content/08_26/b4090038429655.htm.

Evans, David, and Richard Schmalensee. *Paying with Plastic.* Boston: MIT Press, 1999.

Evans-Pritchard, Ambrose. "EU Refuses Bail-out Package Despite Crisis Fears." *The Telegraph,* September 25, 2008. http://www.telegraph.co.uk/finance/comment/ambroseevans_pritchard/3075180/EU-refuses-bail-out-package-despite-crisis-fears.html?mobile-truc.

Fajnzylber, Pablo, and J. Humberto Lopez. *Close to Home: The Development Impact of Remittances in Latin America.* Washington: International Bank for Reconstruction and Development and World Bank, 2007. http://siteresources.worldbank.org/INTLACOFFICEOFCE/Resources/ClosetoHome_FINAL.pdf.

Financial Times. "U.S. Household Debt: A Frightening Picture." Seeking Alpha, August 26, 2008. http://seekingalpha.com/article/92682-u-s-household-debt-a-frightening-picture.

Frantz, Douglas. "Threat of 'Dirty Bomb' Growing, Officials Say." *Los Angeles Times,* May 9, 2004. http://articles.latimes.com/2004/may/09/world/fg-dirty-bomb9.

Friedman, Thomas L. "The Inflection Is Near?" *New York Times,* March 8, 2009. http://www.nytimes.com/2009/03/08/opinion/08friedman.html.

"Getting Immigration Right." *New York Times,* December 26, 2008. http://www.nytimes.com/2008/12/26/opinion/26fri1.html.

Gogoi, Pallavi. "Gloomy Days Ahead for Retailers." *BusinessWeek,* July 21, 2008. http://www.businessweek.com/bwdaily/dnflash/content/jul2008/db20080718_996200.htm.

Gordon, Jennifer. "Workers Without Borders." *New York Times,* March 10, 2009. http://www.nytimes.com/2009/03/10/opinion/10gordon.html.

Hammer, Kate. "Melamine-Laced Pretzels Found on Store Shelves after Recall." *Globe and Mail,* April 10, 2008. http://www.theglobeandmail.com/servlet/story/RTGAM.20081004.wxmelamine04/BNStory/National/home.

Holley, Denise. "Security Beefed Up at Aid Station." *Nogales International,* March 3, 2009. http://www.nogalesinternational.com/articles/2009/03/03/news/doc49ad4c53a6d13560159111.txt.

Houseman, Susan. "Outsourcing, Offshoring, and Productivity Measurement in U.S. Manufacturing." W.E. Upjohn Institute for Employment Research, April 2007. http://www.upjohninst.org/publications/wp/06-130.pdf.

Institute for Local Self-Reliance. "Impact of Big Box Stores on Jobs and Wages." Big Box Tool Kit, n.d. bigboxtoolkit.com/images/pdf/jobsandwages.pdf.

Jones, Maggie. "Migrants No More." *Mother Jones,* November 2004. http://www.motherjones.com/politics/2004/11/migrants-no-more.

Jones, Yvonne D. *International Remittances: Different Estimation Methodologies Produce Different Results.* Washington: U.S. Government Accountability Office, March 2006. http://www.gao.gov/new.items/d06210.pdf.

Kantor, Andrew. "IKEA Plans to Build factory in Danville, Furnish City with Jobs." *Roanoke Times,* October 13, 2006. http://www.roanoke.com/news/roanoke/wb/86839.

Kindleberger, Charles. *Manias, Panics and Crashes.* New York: John Wiley, 1996.

Kiviat, Barbara. "Misery Loves Company: Negative Equity Edition." *Time* Curious Capitalist blog, October 31, 2008. http://curiouscapitalist.blogs.time.com/2008/10/31/misery-loves-company-negative-equity-edition/.

Krugman, Paul. "Decade at Bernie's." *New York Times,* February 16, 2009. http://www.nytimes.com/2009/02/16/opinion/16krugman.html.

Labaton, Stephen. "Agency's '04 Rule Let Banks Pile Up New Debt." *New York Times,* October 3, 2008. http://www.nytimes.com/2008/10/03/business/03sec.html.

Leonhardt, David. "Seeing Inflation Only in the Prices That Go Up." *New York Times,* May 7, 2008. http://www.nytimes.com/2008/05/07/business/07leonhardt.html.

Longman, Phillip. *The Return of Thrift.* New York: Free Press, 1996.

Maclennan, Duncan. "Trunks, Tails, and Elephants: Modernising Housing Policies." *European Journal of Housing Policy* 8, no. 4 (December 2008): 423–40.

Marcus, Daniel. "Live Richly, and Prosper." Flow TV, May 27, 2005. http://flowtv.org/?p=580.

McCombs, Brady. "Abuse Tales Hard to Dispel: Critics Call Short-term Custody 'a Black Hole' for Immigrants; US Denies Claims." *Arizona Daily Star,* October 19, 2008.

Meier, Barry. "Consumer's World: To Insure Toy Safety, U.S. Shifts Its Attack." *New York Times,* August 25, 1990. http://www.nytimes.com/1990/08/25/style/consumer-s-world-to-insure-toy-safety-us-shifts-its-attack.html.

Mencimer, Stephanie. "Why Texas Still Holds 'Em." *Mother Jones,* July 2008. http://www.motherjones.com/politics/2008/07/why-texas-still-holds-em.

Minnesota Department of Health. "Child's Death from Lead Poisoning Prompts Recall and Warning about Children's Jewelry." Press release, March 23, 2006. http://www.health.state.mn.us/news/pressrel/lead032306.html.

"Misplaced Fears about Jobs in America." *The Economist,* March 11, 2004. http://www.economist.com/world/unitedstates/displayStory.cfm?story_id=2501977.

Mitchell, Stacy. *Big Box Swindle: The True Cost of Mega-retailers and the Fight for America's Independent Business.* Boston: Beacon Press, 2006.

Morris, Charles. *The Trillion Dollar Meltdown: Easy Money, High Rollers, and the Great Credit Crash.* New York: Public Affairs, 2008.

Otsuma, Mayumi. "Japan Wholesale Inflation Eases as Oil Prices Drop."

Bloomberg.com, September 9, 2008. http://www.bloomberg.com/apps/
news?pid=20601068&sid=aams5x0rUAac&refer=home.

Qiang, Li. "Textile Sweatshops; Adidas, Bali Intimates, Hanesbrands Inc., Piege
Co (Felina Lingerie), Quiksilver, Regina Miracle Speedo, Walcoal America
Inc., and Wal-Mart Made in China." China Labor Watch, November 20, 2007.
http://www.chinalaborwatch.org/200711204textile.htm.

Quint, Mitchell, and Dermot Shorten. "China's Gold Rush: Should You Make the
Journey East?" Booz Allen Hamilton, January 11, 2004. http://www.boozallen
.com/media/file/143177.pdf.

Ratha, Dilip. "Remittance Flows to Developing Countries Are Estimated to
Exceed $300 Billion in 2008." World Bank People Move blog, February 18,
2009. http://peoplemove.worldbank.org/en/content/remittance-flows-to-
developing-countries.

Ratha, Dilip, and Maurice Schiff. "Migration and Remittances." World Bank,
September 2008. http://web.worldbank.org/WBSITE/EXTERNAL/NEWS/
0,,contentMDK:20648762~menuPK:34480~pagePK:64257043~piPK:437376~
theSitePK:4607,00.html.

Reuters. "Uzbekistan: Wal-Mart Bans Cotton." *New York Times,* October 1, 2008.
http://www.nytimes.com/2008/10/01/business/worldbusiness/
01fobriefs-WALMARTBANSC_BRF.html.

Rinaldi, Laura, and Alicia Sanchis-Arellano. "Household Debt Sustainability:
What Explains Household Non-performing Loans?" ECB [European Central
Bank] Working Paper 570, 2006. http://ec.europa.eu/economy_finance/
events/2006/arc2006/household_debt_sustainability_en.pdf.

Schlisserman, Courtney. "U.S. Import Prices Drop 0.2%; Down 0.6% Excluding
Oil." Bloomberg.com, March 13, 2009. http://www.bloomberg.com/apps/news
?pid=20601087&sid=addHCIGsLwIw&refer=home.

Scott, Robert E. "The Wal-Mart Effect: Its Chinese Imports Have Displaced
Nearly 200,000 U.S. Jobs." Economic Policy Institute, June 26, 2007.
http://www.epi.org/issuebriefs/235/ib235.pdf.

"Seven Questions: China's Total Toy Recall." *Foreign Policy,* August 2007.
http://www.foreignpolicy.com/story/cms.php?story_id=3960.

Shipler, David. *The Working Poor: Invisible in America.* New York: Knopf, 2004.

Stein, Ben. "In Financial Food Chains, Little Guys Can't Win." *New York Times,*
September 28, 2008. http://www.nytimes.com/2008/09/28/business/28every
.html.

Stiglitz, Joseph. *The Roaring Nineties.* New York: W.W. Norton, 2003.

Swarns, Rachel L. "U.S. Reports Drop in Homeless Population." *New York Times,*
July 30, 2008. http://www.nytimes.com/2008/07/30/us/30homeless.html.

Thottam, Jyoti. "Why Mattel Apologized to China." *Time,* September 21, 2007.
http://www.time.com/time/business/article/0,8599,1664428,00.html.

Tilly, Chris. "Reasons for the Continuing Growth of Part-time Employment." *Monthly Labor Review,* March 1991. http://www.bls.gov/opub/mlr/1991/03/art2full.pdf.

Toossi, Mitra. "A New Look at Long-term Labor Force Projections to 2050." *Monthly Labor Review,* November 2006. http://www.bls.gov/opub/mlr/2006/11/art3full.pdf.

Tully, Shawn. "A Profit Gusher of Epic Proportions." *Fortune,* April 15, 2007. http://money.cnn.com/magazines/fortune/fortune_archive/2007/04/30/8405391/index.htm.

United Nations Centre for Human Settlements. "100 Million Homeless in World: Most Are Women and Dependent Children." Habitat II Conference press release, June 1996. http://www.un.org/Conferences/habitat/unchs/press/women.htm.

U.S. Federal Reserve. "Consumer Credit." Federal Reserve Statistical Release G19, March 6, 2009. http://www.federalreserve.gov/releases/g19/current/default.htm.

"Wal-mart, Carrefour and Metro Find 99 Pct of Chinese Products Qualified.," *Xinhua,* September 27, 2007. news.xinhuanet.com/english/2007-09/27/content_6803552.htm.

Waters, Jennifer. "Economy Forces Major Shift in Spending." *Wall Street Journal,* June 16, 2008. http://online.wsj.com/public/article_print/SB121338190561972555.html.

Weller, Christian E. "Drowning in Debt: America's Middle Class Falls Deeper in Debt as Income Growth Slows and Costs Climb." Center for American Progress, May 2006. http://www.americanprogress.org/kf/boomburden-web.pdf.

Willis, Bob, and Timothy R. Homan. "U.S. Economy: U.S. Consumer Price Gains Accelerate." Bloomberg.com, March 18, 2009. http://www.bloomberg.com/apps/news?pid=20601087&sid=a96UYa3hNIho&refer=home.

Wood, Greg. "High Oil Price Fuels 'Made in America.'" *BBC News,* September 12, 2008. http://news.bbc.co.uk/2/hi/business/7611960.stm.

Wozniak, Lara. "Sorry, Vietnam Is Not the Next China." *BusinessWeek,* May 13, 2008. http://www.businessweek.com/print/globalbiz/content/may2008/gb20080513_415737.htm.

Yardley, Jim. "More Candy from China, Tainted, Is in U.S." *New York Times,* October 2, 2008. http://www.nytimes.com/2008/10/02/world/asia/02milk.html.

———. "Worried Parents in China Wait for Answers on Tainted Formula." *New York Times,* September 18, 2008. http://www.nytimes.com/2008/09/18/world/asia/18china.html.

Zhang, Sheldon. *Smuggling and Trafficking in Human Beings: All Roads Lead to America.* California: Greenwood Publishing, 2007.

Chapter 7: Shock Therapy

Birol, Fatih. "World Energy Outlook 2007: China and India Insights." Climate Action, November 23, 2007. http://www.climateactionprogramme.org/features/article/world_energy_outlook_2007_china_and_india_insights/.

Bloomberg.com. "Barbie Sets Up Shop in Shanghai." *Globe and Mail,* June 3, 2009. http://business.theglobeandmail.com/servlet/story/LAC.20090306.RSECONDARYTICKER06/TPStory/?query.

Bradsher, Keith. "China Losing Taste for Debt from U.S." *New York Times,* January 8, 2009. www.nytimes.com/2009/01/08/business/worldbusiness/08yuan.html.

Brahic, Catherine. "33% of China's Carbon Footprint Blamed on Exports." *New Scientist,* July 28, 2008. http://www.newscientist.com/article/dn14412-33-of-chinas-carbon-footprint-blamed-on-exports.html?feedId=online-news_rss20.

Bromley, Bob, Jesse Row, Matthew Salkeld, Pentti Sjoman, Tim Weis, and Paul Cobb. "Wha Ti Community Energy Plan: Options for Energy Supply and Management for Wha Ti, Northwest Territories." Prepared for the Wha Ti Charter Community by Ecology North and the Pembina Institute, June 2004. http://www.aea.nt.ca/files/COMMUNITY%20ENERGY%20PLANNING/Whati_Plan.pdf.

Canadian Broadcasting Corporation. "Nunavut Braces for Pinch of Gas Price Hike." *CBC News,* June 30, 2008. http://www.cbc.ca/canada/north/story/2008/06/30/nunavut-fuel.html.

Carey, John. "The Real Question: Should Oil Be Cheap?" *Business Week,* July 23, 2008.

Chung, Andrew. "Recession Is Ravaging the World's Billionaires." *The Star,* March 12, 2009. http://www.thestar.com/article/600886.

Donohue, Michael. "Mall of Misfortune." *The National,* June 12, 2008. http://www.thenational.ae/article/20080612/REVIEW/206990272/1042.

Driver, Anna, and Dave Zimmerman. "Worldwide Energy E&P Spending Seen up 20 Pct — Lehman." Reuters, June 6, 2008. http://www.reuters.com/article/OILPRD/idUSN0644385420080606.

Findlay, Ronald, and Kevin O'Rourke. *Power and Plenty: Trade, War, and World Economy in the Second Millennium.* Princeton, NJ: Princeton University Press, 2007.

Fouché, Gwladys. "North-West Passage Is Now Plain Sailing." *The Guardian,* August 28, 2007. http://www.guardian.co.uk/environment/2007/aug/28/climatechange.internationalnews?gusrc=rss&feed=networkfront.

Glaeser, Edward L. "If You Got Money, It's Time to Spend Some." *New York Times* Economix blog, February 17, 2009. http://economix.blogs.nytimes.com/2009/02/17/if-you-got-money-its-time-to-spend-some/?scp=5&sq=Keynes&st=cse.

Grynbaum, Michael M. "Core Inflation Remains Steady, Presenting a Puzzle to the Fed." *New York Times,* October 18, 2007. http://www.nytimes.com/2007/10/18/business/18economy.html.

International Energy Agency. "The Next 10 Years Are Critical: The World Energy Outlook Makes the Case for Stepping up Co-operation with China and India to Address Global Energy Challenges." International Energy Agency, November 7, 2007. http://www.iea.org/textbase/press/pressdetail.asp?PRESS_REL_ID=239.

Jowit, Juliette, and Patrick Wintour. "Cost of Tackling Global Climate Change Has Doubled, Warns Stern." *The Guardian,* June 26, 2008. http://www.guardian.co.uk/environment/2008/jun/26/climatechange.scienceofclimatechange.

Kim, Juli S. "A China Environmental Health Project Research Brief: Transboundary Air Pollution — Will China Choke on Its Success?" Woodrow Wilson International Center for Scholars China Environment Forum, February 2, 2007. http://www.wilsoncenter.org/index.cfm?topic_id=1421&fuseaction=topics.item&news_id=218780.

Leonard, Andrew. "Will China's Poverty Reduction Kill the Planet?" *Salon,* April 19, 2007. http://www.salon.com/tech/htww/2007/04/19/poverty_reduction/.

Macalister, Terry. "Energy Agency Sees Oil Price Rising to $200 a Barrel." *The Guardian,* November 7, 2008. http://www.guardian.co.uk/business/2008/nov/07/oilandgascompanies-energy.

Macklin, Gary. "Volatile Market Forces Produce Mixed Cost Indicators for Food Distributors." *Refrigerated Transporter,* December 1, 2004. http://refrigeratedtrans.com/mag/transportation_volatile_market_forces/.

Morris, Charles. *The Trillion Dollar Meltdown: Easy Money, High Rollers, and the Great Credit Crash.* New York: Public Affairs, 2008.

Mutikani, Lucia. "McCain's China-Free Debt Plan Seen Unrealistic." Reuters, October 3, 2008. http://www.reuters.com/article/vcCandidateFeed2/idUSTRE49281F20081003?sp=true.

Norris, Floyd. "The Upside to Resisting Globalization." *New York Times,* February 5, 2009. http://www.nytimes.com/2009/02/06/business/06norris.html?_r=1&hp.

Pedersen, Brian J. "Mexican Tariffs Hit Southern Arizona Exporters." *Arizona Daily Star,* March 19, 2009. http://www.azstarnet.com/news/284973.

Ratliff, Evan. "One Molecule Could Cure Our Addiction to Oil." *Wired* 15, no. 10 (September 24, 2007). http://www.wired.com/science/planetearth/magazine/15-10/ff_plant.

Sachs, Jeffrey. *Common Wealth: Economics for a Crowded Planet.* New York: Penguin, 2008.

Scoffield, Heather. "There Will Be Blood." *Globe and Mail,* February 24, 2009. http://www.theglobeandmail.com/servlet/story/LAC.20090224.RFERGUSON24/TPStory/?query=niall.

Stiglitz, Joseph. *Making Globalization Work.* New York: W.W. Norton, 2007.

Thompson, John. "Life on Iqaluit's Mean Streets." *Nunatsiaq News,* November 10, 2006. http://www.nunatsiaq.com/archives/61110/news/nunavut/61110_02.html.

Uchitelle, Louis. "Oil Prices Raise Cost of Making Range of Goods." *New York Times,* June 8, 2008. www.nytimes.com/2008/06/08/us/08oil.html.

United Nations Environment Programme. "Global Trends in Sustainable Energy Investment 2008." United Nations Environment Programme. http://sefi.unep .org/fileadmin/media/sefi/docs/publications/Exec_summary.pdf.

United Nations Foundation. "Realizing the Potential of Energy Efficiency: Targets, Policies, and Measures for G8 Countries." Expert Group on Energy Efficiency, 2007. http://www.globalproblems-globalsolutions-files.org/ unf_website/PDF/realizing_potential_energy_efficiency.pdf.

U.S. Department of Energy. "Short-Term Energy Outlook." Energy Information Administration, March 10, 2009. http://www.eia.doe.gov/steo.

———. "U.S. Carbon Dioxide Emissions from Energy Sources: 2007 Flash Estimate." Energy Information Administration, May 2008. http://www.eia .doe.gov/oiaf/1605/flash/pdf/flash.pdf.

Waldie, Paul. "Homeowners Left to 'Hope and Pray' as Foreclosure Filings Soar." *Globe and Mail,* October 1, 2008. http://www.theglobeandmail.com/servlet/ story/LAC.20081001.MELTDOWNSUBPRIME01/TPStory/ ?query=one+in+10+foreclosure.

Watt-Cloutier, Sheila. "Intervention 1: Remarks Made to the Arctic Council Ministerial Meeting, Iceland." Inuit Circumpolar Council Canada, November 24, 2004. http://www.inuitcircumpolar.com/index.php?ID=274&Lang=En.

Weber, Bob. "Exploding Fuel Prices Could Take $100 Million Bite out of Nunavut Budget." redOrbit.com, June 15, 2008. http://www.redorbit.com/news/ business/1433675/exploding_fuel_prices_could_take_100_million_bite_out_ of/index.html.

Westcott, Kathryn. "Plain Sailing on the Northwest Passage." *BBC News,* September 19, 2007. http://news.bbc.co.uk/2/hi/americas/6999078.stm.

World Trade Organization. "WTO: Developing, Transition Economies Cushion Trade Slowdown." Chart 3: Real merchandise trade growth by region, 2007. World Trade Organization, April 17, 2008. http://www.wto.org/english/ news_e/pres08_e/pr520_e.htm#chart3.

ACKNOWLEDGMENTS

More than any other book that I've written, this one was a product of generosity. I could not have managed the book's scope, or even reached completion, if a great many people had not helped along the way.

In the field, I collected information and interviews that formed the core research for this book. In Las Vegas, Athene Kovacic and Sam Bundy introduced me to the ASD/AMD trade show; Danny Kole and other exhibitors made time in the midst of a busy event. Jeff Harrison and Kim Brooke at the University of Arizona opened the door to Tucson's annual Global Retailing Conference. Carrie Fox of Borderlinks guided and translated in Nogales, Mexico. Maryada Vallet of No More Deaths shared research. In Los Angeles, Tom Politeo and Elina Green gave engaged ground tours of the port neighbourhoods, and Arley Baker of the Port of Los Angeles provided a deluxe boat ride amid hulking container ships. Dick McKenna and Manny Aschemeyer gave me a bird's-eye view of L.A.'s harbour from the control room of the Marine Exchange. Paul Connolly of OOCL shipping got me onto the docks in the middle of a busy day.

In Hong Kong, Wing Ah Fung and Andrew McAuley were gracious hosts. Nury Vittachi gave good advice at the Foreign Correspondents' Club. Charles Foran made introductions from Canada. Chris Minz opened up his Shanghai apartment, and journalists Miro Cernetig and Raymond Saint-Pierre were good company in Beijing. Labour activist Han Dongfang illuminated parts of China's mainland. André Alexander toured me around Lhasa's old city, and allowed an interview despite security cameras and plainclothes police. More than a few locals in China, Tibet, and Xinjiang, all who cannot be named, played important roles as hosts, translators, and/or interviewees. Throughout Asia, my wife, Lisa Caton, was a lovely travelling companion and co-conspirator. We also met photographer Justin Guariglia on the roof of the Jokhang Temple in Lhasa. His work is featured in this book, along with that of James Whitlow Delano, acclaimed documentary photographer and fellow traveller.

In Fort McMurray, Bruce Lourie and Tim Gray of the Ivey Foundation hosted a forward-thinking workshop and summit on the future of the tar sands. Suncor somehow engineered a ground tour of its Millennium Mine in which it is nearly impossible for visitors to view the mine itself. Dan Woynillowicz of the Pembina Institute shared useful data; Matt Price gave an excellent aerial survey of the tailings ponds and mining operations. In Fort Chipewyan, Alice Rigney was a great host; Alec Bruno, Mike Mercredi, and Allan Adam all gave interviews on short notice, and Jane Glassco helped with questions. In Alberta's petrochemical zone, Dr. Ramesh Ramachandran of Dow Chemical, as well as Roxanne Good, Al Poole, and Eric Kelusky of Nova Petrochemicals were all forthright and accommodating. Bill Moore-Kilgannon and Don MacNeil did much to introduce me to what petrochemicals, pipelines, and non-renewable resources might mean in the twenty-first century.

While investigating homelessness in Greater Vancouver, several people gave me excellent background interviews: Linda Syssoloff, Verna Semotuk, Peter Fedof, Judy Graves, Jim Green, and Senator Larry Campbell. And my periodic trips to Canada's Arctic to report on climate change and energy development are always highlighted by northern hospitality; thanks to Hans Fast, Hans and Zipporah at Ootooq & Miteq Outfitting, Sheila Watt-Cloutier, David Audlakiak, Wayne Davidson, and David Ooingoot.

I owe an ideas debt to writers like Mike Davis, Thomas Homer-Dixon, Barbara Ehrenreich, and Nelson Lichtenstein. But the primary inspiration behind this book is the principle of dependent origination, represented by a broad collection of teachings on interdependence and causality common to all schools of Buddhism. While any unskilful application of teachings is my sole responsibility, I would like to acknowledge Dharma teachers that have been generous along the way: Achariya Doug Duncan, Lama Gyurme Dorje, Karma Gyurmey Rinpoche, Neten Rinpoche, Tarchin Hearn, Edmund Jones, and the Clear Sky Sangha. Kevin Elander and Hart Lazer shed new light on yogasana.

Early segments of this book first appeared in the *Far Eastern Economic Review, Mother Jones, Fuelling the Future* (edited by Andrew Heintzman and Evan Solomon), the *Georgia Straight,* and *This Magazine.*

ACKNOWLEDGMENTS

I would like to thank Hilary McMahon, my agent at Westwood Creative Artists, who understood this project from the beginning, and, more importantly, stood behind it when things got rough. Chris Bucci, my first editor at McClelland & Stewart, gave as much time and patience as was necessary and did great things to shape it into a workable form. My current editor at M&S, Trena White, was excellent throughout the editorial process, and helped the manuscript reach its potential. Jake Klisivitch at Palgrave Macmillan translated the project into the United States, and brought the book to market despite constraints on time and space. Thanks to all others who typeset, copyedited, sold foreign rights, and couriered proofs.

David Carter, Charlotte Caton, Mike Caton, and Andrew Johnson spent valuable time on book proofs. Keith Dewing contributed some great articles on symbiosis and evolution. Shawna Hansen skillfully transcribed a number of interviews. Fellow writers Andrew Nikiforuk and Chris Turner took time to read the manuscript and offer some encouraging words. Apologies to anyone else I've forgotten to thank.

I would like to formally acknowledge the financial support of the Canada Council, as well as the Dave Greber Freelance Writers Award. A journalism fellowship on homelessness with the Sheldon Chumir Foundation for Ethics and Leadership also contributed research to this book, and I appreciate the ongoing support of foundation president Janet Keeping, as well as former president Marsha Hanen. A research bursary from Public Interest Alberta funded part of my investigation into petrochemicals and pipelines.

In the end, it is my family who contributed the most. Lisa, Addison, and Myles not only tolerated frenzied deadlines, but they supported the book even when its scale broadened and our lives became unwieldy and difficult. It must be mentioned that this book coincided with the critical illness of our eldest son, Addison, and so we thank Dr. Victor Lewis, Dr. Karen Booth, Dr. Gregory Guilcher, and the rest of the staff at the Alberta Children's Hospital. Grandma Charlotte Caton and Uncle Mike Caton lived with us for weeks and months at a stretch, and Grandma Elisabeth Caton and Grandma Carol Laird came for periodic stays. Grandpa Dave Laird and Grandma Marni Laird also made great contributions. With few exceptions, our extended network of family and friends repeatedly delivered meals, LEGO sets, and offered love and encouragement.

When you try to save the life of a child, sooner or later one begins to wonder what kind of world they might inherit. We can't always protect children from disease and misfortune, but we certainly can – and must – engineer better futures. It is this very simple notion that pushed this book to completion.

May any shortcomings or mistakes within this work not be a source of distress. *Sarva Mangalam*

INDEX

packaging, 188; volatility in 2000s, 80, 88
Ford, Henry, 6, 76–77
Fort Chipewyan, Alberta, 207–13, 215–16
Fort McMurray, Alberta, 181–82, 207–8, 215
Foster, Bob, 172
Foxconn, 106–7, 124
France, 6, 22
Friedman, Milton, 32
Fujan province, China, 125
Fung, Victor, 146–47

Gagosian, Robert, 79
Gansu, China, 257
Gantz, David, 280
Gap, 61, 147
Gates, Bill, 72
GATT, 147
General Motors, 76, 217
General Properties, 267
generic brands, 27–28
Geng Jinpin, 252
George, Rick, 179
Gerard, Leo, 38
Germany, 62, 147, 275–76
Gheit, Fadel, 183
Girard, Stephen, 72
Gladney, Dru C., 203
Gladwell, Malcolm, 244
Glaeser, Edward L., 274
globalization: and bargain economy, 46, 98, 279–80; and borderlands, 226, 267, 270–71; causing stagnant income and unemployment, 241–42; China's labour market critical to, 95, 109; dependence on logistics, 138, 145–50, 155–56; dependence on migrants, 227–28; dependence on resources, 184, 268; disconnect between local and global economies, 77, 256; and foreign investment in United States, 131; history of, 278–79, 281;

risks of, 64, 80–82; rooted in developing countries, 108; and service economy, 31; and union woes, 39–41; and unrealistic growth cycles, 7–8, 155–56; waning, 9, 87, 133, 256, 267, 274–75; *see also* deglobalization
goods: as majority of trade, 145; shipped non-assembled, 146; through Southern California, 152–53, 159–63; trade dependence on logistics, 145–46, 154–55
Gou, Terry, 107
Graham, Wade, 172
Green Acres Mall, Long Island, 1–4, 61
Green, Elina, 160–62
greenhouse gas emissions: 85, 143, 176, 180–81, 255; *see also* pollution
Greenspan, Alan, 32, 87
Grom, Charles, 86
Gruen's mall, 69
Guangzhou province, China, 24, 93–94, 99, 201, 278
Gymboree, 147

Hale, Todd, 23
Hamilton, Gary, 22–23
Han Dongfang, 101–3, 109, 122–23, 125
Hanjin Container Lines, 142
Hansen, James, 79–80, 82
Harney, Alexandra, 118
Hatfield, Joe, 101
health care: affordability, 230; cost increases, 230; for migrants in China, 114, 225; supports needed, 246; and unions, 46; and Wal-Mart, 59, 77
heavy metals, 249, 289
Henan province, China, 113
Henry, Sally, 63
Hewlett Packard, 106
Holliday, Chad, 190
Home Depot: at 280 Metro Center, 68; declining profits, 70, 233; and environmental reform, 168; imports

George Webber

GORDON LAIRD is the bestselling author of *Power: Journeys Across an Energy Nation* and *Slumming It at the Rodeo: The Cultural Roots of Canada's Right-Wing Revolution*. His writing and commentary have been featured on CNN, National Public Radio, the BBC, CBC Radio and Television, in *Mother Jones, Maclean's*, the *Globe and Mail, The Huffington Post*, and the *Far Eastern Economic Review*. Winner of several National Magazine Awards, including top honours for investigative reporting, Laird lives in Calgary.

www.gordonlaird.com

Jonathan KELLERMAN

victims

headline

First published in the United States in 2012 by Ballantine Books
an imprint of The Random House Publishing Group,
a division of Random House Inc., New York

First published in Great Britain in 2012
by HEADLINE PUBLISHING GROUP

1

Cataloguing in Publication Data is available from the British Library

ISBN 978 0 7553 7450 2 (Hardback)
ISBN 978 0 7553 7451 9 (Trade paperback)

Typeset in Fournier MT by Palimpsest Book Production Limited,
Falkirk, Stirlingshire

Printed and bound in Australia by Griffin Press

Headline's policy is to use papers that are natural products and made from wood
grown in responsible forests. The logging and manufacturing processes are expected
to conform to the environmental regulations of the country of origin.

HEADLINE PUBLISHING GROUP
An Hachette UK Company
338 Euston Road
London NW1 3BH

www.headline.co.uk
www.hachette.co.uk

The paper this book is printed on is certified against the
Forest Stewardship Council® Standards. Griffin Press holds
FSC chain of custody certification SGS-COC-005088. FSC
promotes environmentally responsible, socially beneficial
and economically viable management of the world's forests

To Libby McGuire

1

THIS ONE was different.

The first hint was Milo's tight-voiced eight a.m. message, stripped of details.

Something I need you to see, Alex. Here's the address.

An hour later, I was showing I.D. to the uniform guarding the tape. He winced. 'Up there, Doctor.' Pointing to the second story of a sky-blue duplex trimmed in chocolate-brown, he dropped a hand to his Sam Browne belt, as if ready for self-defense.

Nice older building, the classic Cal-Spanish architecture, but the color was wrong. So was the silence of the street, sawhorsed at both ends. Three squad cars and a liver-colored LTD were parked haphazardly across the asphalt. No crime lab vans or coroner's vehicles had arrived, yet.

I said, 'Bad?'

The uniform said, 'There's probably a better word for it but that works.'

Milo stood on the landing outside the door doing nothing.

No cigar-smoking or jotting in his pad or grumbling orders. Feet planted, arms at his sides, he stared at some faraway galaxy.

His blue nylon windbreaker bounced sunlight at strange angles. His black hair was limp, his pitted face the color and texture of cottage cheese past its prime. A white shirt had wrinkled to crepe. Wheat-colored cords had slipped beneath his paunch. His tie was a sad shred of poly.

He looked as if he'd dressed wearing a blindfold.

As I climbed the stairs, he didn't acknowledge me.

1

When I was six steps away, he said, 'You made good time.'

'Easy traffic.'

'Sorry,' he said.

'For what?'

'Including you.' He handed me gloves and paper booties.

I held the door for him. He stayed outside.

The woman was at the rear of the apartment's front room, flat on her back. The kitchen behind her was empty, counters bare, an old avocado-colored fridge free of photos or magnets or mementos.

Two doors to the left were shut and yellow-taped. I took that as a *Keep Out*. Drapes were drawn over every window. Fluorescent lighting in the kitchen supplied a nasty pseudo-dawn.

The woman's head was twisted sharply to the right. A swollen tongue hung between slack, bloated lips.

Limp neck. A grotesque position some coroner might label 'incompatible with life'.

Big woman, broad at the shoulders and the hips. Late fifties to early sixties, with an aggressive chin and short, coarse gray hair. Brown sweatpants covered her below the waist. Her feet were bare. Unpolished toenails were clipped short. Grubby soles said bare feet at home was the default.

Above the waistband of the sweats was what remained of a bare torso. Her abdomen had been sliced horizontally below the navel in a crude approximation of a C-section. A vertical slit crossed the lateral incision at the center, creating a star-shaped wound.

The damage brought to mind one of those hard-rubber change purses that relies on surface tension to protect the goodies. Squeeze to create a stellate opening, then reach in and scoop.

The yield from this receptacle was a necklace of intestines placed below the woman's neckline and arranged like a fashionista's puffy scarf. One end terminated at her right clavicle. Bilious streaks ran down her right breast and onto her rib cage. The rest of her viscera had been pulled down into a heap and left near her left hip.

2

The pile rested atop a once-white towel folded double. Below that was a larger maroon towel spread neatly. Four other expanses of terry cloth formed a makeshift tarp that shielded beige wall-to-wall carpeting from biochemical insult. The towels had been arranged precisely, edges overlapping evenly for about an inch. Near the woman's right hip was a pale blue T-shirt, also folded. Spotless.

Doubling the white towel had succeeded in soaking up a good deal of body fluid, but some had leaked into the maroon under-layer. The smell would've been bad enough without the initial stages of decomp.

One of the towels beneath the body bore lettering. Silver bath sheet embroidered *Vita* in white.

Latin or Italian for 'life'. Some monster's notion of irony?

The intestines were green-brown splotched pink in spots, black in others. Matte finish to the casing, some puckering that said they'd been drying for a while. The apartment was cool, a good ten degrees below the pleasant spring weather outside. The rattle of a wheezy A.C. unit in one of the living room windows was inescapable once I noticed it. Noisy apparatus, rusty at the bolts, but efficient enough to leach moisture from the air and slow down the rot.

But rot is inevitable and the woman's color wasn't anything you'd see outside a morgue.

Incompatible with life.

I bent to inspect the wounds. Both slashes were confident swoops unmarred by obvious hesitation marks, shearing smoothly through layers of skin, subcutaneous fat, diaphragmatic muscle.

No abrasions around the genital area and surprisingly little blood for so much brutality. No spatter or spurt or castoff or evidence of a struggle. All those towels; horribly compulsive.

Guesses filled my head with bad pictures.

Extremely sharp blade, probably not serrated. The neck-twist had killed her quickly and she'd been dead during the surgery, the ultimate anesthesia. The killer had stalked her with enough thoroughness to know he'd have her to himself for a while. Once attaining total control, he'd gone about choreographing: laying out the towels, tucking and aligning,

3

achieving a pleasing symmetry. Then he'd laid her down, removed her T-shirt, careful to keep it clean.

Standing back, he'd inspected his prep work. Time for the blade.

Then the real fun: anatomical exploration.

Despite the butchery and the hideous set of her neck, she looked peaceful. For some reason, that made what had been done to her worse.

I scanned the rest of the room. No damage to the front door or any other sign of forced entry. Bare beige walls backed cheap upholstered furniture covered in a puckered ocher fabric that aped brocade but fell short. White ceramic beehive lamps looked as if they'd shatter under a finger-snap.

The dining area was set up with a card table and two folding chairs. A brown cardboard take-out pizza box sat on the table. Someone – probably Milo – had placed a yellow plastic evidence marker nearby. That made me take a closer look.

No brand name on the box, just *PIZZA!* in exuberant red cursive above the caricature of a portly mustachioed chef. Curls of smaller lettering swarmed around the chef's fleshy grin.

Fresh pizza!

Lotta taste!

Ooh la la!

Yum yum!

Bon appétit!

The box was pristine, not a speck of grease or finger-smudge. I bent down to sniff, picked up no pizza aroma. But the decomp had filled my nose; it would be a while before I'd be smelling anything but death.

If this was another type of crime scene, some detective might be making ghoulish jokes about free lunch.

The detective in charge of this scene was a lieutenant who'd seen hundreds of murders, maybe thousands, yet chose to stay outside for a while.

I let loose more mental pictures. Some fiend in a geeky delivery hat ringing the doorbell then managing to talk himself inside.

Watching as the prey went for her purse? Waiting for precisely the right moment before coming up behind her and clamping both his hands on the sides of her head.

Quick blitz of rotation. The spinal cord would separate and that would be it.

Doing it correctly required strength and confidence.

That and the lack of obvious transfer evidence – not even a shoe impression – screamed experience. If there'd been a similar murder in L.A., I hadn't heard about it.

Despite all that meticulousness, the hair around the woman's temples might be a good place to look for transfer DNA. Psychopaths don't sweat much, but you never know.

I examined the room again.

Speaking of purses, hers was nowhere in sight.

Robbery as an afterthought? More likely souvenir-taking was part of the plan.

Edging away from the body, I wondered if the woman's last thoughts had been of crusty dough, mozzarella, a comfy barefoot dinner.

The doorbell ring the last music she'd ever hear.

I stayed in the apartment awhile longer, straining for insight.

The terrible competence of the neck-twist made me wonder about someone with martial arts training.

The embroidered towel bothered me.

Vita. Life.

Had he brought that one but taken the rest from her linen closet?

Yum. Bon appétit. To life.

The decomp reek intensified and my eyes watered and blurred and the necklace of guts morphed into a snake.

Drab constrictor, fat and languid after a big meal.

I could stand around and pretend that this was anything comprehensible, or hurry outside and try to suppress the tide of nausea rising in my own guts.

Not a tough choice.

2

MILO HADN'T moved from his position on the landing. His eyes were back on Planet Earth, watching the street below. Five uniforms were moving from door to door. From the quick pace of the canvass, plenty of no-one-home.

The street was in a working-class neighborhood in the southeastern corner of West L.A. Division. Three blocks east would've made it someone else's problem. Mixed zoning allowed single-family dwellings and duplexes like the one where the woman had been degraded.

Psychopaths are stodgy creatures of routine and I wondered if the killer's comfort zone was so narrow that he lived within the sawhorses.

I caught my breath and worked at settling my stomach while Milo pretended not to notice.

'Yeah, I know,' he finally said. He was apologizing for the second time when a coroner's van drove up and a dark-haired woman in comfortable clothes got out and hurried up the stairs. 'Morning, Milo.'

'Morning, Gloria. All yours.'

'Oh, boy,' she said. 'We talking freaky-bad?'

'I could say I've seen worse, kid, but I'd be lying.'

'Coming from you that gives me the creeps, Milo.'

'Because I'm old?'

'Tsk.' She patted his shoulder. 'Because you're the voice of experience.'

'Some experiences I can do without.'

* * *

People can get used to just about anything. But if your psyche's in good repair, the fix is often temporary.

Soon after receiving my doctorate, I worked as a psychologist on a pediatric cancer ward. It took a month to stop dreaming about sick kids but I was eventually able to do my job with apparent professionalism. Then I left to go into private practice and found myself, years later, on that same ward. Seeing the children with new eyes mocked all the adaptation I thought I'd accomplished and made me want to cry. I went home and dreamed for a long time.

Homicide detectives get 'used' to a regular diet of soul-obliteration. Typically bright and sensitive, they soldier on, but the essence of the job lurks beneath the surface like a land mine. Some D's transfer out. Others stay and find hobbies. Religion works for some, sin for others. Some, like Milo, turn griping into an art form and never pretend it's just another job.

The woman on the towels was different for him and for me. A permanent image bank had lodged in my brain and I knew the same went for him.

Neither of us talked as Gloria worked inside.

Finally, I said, 'You marked the pizza box. It bothers you.'

'Everything about this bothers me.'

'No brand name on the box. Any indies around here deliver?'

He drew out his cell phone, clicked, and produced a page. Phone numbers he'd already downloaded filled the screen and when he scrolled, the listings kept coming.

'Twenty-eight indies in a ten-mile radius and I also checked Domino's and Papa John's and Two Guys. No one dispatched anyone to this address last night and nobody uses that particular box.'

'If she didn't actually call out, why would she let him in?'

'Good question.'

'Who discovered her?'

'Landlord, responding to a complaint she made a few days ago. Hissing toilet, they had an appointment. When she didn't answer, he got annoyed, started to leave. Then he thought better of it because she liked things fixed, used his key.'

'Where is he now?'

He pointed across the street. 'Recuperating with some firewater down in that little Tudor-ish place.'

I found the house. Greenest lawn on the block, beds of flowers. Topiary bushes.

'Anything about him bother you?'

'Not so far. Why?'

'His landscaping says he's a perfectionist.'

'That's a negative?'

'This case, maybe.'

'Well,' he said, 'so far he's just the landlord. Want to know about her?'

'Sure.'

'Her name's Vita Berlin, she's fifty-six, single, lives on some kind of disability.'

'Vita,' I said. 'The towel was hers.'

'*The* towel? This bastard used every damn towel she had in her linen closet.'

'*Vita* means "life" in Latin and Italian. I thought it might be a sick joke.'

'Cute. Anyway, I'm waiting for Mr Belleveaux – the landlord – to calm down so I can question him and find out more about her. What I've learned from prelim snooping in her bedroom and bathroom is if she's got kids she doesn't keep their pictures around and if she had a computer, it was ripped off. Same for a cell phone. My guess is she had neither, the place has a static feel to it. Like she moved in years ago, didn't add any newfangled stuff.'

'I didn't see her purse.'

'On her nightstand.'

'You taped off the bedroom, didn't want me in there?'

'I sure do, but that'll wait until the techies are through. Can't afford to jeopardize any aspect of this.'

'The front room was okay?'

'I knew you'd be careful.'

His logic seemed strained. Insufficient sleep and a bad surprise can do that.

I said, 'Any indication she was heading to the bedroom before he jumped her?'

'No, it's pristine. Why?'

I gave him the delivery tip scenario.

'Going for her purse,' he said. 'Well, I don't know how you'd prove that, Alex. Main thing is he confined himself to the front, didn't move her into the bedroom for anything sexual.'

I said, 'Those towels make me think of a stage. Or a picture frame.'

'Meaning?'

'Showing off his work.'

'Okay . . . what else to tell you . . . her wardrobe's mostly sweats and sneakers, lots of books in her bedroom. Romances and the kinds of mysteries where people talk like Noël Coward twits and the cops are bumbling cretins.'

I wondered out loud about a killer with martial arts skills and when he didn't respond, went on to describe the kill-scene still bouncing around my brain.

He said, 'Sure, why not.'

Agreeable but distracted. Neither of us focusing on the big question.

Why would anyone do something like this to another human being?

Gloria exited the apartment, looking older and paler.

Milo said, 'You okay?'

'I'm fine,' she said. 'No, I'm lying, that was horrible.' Her forehead was moist. She dabbed it with a tissue. 'My God, it's grotesque.'

'Any off-the-cuff impressions?'

'Nothing you probably haven't figured out yourself. Broken neck's my bet for COD, the cutting looks postmortem. The incisions look clean so maybe some training in meat-cutting or a paramedical field but I wouldn't put much stock in that, all kinds of folk can learn to slice. That pizza box mean something to you?'

'Don't know,' said Milo. 'No one admits delivering here.'

'A scam to get himself in?' she said. 'Why would she open the door for a fake pizza guy?'

'Good question, Gloria.'

She shook her head. 'I called for transport. Want me to ask for a priority autopsy?'

'Thanks.'

'You might actually get it because Dr J seems to like you. Also with something this weird, she's bound to be curious.'

A year ago, Milo had solved the murder of a coroner's investigator. Since then Dr Clarice Jernigan, a senior pathologist, had reciprocated with personalized attention when Milo asked for it.

He said, 'Must be my charm and good looks.'

Gloria grinned and patted his shoulder again. 'Anything else, guys? I'm on half-shift due to budgetary constraints, figure to finish my paperwork by one then go cleanse my head with a couple of martinis. Give or take.'

Milo said, 'Make it a double for me.'

I said, 'Was significant blood pooled inside the body cavity?'

Her look said I was being a spoilsport. 'A lot of it was coagulated but yes, that's where most of it was. You figured that because the scene was so clean?'

I nodded. 'It was either that or he found out a way to take it with him.'

Milo said, 'Buckets of blood, lovely.' To Gloria: 'One more question: you recall anything remotely like this in your case files?'

'Nope,' she said. 'But we just cover the county and they say it's a globalized world, right? You could be looking at a traveler.'

Milo glared and trudged down the stairs.

Gloria said, 'Whoa, someone's in a mood.'

I said, 'It's likely to stay that way for a while.'

3

STANLEIGH BELLEVEAUX'S house was as meticulous inside as out.

Cozy, plush-carpeted place set up with doily-protected too-small furniture. The dollhouse feel was heightened by a brass étagère filled with bisque figurines. Another case bore photos of two handsome young men in uniform and an American flag paperweight.

'My wife's thing,' said Belleveaux, wringing his hands. 'The dolls, they're from Germany. She's in Memphis, visiting my mother-in-law.'

He was black, fiftyish, thickset, dressed in a navy polo shirt, pressed khakis, and tan loafers. A fleece of white blanketed his scalp and the bottom half of his face. His nose had been broken a few times. His knuckles were scarred.

'Her mom,' said Milo.

'Pardon?'

'You called her your mother-in-law rather than her mom.'

'Because that's how I think of her. Mother-in-law. Worst person I know. Like the Ernie K-Doe song, but you probably don't remember that.'

Milo hummed a few bars.

Belleveaux smiled weakly. Turned grim and wrung his hands some more. 'I still can't believe what happened to Ms. Berlin. Still can't believe I had to *see* it.' He closed his eyes, opened them. No booze on the table before him, just a can of Diet Coke.

Milo said, 'Change your mind about the Dewar's, huh?'

'It's tempting,' said Belleveaux. 'But a little early in the day, what if I get a call and have to drive?'

11

'Call from who?'

'A tenant. That's my life, sir.'

'How many tenants do you have?'

'The Feldmans down below Ms. Berlin, the Soos and the Kims and the Parks and the other Parks in a triplex I own over near Korea Town. Then I've got a real problem rental down in Willowbrook, inherited from my dad, a nice family, the Rodriguezes, are there now but it's been tough because of the gangster situation.' He rubbed his eyes. 'This is my best neighborhood, I chose to live here, last place I thought I'd have . . . a problem. Still can't believe what I saw, it's like a movie, a bad one, a real horror movie. I want to switch to another channel but what I saw won't budge out of here.' Placing a thumb-tip on his forehead.

'It'll fade,' said Milo. 'Takes time.'

'Guess you'd know about that,' said Belleveaux. 'How much time?'

'Hard to say.'

'It's probably easier for you, this being your job. My job, the worst thing I see is a bat in a garage, sewage leak, mice eating wires.' Frowning. 'Gangsters in the Willowbrook place, but I keep my distance. This was way up close, *too* close.'

'How long have you owned the property across the street?'

'Seven years eight months.'

'That's pretty precise, Mr Belleveaux.'

'I'm a detail-man, Lieutenant. Learned precision in the army, they taught me mechanics, a little mechanical engineering, I didn't need a college degree to accumulate adequate knowledge. Later when I was out and repairing washing machines and dryers for Sears, what the army inculcated in me came in handy: only one way to do a job: right. Machine needs three screws, you don't put in two.'

I said, 'The same goes for boxing.'

'Pardon?'

'Your hands. I used to do karate, you pick up the signs someone else is into martial arts.'

'Martial arts?' said Belleveaux. 'Nah, none of that for me, I just did a little sparring in the army, then a little more when I got out, light welterweight, used to be skinny. Busted my septum three times and my wife, she was my girlfriend back then, said, "Stan, you keep scarring yourself to the point where you're ugly, I'm going to go find myself a pretty boy." She was kidding. Maybe. I wanted out anyway, what kind of life is that, getting knocked around, feeling dizzy for days? The money was terrible.'

He drank some Coke. Licked his lips.

Milo said, 'So what can you tell us about Vita Berlin?'

'What can I tell you,' Belleveaux echoed. 'That's a complicated question.'

'Why's that, sir?'

'She wasn't the easiest . . . okay, look, I don't want to be speaking bad of the dead. 'Specially someone who – what happened to her. No one deserves that. *No* one, no matter what.'

I said, 'She had a difficult personality.'

'So you know what I'm talking about.'

I didn't deny it. 'Being her landlord could get complicated,' I prompted.

Belleveaux picked up the soda can. 'Does what I tell you go in some kind of record?'

Milo said, 'There's a problem with that?'

'I don't want to get sued.'

'By who?'

'Someone in her family.'

'They're difficult as well?'

'Don't know,' said Belleveaux. 'Never met them. I just believe in being prepared, ounce of prevention and all that.'

'No particular reason you're worried about being sued.'

'No, but those kinds of things,' said Belleveaux. 'Traits. Orneriness. Runs in families, right? Like Emmaline. My mother-in-law. Her sisters are all like her, scrappy, always ready to tussle. It's like stepping into a cage of badgers.'

'Vita Berlin threatened to sue you?'

13

'About a million times.'

'What for?'

'Anything that bothered her,' said Belleveaux. 'Leaky roof, she doesn't get a call-back in an hour, I'll sue you. Torn carpet, I'm at risk of tripping and breaking my neck, fix it fast or I'll sue you. That's why I got irked when she demanded I show up for the toilet and wasn't there when she said she'd be. That's why I decided to use my key and go in there and fix it. Even though I knew she'd call me up and bitch about entering the premises without her permission. Which the landlord association says I can do at my discretion for just cause. Which includes reasonable repairs requested by the tenant. Turns out the toilet was fine.'

Milo said, 'You went into the bathroom?'

'I listened while I was looking at her. I know it's crazy but I couldn't move for a few seconds, just stood there trying not to hurl my breakfast. And it was quiet, toilet's out of whack you hear it. So I thought about that: it wasn't even broken.'

I said, 'Vita enjoyed giving you a hard time.'

'Don't know if she enjoyed it, but she sure did it.'

'Did you try to evict her?'

Belleveaux laughed. 'No grounds, that's the way the law works. To get evicted, a tenant's just about got to . . .' He stopped short. 'I was going to say they've got to kill someone. Oh, man, this is terrible.'

I said, 'Seven years, eight months.'

'I bought the building four years five months ago, she came with it. I thought that meant good, long-term stable tenant. Then I learned different. Basically, she thought she owned it and I was her janitor.'

'Entitled,' I said.

'That's a nice word for it,' he said.

'Cranky lady.'

'Okay,' he said, 'I'll come out and say it: she was a miserable specimen, didn't have a good word for anyone. It's like she had bile in her veins instead of blood. My guess is you're not going to have too many people crying. Disgusted, yes, scared, yes. But not crying.'

'Disgusted by . . .'

'What happened to her.' Belleveaux's eyes clamped shut again. The lids twitched. 'Man, *no* one deserves *that.*'

'But no one's going to mourn.'

'Maybe she's got some family who'll mourn,' he said. 'But no one who had anything to do with her is going to say they miss her. I'm not stating that for a fact, I'm just guessing, but I'd put money on my guess. You want to see what I mean, go over to Bijou, it's a coffee shop on Robertson. She ate there from time to time, made their lives miserable. Same for the Feldmans, the downstairs tenants. Nice young couple, they've been here a year, are ready to move 'cause of her.'

'Neighbors' dispute.'

'No dispute, she harassed them. They're on the bottom floor, she's on top but *she's* the one complaining about footsteps. Actually made me come up to her place to listen a bunch of times, all I heard was her bitching, she's saying, "See, hear that, Stan? They're clomping around like barbarians." Then she lies down, puts her ear to the carpet, makes me do it. That position, maybe I pick up a little sound but nothing serious. But I lie, tell her I'll talk to them. Just to keep her out of my hair, you know? I did nothing about it, she dropped it. The next time, it's something else — they fill the trash bins too high, they park their cars wrong, she thinks they snuck in a cat and it's a no-pet building. What happened was there was a stray cat came to the back door, looked like it was starving, they gave it some milk. Which is the human thing to do, right? Now the Feldmans are going to leave for sure and I'll have both units vacant. Should've put my pension money in gold bars or something.'

Milo said, 'Sounds like Vita was a little paranoid.'

'That's a word for it,' said Belleveaux. 'But it was more like she wanted attention and being mean was a way to get it.'

'She have any friends?'

'None I ever saw.'

'And you live across the street.'

'Part of the problem. She knew where to find me. Here I was thinking the building would be perfect, convenient, no need to drive. Next time

I buy, it's in another state. Not that there'll be a next time. Market was up, I'd sell everything.'

'What can you tell us about her daily routine?'

'From what I saw she kept to herself, didn't go out much.'

'Except for meals.'

'Once in a while she'd walk over to Bijou. I know because I've been there myself, saw her a couple times. Cheap and good, I'd be there more but the wife's into cooking, takes lessons, likes to try stuff out. Now it's French, that's why I'm not skinny like I used to be.'

Milo said, 'Vita eat anywhere else besides Bijou?'

'Mostly what I saw was takeout,' said Belleveaux. 'From the boxes she'd throw out in the garbage. I know because she'd miss, I'd have to pick them up. The automated trucks they use nowadays, it's not in the can, it stays there and I don't want rats.'

'What kind of takeout?'

'What I saw was pizza boxes. So I guess she liked pizza.'

'From where?'

'Where? I don't know – I think Domino's, they're the ones in the blue hats, right? Maybe other places, I don't know. It's not like I was checking out her eating habits through the drapes. The less I had to do with her, the better.'

'Did she get pizza delivered last night?'

'Wouldn't know,' said Belleveaux. 'I was at Staples, watching the Lakers take one from Utah. Went with my boys, they're both master sergeants in the army, had leave the same week, we did a basketball thing and later we went to Philippe's for some grub.' He touched his belt buckle. 'Overdid it with the French dip, but how many times do you get to go out with your kids, do guy stuff, everyone's being a grown-up? Got home late, slept late till seven, got her message on the machine, why didn't I come yesterday after the first call, the toilet's busted, it's her right to have a functional toilet, all the fixtures are old and cheap and lousy, if I'm not going to replace them the least I can do is repair them in a timely manner, I'd best be there no later than eight a.m. or she's filing a complaint.'

Milo said, 'What time did she call you?'

'I didn't check.'

'Message still on the machine?'

'Nah, I erased it.'

'Can you narrow it down?'

'Hmm,' said Belleveaux. 'Well, I left for the game around four, stopped by at the Soos' apartment to look at an electrical outlet, so it had to be after that.'

'What time did you get home?'

'Close to midnight. Drove Anthony and Dmitri to where they parked their rental car in the Union Station lot, Anthony drove Dmitri to the airport then he drove himself to Fort Irwin.'

'When you got home were Vita Berlin's lights on?'

'Let's see . . . can't rightly say. She paid her own electric, what she did with her lights was her own business.'

'Where can we find the Feldmans?'

'They're good kids, still don't know about this.'

'Why's that?'

'Probably at work, they're doctors – resident doctors. He's at Cedars, she's somewhere else, maybe the U., I'm not sure.'

'First names?'

'David and Sondra with an *o*. Trust me, they had nothing to do with this.'

'Doctors,' said Milo. Thinking: *surgical cut.*

Stanleigh Belleveaux said, 'Exactly. Respectable.'

4

BY THE time we left Belleveaux's house a crime lab van was parked outside the tape. Two techs, both young men, were inside the apartment. Their kits rested out on the landing. The body remained in place.

Milo said, 'Lance, Kenny.'

'Lieutenant,' said the taller man. *L. Sakura* on his tag. 'This sure is disgusting.'

K. Flores didn't react.

Milo said, 'Keeps life interesting. Don't let me stop you.'

Flores said, 'How far do you want us to take this?'

'As far as you need to.'

'What I mean, Lieutenant, is there's no sign of disruption in the room, it all seems centered on the body. Obviously we'll print and look for fibers but do you see any reason to luminol?'

Sakura said, 'Looks way too clean even for someone doing a mop-up. No bleach smell, either. We'll check the drains, call in a forensic plumber if the fixtures give us a problem, but we don't see much chance for significant blood evidence.'

'Other than *her* blood,' said Flores. 'Which is probably the small spots on the towel. Even there, whoever did this was super-careful. Probably dabbed as he went and took whatever he used with him.'

'This is a freak,' said Sakura.

Milo said, 'C.I. said most of the blood is pooled inside the body. Let's see what you pull up print- and fiber-wise then we'll talk about spraying.'

Flores said, 'We pulled up one thing so far, probably no big deal.'

18

'What?'

'A note in the bedroom. We left it there.'

After donning new gloves and foot coverings, we followed Flores in while Sakura began fiddling with his kit.

Vita Berlin's sleeping chamber was close, dim, spare, with walls also painted apartment-beige and linens of the same characterless hue. Double bed, no headboard or footboard, no personal touches. The books Milo had described were piled high on a white fiberboard nightstand. The surface of a three-door dresser was bare. Two more beehive lamps.

She hadn't indulged others or herself.

Flores pointed to the foot of the bed where a rumpled scrap of white paper rested. 'It was underneath, I took a photo of it there, then slid it out.'

We kneeled, read. In neat script someone had written:

Dr B. Shacker

Below that, a 310 number. A diagonal line slashed the name. At the bottom of the page, a single word in larger, darker caps:

QUACK!!!

Flores said, 'There's dust and maybe crumbs down there but nothing weird.'

Milo copied down the information. 'Thanks, Kenny, bag it.'

Back on the landing, he said, 'Might as well talk to this doctor.' Half smiling. 'Maybe he's a surgeon.'

He 411'd, got a listing.

'Bernhard Shacker, Ph.D., North Bedford Drive, Beverly Hills. A colleague, Alex: that makes it a bit more interesting, no? Vita obviously had what you guys call issues, maybe she decided to get some help, tried out therapy, changed her mind. What's that phrase you use about screwed-up folk resisting the most?'

19

'Baloney afraid of the slicer.'

'But she got sliced anyway. Maybe Shacker can educate us on her personality. Know him?'

I shook my head.

'Bedford Drive,' he said. 'That's high-ticket Couch Row, seems a little froufrou for someone who lived like Vita did.' Phoning Shacker's number, he listened, frowned, clicked off.

'Recorded spiel,' he said. 'I like your way better.'

I still use an answering service because talking to human beings is at the core of my job. 'You didn't leave a message.'

'Didn't want to scare him off, in case he gets all pissy about confidentiality. Also I figured maybe talking to him is something you could do. One mind-prober to another.'

'While we're at it, we can figure out transmigration of the soul.'

'Wouldn't put it past you, amigo. So you'll do it?'

I smiled.

He said, 'Great, let's check out that restaurant.'

He left his unmarked at the crime scene and we drove west to Robertson in my Seville. Bijou: A Dining Place was a brown-brick storefront set close enough to the 10 Freeway to harvest soot on its signage. The brick was grimy, too, but a picture window sparkled.

The morning special was blueberry pancakes. Posted hours said *Breakfast and Lunch Only, Closed by Three p.m.*

The restaurant's interior said it was probably a venerable diner remodeled to look even older. From the freshness of the green vinyl seating and the laminate tabletops patterned to look like Formica, a recent upgrade. The kind of movie-star headshots you see in dry cleaners hung on the walls, along with black-and-white shots of pre-freeway L.A.

An old man reading *The Wall Street Journal* sat at the counter, nursing coffee and a sweet roll. Three of seven booths were occupied: up in front, two young moms tried to chat while tending to bibbed, squirming toddlers in booster chairs. Behind them, a husky apple-faced man in his thirties ate steak and eggs while penciling a puzzle book. At the back, a brown-uniformed parcel driver small enough to be a jockey worked on a mountain of pancakes while grooving to his iPod. Both men looked up when we entered, returned to their recreation. The women were too busy with their kids to notice.

A waitress, young, blond, shapely, sleeve-tattooed, had the shift to herself. A short-order cook with an Incan face sweated behind the pass-through.

Milo waited until the waitress had refilled Wall Street's coffee before approaching.

She said, 'Sit anywhere you like, guys.'

Her badge chirped *Hedy!* Milo's badge ruined her smile. The old man put his paper aside and eavesdropped.

Hedy said, 'Let me get the owner.'

Milo said, 'Do you know Vita Berlin?'

'She eats here.'

'Regularly?'

'Kind of,' she said. 'Like two times a week?'

The old man said, 'What'd *that* one do, now?'

Milo faced him. 'She died.'

Hedy said, 'Omigod!'

The old man, unperturbed, said, 'How?'

'Unnaturally.'

'What does that mean? Suicide? Accident?' A bushy white eyebrow compressed to the shape of a croquet wicket. 'Worse? Yeah, probably worse if the constabulary's bothering to show up.'

Hedy said, 'Oh, Sam.'

The old man regarded her with pity.

Milo turned to him. 'You knew Vita.'

'Knew enough not to like her. What happened to her – she mouthed off to the wrong guy and he hauled off and bopped her one?'

Hedy said, 'Omigod, Sam, this is terrible. Can I go get Ralph, Officers? He's in back.'

Milo said, 'Ralph's the owner?'

The old man said, 'Of this gourmet establishment.'

21

'Sure.'

Hedy rushed toward the *Exit* sign.

The old man said, 'They've got a thing going. Her and Ralph.'

Milo said, 'Sam?'

'Samuel Lipschitz, certified actuary,' said the old man. 'Blessedly retired.' He wore a burnt-orange cardigan over a white shirt buttoned to the neck, gray hopsack slacks, argyle socks, cordovan lace-ups.

'What was it about Vita you didn't like, Mr Lipschitz?'

'So you're verifying she was murdered.'

Raising his voice on the last word caused the young mothers to look over. The driver and the puzzle-solver didn't react.

Milo said, 'That wouldn't surprise you.'

'Yes and no,' said Lipschitz. 'Yes, because murder's a low-frequency event. No, because, as I said, she had a provocative personality.'

'Who'd she provoke?'

'Anyone she felt like. She was an equal-opportunity harridan.'

'She was disruptive here?'

'She'd come swaggering in like a man, plop down in a booth, and start glaring, like she was just waiting for someone to do something that would give her the excuse to pull a snit. Everyone was wise to her so we ignored her. She'd sulk, order her food, eat, sulk some more, pay and leave.'

Lipschitz chuckled.

'So she really pushed someone too far, ay? How'd they do it? Where'd they do it?'

'I can't get into that, sir.'

'Just tell me one thing: was it around here? I don't live in the neighborhood anymore, moved to Alhambra when I retired. But I come back to this place because I like the pastries, they get 'em from a Danish baker all the way out in Covina. So if there's something I should worry about personal-security-wise, I'd appreciate your telling me. I'm seventy-four, would like to squeeze in a few more years.'

'From what we've seen, sir, there's nothing for you to worry about.'

'That's ambiguous to the point of being meaningless,' said Lipschitz.

'It wasn't a street crime. It doesn't appear connected to gangs or a robbery.'

'When did it happen?'

'Sometime last night.'

'I come here during the day I should be fine?'

'Mr Lipschitz, is there anything else you can tell us about Vita?'

'Other than her being abrasive and antisocial? I did hear about something but I didn't witness it firsthand. A confrontation, right here. Four, five days ago, I was in Palm Springs visiting my son. Missed my pastry and all the excitement.'

'Who told you about it?'

'Ralph — here he is, let him tell you himself.'

Ralph Veronese was no older than thirty, tall and borderline-emaciated with long, thick dark hair, a rock star's cheekbones and slouchy stance. He wore a black bowling shirt, low-slung skinny jeans, work boots, a diamond stud in his left lobe. One arm was brocaded in blue ink.

His hands were rough, his voice soft. He asked if we could speak outside and when Milo assented, voiced his thanks profusely and guided us through the café to a rear alley. A red van occupied the single parking slot.

'Hedy just told me about Vita. I can't believe it.'

'You don't see anyone wanting to hurt her?'

'No, it's not that. I mean I'm not saying someone would hurt her, it's just . . . someone you know. She was here a couple of days ago.'

'She was a regular?'

'Two, three times a week.'

'Big fan of the food.'

Veronese didn't answer.

Milo said, 'Something must've drawn her here.'

'She could walk from her house. That's what she told me once. "It's not like you're a great chef, I don't have to waste gas." I said, "And hopefully we won't give you any." She didn't laugh. She never laughed.'

'Cranky lady.'

'Oh, yeah.'

'Mr Lipschitz said she'd had some kind of confrontation here a few days ago.'

Veronese rotated his earring. 'I'm sure that had nothing to do with what happened to her.'

'Why's that, Mr Veronese?'

'Mr Veronese was my grandfather, Ralph's fine . . . yeah, Vita had a tough personality but I just can't see anything that happened here being relevant.'

'Tell us about the confrontation, Ralph.'

He sighed. 'There was no excuse for her behavior but I don't even know the people's names, it was the first time they were here!'

'What happened?'

'These people came in with their kid. Vita was already here, reading the *Times* that she always borrows from us and eating away.'

'How many people?'

'Mom, dad, the kid was little – four, five, I'm not good with ages.' Veronese tugged at a forelock, positioned it over his left eyebrow. 'Bald. The kid. Skinny, these humongous eyes. Like you see on those ads for starving kids?' He tapped the crook of one arm. 'Big bandage here. Like she got stuck with a shot, it was a she, a little girl.'

I said, 'Sounds like a sick little girl.'

'Exactly, I figured cancer or something,' said Veronese. He sighed. 'See something like that, makes you want to cry.'

I said, 'Vita didn't cry.'

'Oh, man.' His voice tightened. 'I knew she was a pain in the ass but no way I figured something like that would happen. If I had, I'da seated them far from her. I seated them right next to her, make it easy for Hedy, you know?'

'Vita wasn't happy about that?'

'At first she didn't seem to notice them, she's reading and eating, everything's copacetic. Then the kid starts making noises. Not being annoying, like a moan, you know? Like she's hurting, like something hurts. The parents are leaning over, whispering. Trying to comfort her,

I guess. It goes on for a while. The moaning. Then the kid quiets down. Then she moans again and Vita puts down her paper, gives her the eye, you know?'

'Angry.'

'Angry with sharp eyes,' said Veronese. 'What do they call it, dagger eyes? Like you can stab someone with them? My grandmother used to say that, "Don't be shooting me those dagger eyes, you gonna draw my blood." Vita's doing that, the dagger eyes. Right at the kid. The parents aren't noticing, they're concentrating on the kid. Finally, she quiets down again, Hedy takes their order, offers the kid a donut but the parents say the kid's stomach can't take it. Vita mutters something, the father looks over, Vita glares at him, goes back behind her paper. Then the kid starts moaning again, a little louder. The father walks to the counter and asks me for some ice cream. Like he's figuring that might calm the kid down. I say you bet and fix a double scoop, he goes back, tries to feed the kid the ice cream, she tastes it but then she's not having it. Starts crying *again*. All of a sudden, Vita's out of her booth, like this.' He clamped a hand on each hip. 'Looking down at them, like they're evil. Then she says something, then the kid's father is up on his feet, too, and they're going at each other.'

'Going how?'

'Arguing, I couldn't hear what, 'cause I had gone back to the kitchen, same for Hedy, so all we heard was some kind of commotion. I thought something had happened to the kid, a medical emergency. So I rush back and the father and Vita are in each other's faces and he looks ready to – he's really pissed off but his wife grabs his arm, holds him back. Vita says something that makes him pull his arm free, he raises a fist. Just holds it there. Shaking. All of him is shaking. Then he calms down, swoops up the kid, and they head for the door. Funny thing is, now the kid's calm. Like nothing ever happened.'

Another earring-tug. 'I rush out, ask if there's something I can do. I felt like shit, a sick kid, you know? It wasn't her fault she didn't feel

25

good. Father looks at me, shakes his head, they drive off. I go back inside, Vita's back in her booth, smiling. Says, "Some people have no class, I told them why would you people think the rest of the world wants to see your sick little brat, ruin their appetite? Sick people belong in hospitals, not restaurants."'

Milo said, 'Describe these people.'

'Thirty-five, forty,' said Veronese. 'Nicely dressed.' Looking away.

I said, 'Something else?'

'Black.'

'That "you people" part probably didn't go over well.'

'Yeah,' said Veronese, 'that was evil.'

'Did Vita show other signs of racism?'

'Nah, she hated everyone.' He frowned. 'Would've loved to toss her but she sues people, it's all I can do to keep this place afloat, last thing I need is to be sued.'

'Who'd she sue?'

'The place she used to work, some kind of discrimination, they paid her off, that's how she lives.'

'Who told you?'

'She did. Bragging.'

Milo said, 'The people she had a to-do with. Thirty-five to forty, well dressed, and black. What else?'

'They drove a Mercedes. Not a big one, small station wagon.' Veronese scratched at his hairline. 'Silver. I think. I'm sure they had nothing to do with it.'

'Why's that?'

'How would they know who she was, where to find her?'

'Maybe they knew her before.'

'Didn't seem that way,' said Veronese. 'I mean they didn't use names or anything.'

'Who else has Vita had words with?'

'Everyone leaves her alone.'

'Big tipper, huh?'

'You kidding? – oh, yeah, you are. Her top rate's ten percent and for each thing that pisses her off, she drops a percent. And tells you. Hedy laughs about it, only reason she's here is to do me a favor, her main thing's singing, she sings in a band. I play bass behind her.' Smiling. 'I like looking at the back of her.'

5

WE DROVE back to the crime scene. The coroner's van had taken the body. Sakura and Flores were still busy at work, scraping, diluting, bagging, tagging.

'Lots of prints,' said Sakura, 'where you'd expect them to be. Nothing on the doorknob, that's wiped clean. We got a few hairs off the towels, gray, consistent with hers. We did find more blood on the towels – tiny little specks tucked into the nap. Same for the carpet, we'll cut out squares. If he nicked himself operating on her, you could get lucky.'

Milo said, 'From your mouth to the Evidence God's ears.'

Flores said, 'The sink drain's kind of tricky, we are going to call in the plumber. Could take a couple of days.'

'Whatever it takes, guys. Anything else?'

'I don't want to tell you your business, Lieutenant, but it was me, I'd put in for a tox screen super-stat.'

'You think she was doped?'

'This little resistance, maybe the offender used something on her – like an anesthetic. Something that didn't need to be injected, like chloroform or ether, because we didn't find any needle marks. But maybe she medicated herself and that made his job easy. We found booze bottles under her bathroom sink when we were checking out the plumbing. Stashed at the back behind rolls of toilet paper.'

Reaching into an evidence bag, he drew out two 177ml Jack Daniel's bottles, one sealed, the other down a third.

I said, 'No booze anywhere else?'

'Nowhere.'

Sakura said, 'Big bottles, she bought in bulk.'

I said, 'She lived alone but hid her habit.'

'Living alone doesn't mean she drank alone,' said Milo.

'Then why hide the booze?'

He had no answer for that and it made him frown.

I said, 'If she did have a drinking pal, it was someone who wouldn't pry in the bathroom.'

'Meaning?'

'No intimacy.'

'Behind toilet paper's not the first place anyone would look. And if she was a solitary drinker, why bother to conceal?'

'Hiding a habit from herself,' I said. 'Someone who needed to think of herself as totally in control. And righteous.'

That didn't impress anyone.

Flores said, 'What's your take on the broken neck, Lieutenant, some sort of karate move?'

'I should be checking out dojos? Asking if they have anyone likes also to cut people up and play with their guts.' He turned to the pizza box. 'You guys ready to open it up?'

'Sure,' said Sakura. 'We already dusted, no prints or anything else. Didn't feel like there was any pizza in there. Or anything else.'

'Pop it.'

Flores pried open the top.

Empty but on the bottom surface of the box a piece of plain white paper had been Scotch-taped, margins precise, just like the towels beneath the body. In the center of the paper someone had computer-printed in a large bold-faced font:

?

Milo flushed a deeper red than I'd ever seen. A pulse in his neck raced. For a moment I was worried about his health.

Then he grinned and some of the color faded. Like a joke had just been played on him and he was determined to be a good sport.

He said, 'What's this, a fucking challenge? Fine. Game on, you bastard.' To the techs: 'Print every damn surface of this. Look for spots where someone would be likely to screw up and leave a partial. You don't find anything, do it again. You tell me there's nothing, I want it to really *be* nothing.'

Flores said, 'Yes, sir.'

Sakura said, 'You bet.'

Milo walked me to my car, keeping slightly ahead and making me feel I was being ushered away. He leaned in when I started up the engine.

'Thanks for showing up. I'm gonna be tied up with basics: her bank, her phone records, finding next of kin. I'm also gonna try for a face-to-face with the two doctor neighbors, I get lucky they'll turn out to be Jack the Ripper and his nefarious little Jill. Meanwhile, if you could try that shrink – Shacker.'

'I'll call him when I get home.'

'Thanks. What you said before, the part about Vita wanting to feel in control, I agree with. Righteous, I'm not so sure. What kind of morally upright person unloads on a little sick kid?'

I said, 'Righteous is a broad category. She could've seen herself as the guardian of all that's proper. Restaurants are for eating, hospitals are for sick people, disease is unappetizing, stay away. It's a common feeling. Most people are a lot more subtle but you'd be surprised how often sick people get stigmatized. Back when I worked in oncology, families talked about it all the time.'

He shook his head. 'However she *felt* about herself, she was a major-league jerk and that means the suspect list just expanded to the entire goddamn universe.'

I shifted into Drive.

He said, 'Are there diseases other than cancer that can cause baldness?'

'A few,' I said, 'but cancer would be my guess.'

'And if the kid had cancer there's a good chance she'd be treated at your old turf.'

Western Pediatric Medical, where I'd trained and worked and learned which questions to ask, which to ignore.

I said, 'It's the best place in town.'

'Hmm.'

I said, 'Sorry, no.'

'No, what?'

'You're my pal but I'm not going snooping in the oncology files.'

He poked his chest. 'I would ask for such a thing? Now I know what you *really* think of me.'

'I think you're being your usual ace-detective self.'

His nostrils flared. 'Oh, man, we go too far back to spread the bullshit. Yeah, I'd love for you to dig around. You can't do it, even discreetly?'

'There's no way to do it discreetly. And even if there was, I wouldn't want to be the one pointing a finger at a family that's had more than enough to cope with.'

He exhaled. 'Yeah, yeah, I'm thinking like a hunter, not a human being.'

'You're unlikely to be losing a lead, Big Guy. Like Veronese said, no way for them to know who Vita was and where she lived.'

'Unless,' he said, 'they live in the neighborhood and happened to spot her and were still pissed and decided to act.'

'They go back and carve her up?' I said. 'That's one helluva grudge.'

'True but dealing with a high level of stress could kick up the frustration level, right? What if the poor little thing passed away shortly after the confrontation? That would jam one helluva memory into Mommy and Daddy's heads. Daddy stewed on it, started eating himself up. Eating his guts out. So to speak. He spots Vita, maybe she even snots off again. He decides to — whatever you guys call it — displace his anger.'

'That's what we call it.' And I'd seen plenty of it. Families railing against hospital food, a misspoken phrase, anything but the core issue because you can only deal with so much. More than once I'd been called

31

to ease a weapon away from a grieving father. But nothing at the level of the savagery visited upon Vita Berlin and I said so.

Milo said, 'So if I wanna go there, I'm on my own.'

'Where I'm going is phoning Dr Shacker. If he has an opening, I'll prioritize a meeting.'

'Thanks.'

'No problem.'

'Oh, there are plenty of problems,' he said. 'But they're all mine.'

6

I DROVE home thinking about the horror, tried to switch off The Unthinkable Channel.

The body floated back into my head.

Switching on the radio, I amped the volume to ear-bruise. Knowing that each thunder-chunk of noise was ripping loose tiny hairs in my auditory canal but figuring a little hearing loss was worth it. But station-surfing fed me a bland stew of passionless jingly crap and nerve-scraping chatter that failed to do the trick, so I pulled over, popped the trunk, took out a battered black vinyl case I hadn't touched in a long time.

Audio cassettes.

To anyone under thirty, as relevant as wax cylinders. The Seville has a different opinion. She's a '79 who rumbled out of Detroit a few months before Detroit turned her successors into Bloatmobiles. Fifteen thousand miles on the third engine with an enhanced suspension. Regular oil and filter changes keep her appeased. I retrofitted a CD player years ago, a hands-off phone system recently. But I've resisted an MP3 and kept the original tape deck in place because back when I was a grad student tapes were a major luxury and I've got lots of them, purchased secondhand back when that mattered.

As I got back in the car, the growling in my head grew thunderous. I've seen a lot of bad things and I don't get that way often but I'm pretty sure where the noise comes from: hiding from my father when he drank too much and decided someone needed to be punished. Blocking the *bump-bump* of my racing heart with imaginary white noise.

33

But now I couldn't turn it off and just as amphetamines quiet a hyperactive mind, my consciousness craved something loud and dark and aggressively competitive.

Thrash metal might've been nice but I'd never bought any. I flipped through tapes, found something promising: ZZ Top. *Eliminator.*

I slipped the tape into the deck, started up the car, resumed the drive home. Covered a block and cranked the music louder.

Minimalistic guitar, truck-engine drum, and ominous synthesizer backup worked pretty well. Then I turned off Sunset and got close to home and the peace and beauty of Beverly Glen, the sinuous silence of the old bridal path leading up to my pretty white house, the prospect of kissing my beautiful girlfriend, patting my adorable dog, feeding the pretty fish in my pond, sparked a sly little voice:

Nice life, huh?

Then: malevolent laughter.

The house was empty and sun-suffused. Wood floors tom-tommed as I trudged to my office and left a collegial message for Dr Bernhard Shacker. His soft, reassuring, recorded voice promised he'd get back to me as soon as possible. The kind of voice you believed. I made coffee, drank two cups without tasting, went out back and tossed pellets to the koi and tried to appreciate their slurpy gratitude and continued on to the tree-shrouded studio out back.

A saw-buzz sounded through an open window. Beautiful Girlfriend was goggled and masked and brightened by skylights set into the high sloping ceiling as she eased a piece of rosewood through a band saw. Long auburn curls were bunched under a red bandanna. Her hands were coated with purplish dust.

Adorable Dog crouched a few feet away, nibbling on one of the barbecue-sauce-crusted bones Girlfriend prepares for her with customary meticulousness.

Girlfriend smiled, kept her hands working. Dog waddled over and kissed my hand.

The saw rasped as it ate hardwood. Loud, nasty. Good.

I sat with Blanche on my lap until Robin finished working, rubbing a knobby little French bulldog head. Robin switched off the saw, placed the guitar-shaped slab on her worktable, pushed up the goggles, and lowered the mask. She had on red overalls, a black T-shirt, black-and-white Keds.

I placed Blanche on the floor and she followed me to the bench. Robin and I hugged and kissed and she mussed my hair the way I like.

'How'd it go, baby?'

I touched the rosewood. 'Nice grain.'

'One of those days?' she said.

How much I talk about cases has always been an issue for us. I've progressed from shutting her out completely to parceling the information I think she can handle. Sometimes it works in Milo's favor because Robin is smart and able to bring in an outsider's perspective.

As if I'm an insider. I'm not sure what I am.

I said, 'Definitely one of those.'

She touched my face. 'You're a little pale. Have you eaten?'

'Bagel before.'

'Want something now?'

'Maybe later.'

'If you change your mind,' she said.

'About food?'

'About anything.'

'Sure.' I kissed her forehead.

She eyed the rosewood. 'I guess I should get back to this.'

I said, 'Dinner will probably work. Maybe a little on the late side.'

'Sounds good.'

'If you get hungry sooner, I'm flexible.'

'You bet,' she said.

As I turned to leave, she touched my face. Her almond eyes were soft with compassion. 'The bad days, long-term planning doesn't work so well.'

I returned to my office. No call-back from Dr Shacker. I did some paperwork, paid some bills, got on the computer.

A search of *disemboweling* and *murder* pulled up a disquieting mountain of hits: just under a hundred thousand. Nearly all were irrelevant, resulting from the use of both words in complex sentences, song lyrics by deservedly obscure bands, political hyperbole by blogo-simps who've never lived with anything worse than a paper cut. *('The current administration is disemboweling civil liberties and committing premeditated murder on personal liberties with the bloody abandon of a serial killer.')*

The literal murders I found were mostly single-victim crimes: stalking outrages fueled by sexual fantasy or long-simmering resentment before building to a starburst of violence that led to mutilation and sometimes cannibalism. The crimes were generally carried out carelessly and solves were quick. In several cases, floridly psychotic suspects turned them-selves in. In one instance, an offender dropped a human liver on the desk of a police receptionist and begged to be arrested because he'd done a 'bad thing'.

The few open cases were of the historical variety, most notably Jack the Ripper.

The scourge of Whitechapel had engaged in abdominal mutilation and organ theft, but differences outweighed any similarities to the meticulously organized degradation visited upon Vita Berlin.

Vita's abrasive personality said this could very well be a one-off.

I hoped to God it had nothing to do with the child she'd humiliated.

I surfed a bit more, trying *abdominal mutilation, visceral display, intestinal wounds,* had gotten nowhere when my service called.

'Dr Delaware, it's Louise. A Dr Shacker just called, returning yours.'

'Thanks.'

'He's one of you, right? A psychologist.'

'Good guess, Louise.'

'Actually, it's more than a guess, Dr Delaware, it's intuition. I've been doing this a long time.'

'We all sound alike?'

'Actually you kind of do,' she said. 'No offense, I mean that in a good way. You guys tend to be calm and patient. Surgeons don't sound like that. Anyway, he seemed like a nice guy. Have a good day, Dr Delaware.'

A pleasant, boyish voice said, 'Bern Shacker.'

'Alex Delaware, thanks for calling back.'

'No problem,' he said. 'You said this was about Vita. Does that mean you're the lucky guy treating her now?'

'I'm afraid no one's treating her.'

'Oh?'

'She's been murdered.'

'My God. What happened?'

I gave him the basics.

He said, 'That's dreadful, absolutely dreadful. Murdered . . . and you're calling me because . . .'

Because Vita had labeled him a quack. I said, 'She had your card in her apartment.'

'Did she . . . her apartment? I'm a little – you said you were a psychologist. Why would you be in her apartment? And why, for that matter, are you following up on a murder?'

'I consult to the police and the detective in charge asked me to call you. One shrink to another.'

'Shrink,' he said. 'Unfortunate term . . . well, I don't really – I didn't exactly engage in long-term therapy with Vita – this is a bit complicated. I need to make a call or two before we go any further.'

'Death and confidentiality,' I said. 'The rules change every year.'

'True, but it's not only that,' said Shacker. 'Vita wasn't a typical therapy patient. I'm not trying to be mysterious but I can't say more until I get clearance. If I do, we can chat.'

'Appreciate it, Dr Shacker.'

'Murder,' he said. 'Unbelievable. Where are you located?'

'The Westside.'

'I'm in Beverly Hills. If we do talk, would you mind it being face-to-face? So I can document the conversation?'

37

'That would be fine.'
'I'll get back to you.'

Forty-three minutes later, he was true to his word. 'Alex? This is Bern. The insurance attorneys have cleared me and so did my personal attorney. I've got an opening at six. Does that work for you?'
'Perfectly.'
'Perfectly,' he echoed. 'You sound like a positive person.'
As if he'd just uncovered a character flaw.
'I try.'
'Try,' said Shacker, 'is all we can do.'

7

SHACKER'S BUILDING was three stories of lime and brick in the midst of Beverly Hills' business district. Glossy navy carpeting smothered footsteps. Walls were paneled in bleached oak. A pharmacy calling itself a Dispensing Apothecarie and designed to look Victorian took up a quarter of the ground floor. The rest of the tenants were M.D.s, D.D.S.s, a few other psychologists.

B. Shacker, Ph.D., Suite 207.

His waiting room was tiny, white, and set up with three friendly chairs and a wall-stack of magazines. Soft new-age music played from somewhere. A two-bulb panel sat to the left of the inner door. Red for in session, green for free. Red was illuminated but moments after I sat down, it went dark.

The door opened. An arm extended. 'Alex? Bern Shacker.'

The body attached to the arm was five six, thin, narrow-shouldered. The handshake offered was firm, dry, solid.

Shacker looked around fifty. A fine-boned, rosy-cheeked face was topped by thinning chestnut hair laced with silver and styled in a not-too-bad comb-over. Prominent ears and a slightly crooked pug nose gave him an elfin look. His eyes were soft, hazel, vaguely rueful. He wore a gray V-neck sweater over a black shirt, charcoal slacks, black loafers. The sleeves of the sweater were pushed to his elbows. Black shirt-cuffs overlapped the edges.

'Thanks for taking the time, Bern.'

'Please, come in.'

The treatment room was painted pale aqua, carpeted in a darker variant of the same hue, dimmed by brown silk drapes shielding the window that looked out to Bedford Drive. Not a trace of street noise; double- or triple-glazed glass. The requisite professional paper adorned the wall behind a modest walnut desk: doctorate, intern-ship, postdoc, license. The only thing mildly interesting was a Ph.D. from the University of Louvain in Belgium.

Shacker said, 'My Catholic days,' and smiled.

The wall to the left of the desk bore the auxiliary door that had allowed Shacker's patient to exit into the hallway without encountering me. Next to that hung a chrome-framed cubist print of fruit and bread. Two Scandinavian leather chairs sat in front of the desk, facing each other. Shacker motioned me to one, took the other.

He crossed a leg, tugged his trousers up, flashed argyle sock. 'Over the phone I mentioned insurance lawyers. They're the ones who sent Vita to me.'

'Therapy was part of a settlement?'

'Three years ago she sued her employer. The case dragged on. Finally the employer's coverer was ready to settle but insisted upon a psych evaluation. Insurance work isn't my usual thing but I'd treated an individual with a connection to the insurer – obviously I can't say more – and was asked to see Vita.'

I said, 'What was the purpose of the evaluation?'

'To see if she was malingering.'

'She was claiming some sort of emotional damage?'

'Supposedly she'd been bullied at work and the company hadn't done enough to ensure a hostility-free work environment.'

'What company are we talking about?'

Shacker recrossed his legs. 'I'm sorry, I can't give you that, one condition of the settlement was a ban on discussion by both sides. What I can tell you is that it was an insurance company. Health insurance, to be exact. Vita worked for them as a screener.'

'She decided who got care and who didn't?'

'The company would call it managing the flow of treatment requests.'

'Was she a nurse?'

'She'd had two years of secretarial school and her employment history consisted of nonmedical clerical positions.'

'That qualified her to decide who got to talk to a doctor?'

'Who got to talk to a *nurse*,' he said. 'She was a *pre*-screening screener. It's called diagnosis-specific utilization management and yes, it's atrocious. Vita described working at a huge phone-bank, claimed she'd been provided scripts to read from. Certain conditions were to be ignored, for others she'd suggest an over-the-counter remedy. She was given a list of various call-back protocols – a week for this, a month for that. Acute conditions were to be referred to local emergency rooms, serious diagnoses were put on hold as she pretended to search for the next available nurse.'

I said, 'Telemarketing in reverse: don't use our product.'

Shacker said, 'This is what it's come to. What was different about Vita was that she loved her job. Getting back at "weaklings" and "fakers".'

I said, 'That didn't apply to her post-traumatic symptoms.'

He smiled. 'What can I tell you?'

'What kind of bullying are we talking about?'

'No physical intimidation, just pranks and ridicule from some of her co-workers. Vita said she complained repeatedly to her supervisors but was ignored. Her suit was for five million dollars.'

'High-priced ridicule. What were her symptoms?'

'Difficulty concentrating, insomnia, appetite loss, stomach problems, aches and pains. Ambiguous things unlikely to show up on a medical exam but impossible to disprove. Since the alleged root cause was emotional trauma, the health insurer's casualty insurer wanted an official opinion as to her psychological status.'

'What did you tell them?'

'That her claims couldn't be validated or invalidated and that she came across as a hostile individual. I didn't offer a diagnosis as it wasn't requested. Had I been asked, I suppose I could've dug around the DSM for something that fit, but I'm not one of those therapists who feel bad behavior's a disease.'

'What was Vita's bad behavior?'

He folded his arms across his chest. 'May I tell you something in utter confidence, Alex? Really, I don't want this entered in any official record.'

'Absolutely.'

'Thank you.' He chewed his lip, played with a sleeve. 'Vita was quite possibly the least pleasant person I've ever met. I know we're not supposed to judge, but let's face it, we do. It didn't help that she had no motivation to cooperate and regarded our profession with obvious disdain. Most of our sessions consisted of her complaining that I was wasting her time. That anyone with half a brain could see she'd suffered grievous injury. She just about came out and called me a quack. Now you tell me she's been murdered. Was there evidence of rage? Because I can see her inciting someone's anger past the point of no return.'

'I'm also limited in what I can say, Bern.'

'I see . . . all right. Then that's really all I can tell you.'

'Could we go back to her lawsuit? What kind of pranks and ridicule did she say she'd experienced?'

'Gluing her desk drawer shut, hiding her headset, making off with her snacks. She claimed she overheard people referring to her as the "Mad Cow" and "Grumpy Gertie".'

'Claimed,' I said. 'You think she was pouring it on.'

'I have no doubt she wasn't popular but all I had to go on was her self-report. The question in my mind was what role did her behavior play in provoking hostility? But figuring that out wasn't my job. I was asked to render an opinion about her faking and couldn't. Apparently that was enough because the settlement went through.'

'How much of the five million did she get?'

'I wasn't privy to details but the lawyer said it was considerably less – under a million.'

'Pretty nice payoff for having your drawers glued.'

Shacker stifled a laugh that pitched his spare frame forward, as if he'd been shoved from behind. 'Forgive me, this is a terrible situation. But what you just said – "Having her drawers glued." I'm no Freudian, but that's some image, no? And you could certainly describe Vita as being sealed up. In every way.'

'No sex life?'

'Nonexistent sex life and social life, according to her. She said she preferred it that way. Was that true or merely rationalization? I don't know. In fact, I can't say anything about her with confidence because I never got to see her long enough to break through the resistance. In the end, it didn't matter: she got what she wanted. That's the world we're living in, Alex. Genuinely sick people encounter the likes of Vita who block their treatment and big money's doled out for exaggerated claims because it's cheaper to settle.'

'What's the name of the lawyer who represented her?'

'I asked for official documents but never got them, had to work from a case summary provided by the casualty insurers.'

'Why all the hush-hush?'

'Their position was I needed to be viewed as objective in case my conclusions were called into question.'

The regretful look in his eyes deepened. 'Looking back, sure, I was used. I'll never repeat the experience.'

'What kind of personal information did Vita give you?'

'Not much, taking a history was an ordeal,' he said. 'I did get her to grudgingly admit to a difficult childhood. But once again, can we be sure Vita didn't bring some of that upon herself?'

'Cranky kid.'

'I've come to appreciate the importance of temperament. We're all dealt set hands, the key is how we play them. After observing Vita Berlin as a middle-aged woman it's hard to imagine her as a sweet, cheerful child. But I could be wrong. Perhaps something turned her sour.'

'Was she ever married?'

'She admitted to an early marriage but refused to talk about it. There was one sibling, a sister, they grew up near Chicago. Vita moved to L.A. ten years ago because she hated the weather in the Midwest. But she hated L.A., too. Everyone was stupid, superficial. Anything else — oh, yes, she never had children, detested kids, called them wastes of

43

sperm and eggs – her phrasing. So how long have you worked for the police?'

'I'm not on payroll, more of an independent contractor.'

'Sounds interesting,' said Shacker. 'Seeing the dark side and all that. Though I'm not sure I could handle it. To tell the truth, I'm really not that curious about horrible things. All those terrible dyssynchronies.'

'Me, neither,' I lied. 'It's the solution that's gratifying.'

'My impression is that profiling has turned out to be quite a dud.'

'Cookbooking never works. Could I ask you a few more questions about Vita?'

'Such as?'

'Did she have friends or outside interests?'

'My impression is she was somewhat of a homebody.'

'Did you pick up any signs of substance abuse?'

'No. Why?'

'The police found a couple of bulk-sized whiskey bottles in her apartment. Hidden.'

'Did they? Well, that's humbling, Alex, I never caught that. Not that I could be expected to, given her resistance.' He looked at his watch. 'If there's nothing else—'

'How many sessions did she have?'

'A few – six, seven.'

'Do you have her chart here?'

'The insurance company took possession of all records.'

His desk phone rang. He went over and picked it up. 'Dr Shacker . . . oh, hi . . . well, I could squeeze you in today if that would work . . . yes, of course, it's my pleasure, we'll go over all of that once you're here.'

Hanging up, he said, 'There's one more thing, Alex. I probably shouldn't be telling you, but I will. She mentioned the name of one of the people who'd harassed her. Samantha, no last name. Might that help?'

'It might. Thanks.'

'No problem. Now back to doing what we were trained for, eh? Nice to meet you, Alex.'

8

WALKING TO the Seville, I thought about the question mark in the pizza box. An old case I'd forgotten.

Milo had assumed a taunt but maybe a question really had been posed. I called his office. He said, 'You get an appointment with that shrink?'

'Just finished meeting with him.' I summed up.

'Post-traumatic hoohah and a bully named Samantha? It's a start, thank you, Doctor.'

'Unfortunately, Shacker's bound by a confidentiality clause, couldn't tell me what company Vita worked for.'

He said, 'Well-Start Health Management and Assurance. "Your well-being is where we start."'

'Oh.'

'Found some of her papers tucked in a kitchen cabinet, including five years of tax returns. She spent two of them at Well-Start, did temp office jobs before that, averaged around thirty G a year. Last year she deposited five hundred eighty-three G in a brokerage account, which threw me, but now it makes sense: a fat, onetime settlement. The money's been sitting in preferred stock paying around six percent interest. A little over thirty-three G a year, so she was getting paid more not to work.'

I said, 'It sounds like a job she could've enjoyed.'

He said, 'The chance to torment people every day? Fits what we know about her. I'm gonna try and find this Samantha, work my way through everyone Vita accused of harassing her. Meanwhile Reed and

Binchy are visiting every damn pizza joint in a ten-mile radius, see if they can find someone who uses those boxes. I put in a call to the manufacturer, maybe they ship to private parties as well and I'll get lucky and they'll find some weirdo put in an order. Any other insights?'

'That question mark,' I said. 'I'm not sure it was a taunt.'

'What then?'

'Maybe our bad guy was referring to himself: *I'm curious.*'

'About what?'

'The mysteries of the human body.'

'A do-it-yourself anatomy lesson? Seemed more to me like abusing the victim.'

'Could be.'

'You really see this as mining for gore?'

'The way everything was ordered, the meticulous cleanup reminded me of a patient I saw years ago, when I was a postdoc. Ten-year-old boy, extremely bright, polite, well behaved. No problems at all other than some pretty freaky cruelty to animals. Sadistic psychopaths often start by torturing small critters but this kid didn't seem to derive any pleasure from dominance or inflicting pain. He'd capture mice and squirrels in humane traps, hold gasoline-soaked rags over their noses till they died, make sure never to bruise them. "I hold them just hard enough," he told me. "I never hurt them, that would be wrong." Their death throes bothered him. He shuddered when I asked him about it. But he viewed his hobby as a legitimate science experiment. He dissected meticulously, removed every organ, studied, sketched. Both parents worked full-time, had no idea. His babysitter found him conducting surgery behind the garage and freaked out. As did Mom and Dad. The adult reactions frightened him and he refused to talk about anything he'd done so they sent him to Langley Porter and I got the case. Eventually I got him to talk, but it took months. He really didn't understand what the fuss was about. He'd been taught that curiosity was a good thing and he was curious about what made animals "work". Dad was a physicist, Mom a microbiologist, science was the family religion, how was he any different from them? The truth was, both parents had odd personalities – what would now be called Asperger spectrum – and Kevin really *wasn't* much different.'

'What'd you do with him?'

'I arranged for anatomy lessons from one of the pathology fellows, had his parents buy him books on the subject, and got him to pledge to limit his interest to reading. He agreed reluctantly but let me know that once he was old enough to take biology with a lab he'd be doing the same exact thing and everyone would think he was smart.'

'Maybe we should find out what happened to this little genius.'

'What happened to him is when he was seventeen he went hiking in the Sierras looking for specimens, fell off a cliff, and died. His mother thought I deserved to know because I was one of the few people Kevin talked about with any positivity.'

'So maybe I've got myself a Kevinoid who never got help.'

'A grown-up Kevinoid still stuck in a childhood that could range from eccentric to highly disordered. The urges are durable and now he's got the maturity and the physical strength to pull off a grand expedition. The precision I saw suggests he's done it before, but I haven't been able to find anything similar. So maybe up until this point he's adopted the optimal strategy: hide or get rid of the body.'

'Why switch to show-and-tell with Vita?'

'He's bored, needs a bigger thrill. Or the killing had to do with Vita, specifically. If you can find the ex-husband or the sister, they might shed some light on it.'

He said, 'Sure, but first let's see what mean ol' Samantha has to say for herself.'

Armed with the fact that Vita had worked for Well-Start, finding her tormentor was easy.

During the time it took Robin to shower, I pulled up several photos on the company's employee website, including a group shot, from last year's 'Quality Control Department' Christmas party.

Twenty-two unremarkable human beings who got paid to make life difficult for sick people. Not a set of horns in sight. No evidence of guilt eroding holiday spirit.

Samantha Pelleter was chairperson of the Celebration Committee and she appeared in three photos.

Short, pudgy, fortyish, blond. Mile-wide grin.

Being elected or appointed chairperson implied she had leadership qualities and that wasn't at odds with her playing a dominant role in any harassment. But no way was she big enough to overpower a woman as substantial as Vita.

Leadership could also mean subordinates.

I called Milo again. He said, 'Just found her myself, meeting her tomorrow at eleven. I'm assuming you don't want to miss the fun?'

'Where's it happening?'

'Her place, she's on reduced hours due to budget issues. Sounded scared witless about being contacted by the police but didn't put up a fuss. As to her curiosity level, we'll see. Meanwhile, mine's spiking out of control.'

9

HE PICKED me up the following morning. 'Got your earplugs? She lives right near the airport, I'm talking flight-path hell. This is probably why.'

He handed me two sheets of paper. The first contained Samantha Pelleter's credit report. Two bankruptcies in the last ten years, a fore-closed house in San Fernando, a slew of confiscated credit cards. The second page bore his handwritten notes: Pelleter had no criminal record, owned no property. County records pulled up a divorce six months prior to losing her home.

'Her title's a mouthful,' he said. 'Qualification consultant. Looks like that and chairing the company party supplied more ego dollars than the real stuff. This is a lady on the downslide and I'm wondering if that's related to some sort of serious mental problem.'

'I found a picture of her. She's small.'

'I know, got her stats. So she's got a large friend. Maybe someone else at Well-Start who Vita accused.'

'A revenge killing?'

'Talk about a classic motive.'

'Maybe.'

'You don't think so.'

'Don't know enough to think.'

He laughed. 'Like the engine ever stops running.'

Samantha Pelleter lived in a two-story, block-wide apartment building within walking distance of Sepulveda Boulevard. Aging stucco was the color of freezer-burned chicken. Incoming planes descended at angles that seemed too acute, casting terrible shadows, turning conversation moot. The air smelled of jet fuel. Not a tree in sight.

Pelleter lived in a ground-floor flat on the west end of the complex. The half-second lapse between buzzer-push and open door said she'd been waiting for us. From the look in her eyes and a freshly gnawed thumbnail, not a relaxed wait.

Milo introduced himself.

She said, 'Sure, sure, come in. Please.'

The apartment was small, dim, generically furnished, not dissimilar to Vita Berlin's place.

The woman Vita had accused of masterminding harassment was a shrunken figure with a quavering voice and the slumped-shouldered resignation of a child waiting to be slapped. Watery eyes were blue and so was her expression. Blond had mostly ceded to gray. Her haircut was short, ragged, probably a do-it-yourself. She fooled with the hem of a faded red sweatshirt. A misshapen glass pendant hanging from a thin black cord was her sole adornment. The glass was chipped at one end.

Brushing off the seats of the folding chairs she offered us, she hustled to a cluttered kitchenette, returned with a plastic tray bearing a pitcher, two cups, a jar of instant coffee, a pair of tea bags, loose packets of sugar and sweetener.

'Hot water,' she said. 'So you guys can have coffee or tea whatever. All's I have is decaf, sorry.'

'Thanks, Ms. Pelleter,' said Milo, but he didn't touch anything on the tray and neither did I.

She said, 'Oh, I forgot the cookies,' and turned back.

Milo placed a gentle hand atop her forearm. That was enough to freeze her in place. The blue eyes turned huge.

'Not necessary, Ms. Pelleter, but thanks again. Now please sit down so we can chat.'

She tugged an index finger as if trying to remove a nonexistent ring. Complied. 'Chat about Vita? I don't get it, all that happened last year, it was supposed to be over.'

'The lawsuit.'

'Not allowed to talk about it, sorry.'

I said, 'Must've been an ordeal.'

'Not for her, she got rich. The rest of us – no, no, I can't talk about it.'

'Her accusations were false?'

'Totally, totally, totally. I never did anything to her.'

'What about other people at Well-Start?'

'I – they – Vita was the most – I'm sorry, I'm not allowed to discuss it. I'm really not.'

I said, 'From what we've heard, Vita had trouble getting along with everyone.'

'Ain't that the freakin' truth,' said Samantha Pelleter. Blushing. 'Pardon my language. But she makes me so . . . frustrated.'

'Makes you? You're still in contact?'

'Huh? Oh, no, no way. I haven't seen her since. And I *really* can't talk about it. The lawyers said anyone who stepped out of line was finished, it had already cost the company—' She placed a finger over her lips. 'I don't know what's wrong with me, I keep going back to it.'

'It upset you,' I said.

'Yes, but I'm sorry, I can't. I need my job, I need it bad. As is, they cut us back to twenty-five hours a week. So please. I'm sorry if you wasted your time, but I *can't.*'

I said, 'How about we talk about Vita apart from the lawsuit?'

'I don't know anything about Vita apart from the lawsuit. What's going on, anyway? Is she claiming something else? Not happy with what she got? That's crazy, she's the only one who came out ahead.'

'Was anyone fired because of her?'

Samantha Pelleter shook her head. 'The company didn't want more lawsuits. But none of us got bonuses.'

'Meanwhile, Vita's rich.'

'Bitch,' she said. 'I still don't get what this is about.'

I turned to Milo.

He said, 'Vita's gotten herself in trouble.'

51

'Oh,' said Samantha Pelleter. 'Oh, wow.' New, improved brand of smile. She went into the kitchenette, returned with a box of Oreos, picked one out of the box, and nibbled. 'You're saying she tried to con someone else with false accusations and got caught? You want me to say she was a con? I'd love to help you guys, but I can't.'

'She was a big-time liar, huh?'

'You have no idea.'

'What else did she lie about besides the lawsuit?'

'We have scripts, are supposed to stick to them. Did that matter to Vita? Not a chance.'

'She improvised.'

'Oh, boy did she. Like with a flu-type thing we're supposed to start by having them list all their symptoms. We take our time so if it's not serious just their talking about it will show them it's no big deal and they'll change their mind about wanting an appointment. If they don't, we suggest over-the-counter meds. And drinking fluids, because let's face it, that's enough in most cases. If they get stubborn or call back, we ask if they've got a fever and if they don't, we tell them they're probably getting better, time will heal, but if they really need an appointment we've got one but it's during working hours. After they've been cleared by the nurse. If they want to pursue that, we put them on the nurse's call-back list. It's a system, you know?'

'Vita wasn't satisfied with that.'

'Vita would throw in her own stuff. Give them advice. Like try getting your mind off your problems. Concentrate on something else, stress is the cause of most symptoms, take a look at yours. Once I actually heard her tell someone to suck it up, colds were no big deal. That kind of thing.'

I said, 'How'd people react?'

She said, 'They didn't like it. Sometimes Vita would just hang up on them before they could complain, sometimes she'd stay on the line and let them complain. Holding the phone like this.' Stretching her arm. 'Away from her ear, you know. You could hear noise coming out of the phone like *chirp chirp chirp*. Vita just smiled and let them go on.'

'Enjoying herself.'

'She's one of the meanest people I ever met.'

'Did policyholders complain about her?'

'I'm sure they tried but it would be tough. We never give our names out and our extensions are switched all the time so no one gets the same consultant twice.'

'High level of customer service,' I said.

'It's to keep costs down,' she said. 'So really sick people can get care.'

'You saw Vita improvise. Meaning you sat near her.'

'Right next to her. If I was smart, I'd have kept my darn mouth shut. But it bothered me, doing her own thing, so I said something to her.'

'What'd you say?'

'"You know, Vita, you really shouldn't leave the script."' She winced. I said, 'She didn't take that well.'

'Actually, she ignored me, like I wasn't even there – talk to the hand. But a few days later she looked real mad so she must've found out.'

'Found out what?'

Pelleter looked to the side. 'I was stupid. Because I cared.'

'You talked to someone else.'

'Not a supervisor, just one of the other consultants and they must've snitched because Vita got called in to a supervisor and when she got back to her cubicle she had a crazy look in her eyes, boiling mad. Nothing happened until after the first break but then all of a sudden she's all over me, claiming I'm – a bunch of us – are bullies, we've never treated her like a human being, are out to persecute her.'

'How'd you react to that?'

'I didn't do anything, I was so freaked out. But no, I can't talk about it. Please. No more questions.'

Milo leaned in close. 'Samantha, I promise you nothing you say will get back to the lawyers.'

'How can I be sure? I never really snitched on Vita but she thought I did and that's what started the whole thing.'

He edged within an inch of her knees. 'We know how to keep a secret, Samantha.'

'Whatever . . . so what kind of con did she try this time?'

'I know you didn't harass her, Samantha, but did she have any particular problems with another consultant?'

'No one likes her, what goes around comes around.'

'Any special bad karma with someone else at work?'

'Everyone avoided her,' she said. 'But no one bullied her. No one. What'd she do that you're so interested?'

'Nothing.'

'Nothing? You said she was in trouble.'

'She is, Samantha. The worst kind of trouble.'

'I don't understand.'

'She's dead, Samantha.'

'Huh? What? How?'

'Someone killed her.'

'What're you *saying*? That's crazy!'

Milo didn't reply.

She made a run for the kitchenette, stared at the fridge, returned, wringing her hands. 'Killed? Oh my God oh my God oh my God. *Killed?* Really? Someone *killed* her? Who? When?'

'Who we don't know. When was the night before last, Samantha.'

'So then why are you – oh, no, no, *God* no, not that, you can't believe I'd ever – no, it wasn't like that. I mean I don't – didn't like her but that? No no no no no. No uh-uh. *No.*'

'We're talking to everyone in Vita's past.'

'I'm not in her past! Please. I can't stand this!'

'Sorry to upset you, Samantha—'

'I am upset. I'm totally upset. That you would *think* that? That you would—'

'Please sit back down, Samantha, so we can clear this up quickly and be out of your way.'

He motioned toward the chair she'd vacated. She stared, sank down. 'I really can't take any more stress. I'm like at the end of my – my freakin' husband cheated on me with who was supposed to be my freakin' friend. Then he left me with a pile of debt I didn't even know

54

about that lost me my house and screwed up my credit. Do you know what I used to have? A three-bedroom house in Tujunga, I used to have a horse I rode out in Shadow Hills. I used to have a Jeep Wagoneer. Now you're coming here and thinking terrible things about me and if you go to the company and say those things I won't even have my *job*!'

Milo said, 'No one suspects you, Samantha, this is routine. Which is why I need to ask you – even though it's a crazy question – where were you the night before last?'

'Where was I? I was here. I don't go anywhere, it takes money to go anywhere. I watched TV. I used to have a fifty-inch flat-screen. Now I have a little computer screen in my bedroom, everything's tiny, my whole freakin' world's tiny.'

Covering her mouth with her hands, she wept.

Maybe the closest to mourning Vita Berlin would merit.

Milo fetched her water and when she stopped crying, eased the glass toward her lips while resting a big paw on her forearm.

She drank. Wiped her eyes. 'Thank you.'

'Thank you for putting up with us, Samantha. Now please give us the names of the other people Vita claimed had harassed her.'

I expected resistance but Samantha Pelleter's mouth set crookedly. This smile was hard to characterize.

'You bet,' she said. 'I'll write you out a list. Time to look out for myself, I don't care about anyone else's issues.'

From a kitchenette drawer, she retrieved a scrap of paper and a pen. Writing quickly, she presented the list to Milo as if it were a school project.

1. Cleve Dawkins
2. Andrew Montoya
3. Candace Baumgartner
4. Zane Banion

'Appreciate it, Samantha. Are any of these people unusually strong?'

'Sure,' she said. 'Zane is big and strong. He's fat, but he used to play football. And Andrew's into fitness. He bikes to work, says if people took care of themselves they wouldn't get sick in the first place.'

'What about Cleve and Candace?'

'They're regular.'

'They stick to the script.'

'We all do,' she said. 'That's the point.'

Milo drove north on Sepulveda. 'Little Miss Sealed Lips, but get her feeling threatened and she rats out her work buddies. Any alarm bells go off?'

'As a psychologist, her fragility bothers me. As your lackey, I don't see her as a serious suspect.'

'Lackey? And here I was thinking sage or pundit.'

'Well,' I said, 'once upon a time there was a particularly obnoxious rooster who wouldn't stop hassling the hens in the barnyard. Finally, the farmer was forced to take action. He castrated the rooster and turned him into a pundit.'

He laughed. 'Sage, then. Unless you've got a story about that.'

'Once upon a time, there was an obnoxious rooster . . .'

'Fine form. Anyway, I agree. If anyone lacks the nerve, the physical ability, and the smarts to do what was done to Vita, it's ol' Samantha. But maybe one of the other jokers at Well-Start will turn out to be more interesting.'

He called Moe Reed, passed the four names along, ordered background checks.

Reed said, 'Will do. I had no luck with the pizza box so far but Sean's still out there. You got a call from the coroners, labs are back on Berlin.'

'Too quick for a tox.'

'Guess they prioritized, Loo.'

'I'm talking scientifically, Moses.'

'Yeah, I guess that's true,' said Reed. 'Okay, I'll run these jokers through, get back to you if I learn anything.'

Clicking off, Milo punched in a preset number.

Dr Clarice Jernigan said, 'Hi, there.'

'Labs are back so soon?'

'Who told you that?'

'That was the message I got.'

'Wonderful,' said Jernigan. 'New secretary, she watches too much TV, likes to throw the jargon around. No, sorry to get your hopes up, Milo. Full labs will take weeks. But I *was* calling about your victim's blood alcohol and with that, you might not need the tox. She pulled a level of .26, more than thrice the legal limit. Even being the serious alcoholic her liver says she was, she'd have been pretty vulnerable. So there'd be no need to use anything else to subdue her.'

'Drunk,' he said.

'As the perennial black-and-white-striped mammal.'

'Her liver,' he said. 'You've done the autopsy?'

'Not yet, but I was able to do a visual on a few organs, courtesy of your killer. Once we got rid of all the congealed blood. Which by my estimate was nearly all she started out with. Meaning your offender was meticulous, barely spilled a drop.'

'Someone with medical training?'

'I can't exclude it but no, you wouldn't need anything close to that level of skill.'

'What would you need?'

'The strength and confidence to perform two major incisions with a really sharp blade and a strong enough stomach to snip the intestines free. A butcher could do it. A deer hunter could do it. So could anyone with a warped mind and the wrong kind of knowledge. Which you can get off the Internet, if so inclined. In any event, I didn't need to dissect the liver to know it was seriously cirrhotic. Most of the darn thing was fatty and gray, not a pretty thing to behold. But as I said, even with her being a lush, a .26 could've seriously affected her judgment, reaction time, coordination, and strength. A cinch to overpower. Ask Dr Delaware next time you speak to him. He can probably give you some behavioral parameters.'

I said, 'I'm here, Clarice.'

'Oh, hi. You concur?'

'Completely.'

'Great,' she said. 'It's nice when there's peace in the valley. Milo, I'll do my best to get the autopsy done by tomorrow. I'll be traveling so one of my people will do the actual cutting, but I'll keep an eye on it.'

'Thanks.'

'That said, don't be expecting any profound conclusions. She died from a broken neck, was well dead before he cut her up.'

'How long is well dead?'

'Enough time for the blood to settle, which is minutes, not hours. I'm picturing your creep sitting there, waiting, that was a big part of his fun. What do you think, Alex?'

'Makes sense.'

'Oh, if my teenagers could hear this. Mommy's not always wrong. Bye, guys.'

10

For three days, I heard nothing from Milo. On the fourth morning, he came to the house, vinyl attaché in hand, wearing a black poly suit with lapels from two decades ago and a pumpkin-orange tie and muttering, 'Yeah, yeah, happy Halloween.' He flicked a pocket flap that buttoned. 'Vintage. Live long enough, everything comes back.'

Hard to read his emotions. He cruised past me into the kitchen, did his usual surveillance. Robin and I had been going out to dinner regularly so the fridge was light on leftovers. He made do with beer, bread, mayo, hot sauce, barbecue sauce, steak sauce, mustard, ground horseradish sauce, and three long-forgotten lamb sausages yanked from the back of the freezer that he microwaved into submission.

After several gulps of haphazard sandwich, he took a long swig of Grolsch. 'Good morning, boys and girls, can you spell futility?'

Another long swallow of beer. 'No one local uses that type of pizza box and all the alleged Well-Start bullies have alibis. None of them looked good, anyway. The female is pushing sixty, was babysitting her grandkid, the physical fitness guy was on a nighttime mountain bike ride in Griffith Park vouched for by members of his cycling club, the supposedly big strong guy is big but not strong – close to four hundred and uses a cane and an inhaler and the night of the murder he was at his grandmother's birthday party, verified by the waiter who served his table. The last guy wears Coke-bottle glasses and weighs in at maybe a hundred twenty and he was at the E.R. with one of his kids. Some sort of allergic reaction to shrimp, the nurse and the on-call resident say neither he nor his wife ever left the kid's side and she was hospitalized overnight.'

He swigged, put the bottle down. 'I resisted the temptation to ask if Daddy had pre-screened the kid so she could get treated. They all claimed to be blindsided by the lawsuit, refused to talk about details. I tried to reach someone at Well-Start's corporate headquarters, big surprise, they stonewalled. I put Sean on it 'cause he's got a high tolerance for failure and boredom and dealing with robotic turd-brains.'

He constructed another teetering sandwich, polished it off. 'Autopsy results came in early this morning. Like Clarice said, no surprises.'

He ripped a slice of bread in half, balled it up, consumed. 'Where's Robin?'

'Working out back.'

'Must be nice to be productive. I located Vita's sister using phone records. Had to go back nearly a month to find an Illinois number, so we're not talking regular contact. The sister – Patricia's her name – lives in Evanston and the call was her phoning Vita on her birthday. Which, she made sure to tell me, Vita would never do for her.'

'Was that after she found out Vita was dead or before?'

'After.'

'Not exactly sentimental,' I said. 'How'd she react to the news?'

'She was shocked but it wore off and she got pretty dispassionate. Analytic, like, "Hmm, who would do something so terrible?" And she had a quick answer: "If I was a betting woman, I'd say Jay, he despised Vita."'

'The ex-husband?'

'Bingo, that's why everyone calls you Doctor and bows and scrapes when you enter a room. Jay is one Jackson J. Sloat. He and Vita divorced fifteen years ago but Patricia said the financial battle went on long after. Turns out he's got a record with some violence in it, lives here in L.A. Los Feliz, which is at most a forty-minute drive to Vita's place.'

I said, 'They hated each other, got divorced, but moved to the same city?'

'Funny about that, huh? So maybe it's one of those obsessive, love-hate things. A drop-in on ol' Jay is clearly the next step but if he is our bad guy he could be smart and manipulative and as the ex he could be expecting us. So I figured I'd tap your ample brain for strategy.'

'When were you planning on talking to him?'

'Soon as you finish opining. He works in Brentwood, hopefully he's there or home.'

'What does he do for a living?'

'Salesman at a high-end clothing store.' He retrieved his notepad from the attaché. 'Domenico Valli.'

I said, 'That's why you got spiffed up.'

'Just the opposite.' He rubbed a lapel, ended up with brittle threads on his fingertips. 'I come in like this, he'll feel superior, maybe let his guard down.'

I laughed. 'What kind of record does Sloat have?'

'Some lightweight vehicular stuff – operating without a license, the requisite DUIs every self-respecting marginal character needs for self-validation. The serious stuff is two ag assaults, one with a crowbar.'

'Who was the victim?'

'Guy at a drinking establishment, he and Sloat had words, Sloat followed him outside. Sloat brained him but also received some fairly serious injuries. That enabled him to claim self-defense and maybe there was something to it because charges were dropped. The other case was similar but it happened inside a bar. That time Sloat used his fists. He got pled down, received ninety days at County, served twenty-six.'

'Enough violence to be worrisome,' I said. 'Two incidents in bars could mean he's got a drinking problem – maybe what he and Vita had in common. More important, he'd be familiar with Vita's drinking habits, know she was a nighttime boozer, would be vulnerable. And if there was a love-hate relationship, he could've wheedled his way into the apartment.'

'Arrives with what looks like a pizza,' he said. '"Hi, honey, I miss you. Remember how we used to share an extra-large pepperoni with sausage?"'

He rolled the beer bottle between his hands. 'Everything we know about Vita said she was distrustful, maybe borderline-paranoid. You think she'd fall for that?'

'With the help of Jack Daniel's and old-times' sake?' I said. 'Maybe.'

'Real old times. My phone subpoena covered eighteen months of her records and his number's not on it.'

'What about a different type of contact?' I said. 'Vita used the court system at least once and got rewarded.'

'She's still dragging him to court? Yeah, that might kick up the anger level.'

He called Deputy D.A. John Nguyen, asked for a quick scan of any legal proceedings between Vita Gertrude Berlin and Jackson Junius Sloat.

Nguyen said, 'A quick one I can do for the last five years.'

'That'll work, John.'

'Hold on . . . nope, nothing here. Berlin's your nasty one, right? How's that going?'

'Nothing profound.'

'There's been talk in the office, all that weirdness could be the first installment of a whacko serial.'

'Thought you were my friend, John.'

'I'm not wishing it on you, just repeating what I heard. And the leak didn't start with us. Are there any looser-lipped dudes than cops?'

'Wish I could argue with that,' said Milo. 'Anything else I should know about?'

'Some of our guys are hoping it will go serial so they can jockey to take it and career-build.'

'But if you want it, you'll get it.'

Nguyen laughed. 'With Bob Ivey retiring I really am the Senior Junior Dude, meaning even if the boss takes it officially I'm doing the real work. So keep me posted.'

'Long as you pray for me, John. Little offering to Buddha's fine.'

'I'm an atheist.'

'I'll take whatever I can get.'

11

WHILE HE ate and washed the dishes, I gave him my best guesses about how to approach Jay Sloat: keep it nonthreatening, preface the news of Vita's murder by emphasizing that Sloat was not a suspect, just someone Milo was turning to for valuable information.

However Sloat reacted verbally, his body language would be the thing to watch. Criminal psychopaths operate with lower anxiety levels than the rest of us but it's a myth that they lack emotion. The smartest, coldest antisocials avoid violence completely because violence is a stupid strategy. Look for their smiling faces on election posters. But those a notch lower on the IQ scale often need to prep before indulging their urges with alcohol or dope or by chanting internal rage mantras that provide self-justification.

So if Jay Sloat was anything but the coldest of killers and had carved up his ex, simply bringing up the topic could result in some sort of physical tell: sudden rise in neck pulse, constricted pupils, muscular tension, the merest hint of moisture around the hairline, an increase in blink rate.

Milo said, 'I'm the polygraph.'

I said, 'Isn't that what you do anyway?'

'What if Sloat doesn't respond?'

'Then that tells us something about him.'

Nothing he didn't already know but he seemed more relaxed as he drove to Brentwood. Maybe it was the sandwiches.

* * *

Domenico Valli Men's Couture was located on 26th Street, just south of San Vicente, directly across from the Brentwood Country Mart, bordered by a restaurant run by the latest celebrity chef and another clothing store that hawked four-figure outfits for trust-fund toddlers.

The haberdashery was paneled in violin-grain maple and floored in skinny-plank black oak. Subdued techno pulsed from the sound system. Light was courtesy of stainless-steel gallery tracks. The goods were sparingly displayed, like works of art. A few suits, a smattering of sport coats, small steel tables that would've felt comfortable in the morgue stocked like altars with offerings of cashmere and brocade. A wall rack featured gleaming handmade shoes and boots, black velvet slippers with gold crests on the toes.

No shoppers were availing themselves of all that chic. A man sat behind a steel desk, doing paperwork. Big, fiftyish, with broad shoulders, he had a long sunlamped face defined by a wide, meaty nose. A steel-gray Caesar-do tried but failed to cover a receding hairline. A bushy white soul patch sprouted under hyphen lips, bristly and stiff as icicles.

He looked up. 'Help you guys?'

'We're looking for Jay Sloat.'

His eyes narrowed and he stood and stepped around the desk. Just a touch under Milo's six three and nearly as bulky, he wore a faded, untucked blue chambray shirt with pearl buttons, stovepipe black jeans, gray suede needle-toe boots, a diamond in his left earlobe. Lots of muscle but also some middle-aged padding.

'Don't bother telling me, you're obviously cops. I haven't done anything, so what gives?'

Broad, faintly Slavic midwestern intonation.

'Lieutenant Sturgis, Mr Sloat.' Milo extended his hand. Sloat studied it for a second, endured a brief clasp before retrieving his big paw. 'Okay, now we're all BFFs. Could you please tell me what's going on?'

'Sorry if this is upsetting you, Mr Sloat. It's certainly not our intention.'

'It's not upsetting me,' said Sloat. 'I mean I'm not worried personally because I know I haven't done anything. I just don't get why the cops are here when I'm trying to work.' He frowned. 'Oh, man, don't tell me it's something to do with George. If it is, I can't help you, I just work for the guy.'

Milo didn't answer.

Jay Sloat pressed his palms together prayerfully. 'Tell me it ain't so, guys, okay? I need this job.'

'It ain't so. George is the owner?'

Sloat relaxed, exhaled. 'So it's not about that. Excellent. Okay, then what's up?'

Milo repeated the question.

Sloat said, 'Yeah, he's the owner. George Hassan. He's really an okay guy.'

'Why would we be looking for him?'

'No reason.'

'No reason, but he's the first one you thought of.'

Sloat's brown eyes turned piggishly small as they studied Milo, then me, then Milo again. 'George is going through a complicated divorce and she keeps claiming he's holding back on her. She's threatening to close down the business if he doesn't open the books. Last week, she sent around a private investigator pretending to be a customer, dude's dressed like a dork, starts asking me if I have more of these nice worsted suits in the back. *Worsted*. What a doofus. I said, "Hey, Dan Tana, if you actually want to try something on, let's do it, if this is a game, go play it elsewhere." Guy turned white and got the fuck out.'

Sloat grinned and winked. His bronzed face was smoother than when we'd entered; recounting his dominance put him back in his comfort zone.

Milo said, 'I hear you. Well, this has nothing to do with George.'

'What then?'

'It's about your ex-wife.'

Sloat's jaw muscles swelled. His pupils expanded. 'Vita? What about her?'

'She's dead.'

'Dead,' said Sloat. 'As in police dead? Oh, man. What happened?'

'Someone murdered her.'

'Yeah, I got that. I mean who, how, when?'

Milo ticked his fingers. 'Don't know, nasty, five nights ago.'

Sloat stroked his soul patch. 'Wo-ho,' he said, in a soft, almost boyish voice. 'Someone finally did the bitch.'

We didn't respond.

He said, 'I need a cigarette, let's go outside.'

Milo said, 'Let's.'

Grabbing a pack of wheat-colored Nat Shermans from the steel desk, Jay Sloat led us out of the store to the curb, where he positioned himself in front of the display window and lit up with a gold-plated lighter. 'Can't smoke inside, George doesn't want odor on the merchandise.'

Milo waited until he'd puffed a third of the cigarette before speaking. 'Someone did the bitch. So for you it's not bad news.'

'Me and Vita broke up a long time ago.'

'Fifteen years ago.' Milo cited the date of the final decree.

The detail caused Sloat to recoil. 'What, you guys are looking into my past?'

'We've researched Vita, Mr Sloat. Your name came up.'

'So you know about my arrests.'

'We do.'

'Then you also know they were bullshit. Dorks asking for trouble and getting it.'

Neither of us argued.

Sloat said, 'I watch those shows, I get it, I'm the ex, you think I did it.'

'What shows?'

'Crime – true crap, puts me to sleep at night.' Sloat grinned. 'When I don't have help getting some nighty-night.'

'You get help often?'

'Get pussy as often as I can, good for the complexion.' He laughed. 'Got it every night last week, including five nights ago.'

'From who?'

'A chick who rode me like a rodeo horse and righteously blew my mind.'

'How about a name?'

'How about she's married.'

'We're discreet, Jay.'

'Yeah, I bet. On those shows, cops make promises and break them. And anyway, why do I need an alibi? Like you said, it was fifteen years ago. Whatever Vita did since then was out of my life.'

'Fifteen years ago was the divorce,' said Milo. 'Our research says the war kept going.'

'Okay,' said Sloat, 'so she kept jerking me around for another few. But then it ended. I haven't seen Vita in a long time.'

'How long is "another few", Jay?'

'Let's see . . . last time the bitch took me to court was . . . I'd have to say six, maybe seven years ago.'

That matched Nguyen's failing to come up with anything for five.

'What'd she want?'

'What do you think? More money.'

'She get it?'

'She got some,' said Sloat. 'It's not like I had that much to give.'

'When's the last time you actually saw her?'

'Right after. Maybe a month. She jerks me around in court, then has the nerve to drop in, middle of the night.'

'What for?'

'What do you think? You go to Jay, you want to play.'

Milo said, 'She sues you then does a booty-call.'

'She was crazy,' said Sloat. 'Also, old habits die hard.' He puffed out his chest. 'I'm a tough habit to break.'

He laughed, smoked greedily. Dry hairline, steady hands, steady lips.

I said, 'You're a tough habit to break but for six, seven years Vita managed.'

Sloat's face darkened. 'She didn't end it, I did. That time she dropped over, I wouldn't let her in, told her she ever did that again I'd get a restraining order and sue her ass so fast she wouldn't know what was reaming her. She knew I meant it, I'm not a guy takes bullshit.'

'Like those guys in the bar.'

'You got it,' said Sloat, 'and I ain't embarrassed about it. Back in Chicago I used to work dispatch for a trucking company. They fucked me over, giving the good shifts to some loser who bribed the supervisor, wanting me to work night shift even though I'd been there ten years. I sued and won. Another time one of our *dark*-skinned brothers dented my car, I had this little Benz convertible, gray on gray, sweet drive, this *dusky* fellow isn't looking where he's going, pow. Everyone said don't hassle, those types never have insurance, it's a lost cause. I said screw that, sued his ass, my lawyer found out his mother owned a house, had given the dude a share. We attached Mommy's house, moved to evict her, he paid up.'

'You like the court system.'

'What I like is protecting my rights. Which I know I got, right now. In terms of talking to you guys, I don't have to say squat. But it's cool, you don't bother me. I had nothing to do with Vita getting killed. Trust me, the way Vita was, she'd have no trouble arranging it all by herself.'

'You think she organized her own murder?'

'No, no, what I'm saying is Vita was the biggest bitch this side of . . . I don't know, Cruella Whatshername? From the cartoon? There'd be tons of people she pissed off. All Vita had to do was go on being Vita. Eventually someone was gonna get pissed off.'

'Any suggestions as to who?'

'Nah, Vita was out of my life, I don't have a clue who she was hanging with.'

'Think back,' I said. 'When you were still seeing her. Did she have any enemies?'

'Enemies?' said Sloat. 'Walk down the street and pick people at random. To know her was to hate the bitch.'

'You married her.'

'When I married her, I dug her. *Then* I hated her.'

'She was different back then.'

'Nope,' said Sloat. 'Only I thought she was. She conned me, you know?'

'Being nice,' I said.

'Nah, Vita was never nice. But she hid what a bitch she was by being quiet about it, you know?'

'How?'

'By being cold. Super-frosty, she'd give you this look, this *I'm-a-bitch-but-I'll-still-suck-your-cock* look. And she did. There was a time she had talent, still looked pretty good. Tall and cold with sharp edges, I used to call her Miss Everest. Then she stopped faking it. Why bother when you can be a total bitch?'

'The attraction wore off.'

'I was attracted to her tits,' said Sloat. 'She had a nice face, too. She took care of herself, plucking the eyebrows, wearing the makeup, doing the platinum-blond hair. Like that actress. Novak, Kim Novak. People old enough to remember said she looked like Kim Novak. I went to see *Vertigo*. Novak was a helluva lot hotter, give me ten Vitas for one Kim Novak, you'll still owe me change. But Vita was cute, I'll grant her that. Good where it counted, also. That part she kept up, even after we broke up. I'll grant her that.'

'Sexy,' I said.

'Sexy is a chick hungry to do you. Vita was in the mood, she'd pop you quick. Problem is she got old and fat, stopped dyeing the hair, stopped taking care of herself, the drinking got worse.' Sticking out his tongue. 'Her breath stunk, she was a mess. So even if she wanted to jump your bones, you didn't want those bones jumped. Finally, I said no more. Life's too short, you know?'

Milo said, 'We sure do.'

'Bet you do,' said Sloat. 'Listen, I'm not going to stand here and lie and tell you I give a shit when I don't. Vita tried to take everything I owned. Including the Benz I went to all that trouble to get fixed. Including half any money I made until I went totally broke and stopped working long enough to convince her I wasn't worth going after. I haven't seen her in, like I said, seven years. But at the back of my head

69

is always this thought, she's going to come back. Like those guys in the
horror movies – the dude in the leather mask. So it's obvious I didn't
kill her. Why would I ruin my life for her?'

I said, 'One thing you had in common: Vita also liked using the court
system?'

'Just against me.'

'She never sued anyone else?'

'Nah,' said Sloat. 'She was a wimp. Like when I went after that black
guy, she's yelling at me, "What if he's a gang member, the car isn't
worth it." Which didn't stop *her* from going after it, years later. Same
thing with suing the trucking company. "Don't do it, Jay, they could
be Mafia, it's not worth it." I said, "To you it's not worth it, to me it
is. Rights are rights, that's why we fight wars."'

Milo said, 'You were in the service?'

'My dad was. Three years in Europe. So can I go back to work?'

Still no anxiety tell. Milo said, 'What you're saying makes sense, Jay.
On the other hand, you hated her, you're clearly not upset she's dead,
and you won't back up your alibi.'

'I can back it up but I don't want to.'

'Why?'

Sloat looked over his shoulder, through the glass, at the interior of
the store.

Milo said, 'Don't worry, no customers.'

'I know that. There's never any.'

I said, 'The cowgirl has something to do with the shop.'

Rapid constriction of pupil. A carotid pulse sprang into action.

Milo saw it. 'Give us a name, Jay, or we're going to develop a chronic
interest in menswear.'

Sloat blew out acrid tobacco-air. 'Aw, man.'

Milo said, 'We're talking murder, Jay—'

'I know, I know – okay but swear to keep it secret.'

'We don't swear, Jay. We don't even promise. But unless there's some
reason to go public, we won't.'

'What kind of reason? I didn't kill Vita!'

'Then you'll have no problem, Jay.'

Sloat sucked down half an inch of cigarette. 'Okay, okay, it's Nina. Nina Hassan.'

'George's ex.'

'He finds out, he'll fire my ass and roast my balls on one of those shish-kebab thingies.'

Milo pulled out his pad. 'What's her number?'

'You have to write it down?'

'Phone number, Jay.'

'You actually have to call her?'

Milo stared him down.

Sloat gave up the number. 'Just don't say what I said about her. Being a cowgirl.'

'That I can promise you.'

'She's hot,' said Sloat. 'You see her, you'll understand.'

'Looking forward to it, Jay.'

'I need this job, guys.'

'You also need to be cleared as a suspect.'

'What suspect, I didn't do squat to Vita.'

'Hopefully Nina will confirm that, Jay. Hopefully we'll believe her.'

'Why wouldn't you believe her?'

'Maybe she's so crazy about you, she'd lie.'

'She digs me,' said Sloat. 'But she ain't going to lie.'

'It's really important, Jay, that you don't call her before we show up. We're gonna check phone records, so we'll know.'

'Yeah, yeah sure.' His neck pulse hammered away. Shifty eyes said Milo had altered his plans.

I said, 'How long were you and Vita married?'

'Six years.'

'No kids.'

'We didn't want. Both of us.'

'Not into kids.'

'Kids are a pain,' said Sloat. 'So when're you seeing Nina?'

Milo said, 'When we're ready.'

71

'She'll clear me. She'll impress you, she's a very impressive girl.'
'Bye, Jay.'
Jay Sloat said, 'You absolutely need to talk to her?'
We walked away from him.

Milo looked up Nina Hassan's address, found it on the western edge of
Bel Air, a short drive away.
'Vita and Jay,' he said, heading east on Sunset. 'Thank God those
two didn't breed. So what do you think of him?'
I said, 'Unless he's Oscar-caliber, I don't see it.'
'Me, neither.'
Half a mile later: 'Screw those D.A. ghouls, this isn't going serial,
it's gonna be one of those wrong-time, wrong-place things. Vita finally
ticked off the wrong guy. Speaking of which, I did sic Reed on Western
Peds, see if he could come up with any oncology parents with bad
tempers. Specifically, black parents.'
'You're telling me this because . . .'
'I'm telling you in the spirit of openness.'
I said, 'Do what you need to do.'
'No one would tell him anything.'
'Good.'
'I figured you'd say that.'

12

Nina Hassan's house in the Bel Air hills was sleek, contemporary, gorgeous.

Just like her.

She eased open one of the twin brushed-copper double doors, regarded us as if we were salesmen. Late thirties with velvety skin a tad darker than the doors, she sported a mauve top that revealed an inch of hard belly, a pair of sprayed-on white jeans, silver sandals that revealed pampered, lavender-nailed feet. Her face was heart-shaped, topped by a cloud of black waves and curls. A full nose was graced by a cute little upward sweep at the tip. Probably surgical, but well done. Massive white hoops hung from seashell ears. A long, smooth neck swooped to a pair of high-end collarbones.

Milo flashed the badge.

'Yes? And?' Her eyes were a uniform black, defying analysis of her pupils.

'We'd like to talk to you about Jay Sloat.'

'Him? He's not okay?' As if inquiring about the weather.

'Why wouldn't he be okay?'

'My husband,' said Nina Hassan. 'He's not human, he's an animal.'

'Jay's fine. May we come in, Mrs Hassan?'

She didn't budge. 'Call me Nina. I'm getting rid of *that* name as soon as the divorce is final. What's with Jay?'

'We need to know the last time you saw him.'

'Why?'

'His ex-wife was murdered.'

'Ex-wife? Jay was married?'

'A while back, ma'am.'

'He said he was never married.'

Milo said, 'It was a long time ago.'

'Doesn't matter,' she said. 'I don't put up with lies.' Her hand slashed air. 'What, you think he killed her?'

'No, ma'am. These are what we call routine questions.'

'Nina,' she said. 'I don't like ma'am. Too old. Too . . . ma'am-ish.'

A Maserati coupé purred past the house. The woman behind the wheel slowed to study us. Thin, blond, steely as the car. Nina Hassan waved gaily.

Milo said, 'It's better if we talk inside.'

Hassan's turn to study us. 'How do I know you're really the police?'

'Would you like another look at my—'

'Anyone can make a badge.'

'Who else would we be?'

'Scumbags hired by George.'

'George is your ex?'

'My scumbag ex. He's always sending them around, trying to find something he can use against me. I sleep with Jay? So what? George sleeps with young girls – maybe you should investigate him, he says they're twenty, maybe they're younger.'

She tapped a foot. 'What am I supposed to do, sit around like his mother and have no fun and tell stories from the old country?'

Milo said, 'Sounds like good riddance, Nina, but we're investigating a murder, so if you can remember the last time you were with Jay, that would be helpful.'

'Ex-wife,' she said. 'Liar – was she hot?'

'The way we found her, not in the least. Can you remember?'

'Of course I can remember, I'm not old. The last time was . . . two nights ago.' She smiled. 'Every night until two nights ago. Then I told him I needed a rest.'

'Five nights ago, as well?'

'I just told you: every night.'

'What time?'

'Jay comes over after work, five thirty, five forty.'

'How long does he stay?'

'Long as I want him to.' Her head drew back. She laughed. 'That's a cheeky question.'

'Pardon?'

'You want to know do we do it all night. Why's that your business?'

'Sorry for any misunderstanding,' said Milo. 'What I'm after is can Jay's whereabouts be accounted for five nights ago.'

'Five nights,' said Nina Hassan. 'Wait out here.'

She returned moments later with a receipt. 'Here it is, five nights ago: takeout from Chinois. I keep everything for documentation. So that bastard has to pay what he deserves.'

'Takeout from—'

'For two people,' she said. 'Me and Jay. He tried to get me to eat chicken feet. Yuck.'

'He was here all night.'

'You bet,' said Nina Hassan, winking. 'He was too tired to leave.'

'Okay, thanks.'

'I helped him out, huh? Too bad. I don't like liars.' She tossed her hair. 'But I tell it like it is, that's how to handle all of you boys. Buh-*bye*.'

Stepping back into her house, she nudged the door shut with a manicured finger.

We drove back to Sunset, passing big houses, small dogs leading maids, gardeners blowing dirt with airguns.

Milo said, 'Scratch the ex, why should life be logical? But it's got to be someone else Vita really got to. Too bad she didn't leave an enemy list.'

'That's for presidents.'

He harrumphed. 'Incriminating tapes would be nice, too. Okay, I'll drop you back home, go enjoy your life while we poor civil servants toil. Not that I'm passive-aggressive.'

Just as we approached the Glen, his cell played Mahler and he switched to speaker.

Sean Binchy said, 'Loot—'

'You found a pizza psycho.'

'Unfortunately no, but there is something you're going to want to—'

'What?'

'There's another one.'

13

THE MAN'S shirt was folded neatly by his side. His pants and underwear had been lowered to mid-thigh, arranged neatly, no rumpling. He lay on his back, ten feet to the west of a dirt entry road, in a clearing created by a seven-foot gap in a long hedge of oleander.

Toxic plant. For the person who'd snapped the man's neck, perfect cover.

No towels under this body. A blue tarp had been spread neatly.

A few blood specks dotted plastic and dry dirt, a bit more than at Vita Berlin's apartment, but nothing extensive and no castoff, low- or high-velocity. The earth surrounding the tarp had been smoothed free of footprints.

The man's degradation mimicked Vita's. Broken neck, same change-purse incision pattern, identical display of scooped-out viscera.

The kill-spot was off Temescal Canyon in Pacific Palisades, a quarter mile into the grounds of a former summer camp occasionally used for film shoots but for the most part abandoned. An old wire gate spanning pitted asphalt was hinged to a wooden post. A second post had rotted and crumbled and access was as easy as walking in.

The lack of security was a joke with the locals, according to the first uniform on the scene.

'A few of them bitch about it, Lieutenant, but mostly they like it. Because it's like having an extra park and you know the type of people who live here.'

Her name was Cheryl Gates. She was tall, blonde, square-shouldered,

77

falcon-eyed. Outwardly unaffected by what she'd discovered on routine patrol. By what she and Milo and I were looking at through the gap in the oleander.

Milo said, 'Rich folk.'

'Rich and entitled and *connected* folk, sir. By that I mean Deputy Chief Salmon's sister lives not far away so my instruction is to drive by every day. Takes up time but it is kind of pretty. And nothing much ever happens. One time I found a boy and a girl, sixteen, went overboard with E and tequila, spent the night next to the barbecues up there, buck naked, totally wasted. Funny thing was, neither family reported them missing. All the parents in Europe or wherever. Sometimes I find bottles, roaches, condoms, food wrappers. But nothing serious.'

Outwardly unaffected but talking fast, a bit too loud.

Milo said, 'The spot you found my victim, is that part of your routine?'

'Yes, sir. I figure it's a good place for some homeless type to crash and God forbid the locals should be surprised by some wild-eyed whack when they stroll in with their poodles.'

'Come across any whacks recently?'

'No, sir. When I find them and it's only once in a while, it's always up there, near those barbecues. They like to cook, fix themselves a hot meal. Which is a risk – fires, and all that. So I warn them and I've never had one come back twice. But I figure better safe than sorry, so yes, I do check it daily. Which is how I found your vic.'

'Any particular whack you think I should be looking into?'

'Doubt it, sir,' said Gates. 'These aren't aggressive guys, just the opposite. Passive, out of it, messed up physically.' She eyed the body. 'I'm no expert but that looks pretty organized. The way the dirt's kinda been swept up? I mean that's just my impression.'

'Makes sense,' said Milo. 'Thanks for holding the scene.'

'Doing what I'm supposed to, sir. Once backup arrived I stayed right here and had Officers Ruiz and Oliphant check the grounds. Looking just for obvious stuff, we didn't want to mess anything up. They found nothing, sir, and there's no exit out of here other than the way you come in. So I'm pretty confident we didn't miss any suspect hiding out.'

'Good work.'

'So what do you think, sir, was this a sex thing? Those pants down, maybe some gay thing that got crazy?'

'Could be.'

'With a sex thing, though,' said Gates, 'wouldn't you see direct involvement of the genitals, not just . . . that?'

'There are no rules, Officer.'

Gates tucked a strand of blond hair behind her ear. 'Of course, sir. I'd best be leaving you to go about your business. If there's nothing else.'

'We're fine, Officer. Hope tomorrow morning's more pleasant.'

Gates stood taller. 'Actually, sir, and this is probably an inopportune time to say so but I've been thinking about applying to be a D. Would you recommend that?'

'You're observant, Officer Gates. Go for it and good luck.'

'Same to you, sir. On the case, I mean.'

Sean Binchy and Moe Reed and three other uniforms remained stationed at the entrance, guarding the road between Sunset and the broken gate. The coroner's investigator hadn't arrived so all we could do was stand at the mouth of the clearing and peer in.

The man was middle-aged – closer to fifty-five than forty-five – with thick curly hair, pewter on top, silver at the sides. So tightly coiled it showed no sign of disarray.

Not so for the head and neck below the hair.

Incompatible with life.

Not a particularly memorable-looking man. Average height, average build, average everything. The pants were cotton, medium beige, pressed, pleated, cuffed. Clean where blood hadn't intruded. The shirt was nut-brown, a polo, folded in a way that obscured any logo. His shoes were white Nikes with well-worn soles. A runner or a serious walker? No car parked near the entrance fit with that.

Blue socks clashed. He hadn't figured on being inspected.

I'd approached the scene expecting to react more strongly than I had to Vita Berlin's corpse. The opposite occurred: taking in the butchery released an odd, detergent wash of calm that settled my nervous system.

Getting used to it?

Maybe that was the worst part of it.

Milo said, 'No pizza box, guess that's not part of the signature. So maybe it's just something the bastard came upon and used for Vita, not tracing it won't be any big deal . . . poor devil, I hope he was a total sonofabitch, Vita's spiritual brother.'

A female voice said, 'Hi, again. Unfortunately.'

The C.I. named Gloria walked between us and gazed into the opening. 'Good God.' She gloved up and covered her feet with paper booties, stepped in, got to work.

A wallet emerged from the right rear pocket of the man's khakis. A driver's license I.D.'d him as Marlon Quigg, fifty-six, with an address on Sunset, a mile or two east of the campground. A unit number said condo or apartment. We'd passed some nice buildings on the way over, neatly kept places on the south side of the boulevard, some affording ocean views.

Five eight, one sixty-eight, gray hair, brown eyes, needs corrective lenses.

Gloria checked his eyes. 'Contacts are still in there. Kind of surprising considering the force it took to snap the neck.'

I said, 'They could've fallen out and the killer put them back. He's all about order.'

She thought about that. Tweezed out the tiny clear disks, bagged and tagged.

Armed with a name, Milo got busy learning about his victim. Quigg's ride was a three-year-old Kia. No wants or warrants or brushes with the criminal justice system.

The wallet held seventy-three dollars in cash and three credit cards. Two snapshots remained in plastic sleeves. One featured Quigg and a smallish, dark-haired woman around his age, the other showed the couple with a pair of brunettes in their early twenties. One girl resembled Quigg, down to the tight, curly hair. The other could've been anyone's progeny but her arm rested on the shoulder of the older woman, so the reasonable guess was Daughter Number Two.

Both shots were studio poses, backdropped by green faux-marble. Everyone dressed up, a little stiff and uncertain, but smiling.

Gloria said, 'He's not wearing a watch . . . no pale stripe on his arm, either, so maybe he wasn't a time-bound Type A.'

'Or he took off his watch when he walked,' said Milo.

I said, 'The soles of his shoes say he liked to cover ground.'

'They do,' said Gloria, 'but why come in here? It'd be kind of spooky in the dark, no?'

Milo said, 'The locals consider it their private park. He lives close, maybe felt it was safe.'

'Okay . . . but maybe he was meeting someone.' She shifted uncomfortably. 'The way the pants are . . . you know.'

'Anything's possible, kid.'

'Though I guess with something sexual you'd expect the genitals to be attacked.' She looked at me.

I said, 'Same answer.'

She checked the pants, using a magnifier. 'Well, look at this, I've got foreign hairs . . . whole bunch of them . . . long ones . . . blond.'

Milo kneeled down beside her, plucked several filaments with latex-sheathed fingers that looked too big and thick for the task. Holding the hairs up to the light, he squinted. Sniffed. 'Maybe Marilyn Monroe came back from the grave to do him but they look kinda coarse and I'm picking up doggy odor.'

Gloria said, 'My nose is stuffed.' She tried anyway. 'Sorry, I'm not picking up anything but you could be right about the texture.' Smiling. 'Unless someone's using a real bad conditioner.'

She produced an evidence bag. 'I know the techies generally do hair unless we're running drug screens on the shaft, but we happen to have an intern from the U. doing DNA analysis on all kinds of critters. Want me to take it, maybe I can get you something on species and breed?'

'Appreciate it.'

Gloria took another look at Quigg. 'Poor guy goes out for his nightly

81

dog-walk and this happens?' Frowning. 'So where's the canine in question? Maybe Fido got left at home.'

Milo said, 'Or maybe our bad guy took a live trophy.'

'Rover stands by and watches his master get murdered and then goes off willingly with the perpetrator? Not a protective breed, that's for sure.' Catching her breath. 'Or the poor thing's lying somewhere looking like Mr Quigg.'

'Uniforms checked the immediate area but we'll go over it again after the techies arrive.'

Gloria scanned the dirt. 'Don't see any prints in here, dog or human.'

'Our bad guy cleaned up carefully.'

'Just like the first time,' she said. 'To me that makes it even more repulsive.'

I said, 'I don't see him cleaning every inch of ground all the way to Sunset.'

Milo cell-phoned Reed. 'Moses, keep the entire area tight, no one in or out until whoever's on duty helps you examine every inch of dirt between Sunset and the gate for prints. I'm talking tire, foot, paw, anything.'

Clicked off without waiting for an answer.

Gloria bent back down and turned out Marlon Quigg's remaining pants pockets. 'Empty.' Back on her feet, she photographed the scene at multiple angles, ending with close-ups of the folded brown shirt.

She inspected the label. 'Macy's generic, size M.'

No blood; the garment had been removed prior to the cutting.

She got back down near the body, started rolling it. Stopped and reached under and drew something out.

Piece of paper, folded into a packet, corners perfectly square.

She photographed it closed, then placed a sterile cloth under it and spread it open.

White, standard letter size. In the center, a simple message:

?

14

MARLON QUIGG'S apartment was in one of the nice buildings we'd passed.

A nearby traffic light would've provided easy crossing of Sunset. The walk to Temescal Canyon would've been pleasant.

The complex was designed to resemble an enormous hacienda, tricked out with a too-red tile roof, a false bell tower, and a front loggia that shaded arched entry doors. A tile-roofed carport faced the main structure across a broad, flagstone court.

Eight slots in the port. Quigg's Kia sat in Number Two. *Quigg, B and M* appeared on Unit Two's mailbox.

Ground-floor unit in the middle of the building. I recognized the woman who answered the door because I'd just seen her photo.

Milo said, 'Mrs Quigg?'

'Yes, yes, I'm Belle. You found them?'

'Them?'

'Marlon and Louie.'

'We found Mr Quigg.'

'Not Louie? Marlon went out walking him last night, they never came back. I've been frantic, when I called you people, you said it couldn't be a missing person until—' She stopped, put a hand to her mouth. 'Marlon's okay?'

Milo sighed. 'I'm sorry, he's not.'

'He's hurt?'

'Ma'am, this is hard to—'

Belle Quigg said, 'Oh, no, oh *no no no no no.*'

83

'I'm so sorry, Mrs Quigg—'

She raised her hands and yanked down, as if tugging clouds from a cruel clear sky. Glared at us. Gasped. Then she began beating Milo on the chest.

Small woman pummeling big man isn't much of an assault. Milo bore it until she ran out of steam and dropped her fists to her side.

'Mrs Qui—'

Her head flopped to one side, skin blanched to a bad shade of gray. Eyes rolling upward, she rasped once before pitching backward. Both of us lunged; we each caught an arm, eased her inside her home.

She woke up on the way to the nearest armchair. Milo stayed with her while I fetched water.

When I held the glass to her lips, her mouth opened with all the volition of a marionette. I took her pulse. Slow, but steady.

I eased more water into her mouth. She dribbled. Put her head back. The eyes rolled again.

After a few seconds, her pulse normalized and some color returned to her face. She stared up at us. 'What?'

Milo held her hand. 'I'm Lieutenant Sturgis—'

She said, 'Oh. You. So where's Louie?'

It took another few minutes for her to settle into grief-stricken numbness.

Milo sat holding her hand; I worked the water glass. When she said, 'No more,' I returned the glass to the kitchen.

Spacious sunlit kitchen, shiny granite, stainless steel. The rest of the apartment was done up nicely, too, furnished with timeless furniture, maybe a few real antiques, unremarkable but inoffensive seascapes. A double set of sliding glass doors granted an oblique view of blue swimming pool bleeding to bluer Pacific. The sky was clear, the grass around the pool was clipped, birds flew, a squirrel scampered up a magnificent Canary Island pine.

Marlon Quigg had arrived at a nice place in middle age.

At least one person cared about him. I knew I shouldn't be judging but that made his monstrous end seem even worse than Vita's.

Belle Quigg said, 'Oh, God, God, Louie's probably . . . also gone.'

'Louie's your dog,' said Milo.

'More like Marlon's dog, the two of them were like . . . we got him as a rescue, Louie loved everyone but mostly he loved Marlon. I loved Marlon. Britt and Sarah loved Marlon, *everyone* loved Marlon.'

She grabbed Milo's sleeve. 'Who would hurt him — was he robbed?'

'It doesn't look that way, ma'am.'

'What, then? What? Who would do this? Who?'

'We're gonna work real hard to find out, ma'am. I'm sorry to have to be the one to deliver such terrible news and I know this isn't a good time but if I could ask you some questions?'

'What kind of questions?'

'The more we know about Marlon the better we can do our job.'

'I *love* Marlon. We've been together twenty-six — oh, God, our anniversary is next week. I already made reservations. What am I going to do?'

Two bouts of sobbing later, Milo said, 'What kind of work did Marlon do?'

'Work?' said Belle Quigg. 'Yes, he worked, of course he worked, Marlon wasn't a bum — why, did one of those bums kill him?'

'Those bums?'

'They call them homeless, I call them bums because that's what they are. You see them at Sunset and PCH, panhandling, drunk. The light's long, gives them plenty of time to come up and beg. I never give them a dime. Marlon always gave them something.'

'Why would you suspect one of them?'

'Because they're bums,' said Belle Quigg. 'I always told Marlon that. Don't encourage them. He has a soft heart.'

'The crime occurred over in Temescal Canyon—'

'The Little Indians Camp! I *told* Marlon not to walk there at night! That just proves what I was saying. Anyone can walk in, what's to stop a bum? You want to find them? Go down to Sunset and PCH.'

'We'll definitely check that out, ma'am. Is there anyone else we should be thinking of?'

'What do you mean?'

'Anyone Marlon might've had conflict with, say at work?'

'Never.'

'What kind of work did he do?'

'Marlon was an accountant.'

'Where?'

'Peterson, Danville and Shapiro in Century City. He handled one major client, the Happy Boy supermarket chain. Marlon did a great job, always got the best performance ratings.'

'How long had he been working there?'

'Fifteen years,' she said. 'Before that he worked for the city – DWP – but only for a year, while he was waiting to take his CPA. Before that, he was a teacher. He worked with disabled children.'

'Before he picked up the Happy Boy account did he work with any insurance companies?'

'Happy Boy has been his assignment right from the beginning. They're a huge chain, it's all Marlon can do to keep up with their taxes.'

'So no problems at work.'

'Why would there be a problem? No, of course not, this had nothing to do with Marlon, Marlon's the best.'

'And obviously your personal life is great.'

'Better than great,' said Belle Quigg. 'It's . . . excellent.' Her lips parted. Color began leeching again. 'I'm going to have to tell Britt and Sar— Oh God, how can I do that—'

'How old are they?'

'Britt's eighteen, Sarah's twenty-two.'

'Are they close by?'

Head shake. 'Britt's in Colorado, Sarah's in . . . I . . . where is she, that place underneath Colorado . . .' Her face screwed up. 'It's on the tip of my . . . that place . . .'

I said, 'New Mexico.'

'New Mexico. She's in Gallup, it sounds like horses running around, that's how I remember it. She's there because her boyfriend lives in Gallup, so she does, too. She used to drive a car, now she rides a lot of horses, it's a ranch, one of those ranches. Britt's not married, I hope she will be but she's not, she lives in Colorado. Vail. She works as a waitress, gets real busy when it's ski season. She skis, Sarah rides horses. They're beautiful girls — how am I going to *tell* them!'

'If you'd like us to stick around while you call—'

'No, no no, *you* call.'

'You're sure, ma'am?'

'It's your job,' said Belle Quigg. 'Everyone needs to do their job.'

She turned silent, almost stuporous, as Milo phoned her daughters. The conversations were brief, terrible, and every second seemed to diminish him. If Belle Quigg had eavesdropped, she showed no signs of reacting.

He sat back down. 'Sarah would like to talk to you, Mrs Quigg.'

'Britt, too?'

'Britt will call you back when she composes herself.'

'Composes,' said Belle Quigg. 'Like a composition. She was always good in English.'

'Will you speak with Sarah?'

'No, no, no, tell her I'll call back. I need to sleep. I need to sleep forever.'

'Is there someone, a friend, a neighbor, that we could call to come over to be with you?'

'Be with me while I sleep?'

'To offer support, ma'am.'

'I'm fine, I just want to die in peace.'

I returned to the kitchen, looked for an address book, found a cell phone. A scan of recent calls listed a speed-dial number for Letty. I phoned it.

A woman said, 'Belle?'

I said, 'I'm calling on Belle's behalf.'

It took a while to clarify, longer until Letty Pomeroy stopped gasping, but she agreed readily to come over to take care of her friend.

'Are you nearby?'

'Like a five-minute drive.'

'We really appreciate it, Mrs Pomeroy.'

'Of course. Marlon's really . . .'

'I'm afraid so.'

'That's crazy — do you know who did it?'

'Not yet.'

'Where did it happen?'

'In Temescal Canyon.'

'Where Marlon walked Louie.'

'That's common knowledge?'

'Anyone who knows Marlon knows he likes to walk Louie there. Because he didn't need to clean up after Louie, it's so . . . rural. I mean I guess officially he did but . . . was Louie also . . .'

'Louie's missing.'

'Figures,' said Letty Pomeroy. 'That he wouldn't protect Marlon.'

'Pushover?'

'Moron.'

'What kind of breed is he?'

'Golden retriever. Or maybe a retriever mix. Mixed-up is more like it, that has to be the dumbest animal I've ever encountered. You could step on him, he'd grin up at you like the village idiot. Kind of like Marlon, I guess. No, that came out wrong, I'm not saying Marlon was stupid, God forbid no, Marlon was smart, he was a bright man, very mathematical.'

'But easygoing,' I said.

'*That's* what I meant. Marlon was the easiest-going guy, I can't believe someone would hurt him. I mean *Marlon*, for God's sake. He was the original bleeding heart. That's how he got Louie, no one wanted to adopt Louie, probably because he's so dim. My husband and I used to call him the Dumb Blond. A breathing, pooping throw rug. Anyone who'd steal that mutt is a worse idiot . . . sorry, I'm ranting, I still can't believe this. Someone actually hurt *Marlon*. Unbelievable.'

'Mrs Quigg's pretty traumatized, if you think you're up to coming over right now—'

'I'll be there in a jif.'

Back in the living room, Belle Quigg was resting her head on Milo's shoulder. Eyes closed, maybe sleeping, maybe withdrawing deeper than slumber. She'd caught him in an awkward position but he didn't budge.

I told him a friend would be showing up shortly.

Belle Quigg stirred.

Milo said, 'Ma'am?'

'Huh?'

'If you can handle a few more questions.'

Her eyes opened. 'Whu?'

'Is the name Vita Berlin familiar?'

'Like the city?'

'Yes.'

'No.'

'Not familiar with Vita Berlin?'

'Sounds like a food supplement.'

'What about an insurance company named Well-Start?'

'Huh?'

He repeated the name.

'We use Allstate.'

'Allstate's casualty, Well-Start does health insurance.'

'We use one of the blue ones, Marlon paid all the bills.'

'So neither Vita Berlin or Well-Start rings a bell.'

'No.' Flash of clarity. She sat up but remained pressed against him. 'No. Neither. Why?'

'Just routine questions.'

Smiling, the new widow placed a hand on his chest. Snuggling closer, she said, 'You're so *big*.'

15

Two women entered the Quigg condo. First through the door was a tall buxom redhead with short, feathered hair, wearing a green sweater over a black unitard and red Chinese slippers. She announced herself as Letty, identified her shorter, sweats-attired companion as 'Sally Ritter, she's also a friend.'

Belle Quigg didn't react. Her eyes were open but they'd been blank for the last quarter hour. One hand continued to grip Milo's wrist. The other rested on his chest.

Letty Pomeroy said, 'Oh, honey!' and surged forward.

Milo manage to extricate himself and stretch.

Sally Ritter said, 'So what exactly happened?'

I said, 'I've explained to Ms. Pomeroy.'

'From what she told me on the way over, that's not much.'

Milo said, 'We don't know much, that's why we need to investigate. Thanks, ladies.' He headed for the door.

Belle Quigg said, 'Wait.'

Everyone looked at her.

'You've remembered something, ma'am?'

She shook her head. 'But *everyone* should stay.'

Milo started up the engine before closing the driver's door, sped onto Sunset. Crossing the next intersection on an iffy amber evoked honks and curses. He said, 'Sue me,' and steered with one finger as he celled Moe Reed.

'Any shoe prints out front?'

Reed's voice came on speaker, grainy but audible. 'A few closer to the gate like you suggested. Techies arrived just after you left and I had them cast. Unfortunately, nothing was clear enough, all they got is an approximation of shoe size.'

'Which is?'

'We're talking at least five different sets, ranging from small to big.'

'What about tire tracks?'

'I really have to be the one to tell you, huh?'

'That bad?'

'No tracks whatsoever, Loo. Whoever sliced that poor guy up either walked in and out or he parked somewhere in the surrounding neighborhood. Street parking is illegal after eight p.m., any vehicle would've stood out and the locals would've probably complained. I checked with Traffic. No one called in anything and no tickets were issued last night.'

'Have the uniforms canvass the entire grounds again.'

'Uniforms just finished canvassing a second time. Nothing.'

'Do it a third time. You supervise. Have Sean participate, sometimes he notices things.'

'Sean's doing a door-to-door with the nearest neighbors.'

'You, then. Make sure it's done right.'

'Yes, sir.'

'I'm not only talking juicy obvious evidence, Moses. I'm talking random trash, a bottle, a candy wrapper. Anything but the damn trees and shrubs and rocks that God put there.'

'Only different thing that came up the second time was a dead snake near an empty garbage can. California king, a baby, pretty little thing, with blue and yellow and red stripes. And I'm not sure you can call that out of place.'

'Didn't know you watched Animal Planet, kid. Bring me a cobra and I'll be impressed.'

Reed laughed. 'Really was a nice snake, poor thing.'

Milo ended the call; a second later it beeped Brahms. 'Sturgis . . . oh, hi. Thanks for calling back . . . sure . . . actually

91

I understand the whole schedule thing, a good friend of mine's a physician . . . Richard Silverman, he's also at Cedars . . . you do? Yes, he is. So when can I speak to both of you? Sooner's better than later . . . I see. Well, that's fine, just give me your room number. Great, see you in twenty.'

He accelerated, zoomed around curves. The unmarked's loose suspension griped. He kept racing, zipping past the tree-shrouded northern border of the U.'s massive campus.

I said, 'Vita's downstairs neighbors?'

'The Drs Feldman. That was the male half. They both just got off call, found out about Vita, and are too freaked out to return home. So they're staying at the Sofitel across from Cedars.'

I said, 'Freaked out because they know something or just general anxiety?'

'We'll find out soon enough, I'm headed straight there. Any thoughts about poor Mr Quigg?'

I repeated what Letty Pomeroy had told me.

'Mr Nice Guy,' he growled, as if that was the gravest personality flaw of all. 'Maybe too trusting?'

'Sounds like Louie sure was. No protective instinct at all.'

'And now he's probably lying in a ditch with his own guts churned up. What the hell's going on, Alex? One victim's the most hated woman in Southern California, the other's ready to be sainted. There's a rational pattern for you.'

I said, 'Only thing I can see in common is they were about the same age.'

'A psycho who targets aging boomers? Now all I have to do is keep a close watch on a few million potential carvees. Hell, Alex, maybe I sic AARP on the damn case. Here I'd convinced myself this had something to do with Vita specifically. Now I'm picking up that random stench. Or something so crazy it might as well be random. Please tell me I'm wrong.'

'Too much planning went into the killings for a random strike. Same goes for the cleanup and sitting by the bodies until they were safely dead before mutilating.'

'So something nuts. Wonderful.'

'Calculated evil, not insanity. My bet is Vita and Quigg were both stalked. Vita was a stay-at-home who went out to shop and eat. Quigg took the same walk with his dog every night.'

'Creatures of habit,' he said. 'Fine, but what made them targets? Vita pissing off some psycho I can see. But mild-mannered Marlon? So maybe Quigg's not as perfect as his wife made out. You have time to revisit her? Maybe she'll give something up.'

'I have time, but she sure seemed to like your big manly chest.'

'Hate to deprive her but you'll be an excellent second choice.'

A mile later, he said: 'The dog bothers me. So he's no pit bull. But standing around while Quigg got butchered?'

I said, 'All the killer needed to do was incapacitate Quigg then tie the dog's leash to a branch or pin it under a rock. If Louie did react to seeing his master die horribly, that could've heightened the pleasure.'

'A sadist.'

'With a captive audience.'

'Think the dog's dead or a live trophy?'

'Could go either way.'

'Either,' he said. 'God, I hate that word.'

16

DR DAVID FELDMAN sat on the edge of the hotel bed. Dr Sondra Feldman sat so close the two of them looked glued together. The room was compact, tidy, air-conditioned frigid.

He was thirty or so, tall, thin, and long-limbed as an egret, with wavy black hair and the anxious nobility of a Velasquez prince. His wife, pretty and grave with nervous hands and straight black hair, could've been mistaken for his sib.

They'd insisted that Milo slip I.D. under the door before unlatching. The chain had remained in place while two sets of eyes checked us over through the crack.

After letting us in, Sondra Feldman bolted and rechained and David Feldman double-checked the strength of the hardware. Both Feldmans wore jeans, sneakers, and polo shirts, hers a pink Ralph Lauren Polo, his a sky-blue Lacoste. Their white coats were draped individually over separate chair-backs. A bowl of fruit on a nightstand was untouched. A bottle of Merlot had been touched to half empty.

Sondra Feldman saw me looking at the wine. 'We thought it might help but it was all we could do to hold it down.'

Milo said, 'Thanks for getting back to me.'

David Feldman said, 'We're hoping you can protect us. Or is that unrealistic?'

'You think you're in danger?'

'A neighbor gets murdered right above us? Wouldn't you consider that danger?'

Sondra said, 'There's no alarm system in the apartment. That always bothered me.'

'Have you had security problems?'

'No, but we're into prevention not treatment. We talked to Stanleigh – Mr Belleveaux. He was reluctant to install anything for a one-year lease.'

David said, 'For lack of contradictory data, we're assuming we're in danger. We'll be moving soon as we find another place but at some point, we'll need to go back to retrieve our stuff. Is there any way we could receive some sort of police escort? I know we're not celebs and the city's tight financially, but we're not asking for anything extensive, maybe one cop.'

Milo said, 'Until you find a new place, you'll be staying here?'

Sondra frowned. 'The cost is crazy and we get what, two hundred square feet?'

David said, 'We both have tons of loans. Stanleigh's place seemed like a great deal because he was friendly and honest and it was reasonably close to both our work. But after this? Not a chance.'

'You're a resident at Cedars?'

'And Sonny's at the U.'

The mention of work seemed to relax them. I said, 'What are your specialties?'

'I'm in medicine, want to do a gastro fellowship. Sonny's pediatrics.'

Sondra Feldman said, 'Can we interpret your not answering the request for an escort as a no?'

Milo said, 'Not at all. Once you're ready, get in touch. If I can't accompany you myself, I'll get someone else.'

'You'd do that?'

'Sure. I'll be back to the scene several times, anyway.'

The Feldmans exchanged quick rabbity looks. Sondra said, 'Well, thank you.'

Milo said, 'Hey, a neighbor murdered is heavy-duty, I don't blame you for being on edge. But is there some specific reason you feel you might be targeted?'

Another exchange of jumpy eye-language.

David said, 'We may just be paranoid, but we think we might have seen something.'

Sondra said, 'Some*one*. The first time was around three weeks ago. Davey saw him – you tell them, honey.'

David nodded. 'I can't be sure exactly when this was, given our sleep patterns, time blurs. We get home, take Ambien, collapse. The only reason I noticed him in the first place was the neighborhood's generally quiet, you never see anyone out past five. Not like Philly, we lived in City Center, there was street life all the time.'

Sondra said, 'The second time was maybe two weeks ago and I was the one who saw him. Davey hadn't told me he saw him so I never mentioned it. It was only after what happened to Vita that we compared notes.'

Milo said, 'Who's him?'

She said, 'Before we get into it, Lieutenant, we need to feel certain we're doing the right thing.'

'Believe me, Doctor, you are.'

'We don't mean morally, we mean personal-safety-wise. What if it gets back to him that we played a role in his apprehension and he comes after us?'

'Dr Feldman, we're a long way from that.'

'We're just saying,' said Sondra. 'Once we pass along information we're part of the process. There'll be no way to get *un*involved.'

Milo said, 'I appreciate your concern but I've been doing this a long time and I've never had someone in your situation harmed.'

David said, 'Please excuse us for not finding that comforting. There's always a first time.'

I said, 'You returned Lieutenant Sturgis's call. That wasn't just to ask for a police escort to pick up your stuff.'

'That's true,' said David. 'We wanted to do the right thing. But then we got to discussing it.'

'A criminal investigation is a complex process. Before anyone's apprehended, let alone charged and brought to trial, there'll be thousands of bits of data added to the pile. Your contribution won't stand out.'

Sondra said, 'You sound like my father. He's a psych prof, always dissecting things logically.'

'What does your father think you should do?'

'I haven't told him! Neither of us has told anyone.'

David said, 'If he knew, he'd be here on the next plane. Trying to run things, telling us, "See, I was right, you should've stayed in Philly."' She smiled. 'Your mom, too.'

'In spades. Meddle-city.'

They held hands.

I said, 'Who'd you both see?'

Sondra said, 'If our contribution's so insignificant, you probably don't need us in the first place.'

'Not insignificant,' I said. 'But not conspicuous, either. Isn't medicine like that? You don't always know what will work?'

David said, 'We'd like to think medicine can be pretty scientific.'

'We'd like to think criminal investigations can be scientific but reality doesn't always cooperate. The information you have may turn out to be irrelevant. But if it narrows things down, it could help.'

Sondra said, 'Okay, fine.'

'Sonny?'

'It's the right thing, Davey. Let's just get it over with.'

He inhaled, massaged the little crocodile snarling at his left breast. 'I was coming home from work around a month ago, saw a guy across the street. It was at night but I could see him, I guess there were stars out, I really don't know. My initial impression was he was staring at our building. Up, at the second story.'

I said, 'Vita's apartment.'

'I can't swear to it but from the way his neck was tilted that's what it seemed like. I found that curious because in all the time we'd been there, we never saw Vita have a visitor. I suppose it's possible she entertained during the day when we were gone. But all the times we were home during the day, we never saw anyone.'

'Total loner,' said Sondra. 'No surprise.'

'Why's that?'

'Her personality.'

'Abrasive, combative, obnoxious, pick your adjective,' said David. 'She's on top, we're on bottom, if anyone's going to hear footsteps it's us. But we never complained and trust me, her steps were heavy, she wasn't exactly a fashion model. Sometimes, after we'd been on call, it was hell being woken up by her clomping around.'

Sondra said, 'It seemed to happen a *lot* when we came back from call.'

Milo said, 'You think she was trying to bug you?'

'We wondered.'

David said, 'We didn't get into it with her, what's the point? Then she goes and complains to Stanleigh about us.'

Sondra said, 'How can you hear footsteps from downstairs? Plus we always go barefoot. Plus we're careful. Stanleigh was cool, said he was sorry. Obviously he was paying lip service. After that, anytime we'd see Vita she'd give us the stink eye.'

David said, 'Anyway, back to the salient issue: she never once had a visitor that we saw and now some guy was looking up at her place.'

I said, 'From across the street.'

'He took off the moment he saw me watching him.'

'What did he look like?'

'White, maybe five eleven. What I did find unusual was how he was dressed. It was a warm day but he was wearing a coat. No one wears coats in L.A., I brought one from Philly, it's still in a garment bag.'

'What kind of coat?'

'Kind of bulky. Or maybe he was bulky and filled it out.'

Sondra said, 'Given the benefit of hindsight, maybe he chose a bulky garment in order to conceal a gun. Was she shot?'

Milo said, 'She was stabbed.'

She gripped her husband's arm. 'God, even if we had been there, it could've gone on right under our noses and we might not have heard it. That's *repellent*.'

I said, 'What else can you remember about this person, David?'

'That's it.'

'What was his age?'

'I really can't say.'

'When he left how did he move?'

He thought. 'He didn't limp if that's what you're getting at . . . didn't move like an old guy, so probably not too old. I wasn't close enough to get details. I was more concerned about what he was doing there. In fact, I wasn't really worried, more like curious. It's when he got out of there that I started to wonder.'

Milo said, 'Think he was younger than fifty?'

'Hmm . . . probably.'

'Younger than forty?'

'That I can't tell you.'

'If you had to guess.'

'Twenties or thirties,' he said. 'And I don't even know why I'm saying that.'

'Fair enough.' Milo turned to Sondra.

She said, 'Three weeks ago – I know that because I was rotating at a clinic in Palmdale, too far to commute so mostly I slept out there but that night I got off early and David was on call and I wanted to clean up the apartment. So that would make it a week or two after Davey saw him. It was also at night, nine-ish, I'd gotten home at eight, eaten, showered, was doing some puttering, it relaxes me. Part of that was emptying the trash baskets into a big garbage bag and taking them out to the alley.'

She bit her lip. 'In retrospect, it's terrifying.'

I said, 'Someone was in the alley.'

She nodded. 'Not near our garbage, near the garbage next door. I must've spooked him because as soon as I got to our garbage, I heard footsteps. Then I saw him running. That freaked me out. Not only had he been there and I was unaware, but the fact that he ran away. Why would you run if you weren't up to no good? He ran fast, west up the alley. Some of the properties have security lights and as he passed under them I could see his form diminishing. Could see his coat billowing. That's why I know – I think – it's the same person Davey saw. It was a warm night, why wear a coat? I can't give you his age, saw him from the distance and from the back. But from the way he moved – more like a bear than a deer – I got the feeling he was kind of husky, the bulk just wasn't the coat. Do you think Vita's murder had to do with her specifically?'

Milo said, 'As opposed to?'

'A random psychopath.'

David said, 'Obviously we'd rather it be something specific and not some sexual predator targeting all women.'

Sondra said, 'That night, when I went down to the garbage, it really was warm. I had on a tank top and shorts. And I'm not sure I drew all the drapes on our windows.'

Her eyes teared up.

Milo said, 'We have no evidence he was after anyone at the building other than Vita.'

'Okay,' she said. Her tone belied any confidence.

David said, 'No matter, we're out of there.'

I said, 'Sonny, when you saw this person running away, what did you do?'

'I hurried back inside.'

'The only rational response,' said David.

Her eyes shot to the left.

I said, 'Did you look around at all before you hurried back?'

David said, 'Why would she?'

Sondra said, 'Actually . . .'

David stared at her.

'Just for a second, Davey. I was frightened but I was also curious, what would someone be doing there? I wanted to see if he left something. Some kind of evidence. So I'd have something to report to the police if he came back.'

'Wow,' said David. 'Wow-ow.'

'It's okay, hon, he was long gone, there was absolutely no danger. I only looked around a bit and then I went right back inside.'

I said, 'What'd you see?'

'Not much. There was a box on the ground so I assumed he'd been rooting around in the trash. I wondered if he was just a homeless guy scrounging for something to eat. That could explain the coat. When I rotated through Psych they told us schizophrenics sometimes dressed way too heavy.'

'What kind of box?'

'A pizza box, empty. I know that because I picked it up and put it in the trash and from the weight you could tell it was empty.'

David said, 'Ugh, time for Purell.'

She shot him a sharp look. 'Like I didn't?'

'I'm kidding.'

Milo said, 'Any markings on the pizza box?'

'I didn't notice. Why? Does pizza have something to do with Vita?'

Milo said, 'Nope.'

'So maybe,' said Sondra, 'he was just a mentally disturbed homeless guy Dumpster-diving, no big deal.'

'Anything else?'

Twin head shakes.

'Okay, thanks, here's my card and when you need that escort, give me a ring.'

Both Feldmans stood. He was an easy six four, she was four inches shorter. One day they might breed and create a brainy power forward.

As we headed for the door, I said, 'Philly as in Penn?'

Sondra said, 'Undergrad and med school for me, med school for Davey, he did undergrad at Princeton.'

David allowed himself a smile. 'We come across as Ivy League twits?'

'You come across as serious thinkers.'

'Thanks,' he said. 'I think.'

'Thinking,' said his wife, 'can be a big pain.'

17

MILO HAD his phone out before beginning the drive back to the station. He started with Moe Reed, checking again on the campgrounds.

Reed said, 'Nothing, but Sean has something for you.'

Sean Binchy came on. 'A neighbor thinks she saw someone lurking three days ago. White, indeterminate age, wore a coat, which she thought was weird, seeing as it was a warm night.'

'What kind of coat?'

'I didn't ask. Is that important?'

'Maybe.' He recounted the Feldmans' sightings, Sondra's theory about a concealed weapon.

'Oh, boy,' said Binchy. 'I'll go back and requestion her.'

'No need,' said Milo. 'Give me her info.'

We sped to Temescal Canyon.

The house was a wood-sided, two-story Craftsman on a generous lot due west and slightly north of the campground entrance, separated from the road by a densely planted berm. Plenty of hiding places among trees and shrubs.

Not ideal for a woman living alone, and that's what the informant turned out to be. Stunning, fortyish, athletically built, she responded to Milo's I.D. with, 'Hi, Milo B. Sturgis, I'm Erica A. Vail.'

Stepping out onto her lawn, she bent to pluck a dead bud from an azalea bush. She wore a skimpy black top, leggings in a curious shade of green that took on pink highlights when the sun hit the fabric at a certain angle, pink Vans. Her hair was huge, dark, artfully mussed. A diamond chip pierced her left nostril.

'I don't know what I can add to what I told that young cop. Didn't know you guys could be so hip. Spiky hair, that whole surfer thing, Doc Martens. Someone brought that to me in a script I'd tell them to get authentic. But apparently I need to be more broad-minded.'

'You're a director?'

'Producer.' She name-dropped a comedy series that had been off the air for five years, added the fact that she had three pilots in development for three separate networks.

'Glad Detective Binchy was helpful,' said Milo. 'I'm his boss.'

Erica Vail flashed blindingly white teeth. 'I merit the boss? Flattered. Maybe you'll be a little more forthcoming. Who exactly got killed?'

'A man who lives nearby.'

'How nearby?'

'Couple of miles.'

'By lives do you mean actually lives, like in a house? Or one of those homeless guys who congregate at PCH?'

'He had a home. His name was Marlon Quigg.'

'Never heard of him,' she said. 'I'd figured it for a homeless guy, once in a while they wander in. But when one of us asks them to leave we've never had a problem – did one of them kill Mr Quigg?'

'Too early to say, Ms Vail.'

'The guy I saw didn't impress me as homeless. Too healthy-looking. Even a little on the heavy side.'

'Tell us about it.'

'Sure,' said Erica Vail, bright-eyed, cheerful. 'Three nights ago, must've been close to ten, I came out and there he was.' Pointing to the berm. 'I was just about where I am now and I could see him because the moon was fat, it created kind of a halo around him.' She smiled. 'Almost a special-effects thing, forgive me, I tend to think in terms of movie frames.'

Milo said, 'You don't seem upset.'

'About the murder or seeing him?'

103

'Either.'

'The murder doesn't bother me because it's too abstract and back in a former life I was a surgical nurse, including duty in Afghanistan. So it takes a lot to gross me out. Seeing him didn't bother me because of Bella.'

'Who's Bella?'

She jogged back inside her house, returned moments later with a beast in tow.

At least a hundred fifty pounds of defined blue-gray muscle was graced by a massive, blunt-nosed head. Spots of gold accented the brow above the small, watchful eyes, same for the bottoms of the legs. A color-morphed rottweiler. But bigger and leggier than a rottweiler with a tail docked to a stub and ears cropped to pointy remnants. Circling a tree-trunk neck was a stainless-steel pinch collar tethered to a stout leather leash.

'Say hello to the nice policemen, Bella.'

The dog's lips drew back, baring lion-sized fangs. A low but thunderous noise – abdominal, menacing – emerged from its maws.

Erica Vail said, 'Apart from me, Bella doesn't like people.'

As if on cue, the dog lunged at us. Even with a pinch chain, Erica Vail had to labor to hold her at bay.

Erica Vail laughed. 'Men, in particular. She was my present to myself after my divorce.'

'What's her breed?' I said.

'Cane Corso. Combination of Roman war dog and some sort of Sicilian hound. Back in the old country they guard Mafia estates and hunt boar.'

Bella growled.

'I am woman, hear me roar,' said Milo.

Erica Vail laughed. 'You can see why Mr Lurker didn't bother me. Bella smelled him when she was still in the house. That's why I came out, she was getting all restless, whining near the door. Once we got out she went straight for him, would've had him for a snack if I hadn't been able to hold her back.'

'How'd he react?'

'That's the funny thing,' she said. 'Most people see Bella coming, they cross the street. This idiot just stood there. Maybe he was trying to prove how macho he was. But it was stupid, Bella pulls hard enough, I'm not sacrificing my shoulder.'

She tossed her hair, loosened her grip on the dog. Bella edged closer. I tried a closed-mouth smile; some dogs view teeth as a threat. She cocked her head, not unlike Blanche when she's thinking. Favored me with a long stare and settled for aloof condescension.

Erica Vail said, 'I was about to warn the fool when he finally got smart and split.'

Milo said, 'Which way did he go?'

'Down the street, that way – south. If he'd disappeared into the berm I'd have called you guys.'

'Anything else you remember about him?'

'I figured him for a perv because he was wearing a coat. You know, a yanker, Joe Raincoat.'

'Exhibitionist,' said Milo.

'Exhibitionists I'm used to,' said Vail. 'See 'em every day on the set. So what, you think he killed Mr Quigg?'

'We're just starting to investigate. How big was the guy you saw?'

'Average size.' Tapping my shoulder. 'More like him than you.'

'What about the coat?'

'Knee-length. He wore it open, that's another.'

'You could tell it was open because—'

'The shape, too wide to be zipped up. I got the impression of bulk, so nothing like microfiber. Hope you catch whoever killed that poor man. Bella and I are going back inside to read scripts.'

The dog had sidled close. I ventured a pet of her head. She purred.

Erica Vail stared at me. 'Unbelievable, she never likes guys.' Smiling. 'You married?'

Milo said, 'What kind of scripts does Bella like?'

'She's eclectic,' said Vail. 'But discerning. If she doesn't whine at a page of dialogue, I give it a second look. The caliber of stuff I'm getting lately, she whines plenty.'

18

OVER THE next few days, data trickled in.

Neither of Marlon Quigg's daughters had any idea who'd want to harm their father. The same went for family friends Milo and Reed and Binchy interviewed. Belle Quigg, requestioned through a fog of sedation, repeated a mantra: everyone loved Marlon, this had to be a maniac.

Animal Control reported thirty-three dead canines collected across the county since Quigg's murder. Milo and the young Ds took the time to check each one. None was Louie.

Most of the dogs had been abandoned and had died of malnutrition or disease or from being hit by cars. A golden retriever mix discovered on a Canoga Park side street had been shot in the head, execution-style, and Milo took the time to contact its owners. Two college girls had shared Maximilian; both were bereft and guilt-stricken. The ex-boyfriend of one young woman was their prime suspect and a background check revealed a husky thirty-year-old with a misdemeanor record of assaults and disorderly conduct.

Milo grew excited and looked for the man. He turned out to have been on the open sea for seven months, working as a deckhand on a commercial freighter on its way to Japan.

The shelter where Marlon Quigg had adopted Louie employed no one who matched the description of the broadly built white man seen lurking near both murder scenes. With the exception of a Vietnamese American high school student and two octogenarian retirees, the staff was exclusively female.

The woman who'd handled Louie's paperwork recalled Marlon Quigg because he'd been so easy to deal with and opined that he'd seemed the perfect match for Louie: quiet, laid-back, no-fuss kind of guy.

I thought: *Easy victim.*

Binchy and Reed visited other shelters with no better results.

Inspection of Quigg's phone and financial records revealed nothing suspicious. An additional search of the campgrounds and interviews with a score of homeless people congregating near PCH and Sunset were futile, though one of the panhandlers, a wild-eyed, gap-toothed woman named Aggie, was certain Quigg had once driven by and given her fifty dollars.

Milo said, 'Big haul.'

'Oh, yeah, he was great.'

'What kind of car was he driving, Aggie?'

'What else? Big Rolls-Royce. Like I say, some of those rich folk are nice!'

Quigg's autopsy and lab results came in.

A significant bruise where the back of the neck met the skull suggested he'd been subjected to a single hard blow from behind. The C.I. hadn't caught it at the scene because Quigg's thick hair concealed it. Not a fatal blow but hard enough to stun.

No human hairs other than Quigg's had been found on his person but Louie had shed a few more strands onto his master's shirt. Three additional fibers turned out to be synthetic sheepskin.

I said, 'Our bad guy wears a bulky coat. Maybe it's a cheap shearling.'

'Dressed for the hunt . . . in Montana . . . may-be.' Milo scrawled in his pad. 'What do you think of that head wound?'

I said, 'Classic sneak-attack sucker punch. Vita didn't need to be blitzed because she was reeling drunk and the pizza ruse caught her off guard. If the killer's the guy Erica Vail saw, he was near the scene three days before he did Quigg. Quigg's walks were predictable, it wouldn't have been much of a challenge to pretend to be taking a walk himself. Pass by and smile and wave, maybe even stop to pet Louie.'

'Friendly stalking,' he said. 'Till it's not.'

'I'd go back to Belle Quigg and ask if Marlon ever mentioned encountering anyone during his walks.'

More writing. 'On my list . . . so we have a good idea how each of them was done. But that still begs the big question: what turned them into victims? There's got to be something in common but hell if I can find it. I was hoping it would be Vita's lawsuit but it's not shaping up that way. The suits at Well-Start ended up being a lot more forthcoming than I expected. Not because they're nice guys, because Vita's murder has them worried the original gag order will be rescinded, they'll have to deal with a whole bunch of bad publicity. They actually sent a lawyer over yesterday and she showed me a lot of paper: the prelim motions, all the interviews with the accused co-workers, Shacker's report. Which came across as a lot of shrinky bullshit, no offense. But all in all, nothing new and the mouthpiece swore the company had no connection with Quigg. I didn't take her word for it, emailed Well-Start's CEO's second in command in Hartford, Connecticut. He called me personally, gave me the name of the accounting firm that does their books, greased the skids so they'd talk to me. They'd never hired Quigg nor, to their knowledge, had Quigg ever applied for a job. That was backed up by Mrs Quigg. Marlon wasn't a "seeker". Happy with the status quo and figuring on retiring in a few years. Despite *that*, I got hold of Quigg's boss at the CPA firm and probed about Quigg doing insurance work. The firm does some but not for Well-Start and not for Well-Start's liability carrier. And even if they had, Quigg wouldn't have been assigned to it, he was more than busy with his supermarket account. He described ol' Marlon the way everyone else has: pleasant, compliant, even-tempered. So why were the two of them singled out? Or maybe there is no X factor and this bastard drives around, spots random prey, stalks and studies and sets up the hunt.'

Nothing about this kind of murder was ever random but it wasn't the time to say so.

'Meanwhile,' he said, 'both cases are thawing out fast. Bastard quits right now, he may get away with it.'

He needn't have worried about that.

19

THE FOLLOWING day, Milo's mood lifted from subterranean to glum.

Belle Quigg had remembered a 'nice young fellow' Marlon had met during his nightly walk.

Louie had 'taken' to the man, a clear sign to Quigg that he was a person of sterling character.

Milo hmmphed. 'Because we all know dogs are such great judges.' He spooned lentils onto a hillock of basmati rice. Sucked-out lobster claws were heaped in front of him, a gruesome display if you thought too much about it.

We were at his usual corner table at Café Moghul, an Indian restaurant around the corner from the station that serves as his second office. Over the years he'd handled a few disruptive psychotics wandering in from Santa Monica Boulevard. The owner, a sweet bespectacled woman who never wears the same sari twice, views him as Lord Protector and feeds him accordingly.

Today it was the lobster, plus tandoori lamb and a farm-plot's worth of slow-cooked vegetables enriched by clarified butter. He'd downed six glasses of iced clove tea.

With nowhere to go on the murders, I figured it for an easy day and was nursing my second Grolsch. 'Marlon say anything else about this nice fellow?'

'If he did, Belle doesn't remember. By the way, I talked to a fabric analyst at the lab and the synthetic fleece found on Quigg would definitely be consistent with a low-budget shearling-type lining. Not that it leads me anywhere.'

I said, 'You heard what David Feldman said: he still hasn't unwrapped his winter coat. The fact that our boy wears his could mean he's originally from a cold climate.'

'Or just rummaged at the right thrift shop. But if I come across a dogsled and mittens, I'll go with that. I find the fact that Quigg could've been primed for days hugely creepy. Like those wasps, stroking caterpillars into a stupor before they plunge the stinger.'

I said, 'Priming could serve an additional purpose: we've got a wasp who enjoys playing with his food.'

'Joy of the hunt.'

'A shearling might be something a hunter would own.'

'Homicidal fore-prey.' His laughter was harsh. The woman in the sari glided over. Today's garment was a celebration of turquoise and coral-pink and saffron-yellow. The pink matched her eyeglass frames.

'You are enjoying?'

'As always.'

'More lobster?'

Milo patted his paunch. 'Couldn't handle another bite. I've already demolished an entire coral reef.'

She was confused by the reference, covered with a smile. 'You want more, tell me please, Lieutenant.'

'Will do, but honestly, I'm done.'

'Not totally done,' she said. 'Dessert.'

'Hmm,' he said. '*Gulab jamun* sounds good.'

'Very fine.' She glided away moving her lips. I caught two words: 'My lieutenant.'

Milo caught nothing because his phone was vibrating on the table. When he processed the digital readout, his shoulders dropped.

'Sturgis, sir. Oh, hi, Maria . . . oh. Jesu— When? Oh. Okay. Yeah. Right away.'

Pushing away from the table, he threw cash down, swiped his chin viciously with a napkin. As I followed his trot for the door, the woman in the sari emerged from the kitchen bearing a platter of dough balls glazed with rosewater syrup and two bowls filled to the brim with rice pudding.

'There's *kir*, too,' she said. 'For extra sweet.'

'Unfortunately, life isn't,' said Milo, shoving the door open and leaving me to catch it.

He race-walked south on Butler, heading back to the station, flushed and breathing hard and wiping his face and grinding his teeth.

I said, 'What's up?'

'What do you think?'

'Maria Thomas is a pencil-pusher. Something mindlessly bureaucratic, like a meeting you've been avoiding?'

He stopped short, wiped his face so hard it was almost a slap.

'Our bad boy's back in action and instead of calling me, the watch commander went straight to His Splendiferousness. Who handed off to Maria because he didn't want to hear the sound of my voice. Obviously I've been under the microscope on these murders and not engendering confidence. I'm heading over to the scene now. Don't be surprised if they yank me off.'

He resumed his march.

I said, 'Who's the victim?'

His jaw was tight; the answer came out hoarse and strangled.

'Think plural. This time the bastard doubled his fun.'

The house was a low, wide ranch on a street of similar structures in a no-name neighborhood of West L.A.

The man had been found in the backyard, lying on his stomach, wearing a black silk bathrobe. Deep stab wounds concentrated in a tight circle at the center of his chest. A couple of coup de grâce throat slashes had severed the right jugular and carotid and the trachea.

No disembowelment, nothing similar to Vita and Quigg. I watched as Milo examined the body.

The man's hair was long, dark, and wavy. His mustache was clipped precisely. Thirty to forty, good-sized, well muscled.

No effort to clean up the blood; the grass beneath the body was glazed a slick, unpleasant brown. No shredded lawn or damaged shrubs or other sign of struggle.

No blow from behind; this time, the C.I. had probed under the hair immediately, found no swelling or bruising.

The killer had taken on a serious foe face-to-face, dispatched him easily.

Maybe darkness had been his ally.

Milo circled the body for the fourth time.

The crime scene techs had finished their initial work and were waiting for him before leaving. Deputy Chief Maria Thomas had taken her time calling him to the scene.

Out in front of the house, the coroner's van was waiting to transport.

Nice, sunny day on the Westside. The yard where the man in the robe lay dead was ringed with high block walls laced with trumpet vine. In Missouri, where I'd grown up, no one bothered with fences and a kid could pretend he owned the world. Behind our rattrap house was a dense black forest that yielded an occasional dead animal and two human corpses. The first had been a hunter, shot accidentally by a buddy. The second had been a little girl, five years old, my age at the time. I supposed freedom could be the stuff of bad dreams but right now this boxy, confined space felt oppressive. Why was I thinking about that?

Because I had nothing constructive to offer.

Milo completed another circle before heading for Maria Thomas.

The D.C. had positioned herself midway up the blue house's driveway, on the near side of two parked vehicles. Sheltered from the ugliness, she made love to her cell phone.

Blond-coiffed and trim with a preference for tailored suits, Maria had been a captain when I'd met her a couple of years ago. Well spoken, cautious, decorous, she was the ideal corporate cog. The only time I'd seen her in action, she'd screwed up big-time by usurping a detective's role, leading to the death of a suspect in an interview room.

Somehow that disaster had earned her a promotion.

She kept Milo waiting as she talked, finally pointed to the house's rear door but didn't end the conversation.

Milo and I made our way through the bright, neatly kept house. The laundry room and the kitchen and the living room appeared untouched, no blood from the yard tracked in.

The kitchen smelled of cinnamon.

Everything neat and clean and normal.

The master bedroom was another story.

The woman lay on her back atop a queen-size bed. Her hair was short and wavy, a careful blend of several shades of subdued caramel. Her left hand was tethered to a brass headboard with a blue necktie. The tie's label was visible. Gucci.

No towels or tarp had been spread underneath her naked body. A few ruby specks dotted pale blue sheets, but no arterial explosion or castoff or significant leakage.

Waiting until every organ system had shut down before doing his thing.

The exact same thing he'd done to Vita Berlin and Marlon Quigg.

This woman's eyes were wide open, maybe positioned that way postmortem or perhaps they'd opened spasmodically and stayed that way.

Big and gray and artfully shadowed, the lashes enriched with mascara.

Disturbingly lifelike despite the impossible angle of her broken neck and putrid guts piled up in grotesque decoration.

On the carpet next to the bed was a filmy, pink negligee. The woman's nails were silver nacre, her toes, claret.

Just beneath the baby toe of her left foot was a sheet of white paper.

?

Milo growled. 'You're getting boring, asshole.'

The uniform by the door said, 'Pardon?'

Milo ignored him and took in the room.

I was already scanning the space for the second time, concentrating on the left-hand nightstand where a pair of frilly pink panties draped a lamp shade. Spread across the stand was a careless array: a tube of Love Jam apricot-flavored lubricant, a package of ribbed condoms, an unopened bottle of Sauvignon Blanc, a corkscrew, two wineglasses.

A similar lamp graced the other stand, minus the undergarment. The only object it housed besides the lamp was a silver-framed photo.

Good-looking couple. Tux and wedding dress, big smiles as they cut into a four-tiered cake festooned with yellow sugar roses.

No younger than they appeared now. Newlyweds?

A ceiling lamp glowed faint orange. A dimmer switch near the bed was set on low.

Romantic lighting.

The scene shot into my head, as surely as if I'd scripted it.

The two of them retire for bed, counting on a night of romance.

One or both of them hears something out back.

They ignore it because you can't go check on every little leaf-rustle and imagined intrusion.

They hear it again.

Someone – some*thing* – out in the yard?

No big deal, at worst a raccoon or a possum or a skunk. Or just a stray cat or dog, that had happened before.

They hear it again.

A faint scratching. Rustling of foliage.

Again.

Too enduring to be ignored.

Is there really something out there, honey?

No prob, I'll check.

Be careful.

I'm sure it's nothing.

He throws on his robe, goes to check it out. Because that's what husbands do.

She waits, thinking it's nice to be married, have someone to squish bugs and play Protector.

Lying back, she relaxes, anticipating deliciousness.

He doesn't return quickly the way he usually docs.

The moments pile up.

She begins to wonder.

Don't be silly, maybe he really did encounter a critter and had to deal with it.

Hopefully not a raccoon, they carry rabies. And get mean when cornered.

But no sound of struggle, so maybe he's just being careful.

The notion of her darling and a critter makes her smile. So . . . primal. He'll be careful, he always is, and it'll turn out to be one of those funny stories they'll tell their grandchildren.

But it *is* taking a long time . . .

More time passes.

She calls his name.

Silence.

Then, the door closes. Good. Everything's fine, maybe he'll come in with one of his yummy surprises. Last time it was Godiva chocolate.

This time it could be another treat. Food or otherwise . . .

She closes her eyes, arranges herself the way he likes. The comforting sound of male footsteps grows louder.

She loves that sound.

She coos his name.

Silence.

Or perhaps a vague masculine grunt.

Baby's playing Caveman. Excellent, this is going to be one of *those* nights.

Something *not* to tell the grandchildren.

She smiles. Purrs.

Positions herself a little racier than usual, creating sublime invitation.

He's in the room, now. She hears his breathing intensify.

'Baby,' she says.

Silence.

Fine, *that* game.

He's right next to her, she senses him, feels his heat. But . . .

Something different.

She opens her eyes.

Everything changes.

Papers in the desk of the home office next to the bedroom conformed to DMV info.

Barron and Glenda Parnell.

He'd lived just over two months past his thirty-sixth birthday. She'd made it thirteen months longer.

A picture I.D. badge from North Hollywood Day Hospital tagged her as *G. A. Usfel-Parnell, M.D. Nuclear Medicine*. In the picture, she was grave, still pretty, wearing big, rimless glasses. Milo found them in a nightstand drawer.

I wondered about the extent of Dr Glenda Parnell's visual impairment. What had she actually seen when she'd opened her eyes?

Had she ever really focused?

Trembled at the horror but composed herself sufficiently to bargain?

Fear about her husband's fate would have shaken her, but perhaps she'd been able to put that aside, sufficiently adrenalized to concentrate on her own survival.

Had the killer pretended to go along as he had her tie her own arm to the bedpost? Or had he relied, at the outset, on terror and intimidation?

Had she sensed it was futile the moment he'd breached the door? Complied out of self-preservation as well as love for Barron, hoping cooperation would spare both of them?

If so, she'd spoken a completely different language from the killer. To him, Barron was nothing more than an obstacle to overcome.

He'd pulled the prelim off perfectly, drawing the guy into his trap. Now the fun part.

Once prints had been taken, Milo gloved up and gave the office desk a thorough search. Glenda Parnell's malpractice insurance was paid up, as were her subscriptions to several medical journals. Mail addressed to Barron Parnell appended CFP to his name. A mailer from a brokerage house expanded that to Certified Financial Planner.

So did a letter from an attorney representing the Cameron Family Trust that specified malfeasance and 'incautious' investing.

The date was nineteen months ago. Milo copied down the particulars.

Further excavation of the desk drawers indicated Parnell worked out of the home with no apparent clients other than himself and his wife. He'd done well, amassing just over a million dollars in a stock account, two hundred thousand more in a corporate bond account, just under ten thousand in a joint savings-checking account.

The two vehicles parked in the driveway were a three-year-old yellow Porsche Cayman registered to Barron and a gray Infiniti QX registered to Glenda. Both had been recently washed and appeared undisturbed.

Also unmolested was a pricey bank of computers in the office, some serious jewelry in a leather box barely concealed behind blankets in the linen closet, a case of sparkling Christofle silverware in the pantry, a home entertainment system in the living room that included a sixty-inch plasma TV.

We returned to the bedroom. In Barron's sock drawer, Milo found a silver-framed glamour shot of Glenda. Fuzzy focus, the suggestion of nudity, cornucopia of cleavage, glistening teeth.

To Barry Boo from Sweet Gee. Love 4ever. Happy anniversary. XXXX
The inscribed date was forty-two days ago.
Maria Thomas stuck her head in the room. 'Anything?'
Milo shook his head.
'Got a sec?'
'Yeah.' He might've been agreeing to do-it-yourself root canal.

* * *

118

The three of us powwowed in the Parnells' spotless kitchen. Someone had put money into the décor: matte-black Euro cabinets trimmed in chrome, white marble counters that appeared unused, copper pots hanging from a cast-iron ceiling rack, everything else brushed steel.

Maria Thomas plinked a counter with a fingernail. 'Marble's good for rolling pastry dough, not cooking. No one did serious food, here.'

'Didn't know you were into the culinary arts, Maria.'

'I'm not, my daughter is. That translates to she's the one gets addicted to *Top Chef*, I'm the one pays tuition at some overpriced institute in New York. Now she wants to spend next summer in France, learning how to properly slice onions. This is a kid who survived the first four years of her life on hot dogs and chocolate milk.'

She fingered a crisp tweed lapel. Her hair was sprayed in place. Not helmet-stiff, a higher level of fixative that lent the illusion of softness. An expensive-looking phone dangled from her other hand. 'Some mess, huh?'

Milo said, 'It's a step up.'

'From what?'

'Not from, for,' he said. 'The offender. He took risks with the husband in order to get to the wife. Earned himself a two-fer, kicked up the thrill level. But you know that, already. Seeing as you've been here for a while.'

She stared at him. 'Someone's touchy.'

He turned his back on her. Interesting move; she outranked him significantly. He'd been there when she'd screwed up, had never exploited it. Maybe Maria figured that gave him a certain power. Maybe that would eventually work against him.

'Okay,' she said, 'let's clear the air right now so we can go about our respective businesses?'

'Thought we were in the same business.'

Thomas's gray eyes turned to pond pebbles. 'I'm here because the chief has been following this since the second one, Mister' – consulting her phone – 'Quigg. The reason the chief was informed early is someone thought a serial pattern might be forming and that the details were sufficiently out of the ordinary for the chief to need to be apprised. Don't ask who informed him, that's irrelevant.'

'I couldn't care less about any of that, Maria, all I want to do is clear four murders.'

'That's what we all want. Think there's a remote chance of your accomplishing it anytime in the near future?'

'You betcha, boss,' he said. 'Everything will be gift-wrapped and presented for your approval by' – reading his Timex – 'nine forty-three tonight. Give or take a nanosecond. Also on the schedule is the capture of Osama's entire organization but in the meantime be sure to warn His Amazingness to treat any packages from Pakistan with caution.'

'Hey—'

'Is there a remote chance? What kind of *question* is that, Maria? You think this is writing traffic tickets?'

'Ah, the temper.' She winked. 'The classic *Irish* temper and I can say that because half my family traces back to County Derry.'

'Whoopee for genealogy, Maria. Is there a point to this conversation?'

Thomas caressed marble, ran a finger under the counter rim. 'Indulge yourself, Milo, keep venting. Get all the bad feeling out so we can both do our jobs like grown-ups.'

She turned to me, seeking confirmation of something.

I kept studying the double-wide refrigerator. No magnets, no memos or photos. Nothing like a blank panel of steel to keep one fascinated.

Maria Thomas turned back to Milo. 'You bet it's a reasonable question. When's the last time you dealt with a serial remotely similar to this, Milo? A necktie of guts? Jesus, it's beyond disgusting.'

He didn't answer.

She said, 'I can't see any common thread among the victims other than they're all white. Can you?'

'Not yet.'

'Not yet,' she repeated. To me: '*You* ever see anything like this? A sexual psychopath who throws such a wide net?'

Milo said, 'It's not necessarily sexual.'

'Then what?'

'Some kind of grudge. The first victim was engaged in a big-time lawsuit and I just found a financial complaint in Mr Parnell's desk.'

'I saw that,' she said. 'You can't seriously think a money thing led to *that*. And what about Mr Quigg? He sue anyone or vice versa?'

'Nothing's come up yet.'

'You should've checked his financials.'

'I have.'

'And you haven't found anything. So the answer's no, not "nothing's come up". Meaning there's no common thread. Meaning a money thing's less than unlikely. You go along with his theory, Dr Delaware? You don't see this as a sexual psychopath?'

'Can't say.'

'Can't or won't?'

'I don't see the point of guessing.'

'So far I've heard nothing but guessing – all right, enough of this pleasantry. I'm expected to go back to the boss and report something. What do *you* suggest, Milo?'

Milo said, 'Tell him each time the killer strikes he increases the possibility of a lead. In the meantime, I'll be concentrating on the Parnells.'

'Each time,' she said. 'Maybe by the time we get ten, eleven victims, we'll be in great shape. Very reassuring.'

Milo grinned in that lupine way: teeth bared in anticipation of ripping flesh.

Maria Thomas said, 'you always see humor when no one else does. When were you planning to go to the public?'

'His Perfectness thinks I should?'

'Word to the wise, Milo: you really need to stop with the obnoxious nicknames, one day it'll get back to him.'

'He doesn't like being perfect?'

'The *public*. *When?*'

'I hadn't thought about it.'

'No? That's too bad because the chief thinks it might be useful.' She looked over her shoulder, in the direction of the bedroom. 'Given the steadily rising corpse count. And something tells me he won't find your lassitude reassuring.'

Milo walked away from her again. Her face tensed with anger but before she could speak, he circled back. 'Okay, here's something to tell him: if this *was* a confirmed sexually motivated psychopath, some rapist who escalated to murder, I'd have been talking to Public Affairs as soon as the second one surfaced, hoping an earlier, live victim would come forth. The same goes for a serial asshole targeting a specific victim population – hookers, convenience clerks, whatever. In that case there'd be a moral as well as a practical benefit: letting high-risk targets know so they can protect themselves. But what do we go public on, here, Maria? A bogeyman stalking and butchering random citizens? That risks setting off a panic with very little upside.'

'What's your alternative?' she said. 'A nice collection of murder books?'

'I haven't even started working these two victims. Maybe I'll learn something that will change everything. If you let me do the damn job.'

'*I'm* holding you back?'

'Wasting time explaining myself is holding me back.'

'Oh, so you're different from anyone else?' Back to me: 'What's with the question mark on these two, Doctor?'

I said, 'The same thing was left with the first two victims.'

She blinked. 'Yes, of course. So what does it mean?'

'Could be a taunt,' I said.

Milo smiled. 'Or our bad boy's expressing his curiosity.'

'About what?' said Thomas.

'The mysteries of the human body.'

'That's grotesque. You know what *I* thought when I saw it? Some weird mystical symbolism, like the Zodiac used to send. You look into any witchcraft angles?'

'I'm open to anything, Maria.'

'Meaning you haven't. And you're opposed to going public. How many bodies will it take to get you flexible?'

'If nothing on these two—'

'Good,' she said. 'You're open-minded when forced to be. He'll be happy to hear it. He respects you, you know.'

'I'm touched.'

'You really should be. Get back to me if you learn something. Sooner rather than later.'

'You're the glove,' said Milo.

'Pardon.'

'He doesn't want to dirty his hands so he gloves up.'

Maria Thomas examined her spotless, manicured digits. 'You have a way with words. Sure, view me as a glove. And bear in mind that finger-poking can be painful.'

20

THOMAS LEFT the scene scolding her phone. Drove off in a sparkling blue city sedan.

Milo said, 'Before she stuck her nose in, I was thinking about going public at some point. But right now I don't see what it'll accomplish and the panic thing's an issue.'

I said, 'If you release any data, I'd choose the question marks. They're unique to our bad guy, might jog someone's memory.'

He shuffled over to the Parnells' cars, looked inside. 'I don't make some kind of progress soon, the decision won't be mine. You got the point of Thomas showing up.'

'Behave or else.'

'More than that. The chief smells a big-time loser in these cases so he's keeping his distance.' He flipped his pad open. 'Where's that lawyer who threatened Barron Parnell . . . here we go, "William Leventhal, Esquire, representing the Cameron Family Trust". Sounds like a big money deal, let's see if this legal eagle earned his cut.'

William B. Leventhal ran a one-man practice on Olympic near Sepulveda.

On the way over, Milo said, 'Booze and surprise for Vita, sucker punch for Marlon. Now he does two young healthy ones.'

I said, 'Same basic technique: surprise supplemented this time by darkness. Barron was the serious threat so he was drawn outside, blitzed, and stabbed to death. But no surgery, not even later when our bad guy had a chance. That says Glenda was the primary target and with Barron

124

unlocking the door, she was easy prey. Also, her glasses were off because the two of them were planning a romantic evening and the room was dim, leading to a loss of focus. Before she had time to figure out what was going on, he was in charge. We know he stalked his first two victims, so he probably did the same with her.'

'You don't see it as a two-fer? Doubling his pleasure?'

'Upping the body count was a bonus, but I think Barron was a hurdle to jump so he could get to Glenda.'

'So I'm wasting my time with Leventhal.'

'Only one way to find out,' I said.

The lawyer's front office staff was a woman in her seventies at a hundred-year-old desk. A brass nameplate said *Miss Dorothy Band, Exec. Secy. to Mr Wm. B. Leventhal.* An IBM Selectric took up half her desk. Near the machine sat a precisely cornered stack of elegant beige stationery, a shorter pile of carbon paper, and a Bakelite intercom box that predated the Truman administration.

Unflustered by our drop-in, Miss Dorothy Band pressed a button on the box. 'Mr L, police to see you.'

The machine barked back: 'I paid those tickets.'

'They say it's about the Cameron case.'

'What about it?'

'They say they need to talk to you directly.'

'That's a civil case, none of their business.'

'Sir . . .'

'Fine. See-*yend* them in.'

The trek to Leventhal's inner sanctum took us past a vast law library. A man was there to greet us, a good ten years older than Dorothy Band. Short, thick, and broad-shouldered, William Leventhal had bright, burnt-chocolate eyes, white hair still tinged rusty in spots. An uncannily deep voice said, 'Police. Heh. C'mon in.'

Leventhal's office was vast, wood-paneled, shag-carpeted in the precise green of pimiento olives, redolent of dill pickles and old paper and musky aftershave. Heat streamed from a floor vent, creating a tropical ambience. William B. Leventhal wore a three-piece English-cut herringbone suit of heavy tweed, a starched white shirt, and a bolo tie held in place by a mammoth nugget of amethyst.

Not a trace of sweat on his plump face. A tweedy leprechaun, he lowered himself into a tufted leather chair commodious enough to harbor a panda. 'The girl informs me this is about Cameron.'

Milo started to explain.

Leventhal said, 'Murder? You won't find the solution here. Never met Parnell, never even deposed him. Heh.'

'You sent him a letter—'

'He was named along with everyone else in that firm. The case settled. *Finis.* Good-bye.'

'What firm is that, sir?'

'"Sir,"' said Leventhal. 'A kid with manners, I like that. If you must know, the miscreants in question are Lakewood, Parriser and DiBono, alleged money managers. Parnell worked there as a fixed-income specialist. In plain terms, boys, he bought bonds for rich people.'

'The Cameron Trust is—'

'An inspired creation that has allowed two generations of not-too-bright Camerons to avoid gainful employment.'

'Parnell's investments didn't do well?'

'They did fine,' said Leventhal. 'Though a trained parakeet could've handled the task. We're talking triple-A conservative investments, you read a daily list and pick. Or peck, if you're a parakeet. Heh.'

'Then why did you—'

'In order to proceed optimally against the *primary* scoundrels, I was required to name everyone through whose hands Cameron money had passed.' He rubbed chubby palms together. 'I got to sue their office manager, their Human Resources person, their bookkeepers. The cleaning crew's fortunate they weren't named. Heh.'

'The scoundrels were—'

'Lakewood.' Leventhal ticked a finger. 'DiBono. Parriser. Not necessarily in that order.'

'What I'm getting at,' said Milo, 'is the nature of their scam—'

'No scam,' said Leventhal. 'I never said scam, no, no, no, no-*ooow*. A clear case of deceit would've been easy to ferret out. No, these geniuses were subtle. Promising verbally to invest in secure products but engaging in all sorts of risky nonsense. Commodity futures, derivatives, inadequately secured real estate loans. The veneer of solidity but once you looked closely, a house of cards.' He winked. 'I sued their outside accountant. Brought the lot of them to their knees.'

'So the Camerons never lost money.'

'Preventive medicine, boys. The rascals tried to claim that the original terms of the trust gave them lifetime control. I put the lie to that notion.'

The left side of Leventhal's mouth rose. 'And now the Camerons remain free to avoid honest labor.'

'Congratulations,' said Milo.

'Virtue is its own reward, young man. No, actually a fat contingency commission is far better recompense. So. Who murdered poor Mr Parnell? Whom I've never met.'

'That's what we're trying to find out.'

'Well, you won't find out here. Was the wife involved?'

'Why do you ask that?'

'Because she was a battle-ax. I say that because when we served Parnell, she was abusive to the server. He described her with the B word but I'll stick with "battle-ax" because memories of my mother washing my mouth out with soap still linger.'

'The process server told you this?'

'He's my great-grandson, of course he told me.'

'We'd like to speak with him.'

'Suit yourselves,' said Leventhal, rattling off an international number. 'That's England, Brian's international cell phone. Brian Cohn, no *e*. Cambridge University, he's on fellowship. International relations, whatever that is. Jesus College. Brian Cohn at Jesus College. Heh. Tell him he owes me ten hours of work. You're thinking the wife was involved?'

'She was definitely involved,' said Milo. 'She's also dead.'

'I see . . . did her death occur within the same approximate time frame as Mr Parnell's?'

'Yes, sir.'

'Both bodies at the scene?'

'Sir—'

'I'll take that as a yes,' said Leventhal. 'Wouldn't the obvious answer be murder-suicide?'

'Why would you think that, sir?'

'Because when a couple expires in a near-simultaneous manner, we always zeroed in on the murder-suicide angle and we were almost invariably correct. I'm referring to back in the day. When I did criminal prosecution at the Brooklyn D.A. Two bodies, weapon on the scene, first thing we'd look for was one party going berserk and victimizing the alleged loved one. You could put money on it. Sometimes we did. Office pools and such.'

'That didn't happen here, Mr Leventhal.'

'You're certain.'

'We are.'

'Okay, hmm . . . did the wife have a boyfriend? Did *he* have a *girl-friend*? Was money taken? Jewelry, other valuables? Do acquaintances imply loss of mental control for one of the parties – some sort of personality disintegration? How were the two of them dispatched? Gun? Knife? Blunt object? None of the above?'

Milo said, 'Sorry, we can't—'

'Of course you can't,' said Leventhal. 'Because if you could you might stumble upon someone with half a brain, sixty-two years of legal experience, one-third of that prosecutorial. But why make your life easier?'

He sprang up and waved us to the door. 'Despite your reticence, I'll reiterate some sage advice, boys: check out the wife. Even without a murder-suicide angle, we always hurt the one we love. And someone as short-tempered as her was bound to evoke hostility. Take a close look to see if she'd engaged in any sort of emotional dustup recently. If you find out she had a boyfriend to boot, we're talking emotional TNT.'

'Thanks for the tip, sir.'

'No problem,' said Leventhal. 'I won't even bill you.'

Milo called Cambridge from the car. Brian Cohn picked up, sounding hung-over. 'Yuh?'

Milo explained.

Cohn said, 'This is England, man, you know what time it is?' He coughed, cleared his throat. Phlegm-laden laughter. 'Oh, man, there he goes again.'

'Who?'

'Wild Bill. Aka Greatest-Grandpa. *He* gets up at four a.m. so we all have to.'

'He's quite a guy. Says you owe him—'

'Ten hours of work, yada yada yada. By his calculation. Which was probably done on an abacus.' Cohn laughed again. A female voice sounded in the background. 'One sec, babe.' Yawn. 'Okay, I'm quasi-awake, what do you need to know about that crazy shrew?'

'Tell us about your encounter.'

'Why?'

'She's dead.'

'Oh. That's too bad. Even for someone like that.'

Milo said, 'Like what?'

'Hostile. No one likes to be served but the worst you usually get is a sneer, some cursing. She came to the door wearing her white coat; I figured, good, a doctor, someone rational. Because plenty of times you're dealing with Neanderthals. This was one of those deals where I didn't need to hand it to Parnell personally, just ascertain his primary residence and verify that someone had accepted it. I used the flower ruse, bought some cheap ones at the supermarket. She came to the door, said, "Is this from Barry? Hold on, I'll get you a tip." I said not necessary, handed her the papers, informed her she'd just accepted service, and split. She came after me, running into the street, screaming I'm a lowlife. Then she grabbed me by the shoulder, tried to force the paper back on me. First time anyone ever got physical other than one drunk guy and that time I was prepared, took a friend who played halfback at the U. From a woman, let alone a doctor, I wasn't ready for it, I'm trying to peel her off me, her nails are digging in my arm, the papers are flying all over the place. Finally, I free myself and get the hell out of there. So what, she pissed someone off and they killed her?'

'Don't know, yet.'

'Well,' said Brian Cohn. 'I'd sure look into that possibility.'

As we drove away from Leventhal's building, Milo said, 'Another tough personality, shades of Vita. Without Quigg stuck between the two of them I'd say we had ourselves a nice little pattern: women with short fuses.'

'Be interesting to see if Glenda's co-workers saw her that way.'

'Interesting would be okay,' he said. 'Intriguing would be better.'

21

NORTH HOLLYWOOD Day Hospital was an off-white sugar cube on a marginal block of Lankershim Boulevard. Windows were barred. A bearish uniformed guard lurked near the front door, smoking.

Bordering the building were storefront offices catering to personal injury lawyers, physicians and chiropractors specializing in 'Industrial Rehabilitation,' and medical equipment suppliers. The largest concern, double-wide and neon-lit, advertised walk-in occupational and physical therapy.

Welcome to Slip-and-Fall Heaven.

Milo said, 'Lordy, my sacroiliac is a-throbbin',' as he pulled into a loading zone and left a long-expired crime scene parking card on the dash.

The guard studied our approach above a smog-burst of tobacco. When we got close, he stepped in front of the door and folded his arms across his chest.

Milo said, 'You're kidding.'

'Huh?'

'A pro like you can't sniff out a big clue?'

'Wuh clue?'

'We ain't selling catheters, Marshal Dillon.' Out came the badge. The guard shifted just wide enough to clear the entry.

'Fast learner,' said Milo and we strode past him.

The waiting area was bright, stuffy, standing room only. Despair vied with boredom for the dominant emotion. Wheelchairs, walkers, oxygen

131

tanks abounded. Anyone who seemed physically okay looked psychologically stricken. All the joy of death row.

The queue at the reception window was a dozen deep. Milo pushed past and rapped his knuckles on the glass. The woman on the other side kept clicking computer keys.

He rapped again.

Her eyes remained on her keyboard.

Third time's the charm. She snapped, 'Just hold on!' A speaker box transformed her voice into something metallic and unwelcoming. Or maybe that was just her.

Milo banged hard enough to vibrate the glass and the receptionist wheeled, teeth bared, ready to confront. The badge silenced her and she took it out on a button under her desktop, stabbing viciously. A door on the far side of the waiting room gave off a loud *click*.

Someone said, 'How come he gets to jump?'

Milo said, 'Because I'm handsome.'

Another large but soft guard waited on the other side. Behind him was a beige corridor lined with doors the same color. Identical hue, also, for the vinyl flooring and the plastic signs directing the infirm toward Exam 1, Exam 2 . . . Ecru faces on the patients, as well. Welcome to Planet Bread Dough.

'Police, what for?' said the guard.

'I need to talk to Dr Glenda Usfel-Parnell's boss.'

The guard's lips moved as he tried to get his mouth around the hyphenation.

Milo said, 'Get me the head of nuclear medicine.'

The guard reached into his pocket and drew out a wilted piece of paper. 'Um . . . that's . . . Usfel, G.'

'Not anymore. Who's her boss?'

'I dunno.'

'How long you been working here?'

'Three weeks tomorrow.'

'You know Dr Usfel?'

'You don't hardly see the doctors, they go in and out through there.' Pointing to a door at the end of the hallway.

'Who's the big boss?'

'That would be Mr Ostrovine.'

'That would be who you go find.'

The man who burst through the rear door wore a too-snug gray suit of ambiguous cloth, a blue shirt with a high, stiff collar, and a pink paisley tie that had never gone near a silkworm. With better fabrics, the result would've been foppish. This screamed *Trying Too Hard*.

The same went for fruity aftershave, a scary tan, and a toupee that landed well short of possible. 'Mick Ostrovine. How can I help you?'

'We're here about Dr Usfel.'

'What about her?'

'She's deceased.'

Ostrovine's spray tan drained to the ambient beige. 'Glenda? She worked a double shift yesterday, she was fine, what happened?'

'Someone broke into her home and killed her.'

'Oh my God, that's insane. Her home? Some kind of home invasion?'

'We're sorting things out, Mr Ostrovine.'

A nearby door opened, silent as the gill-slit on a shark. A heavy woman in scrubs pushed a wheelchair toward us. Her passenger was an ancient man wrapped in a blanket, hairless, blue-veined, slumped, barely conscious.

'Hey, Mr O,' she said. 'Got all them tests run, taking him to the physical therapy for that exercise.'

'Sure, sure,' said Ostrovine.

His abruptness made her blink. As the chair rolled past, another exam room disgorged a burly man brandishing a crutch. The implement was tucked under one arm. He took a couple of unaided steps, saw us, placed his weight on the device, and assumed an exaggerated limp.

'Mr O,' he said. 'Gonna get myself some hydrotherapy.'

'Good, good,' said Ostrovine.

When a third door opened and a twenty-year-old girl came skipping out waving a shiny chromium cane like a cheerleader's baton, Milo said, 'Could we go somewhere to talk?' Nudging me. *You know hospitals, handle this.*

Ostrovine's office was a beige rectangle that faced the parking lot. The rest of the hospital's rear section housed orthopedics, nuclear medicine, physical medicine, anesthesiology, radiology.

Not a bed in sight.

I said, 'You do outpatient care.'

'We're adjunctive,' said Ostrovine, settling behind a desk, bare but for a laptop. The room looked unused.

'Meaning . . .'

'We fill a niche.'

'What's that?'

Ostrovine sighed. 'We're better equipped than a clinic and more efficiently specialized than a larger institution. We don't do E.R. so that frees us up for other modes of delivery. Our primary specialty is aftercare: pain management, disability evaluation, lifestyle readjustment.'

'What was Dr Usfel's specialty?'

'Glenda ran nuke med. That's cutting-edge technology assessing how parts of the body are actually working. As opposed to conventional radiology, which is primarily static, nuke uses dyes, radio-isotopes to capture ongoing function.'

He shook his head and the toupee shifted downward. He nudged it back in place without a trace of self-consciousness. 'Glenda was terrific. This is horrible.'

I said, 'How'd she get along with patients and staff?'

'Everyone here gets along.'

'Did she have an easygoing personality?'

Ostrovine's jaw rotated, settled slightly left of center. 'What are you getting at?'

'We've heard she could display a bit of temper.'

'I don't know what you heard but it doesn't apply to her performance here.'

'So anyone we talk to here is going to tell us she was easygoing.'

He unbuttoned his suit jacket, let out an inch of abdomen, sucked it back in, refastened. 'Glenda was businesslike.'

'Efficient but not touchy-feely.'

'She never had a problem with anyone.'

I said, 'You can't think of anyone who'd resent her.'

'I cannot.'

'Who are her friends here?'

He thought. 'I suppose she didn't socialize much on the job. We're task-oriented, anyway. A lot of our employees are floats.'

'Who'd she work with most closely?'

'That would be her technicians.'

'We'd like to talk to them.'

Ostrovine opened the laptop, typed. 'The tech on duty today is Cheryl Wannamaker. She's fairly new, I doubt she can tell you much.'

'We'll give her a try, anyway. And please give us the names of the others.'

'What makes you think Glenda's work had anything to do with what happened to her?'

'We need to look at everything.'

'I suppose,' said Ostrovine, 'but in this case you'd be best off looking outside the workplace. We're low on drama, run a business, not a production company.'

'Insurance business?'

'The business of wellness often involves third-party payment.'

'Do you deal a lot with Well-Start?'

'We deal with everyone.'

'If I give you some names could you check if they've been your patients?'

'Impossible,' said Ostrovine. 'Confidentiality's our first command-ment.'

'How about checking and if the names aren't there we won't have to come back with subpoenas.'

'I'm afraid I can't do that.'

'I understand. As I'm sure you will when we show up with the appropriate paperwork and all those tasks you're oriented toward come to a grinding halt.'

Ostrovine flashed oversized dental caps. 'Is this really necessary, guys? I'm sure Glenda's . . . tragedy had nothing to do with work.'

Milo said, 'Maybe you should switch careers and become a detective.'

'Fine, give me those names. But if they are here, I can't give you details.'

'Vita Berlin.'

Keyboard arpeggio. Sigh of relief. 'No. Next.'

'Marlon Quigg.'

'No, again. Now, if there's nothing more—'

'Dr Usfel's techs.'

'Oh,' said Ostrovine. 'That. Fine. I'll call Cheryl for you.'

Cheryl Wannamaker was young, stoic, dreadlocked, with a Jamaican lilt to her speech. We talked to her in the parking lot, near a black Mercedes parked in *M. Ostrovine*'s spot.

The news of Glenda Usfel-Parnell's death seemed not to impact her immediately. Then her eyes got wet and her chin shook. 'Another one.'

'Ma'am?' said Milo.

'Lost my nephew,' she said. 'Two weeks ago. Hit by a drunk driver.'

'I'm so sorry.'

'DeJon was twelve.' She wiped her eyes. 'Now Dr U. This world. Dear God.'

'How long did you work with Dr U?'

'Five weeks.'

'Anyone have a beef with her?'

'Not that I saw.'

'What kind of person was she?'

'She was an okay person,' said Cheryl Wannamaker.

'Friendly?'

'Sure.' She smiled. 'Actually, not so much. She was all about let's get the work done and go home.'

'Not a lot of chitchat.'

'No chitchat at all, sir.'

'That create tension?'

'Not for me,' said Wannamaker. 'I don't like wasting time.'

'What about others?'

'Everything seemed okay.'

'We've heard she had a temper.'

'Well,' said Wannamaker, 'she kind of did.'

'Who'd she get mad at?'

'Not mad, more like . . . grumpy. When things got backed up, when people didn't do what she wanted.'

'How'd she show her grumpiness?'

'She'd get all quiet.' Cheryl Wannamaker licked her lips. 'Too quiet, like a kettle gonna overflow.'

'What happened when she overflowed?'

'She never did. She just got that heavy quiet thing going. You'd talk to her, she wouldn't answer, even though you knew she heard you. So you just guessed what she wanted and hoped it *was* what she wanted.'

'You never saw her go off on anyone?'

'Never,' she said. 'But I heard someone went off on her.'

'Who?'

'Some patient,' said Wannamaker. 'Before my time, I just heard about it.'

'What'd you hear?'

'Someone lost it in the scan room.'

'Who told you?'

'Margaret,' she said. 'Margaret Wheeling, she's on when I'm off.'

'How long before you arrived did this happen?'

'I couldn't say.'

'But people were still talking about it when you began work.'

'No, just Margaret. To educate me.'

'About?'

'Dr U, what she was like. How she could be tough. When the patient went off on her, she didn't back down, stood right up to him and said, "Calm down or leave right now." And he did. Margaret was saying we all needed to be assertive like that because you never know what's going to walk in.'

'Did that patient ever show up again?'

'Couldn't tell you, sir.'

'Margaret tell you anything else about Dr Usfel?'

'She said when Doctor gets quiet, give her space.'

'Where can we find Margaret?'

'Right here,' said Cheryl Wannamaker, producing a cell phone. 'I have her number.'

Margaret Wheeling lived a quarter hour from her job, in a town house on Laurel Canyon just north of Riverside. She opened the door holding a glass of ice water. Milo gave her the news gently.

She said, 'Oh my God.'

'I'm sorry to have to tell you.'

'Dr U,' she said. 'Glenda . . . come in.'

Rawboned and ruddy with curly gray hair and unadorned yellow-gray eyes, she led us to a living room heavy on golden maple furniture and needlepoint pillows. Toby mugs filled a glass-front cabinet. Another was chocked with souvenir ashtrays with an emphasis on national parks and Nevada casinos. A jowly man sat drowsing on a sofa, sports pages spread on his lap.

'My husband,' said Margaret Wheeling, sounding proud of the fact. She kissed his forehead lightly. 'Don, they're here.'

Don Wheeling blinked, stood, shook our hands. She told him about Glenda Usfel. He said, 'You're kidding.'

'Oh, Don, isn't that horrid?'

He cupped the bottom of her chin. 'You be okay, Meg?'

'I'll be fine. Go use the bedroom, take a real nap.'

'You need me, you know where to find me, Meg.'

When he was gone, she said, 'Don was in law enforcement, rode a motorcycle for Tulsa PD for a year, back when he was right out of the service. By the time I met him he was already in asphalt and concrete. Please sit. Some cookies? Coffee, tea, soda?'

'No, thanks,' said Milo.

Margaret Wheeling said, 'Dr U murdered. I still can't believe it. You have any idea who did it?'

'Unfortunately, we don't. Cheryl Wannamaker told us about a patient who gave Dr U a hassle.'

'That small thing? Why would anyone kill over something like that?'

'Tell us about it.'

'It was stupid,' said Wheeling. 'One of those stupid things. Dr U keeps the temp low in the scan room. For the machines. This idiot got all huffy because we didn't have blankets. Because the linen service hadn't delivered that morning, not our fault. I tried to explain to him but he got abusive.'

'Abusive, how?'

'Cursing me out, saying I was stupid. Like it's my fault the service screwed up.'

'What'd you do?'

'Called Dr U,' she said. 'She makes decisions, I just follow directions.'

'Then what happened?'

'He started in with her. "I'm cold, you should have a blanket." A grown man but he acted like a spoiled kid. She told him to calm down, it's not the end of the world, we'll do the procedure quickly and get you out of here. He called her the same names he called me. That was it for Dr U. She went up to him, told him off. Not loud, but firm.'

'What'd she say?'

'That his behavior was out of line and he needed to leave. *Now.*'

I said, 'No second chance.'

'He had his chance,' said Wheeling. 'We had a waiting room full of scans, who needed him? The idiot probably thought her being a woman he could intimidate her. It was a little chilly, sure, but it's not like he didn't have insulation.'

'What do you mean?'

'Plenty of body fat. And obviously he wasn't screwed on too tight because he came in wearing a heavy coat and it wasn't cold outside, just the opposite. Not that at first he looked like a weirdo. That being the case I'd have called security from the beginning. He seemed okay. Real quiet. Then it was just like he . . . came apart.'

'Do you call security a lot?'

'When I need to. We get all types.'

'But this guy set off no warning bells.'

'I guess I should've noticed that crazy coat, but I'm not looking at them, I'm checking the machines.'

'He came apart.'

'Went from normal to ticked off like *that*.' Snapping her fingers.

'Scary,' I said. 'But Dr Usfel handled it.'

'She's tough, went to med school in Guadalajara, Mexico, told me she saw things there you wouldn't see in the States. You don't really think that guy had anything to do with it? I mean how would he find her? And this was like two months ago. And he never came back.'

I said, 'What else can you tell us about him?'

'Just what I told you. White, normal-looking, thirty, thirty-five.'

'Clean-shaven?'

'Yup.'

'Hair?'

'Brown. Short. Pretty neat appearance, actually. Except for that crazy coat, we're talking heavy-duty winter wear, one of those shearlings.'

'What color?'

'Some kind of brown. I think.'

'Any distinguishing marks? Like scars, tattoos, unusual features?'

She thought. 'No, he looked like a regular person.'

'To get scanned he'd need paperwork. Did you see his?'

'We don't see paperwork, the front desk handles all that. They come in with a day-chart that has an I.D. number, not even a name.'

I said, 'What procedure was he sent for?'

'Who remembers?'

I gave her time.

She shook her head. 'I'm not sure I even looked.'

Milo said, 'How about you sit down with an artist and help produce a drawing?'

'You're saying it *was* him?'

'No, ma'am, but we've got to nail down every detail we can if we're gonna solve Dr Usfel's murder.'

'My name wouldn't be on it, right?' she said. 'The drawing?'

'Of course not.'

'Really, you'd be wasting your time. All I'd tell an artist is what I just told you.'

'Would you be willing to give it a try? To help us out?'

'I can totally keep myself out of it?'

'Absolutely.'

She crossed a leg, scratched a bare ankle. 'You really think it's important?'

'Honestly, Ms Wheeling, we don't know. But unless you can tell us of some other person Dr U had problems with, we've got to follow up.'

'What kind of person would go kill someone over a small thing?'

'Not a normal person.'

'That's for sure . . . an artist? I don't know.'

Milo said, 'Back when Don was in law enforcement, I'll bet he appreciated any help he could get.'

'I suppose,' said Margaret Wheeling. 'Okay, I'll try. But you're wasting your time, he just looked like a regular person.'

22

Wʜᴇᴇʟɪɴɢ's ᴅᴏᴏʀ closed behind us and we headed for the unmarked.

Milo said, 'Heavyset guy in a shearling. Usfel pissed him off royally, no doubt Vita did, too.' He frowned. 'And somehow nice Mr Quigg managed to get on his bad side.'

I said, 'His confrontation with Usfel was a brief onetimer that took on huge proportions in his mind only. So his brushes with the others wouldn't need to be dramatic.'

'Touchy fellow.'

'Leading to increased element of surprise.' We got in the car. I said, 'One thing different about Usfel is he tied her up. Maybe because he'd seen her in action, knew she was tough enough to be a threat.'

'Not so tough that she didn't give in easily, Alex. There was no sign of struggle in that bedroom.'

'He could have controlled her with a gun. She probably expected to be raped, figured on negotiating her life, had no idea what he was really after.'

'If he used a gun on Usfel, he could've done the same for the others. Knock knock, pizza delivery, here's my little steel friend. Vita being drunk would have made his job easier. And a guy like Quigg wouldn't have fought back. Okay, let's put a face on this choirboy.'

He called Alex Shimoff, a Hollenbeck detective with serious artistic talent whom he'd used before. When Shimoff's cell and home lines didn't pick up, he left a message and tried Petra Connor at Hollywood Division. Same story.

142

He turned on the engine. 'I don't get my blankie, I gut you. There's a reasonable motive.'

I said, 'That place is an insurance mill and Vita was involved in a lawsuit. Maybe she and Shearling met there or at a place like it. Though Vita's alleged damages were emotional; she wouldn't have needed any scans and I can't see Well-Start paying for them.'

'Maybe her lawyer had a deal with Ostrovine or someone like him. Problem is I can't find out who handled the suit. Well-Start won't say and because it settled early, nothing was filed. I'll try them again.'

He headed for the station. A few miles later, I thought of something. 'Wanting a blanket even though he's overdressed could be a psychiatric issue. But it could also mean his temperature regulation really is off. And that could be due to a physical condition.'

'Such as?'

'The first thing that comes to mind is low thyroid function. Nothing severe enough to incapacitate him but just enough to make him put on a few pounds and feel chilly. And hypothyroidism can also increase irritability.'

'Perfect,' he said. 'He ever gets caught, some lawyer claims diminished capacity due to bad glands. I like the other thing you said: he and Vita crossed paths during some medical procedure. A waiting room spat. Given Vita's level of tact, I can see her dissing his damn coat and that being enough.'

'Was there anything in the paper Well-Start showed you that said she got medically evaluated?'

'Nope, but who knows? Hell, given the fact that this guy's obviously unbalanced, maybe he and Vita ran into each other at Shacker's office.'

'Shacker's got a separate exit so patients don't cross paths, but anything's possible.'

'Why don't you call him, see if he knows Shearling.'

'He wasn't that comfortable talking about Vita and asking him to identify a patient would be off the table, ethically, unless you could show imminent danger to a specific person.'

'The specific person's his next damn victim . . . yeah, you're right but bug him anyway. I need to do *something*.'

I made the call, left a message on Shacker's voicemail.

He said, 'Thanks. Any other ideas?'

I said, 'Ostrovine buckled when we threatened to shut him down for a day. If he was lying about Vita, maybe he'll eventually give up the info.'

'Let's go back there,' he said, hanging a U. 'He balks, I'll grab that stupid rug on his head and hold it for ransom.'

This time, Ostrovine kept us waiting for twenty minutes.

When we entered his office, there were papers on the desk. Columns of numbers, probably financial spreadsheets. He put down a gold Cross pen and said, 'What now, Lieutenant?'

Milo told him.

'You're kidding.'

'Nothing funny about Dr Usfel's murder, sir.'

'Of course not,' said Ostrovine. 'But I can't help you. First of all, I've never heard about any confrontation between Glenda and any patient. Second, I still don't believe Glenda's death had anything to do with her work here. And third, like I told you, I have no knowledge of anyone named Vita Berlin.'

'We know a confrontation occurred,' said Milo. 'How come there wasn't a report?'

'Obviously, Dr Usfel never informed security of the need for one because she viewed it as insignificant.' Ostrovine laid his hands flat on the desk. Milo had pulled his chair close. The wig was in reach of his long arm. 'And frankly, so do I.'

'Who referred this guy to you?'

'How can I tell you that when I don't even know his name?'

'Check the patient list for that day.'

'He wouldn't be on there because incompletes aren't recorded.'

'Not even their referrals?'

'Not anything,' said Ostrovine. 'Why would we pile up extraneous data? As is, we've got storage issues.'

'What if the patient was referred for another procedure that was completed?'

'You're asking me to examine my entire patient database.'

'Just white males seen two months ago, give or take two weeks either way.'

'That's huge,' said Ostrovine. 'And what will I be looking for? Inappropriate clothing? We don't list attire in our charts.'

'Just tease out white males in a particular age range and we'll take it from there.'

'No can do, Lieutenant. Even if we had the manpower for that kind of scavenger hunt, we're legally forbidden.'

'In terms of manpower, I can send you a couple of detectives.'

'That's generous of you,' said Ostrovine, 'but it doesn't solve the main problem: rooting around in patient records without clear justification is illegal.'

Milo waited.

Ostrovine fiddled with his pen, placed his hand on his toupee, as if anticipating attack. 'Look, guys, Glenda was one of ours, her death is a tragedy and if I could help you, I'd jump at the opportunity. But I can't. You have to understand.'

'Then we'll have to go the subpoena route, sir. Which would cause all those delays we discussed before.'

Ostrovine clicked his tongue. 'We didn't discuss anything, Lieutenant Sturgis. You threatened me. I understand that you've got an important job to do. But further intimidation is not going to work. I've talked to our attorneys and they say it'll never get that far.'

Milo stood. 'Guess we'll just have to see.'

'We won't see anything, Lieutenant. The rules are clear. I'm sorry, I really am. But what took place in the scan room was just one of those things.'

'Business as usual.'

'People as usual,' said Ostrovine. 'Put enough of them together and heads will bump. That's a far cry from murder.'

'Human nature,' said Milo. 'You learn about it from all those insurance scams you do?'

Ostrovine's smile sped toward sincere, screeched to a halt just short of the goal. 'I learned about it from reality.'

On the way back to the station, Dr Bern Shacker returned my call.

Ten to the hour; catching up between patients.

I thanked him. He said, 'The police have caught someone?'

'They may have a lead.' I described the man in the shearling.

Silence.

'Doctor—'

'But no one's been caught. So you're telling me this because . . .'

'We're wondering if Vita crossed paths with him. Perhaps during an evaluation. I don't want to put you in a bind but it could be a *Tarasoff* situation.'

'Imminent danger?' he said. 'To whom?'

'He's killed two other people.'

'That's horrible but obviously they're no longer in danger.'

'It's a tough situation, Bern.'

'I know, I know. Dreadful. Well, fortunately he isn't a patient of mine. No one in my practice dresses like that.'

'Okay, thanks.'

'Self-swaddling,' he said. 'That smells a bit like schizophrenia, no?'

'Or a medical problem.'

'Such as?'

'Hypothyroidism.'

'Hmm . . . interesting. Yes, I suppose so. But I'd still lean toward the psychological. In view of what he's done. And it sounds as if he's reacting to threat. At the core, psychotics are helpless, no? Fear biters, not attack dogs.'

'True.'

'What a mess,' said Shacker. 'Poor Vita. All the others, as well.'

* * *

Just before we turned onto Butler, Alex Shimoff called back.

'You need another masterpiece, Lieutenant?'

'You're the man, Detective.'

'Last time was easy,' said Shimoff. 'Dr Delaware's girlfriend had a good eye for detail, she gave me a lot to work with.'

'Nothing like a challenge,' said Milo.

'I'm married with children, I know about challenge. Sure, what's your schedule?'

'I'll get back to you with a time and place.'

'Tomorrow would be good,' said Shimoff. 'Got a day off, my wife wants me to take her shopping, you can help me get out of it.'

Back at his desk, Milo phoned D.C. Maria Thomas, told her of his intention to release a suspect drawing and the question marks to the media, asked her to facilitate with Public Affairs.

She said, 'Cart before horse, Milo.'

'Pardon?'

'Go get your rendering but nothing gets facilitated until the basic decision is reified. That's a fancy word for it turns real. That means the chief clears it.'

'His orders?'

'Do anyone else's matter?'

She hung up. Milo cursed and called Margaret Wheeling. She'd had enough time to retreat from the offer to cooperate, claimed she really hadn't seen the man in the shearling well enough to be useful. He worked with her for a while to get her to agree to the sit-down with Shimoff.

He was reaching for a panatela when his phone rang. 'Homicide, Sturgis.'

'Better be,' said a raspy, Brooklyn-tinged voice. 'This is *your* fucking extension.'

'Afternoon, sir.'

The chief said, 'When all else fails go the artistic route?'

'Whatever works, sir.'

147

'You have enough to turn out a decent enough drawing? 'Cause we probably won't get more than one bite of the apple and I don't want to waste it on some ambiguous bullshit.'

'Me neither, sir, but at this point—'

'Nothing else has worked, you're stuck, you're freaking out about more victims popping up. I *get* it, Sturgis. Which is why I swallowed my pride and put in a call to a guy I know at the Bureau who is a lard-ass pencil-pusher but used to be a behavioral sciences honcho at Quantico. Not that I think their bullshit profiles are more than a carny show, which is why I called him personally, said forget your stupid questionnaire and just give me something off the top of your head about a loony who snaps necks then cuts out guts and plays with them. He gave me big-time Ph.D. wisdom, so now you're going to hear it: white male, twenty-five to fifty, probably a loner, probably doesn't have a happy domestic life, probably going to be living in a weird home situation, probably jacks off when he thinks about what he did. That any worse than what Delaware's given you so far? So what does this suspect whose image you want to foist on a neurotic public look like?'

'White, thirty to forty.'

'There you go,' said the chief. 'Science.'

Milo said, 'He wears a heavy coat in all sorts of weather.'

'Big deal, he's concealing a weapon.'

'That could be part of it, sir, but Dr Delaware says it could be a sign of mental illness.'

'Does he?' The chief laughed. 'Big fucking genius. I'd say ripping people's intestines out covers that base pretty well.'

I said, 'It sure does.'

Silence.

'I figured you were there, Doctor. How's life treating you?'

'Fine.'

'That makes one of us. Charlie sends his regards.'

Charlie was his son and the regards part was a lie. A brilliant, alien-ated kid, he'd asked me to write a college recommendation, emailed me a couple of times a month from the seminary he was using to defer college.

He hated, loved, feared his father, would never use him for a messenger.

I said, 'Hope he's doing well.'

'He's being Charlie. By the way, the department still owes you some consult money on the last one.'

'True.'

'You haven't bugged my office about it.'

'Would it have helped?'

Dead air. 'Your loyalty in the face of our bureaucratic ineptitude is laudable, Doc. So you concur that broadcasting this lunatic's face is a good idea?'

'I think if we keep the information tight it's got potential.'

'What does tight mean?'

'Limit it to the artist rendering and the question marks and don't let on that anyone could theoretically be a victim.'

'Yeah, that would set off some skivvy-soiling panic, wouldn't it? Speaking of those question marks, what the hell do they mean? The FBI guy said he'd never seen that before. Checked his files and there was nothing. Only similar gutting was Jack the Ripper and there were enough differences between our boy and Jack to make that avenue a dead end.'

'Don't know.'

'Don't know what?'

'What the question marks mean.'

'So much for higher education . . . what do you think about releasing details on the coat? Could jog some citizen's memory.'

'It might also cause the bad guy to ditch the coat and you'd lose potential evidence.'

Silence. 'Yeah, there could be spatter on the fucking thing, gut juice, whatever. Okay, keep it tight. But you could still be screwed – I'm talking to you, Sturgis. He sees himself on the six o'clock, he rabbits.'

'There's always that chance, sir.'

Another silence, longer.

The chief said, 'Doctor, what's your take on another victim coming up sooner rather than later?'

'Hard to say.'

'That all you do? Sidestep questions?'

'That's a poser, Chief.'

'Shrink humor,' he said. 'I wouldn't count on getting a sitcom anytime in the near future. You still awake, Sturgis?'

'Wide awake.'

'Stay that way.'

'God forbid I should sleep, sir.'

'More to the point,' said the chief. '*I* forbid.'

23

ALEX SHIMOFF delivered his rendering to Milo's office the following afternoon.

'Don't tell anyone who did this,' he said. 'This is garbage.'

The last time he'd sat down to draw for Milo, Shimoff had produced a stunningly accurate re-creation of a girl whose face had been blown off. What he presented this time was an ambiguous pale disk filled with bland, male features.

Color it yellow you'd have Mr Happy Face's noncommittal brother.

And yet, it twanged a memory synapse deep in my brain.

Had I seen him before? Mental scouring produced nothing.

Milo told Shimoff, 'Thanks, kid.'

'Don't thank me for doing crap, El Tee. That Wheeling lady couldn't come up with anything useful. I hate the computer Identi-Kit but after she gave me nothing I tried it. She said it confused her more, too many choices. She couldn't even respond to my questions. Wider, longer, rounder, nothing. She claimed she barely saw the guy.'

'Did she seem scared?' I said.

'Maybe,' said Shimoff. 'Or she's just stupid and can't process visually.'

Milo studied the likeness. 'It's better than what we had before.'

Shimoff looked ready to vomit. 'It's any pie-faced white guy.'

'Hey, kiddo, maybe this is what he actually looks like. Like that cartoon, the kid brings in a stick figure drawing of his family, on parent-teacher day stick figures show up?'

Shimoff wasn't amused.

I tried again to figure out why the crude drawing gnawed at me. Blank mental screen.

Shimoff said, 'At art school I could get away sometimes with jokes. Real life? It sucks to turn out garbage. Top of that, I still have to take my wife shopping tonight.'

Clenching his fists, he left.

Milo murmured, 'Creative types,' and took the photo to the big detective room where he told Moe Reed to scan and email it to Maria Thomas.

That evening at six the rendering was featured on the news, along with a sketchy tale of a Westside home invader who broke his victims' necks and left behind a **?** calling card. Ambiguity made the story more frightening and the phones began ringing seconds after the ensuing commercial.

By six fifteen, Milo had commandeered Moe Reed and Sean Binchy to help work the lines. He moved out of his office and took a desk in the big D-room left unoccupied by a daywatch detective on sick leave. Manipulating three separate lines himself, pushing buttons like a concertina player, he kept the conversations brief, took a few notes, the most frequent notation being 'B.S.' followed by 'schizo', 'ESP', and 'prank'. Reed's dominant notation was 'neg.', Binchy's, 't.n.g'. When Sean saw me trying to figure that out, he cupped his hand over the receiver, smiled, and said, 'Totally no good.'

I heard Reed say, 'Yes, I understand, ma'am, but you live in Bakersfield, there's no reason to be worried.'

Binchy: 'Absolutely, sir. There's no indication he has anything against Samoans.'

Milo: 'I know about the Chance cards in Monopoly. No, there wasn't one.'

Slipping out of the room, I drove home thinking about victims.

Robin said, 'No blanket? Doesn't take much to set this maniac off.'

We sat near the pond, tossing pellets at the fish, Blanche wedged between us, snoring lightly. I'd finished a couple ounces of Chivas, was nursing the ice. Robin hadn't made much headway with a glass of Riesling. The night smelled of ozone and jasmine. The sky was charcoal felt stretched tight. A few stars peeked through like ice-pick wounds.

She said, 'She kicks him out of the clinic and he comes back to get her months later?'

I said, 'Maybe he took his time because planning was part of the fun. For all I know, he set up the confrontation.'

'To give himself an excuse?'

'Even psychopaths need to self-justify and I don't think his real motive is avenging insult. It's got to be rooted in fantasies he's had since childhood but he frames his victims as bad people so he can feel righteous. Glenda Usfel maintained control by being the alpha female only this time it backfired. The same probably went for Berlin. Spreading bad cheer was her hobby but she tried it with the wrong guy. What doesn't fit is brutalizing Marlon Quigg, who's described by everyone as the mildest man on the planet.'

'Maybe he wasn't always that way.'

'Reformed crank?'

'People can change.' She smiled. 'Someone once told me that. What did Quigg do for a living?'

'Accountant.'

'Not an IRS auditor by any chance?'

'Not even close, just a cog in a big firm, sat at his desk and number-crunched for a big grocery chain.'

'Someone didn't like the tomatoes, they wouldn't take it out on him. Did he have any outside interests?'

'No one's mentioned any. Family man, walked his dog, led a quiet life. Before that he taught disabled kids. We're talking a softie, Rob. Totally different from the other two victims.'

'Interesting switch,' she said.

'What is?'

'Trading a job where you're constantly dealing with people for one where you stare at ledgers all day.'

'His wife said the money wasn't there so he took the CPA exam.'

'I'm sure that's it.'

'You have your doubts?'

'It just seems like a radical shift, Alex, but money is important.'

I thought about that. 'Something happened when Quigg was teaching that pushed him in a totally different direction?'

'You just said the killer's motive goes back to childhood. "Disabled kids" covers a lot of territory.'

'A student with serious psychiatric issues,' I said. 'Revenge on the teacher? Oh, man.'

She said, 'What if Quigg left teaching because he encountered a student who scared him out of the profession? I know it's far-fetched but you just said this guy loves the thrill of the hunt. What if now that he's an adult, he's decided to revisit old enemies?'

The sky seemed to darken and drop, stars receding. Robin tried to flex her fingers and I realized I was squeezing her hand and let go.

'I'm just tossing stuff out,' she said, raising the wineglass to her lips. Good vintage but tonight it evoked a frown and she put it aside. 'Let's change the subject.'

I said, 'Mind if I make a call?'

Belle Quigg said, '*Who* is this?'

I repeated my name. 'I was at your home the other day, and also with Lieutenant Sturgis.'

'Oh. You're the other one. Has something happened about Marlon?'

'I have a few more questions, Mrs Quigg. How long ago did Marlon teach school?'

'A long time. Why?'

'We're being thorough.'

'I don't understand.'

I said, 'The more we know about Marlon, the better our chances of catching whoever did that to him.'

'Did that,' she said. 'You can say killed. *I* say it. I *think* it. I think it all the time.'

I didn't answer.

She said, 'I don't see what his teaching has to do with it. That was years ago. This is a madman who killed Marlon and Louie, and it had nothing to do with anything Marlon did or said.'

'I'm sure you're right, ma'am, but if you could—'

'Marlon didn't teach at a school, he taught at a hospital. Ventura State.'

Once the largest psychiatric facility in the state, long-shuttered. 'How long ago?'

'This was before we got married, I'd just met him and he told me he used to be a teacher, so . . . at least twenty-four years ago.'

'What kind of disabled children did he teach?'

'He just said disabled,' she said. 'He didn't talk much about it and I wasn't that curious, that kind of thing's not for me. Marlon said the reason he quit was the pay was awful, that's why he was doing book-keeping for the city, studying for his CPA. Also he found out the hospital was closing down, told me years later that's the real reason he quit, he didn't want to be left stranded.'

'How'd he feel about the closure?'

'It bothered him. Because of the kids. He said, "Where will they go, Belle?" That was Marlon. He *cared*.'

24

NICE-GUY MARLON Quigg had lied to his wife.

There had been no plans to close Ventura State back when he worked there.

I knew that because I'd been there weeks before the hospital had emptied, hired by a law firm representing two wards of wheelchair-bound, minimally functioning children facing a terrifyingly ambiguous future. I evaluated each patient and made detailed recommendations for the aftercare promised by the state. Some of what I advised was put into effect. Mostly the state reneged.

Several years before that, well after Quigg had already quit, I'd rotated through as an intern, augmenting my training at Langley Porter with a month of observation at the largest mental hospital west of the Mississippi.

That spring, I'd set out from San Francisco at sundown, slept on the beach in San Simeon and watched elephant seals lolling, ended up in Camarillo by midmorning where I showered and dressed in the restroom of a public beach, checked my map, and got back on the freeway.

A poorly marked road slanting east of the 101 had guided me inland over a dry creek, past empty fields, copses of native sycamore and oak, and Australian eucalyptus that had long made themselves comfortable in Southern California. For the next few miles nothing hinted at the hospital's presence. Then a twenty-foot gate of heavy-duty iron painted red snapped into view just around a severe bend and forced me to brake hard.

A watchful guard checked my I.D., frowned, pointed to a *Five MPH* sign, and buzzed me through. Snailing through more twisting, shaded road, I came to a stop at the mouth of a stadium-worthy parking lot full of cars. Rising behind the auto glare were buildings sheathed in dun stucco and prettied by moldings, medallions, pediments, and arched loggias. Most of the windows were grilled in that same rusty red.

City of the Sad.

Decades before, Ventura State had gained infamy as a place where anything went if a doctor said so. A host of horrors had taken place behind its walls until World War II drew the doctors to Europe and the Pacific, and the Holocaust got people thinking harder about degradation of personal liberty: lobotomies and other untested surgeries, crude versions of shock and insulin therapy, forced commitment of those labeled a nuisance, forced sterilizations of those deemed unfit to breed. Reforms had been drastic and thorough and the hospital had gained a reputation for enlightenment and humanism; I was eager to experience a new clinical setting and to be back in Southern California.

I spent my first two days in orientation sessions delivered by a nursing supervisor, accompanied by freshly minted psychiatric residents, other psychology interns, new-hire nurses and orderlies. Once educated, we were free to explore the grounds, with the exception of the easternmost end where a compound marked *Specialized Care* sat. An orderly asked the training nurse what specialized meant. She said, 'Unique situations, it varies,' and went on to the next topic.

With hours to go before my first assignment, I wandered the campus staggered by the dimensions and ambitions of the place. The near-worshipful silence of the other rookies as they explored told me I wasn't alone in my reaction.

Built in the twenties as the California State Mental Hygiene Sanitarium at Ventura, the place that had come to be known as V-State was graced by a combination of Old World craftsmanship and New Deal optimism that had created some of the finest public buildings in the state. In the case of the hospital, that meant twenty-eight buildings on over two hundred fifty acres. Pink flagstone pathways slinked through the grounds like rosy streams, flower beds were riotous with color, shrubs appeared trimmed by nail scissors. The entire property sat in a shallow valley graced by fog-capped mountains on three sides.

Auxiliary structures on the west end kept the hospital self-sufficient: refrigeration house, butcher, dairy, vegetable and fruit gardens, bowling alley, two movie theaters and a concert stage, employee dorms, on-site police and fire departments. Self-sufficiency was partly the product of noble rehabilitative intentions. It also shielded the rest of Ventura County from neighbors locked up by reason of insanity, deficiency, and 'unique situations'.

I spent my entire month with children more advanced than the unfortunates I evaluated years later but still too impaired to handle school. More often than not an organic factor was at play: seizure disorders, post-encephalitic brain injury, genetic syndromes, and puzzling groups of symptoms that, decades later, would be labeled autism-spectrum disorder but were classified back then by a variety of terms. The one I remembered was 'idiopathic neurosocial irregularity'.

I spent sixty hours a week honing my observational skills, doing some testing, and receiving solid training in child psychopathology, play therapy, cognitive restructuring, and applied behavioral analysis. Most important, I learned humility and the value of reserving judgment. V-State was no place for those craving heroism; when improvement occurred it was gradual and minuscule. I learned to fuel each day with a mantra:

Keep your goals specific and realistic, be happy when anything goes well.

At first glance, the hospital was a pastoral retreat from reality but I came to learn that turgid silence could be shattered without warning by screams and mewls and the crack of what sounded like wood on flesh from the easternmost tip of the campus.

Specialized Care was a hospital within a hospital, a cluster of low, mean structures nudging up against an eastern butte of granite, sectioned by the ever-present red iron fencing topped by razor wire. The bars were stouter, the windows skimpier. Behind the fence, uniformed guards patrolled irregularly. Mostly, the surrounding yard was unoccupied. Never once did I spot a patient.

One day I asked my supervisor what went on there.

An elegant, gray-haired psychologist, Gertrude Vanderveul was American but British-trained at the Maudsley Hospital, fond of beautifully tailored suits and inexpensive, sensible shoes, passionate about Mahler but otherwise dismissive of post-Bach music, a former research assistant to Anna Freud during the London years. (*'Lovely woman but far too attached to Daddy to acquire a conventional social life.'*)

The day I posed the question, Gertrude was supervising me outdoors because the weather was perfect. We walked the hospital grounds under a cloudless sky, the air fragrant as fresh laundry, drinking coffee and reviewing my cases. That done, she shifted the focus to a discussion of the limitations of Piaget's methodology, encouraging me to give my opinions.

'Excellent,' she said. 'Your insights are acute.'

'Thanks,' I said. 'Could I ask you about Specialized Care?'

She didn't answer.

Thinking she hadn't heard, I began to repeat myself. She held up a silencing finger and we continued our stroll.

A few moments later she said, 'That place isn't for you, dear boy.'

'I'm too green?'

'There's that,' she said. 'Also, I like you.'

When I didn't reply, she said, 'Trust me on this, Alex.'

Had Marlon Quigg learned the same thing through direct experience?

Interesting career switch.

Smart girl, Robin.

I went out back to tell her she might be onto something but she'd left the pond and her studio windows were lit and I could hear the whir of a saw. I returned to my office and phoned Milo.

'Quigg didn't teach at a school, he worked at Ventura State Hospital.'

'Okay.' Distracted.

I said, 'He may have given his wife a phony reason for changing careers and that makes me wonder if something — or someone — at V-State scared him.'

159

I recounted the unsettling sounds I'd heard from Specialized Care, Gertrude's protectiveness. 'That could be Quigg's connection.'

He said, 'Patient with an old grudge? How long ago are we talking, Alex?'

'Quigg was out of there twenty-four years ago but our guy could have a long memory.'

'Twenty-four years and something sets him off?'

'Killing sets him off,' I said. 'He got into the swing, thought back to his bad old days at V-State.'

'Kill Teach. So Quigg wasn't such a softie back then?'

'Not necessarily. For someone with paranoid tendencies it could've been a wrong look, anything.'

'Wonderful . . . but other than you think Quigg fibbed, there's no proof he actually worked that special ward.'

'Not yet, but I'll keep digging.'

'Fine. Let's talk after I get back.'

'Where you going?'

'To meet Victim Number Five.'

'Oh, no. When?'

'Body just turned up. This time it was Hollywood Division that got lucky. Petra caught it. She's a tough girl but she sounded pretty shaken. I'm on my way over now.'

'What's the address?'

'Don't bother,' he said. 'It's already a circus and you know what you're gonna see.'

'Okay.'

He exhaled. 'Look, I'm not sure I'm gonna be kept on, word is His Grandiloquence is "reassessing". So there's no sense you ruining your night. Top of that, I'm fielding a pile of useless tips and I have a sit-down with Usfel's and Parnell's families at an airport hotel first thing tomorrow morning. Both sets of parents, this is gonna be rollicking.'

A murder so soon after the media play felt like a taunt and I reassessed my theory about the question marks, figured Milo had been right. I went to my office, sat at the computer, and shuffled varying combinations of *ventura state hospital criminally insane child murderer young disembowel question mark.* When that pulled up nothing useful, I spent some time wondering if Shimoff's drawing had stimulated my memory because, years ago, I'd seen a younger version of the round-faced man on the grounds of V-State.

A patient I'd worked with? Or just passed in the wards? A dangerous kid who'd eluded Specialized Care because he'd been smooth enough to fool the staff and remain on an open ward?

Hospital teachers spent more time with patients than anyone. Had Marlon Quigg noticed something about a deeply disturbed boy that everyone else had missed? Had he spoken up and convinced the doctors about the need for extreme confinement?

Motive for a major-league grudge.

But Milo's question remained: why wait so long to wreak vengeance?

Because the dangerous kid had turned into a truly frightening adult and had been locked up all these years.

Now released, he sets about righting wrongs. Locating Quigg, stalking him, grooming him with cordial greetings during Quigg's dog-walk in the park.

Recognizing Quigg but no reason for Quigg to associate a child with a grown man in a shearling.

?

Guess why I'm doing this.

Ha ha ha.

Gertrude Vanderveul had known enough about what went on at Specialized Care to keep me away.

Trust me on this, Alex.

Maybe now she'd agree to tell me why.

I looked for her in cyberspace, starting with the APA directory and the state psychology board website and fanning out from there.

She wasn't listed anywhere, but a Magnus Vanderveul, M.D., practiced ophthalmology in Seattle. Maybe kin, maybe not, and too late in the day to find out. I played with the computer some more, hit nothing but sour notes, was feeling cranky when Robin and Blanche returned to the house, worked hard at faking pleasant.

Blanche sensed my true mood right away but she licked my hand and nuzzled my leg, a cobby little wrinkly bundle of empathy.

Robin was there a second later. 'What's the matter?'

I told her about Quigg's lie. 'You might have put it together, Lady Sherlock.'

She said, 'What kind of things did the scariest kids do?'

'Don't know because I never saw them.' I described Specialized Care, Gertrude's protectiveness. 'Couldn't get her to explain. I'm trying to locate her, maybe she'll be more open.'

'Work on her maternal instincts.'

'How so?'

'Tell her all you've accomplished. Make her proud. And confident.'

Milo hadn't gotten in touch by ten the following morning. Nothing about the latest victim appeared in the news and I figured the chief had kept things tight.

I tried Dr Magnus Vanderveul's office in Seattle. A woman answered, 'LASIK by Design.'

Doctor was busy with procedures all day but if I wanted information about myopia or presbyopia she'd be happy to transfer me to an educational recording.

'Appreciate that but I need to speak to Dr Vanderveul personally.'

'Regarding?'

'His mother and I are old friends and I'm trying to get in touch with her.'

'I'm afraid that's impossible,' said the receptionist. 'She passed last year. Doctor flew to the funeral.'

'I'm sorry,' I said, feeling that on multiple levels. 'Where was the funeral?'

A second of silence. 'Sir, I'll give him your message. Bye, now.'

I found the death certificate. Palm Beach, Florida. Downloaded the obituary from the archives of a local paper.

Professor Gertrude Vanderveul had succumbed to a brief illness. Her tenure at V-State was noted, as was a subsequent move to Connecticut to teach at the university level. She'd published a book on child psychotherapy and served as a consultant to a White House commission on foster care. Ten years ago, she'd relocated to Florida where she'd advised various welfare agencies and pursued a lifelong interest in lily cultivation. Predeceased decades ago by an orchestra conductor husband, she was survived by a son, Dr Magnus Vanderveul, of Redmond, Washington, daughters Dr Trude Prosser of Glendale, California, and Dr Ava McClatchey of Vero Beach, and eight grandchildren.

Contributions to the Florida Foundation for Child Development were requested in lieu of flowers.

Trude Prosser practiced clinical neuropsychology from a Brand Boulevard office. A voicemail greeting recited by an automated voice greeted me. Same deal at Ava McClatchey's obstetrics group.

Having left messages for all three of Gertrude's erudite progeny, I went for a run, wondering if any of them would bother to call.

By the time I returned, all three had.

Keeping it local, I started with Trude. This time she picked up, announcing 'Dr Prosser' in a sweet girlish voice.

'This is Alex Delaware. Thanks for getting back.'

'You were one of Mother's students.' Statement, not a question.

'She supervised me during an internship rotation. She was a wonderful teacher.'

'Yes, she was,' said Trude Prosser. 'How can I help you?'

I started to explain.

She said, 'Did Mother ever talk about a murderous little monster? No, she never talked about *any* of her patients. And I should tell you that while I don't know you, I know *about* you through Mother. She found what you do now quite fascinating. The investigative work.'

163

'I had no idea she was aware of it.'

'Quite aware. She read about some case in the paper and remembered you. We were having lunch and she pointed to your name. Quite tickled, really. "This was one of my trainees, Trude. Bright boy, very inquisitive. I kept him away from the nasty stuff but apparently I only whetted his appetite."'

'Any idea what she was protecting me from?' I said.

'I assumed the dangerous patients.'

'In Specialized Care.'

'Mother felt they were untreatable. That nothing psychology or psychiatry had to offer could put a dent in personality issues of that severity.'

'Did she herself ever work with patients there?'

'If she did, she never shared that,' said Trude Prosser. 'Not only was she ethical, she avoided talking to us about work, in general. But she was at V-State for years, so it's possible she circulated there. How much time did you spend with her, Alex?'

'A memorable month,' I said.

'She was a wonderful mother. Father died when we were young and she raised us by herself. One of my brother's teachers once asked her what the secret was to raising such well-behaved kids, did she have some kind of psychological formula?'

She laughed. 'The truth is, at home we were wild animals but we knew enough to fake it on the outside. Mother nodded gravely and told the woman, "It's very simple. I lock them in a root cellar and feed them crusts and stagnant water." The poor thing nearly fell over before she realized Mother was having her on. Anyway, sorry I can't help more.'

'This is going to sound strange, but did the issue of question marks ever come up?'

'Pardon?'

'A child who drew question marks. Did your mother ever allude to something like that?'

'No,' she said. 'Really, Mother's patients never came up, period. She was ironclad about confidentiality.'

'Did she ever mention a teacher named Marlon Quigg?'

'Marlon,' she said. 'Like the fish. Now, that I can say yes to. I remember the name because it became a bit of family entertainment. Mag – my brother – was home from college and had quickly regressed to being a loudmouthed oaf. So when Mother announced that someone named Marlon was coming over, could we please make ourselves scarce and not intrude, it was an obvious cue for Mag to get obnoxious. Insisting to Mother we should ply Mr Fish with tuna salad and watch him wax cannibalistic. Of course Ava – my sister – and I thought that was hilarious, though we were old enough not to act like blithering idiots. But Mag brought that out in us, when he was home, we all regressed. And of course that spurred Mag on and he began making more terrible puns – Marlon had no sole, Marlon was getting crabby, what a shrimp. Et cetera. When Mother stopped laughing, she demanded that we not show our faces until the poor boy left because he was a teacher at V-State going through a rough patch and needed some bucking up.'

'She called Quigg a boy?'

'Hmm,' said Trude Prosser. 'It was long ago, but I believe I'm recalling accurately. He wasn't of course, he must've been a man. Being a teacher. But perhaps his vulnerability made her think of him as a child. Anyway, we knew better than to mess with Mother when she was waxing clinically protective, so we went to a movie and by the time we got back, it was just Mother in the house.'

'Did Quigg ever show up again?'

'If he did, I'm unaware. You're wondering if something happened back then that ties in to his murder? Some homicidal patient killed him after all these years?'

'Right now the investigation's pretty much dead-ended so we're looking at everything. Is there anyone else I might talk to who'd remember those days at V-State?'

'Mother's boss was a psychiatrist named Emil Cahane. I think he was the assistant director of the hospital, or something along those lines.' She spelled the name. 'I met him a couple of times – Christmas parties,

165

that kind of thing. He came for dinner a few times. He was older than Mother, would be well into his eighties by now.'

'Did you know any of her other students?'

'She never brought students home. Or talked about them. Until she pointed out that article in the paper, I'd never heard of you.'

'So no staff person ever visited other than Marlon Quigg and Dr Cahane?'

'Dr Cahane coming for dinner was more social,' she said. 'Besides that, nothing.'

'She told you Quigg was having a rough patch.'

'That could mean anything, I suppose. But now that I think about it, for Mother to bend her rules it must've been serious. So perhaps you're onto something. But someone bearing a grudge that long? Goodness, that's grisly.'

I said, 'Your brother and sister also called me back. Think they might have something to add?'

'Mag's a bit older so perhaps his perspective would be different, but by then he really wasn't around very much. Ava's the youngest, I doubt she'd know anything I don't but give her a try.'

'I appreciate your taking the time.'

'I appreciate your getting me to talk about Mother.'

Dr Ava McClatchey said, 'Trude just called me. At first I didn't even remember the guy's visit. Once Trude reminded me of Mag's stupid fish puns, I got a vague memory but nothing Trude didn't already tell you. Got a C-section to do. Good luck.'

Dr Magnus Vanderveul said, 'Nope, we went to the movies before the fellow came over and he was gone when we came back. I did start to torment Mother with more fish puns – was he gone because she was into catch and release.' He chuckled. 'The look on her face told me to cool it.'

'Upset?'

'Bothered,' he said. 'Now that I think about it, that was odd. Mother was Superwoman, it took a lot to bother her.'

25

I'D NEVER met Dr Emil Cahane. No reason for the hospital's deputy director to have contact with a floating intern.

If I got lucky, that would change soon.

Cahane wasn't listed in any public directories nor was he a member of the American Psychiatric Association, any psychoanalytic institutes, or scientific interest groups. No active medical license in California; same for the neighboring states. I checked East Coast locales with high concentrations of psychiatrists. Nothing in New England, New York, Pennsylvania, Illinois, New Jersey. Florida, where Gertrude had ended up.

Nothing.

Well into his eighties. The worst-case scenario loomed.

Then a search using Cahane's name pulled up a career achievement award he'd received from the L.A. Mental Health Commission eighteen months ago.

An accompanying photo revealed a thin, hawkish white-haired man with a crooked smile and a listing physique that suggested a stroke or other injury.

Cahane's listed accomplishments included his years at V-State, two decades of volunteer work with abused children, foster families, and the offspring of military veterans. He'd researched post-traumatic stress disorder, closed head injuries, and integrated methods of pain control, had endowed a study of the emotional effects of prolonged parental separation at the med school cross-town where he held a clinical professorship.

The same med school had graced me with an identical title.

Twenty years of volunteer work said he'd left V-State a few years after Marlon Quigg.

I phoned the med school, got a receptionist who knew me, and asked for a current address and number for Cahane.

'Here you go, Doctor.'

Ventura Boulevard address in Encino. That had to be office space.

No active license but working? At what?

A woman answered crisply: 'Cahane and Geraldo, how may I help you?'

'This is Dr Delaware calling Dr Cahane?'

'This is the office of *Mister* Michael Cahane.'

'He's a lawyer?'

'Business manager.'

'I got this number from the medical school.'

'The medical school – oh,' she said. 'Mr Cahane's uncle uses us as a mail-drop.'

'Dr Emil Cahane.'

'What is it exactly that you want?'

'I trained under Dr Cahane at Ventura State Hospital and was looking to get in touch.'

'I couldn't give out his personal information.'

'Could I speak with Mr Cahane?'

'In a meeting.'

'When will he be free?'

'How about I give him your number.' Statement, no question.

'Thanks. Please let Dr Cahane know that another staffer from the hospital passed away and I thought he might want to know. Marlon Quigg.'

'How sad,' she said, without emotion. 'You get to an age and your friends start dropping off.'

The phone rang nine minutes later. I picked it up, ready with my sales pitch for Dr Cahane.

Milo said, 'Petra and I are having a skull session, feel free.'

'When and where?'

'In an hour, the usual place.'

Café Moghul was empty but for two slumping detectives.

Milo's Everest of tandoori lamb was untouched. Ditto, Petra Connor's seafood salad.

His greeting was a choppy wave that could be misinterpreted as apathy. Petra managed a half smile. I sat down.

Petra's a young, bright homicide D working Hollywood Division, a former commercial artist with an especially keen eye and a quiet, thoughtful manner that some mistake for iciness.

She's got the kind of slender, angular good looks that, rightly or wrongly, imply confidence and imperturbability. Thick, straight black hair cut in a functional wedge is never mussed. Her makeup's minimal but artful, her eyes clear and dark. She dresses in tailored black or navy pantsuits and moves with economy. Listens more than she talks. All in all, she comes across as the girl everyone looked up to in high school. Over the years, she'd let out enough personal details to tell me it hadn't been that easy.

Today her lips were pallid and parched, her eyes red-rimmed. Every hair remained in place but her hands clasped each other with enough force to blanch fine-boned knuckles. One cuticle was raw.

She looked as if she'd been on a long, harrowing journey.

Seeing it.

She loosened her hands, placed them flat on the table. Milo rubbed the side of his nose. A bespectacled woman came over in a swoosh of red sari silk and asked what she could get me. I ordered iced tea. Petra ate a lettuce leaf and checked a cell phone that didn't need checking.

Milo dared to fork some lamb into his mouth, grimaced as if he'd just swallowed vomit. He shoved the platter away, ran a finger under his belt, pushed his chair back a few inches, distancing himself from the notion of eating.

He looked at Petra.

She said, 'Go ahead.'

He said, 'Number Five is a poor soul named Lemuel Eccles, male Cauc, sixty-seven. Homeless street person, crashed in various alleys, one of which served as his final resting place. East Hollywood, specifically: just north of the Boulevard, just shy of Western, behind an auto parts store.'

I said, 'Who found him?'

'Private garbage service. Eccles was left next to a Dumpster.'

'Same technique?'

Petra flinched and muttered 'Dear God' before looking away. 'Patrol knew Eccles, he's got an extensive record. Aggressive panhandling, shoplifting, drunk and disorderly, creating a disturbance for shoving a tourist, he was in and out of County.'

'Your basic revolving-door juicehead nuisance,' said Milo.

She said, 'Obviously, someone thought he was more than a nuisance. To do *that* to him.'

'Not necessarily,' I said.

Both of them stared at me.

'Things we'd consider petty could loom huge in our boy's mind. Righting wrongs, real or imaginary, gives him justification to act out his body-exploration fantasies.'

Petra said, 'People irk him so he *guts* them? Insane.'

Milo patted my shoulder. 'Ergo *his* presence.'

She closed her eyes, massaged the lids, exhaled long and slow.

I said, 'Glenda Usfel kicked him out of the clinic. Vita Berlin was constitutionally nasty, it's not hard to imagine her getting in his face. And Mr Eccles's tendency to beg with a heavy hand and become rowdy while drunk would fit, too. Most people would walk away. Shearling took another approach. That section of Hollywood's commercial and industrial. Meaning at night there wouldn't be a lot of people around. An elderly wino snoozing in the alley would've been easy prey. Were there any other wounds besides the abdominal incisions?'

Petra said, 'Black-and-blue mark on his upper lip, right under the nose.'

'A cold-cock, like Marlon Quigg, but from the front because Eccles was probably inebriated. Or sleeping in the alley.'

'Could be, but Eccles's entire body was full of bruises and most of them looked old. Maybe bleeding issues due to alcohol, or he bumped into things.'

Milo said, 'To me the lip bruise looked fresher, I'm betting on a cold-cock while he was out of it.'

'Or,' said Petra, 'Eccles heard the bad guy approaching, stirred, and got sent back to slumberland.'

'Fine,' said Milo, 'once again we're getting a notion of how but the why's still far from clear. Not that I don't buy your theory about over-reacting to small slights, Alex. Giving himself an excuse to do what he loves to do. But Marlon Quigg doesn't fit any of that. Unless you found out he taught Shearling when Shearling was a tyke, rapped his knuckles with a steel ruler or something.'

'Not there yet, but I'm getting closer.' I told them what I'd learned from the Vanderveul children.

Milo said, 'Quigg pays her a visit for moral support? That could mean anything.'

'Not in Gertrude's case,' I said. 'She was adamant about separating work from her home life, had never entertained anyone else from the hospital in that manner. So whatever Quigg had on his mind was serious. And she made sure her kids weren't around to hear it.'

'Heavy-duty therapy.'

'Maybe heavy-duty advice,' I said. 'Like telling Quigg to quit the hospital. And shortly after, he did. Left teaching completely and took up a whole new profession and lied to his wife about his reason.'

Petra said, 'Something happened at work that freaked him out.'

'What if he came upon a patient committing acts that alarmed him and warned the staff about it? If he was ignored that could've been extremely upsetting. If he wasn't, it could've gotten the patient a transfer to Specialized Care and earned Quigg a serious enemy.'

I described the layout of the ward behind the fence. Curdled silence broken by the occasional ragged noise.

171

'If Quigg succeeded in having a child moved there, it would've brought about a profound shift in quality of life, trading an open therapeutic environment for what was essentially a prison. Possibly for years.'

'The main hospital was that cushy?' said Milo.

'There were a few locked wards but they were used for the patients' safety, profoundly delayed individuals who'd hurt themselves if allowed to wander. Specialized Care was designed with everyone *else's* safety in mind.'

'Shackles and rubber rooms?'

'I never found out what went on there because Gertrude wouldn't let me near the place. Because she liked me.'

'They have teachers there?'

'Same answer. I couldn't say.'

Petra said, 'Well, something bothered Quigg enough to get him out of that place. How old of a scary kid would we be talking about?'

'The few descriptions we have of our suspect are a man in his thirties and Quigg left V-State twenty-four years ago, so probably a preteen or an early adolescent. The hospital closed down ten years ago. If he was kept there until the end, we're talking a disturbed, angry man in his twenties possibly released to the streets. Or it took him this long to act out because he wasn't released, he was transferred to Atascadero or Starkweather before finally earning his freedom.'

'Or,' said Milo, 'he's been out for a while and these aren't his only murders.'

Petra said, 'Other surgeries,' and shook her head. 'No one including the Feebies has seen anything like his pattern.'

'Not every murder gets discovered, kid.'

'For ten years he's careful and conceals his handiwork, then all of a sudden he goes public?'

'It happens,' said Milo. 'They get confident.'

'Or,' I said, 'they start to get bored and need more stimulation.'

Milo pulled out his phone. 'Let's find this psychiatrist – Cahane.' He called in a real estate search. Negative.

Petra said, 'He's in his eighties, could be in some kind of assisted living.'

Milo said, 'Hopefully he's not too senile to help us.'

I said, 'If he doesn't pan out, there are others who might know — someone who actually worked in Specialized.'

Petra said, 'We could look for old hospital personnel records.' Producing a tube of MAC lipstick from her purse, she refreshed. Smiled. 'Being de-*tec*tives and all.'

As we left the restaurant, both their phones went off simultaneously. Not coincidence; two minions from the chief's office were ordering them downtown immediately for a 'planning session'.

As we headed for the West L.A. parking lot, Petra's cell chirped again. This time the call was from her partner, Raul Biro, back at his desk in Hollywood Division.

He'd located Lemuel Eccles's son, an attorney from San Diego. Because of the distance, Biro had done a telephonic notification. But Lem Jr. had business in San Gabriel tomorrow and would stop in L.A. for a face-to-face.

Petra said, 'We can do the interview together, Big Guy, or if you're tied up, I'll handle it. Assuming we don't get "planned" off the case.'

'Assuming,' said Milo. They walked off wordlessly, a bear and a gazelle.

Five paces later, Petra stopped and looked back. 'Thanks for the ideas, Alex.'

Without breaking step, Milo bellowed, 'I second the motion.'

26

I GOT home prepared to examine Ventura State Hospital's history, seeking out anyone who could tell me about the patients in Specialized Care.

One curious boy, in particular.

If that failed, I'd press Emil Cahane's nephew to gain access to the psychiatrist. As I settled in my chair, my service called in. 'I have a Dr Angel on the line, she says it's important.'

Donna Angel and I go way back, to my first job fresh out of training, working the cancer ward at Western Pediatric. Donna had been an oncology fellow, one of the best, and the department had asked her to stay on as a faculty member. After I went into private practice, she referred occasional patients, always with insight and wisdom.

Picking up a new patient right now would be a distraction but sick kids never lost their priority. I said, 'Put her through.'

'Good to talk to you, Alex.' Donna's Tallulah voice was even huskier than usual. When I'd met her, she smoked, a habit picked up in college. It had taken years for her to quit; I hoped the vocal change meant nothing.

She coughed. 'Darn cold, kids are like petri dishes for viruses.'

I said, 'Heal up. What's new?'

'I've got someone you should meet.'

'Sure.'

'Not a referral,' she said. 'This time I'm helping you.'

She told me about it.

I said, 'When?'

'Right now, if you can swing it. There's some . . . eagerness at play.'

I made the drive to Sunset and Vermont in a little under an hour. Western Pediatric Medical Center was in its usual state of demolition and construction: another gleaming building rising from a rebar-lined maw, new marble on the façade, chronic deficits be damned.

The campus was a vein of noble intention in the drab bedrock that was East Hollywood. Half a mile to the north, Lemuel Eccles had been savaged and dumped. No time to ponder coincidence or karma or metaphysics.

I parked in the doctors' lot, rode to the fifth floor of a glass-fronted structure named after a long-dead benefactor, smiled my way past the hem-onc receptionist, and knocked on Donna's door.

She opened before my knuckles left the wood, hugged me and guided me inside.

Her desk was the usual clutter. A man stood next to one of two visitors' chairs.

'Dr Delaware, this is Mr Banforth.'

'John,' said the man, extending a hand.

'Thanks for seeing me.'

'Maybe I should be thanking you.'

Banforth waited for me to sit before lowering himself into the chair.

Thirty-five or so, he was six feet tall, solidly built, black, with close-cropped hair graying early and tortoiseshell eyeglasses resting on a small, straight nose. He wore a brown cashmere crewneck, mocha slacks, mahogany suede running shoes. A golf-ball pin was fastened to the left breast of the sweater. A thin gold chain around his neck held two tiny figurines. Outlines of a boy and a girl.

Donna said, 'I'll leave you two to talk,' and headed for the door.

When it closed, John Banforth said, 'This has been weighing on me.' He crossed his legs, frowned as if anything close to relaxation felt wrong, and planted both feet on the floor.

'Okay,' he said, 'here goes.' Inhaling. 'As Dr Angel told you, my daughter Cerise is her patient. She's five years old, her diagnosis is Wilms' tumor, she was diagnosed at Stage Three, one of her kidneys had to be removed, and we thought we were going to lose her. But she's doing great now, really responding to treatment and we firmly believe, all of us, including Dr Angel, that she's going to live to a ripe old age.'

'That's fantastic.'

'I can't say enough about Dr Angel. If anyone fits their name, it's her . . . but it's still an ordeal. Cerise's treatment. Her body's sensitive, she reacts to everything. A few weeks ago, she finished another course, had to be hospitalized until her labs stabilized. Finally, we were able to take her home. We live in Playa Del Rey and were on the freeway when Cerise started crying, she was hungry. I got off at the next exit, which was Robertson, mostly fast-food places then this café – Bijou – that looked nice. If Cerise was going to eat, we wanted it to be good quality. Also, to be honest, it was lunchtime, my wife and I figured we'd eat, too. Madeleine's a dance instructor, I'm a golf pro, we try to keep in shape.'

'Makes sense.'

'So we went in and ordered some food and everything was going okay, then Cerise got cranky. I guess we should've taken her home right then and there but her labs were really good . . . your kid goes through hell, she wants something, you give it to her, right?'

'Of course.'

'Still,' said Banforth. 'We should've known, because sometimes after treatment, Cerise overestimates her strength.' His eyes watered. 'She's been through hell but she's always trying to be strong.'

Fishing out a wallet, he showed me photos. A chubby-cheeked little girl sporting a mass of brass-colored ringlets, then the same child barely older, bald, paler, *why-me* eyes rendered huge by the shrinkage of the surrounding face.

I said, 'She's adorable,' was surprised by the catch in my voice.

'You see what I mean, it tugs at your heart, you say yes maybe when you shouldn't.'

'Of course.'

'So that's what we did and everything was okay for a while, then Cerise started to get super-cranky. Moaning, at first we thought she was in pain, but when we asked she said no but she couldn't tell us what was bothering her, sometimes I think she really doesn't know. Then all of a sudden she said what would make her happy was ice cream. Normally she gets ice cream once she's finished her dinner, but . . .'

He made another attempt to cross his legs. Same discomfort and reversal. 'Yes, we spoil her. Jared – our son, he's ten – complains about it all the time. But with everything Cerise has gone through . . . anyway, we ordered ice cream but when it arrived Cerise changed her mind, started making noise again, the waitress came over and asked if she wanted a fresh donut, she said yes.'

Banforth's forehead had slicked. He dabbed with a linen handkerchief. 'Sure, she manipulates us. We figure it's the only power she has, when she's out of the woods, we'll start to . . . anyway, at this point we're thinking we definitely need to pay and leave but before I get my wallet out, the woman in the next booth shoots up like she's been bitten in the butt, stamps over and glares down at Cerise. Like she hates her. Cerise is sensitive, she freaks out, starts wailing. A normal person would realize and back off. Not this one, she actually glares *harder*. Like she's trying to break Cerise's spirit, just break her in two, you know?'

'Unbelievable,' I said.

'My wife and I are too shocked to react. This woman evil-eyes me. I say, "What's the problem?" She says, "You people are. Sick people eat in hospitals not restaurants." I'm tongue-tied, I mean I can't believe what I just heard, but Madeleine, she's always rational, she starts to explain and this crazy woman, this *terrible* woman, waves her off and says, "*You* people. What makes you think it's okay to inflict your brat on the rest of us?" And I just lost it, I mean I really lost it.'

Banforth looked at the floor. 'I should've known better. I was in the military, trained to withstand pressure. But this was my *kid*. Calling Cerise a *brat*. It was like she was mixing up some explosive to make me blow and I *understood* that but still I *lost* it. Didn't touch her, that crazy I'm not but I jumped up, got in her face, I tell you, Doctor, I was *this*

177

close to doing something stupid but fortunately my army training helped. Also Madeleine's got hold of my hand and she's begging me to back off. So I did and the bitch went back to her booth but she kept on smirking at us. Like she won. We got the hell out of there, all three of us are real quiet. Including Cerise. But when we got home, she said, "I make everything bad." And oh, man, Madeleine and I just lost it in a whole different way. After Cerise went down for a nap we collapsed and bawled like babies.'

'I'm so sorry you had to go through that.'

'Yeah, it sucked. But we're okay, now. And you know what, the next day, Cerise was fine, like it never happened.' He shrugged. 'We roll with the punches. Cerise shows us the way.'

He fingered the chain, found the child figurines and touched each one.

'So why,' he said, 'did I tell Dr Angel I wanted to talk to you? Actually, it was her idea after I told her another part of the story, how it was weighing on me. She said she knew a doctor used to work here now works with that particular detective – I'm getting ahead of myself.'

A third leg-crossing endured but Banforth still looked as if he'd been forced into a painful contortion. 'Here's the part that's going to sound weird. I went back there, Doc.'

'To Bijou.'

'A couple days later. I know it sounds crazy but I'd composed myself, thought maybe I'd go back and if by some chance she was there, I'd try to talk to her rationally. Educate her, you know? About sick kids, how you need to be flexible. I wanted to make it right – to be rational with her no matter how she behaved. So I could prove to myself I had it together.'

He looked to the side. 'It was stupid, what can I say? Anyway, I went in and the owner – a long-haired guy with an earring – recognized me and was real nice, saying my family was welcome back anytime, he felt awful about what happened. I thanked him and then I asked if that woman ever came back, maybe one day I could explain to her about sick kids – keeping it friendly. And he got this weird expression and said, "Vita? She was murdered." I said, "Oh, crap, when?" He said a few days after you were here. I'm speechless. I leave. But later, driving to work, I remember something that happened the day this Vita started up with us. I put it aside, for sure it's nothing. But it stays in my head and I can't stop thinking about it and finally I tell Dr Angel.'

I waited.

John Banforth said, 'When we left and reached our car a guy came out behind us. At first he walked the other way. Then he turned and walked toward us, I'm thinking oh no, another nutcase, so I hustle to get Cerise and Madeleine into the car. He comes closer and he's smiling but I don't know if it's a friendly smile or a crazy smile, sometimes you can't tell. I must've tensed up because he stops a few feet away and does this.'

He held both palms frontward. 'Like *I come in peace*. I stay on my guard anyway and he winks and smiles. Friendly but also weird, I can't tell you why I felt that, he just creeped me out. Then he winks again and gives the V-sign for victory and he walks away. It confused me and creeped me out but my mind was on getting home and settling Cerise. But when I found out this Vita got murdered, I start wondering but I'm like no way, he was just reassuring us, being a nice guy. But the V-sign didn't fit that, it was like he was saying we were on the same team and we'd won. And that didn't make sense. So it started bothering me, what if he thought he was doing us a favor? It's probably nothing, I tend to dwell on stuff. I actually called the police and asked who's handling the murder of a woman named Vita. It took them a while but finally they said Detective Sturgis, we'll put you through. I hung up, figured they'd trace me, I'd get a call-back. But it never happened.'

'Police lines don't have caller I.D.,' I said. 'So people won't be inhibited about giving tips.'

'Oh . . . makes sense. Anyway, I couldn't stop wondering if he actually *did* it, some crazy sonofabitch who thought we were on the same side. Finally, I told Dr Angel and she said funny thing, you worked with that exact detective and I said, "Whoa, karma, I definitely need to get this off my chest."'

Shrugging. 'So here we are, Doc.'

'Thanks for getting in touch. What did the guy look like?'

'So it *is* relevant,' said Banforth. 'Damn.'

'Not necessarily, John. At this point, the cops look at everything.'

'They don't have a suspect?'

'They've got various bits of information that may or may not be important. What did he look like?'

'White guy,' he said. 'Around thirty-five, forty. Heavyset, kind of a round face, that's about it.'

'Hair color?'

'Brown – short, like it was growing back from a buzz.'

'Eye color?'

'Couldn't tell you.'

'He never spoke.'

'Nope, just the wink and the V-sign. It's not like evidence, that's why I tried to put it aside.'

'Your first impression was something about him seemed off.'

'But I can't tell you why, sorry.'

I gave him time. He shook his head.

'How was he dressed?'

'In a coat. Like a winter coat, even though it was a warm day – *that's* different, I guess. Maybe that's what seemed off?'

'What kind of coat?'

'One of those fleece-lined things,' said Banforth. 'Brown on the outside, maybe suede, maybe cloth, I wasn't paying attention. Oh, yeah, something else: he was carrying a book. Like students do but he didn't look like a student.'

'What kind of book?'

'Not a hardcover – more like a magazine, actually. Maybe some sort of puzzle magazine because it had a big question mark on the cover?'

My heart raced. Now I knew why Alex Shimoff's sketch had tweaked my brain.

The morning after the murder, when Milo and I had visited Bijou, an apple-faced man had been there.

Sitting in a booth behind the soccer moms and their toddlers.

Eating steak and eggs, a book in front of him, penciling a puzzle.

Enjoying a hearty breakfast hours after he'd gutted Vita.

John Banforth said, 'Doc?'

'You did the right thing.'

'He's the guy? Oh, man.'

'Not necessarily but it's a lead and Detective Sturgis needs anything he can get.'

'Well okay, then, I feel better not wasting anyone's time.'

'Would you mind sitting with a police sketch artist? So we can get a clearer image?'

'They still do that? Thought everything was computers.'

'They still do.'

'An artist, huh? Would my name have to be on it?'

'No.'

'Then guess so,' he said. 'If you can fit it to my schedule. And if Madeleine doesn't know, she has no idea about any of this, including the fact that I'm here.'

'We'll do it at your convenience.'

'All right, here's my business card, call the top number, it's my reservation line for lessons.'

'Thanks very much.'

'Just doing what I had to.'

We headed for the door. He got there first, stopped. 'She was a nasty one. That Vita. Madeleine and I took to calling her the Evil One. As in wonder who the Evil One's tormenting now. We turned it into a joke. To ease what happened. But I guess no one deserves to be murdered.'

His voice wavered on 'guess'.

27

On the way home, I detoured and drove through Vita Berlin's neighborhood, rolling through sunlit streets and shadowed alleys, searching for a man dressed too heavily for the weather. When four circuits produced nothing, I headed to Bijou.

It was just past the three o'clock closing time. The storefront window afforded a view of Ralph Veronese sweeping up, his long hair bunched in a topknot that was part girlie, part Samurai warrior. I rapped on the glass. Without breaking rhythm, he pointed to the *Closed* sign. I rapped harder and he looked up.

He cracked the door halfway, propped his broom against the jamb. 'Hey.'

'I'm doing follow-up on Vita.'

'You caught the guy?'

'Not yet. I want to ask you about a customer I noticed the first time I was here.' I described Shearling.

'Nope, doesn't ring a bell.'

'He's been here at least twice.'

'Twice doesn't make him a regular. Half the time I'm in back.'

'He sat in that corner booth, eating steak and eggs, worked on a puzzle book.'

Veronese said, 'Oh.'

'You remember him.'

'Not so much him, I remember the book. Thinking here's another camper, going to use us as the public library. But then he ordered.

182

Campers just like to stretch out a coffee, bring their laptops, gripe when they find out we don't have wireless.'

'Has he been here any other times?'

'Not that I know of.'

'How about checking your receipts for both the days we know he was here?'

'Receipts are with my bookkeeper, I send paperwork to her every Friday.'

'Then please call her.'

He dialed a preset number, spoke to someone named Amy, hung up.

'She says it's already in the storage bin, she can try to find it but it'll take time.'

'Sooner's better than later, Ralph.'

'She charges me by the hour.'

'Send me the bill.'

'You're serious?'

'You bet.'

He texted Amy.

I said, 'You're in the back but Hedy's always out front. Please get her on the line for me and if you can't reach her, give me her number.'

'Her number's my number,' said Veronese. 'We're thinking of getting married.'

'Congratulations.'

I pointed to his phone. He reached Hedy, explained, passed it over.

She said, 'The guy with the puzzle book? Sure, I remember him. But I have to tell you, he paid cash. I know for sure because it was all singles and a lot of coins. Like he busted open his piggy bank.'

'What else can you say about him?'

'Um . . . he cleaned his plate . . . didn't talk except to order . . . had kind of a girlie voice – high-pitched, didn't fit his body, he's kind of a football-player type, you know?'

'Not much for conversation.'

'Kept his head in that book even when he was eating.'

'What kind of puzzles was he working on?'

'Couldn't tell you. You're thinking he's the one who killed Vita?'

'He's someone we want to talk to.'

'Because he's a little off?'

'Off how?'

'You know, mentally.'

'He impressed you that way?'

'I'm no shrink,' she said, 'but he just wasn't . . . like he never made eye contact. Kind of mumbled. In that high voice. Like he was trying to whisper – to like stay in the background.'

'Not sociable.'

'Exactly. Just the opposite. Like *I want to be in my own world*. So I respected that, my job you have to be a shrink.'

'Anything else about him strike you as odd?'

'His clothes. It's pretty warm inside Bijou, we don't have the best A.C. and he's wearing this fleece-lined shearling. I've got one of those in my closet from when I lived in Pittsburgh, haven't used it once since I moved to L.A.'

'Was he sweating?'

'Hmm . . . I don't think so – oh, yeah, one more thing, he had a scar. In the front of his neck, like at the bottom. Nothing gross, like a white line running across his neck.'

'Across the Adam's apple?'

'Lower, in the soft part. Like someone cut him a long time ago but it healed up pretty good.'

'Any other marks?'

'Not that I saw.'

'Tattoos?'

'If he has 'em, they were covered up. *He* was pretty much covered up.'

'What else was he wearing besides the shearling?'

'You think he's the one?' she said. 'That kind of freaks me out. What if he comes in again?'

'No reason to worry, but if that happens just call this number.' I recited Milo's extension.

Hedy said, 'Got it. What else was he wearing? I guess he had a shirt on underneath but I wasn't paying attention. Sorry, the shearling's all I noticed. Because it was out of place. Mostly I was concentrating on getting the orders right. You want to know exactly what his order was, I can tell you: steak and scramble with onions and mushrooms, steak medium, no instructions on the scramble. He left like a ten percent tip, all coins, but I didn't mind. Because it wasn't like he was trying to be a jerk, you know.'

'More like he didn't know better,' I said.

'Exactly,' she said. 'A little out of it. You feel sorry for those people.'

I drove a mile north to a newspaper stand I knew on Robertson near Pico. The primary merchandise was a mix of fan mags and porn. Small selection of puzzle books in a corner.

Nothing with a question mark on the cover. I flashed my dubious consultant's I.D. to the Sikh proprietor and described Shearling.

He said, 'No, sir, I don't know him.'

I gave him Milo's card, anyway, asked him to call if Shearling showed up. 'He might buy a puzzle book.'

He smiled as if it was a perfectly reasonable request. 'Certainly, sir, anything to help.'

Good attitude, so I spent ten bucks on a glossy design magazine. Robin likes looking at dream houses.

I tried Milo again from the car, then Petra, and when she was also out I switched to Raul Biro. His voicemail answered but I left no message.

Was Shearling's presence at Bijou evidence of long-term stalking, or had he happened upon the café, seen Vita torment Cerise Banforth, and decided she merited execution? If the latter, maybe he lived nearby. Reversing direction on Robertson, I gave Vita's neighborhood another try, starting with her street.

Stanleigh Belleveaux was outside, watering his shrubs. A *For Lease* sign was staked on the lawn of the duplex. Two vacant units. I drove

185

slowly enough for Belleveaux to notice but he didn't look up and I continued south.

No sign of a man in a shearling and other than a young woman wheeling a baby in a stroller, all the activity was automotive: people pulling in and out of driveways. A door opened and a beanpole kid came out with a basketball, began shooting hoops.

Everything back to normal. People need to believe in normal.

It was close to eleven p.m. when Milo called.

'Still on the case and so is Petra.'

'Congratulations.'

'Or condolences. His Magnanimousness made it painfully clear I didn't deserve it but starting from scratch ran the risk of "butt-fucking this one into oblivion".'

I said, 'Next Christmas, he'll be Santa at the office party.'

He laughed. 'Petra and I know the real reason he's not shifting gears to Robbery-Homicide. Any hotshots who aren't already on long-termers are being flown to Arizona courtesy the taxpayers for a confab on Mexican drug cartels, gonna be PowerPoint galore. What's up?'

I told him about John Banforth, Shearling's presence at Bijou hours after Vita's murder, Hedy's description.

'A nutcase with a taste for steak.'

'Plus the way he ate – fixed on his food – smacks of an institutional background. Thirty-five to forty means that back when Quigg was working at V-State, he'd have been eleven to sixteen.'

'A kid,' he said. 'But scary enough to be transferred to Specialized Care.'

'I'm also convinced of the thyroid angle. The waitress noticed a neck scar. So maybe a thyroid scan's what brought him to North Hollywood Day. The most common reason for a thyroidectomy is cancer. There are also immune disorders that can justify it, like Hashimoto's disease. Whatever the reason, he'd need to take a daily pill to regulate his metabolism. Sometimes dosages can be tricky and if he's a street guy, he may not be getting optimal care. That could explain feeling cold and putting on a few pounds.'

'Cancer?' he said. 'Now I'm dealing with a psycho with serious sympathy issues?'

'Thyroid cancer's one of the most curable malignancies. He'd have the potential to live to a ripe old age.'

'Except his chemistry's off.'

'Which would explain the scan. He needs his prescription renewed, would have to see a doctor at some point. A physician who picked up on his symptoms and found out he hadn't been followed up regularly might want comprehensive data before adjusting his dosage. North Hollywood Day is an insurance mill but no doubt they see lots of Medi-Cal patients, so a referral there makes sense.'

'He comes in to get nuked, gets on Glenda Usfel's bad side, she boots his ass out.'

'Wrong guy to boot.'

'"Ladies and gentlemen of the jury, yes my client's a bit touchy but not only is he certifiably loony, his glands are out of whack and he endured the big C."'

'Cart before the horse, Big Guy.'

'Yeah, yeah, find him first. Before someone *else* gets on his bad side. So where do I go with this thyroid stuff, Alex? Call every endocrinologist in town?'

'They're unlikely to talk to you but the general public won't have those compunctions. Have John Banforth sit down with Shimoff and work up a better likeness. If Banforth can't give enough details, I'll try to fill them in because I got a decent look at the guy. That and the scar, the coat, and the puzzle book could tweak someone's memory. Even if he's underground, he's got to surface occasionally. Assuming he's got an institutional background, I'd also check health clinics, welfare offices, halfway houses, and aftercare facilities near each of the murder sites. He paid for his meal with coins, I doubt that's interest from a brokerage account.'

'On the dole,' he said. 'Or he panhandles. Like Eccles. Hell, maybe that's why he *did* Eccles: the two of them got into a competitive thing and Shearling decided to engage in unfair business practices . . . okay, I'll get Banforth and Shimoff together. This is helpful, amigo.'

'One more thing,' I said. 'Check out newsstands, see if anyone sells a puzzle book with a question mark on the cover. The one near Vita's scene doesn't but there are plenty of others.'

'There's a big one off Hollywood Boulevard, not that far from where Lem Eccles got it. Speaking of which, Jernigan called on Eccles's autopsy. The bruise on Eccles's lip was from a hard blow or a kick, most likely a kick from a blunt-toed shoe. Not severe enough to be lethal but it could've stunned him. Other than that, the details are like the others. Eccles's son's trip to L.A. is tomorrow. Want to be there?'

'Wouldn't miss it.'

28

LEMUEL ECCLES JR, aka 'Lee', was thirty-eight and rock-jawed, with meaty shoulders, blue eyes that tended to wander, and longish light brown hair lightened to blond at the tips.

Your basic aging surfer. This one sported a manicure, a two-thousand-dollar charcoal chalk-stripe suit, a purple Hermès tie, a canary-and-violet pocket square.

His card said he was an attorney specializing in real estate.

Milo said, 'Leases and mortgages?'

Eccles said, 'Used to be, now it's evictions and foreclosures. Basically I'm a vulture.' His smile was practiced and pretty, but lacked staying power. We'd been in the interview room for less than a minute. Eccles had spent most of that time sneaking glances at Petra Connor.

Easy to see why, especially given the competition. Her lips had moistened since yesterday, her eyes were clear, her skin tone had warmed. She wore a simple gold chain and diamond-chip ear-studs. The drape of her black pantsuit was even better than that of Lee Eccles's suit.

The first few times she caught Eccles checking her out, she pretended not to notice. Finally, she smiled at him and edged closer.

She's in a committed relationship with a former detective named Eric Stahl, but you use what you have.

Milo sniffed the chemistry early on and let her take the interview.

'Lee,' she said, as if savoring the word, 'we're so sorry about your dad.'

'Thanks. Appreciate it.' Eccles loosened a jacket button. 'I guess I

189

shouldn't be totally surprised because he led what you guys would call a high-risk life. But still . . .'

'You can never be prepared for something like this, Lee.'

Eccles's eyes filmed a bit. A tissue box sat nearby. Petra didn't offer it. No sense highlighting vulnerability.

Eccles used his pocket square to swipe quickly, took the time to refold and put the handkerchief back with four points showing. 'What exactly happened?'

Petra said, 'Your dad was murdered and we're determined to catch the bad guy. Anything you can tell us will be a big help.'

'The first thing you need to know,' said Eccles, 'is he was crazy. I mean that literally. Paranoid schizophrenic, he was diagnosed years ago, not long after I was born. He and my mom divorced when I was four and I rarely saw him. After I got out of law school, he found me somehow and dropped in at my office. I was foolish enough to bring him home. It didn't take long for things to get hairy. Right from the beginning he scared Tracy – my wife. He ended up scaring me, too.'

'In what way, Lee?'

'He wasn't actually violent but the threat of violence always seemed to hover around him and in a sense that was even worse. The look in his eyes, the way he'd suddenly go silent in the midst of a conversation. Then one time, we let him sleep over and he punched holes in the wall. Woke us up in the middle of the night, we were terrified. When I went in to see what was wrong, he was sitting on the floor, huddled in a corner, claimed he'd fended off an intruder. But the alarm was still on, no one had gotten in. I finally calmed him down and left. Later, I heard him crying in bed.'

'What an ordeal,' said Petra.

'I learned that it kicked in when he drank. Problem is, that was often. Eventually, Tracy and I agreed: no more visits, we really needed to cut him off. The next time he showed up we told him and he got pissed off and cussed us out. I offered to rent him a motel for as long as he needed and we could still see each other during the day. That pissed him off even more, he stormed off. A few weeks later he showed up and tried to force himself inside the house – pushed the door as I held it. That's when I decided to have him committed. I tried three separate times. For his sake as much as for ours, he needed to be cared for in a supervised setting, not drift around on the street. Each time I showed up in court, some do-gooder Legal Aid type was there to block me. Some asshole who'd never met him but claimed to be defending his rights. Apparently they scan the dockets and even when someone's only requesting a seventy-two-hour hold, they come to make trouble.'

'Oh, man,' said Petra.

Lee Eccles said, 'I'm talking publicly funded wienies who know all the angles and brain-dead judges they probably take out to lunch. I'm an attorney and I still couldn't get it done. After the third time, I talked to a buddy who does health law and he said don't waste your time and money, until he actually assaults – which means drawing blood – or makes a suicide attempt, it's not going to happen. Even then, all they're going to do is warehouse him for a couple of days and turn him loose.'

'Not enough imminent danger,' said Petra.

'What a crock. The mere fact he was living on the street put him in imminent danger. *Obviously*.' His strong jaw shifted to the side. Settled back in place. 'You know what I'd like to do? Haul one of those wienies over to the morgue and show them what their meddling accomplished.'

He tugged at his tie knot. 'Do you have any idea who did this to him?'

Him. He. No Dad, Pops, Father, the Old Man.

'Unfortunately not yet, Lee. Do you?'

'I wish. Where was he killed?'

'In an alley near Hollywood and Western.'

'Oh, Jesus,' said Eccles. 'That's right where I dropped him off when I bailed him out of jail.'

'When was that, Lee?'

'About a month ago, he'd gotten busted for pushing someone while panhandling. He used his call to beg me to get him out. I figured he'd get out anyway, be pissed if I didn't help him so I paid the bail and picked him up and dropped him where he wanted to be dropped. Where he *instructed* me to drop him. Like I'm his limo driver. So that's where it happened?'

Petra said, 'Did you observe where he went after you dropped him off?'

'No, I just booked out of there as fast as I could.'

'Did you notice him making any contact with someone?'

'No. But something just occurred to me, it's probably psychotic delusion but I might as well tell you. On the ride from the jail he got on one of his rants about some guy hassling him, he was scared. Then he got all paranoid with me, I was a goddamn lawyer, lawyers ran the system, why couldn't I help him? I said if he was scared I could find him somewhere to stay. He went ballistic, accused me of wanting to lock him up in some "loony bin" and throw away the key, I was like all lawyers, a scumbag. I said, "You're the one complaining someone's after you, I'm just trying to help." That made him clam up, ignore me totally. When I reached where he wanted, he said, "Stop here," and he got out, didn't bother to look back.'

Petra said, 'Who'd he say was he scared of?'

'Trust me, it was delusional. An old delusion.'

'What do you mean?'

'This guy he complained about didn't exist. He's been bitching about it my whole life. According to my mother since he actually *was* locked up in a mental hospital.'

'Where's that?' said Petra.

'A place that no longer exists,' said Lee Eccles. 'Ventura State Hospital, he got committed for an indefinite term but was out in pretty short time according to my mother. Back then it was easier to commit someone, a judge put him in after he busted some guy's jaw in a bar, got on the stand and claimed the guy was implanting radio speakers in his head.'

'How long ago was this, Lee?'

'Let's see, I was thirteen . . . no, fourteen, I was playing baseball, which means I was in high school. So twenty-three years ago. I remember the baseball part because I was always worried he'd show up at a game and embarrass me.'

'So what's the old delusion?'

'While he was locked up, one of the guards supposedly killed his wife. Not my mother, not even a real wife, some woman he'd been living with, a barfly like him.'

'Where was he living before he was committed?'

'Oxnard. We were in Santa Monica, which sounds far enough but the things Mom told me, I was always worried he'd show up. So was she, she moved us down to O.C., trying to put some distance between us.'

'This woman who was allegedly murdered,' said Petra. 'Did your mom mention her name?'

'I think Mom said Rosetta. Or Rosita, I don't know. But don't waste your time, Detective. The story was insane. Like a guard could poison someone? Or want to? I'm not sure the woman even existed. Or if she did, that what happened to her is what he told Mom.'

'What's that?'

'Rosita comes to visit him, leaves, drops dead in the parking lot. He knows this guard did it to get back at him. Why I can't tell you. Anyway, now it's the same person who's bothering him in Hollywood and I'm supposed to do something about it because I'm a lawyer.'

'This imaginary person has a name.'

'Petty,' he said. 'Or maybe it was Pitty. My father was originally from Oklahoma, had a twang that got worse when he was agitated. His story was the guy's popping up on the street, following him, giving him quote unquote X-ray eyes. It was a ridiculous story all those years ago and didn't get better in the retelling but I figure you should know everything.'

'Appreciate it, Lee,' said Petra. 'Would you mind if we talked to your mother? Just to fill in details?'

'I'd love if you'd talk to her because that would mean she's alive. Unfortunately, Parkinson's disease had other ideas.'

'I'm so sorry.'

193

'So am I, Detective. They say you don't grow up until you lose your parents. Frankly, I'd prefer to be immature.'

Petra's mother had died giving birth to her. Her father had succumbed a few years back. She said, 'I've heard that.'

Eccles stood, checked the folds of his hankie.

'I guess,' he said, 'I'm responsible for the body.'

A uniformed officer saw Lee Eccles out.

Petra said, 'He has no idea what he just gave us. Marlon Quigg worked at that hospital at the same time Lem Eccles was committed there. Looks like you were right about some sort of ancient history, Alex.'

I said, 'Maybe for those two but I can't see Vita and Glenda Usfel connected to V-State that long ago. Usfel was a young child and Vita grew up in Chicago.'

'Fine,' said Milo. 'So their problems with Mr Shearling were more recent, he's an equal-opportunity disemboweler.'

Petra said, 'Eccles Junior is one angry man, that boy did not like his daddy. Can't say that I blame him but he's lucky Daddy's murder is part of a serial because if I picked it up as a one-shot I'd be looking at him as my prime. And if Eccles alienated his own offspring that thoroughly, imagine what he could evoke in a homicidal maniac. Especially if the two of them went way back to V-State.'

Milo said, 'Mr Crazy, meet Mr Curious. Where do we go with this Pitty-Patty-Petty dude? If any of it's true, we've got complications because Shearling's too young to have worked as a guard twenty-three years ago.'

I said, 'The story could be partially true. Eccles knew someone named Pitty years ago, convinced himself the guy was after him. He notices someone stalking him and resurrects his old personal bogeyman.'

'You believe the stalking part?' said Petra.

'Eccles was murdered.'

Milo said, 'The bumper sticker.'

'What?'

'Even paranoids have enemies.'

She laughed.

Milo said, 'Even if Pitty did exist, Alex is probably right and he's irrelevant. Eccles was schizo, had a fixation, flashed back to it. Or Pitty's a squid in a three-piece suit or some other figment. In any event, we've got multiple sightings of Shearling.'

Petra said, 'If Shearling was a patient at V-State, we might be able to find some known associates, family, anything that could lead us to him. Any word back from that psychiatrist, Alex?'

'No.'

Milo said, 'Got his address just before Eccles Junior showed up. Social Security records, don't ask.'

She said, 'Excellent. Let's pay him a visit, Big Guy.'

'I don't know. He's under no obligation to let us past the door let alone cough up patient info. We get heavy-handed, he invokes the doctor confidentiality thing. So my vote's for having Alex try first, shrink-to-shrink.'

Petra looked at me.

I said, 'He could refuse me, too, but sure.'

Milo fished out a scrap of paper and handed it over. Van Nuys address, 818 landline.

'Meanwhile, we can have Shimoff do a better drawing with Banforth and push to get it on the media along with the new info. I've got Sean and Moe checking out newsstands and bookstores, see if anyone remembers an asshole buying puzzle books.'

Petra said, 'Raul's been talking to street people but so far no one had a special beef with Eccles, basically everyone thought he was a general pain.' Smiling. 'I'll tell him to look for a cephalopod in a suit.'

I said, 'Eccles's last arrest, the one his son bailed him out for, was for shoving a tourist. Have you looked at the arrest report?'

'I read the summary. Your basic citizen versus nutcase.'

'Citizen have a name?'

'I didn't make note of it. Why?'

'Maybe it's worthwhile. On the off chance that it was Shearling.'

'Nutcase versus nutcase?' said Milo.

'Flagrant psychotic versus someone able to maintain outward control,' I said. 'What was the exact nature of the charge?'

Petra said, 'Eccles tried to get money from a tourist, the tourist resisted, Eccles did some screaming and pushing and shoving.'

'Did the tourist phone in the complaint?'

'No, someone on the street did and a car was a block away.'

I said, 'Think what the officers would've found: a he said–he said between a quiet young man and an angry alcoholic with a record for aggressive panhandling whom they knew as a neighborhood nuisance.'

Milo said, 'Shearling's able to fake normal.'

'Five murders without a trace of physical evidence says he's organized, meticulous, able to slip in and out without setting off alarms. He impressed Hedy the waitress as eccentric but didn't scare her. John Banforth thought his behavior was odd but it didn't trouble him too much until he learned of Vita's murder. So we're talking someone who's not overwhelmingly threatening. When contrasted with Eccles's ravings, there's no doubt who the cops would've seen as the offender.'

'Monster trumps maniac,' she said. 'Okay, I'll check the complete report. And as long as we're dotting *i*'s, I'm going to call Oxnard PD and see if I can dig up something about this Rosetta woman.' Winking. 'The bumper sticker and all that.'

The three of us headed for the exit.

'Crazy,' said Milo. 'The only time I like it is when Patsy Cline's singing about it.'

29

CAUGHT IN a traffic jam on Wilshire and Westwood, I phoned my service.

Three calls, none of them from Emil Cahane.

I tried the Valley number Milo had given me. No answer.

When I got home, I began working the computer, searching for staff lists at V-State and finally coming upon an old one that listed Cahane as deputy director with one person above him, Dr Saul Landesberg.

A search using Landesberg's name pulled up a four-year-old obituary.

Him, Gertrude, I wasn't even sure if Cahane was coherent.

Ancient history. But not to a man in a fleece-lined coat.

Robin was working out back. I dropped in, kissed her, petted Blanche, engaged in a brief discussion of dinner. Yes, Japanese sounded fine, maybe we'd splurge on Matsuhisa.

When I returned to my office, the phone was ringing.

Milo said, 'Guess what, we actually learned some stuff. A clerk at a stand on San Vicente in Brentwood told Reed he sold an armload of puzzle books to someone about a week ago. Unfortunately, he remembers the books, not the purchaser. Who cleaned him out. And paid with small bills and coins.'

I said, 'Go west from that location, hook north to Sunset and keep going, you'll reach Quigg's apartment. Couple of miles farther, you're at Temescal Canyon.'

'Stocking up on reading material for a thorough surveillance? Interesting . . . The second thing is Petra found out from Oxnard that there really was a Rosetta who died in the parking lot at V-State, last name Macomber. She lived in a public housing project, had coke and booze issues. So Eccles had at least some reality testing, but there was no evidence it was murder, more likely a heart attack.'

'Not a scratch on her,' I said. 'That's why Eccles thought she'd been poisoned. Was she visiting him?'

'The cop Petra talked to didn't know, only reason he remembered was he'd patrolled near the hospital, was called to the scene by their on-site security. Thought it was ironic for someone to walk out of a hospital and keel over. Even though it wasn't *that* kind of hospital. The last bit of news is Shimoff's second drawing is much more detailed than the one he did with Wheeling, I'm working on getting it to the media. So thanks for directing us to Mr Banforth. Anything from Cahane?'

'Not yet.'

'He gets back to you, fine. He doesn't, we'll figure out what to do. Sayonara.'

I returned to the list of V-State senior staffers, tried the next name, the head social worker, a Helen Barofsky. Her personal data had managed to elude me for nearly an hour by the time my service rang in.

'A Dr Cahane called,' said the operator. 'He said it wasn't an emergency.'

Depends on your definition.

The number she gave me matched the one I'd received from Milo. I waited seven rings before a soft voice said, 'Yes?'

'Dr Cahane? This is Alex Delaware returning—'

'Dr Delaware.' Soft, wispy voice, tremulous at the tail end of each word, like an amp set on slow vibrato. 'I'm afraid your name isn't familiar.'

'No reason it should be,' I said. 'I floated through V-State years ago as an intern. Gertrude Vanderveul was my supervisor. Years later, when the hospital closed down, I did some consulting on getting the patients in E Ward some decent aftercare.'

'Aftercare,' he said. 'Promises were made, weren't they?' Sigh. 'I was gone by then. Gertrude . . . have you been in contact with her?'

'Unfortunately, she passed away.'

'Oh. How terrible, she was young.' A beat. 'Relatively . . . my nephew's secretary said something about a Mr Quib passing but I can't say I know who that is, either.'

'Marlon Quigg.' I spelled it.

'No, sorry, doesn't ring a bell.'

Yet he'd returned my call.

As if reading my mind, he said, 'I responded to your message because at my age any bit of novelty is welcome. In any event, sorry I couldn't be more helpful.'

'Marlon Quigg worked as a teacher at V-State during your tenure.'

'We employed many teachers,' said Cahane. 'At the height of our glory, we were quite the enlightened institution.'

'This teacher was murdered and the police have reason to believe his death relates to his work at the hospital.'

Silence.

'Dr Cahane?'

'This is a bit to digest, Dr Delaware. The police have reason to believe, yet they're not calling me, you are.'

'I work with them.'

'In what capacity?'

'A consultant.'

'Meaning?'

'Sometimes they think psychology has something to offer. Could you spare a few minutes to meet?'

'Hmm,' he said. 'And if I phoned the police, Alex, they'd confirm that you're a consultant?'

I rattled off Milo's name, rank, and private number. 'He'd be more than happy to speak to you, Doctor. He's the one who asked me to get in contact with you.'

'Why is that?'

'You were the deputy director at V-State when Marlon Quigg worked there, had access to information.'

'Patient information?'

'Specifically dangerous patients.'

'That, as I'm sure you know, raises all kinds of issues.'

'The situation,' I said, 'is way beyond *Tarasoff*. We're not talking imminent danger, we're talking empirical brutality with a significant risk of more.'

'That sounds rather dramatic.'

'I saw the body, Dr Cahane.'

Silence.

He said, 'What exactly are you looking for?'

'The identity of a child Quigg was teaching whose behavior frightened him, perhaps to the point of suggesting a transfer to Specialized Care.'

'And this person killed him?' said Cahane. 'All these years later?'

'It's possible.'

'You're supposing, you really don't know.'

'If I knew I wouldn't need to speak to you, Dr Cahane.'

'Specialized Care,' he said. 'Did you ever rotate through there?'

'Gertrude felt I shouldn't.'

'Why was that?'

'She said it was because she liked me.'

'I see . . . well, there are always judgments to make and for the most part Gertrude made sound ones. But Special-C wasn't a hellhole, far from it. Whatever steps were taken to control patients were taken judiciously.'

'This isn't about hospital procedure, Dr Cahane. It's about a particularly calculating, vicious murderer acting out years of resentment and fantasy.'

'Why exactly do the police believe Mr Quigg's death had something to do with a patient at V-State?'

Because I told them so.

I said, 'It's complex. Could we meet face-to-face?'

'You want a prolonged opportunity to convince me.'

'I don't think you'll need much convincing.'

'Why's that?'

'Something was left on Mr Quigg's body,' I said. 'A piece of paper upon which the killer had printed a question mark.'

I could hear Cahane's breathing, rapid and shallow.

Finally, he said, 'I don't drive anymore. You'd need to come to me.'

The address Milo gave me matched an apartment building a few miles east of Cahane's nephew's office in Encino, a plain-faced, two-story rhombus stuccoed the color of raspberry yogurt and planted with yuccas, palms, and enough agave to cook up a year's worth of margaritas.

The freeway passed within a couple of blocks, its roar the awakening yawn of an especially cranky ogre. The building's front door was closed but unlocked. The center-spine hallway was freshly painted and immaculately maintained.

Five units above, five below. Cahane's flat was ground floor rear. As I approached the door, the ogre's growl muted to a disgruntled hum. I knocked.

'Open.'

Cahane sat ten feet away in a scarred leather easy chair that faced the door. His body tilted to the left. His face was even thinner than in the tribute photo, white hair longer and shaggier, a couple days' worth of stubble snowing chin and cheeks. He had long legs and arms, not much upper body, was dressed in a clean white shirt and pressed navy slacks under a fuzzy plaid bathrobe. Black suede slippers that had once been expensive fit over white socks that hadn't been. A mahogany piecrust table held a cup of still-steaming tea and a book. Evelyn Waugh's hilarious take on travel.

Extending a quivering hand, he said, 'Forgive me for not rising but the joints aren't cooperating today.'

His palm was cool and waxy, his grip surprisingly strong but contact was as brief as he could manage without being rude. He shook his head. 'Can't say I remember you.'

201

'No reason—'

'Sometimes images register anyway. Would you care for something to drink?' Pointing to a kitchen behind the front room. 'I've got soda and juice and the kettle's still warm. Even bourbon, if you'd like.'

'I'm fine.'

'Then please sit.'

No puzzle about where to settle. The sole option was a blue brocade sofa pushed to the wall opposite Cahane's chair. Like the slippers, it looked pricey but worn. Same for the piecrust table and the Persian rug that stretched unevenly atop soot-colored wall-to-wall. Disparate bookcases covered every inch of wall space save for doorways into the kitchen and the bedroom. Every case was full and some shelves were double-stacked.

A quick scan of the titles showed Cahane's reading taste to be unclassifiable: history, geography, religion, photography, physics, gardening, cooking, a wide range of fiction, political satire. Two shelves directly behind his chair held volumes on psychology and psychiatry. Basic stuff and not much of it, considering.

Chair, beverage, robe and slippers, reading material. He had enough money to endow a program, had pruned to the basics.

He kept studying my face, as if trying to retrieve a memory. Or just reverting to what he'd learned in school.

When in doubt, do nothing.

I half expected to be presented a Rorschach card.

I said, 'Doctor—'

'Tell me about Marlon Quigg's end.'

I described the murder, giving him the level of detail I figured Milo would approve. Wanting to communicate the horror without divulging too much and making sure not to mention the other victims lest Cahane interpret that as pointing away from V-State.

He said, 'That is beyond brutal.'

'Does the question mark mean anything to you, Dr Cahane?'

His lips folded inward. He rubbed chin stubble. 'How about fetching that bourbon? Bring two glasses.'

* * *

202

The kitchen was as spare as the front room, clean but shabby. The glasses were cut crystal, the bourbon was Knob Creek.

Cahane said, 'A finger and a half for me, calibrate your own dosage.'

I allotted myself a thin amber stripe. We clinked crystal. No one toasted.

I sat down and watched him drain his glass in two swallows. He rubbed his stubble again. 'You're wondering why I live this way.'

'It wasn't the first thing on my mind.'

'But you are curious.'

I didn't argue.

He said, 'Like most people, I spent quite a bit of my adult life accumulating things. After my wife died I began to feel smothered by things so I gave most of them away. I'm not stupid or impulsive, nor am I ruled by neurotic anhedonia. I held on to enough passive income to ensure freedom from worry. It was an experiment, really. To see how it felt to cleanse oneself of the rococo trim we think we crave. Sometimes I miss my big house, my cars, my art. Mostly, I do not.'

Long monologue. Probably a stall. I had no choice but to listen.

Cahane said, 'You've put me in a difficult position. You've come to me with nothing more than hypotheses. Granted, hypotheses are often based on logic but the problem is you don't have facts and now you're asking me to break confidentiality.'

'Your position at V-State wouldn't necessarily obligate you to confidentiality,' I said.

His eyebrows dipped. 'What do you mean?'

'A case can be made that administrators aren't bound the way clinicians are. Of course, if you did treat the person in question, that assertion might be challenged.'

He lifted his empty glass. 'Would you mind fetching the bottle?'

I complied and he poured himself another two fingers, finished half. His eyes had grown restless. He closed them. His hands had begun to shake. Then they stilled and he didn't move.

I waited.

For a moment I thought he'd fallen asleep.

The eyes opened. He looked at me sadly and I braced myself for refusal.

'There was a boy,' he said. 'A curious boy.'

204

30

EMIL CAHANE poured another half inch of bourbon. Studying the liquid as if it held both promise and threat, he took a tentative sip then swigged like a sot.

His head tilted up at the ceiling. His eyes closed. His breathing grew rapid.

'All right,' he said. But he spent another half minute sitting there. Then: 'This child, this . . . unusual boy was sent to us from another state. No sense specifying, it doesn't matter. They had no idea how to deal with him and we were considered among the best. He arrived in a pale green sedan . . . a Ford . . . he was accompanied by two state troopers. Large men, it emphasized how small he was. I tried to interview him but he wouldn't talk. I placed him in G Building. Perhaps you remember it.'

I'd spent most of my time there. 'An open ward rather than Specialized Care.'

'There were no youngsters in Specialized Care,' said Cahane. 'I felt it would've been barbaric to subject someone of that age to the offenders housed there. We're talking murderers, rapists, necrophiles, cannibals. Psychotics judged too disturbed for the prison system and sheltered from the outside world for their sake and ours.' He massaged his empty glass. 'This was a *child*.'

'How old was he?'

He shifted in his chair. 'Young.'

'Pre-adolescent?'

'Eleven,' he said. 'You can see how we were faced with a unique set of circumstances. He had his own room in G with an atmosphere that emphasized treatment, not confinement. You remember the array of services we offered. He made good use of our programs, caused no trouble whatsoever.'

I said, 'His crime justified Specialized Care but his age complicated matters.'

He shot me a sharp look. 'You're trying to draw out details I'm not sure I'm willing to offer.'

'I appreciate your talking with me, Dr Cahane, but without details—'

'If I'm not performing to your satisfaction, feel free to walk through that door.'

I sat there.

'I apologize,' he said. 'I'm having a difficult time with this.'

'I can understand that.'

'With all due respect, Dr Delaware, you really can't understand. You're assuming I'm waffling because of medico-legal constraints but that's not it.'

He poured yet more bourbon, tossed it back. Tamped white hair, succeeded only in mussing the long, brittle strands. His eyes had pinkened. His lips vibrated. He looked like an old, wild man.

'I'm too old to care about the medico-legal system. My reservations are selfish: covering my geriatric buttocks.'

'You think you screwed up.'

'I don't think. I know, Dr Delaware.'

'With patients like that, it's often impossible to know—'

He waved me quiet. 'Thanks for the attempt at empathy but you can't know. That place was a city. The director was a do-nothing ass and that left me the mayor. The buck stopped at me.'

Tears filled his eyes.

I said, 'Still—'

'Please. Stop.' The soft voice, the sympathetic look. 'Even if you are being sincere and not using rapport to crack me open, sympathy without context churns my bowels.'

I said, 'Let's talk about him. What did he do at eleven that his home state couldn't handle?'

'Eleven,' he said, 'and every bit a child. A small, soft, prepubescent boy with a soft voice and soft little hands and soft, outwardly innocent eyes. I held his hand as I led him to the room that would be his new home. He clutched me with fear. Sweaty. "When can I go back?" I had no comforting answer but I never lie so I did what we mind-science types do when we're flummoxed. I veered into bland reassurances – he'd be comfortable, we'd take good care of him. Then I used another tactic: peppered him with questions so I wouldn't have to provide answers. What did he like to eat? What did he do for fun? He turned silent, and slumped as if he'd given up. But he marched on like a good little soldier, sat on his bed and picked up one of the books we provided and began reading. I stuck around but he ignored me. Finally, I asked if there was anything he needed and he looked up and smiled and said, "No, thank you, sir, I'm fine."'

Cahane winced. 'After that, I resorted to cowardice. Inquiring periodically about his progress but having no direct contact with him. The official reason was it wasn't part of my job description, by that time I was essentially an administrator, saw no patients whatsoever. The real reason, of course, is I had nothing to offer him, didn't want to be reminded of that.'

'He confused you.'

Instead of responding to that, he said, 'I did keep tabs on him. The consensus was that he was doing better than expected. No problems at all, really.'

Bracing his hands on the arms of his chair, he tried to get up, fell back and gave a sick smile. When I moved to help him, he said, 'I'm fine,' and struggled to his feet. 'Bathroom.' Tottering, he trudged through the doorway that bisected his bookshelves.

Ten minutes passed before a toilet flushed and sink-water burbled. When he returned, his color had deepened and his hands were trembling.

Settling back down, he said, 'So he was doing fine. Then he wasn't. Or so I was told.'

'By Marlon Quigg.'

'By a senior staff member who'd been informed by an intern who'd been informed by a teacher.' He sighed. 'Yes, your Mr Quigg, one of those breathlessly idealistic young men who thought he'd found a calling.'

'What did he report?'

'Regression,' said Cahane. 'Severe behavioral regression.'

'Back to what brought the boy to you.'

'Dear God,' said Cahane. He laughed oddly.

I said, 'Anatomical curiosity?'

His hands pressed together. He mumbled.

I said, 'What was his original crime?'

Cahane shook a finger at me. I expected reproach. The finger curled, arced back toward him, hooked in an ear. He sat back. 'He killed his mother. Shot her in the back of the head as she watched television. No one missed her at the farm where she cleaned barns because it was the weekend. She didn't socialize much, it was just her and him, their home in Kan— They lived in a trailer at the edge of the farm.'

'He stayed with her corpse.'

Nod.

I went on, 'Once he was sure she was dead he used a knife.'

'Knives,' said Cahane. 'From the kitchen. Carving tools, as well, a Christmas gift from her. So he could whittle. He used a whetstone she'd employed when she slaughtered chickens that she brought home for their dinner. She used to slaughter the birds in front of him, wasted nothing, reserved the blood for sausage. When the police finally found her, the stench was overpowering. But he didn't seem to mind, displayed no emotion at all. The police were stunned, didn't know where to take him and ended up using a locked room at a local clinic. Because the jail was filled with adult criminals, no one knew what would happen to him in that environment. He didn't protest. He was a polite boy. Later, when one of the nurses asked him why he'd stayed with the body he said he'd been trying to know her better.'

I described the wounds Shearling had left on Quigg.

He said, 'The troopers who brought him also brought crime scene photos from the trailer. When I'm feeling remorseful about something, I dial those images up and make myself downright miserable. The home was a sty, utter disorder. But not his room, his room was neat. He'd decorated the walls. Anatomical charts. Hanging everywhere. Where a child that age would obtain such things baffled me. The police hadn't been interested enough to ask but I pressed them and they made inquiries. A physician, a general practitioner to whom the boy had been taken far too infrequently, had befriended him. Because he seemed like such a *good* little boy with his interest in biology. Might very well make a *splendid* doctor, one day.'

'What do you know about his mother?'

'Reclusive, hardworking. She'd moved to town from parts unknown with a two-year-old, got the job cleaning barns and kept it. The trailer she lived in was at the far end of a wheat field. Owned by the farmer and she was allowed to live there gratis.'

'Was there evidence of premeditation?'

'He shot her while she was watching her favorite TV show. Apart from that, I couldn't say.'

'Any remorse?'

'No.'

'How was she discovered?'

'On Monday she didn't show up for work. The first time she'd ever missed, she was dependable, you could set your clock by her. She had no phone so a farmhand went to check, smelled the stench, and cracked the door and saw her. The boy was sitting next to her. Exploring. He'd fixed himself a sandwich. Peanut butter but no jelly.' He smiled. 'The details policemen put in their reports. They found a few smudges on the charts in his room, didn't know what to make of that. My guess is he was looking for confirmation. Between what was on the chart and what he'd . . . palpated. Her intestines, in particular, seemed . . . of interest.'

209

I said, 'Homeschooling himself in biology. Kansas couldn't deal so you got him.'

'Several institutions were solicited and refused. We accepted him because I was arrogant. I'm sure you're familiar with V-State's history, all those terrible things carried out in the name of medicine. By the time I got there – the reason I went there – all that had been expunged and we had a well-justified reputation for being humane.' He studied me. 'When you were there did you find indications to the contrary?'

'Not at all. I got great training.'

'Glad to hear you say that. Glad and proud . . . there was the notion that he wouldn't be safe in Kansas. Too much notoriety.'

'What caused Marlon Quigg to be concerned?'

'I'm sure you recall the beauty of our grounds.'

Apparent non sequitur. I nodded.

He said, '*Pastoral* was a term I heard bandied about quite often. Abundant flora *and* fauna.'

I said, 'Animals. He trapped them. Resumed exploring.'

'Small animals,' said Cahane. 'Analysis of the bones identified squirrels, mice, lizards. A garter snake. A stray cat. Birds, as well, we never figured out how he caught them. Caught any of them. He was clever enough to conceal his handiwork for months. Found a quiet spot behind a remote storage shed, conducted his experiments, buried the remains and tidied the ground. He'd been allowed to leave the ward for two hours a day, once in the morning, once before dinner. From the body count, we estimated he worked with one creature a day.'

Tidying. I thought of the clean dirt at Marlon Quigg's kill-site. 'How was he discovered?'

'Young Mr Quigg had grown suspicious and chose to follow him one evening. The chosen creature was a baby mole.'

'What made Quigg suspicious?'

'The boy had grown uncommunicative, even surly. Should someone else have noticed? Perhaps. What can I tell you?'

'Teachers and nurses spend a lot more time with patients than we do.'

'They do . . . In any event, faced with a new set of facts, we needed to shift our paradigm but we weren't sure how. Some of the staff, most vocally Marlon Quigg, agitated for an immediate transfer to Specialized Care. Others disagreed.'

Cahane's eyes shifted to the right. 'I listened to everyone, said I'd take some time and decide. As if I was being deliberative. The truth was I was unable to make a decision. Not only because he posed problems I was ill prepared for. My own life was in shambles. My father had just died, I'd applied for positions at Harvard and UC San Francisco, had been turned down at both places. My marriage was falling apart. There had always been issues but I'd brought them to a head by straying with another woman, a beautiful, brilliant woman but, of course, that doesn't excuse it. In a pathetic attempt to reconcile with my wife, I booked a cruise through the Panama Canal. Even under the guise of sensitivity I was being selfish, because sailing through the canal was something *I'd* always wanted.'

He picked up his glass, changed his mind, put it down hard. 'Twenty-four days on a ship, preceded by several weeks on the Outer Banks of North Carolina because Eleanor hailed from there. I was away from the hospital for forty-three days and during my absence, someone took it upon himself to deal with the boy. The psychologist who'd come to me with Quigg's original complaint. He agreed with Quigg, viewed the boy as untreatable and tainted. His term. He was a foolish, authoritarian man, too confident in his own meager abilities. I'd long had my reservations about him but his credentials, though foreign, were excellent. As a state employee he had all sorts of contractual protection, had never made an error that would jeopardize that.'

Cahane's shaky fingers entangled in his hair. 'Then, he did. And now *this* moment has arrived.'

His eyes lost focus. 'There I was, on a beautiful ship, dining, dancing. Marveling at the canal.' He poured bourbon, spilled some, studied the droplets on his sleeve. 'Dear God.'

I said, 'The boy was sent to Specialized Care.'

'If only that was all of it,' said Cahane. 'That man, that overconfident *ass*, decided – on his own, with no evidence or prior discussion – that

211

the boy's problems were primarily hormonal. *Glandular irregularity* was the way he termed it. Like something out of a Victorian medical book. He prepared papers, had the boy transported to a clinic in Camarillo where he was operated on by a surgeon who lacked the judgment to question the request.'

'Thyroidectomy,' I said.

Cahane's head jerked back. 'You already know?'

'A witness described a scar across the front of his neck.'

He gripped his glass with both hands, hurled it awkwardly across the room. It landed on the carpet, rolled. 'A complete thyroidectomy for absolutely no reason at all. After a week's recuperation, the boy was transferred to Specialized Care. The quack claimed he was looking out for the boy – trying to *regulate* his behavior because clearly nothing else had worked. But I always suspected there was an element of base, vicious revenge.'

'You like to operate, Sonny? See how it feels?'

'One of the animals the boy had chosen to explore had been the fool's unofficial pet. A stray cat that he fed from time to time. Of course he denied that this was all about *helping* the lad. I returned from my cruise, learned what had happened, was horrified, livid at my staff for not intervening. Everyone claimed they'd been unaware. I sat the bastard down, had a long talk with him, told him he was retiring and that if he ever applied for a position at another state hospital, I'd write a letter. He protested, switched to sniveling, tried to bargain, ended up making a pathetic threat: anything he'd done had been under my supervision so I wouldn't escape scrutiny. I called his bluff and he deflated. He was over the hill, anyway. Pushing eighty.'

He smiled. 'Younger than I am today. Some of us rot more quickly than others.'

'Foreign credentials,' I said. 'From where?'

'Belgium.'

My chest tightened. 'University of Louvain?'

Cahane nodded. 'A fussy little twit with a fussy, comical Teutonic accent who wore ridiculous bow ties and slicked his hair and strutted around as if he'd kissed Freud's ring.'

'What was his name?'

Unnecessary request.

Cahane said, 'Why the hell not? His name was Shacker. *Buhrrrn*-hard Shacker. Don't waste your time looking for him, he's quite dead. Suffered a heart attack the day after I fired him, collapsed right in the hospital parking lot. No doubt stress was a factor but those sandwiches he brought to staff lunches couldn't have helped. Fatty pork and the like, slathered with butter.'

'What happened to the boy?'

'Did I remove him from Special-C?' said Cahane. 'That didn't seem advisable, given signs of impending puberty and the enormity of what had been done to him. Instead, I created a custom environment for him within the walls of Special. Kept him out of a barred cell and put him in a locked room that been used for storage but had a window and a nice view of the mountains. We painted it a cheerful blue, moved in a proper bed not a cot, installed wall-to-wall carpeting, a television, a radio, a stereo, audio tapes. It was a nice room.'

'You kept him in Special-C because you expected him to grow increasingly violent.'

'And he defied my expectations, Dr Delaware. Developed into a pleasant, compliant adolescent who spent his days reading. At that point, I was a good deal more hands-on, visiting him, making sure everything was going well. I brought in an endocrinologist to monitor his Synthroid dosage. He responded well to T4 maintenance.'

'Did he receive any psychiatric treatment?'

'He didn't want any and he wasn't displaying symptoms. After what he'd been through, the last thing I wanted to do was coerce. Which isn't to say he wasn't monitored thoroughly. Every effort was made to ensure that he didn't regress.'

'No access to animals.'

'His recreational time was supervised and confined to the Special-C yard. He shot hoops, did calisthenics, walked around. He ate well, groomed himself just fine, denied any delusions or hallucinations.'

'Who supervised him?'

'Guards.'

'Any guard in particular?'

'No.'

'Do you recall a guard named Pitty or Petty?'

'I didn't know any of their names. Why?'

'The name came up.'

'With regard to?'

'A murder.'

'Quigg's?'

'Yes,' I lied.

Cahane stared. 'A murderous *team*?'

'It's possible.'

'Pitty Petty,' he said. 'No, that name isn't familiar to me.'

'What happened to the boy after the hospital closed down?'

'I was gone by then.'

'You have no idea?'

'I was living in another city.'

'Miami?'

He reached for his glass, realized he'd tossed it. Clamped his eyes shut as if in pain, opened them and stared into mine. 'Why would you suggest that?'

I said, 'Gertrude moved to Miami and men have been known to follow beautiful, brilliant women.'

'Gertrude,' he said. 'Did she ever speak of me?'

'Not by name. She did imply she was in love again.'

Another lie, blatant, manipulative. Use what you have.

Emil Cahane sighed. 'No, I moved down here, to L.A. It wasn't until years later that I showed up at her doorstep in Miami. Unannounced, hoping she was still single. I emptied my heart. She let me down easy. Said that what we'd had was wonderful but that was ancient history, there was no looking back. I was utterly crushed but pretended to be valiant, got on the next plane back here. Unable to settle myself, I moved to Colorado, took a job that proved lucrative but unsatisfying, quit, and did the exact same thing. It took four job changes before I realized I was little more than a prescribing robot. I decided to live off my pension and give away most of what I owned. My charity has extended to the point where I need to budget. Ergo, my mansion.'

He laughed. 'Ever the narcissist, I can't refrain from boasting.'

I said, 'Where would you guess the boy went after V-State shut down?'

'Many of the Specialized patients were transferred to other institutions.'

'Which ones?'

'Atascadero, Starkweather. No doubt some of them ended up in prison. That's our system, we're all about punishment.'

'Help me understand the timeline,' I said. 'What year did the boy arrive at V-State?'

'Just over twenty-five years ago.'

'Eleven years old.'

'A few months shy of twelve.'

'How long did he stay on the open ward?'

'A year and some months.'

'So he was thirteen when he got operated on and transferred.' Right around the time Marlon Quigg had left the hospital and abandoned a teaching career.

Had the switch been due to horror at what he'd witnessed behind the shed, or remorse over what his suspicions had led to?

Either way, he'd been called to pay.

I said, 'What's the boy's name?'

Cahane turned away.

'Doctor, I need a name before other people die.'

'People such as myself?'

Ever the narcissist.

'It's possible.'

'Don't worry about me, Dr Delaware. If you're correct that he killed Quigg out of revenge, I can't imagine any personal danger to myself. Because Quigg got the ball rolling, without Quigg none of the rest of it would've ensued. I, on the other hand, did my utmost to help the boy and he recognized that.'

'Providing a nice room.'

'A protective environment that provided security vis-à-vis the other patients.'

'You know he appreciated that because—'

'He thanked me.'

'When?'

'When I told him I was leaving.'

'How old was he, then?'

'Fifteen.'

'Two years in Specialized.'

'In Specialized *technically*,' he said. 'But for all purposes, he had his own private ward. He *thanked* me, Dr Delaware. He'd have no reason to harm me.'

'That assumes rationality on his part.'

'Do you have some concrete evidence that I'm in peril, Dr Delaware?'

'We're talking about a highly disturbed—'

He smirked. 'You're trying to fish out information.'

'This isn't about you,' I said. 'He needs to be stopped. Give me a name.'

I'd raised my voice, put some steel into it. For no obvious reason Cahane brightened. 'Alex, would you be so kind as to check my bathroom? I believe I've left my glasses there and I'd like to spend a pleasant afternoon with Spinoza and Leibniz. Rationality and all that.'

'First tell me—'

'Young man,' he said. 'I don't like being out of focus. Help restore some visual coherence and perhaps we'll chat further.'

I passed through the doorway to the lav. The space was cramped, white tiles crisscrossed by grubby grout. A threadbare gray towel hung from a pebbled glass shower door. The smell was bay rum, cheap soap, faulty plumbing.

No eyeglasses anywhere.

Something white and peaked sat atop the toilet tank.

Piece of paper folded, origami-style, the folds uneven, the flaps wrinkled by unsteady hands. Some sort of small squat animal.

Serrated edges said the paper had been ripped from a spiral notebook. I spotted the book in a ragged wicker basket to the left of the commode, along with a tract on philosophy and several old copies of *Smithsonian*.

Every page of the notebook was blank.

I unfolded. Black ballpoint block printing centered the page, made ragged by several hesitation breaks.

GRANT HUGGLER
(The Curious Boy)

I hurried back to Cahane's living room, note in hand. The big leather chair was empty. Cahane was nowhere in sight.

To the left of the bathroom was a closed door.

I knocked.

No answer.

'Dr Cahane?'

'I need to sleep.'

I turned the knob. Locked. 'Is there anything else you can tell me?'

'I need to sleep.'

'Thank you.'

'I need to sleep.'

31

ALEX SHIMOFF's second drawing aired on the six o'clock news. A bored talking-head noted the suspect's 'winter coat' and a possible history of 'thyroid issues'. Total broadcast time: thirty-two seconds.

I froze the frame. This sketch was lifelike, the broad face impassive.

This was the man I'd seen huddled in a corner booth at Bijou, inches from a group of moms and tots.

Robin said, 'He looks blank. Like something's missing. Or maybe Shimoff didn't have enough to work with.'

'He did.'

She looked at me. I'd already told her some of what Cahane had related. Took it no further.

Blanche studied each of us. We sat there.

Robin said, 'Eleven years old,' and walked out of the room.

Milo'd been off the radar all day but he phoned about an hour after the broadcast. My searches using Grant Huggler's name had proved fruitless.

He said, 'Catch it? Big improvement, no? His Exaltedness pulled strings because "shit needs turning over so it won't stink worse than it already is". Anyway, we've got a piece of fine art, even Shimoff's satisfied. The tip lines just started to light up, so far it's fewer than we got the first time, maybe Joe Public's played out. But Moe caught one worth looking into. Anonymous female caller says a guy fitting Shearling's

218

description received his thyroid prescription at a clinic in Hollywood, she hung up when Reed asked her which one. A place in Hollywood fits a guy on the streets and puts him in proximity to Lem Eccles. All the clinics Petra called are closed until tomorrow, she'll follow up and if God's feeling generous we'll get a name.'

'God loves you,' I said. 'His name's Grant Huggler.'

'*What?*'

I recapped the meeting with Cahane.

He said, 'He leaves it for you to find in the damn bathroom? What was that, pretending he wasn't actually a snitch?'

'He left it folded like origami. Setting up a little production but distancing himself from it. He's a complicated guy, spends a lot of energy on self-justification.'

'Is he a reliable guy?'

'I believe what he told me.'

'Grant Huggler,' he said. 'Eleven years old a quarter century ago makes him thirty-six, which fits our witness reports. Can't be too many with that name, I'm plugging him in now – well looky here, male Cauc, six feet, two thirty-six, picked up five years ago in Morro Bay for trespassing, possible intent to commit burglary . . . a doctor's office, that probably means they nabbed him just as he broke in to score dope . . . which fits with a street guy with psych issues . . . no prison sentence, he got pled down to jail time served . . . here's the mug shot. Long hair, scruffy beard but the face behind all that pelt looks kinda chubby . . . talk about weird eyes. Dead, like he's staring into the Great Abyss.'

'No busts before then?'

'Nope, that's it. Not much of a criminal history for someone who's now a serial gutter.'

I said, 'Morro Bay's not far from Atascadero, which is one of the places dangerous patients were transferred when V-State shut down. A first offense five years ago could mean he was locked up until then. If so, he's been incarcerated for twenty years.'

'Plenty of time to stew.'

'And to fantasize.'

'He'd be treated with meds, right?'

'Possibly.'

'I'm asking that because if it was dope he was after, maybe he got hooked on something, tried to boost from a doctor's office. Though once he got out, wouldn't he be sent to some kind of outpatient facility where he could score legally?'

'That assumes he'd show up,' I said. 'And few patients crave psychotropics, something recreational would be more likely. I'm betting he was noncompliant about aftercare, if for no other reason than he'd want to avoid waiting rooms.'

'Little medical phobia, huh? Yeah, getting your neck sliced for no reason can do that to you – so maybe he was trying to swipe *thyroid* meds because he hated waiting rooms.'

'Anxiety about medical settings could explain being so tense in Glenda Usfel's scan room. Toss in some hormonal irritability, add Usfel's aggressive nature, and you'd have a volatile situation. But he didn't react impulsively, just the opposite. He bided his time, planned, stalked her, took action. I suppose spending most of your life in a highly structured environment could instill patience and an interesting sense of focus.'

'Losing an organ he didn't have to lose,' he said. 'Doing that to a kid. Barbaric. Now he's out, practicing his own brand of surgery.'

'Avenging old wrongs and some new ones,' I said. 'I'd like to know the name of the surgeon who operated on him. All Cahane remembered was that the office was in Camarillo.'

'Another victim before he got to L.A.? No similars have shown up anywhere.'

'One person who did meet an interesting end was the psychologist who orchestrated the thyroidectomy. When Cahane got back, he lost no time firing him and the following day he dropped dead in the hospital parking lot. Apparent heart attack. Sound familiar?'

'Lem Eccles's wife – Rosetta. Oh, Jesus. Eccles was nuts but not wrong?'

'There's more, Big Guy. The psychologist's name was Bernhard Shacker.'

'Same as the guy who analyzed Vita for Well-Start? What the hell's going on? Some sort of identity theft?'

'Has to be,' I said. 'The man I spoke to was in his late forties and the real Shacker was nearly eighty when he keeled over. The real Shacker was Belgian and the diploma I saw in that office was from a university in Belgium. When Shacker – the guy calling himself Shacker – saw me looking at it, he said something about his Catholic phase. Photoshopping fancy-looking paper isn't any big deal.'

'A scamster making it in B.H.?'

'I'm wondering if his transgressions go beyond practicing without a license. Because pulling off the murders would be a lot easier with two people involved.'

'Where'd *that* come from?'

'Eccles's fear of a guard at V-State. Huggler may be your prototypical odd loner but that doesn't preclude someone from gaining his trust. Someone he met while at V-State.'

'Another lunatic?' he said. 'Working as a guard? Now he's palming himself off as a shrink? Good Lord.'

'Faking it would be a lot easier for someone who'd worked on psych wards long enough to soak up the terminology. Eccles was confined at V-State the same time as Huggler. Maybe in Specialized Care because he'd gotten overly aggressive with a judge. There's no reason to think he didn't continue being his usual combative, obnoxious self. That got him on a guard's bad side. But the guard was too clever to face off against Eccles, took it out on Eccles's only visitor. The woman Eccles considered his wife. She really was poisoned and when he got away with it, he did the same to Bernhard Shacker.'

'Get on my bad side, you die,' he said. 'Another touchy one?'

'Common ground for a relationship. Cahane described Huggler as cooperative, compliant. Even so, his recreational time was supervised. For *his* safety. That meant being supervised by a guard whenever he left his room. What if it was the same guard each time and a bond

221

developed? The man passing himself off as Shacker would've been in his twenties back then, perfect age to be a mentor to an isolated adolescent. The bond was solidified forever when he eliminated the man who'd robbed Huggler of a vital organ. And the bond could've remained strong enough for the mentor to travel with Huggler – seeking out a job at Atascadero when Huggler got transferred there.'

'And now they're traveling together.'

'For at least five years,' I said. 'If that's the case, Huggler's not crashing on the street. He's living securely with his self-appointed guardian. Who's making a nice living in a Beverly Hills office. And who could be sending Huggler to inflict his particular brand of curiosity upon those who've gotten on *his* nerves. Case in point, Vita. Huggler witnessed her tormenting the Banforth family but I don't see him as out for truth and justice. More likely he was already at Bijou because he'd been stalking Vita for a while. And the reason for that was Vita had offended Fake Dr Shacker. I know that because he told me she'd just about come out and called him a quack, no one had ever treated him that way. He was bothered. It was the only time he dropped his professional guard.'

'Doing her mean thing,' he said. 'No pity from Pitty. Hold on.' *Click click.* 'No Shacker or Pitty in the files . . . not at DMV, either . . . all I'm finding is the office address on Bedford.'

I said, 'Let's work out a plan tonight, bop over there tomorrow.'

'Analyze the analyst,' he said. 'He's that dangerous, we should bring an army.'

'I figured I'd talk to him, you'd be there for backup.'

'What's your angle?'

'Does he remember anything else about Vita? If it feels right, I'll probe deeper about the quack issue. If not, I'll bring up additional victims, did he have any theories? Get people talking, they make mistakes.'

'Let me call Petra, see what she thinks.'

Six minutes later:

'Poor kid was having some face-time with her lovey-dove at L'Oise in Brentwood. Not far from your place, you mind hosting us in say an hour?'

'No prob.'

'Check with Robin.'

'She'll be fine with it.'

'How do you know?'

'She loves you.'

'Rare lapse of taste on her part,' he said. 'An hour.'

32

PETRA RANG the bell, white paper bag in hand. She had on a sleeveless navy silk sheath, red sandals with heels, strategic pearls, darker-than-usual lipstick. First time I'd seen her in a dress.

Robin said, 'Date night interrupted?'

'Woman plans, God laughs.'

Petra bent to pet Blanche. Blanche rolled on her back, earned a massage.

Petra said, 'We made it through the first course, I took dessert to go.'

I said, 'Want some coffee?'

'Strong, if you don't mind.'

I brewed Kenyan, kicking up the octane. Robin and Petra settled at the table and Petra pulled plastic-topped boxes out of the bag. Assortment of cookies, four slabs of chocolate cake.

Robin said, 'That's more like catering.'

'I brought for everyone, seeing as you guys are donating home and hearth to the dark side.'

A heavy hand pounded the door.

Milo trudged in bearing a brown bag, greasy, flecked with powdered sugar. He scowled. 'Who mugged a pastry chef?'

Robin sniffed the air. 'This Magi brings churros?'

'It seemed like a good idea.' His eyes fixed on the chocolate cake.

'Flourless,' said Petra.

'Got nothing against flour, but why not?'

He put the churros aside, was ingesting cake before his haunches

224

met his chair. Blanche waddled over and nuzzled his ankle. He said, 'Yeah, yeah,' and conceded a rub behind her ear. She purred like a cat. 'Yeah, yeah, again.'

Robin took her cup and headed for the back door. Blanche followed. 'Good luck.'

No one invited her to stay. They like her.

Petra said, 'This fake psychologist is Huggler's confederate, as well as the Pitty character Eccles claimed was stalking him?'

Milo said, 'Working assumption, kid, but it feels right. He steals one identity, why not another? Can't find any "Pitty" in the file, so maybe it's a nickname. Or Eccles was totally delusional and we're wrong.'

She turned to me. 'How did fake-o come across when you talked to him?'

'Pleasant, professional, the right paper on the wall. The only time he stepped out of the role was when he complained that Vita had implied he was a quack. At the time, I took it as collegial banter.'

'Looks like she was right. Sometimes I wonder if those nasty people don't have special insights. Maybe because they see everyone as a threat.'

Milo said, 'But look what happens after they get elected.'

'Good point.' She turned to me. 'You see Vita insulting him as the reason she got killed?'

I nodded. 'His trigger, Huggler's fun. We have two people working in concert, with layers of pathology building on each other. I'm not sure either of *them* understands it fully. At the base is Huggler's fascination with human plumbing and no, I can't tell you how that developed. It's normal for children to wonder how their bodies work and kids who hold on to that curiosity sometimes channel it professionally – become mechanics, engineers, anatomists, surgeons. For a few, interest grows to obsession and gets tangled up with sexuality in a really bad way.'

She said, 'Dahmer, Nilsen, Gein.'

'All of whom were described as odd children but none of whom had especially horrific childhoods,' I said. 'Huggler killing his mother at eleven suggests a less-than-optimal upbringing, but it doesn't come close to explaining the act. Whatever the reason, something short-circuited in his brain and he began pairing sexual gratification with plunging his hands into visceral muck. Being locked up for most of his life made him a prime target for observation and I'm betting one of his sharpest and most frequent observers wasn't a doctor. It was a young man working a low-status job. Someone who'd never be invited to staff meetings but craved authority and had the time to pick up all sorts of interesting things.'

'Doctors come and go,' she said, 'but guards stay on the ward for eight-hour shifts.'

'And this guard's ability to sniff out depravity could've been fine-tuned because he could relate to it on a personal level.'

'His own kinks.'

Milo said, 'Psychopath pheromones. One beast smells another.'

I said, 'Pitty, or whatever his name really is, studied Huggler long enough to become a Huggler scholar. He befriended the boy and a mentor-trainee relationship developed. The boy had finally met someone who appreciated his urges instead of condemning them. Maybe it was Pitty who caught small animals for Huggler to play with.'

'What was the payoff for him?'

'Adulation, subservience, or maybe just having someone like himself to relate to. Given Huggler's age and his apparent adjustment, there was a good chance he'd get out when he became an adult. Then Marlon Quigg ruined everything by exercising his own powers of observation, Huggler was subjected to unnecessary surgery and got put in Specialized Care. If I'm right about his only being out for five or so years, he was shipped off to another hospital, probably Atascadero, and got thoroughly institutionalized. A relationship with someone who claimed to care about him would've been his only link to reality.'

'Pitty moves with him, Pitty's reality becomes his?' said Petra. She shook her head. 'That surgery, talk about institutional abuse. I guess you could see a tit-for-tat: they cut his neck, he breaks other people's necks. But then why haven't we seen any throat-slashing? Wouldn't that be a more direct symbolic revenge?'

'I could theorize for you all day – maybe he chose to avoid slashing because it cut too close to home. So to speak. The truth is we may never know what's been stoking Huggler's engine.'

Milo said, 'V-State closes, mentor follows mentee, mentee finally gets out, mentor turns him into a lethal weapon. That's your layer two?'

I nodded. 'A weapon aimed at people who anger each or both of them. Pitty might not want to soil his own hands but if he's the brittle, power-craving narcissist I think he is, he'd crave payback for slights the rest of us would shrug off.'

Petra said, 'Are we talking something sexual between the two of them?'

'Maybe but not necessarily. It's possible neither of them has anything close to a conventional sex life.'

'People irk me,' Milo said, 'I sic Lil Buddy at them and they become anatomy projects.'

I said, 'And Lil Buddy loves the assignment. That's layer three: a perfect partnership that satisfies both of their needs. Let's start with Vita Berlin: obnoxious, combative, spreading misery wherever she went. Like most bullies she had a keen sense about who'd make a safe victim and the man she knew as Dr Shacker seemed perfect: physically unprepossessing, outwardly mild, and a psychologist – we're expected to be patient, nonjudgmental. Think of the movies you've seen about therapists: most show them as absentminded wimps. Vita may have been forced into sessions with the little wuss in order to collect her insurance settlement but she was damn sure going to have fun along the way. Right from the start she resisted, needled him, finally came out and let him know she thought he was a charlatan. Unfortunately for her, he's anything but nonjudgmental. I wouldn't be surprised if the death sentence was passed the moment the words left her mouth.'

'Call in Huggler,' said Milo. 'Easy hit because fake-o-Shacker had her address, phone number, knew what she looked like.'

I said, 'And despite her resistance she might've given out some personal details during the evaluation that also made stalking her easier. Huggler was spotted lurking near her garbage cans. My guess is he went through them, found her empties, knew she was a serious solitary drinker. If he found pizza boxes, that would also have helped set up the kill. In general, her routine was easy to learn because she rarely went out except for shopping and occasional meals at Bijou.'

'Think Pitty was in on the kill?'

'It's possible he held a gun on the victims, served as a lookout. Two actors would explain no sign of struggle, even from someone as aggressive as Vita.'

Petra said, 'The pizza box ruse was still a gamble, given Vita's temper. What if she was sober enough to make a ruckus?'

I said, '"Oops, gee sorry, ma'am, wrong address." Huggler leaves and they wait for a second chance.'

Milo said, 'Eccles snoozing in the alley would've been a piece of cake. Same for Quigg.'

Petra said, 'If we're right about Quigg, he'd have been *the* major target – the person to blame for everything bad that happened to Huggler. With that kind of rage, why wait five years to get him?'

'Maybe there were other targets just as important – like Shacker – and they're going down a list.'

Milo said, 'Like the doc who actually did the throat-cutting.'

'Oh,' I said.

They looked at me.

'Huggler was busted for trespassing behind a medical office. The police assumed he was about to break in and steal dope. But what if Huggler had a more personal connection to the doctor?'

Milo said, 'Stalking the surgeon. Problem with that is the arrest was in Morro Bay and Huggler's surgery took place a hundred miles away in Camarillo.'

'People move.'

'The same surgeon just happened to live near two hospitals where Huggler was confined?'

I thought about that. 'Maybe Huggler was taken to that particular surgeon because of an arrangement with V-State – some sort of consultancy. When V-State closed the guy went for the same thing at Atascadero.'

Petra said, 'A guy who couldn't make it in private practice. Maybe he had his own issues.'

I said, 'Obviously, he had ethical issues.'

'Going for government dole,' said Milo. 'I guess anything's possible.'

She produced her iPhone, poked and scrolled.

Milo said, 'What's on that?'

'My notes.'

'You're totally digital?'

'I copy stuff from the murder book so I can follow up at home . . . here we go. Huggler was busted at Bayview Surgical Group of San Luis Obispo County. It's the right specialty, isn't it?'

We shifted to my office and I ran a search on Bayview, found no current listings. But a four-year-old item from a San Luis Obispo TV station featured the disappearance of 'local surgeon Dr Louis Wainright, staff member of Bayview Surgical Group. Wainright, 54, was last seen hiking in the foothills above San Luis Obispo with his dog 11 days ago. The doctor's SUV was found in a park service lot but neither he nor his German shorthaired pointer Ned has been seen since.'

Additional hits on the disappearance described futile searches conducted by law enforcement and a cadre of Eagle Scouts. A picture of Wainright showed him grim, gray-haired, and bearded with a strong jaw and outdoor skin.

'Dr Hemingway,' said Petra. 'Walking with his dog, just like Quigg. And our boy has a thing for animals.'

Milo said, 'Let's make sure Wainright didn't eventually show up.'

He phoned the Morro Bay Police Department. A desk officer named Lucchese remembered Wainright because the surgeon had once removed a fatty tumor from his back.

'Good surgeon?'

'Not really,' said Lucchese. 'Left me a lump scar. No bedside manner, either, just get in there and slice. Only reason I used him is he had a contract with the union.'

'Any theories about what happened to him?'

'That was some pretty rough terrain he was climbing. Best guess is he broke a leg or fainted or had a heart attack or a stroke or whatever, lay there without anyone noticing and either died outright or from dehydration or hypothermia. Eventually he probably got taken care of by mountain lions or kye-oats or both.'

'Human suspects were never on the radar?'

'No reason for them to be. Why's this interest you, Lieutenant?'

'A former patient of Wainright's is a suspect in a killing down here.'

'That so. Who?'

'Former inmate at Ventura State in Camarillo, back when Wainright worked there.'

'A nutter? We got plenty of those over at Atascadero and I guess one of them could've known Wainright from there. But those guys never get out, they're the least of our problems.' He chuckled. 'Best therapy: lock 'em up and toss the key.'

'Wainright worked at Atascadero?'

'Part-time,' said Lucchese. 'Guess he had a contract there, too. But there were no escapes around the time he went missing, no alerts, nothing. I'll ask around for you but I won't learn anything.'

Milo thanked him and clicked off.

Petra said, 'Oh, my.'

I said, 'Shacker was first, then as soon as Huggler got out, they went after Wainright. The trespassing bust delayed but didn't deter them. A year later, Wainright was dispatched.'

'Easy to stalk the guy while he hiked,' said Milo. 'Why would he fear a vengeful patient from almost twenty years before?'

'Even Huggler's arrest wouldn't have alerted him. If he even remembered – or knew – Huggler's name. Morro Bay PD figured Huggler for an addict out to score, no reason to I.D. him to Wainright after they picked him up. Even if they had, why would Wainright connect a grown man to a kid he'd operated on years before?'

'Surgeon becomes patient,' said Petra. 'God, how many others are out there?'

Milo said, 'If Huggler and his mentor could wait to handle Wainright and Quigg and whoever else they might've done in between, why'd Shacker have to go right away?'

I said, 'Shacker was a solo act by Pitty so Pitty could prove himself to Huggler and cement their bond. For that, he needed a quick, dramatic result.'

'Look what I did for you, Little Buddy,' said Petra.

'There was also time pressure: Shacker was elderly and he'd just been fired, meaning he would've left town. So Pitty reverted to something that had worked for him a few months before.'

'Poisoning, as in Eccles's lady friend,' said Petra. 'Two people drop dead within moments of leaving the hospital. What kind of poison could be calibrated that precisely?'

I said, 'It wouldn't have to be poison, per se. With a man of Shacker's age and dietary habits, a huge dose of a strong heart stimulant could do the trick. As an alcoholic and a cocaine abuser, Eccles's wife would also be vulnerable to cardiac insult.'

Milo said, 'No poison, per se, means nothing on the tox screen.'

He got up, paced, tugged an earlobe. 'Everything you're saying makes sense, Alex, but unless one of these two monsters confesses, I don't see Men*tor* going down for anything other than I.D. theft and practicing without a license. And Men*tee* could get away clean. He's left no trace evidence and all we have on him are ambiguous sightings and a V-sign he shot to John Banforth that could be interpreted any number of ways.'

I said, 'Find them and separate them. Huggler could be crackable.'

'Your mouth FedExed to God's ears,' said Petra. 'I've got another timing issue: if Pitty got slimed one too many times by Eccles and took it out on Eccles's wife, why wait all these years to get the slimer himself?'

'Maybe he figured he'd get more immediate pleasure from watching Eccles suffer than from dispatching him. From having Eccles know what had happened and being powerless to do anything about it.'

Milo said, 'Who the hell's gonna pay attention to some lunatic's ravings?'

I said, 'Pitty could've planned to do Eccles after Eccles was discharged but Eccles went underground and Pitty couldn't find

231

him. As to why didn't Eccles try to get back at Pitty, maybe his mental illness got in the way — too disturbed and scattered to devise a plan.'

'Or,' said Petra, 'he was scared and got the heck out of Dodge.'

Milo said, 'Then Pitty just happens to spot Eccles years later in Hollyweird?'

I said, 'It's not that big a coincidence. You've got a tip placing Huggler at a Hollywood clinic. The neighborhood's a magnet for drifters and short-term residents. With Shacker renting a Beverly Hills office, I've been figuring him for a nice crib. But maybe he economizes in order to afford that office and he and Huggler are bunking in some pay-by-the-week.'

'On my turf,' said Petra. 'Thrilling.'

Milo said, 'We could write screenplays all night but at this point we don't even know if Huggler was actually transferred to Atascadero, let alone Pitty or whatever his name is moving to be with him. So let's stake out this fake shrink, nab him on I.D. theft, and see what shakes out. B.H. business district is small, we'll need to be subtle, meaning more sets of eyes, extra-low profile. I'm gonna have Moe and Sean with me and whoever B.H. wants to send, assuming they cooperate. Wouldn't mind Raul, either, if it's okay with you.'

Petra made the call. 'Done.'

I said, 'Did you manage to get hold of Eccles's last arrest report?'

'Sure did and the complainant wasn't named Pitty or close. Something Stewart.'

'What'd he list for an address?'

'You really think he could be Pitty?'

'Something about him got Eccles hyped up.'

Back to her iPhone. 'Mr Loyal Steward. With a *d*.' She read off a phone number and a street address and her eyes got tight. 'Main Street, City of Ventura. That's commercial, isn't it?'

'It's also two towns north of Camarillo.'

Her aerial GPS confirmed it. 'Big old parking lot, guys.'

She checked the phone number Loyal Steward had given to the

arresting officers. Inactive, and a call to the phone company revealed it had never been in use.

'Loyal Steward,' said Milo. 'That's gotta be phony.'

I said, 'It's not a name. It's how he sees himself.'

33

Milo played database piano on my computer with the grim concentration of a lonely kid at an arcade.

No residential listings, driver's license, or criminal record for Loyal Steward.

He said, 'Big surprise,' and called Deputy Chief Maria Thomas. She was miffed about being interrupted at home and balked at disturbing the chief. Milo began with tact, eased into bland persistence, ended up with barely veiled menace. Like a lot of bureaucrats, she had a weak will when confronted with dedication.

Within minutes, the chief had phoned Milo and Milo was doing a lot of blank-faced listening. Soon after, a senior Beverly Hills detective named Eaton rang in.

Milo started to explain.

Eaton said, 'It came straight from my boss, like I'm gonna say no?'

When Milo hung up, Petra said, 'Maybe one day *I* can be a *loo*-tenant.'

'That's like wishing for wrinkles, kid.'

Six the following morning found eight people surveilling the office building on Bedford Drive where a yet-to-be-identified man pretended to be Dr Bernhard Shacker. Downtown Beverly Hills was yawning itself awake, vanilla swirls of daylight scratching their way through a gray-satin sky. A few delivery trucks rumbled by. But for a scatter of joggers and put-upon citizens ruled by the intestinal tracts of fluffy dogs, the sidewalks were bare.

BHPD knew the building, couldn't recall a problem there since three years ago when a plastic surgeon and his wife had been hauled off for mutual domestic violence.

'They start whaling on each other in the waiting room,' said B.H. detective Roland Munoz. 'Anorexic women with stitched-up faces are sitting there, freaking out.'

An hour into the watch, a custodian unlocked the building's brass front doors. Tenants had keys and the alarm code and could come and go 24/7 but none had appeared after nine the night before when Munoz and Detective Richard Eaton had earned overtime watching the last trickle of weary health-care providers, none of them Shacker, exiting. Between nine and this morning, hourly drive-bys by B.H. patrol cars had spotted no activity in or around the structure. Not an ironclad assurance, but confidence was high that the identity thief had yet to appear.

The rear alley door was also key-operated and Sean Binchy watched it from the front seat of a borrowed Con Edison van, accompanied by Munoz, a jovial man whose mood was even rosier because he'd rather be doing this than responding to false intruder calls phoned in by hysterical rich people. Lost cats, too; last week a woman on North Linden Drive had 911'd on 'Melissa'. Making her sound like a human in jeopardy, not an Angora up a tree.

The building offered no on-site parking but doctors and their staffs got a discount at the private pay facility two doors south that opened at six thirty. This early, plenty of metered street parking remained available but only seven vehicles had seized the opportunity. Milo ran the tags. Nothing interesting.

He and I were stationed on the east side of Bedford Drive, twenty yards north of the brass doors, in a silver, black-windowed Mercedes 500 that he'd borrowed from the LAPD confiscation lot. The former owner was an Ecstasy dealer from Torrance. The interior was spotless black calfskin, the brightwork polished steel, the white bunny-rabbit headliner and matching carpeting sucked free of lint. A strong shampoo fragrance lingered, mixed in with the smell of honey-roasted peanuts.

Milo had told me to 'dress B.H.'.

'Meaning?'

'Knock yourself out so you blend in with the hoohahs.'

The best I could come up with was jeans and a gray wool pullover emblazoned with an Italian designer's surname. The sweater was a ten-year-old gift from the sister I never saw. Other people's names on my clothing make me feel like an impostor; this was the first time I'd worn it.

Milo's costume consisted of a royal-blue velour tracksuit piped with thick strands of silver lamé resembling rivulets of mercury. Oversized designer logo on the sleeves and on one thigh, some sort of hip-hop artiste I'd never heard of. The outfit managed to be too large for him, settled in folds, tucks, and wrinkles a Shar-Pei would covet.

I'd controlled myself but now I said, 'Congrats.'

'For what?'

'High-bidding on Suge Knight's storage bin.'

'Hmmph. Got it at the Barneys sale. VIP night, if you will. In case you find that relevant.'

'My job, everything's relevant. How'd you get vipped?'

'Store manager was in a car crash, Rick saved his nose.'

A slim, dark figure zipped past us, heading north.

Petra dressed in black bicycle pants and pullover neared completion of her second square-block jog. The role Milo had assigned her was a variant of her normal morning routine and she ran like she meant it.

Up near Wilshire, a grubby homeless person in shapeless gray-brown tatters shuffled, bobbed his ski-capped head, gazed up at the morning sun, jaywalked east.

Moe Reed had volunteered for that part.

Milo'd said, 'Clean-cut kid like you?'

'I did it last year, El Tee. Checking out a bad guy in Hollywood.'

Petra had said, 'He was convincing, trust me.'

'Fine,' said Milo. 'We'll get you some bum duds.'

'No need,' said Reed. 'Still have the threads from last year.'

'Wash 'em?'

'Sure.'

'Then you won't be authentic, but hey, go for it.'

Observers Seven and Eight were two female B.H. officers patrolling in a black-and-white on a ten-minute circuit. Shimoff's second drawing of Grant 'Shearling' Huggler was taped to their dashboard along with a description of faux-Dr-Shacker that I'd supplied. Nothing unusual about a conspicuous police presence in Beverly Hills. Response time was three minutes and citizens liked seeing their protectors.

By six thirty, the pay lot had opened and cars trickled in. Thirteen more street spots had been taken. Every tag checked out clean except for a woman with an address on South Doheny Drive who owed over six hundred bucks in parking tickets. This morning, her Lexus was being driven by an Asian woman in a white housekeeper's uniform doing a pickup at the deli on the corner.

No sign of either suspect and that remained the status by eight a.m. when patients began showing up at the brass doors.

Same for nine a.m., ten, ten thirty.

Milo yawned, turned to me. 'When you were in practice when did you start work?'

'Depended,' I said.

'On what?'

'The patient load, emergencies, court. Maybe all he does is insurance work. That could mean easy hours.'

'Insurance companies hire a murderous fraud.' He smiled. 'Maybe he put that on his application.'

He got out, loped to the deli, ordered something, and scanned the three customers at the counter. A few minutes later, he returned with bagels and overboiled coffee. We ate and drank and lapsed into silence.

At eleven a.m., he stretched and yawned again and said, 'Enough.' Radioing Reed, he instructed the young detective to alter his bum-shamble from Wilshire to Bedford where he could keep an eye on the building's entrance. Then he informed everyone else that he was going inside to have a look.

I said, 'I'll go, too. I can point him out to you.'

He thought about that. 'Doubt he's in there but sure.'

As we walked through the blue-carpeted, oak-paneled hallway, his oversized tracksuit flapped, eliciting a few amused looks.

My designer sweater didn't seem overly humorous but two young women in nurses' uniforms smiled at me then broke into muted giggles as I passed.

Just a coupla wannabe clowns providing comic relief.

We took the stairs to the second floor where Milo cracked the door and scanned the corridor.

Suite 207 was just a few feet away.

The nameplate on Shacker's door was gone.

He went and had a close look, waved me over. The glue outlines surrounding the sign were visible. Recent removal.

'Shimoff's too good an artist,' he said. 'Bastard saw his prodigy's face on TV, burrowed straight underground.'

He radioed the detail, told them the suspects were unlikely to show but to stay in place, anyway. We took the stairs back down, searched the directory for the building's manager, found no listing. A clerk at the ground-floor *Dispensing Apothecarie* had a business card on file.

Nourzadeh Realty, headquartered in a building on Camden Drive, right around the corner. The name on the card was the managing partner, Ali Nourzadeh. He wasn't in and Milo spoke to a secretary.

Ten minutes later, a young woman in a red cowl-neck cashmere sweater studded with rhinestones at neck and cuffs, black tights, and three-inch heels arrived with a ring of keys big enough to burglarize a suburb.

'I'm Donna Nourzadeh. What seems to be the problem?'

Milo flashed his card, pointed to the glue-frame. 'Unless your signs tend to fall off, looks like your tenant cut out.'

'Darn,' she said. 'You're sure?'

'No, but let's have a look inside.'

'I don't know if I can do that.'

'Why not?'

'The tenant has rights.'

'Not if he abandoned the office.'

'We don't know that.'

'We will once we go in.'

'Hmm.'

'Donna, how long has Dr Shacker been renting?'

'Seven months.'

Shortly before he'd screened Vita Berlin using fake credentials. Maybe he'd offered Well-Start a bargain fee that got them slavering.

Milo said, 'Was he a good tenant?'

Donna Nourzadeh thought about that. 'We never heard any complaints from him and he paid six months up front.'

'How much was that?'

'Twenty-four thousand.'

Milo eyed the keys.

Donna Nourzadeh said, 'He did something?'

'Quite likely.'

'You don't need a warrant?'

'Like I said, if Dr Shacker left prematurely, you control the premises and all I need is your permission.'

'Hmm.'

'Call your boss,' said Milo. 'Please.'

She complied, spoke in Farsi, selected a key, and moved toward the lock. Milo stilled her with a big index finger atop a small wrist. 'Better I do it.'

'What do I do in the meantime?'

'Other business.'

He took the key. She hurried away.

The tiny white waiting room was unchanged from the time I'd seen it. Same trio of chairs, identical magazines.

Same new-age music, some sort of digitalized harp solo streaming at low volume.

The red light on the two-bulb panel was lit. In session.

Milo freed his 9mm, approached the door to the inner office and knocked.

No answer. He rapped again, tried the doorknob. It rotated with a squeal.

Stepping to the left of the door, he called out, 'Doctor?'

No answer.

Louder: 'Dr Shacker?'

The music switched to flute, a nasal arpeggio, vibrating with the subtlety of a human voice.

An unhappy human, keening, whining.

Milo nudged the door another inch with his toe. Waited. Afforded himself another half inch and peeked through.

Cherry-sized lumps sprouted along his jawline. His teeth clicked as he holstered his gun.

He motioned me to follow him in.

34

DRAPES WERE drawn on the window overlooking Bedford Drive. Low-voltage light from a desk lamp turned the pale aqua walls grayish blue.

The walnut desk was bare. The same diplomas remained affixed to the walls.

He had no further need for them, had moved on to another role.

In reduced light, the cubist print of fruit and bread looked drab and cheap. The Scandinavian chairs had been nudged closer together, set for an intimate chat.

One chair was bare.

Something occupied its mate.

Milo flicked on the ceiling light and we had a look.

A mason jar filled with clear, greasy liquid was propped against the chair-back.

Floating inside were two grayish round things.

Milo gloved up, kneeled, lifted the jar. One of the orbs shifted, exposing additional color: pale blue dot centered by a black sphere. Pinkish strands streamed like tiny worms from the other side.

He shifted the jar again and the second orb bounced and turned, showed the same decoration, the same fuzzy pink filaments.

A pair of eyeballs. Human. Oversized pearl onions bobbing in a horrific cocktail.

Milo put the jar where it had originally sat, called for a crime scene crew, priority.

As he radioed the others, I noticed a discordant detail across the room.

The largest diploma, placed dead center behind the desk chair, had been altered. When I'd seen it, it had verified Bernhard Shacker's doctorate from the University of Louvain.

Now a sheet of white paper blocked that boast.

I walked over.

Glue marks were evident at the periphery of the glass, bubbling the underside of the sheet.

Blank, white rectangle, but for a single message:

?

35

A CORONER'S investigator named Rubenfeld took possession of the jar.

'Never seen that before,' he said. 'Always a first time.'

Milo said, 'Any way to tell how long they've been in there?'

Rubenfeld squinted. 'If the fluid was real old I'd expect more discoloration, but can't really say.' He bobbled the jar gently. 'The severed ends are a little faded out — that's small blood vessels you're seeing, look like feathers . . . the eyes themselves seem a little rubbery, no? That could mean they've been preserved for a while, could be lab specimens.'

'They're specimens all right,' said Milo, 'but not from a lab.'

Rubenfeld licked his lips. 'Giving time estimates of body parts really isn't my pay grade, Lieutenant. Maybe Dr Jernigan will be able to tell you.' He glanced back at the chair. 'One thing you can be pretty sure of. That blue in the irises, your victim's probably Caucasian.'

'Thanks for the tip,' said Milo. Well before the crime scene crew arrived, he'd obtained a readout of Dr Louis Wainright's last recorded California driver's license. Blue eyes, no need for corrective lenses.

Rubenfeld swung the carrier gently. 'Least I don't need a gurney.'

Milo got the cleaning schedule from Donna Nourzadeh. The suites were tended to weekly by a crew of five, but this week there'd been a delay and no office had been touched for three nights.

'Scheduling issues,' she said. 'Now, if you don't need me . . .'

Milo let her go, turned to me. 'Sometime during the last seventy-two hours, the bastard planted the jar.'

I thought: he'd displayed the eyes, expecting to be discovered. Left the question mark behind to confirm his connection to the murders.

Boasting. Unworried; because he was on to a new phase?

Whatever his intentions, the man who called himself Shacker had cleaned up with care, vacuuming the rugs so thoroughly that the crime scene techs pulled up only a few crumbs. Hard surfaces had been wiped free of prints, including in places where you'd expect to find them.

The crime scene crew began to lose energy as it went through the final motions.

Then one of the techs said, 'Hey!' and brandished a tape she'd pulled off the glass fronting one of the diplomas.

Shacker's date-altered psychology license, positioned to the left of the papered-over diploma, Photoshopped on good-quality paper. Even up close, the forgery was convincing.

The tech held the tape up to the light. Nice clear pattern of ridges and swirls lifted from the upper right-hand corner of the pane.

'Looks like a thumb and a finger,' said the tech. 'Like someone leaned on it.'

I pointed to the page with the question mark. 'Maybe to catch his balance while gluing that.'

'Or it's just from the cleaning crew,' said Milo.

'Aw c'mon, Lieutenant,' the tech said. 'Think positive.'

'Okay,' he said. 'How's this: I've got a pension plan, might live long enough to use some of it.'

The AFIS match to the latent came back at seven thirteen p.m. Hand-delivered by Sean Binchy to Milo as he presided over a tableful of food at Café Moghul. Petra, Moe Reed, Raul Biro, and I sat around the table. Everyone was hungry in a frustrated, miserably compulsive way, putting away lamb and rice and lentils and vegetables without tasting much.

Milo read the report, bared his teeth, passed it on.

James Pittson Harrie, male Caucasian, forty-six, had been

fingerprinted upon joining the staff of Ventura State Hospital a little over twenty-five years ago.

Harrie's five-year-old DMV shot featured the smiling visage of the elfin-faced, rosy-cheeked man I'd met. Slightly longer hair made for a less artful comb-over. Five six, one forty.

One of the few who didn't bother to fib about his stats. Honor among fiends?

Harrie's listed address was a P.O.B. in Oxnard.

Sean said, 'Already checked and it's a parcel shipping outlet in a strip mall. They're still in business but they haven't had boxes for five years, well before Harrie used it. I'm thinking he lived in or around that general area, lied to stay off the grid.'

I said, 'Oxnard's one town north of Camarillo and one below Ventura, where he also lied about living as Loyal Steward.'

Biro said, 'Everything's revolving around the beach towns. Returning to roost?'

I nodded.

Sean said, 'His last registered ride is a fifteen-year-old blue Acura but he hasn't paid his regs for years, got his license suspended. Want me to put a BOLO on the tags anyway?'

'You bet,' said Milo. 'Good work, kid. Wanna join us for some grub?'

'Thanks but I'd rather be working.' Binchy blushed. 'Not that you guys aren't working.'

Milo said, 'Go be productive, Sean,' and Binchy hurried out of the restaurant.

Petra studied James Pittson Harrie's photo. 'Aka Pitty. Finally we have a face and a name. Don't imagine driving illegally weighs on someone like that, but if he was stupid enough to hold on to his old wheels and keep expired tags on, that BOLO could be exactly what we need.'

Milo cracked his knuckles. 'Where the hell are the two of them *crashing*?'

'Like Raul said, the beach towns keep popping up, but that wouldn't stop them from drifting down here to do their dirty work and sticking around for a while.'

I said, 'If Harrie moved to Atascadero after Huggler got transferred there, maybe he listed a forwarding when he left.'

A call to the hospital was fruitless, two records clerks and a supervisor claiming old personnel records couldn't be accessed until business hours began the following morning.

'Even with that, don't get your hopes up,' said the supervisor. 'We've got major storage issues, don't hold on to everything.'

A second intrusion into Maria Thomas's domestic life resulted in a call from Atascadero's deputy director of Human Resources who'd somehow managed to pull Harrie's employment application during non-business hours.

Milo got the restaurant's fax number from the woman in the sari and told him to send everything he had. He asked a few more questions, scrawled unreadable notes, thanked the man and hung up and began reciting.

On his Atascadero application, James Pittson Harrie had claimed a B.A. in psychology from the University of Oregon in Eugene. For one year after graduation, he'd worked as a veterinary technician at a local animal hospital, then moved to Camarillo where he applied to be a psychiatry tech at V-State.

'From four legs to two legs,' said Petra. 'Maybe Harrie's the one who likes dogs, that's why they take them.'

Reed said, 'The question is likes them for what?'

'Ugh.'

Milo read on. 'He didn't receive a tech job but they did hire him as a janitor. Looks like he did that for thirteen, fourteen months, got promoted to custodial officer, level one. Custodial as in guard, not as in sweeping up . . . that seems to be as high as he got there, but then he moved to Atascadero as part of a compensation program: staffers who'd lost their jobs at V-State were given priority at other state facilities. And Atascadero granted his wish, he came on as a psychiatric technician, level one. The HR guy insisted they have no records of which specific wards he worked but he must've performed okay because he got promoted to level three and left voluntarily a little over five years ago. Which happens to be shortly before Grant Huggler was discharged. And guess who stayed on? Dr Louis Wainright. Guy had a half-time consultancy with Atascadero, doing outpatient surgical procedures. Received the same transfer courtesy.'

I said, 'How long after Harrie resigned was Huggler arrested behind Wainright's office?'

Milo squinted to decipher his own shorthand. 'Looks like . . . three days. Guess they got right to work.'

Reed said, 'Anyone want to lay odds on who bailed Huggler out?'

Petra said, 'That leaves four years until they did Vita. Way too long for there to be no one else.'

Reed said, 'Maybe another doctor was involved in Huggler's surgery. An anesthesiologist or a nurse?'

I said, 'Bodies never showed up because at that point Huggler and Harrie were still concealing their handiwork. I'd concentrate on disappearances between Morro Bay and Camarillo, anyone with a health-care job.'

Milo said, 'Wainright gave up whatever private practice he had in Camarillo to keep working for the state. Unbeknownst to him, he made Harrie and Huggler's job easy.'

'But Harrie and Huggler still waited until Huggler got out to do him,' said Petra. 'Fifteen years of waiting?'

I said, 'The key, at that point, was for Huggler to be directly involved. Think of it as therapy.'

Biro toyed with his food. 'Wonder if those eyes are Wainright's.'

Petra said, 'Anyone here want to volunteer approaching Wainright's family and explaining why we want their DNA?'

'Even worse,' said Reed, 'we do it and the eyes turn out not to be Wainright's.'

Milo said, 'Enough banter, kiddies. Still hungry, Raul?'

Biro looked at his plate. 'Nah, I'm finished.'

'Then how about starting with the calls, from Morro south, anyone with a medical background disappearing between Wainright's final hike and Vita Berlin's murder.'

'You bet.' He walked to a corner of the restaurant.

The woman in the sari came over with a silver tray. 'Faxes for you, Lieutenant.'

'Nothing like dessert.' Milo scanned the material, handed it to Petra, who did the same and passed it on.

James Pittson Harrie's Atascadero personnel photo portrayed a young man with long, thick, straight hair draping his brow from hairline to eye-ridge. Much of the remaining facial space was taken up by a dense beard.

Hippie in a uniform.

Grant Huggler's patient I.D. showed him with even longer hair and a patchy beard long enough to conceal his top shirt button.

Moe Reed said, 'Wainright was last seen in the mountains and these two look like mountain men. Maybe they camped up there, were ready for him.'

Milo compared the photo with Harrie's driver's license. 'He cleaned up well enough to fake being a B.H. shrink, got himself insurance gigs. But he had to be doing well before he rented that office because he anted up twenty-four G in cash. So maybe he practiced somewhere else. Or had another scam going.'

I said, 'Or he collects monthly pension checks. As a state employee for over two decades, he'd have a generous payout, maybe a bonus for leaving early. And Huggler would qualify for all sorts of welfare. If the two of them have lived prudently, they could've saved up plenty. And if they are living off the state, the checks get mailed somewhere.'

Milo tried Maria Thomas again, sat there for a while, tapping his fingers on the table. 'Dammit, answer.'

Unanswered prayer; he tried another number. Same result.

Petra said, 'Who was your second choice?'

'His Voluminousness.'

'You have his personal line?'

'I've got a line he sometimes answers.' A 411 got him the pension board's main office in Sacramento. Closed until working hours tomorrow morning.

He cursed, shoveled food.

Biro returned to the table. 'Got an interesting hit in Camarillo, woman named Joanne Morton, eighteen months ago. Went hiking in the foothills, not that far from where V-State used to be and hasn't been seen since. It was initially worked as a low-priority MP then they started considering suicide because Morton had a history of depression and her third divorce had really knocked her low. It was the ex who reported her missing but he didn't stay a suspect for long. Lives in Reno and could account for his whereabouts.'

'Why'd he call?' said Petra.

'Concerned about her. They broke up but it was friendly. He told them Joanne had "issues", he was worried she might hurt herself. And yes, she was a surgical nurse, freelanced around town.'

Reed said, 'If I helped Wainright mutilate kids I might have issues.'

Milo said, 'Was she hiking with a dog?'

'If she was,' said Biro, 'it's not in the report.'

Petra said, 'A pet's not a prereq for getting carved up, it's just a perk for the bad guys. Eighteen months ago. They *are* going down a list.'

'Eighteen months ago,' said Reed, 'leaves plenty of time for someone between Wainright and Morton, or after her and before Berlin.'

I said, 'Or they started off gradually, picked up the pace. Because it's no longer just about revenge.'

'What's it about?' said Milo.

'Recreation.'

No one spoke for several seconds.

Milo said, 'Moe, you and Sean and whoever else you can get who's competent, do a total and comprehensive recanvass of all the murder neighborhoods using the drawing of Huggler and Harrie's DMV photo. Petra, how about you and Raul try to find the clinic where the tipster claimed Huggler got his thyroid meds. That doesn't work out, go back to North Hollywood Day and lean on Mick Ostrovine to produce medical records for Grant Huggler. We know he was there and I'm not buying

249

Ostrovine's hear-no-evil. I'll contact the pension board first thing tomorrow, find out if checks are being mailed to one or both of our creep-os. If I get an address, we reconvene and map out an assault, probably with SWAT. I'll also talk to Jernigan, see if those eyeballs can be DNA'd and if they can, I'll approach Wainright's family.'

He snatched up his phone, called in a DMV on Wainright's nurse, Joanne Morton. 'Brown eyes, so they're not hers. Any questions?'

Without waiting for an answer, he stood, brushed off his trousers, threw money on the table.

When the others reached into their wallets, he said, 'Not a chance.'

Reed said, 'You're always footing the bill, El Tee.'

'Pay me back with good deeds.'

36

PETRA AND Raul Biro divided the assignments. He'd look for free clinics where Grant Huggler might've gotten his prescription, she'd have a go at Mick Ostrovine. Figuring a soft touch might work better with the administrator than another dose of male cop.

Ostrovine sighed a lot, said, 'Here we go again,' paid lip service to patient confidentiality. But sooner than Petra expected he said, 'Oh, all right, come around and look for yourself.'

She crossed to his side of the desk as he opened up some files.

'See?' said Ostrovine, nudging closer and favoring her with a burnt-whiskey whiff of some terrible cologne.

Alphabetized patient records; no Huggler.

'How about James Harrie, with an *i-e*, maybe middle initial *P.*'

Long, theatrical sigh. Ostrovine pecked.

'See? Nothing. It's like I told those first officers, we're not connected to any of this.'

Petra said, 'I'm sure you're right, Mick. But Mr Huggler was definitely here for a thyroid scan.'

'I explained the first time: he never *received* the scan so there'd be no record.'

Petra flashed him her best wholesome smile. 'Just to be sure, Mick, I'd like to show Mr Harrie's photograph and this drawing of Mr Huggler to your staff.'

'Oh, no. We're swamped.'

The horde she'd seen in the waiting room said the mope wasn't lying. 'I know you are, Mick, but I'd *really* appreciate it.'

She showed Ostrovine the images first. The drawing elicited nothing but he blinked at the photo.

Giving him a chance to fill in the blank, she sat back down.

'What?' he said, irritated. Maybe her feminine touch had lost its mojo.

'Never seen him?'

'Not in this world or any other.'

No one on staff recognized either man.

Even Margaret Wheeling, about to prep a sleepy-looking homeless type for a no-doubt-pricey MRI, had seemed confused when shown Alex Shimoff's second drawing.

'Guess so.'

Petra said, 'When you spoke to Lieutenant Sturgis, you were sure you'd met him.'

'Well . . . my drawing was different.'

Like *she* was the artist. Petra said, 'This one doesn't resemble the man who confronted Dr Usfel?'

Wheeling squinted. 'I'd need to put on my glasses.'

You don't need to see accurately when you're magnetizing someone?

'Go right ahead, Ms Wheeling.'

Wheeling let out a long exhalation followed by an eye roll. Another dramatic type; this place was like one of those summer camps for histrionic kids obsessed with musical theater.

Glasses in place, the fool continued to just stand there.

'Ms Wheeling?'

'I think it's him. Maybe. That's the best I can do. It was a long time ago.'

'What about this man? He's a friend of Huggler's.'

Emphatic head shake. 'That I can tell you. Never.'

* * *

Petra reported to Milo.

He said, 'Good work, onward, kid.'

She frowned at the unearned praise.

At Biro's third clinic, the Hollywood Benevolent Health Center, he got as far as a volunteer receptionist. The place was makeshift, set up with rolling partitions and what looked to be pretty tired medical equipment in the basement of a church on Selma just west of Vine. Big old beautiful Catholic church with intricate plaster details and an oak door that had to weigh a ton. Smaller than but not unlike St. Catherine in Riverside where Biro's parents had taken him for Mass when he was a kid.

All that grace and style ended in the basement. The space was dank, windowless, patchily lit by bare bulbs suspended from extension cords stapled to the ceiling. The wires drooped, some of the bulbs were dead. Where the walls weren't chipped white plaster they were rough gray block. Wilting posters about STDs and immunizations and nutrition were taped randomly. Everything in Federal Government Spanish.

The waiting room wasn't a room at all, just a clearing surrounded on three sides by stacks of long, wooden, folded tables. Half of the lawn chairs provided were occupied, all by Latino women who kept their eyes down and pretended not to notice Biro.

As he approached the desk, his spotless beige suit, white shirt, and olive paisley silk tie drew some admiring glances. Then he flashed his badge and someone's breath caught and all eyes shot downward.

Had to be one of those sanctuary deals for undocumenteds. Biro felt like shouting he wasn't La Migra.

One thing in his favor: an Anglo male like Huggler would stand out, maybe this would lead somewhere.

The receptionist was also Hispanic, a well-groomed, dyed blonde in her late twenties, a little extra-curvy in places where that was okay.

No name tag, no welcoming smile.

Raul grinned at her anyway, explained what he needed.

Her face closed up. 'All our doctors are volunteers, they come in and out so I don't know who you'd talk to.'

Raul said, 'The doctor who treated Grant Huggler.'

'I don't know who that is.'

'The doctor or Huggler?'

'Both,' said the receptionist. 'Either.'

'Could you please check your files?'

'We don't have files.'

'What do you mean?'

'Just that. We don't have files.'

'How can you run a clinic without records?'

'There are records,' she said. 'The doctors take them when they leave.'

'Why?'

'The patients are theirs, not ours.'

Biro said, 'Aw c'mon.'

'That's the way we do it,' she said. 'That's the way we've always done it. We're not an official health-care provider.'

'What are you then?'

'A space.'

'A space?'

'The church merely provides access for providers to provide.'

Merely and *access* and *providers* gave that the sound of a prepared speech. This place was definitely set up for illegals. Scared people coming in with God-knows-what diseases, afraid to broach the county system even though no one there asked questions. He glanced at the women in the lawn chairs. They continued to pretend he didn't exist. No one appeared especially sick but you never knew. His mother had just told him about one of her friends visiting relatives in Guadalajara and coming back with tuberculosis.

Telling it, the way she always did, as if Raul had the power to prevent such disasters.

He said, 'No charts here at all?'

The receptionist said, 'Not a one.'

'That sounds a little disorganized, Miss—'

'Actually it's super-organized,' she said, not offering a name. 'So we can multitask.'

'Multitask how?'

'When the church needs to use the space for something else, we wheel everything out of the way.'

'How often do doctors come in and use the space?'

'Most every day.'

'So you don't do much wheeling.'

Shrug.

Raul leaned in and half whispered, 'You've got people waiting but I don't see any doctors.'

'Dr Keefer's due in.'

'When?'

'Soon. But he can't help you.'

'Why's that?'

'He's new. Yesterday was his first day, so he wouldn't know your Mr Whatever.'

'Huggler.'

'Funny name.'

Biro looked at her.

She said, 'I don't know him.'

He gave her a look at his business card.

She said, 'You already showed me your badge, I believe that you're po-lice.'

'See what this says?'

Moment's hesitation. 'Okay.'

'Homicide,' said Biro. 'That's all I care about, solving murders.'

'Okay.'

'Grant Huggler may have a funny name but he's suspected of committing several really nasty murders. He needs to be stopped before he does more damage.'

He glanced back at the waiting women, trying to imply that they could turn up as victims.

The receptionist blinked.

255

He showed her the drawing.

She shook her head. 'Don't know him. We don't want murderers here. If I knew him, I'd tell you.'

'Are you the only receptionist here – what *is* your name?'

'Leticia. No, I'm not. A bunch of us volunteer.'

'How many is a bunch?'

'I don't know.'

He pulled out an enlargement of James Pittson Harrie's lapsed driver's license. 'How about him?'

To Biro's surprise, she went pale.

'What's the matter?'

'He's a doctor.'

'What kind?'

'Mental health,' she said. 'A therapist. He came in to ask questions but he never came back.'

'What kind of questions?'

'Did we do insurance work. He said he had a lot of experience with it, could help if someone needed help with an accident or an injury. I told him we didn't do that here. He gave me his card but I threw it out. I didn't even read his name.'

'But you remember him.'

'We don't usually get doctors walking in to drum up business.'

'What was his attitude?'

'Like a doctor.'

'Meaning?'

'Businesslike. He didn't seem like one of *those* but I guess he was.'

'One of those what?'

'Slip-and-fall scammers. Those we get from time to time. Scouts working for lawyers.'

'Trying to exploit your patients.'

Nod. No attempt to claim they're not *our* patients.

'So Mr Harrie told you he was a psychologist.'

'Or a psychiatrist, I forget. He's not?'

'Nope.'

'Oh.'

'How'd he react when you turned him down?'

'Just said thanks and gave me the card.'

'How long ago did this happen?'

'A while back,' said Leticia. 'Months.'

'How many?'

'I don't know – six, five?'

'That long ago but you remember him.'

'Like I told you, it was unusual,' she said. 'Also, he was Anglo. We don't get too many white guys, period, except for homeless who come in from the boulevard.'

Unzipping his file case, Raul showed her a mug shot of Lemuel Eccles. 'Like him?'

'Sure, that's Lem, he comes in once in a while.'

'For what?'

'You'd have to ask his doctor.'

'Who's that?'

'Dr Mendes.'

'First name?'

'Anna Mendes.'

Raul kept the photo in her face. She turned to the side.

He said, 'So Lem comes in but this white guy' – switching back to the drawing of Huggler – 'you don't know about?'

'Correct. Do these guys know each other or something?'

'You could say that.'

'The other one, too? The psychologist?'

'What else can you tell me about Lem?'

'Just that he comes in,' she said. 'He can be difficult but mostly he's okay.'

'Difficult, how?'

'Nervous, kind of wired. Talks to himself. Like he's crazy.'

'Like?' said Biro.

'We don't judge.'

257

'Do you have a list of the other receptionists?'

'I don't keep any lists and I don't know who they are 'cause when I'm here, they're not.'

'And you all volunteer.'

'Yeah.'

'Through what agency?'

'No agency, I do it for community service.'

She was too old for a high school student, didn't look like an ex-con, any kind of troublemaker. 'What kind of community service are you doing?'

'It's for a class. Urban issues, I'm a senior at Cal State L.A.'

'You think maybe upstairs in the church office they'd have a list?'

'Could be.'

Biro said, 'Okay, I'm going to leave you my card the way Mr Harrie did, but please don't throw it out.'

She hesitated.

'Take it, Leticia. Good people need to be good even when they're not volunteering.'

Her mouth dropped open. Raul began climbing the steps to the church's ground-floor lobby. One of the women in the lawn chairs said something in Spanish. Too soft for Biro to make out the words, but the emotion was obvious.

Relief.

As he headed for the church office a young man in a white coat and carrying a box crossed his path. M. Keefer, M.D. Resident in medicine at County General.

Ninety-hour work weeks but he had time to volunteer.

Raul said, 'Hi, there, Doctor. Ever seen this guy?'

M. Keefer said, 'No, sorry,' and bounced down the stairs.

The church office was locked, the magnificent marble sanctuary unoccupied. Raul returned to his car and got a number for an Anna Q. Mendes, M.D., in Boyle Heights.

This receptionist answered in Spanish and maybe it was Biro

responding in kind, maybe not, but she said, 'Of course,' and a moment later a warm female voice said, 'Dr Mendes, how can I help you?'

She listened to Biro's explanation, said, 'The thyroid case. Sure, I referred him for the scan. He came in for a refill of his Synthroid but his medical history was patchy. He looked a little underdosed to me and he was well overdue for a good look at his neck. He was reluctant but his therapist helped me convince him.'

'His therapist?'

'Some psychologist came with him, I thought that level of care was pretty impressive. Especially because the psychologist's office was in Beverly Hills and Huggler clearly wasn't a paying private patient.'

The ease with which she tossed out facts surprised Biro. Not even an attempt at resistance and he wondered if she'd been the anonymous tipster.

He said, 'Did the psychologist give his name?'

'He did but I can't recall.'

'Dr Shacker?'

'You know, I think that's it,' said Anna Mendes. 'He readily agreed that in order to optimize the dosage we'd need better data. In the meantime, I upped Mr Huggler's dosage a tiny bit and wrote a scrip for three months' worth.'

'Anything else you can tell me about Huggler?'

'You said you were in Homicide,' said Mendes. 'So obviously he killed someone.'

Biro hadn't mentioned Homicide. And *obviously* Huggler could've been a victim as easily as an offender.

Definitely the tipster.

'Looks like that, Doctor.'

'My brother was murdered six years ago,' she said. 'Stupid wrong-address drive-by, the imbeciles shot him with an AK while he slept in his bed.'

'I'm so sorry.'

'They never caught the bastards who did it. That's why I'm talking to you. Someone kills someone, they should get what they deserve. But no, that's really all I can tell you about Huggler.'

'What was his attitude?'

'Quiet, passive, didn't say much, didn't make eye contact. In fact, he was so quiet that even before the therapist – Shacker – came in, I'd started wondering about some sort of mental illness.'

'Could that be because of his thyroid?'

'No way,' she said. 'If he was a bit hypothyroid like I suspected he might slow down a tad, maybe lose some energy, gain some weight, but nothing significant. He might also feel cold, which is the first thing that tipped me off. He was overdressed for the weather, big heavy fleece-lined coat. I never confirmed my hypothesis, though, because he never came back with any lab results.'

'Could we expect him to get sicker?'

'Not if he takes his meds. Even with his old dosage this was no weakling, just the opposite. I checked him out and his muscle tone was really good. Excellent, actually. He had huge muscles. In clothes you couldn't tell, he looked almost pudgy.'

'Overdressed because he felt cold.'

'Or maybe it was a symptom of mental illness, you see that from time to time.'

Biro said, 'Speaking of mental patients, they told me at the clinic that Lem Eccles was your patient.'

'Was? Something happened to him?'

'Afraid so,' said Biro. 'He's dead.'

A beat. 'And that's connected to Huggler?'

'Could be.'

'Oh, wow,' said Mendes. 'Well, if you're going to ask me did I see them together, I didn't.'

'Could you check your records and see if they happened to be at the clinic on the same day?'

'I could, if I was at my other office in Montebello where I keep all the clinic records.'

'Kind of a strange system,' said Biro. 'Doctors taking the paperwork with them.'

'Big pain,' said Mendes, 'but they insist upon it. That way they're not an official clinic, just donate space.'

'In case La Migra asks.'

Mendes laughed. 'It's not very subtle, is it? I don't get involved in any of that. I treat patients, politics isn't my thing.'

'You work there on a volunteer basis.'

She laughed harder. 'Did it look like there was any serious money to be made there? Yes, I volunteer. I was a scholarship student at Immaculate Heart and the archdiocese helped with my med school tuition. They ask for a favor, I say sure. So what did this Huggler actually do?'

'It's nasty,' said Biro.

'Then forget I asked, Detective, I trained at County, saw more than enough nasty. I certainly hope you catch him and if I ever see him again, you'll be the first to know.'

'Couple more things,' said Raul. 'You said Dr Shacker showed up after Huggler. So Huggler came in by himself?'

'Technically I guess he did,' said Mendes. 'A few minutes later, Shacker showed up, said he'd been parking the car. I got the clear impression they'd arrived together. Now if you don't mind, I've got patients waiting.'

Parking the car. Small point to her but Raul's brain was screaming *A Vehicle. Ripe for a BOLO.*

He said, 'One more question. How come you referred Huggler to North Hollywood Day?'

'Because Dr Shacker recommended it. You should get the details from him, he really seemed to care about Huggler. Then again, he'd probably have confidentiality issues. So do I, but murder's different.'

Biro filled Petra in.

She said, 'It's a good bet Shacker spotted Eccles at that clinic. I'll go back to the uniforms who busted Eccles, see if there's anything else they remember about Loyal Steward. And seeing as Harrie directed the doctor to North Hollywood Day and he's an insurance whore and they're an insurance mill, it's obvious my charm didn't work as well with Ostrovine as I thought and he's still holding back. You up for bad-copping him?'

'More than up,' said Raul. 'Raring to go.'

On the way to the Valley, he phoned in and reported to Milo.

Milo said, 'Good work, Raul. Onward.'

I'd just stepped into his office. He wheeled his chair back. 'See how supportive I am with the young'uns?'

'Admirable.'

'Not that anything they've learned adds up to a warm bucket of spit until we locate these freakoids.'

He summarized.

I'd been up late, trying to answer some questions of my own. Mentally reviewing my brief talk with James Harrie to see if I'd missed something.

Understanding why someone like Huggler would welcome Harrie's caretaking but not getting what was in it for Harrie, because if a man that calculated was able to exact his own brand of vengeance, why raise the risk of discovery by collaborating with someone so deeply disturbed?

Engaging in twenty-plus years of what was effectively foster-parenting.

What was in it for the parent?

The small questions had resolved quickly but the big picture remained clouded and I couldn't shake the feeling that I'd made several wrong turns.

I said, 'The pension angle didn't work out?'

'The pension board is absolutely certain that no checks are mailed from any government agency to James P. Harrie, same for the welfare office regarding assistance payments to Grant Huggler. I tried out a whole bunch of spelling variations because paperwork gets messed up.

Even checked under Shacker's name, because he'd also been a state employee, maybe Harrie had stolen his benefits as well as his identity. No such luck, those checks are sent to a cousin in Brussels. So maybe we're dealing with free-enterprise criminals, intent on making it the old-fashioned way.'

I said, 'How much money are we talking about?'

'Best estimate I could get was someone in Harrie's situation could pull a pension of three to four grand a month, depending if he claimed stress or disability. No way to know exactly what Huggler's qualified for, there's an alphabet soup of welfare goodies for someone who knows how to work the system. Top estimate was two or so a month.'

'The two of them pool their funds, they can rake in as much as sixty, seventy thousand a year, tax-free. I don't see them forgoing that, Big Guy, even with Harrie making money as a fake psychologist. He put up serious money for that office, must've started with some sort of stash. So the checks are going somewhere. What if Harrie stole I.D.s other than Shacker's? For himself and for Huggler?'

'Someone cross-checks Social Security numbers, they'd get found out.'

'Big if,' I said. 'But okay, what if they went the legal route and changed their names in court? Any switch for Huggler would have to be within the last four years because he was still using his real name when he got arrested behind Wainright's office.'

'Send the check to Jack the Ripper and his lil pal the Zodiac? Some computer obliges without a squawk? Wonderful.'

He called a Superior Court clerk he'd befriended years ago, hung up looking deflated.

'Guess what? Court orders are no longer required for name changes. All you have to do now is use your new moniker consistently while conducting official business and eventually the new data's "integrated" into the county data bank.'

He yanked a drawer open, snatched a panatela, rolled it, still wrapped, between his fingers. 'But you're right, no way they'd pass up that much easy dough.'

His cell phone played Erik Satie. He barked, 'Sturgis!' Then, in an even louder voice: '*What!*'

He turned scarlet. 'Back *up*, Sean, give me the details.'

He listened for a long time, scrawled notes so angrily the paper tore twice. When he clicked off he was breathing fast.

I said, 'What?'

He shook his head. Attacked the phone with both thumbs.

The image appeared moments later, a grainy gray peep show on the phone's tiny screen.

Tagged at the top with rolling digital time and the I.D. number of a Malibu Sheriff cruiser's dash-cam.

Six thirteen a.m. Malibu. Pacific Coast Highway. Mountains to the east, so north of the Colony where the beach city turns rural.

The deputy, Aaron Sanchez, justifying the stop on the fifteen-year-old Acura.

Not because of the BOLO; the tags matched a recent theft from the Cross Creek shopping center.

Felony stop. Extreme caution.

Six fourteen a.m.: Deputy Sanchez calls for backup. Then (on loud-speaker): 'Exit the vehicle, now, sir, and place your hands on your head.'

No response.

Deputy Sanchez: 'Exit the vehicle immediately, sir, and place—'

Driver's door opens.

A man, small, thin, wearing a sweatshirt and jeans, emerges, places his hands on his head.

Flash of bald spot. Bad comb-over.

Deputy Sanchez exits his own vehicle, gun out, aimed at the driver. 'Walk toward me slowly.'

The man complies.

'Stop.'

The man complies.

'Lie down on the ground.'

The man appears to comply then whips around, pulling something out of his waistband. Crouching, he points.

Deputy Sanchez fires five times.

The man's small frame absorbs each impact, billowing like a sail.

He falls.

Sirens in the distance gain volume.

Backup, no longer needed.

The whole thing has taken less than a minute.

Milo said, 'Bastard. They ran the car, found the BOLO, contacted Binchy because his name was on the request.'

'Was the thing in his hand for real?'

'Nine-millimeter,' he said. 'Unloaded.'

I said, 'Suicide by cop.'

'Whack-job suicide by cop was the Sheriff's initial assumption because Harrie getting that hard-core to avoid a license plate theft rap made no sense. And initially, they saw nothing in Harrie's car to make him squirrelly, just fruits and vegetables and beef jerky and bottled water, probably from one of those stands on the highway. Then they popped the trunk and found a bunch more firearms, ammo, duct tape, rope, handcuffs, knives.'

I said, 'Rape-murder kit.'

'And stains on the carpet presumptive for blood. What they *didn't* find was any sign Harrie was running with an accomplice.'

I said, 'Because Huggler's waiting back home for Harrie to return from his grocery run. Somewhere north of where Harrie was pulled over.'

'That's a lot of territory. What does a kit say to you?'

'None of our victims showed evidence of restraint and none of the females was assaulted or posed sexually. I'd bet on a separate victim pool.'

'Games Harrie played solo.'

'More likely with backup by Huggler.'

'Jesus.'

'It fills in a missing piece,' I said. 'Harrie taking Huggler under his wing because of altruism never made sense. He was attracted to a disturbed child because of a shared fascination with dominance and violence. Think of their relationship as Huggler's alternative therapy: the entire time the staffs at V-State and Atascadero were struggling to devise a treatment plan for him, Harrie was sabotaging them by nurturing Huggler's drives. And coaching Huggler in concealing his bad behavior. When Huggler got transferred, Harrie moved with him. When Huggler finally gained his freedom, he and Harrie embarked on a new life together.'

'Foundation for a wholesome relationship,' he said. 'Too bad Harrie bit it before the two of them could be booked on the talk-show circuit.'

37

SEAN BINCHY'S second call pinpointed the coordinates of the shooting.

James Pittson Harrie had died 3.28 miles above the Colony, leaving 15 or so miles of the beach city and anywhere beyond for a hide-spot.

Milo said, 'Don't see them scoring a pad on the sand or an ocean-view ranch in the hills. But if they're still doing the mountain man bit, they could be squatting in some remote place up in the hills.'

I said, 'I'm certain they're cashing government checks, at some point one or both of them ventures out to get cash. So someone's seen them. My mind keeps fixing on the beach cities above Malibu. Harrie's used two phony addresses we know about, the parking lot on Main Street in Ventura when he told the Hollywood cops he was Loyal Steward and the dead mail-drop in Oxnard for his driver's license. Something in the region attracts him.'

'What attracts me is nailing Huggler before he does more damage. Once the media latch onto Harrie's death — and they will, a cop shooting's always a story — he's bound to rabbit.'

'That assumes Huggler's wired into the media.'

'Why wouldn't he be?'

'Harrie could've made himself Huggler's sole link to the outside world.'

'No MTV for ol' Grant, huh?' he said. 'Keeps his nose buried in puzzle books until Harrie tells him it's time to balance the scales with an anatomy lesson? Even so, Alex, when Harrie doesn't return, Huggler's gonna get antsy. If fear overtakes him, he might reveal himself and get

267

taken down easy. But if he goes the rage-route, more people are gonna die. And those guns in Harrie's trunk might not be the total stash. All I need is a lunatic loaded with heavy-duty firepower.'

Balance the scales.

Unbalanced.

My mind raced. Braked hard.

A warm wave of clarity washed over me. The tickle at the back of my brain, finally gone.

He said, 'You just floated off somewhere.'

'What you just said about balancing the scales reminded me of something Harrie mentioned when I met with him. He asked me about my work with the police then claimed to have no interest in the darker aspects of life. Called them "terrible dyssynchronies". Obviously, he was lying and I think he was playing with me by alluding precisely to what's framed the murders from the onset: achieving equilibrium by symbolically undoing the past. And that might help focus the search for Huggler: start where it all began.'

'V-State,' he said. 'They'd go back there?'

'They would if it was part of Harrie's treatment plan for Huggler.'

'You just said his treatment was encouraging Huggler's gut-games.'

'I did but I was missing something. Harrie really came to see himself as a therapist. Like most psychopaths, he had an inflated belief in his own abilities. No need to actually earn a degree, he was already smarter than the shrinks. So all he had to do was learn enough jargon to impersonate convincingly. And when he went into practice, he started right at the top: high-rent Couch Row. He zeroed in on insurance evaluations because they were lucrative, thin on oversight, and, most important, short term with no clinical demands: patients wouldn't spend enough time with him to get suspicious and he wouldn't be required to actually help anyone.'

'Vita got suspicious.'

'Maybe she sensed something,' I said. 'Or she was just being Vita. Overall, Harrie got away with it and that had to be a massive ego trip. And that led him to see himself as a *master* therapist. With a single long-term patient. Yes, the past five years have been about bloodlust and revenge, but they've also been part of a regimen Harrie devised for Huggler: achieving synchrony by working through old traumas. And what better way to achieve that than by returning triumphant to the place where control was ripped away?'

'Neck-snapping and gut-squishing in the name of self-actualization,' he said. 'The hospital closed down years ago. What's there now?'

'Let's find out.'

Milo typed away. Moments later, we had a capsule history, courtesy of a historical preservation group: the original plan had been to maintain the hospital buildings and convert them to a college campus. Shortage of funds caused that to languish until six years ago when a group of private developers had purchased the site in a sweetheart deal and put up a planned community called SeaBird Estates.

He found the website. 'Luxury living for the discerning? Doesn't sound like our boys would fit in.'

I scrolled. 'It also says "nestled in sylvan surroundings". Enough woodland and our boys could've found refuge.'

He shot to his feet, flung his office door open, paced the corridor a few times, returned.

Using both hands to sketch an imaginary window, he peered through, an artless mime.

'Looks like nice weather for a drive, let's go.'

38

Fifty minutes to Camarillo, courtesy Milo's leaden foot.

The same exit off the 101, the same winding road through old, dense trees.

The same feeling of arriving at a strange place, untested, unsure, ready to be surprised.

What had once been an open field of wildflowers was planted with lemon trees, hundreds of them arranged in rows, the ground cleared of stray fruit. The logo of a citrus collective graced several signs on the borders of the grove. The sky was a perfect, improbable, crayon blue.

Milo sped past the grove. I peered through each row, looking for errant human presence.

Just a tractor, unmanned, at the far end. The next sign appeared half a mile later, lettered in aqua and topped by a rendering of three intense-looking gulls.

SEABIRD ESTATES
A Planned Community

A few yards up, shoulder-high blue gates were hinged to cream-colored stucco posts. Superficially reassuring but a whole different level of security from V-State's twenty-foot blood-red barrier.

Keeping them out was different from keeping them in.

A guard inside a tiny booth was texting. Milo tooted his horn. The guard looked over but his fingers kept working. He slid a window open. Milo's badge pretzeled the guard's lips. 'We didn't call in no problem.'

'No, you didn't. Can we come in, please?'

The guard pondered that. Resuming texting, he stabbed at a button on a built-in console, missed the first time, got it right on the second. The gates swung open.

The main street was Sea Bird Lane. It snaked up a slope that picked up as it climbed. Condos appeared on both sides of the road. Landscaping consisted of predictably placed date palms, red-leaf plum trees, beds of low-maintenance succulents that clung to each curve like green cashmere.

Every building was styled identically: neo-Spanish, cream like the gateposts, red composite roofs trying to pass themselves off as genuine tile.

Superficial resemblance to the old V-State buildings. No bars on these windows. No foot traffic to speak of. During the hospital's tenure, staff and low-risk patients had strolled freely, creating an easy energy. Strangely enough, SeaBird Estates felt more custodial.

Milo drove fifty yards in with a light foot before I spotted an original structure: the mammoth reception hall where I'd been oriented. A sign staked near the entry read *Sea Horse Club House*. As we continued to explore, other hospital structures appeared. *Sea Breeze Card Room. Sea Foam: A Meeting Place.* Former wards and treatment centers and who-knew-what coexisting with new construction. Transplanted smoothly, a wonder of cosmetic surgery.

Finally, a few people showed themselves: white-haired couples, strolling, casually dressed, tan, relaxed. I was wondering if they had any idea of their neighborhood's origins when a red-haired man in a blue poly blazer one size too large, baggy khakis, and ripple-soled shoes stepped into the middle of the road and blocked our progress.

Milo braked. Blazer examined us, then came around to the driver's side. 'Rudy Borchard, head of security. What can I do for you?'

'Milo Sturgis, LAPD. Please to meet you, Rudy.'

Mutual badge-flashes. Borchard's was significantly larger than Milo's, a gold-plated star that evoked the OK Corral. Probably larger than anything Earp had worn because why offer a generous target?

'So,' said Borchard. Tentative, as if he'd only memorized the script this far. He placed a protective finger on the knot of his clip-on tie. His hair was too long in places, too short in others, dyed the color of over-cooked pumpkin. A one-week mustache was a sprinkle of cayenne on a puffy upper lip. 'L.A. police, huh? This ain't L.A.'

'Neither is it Kansas,' said Milo.

Borchard's eyes tilted in confusion. He puffed his chest to compensate. 'We didn't call in any problem.'

'We know, but—'

'It's like this,' Borchard cut in. 'Residents' privacy is real important. I'm talking affluent senior retirees, they want to feel private and safe.'

'Safety's our goal, too, Rudy. That's why we're inquiring about a suspect who might be in the area.'

'A suspect? Here? I don't think so, guys.'

'Hope you're right.'

'*In* the area or just close to the area?'

'Could go either way.'

'Naw, I don't think so,' said Borchard. 'No one gets in here without my say-so.'

Our easy entry put the lie to that. Milo said, 'That's excellent, but we'd still like to have a look.'

Borchard said, 'Who's this suspect?'

Milo showed him the drawing of Huggler.

Borchard said, 'Nope, not here, never been here.'

Milo kept the drawing in Borchard's face. Borchard stepped back. 'I'm telling you nope. Looks like your basic lowlife. Wouldn't last two seconds, here. Do me a favor and put that away, okay? I don't want some resident getting their undies all scrunched.'

'Keep it, Rudy. Should you want to post it, that would be fine.'

Borchard took the drawing, folded, slipped it into his pocket. 'What exactly this lowlife do?'

'Killed a bunch of people.'

The red dots atop Borchard's lip bounced as he chewed air. 'You kidding? No way I'm posting that picture. The residents hear *killed*, someone'll have a heart attack for sure.'

'Rudy,' said Milo, 'if Grant Huggler gets in here, it's gonna be a lot worse than a heart attack.'

'Trust me, he won't.'

'You guys keep it that tight?'

'Tighter than a virgin's — real tight, trust me on that.'

'How many ways are there to get in here?'

'You just saw it.'

'The front gate is all?'

'Basically.'

'Basically but not completely?'

'There's a service entry around the back,' said Borchard, hooking a thumb eastward. 'But that's just deliveries and it's locked twenty-four seven and it's monitored by c-circuit and we know exactly who ingresses and egresses.'

'What comes in that way?'

'Deliveries. Large-scale. Small-scale come through the front, every parcel is checked out before it's delivered.'

'Checked out how?'

'The residents give us authorization to sign for UPS and FedEx and we verify addresses and hand-deliver. That way no one gets bothered, it's all part of the service.'

A honk from behind made us turn. Elderly couple in a white Mercedes itching to proceed. The woman was stoic but the man's mouth worked.

'You better move over,' said Borchard.

Milo pulled to the curb and we got out. The Mercedes passed and Borchard favored the occupants with a wide wave. They ignored him, tooled to the next street, turned left. Sea Cloud Road.

Rudy Borchard said, 'Have a nice day, guys.'

Milo said, 'What constitutes large-scale deliveries?'

'You know, bulk stuff. We're like a town, supplies for the clubhouse and the restaurants – we got two, the formal and the informal – come in all the time. We got nearly eight hundred residents.'

I said, 'The clubhouse is back there. So there's a way for the trucks to approach it from the back and drive straight to the loading dock.'

''Zactly,' said Borchard. 'We can't have semis rumbling through, messing up the pavement, creating a ruckus.'

'Where does the service road connect from?'

'Cuts through the middle.'

'Of what?'

'The rest of the property.'

'There's a section that's not developed?'

''Zactly. Phase Two.'

'When's it going to be developed?'

Borchard shrugged.

Milo said, 'How do you get to the service road without driving through here?'

'You probably took Lewis off the freeway, right? Next time, get off one exit before, then you travel a few streets and go on some farm roads. But trust me, no one's gonna get in that way. And even if they did – and they didn't – there'd be nowhere to hide. Plus the residents have panic buttons in their condos and they can pay extra for portable ones to carry around. We got no problems here. Never.'

Milo said, 'So the delivery road cuts through the back and ends up at a loading dock.'

'Not one dock, a bunch, and there's always people around. Trust me, your lowlife wouldn't last a minute. What even makes you think he's anywhere near here?'

'Because he used to live here.'

'In Camarillo? It's a big place.'

'Not the city, Rudy. Here.'

'Huh? Oh. He was one of those.'

'One of who?'

'A nutter. From when this was a nuthouse.'

I said, 'Do the residents know about that?'

274

Borchard smiled. 'It's not on the brochure but sure, some of them would have to. But no one gives two rats. Because that was a long time ago and now everything's normal and safe. Why would a nutter come back to where he was locked up, anyway? That's not logical. Psychologically speaking.'

Milo suppressed a smile. 'Maybe so, Rudy. How many guys on your security staff?'

'Five. Including me. It's enough, trust me. Nothing happens here. The whole nut thing's a joke to us. Like when something gets dug up.'

'Dug up?'

'When they're doing landscaping,' said Borchard. 'Someone's turning the dirt for plants, whatever, something pops up.'

'Like what?'

'Oh, no, don't go thinking criminal. I'm talking spoons, forks, cups. With the hospital brand on it, this big *VS*. One time some buckles and a strap got dug up, probably from one of those straitjackets.'

'What do you do with all that when you find it?'

'I don't find it, the landscaping crew does. They give it to me and I throw it out, what do you think? It's junk.' Borchard checked his watch. 'Your maniac ain't here but if he shows up I'll take care of it.'

Unbuttoning the oversized jacket, he gave us a view of a holstered Glock.

'Nice piece,' said Milo.

'And I know how to use it.'

'You were in the military?'

Borchard flushed. 'I go to the range. Have a nice day, guys.'

Milo said, 'How about showing us that service road?'

'You're kidding.'

'Just so we can tell the boss we've been careful.'

'Bosses,' said Borchard. 'Yeah, I hear that. Fine, I'll show you, but it's clear on the other end, you don't wanna walk.'

'So we'll drive.'

Borchard eyed the unmarked. 'I'm not getting in the back of that, looks bad to the residents, you know?'

'I promise not to cuff you, Rudy.'

'I like your jokes. Not.' He touched the spot beneath his jacket where the gun was positioned. 'You really need to be doing this?'

'We drove all the way from L.A.'

'So go get a fish taco in town and say you looked.'

Milo smiled.

'Okay, okay, hold on.' A man with a cane was approaching and Borchard hurried to intercept him. Borchard smiled and talked. The man walked away, midsentence, muttering. Borchard shot us an *I-told-you-so* look, disappeared around a leafy turn, and emerged several minutes later driving a canvas-topped golf cart.

'Hop in for the E Ride.'

Milo sat next to him, I took the rear bench. The plastic seat was aqua blue patterned with green herons.

'Guys, I'm only doing this cop-to-cop, trust me your nutter didn't stow away in some eighteen-wheeler. Everything comes from recognized vendors, we log every ingress and egress. Now, if the tunnels were still open, I might consider you have a point, but they're not so you don't.'

'What tunnels?'

'Ha, knew I'd get you with that,' said Borchard, chuckling. 'I'm messing with you, trust me, it's nothing.'

'No tunnels.'

'Not anymore and they're all filled with concrete.'

'None, but they're filled.'

'You know what I mean, you can't go in 'em.'

Milo looked back at me. I shook my head.

Borchard said, 'What it was, back in the day there were these underground passages between some of the hospital buildings. For moving supplies, I guess.' He laughed harder. 'Or maybe they ran the nutters down there for exercise, punishment, whatever. Anyway, when the developers bought the property the county made them fill them all with concrete because of earthquakes. You want to see?'

'Why not?' said Milo, casually.

'Giving you the full tour, gonna be a surcharge.' Laughing and flooring the cart's accelerator, Borchard swung a quick U-turn and headed up the road at five mph. Moments later, he stopped at a side street that led to a clump of condos. Sea Wave Road. Motioning us out, he squatted, parted some bushes. Inlaid in the dirt was a metal disk around six feet in diameter. Painted brown, unmarked, like an oversized manhole cover with two metal eyelets.

'Watch, this is cool.' Looping a finger around one of the eyelets, Borchard tried to lift. The lid didn't budge. He strained. 'Must be stuck or something.'

'Want some help?' said Milo.

'No, no, no.' Borchard used two hands, turned scarlet. The lid lifted an inch and Borchard let go and some sort of pneumatic mechanism kicked in. The lid rose until it was perpendicular with the ground.

Underneath was a circle of concrete. Borchard stood on top of it, jumped like a kid on a trampoline. 'Solid, all the way through. Rebar and concrete, extra-strong to handle the big one.'

'How many openings like this are there, Rudy?'

'Who knows? Most of them are buried over, they run under the condos. It's only when they're in landscaped areas that we find them. I've seen four of those and trust me, they're all solid, like this one.' He jumped twice more. 'Nutter skulking through a tunnel would be a good movie. Unfortunately, this is reality, guys. You really don't want to bother seeing the back fence, do you?'

Milo shrugged. 'What can I tell you, Rudy?'

'Knew you'd say that.'

We put-putted along Sea Bird Lane, switched to Sea Star Drive, reached the rear of the development. The service road was a single lane of asphalt that passed through a high chain-link gate. A closed-circuit camera was bolted to the right-hand post. Through the links a slice of blue sky and brown field and mauve mountains was visible but the broad view afforded only sky above twenty-plus feet of ficus hedge. The trees had been densely planted on both sides of the fence, creating an impenetrable wall of green.

I strained to catch a lateral glimpse but Borchard swung the cart away and drove along the development's south rim, parallel to the hedge. The road continued for several minutes before branching to a three-tine fork.

'Okay? Satisfied?'

Milo said, 'Where do these roads go?'

'They're not roads, they're driveways. That one's to the clubhouse, that's to the recreation center – basically for towels from the linen service – and that one goes to La Mer, which is the formal, open for dinner only, and also to Café Seabird, which is right next door and does three meals a day and also has a tearoom for snacks – what the hell, I'll show you.'

Three loading docks, all of them bolted shut. Not a truck in sight. Despite Borchard's boast of observers everywhere, no workers.

'Quiet day,' said Milo.

'It's always quiet,' said Borchard, as if he regretted the fact. Reversing the car, he headed back toward the front. As we passed the chain-link gate, Milo said, 'Stop for a sec,' and hopped out and peered through.

He came back stoic.

'What'd you see?' said Borchard. 'Empty land, right? No nutters in sight. Can I go on?'

'You keep the disks from that CC camera?'

'Knew you'd ask that. The disk erases itself every twenty-four and we recycle. 'Cause there's never nothing on it. Now I'm taking you back, I already got too many curious residents wanting to know what's up.'

I said, 'What are you going to tell them?'

'That you guys are from the county. Making sure we're earthquake-safe. Which we are. Totally.'

Back at the unmarked, Milo asked Borchard for detailed directions to the undeveloped land.

'Just what I told you.'

'How about if we don't want to get back on the freeway?'

Borchard scratched his head. 'I guess you could, as you get out of here, turn left, then left again. But it's way longer, you're making a big square. Then you have to drive a ways till you see an artichoke field. At least now it's artichokes, sometimes they plant it with something else – when it's onions, trust me you'll smell it. You get to the artichokes, you still keep going and then you'll see a whole bunch of nothing, like you just saw through the back gate.'

He scraped a tooth with a fingernail. 'That's how you'll know you're there. It's a whole lot more nothing than anywhere else around here.'

39

AFTER SEVERAL wrong turns, we found the artichoke field.

The crop was ample but not ready for picking. A solitary man stood sentry near the south edge of the acreage, positioned on a dirt road above a drainage ditch drinking amber-colored soda. Small and dark-skinned, he wore gray work clothes and a broad-brimmed straw hat. When Milo pulled the unmarked within a yard of his feet, he didn't budge.

Human scarecrow. Effective; not a bird in sight.

We got out and he finally turned. The soda was Jarritos Tamarindo. His workshirt had two flap pockets. One was empty, the other sagged under the weight of a cellophane-wrapped half sandwich. Some kind of lunch meat, Spanish writing on the pack.

'*Hola, amigo,*' said Milo.

'*Hola.*'

'Ever see this person?'

The drawing of Huggler evoked a head shake.

Same for the photo of the late James Pittson Harrie.

'Ever see anyone around here?'

'No.'

'Never?'

'No.'

'Okay, *gracias.*'

The man tipped his hat and returned to his post, repositioning himself with his back to the car.

Milo consulted the notes he'd taken from Borchard's sketchy directions, drove another quarter mile, made a turn, came to a stop. 'Guess ol' Rudy was right.'

Humming first seven bars of 'Plenty of Nuthin'', he knuckled an eye.

A vast field stretched west to the twenty-foot ficus hedge and SeaBird's rear gate, thousands of square feet of brambles and weeds, much of it tall as a man. Drought-friendly wildflowers with pinched gray foliage alternated with coarse grass bleached to hay. Ragged bare spots were occupied by shards of rusted metal and tan stucco fragments edged with the snipped ends of chicken wire.

At the far end, a second ficus hedge stood, untrimmed and taller than SeaBird's rear border by a good ten feet. The east end, where Specialized Care had once stood. Behind the wall of green, the foothills sprouted like massive tubers.

We sat in the car, dispirited. The failure of my theory meant Huggler could be anywhere.

Milo said, 'What the hell, we tried.' He lit up a wood-tipped panatela, exhaled acrid smoke through the driver's window and called in for messages, starting with Petra.

The officers who'd arrested Lemuel Eccles thought Complainant Loyal Steward might be James Harrie but they couldn't be positive, they'd been concentrating on the offender not the victim.

Raul Biro had pressured Mick Ostrovine into giving up the truth: yes, 'Dr Shacker' had sent insurance cases to North Hollywood Day. No, there'd been no kickback, he was just another referral source.

Well-Start Insurance was through returning calls.

Biro said, 'There had to be kickbacks. I found out who owns the place, bunch of Russians headquartered in Arcadia and they're billing Medi-Cal gazillions. But I don't see pursuing that unless there's an organized crime aspect to our cases.'

'God forbid,' said Milo.

'That's what I thought. Can't think of anywhere else to go with this, El Tee.'

'Take your girlfriend out to dinner.'

'Don't have one,' said Biro. 'Not this month.'

'Then find one,' said Milo. 'Meal's on me.'

'Why?'

''Cause you do your job and don't bitch.'

'Haven't done much on this one, El Tee.'

'So run a tab.'

Biro laughed and hung up and Milo called the coroner. Dr Jernigan was out but she'd authorized her investigator to summarize James Pittson Harrie's autopsy for Milo. Harrie's heart and lungs and brain had been perforated by five bullets fired from the service gun of Sheriff's Deputy Aaron Sanchez, any of which could've proved fatal. No I.D. had been found on Harrie's person but his fingerprints matched some from twenty-five years ago when he'd begun work as a janitor at V-State.

The human blood in the Acura's trunk came from three separate samples, two type As, one type O. DNA swabs would take a while to analyze but a sex screen had come back female.

Milo hung up and gazed at weed-choked acreage. 'A tunnel would've been nice. When you were here, you never heard of that?'

'No,' I said.

'Why'd you end up here, anyway?'

'To learn.'

'About kids like Huggler?'

'The patients I saw weren't dangerous, not even close.'

'They get better?'

'We made their lives better.'

He said, 'Uh-huh.' His eyes closed. He stretched his long legs, rested his head on the seat-back. Stayed that way for a while. Except for the occasional puff on the cigar, he appeared to be sleeping.

I thought about an unusual child, living in a special room.

Milo shook himself like a wet dog, stubbed the cigar in the ashtray the city officially forbade him from using. 'Let's drive around Camarillo, check out mailbox outlets, shitty motels, and other potential squats.

Afterward we'll celebrate nothing with a nice fish dinner at Andrea in Ventura. Been there?'

'Robin and I went whale-watching last year, it's right near the launch.'

'Rick and I went whale-watching last year, too. Closest we got was when I caught a glimpse of myself in the mirror.'

I was expected to chuckle so I did.

He spit a tobacco shred out the window.

Just as he started up the car, something moved.

40

Blurred movement.

A flickering dot bobbing somewhere past the midpoint of the field's length. Clear of the rear ficus wall but at this distance no way to gauge how far in front.

We watched as the shape bounced above the lower grass, was obscured by taller vegetation.

Up and down, in and out. Sunlight caught the outer edges, limned them gold.

The gold endured. A golden shape. Some sort of animal.

Too large and not furtive enough to be a coyote.

The shape got closer. Lumbering.

A dog. Oblivious to our presence, making its way through the weeds.

Milo and I got out of the car, walked along the border of the field. Got close enough to make out more details.

Sizable dog, obvious golden retriever heritage but too long and narrow in the snout for a purebred. One ear perked, the other flopped.

It stopped to pee. No leg-raising, a brief, submissive squat. Lowering its head, it continued. Stopping, starting, sniffing with no obvious goal. Maybe harking back to some ancient hunting dog imperative.

We kept walking.

The dog looked up, sniffed the air. Turned.

Soft eyes, grizzled muzzle. Not a trace of anxiety.

I said, 'Nice to meet you, Louie.'

* * *

We stood on the roadside as Louie peed again. Squatting longer, he strained to defecate, finally succeeded and pawed the ground before continuing through the field.

A second shape appeared off to his right.

Materializing from nowhere, just as Louie had.

The second dog looked ancient, limping and hobbling as it struggled to catch up with Louie. Tenuous steps alternated with shaky halts. A few seconds of that led to what appeared to be convulsive loss of control that plunged the animal to the ground.

It struggled, moaned, got to its feet, trembling.

Louie turned. Ambled over.

The other dog remained rooted, chest heaving. Louie licked its face. The other dog seemed to revive, managed a few more steps.

Louie and his pal entered a low patch that gave us a clear view. We edged into the field, saw the too-pronounced rib cages of both animals. Louie was underweight, the older dog emaciated with a belly tucked tighter than a greyhound's.

Not the abdomen intended for this breed. What had once been a muscular body was white skin speckled with brown stretched over spindly bones. The head remained noble: brown, with floppy ears, solid bone structure, eyes that appeared vacant but continued to dart around intelligently. A single brown patch ran along a spinal ridge corrugated by age and malnutrition.

German shorthaired pointer.

I said, 'Dr Wainright's hiking buddy, Ned. All these years.'

Milo said, 'They cut up animals but save these two?'

'Boys and their pets.'

Ned paused again, breathing hard, fighting for balance. Louie nuzzled him, sidled up and kept his own body close to that of the pointer, helping the older dog maintain equilibrium. They explored some more, Ned stumbling, Louie there to brace him. Each time the pointer marshaled its energies, Louie rewarded with a lick.

Canine behavior therapist.

For the next quarter hour, we watched both dogs zigzag through the field. If they noticed the unmarked parked off to the side, they gave no indication. One time Louie lifted his head and did seem to be looking at us again, but matter-of-factly, with no alarm.

A trusting creature.

Milo said, 'They've been starved . . . if they're here, he's got to be.' He scanned the horizon, fingers meandering toward his holster. 'C'mon, you sick bastard. Show yourself or I'll sic PETA on you.'

The dogs wandered around a bit more for no apparent reason. Then the pointer squatted, took an interminable time to do its business while Louie stood by patiently.

Louie led Ned along what seemed to be an agonizing trek. Both dogs entered a patch of high grass and faded from view.

Twenty minutes later, they hadn't reappeared.

Milo motioned me forward and we stepped into high grass, focusing on the spot where we'd last seen the dogs. Muting noise by parting handfuls of brush before passing through.

Stopping every ten paces to make sure we weren't being watched.

No sign of the dogs, no sign of any other creature.

A few hundred feet in, the vegetation died and we faced a clearing.

Irregular patch of dirt, twenty or so yards in front of the ficus wall. Smooth, brown, swept clean. Just like Marlon Quigg's kill-spot.

Crossing the patch were two sets of paw prints. Milo kneeled and pointed to the left of the dog tracks. A human shoe print. Several, mostly obscured by the dogs.

I made out the shape of a heel. A boomerang-shaped arc of sole.

Feet facing the road. Someone had left this place.

The dogs' trail ended at a hole in the ground. Not irregular, a perfect circle. Six or so feet in diameter, rimmed with rusty metal.

Yawning mouth, flush to the ground. With the slope of the field and the high foliage, you had to get close to see it.

A tunnel entry, identical to the one Borchard had showed us. In place of a pneumatic lid, this one was wide open.

Milo motioned me back, took out his gun, crept to the opening, and hazarded a look.

His gun-arm grew rigid.

Louie's head sprouted from the opening. He panted, grinned goofily. Unimpressed by Milo's Glock.

Milo waved and Louie emerged, tail wagging. Padding up to Milo, he flipped onto his back in a grand display of surrender.

With his free hand, Milo rubbed Louie's tummy. Louie's eyes clamped shut in ecstasy.

No genius but once a handsome fellow. Now his pelt was gray-tipped and mangy.

Milo motioned for Louie to sit. Louie sat.

Milo tiptoed back to the mouth of the opening.

A sound burst from inside the tunnel, wheezy and wet and amplified by the subterranean tube.

Louie's upright ear stiffened but he remained on his haunches.

Heavy breathing. Scraping.

Ned the pointer stuck his head out.

He studied Milo. Me. Louie.

Louie's composure must have convinced his buddy. The old dog sank down and rested his chin along the rim of the hole.

Milo motioned me over, handed me the keys to the unmarked, gave me my assignment.

The man guarding the artichoke field hadn't budged. I allowed him ten paces of warning before coming up behind him and saying, ''Scuse me.'

He turned as if he'd expected me. Tipped the broad-brimmed hat.

The soda bottle was still in his hand but now it was empty. The sandwich in his pocket was untouched. I showed him the twenty-dollar bill, pointed to the sandwich.

His eyebrows arched. '¿Veinte para esto?'

'Sí.'

He handed me the sandwich.

'Gracias.' I tried to give him the twenty. He shook his head.

I said, *'Por favor,'* dropped the bill in his pocket.

He shrugged and went back to watching the artichokes.

Using the sandwich, Milo coaxed both dogs away from the tunnel hole. He took hold of Louie and I placed my hand on Ned's scruff. Skin and bones was an overstatement. He'd probably once weighed close to seventy pounds, was lucky if he was half of that now. I lifted him gently. Like hoisting a bale of twigs. As I carried him to the car, his head swiveled toward me and I saw that one of his eyes was a gray-blue film stretched over a sunken orbit.

I said, 'You're doing great, guy.'

He moaned, licked my face with a dry, fetid tongue.

Milo was able to guide Louie with the slightest prod of finger behind ear. We put both dogs in the rear of the unmarked, cracked the windows for air. The sandwich wasn't much, just a scanty portion of lunch meat between slices of white bread. But neither pooch griped when Milo broke off small bites and fed them equal amounts.

Louie chewed pretty well but the pointer didn't have too many teeth left and was forced to gum. Unneutered male but well past the point where testosterone made a difference.

We gave them both water from bottles we'd brought for ourselves, made sure they lapped slowly.

Ned rolled onto his back, curled up against the car door. Louie placed his paw on his pal's haunch. They both slipped into sleep, snoring in tandem, a comical waltz-like cadence.

We got out of the car and Milo locked up and turned back to the field of weeds. Homing in on the spot, invisible once more, where the tunnel mouth sat.

'Only one set of shoe prints,' he said. 'Assuming that's Harrie, what're the odds on Huggler still being down there?'

I said, 'Good to excellent. He's getting anxious that Harrie hasn't returned with the groceries but has nowhere to go.'

'So we'll assume he's down there. Problem is there's no way to know where the tunnel leads. What if Borchard's wrong and not all of SeaBird's tunnels are sealed and Huggler's able to get in there?'

'Trust me, I'm head of security and it couldn't happen.'

He laughed. Turned serious. 'You were right. It's all about synchrony.' He looked back at the snoozing dogs. 'Maybe they've got the right idea. Follow your ignorance, reach your bliss.'

We returned to the car and pushed it nose-first into the grass. If Grant Huggler headed for the road he'd eventually spot us. But if he remained near his hideaway, the same geography that blocked the tunnel from view would work in our favor.

If I'd guessed wrong and he'd already wandered away and chose to return from any direction, we'd be a clear target.

We stood next to the car. Milo said, 'Once we get going, mind looking back every so often so I can concentrate on what's ahead?'

'No prob.'

'Lots of probs, but we're solvers.' A bird flew. Seagull soaring westward before passing out of view.

Then nothing.

Milo said, 'Damn oil painting.'

I said, 'The tunnel is where Specialized Care used to stand.'

'Home sweet home.' He gazed through the window crack. 'These two geezers are gonna need medical care.'

A long, sonorous tone issued from the car. Louie farting in B minor.

'Couldn't agree more, pal,' said Milo. 'Unfortunately, Animal Control will have to wait its turn.'

I said, 'Time to call in the human cops?'

'That would be proper procedure, wouldn't it?' He bared his gums. 'The question is what constitutes optimal backup in a situation like this? If I call Camarillo PD and explain the situation, they might be cooperative. Or they might figure since it's their jurisdiction they don't need to listen and end up doing something heavy-handed.'

'Like bringing in SWAT?'

'And/or one of those hostage negotiators who reads from a script, half the time it turns out bad, because let's face it you can't stop someone if they're intent on checking out. And with a loon like Huggler – if he's even in there, God I hope he is – no crash-course in sweet-talk's gonna help, right?'

'Right.'

'They wanna go all military, I can't stop them and then we're stuck with one of those long-term standoffs and Huggler ends up biting it just like Harrie did. Maybe a bunch of cops, too, if he's got firepower down there. With only one way into the tunnel, it's a nightmare. Tear gas could help if it's a short passage but if he's got lots of room to back into, it could get complicated.'

He rubbed his face. 'I couldn't give an iota of rat-shit about Huggler personally but I need to talk to him, find out what Harrie needed a rape kit for, how many DBs haven't we found. Who belonged to those damn eyeballs.'

He phoned Petra again, updated her on the tunnel, told her to clue the other detectives in then make the hour drive to Camarillo with Reed or Binchy or Biro, whoever was closest.

'But don't come out here, stay in town, I'll let you know if I need you.'

'Where exactly are you?' she said.

He told her.

'I know a place not far,' she said. 'Decent pizza, Eric and I go there when we shop the outlets.'

'Eric shops?'

'I shop, he pretends not to hate it. Okay, I'll get there soon as I can, good luck.'

Just as he clicked off, Louie broke wind again.

'What the hell was in that sandwich?'

'Looked like some variant of baloney,' I said.

'We're stuck here long enough, I'm gonna regret sharing.'

41

THE FIRST hour slogged by. The second sloth-crawled.

The dogs alternated among sleep, flatulence, and a mellow, glassy-eyed torpor that evoked a weed-fragrant college dorm room.

Milo said, 'Someone's thinking right,' and closed his eyes.

I was wide awake and I was the one who saw.

Same place, different shape.

Taller than the dogs. Upright. Wearing something brown with a pale collar.

Moving forward. Stopping. Moving again. Stopping.

Facing away from us. So far, so good.

I nudged.

Milo roused, stared. Took hold of his gun, got out of the car, shut the driver's door just shy of latching. Walked forward silently.

He stood, mostly concealed by weeds, as the man in the brown jacket trudged through the field. The man's head stayed canted toward the ground. His pace was deliberate but jerky, broken by frequent stops that seemed to serve no function.

Like a poorly oiled machine.

Milo kept the Glock in his right hand and used his left to part the grass, crouched until he was as high as an average man, and stepped in.

I waited before lowering the car windows a bit more. Not enough for the dogs to get their heads stuck, but sufficient for good ventilation.

They remained drowsy.

I got out.

Backtracking, I mapped out a trajectory that would keep me perpendicular to Milo's hunter's prowl, aiming to cross the field in a way that kept me to the rear of the man in the brown coat, placing him at the apex of a human triangle.

As we converged on the target, Milo pushed forward, unaware of my presence. Then he saw me and froze. Shot me a long stare but made no attempt to wave me back.

Knowing it wouldn't work.

The two of us maintained the same pace. The man in the brown coat kept trudging without an apparent goal. Head down, weaving, lost in some private world. His head was bare, pale, shiny. Shaved recently.

Milo and I got thirty yards behind him, then twenty. I stopped parting the grass and muting the scratchy sound. Making no attempt at quiet.

The man in brown kept pausing, searching the horizon to the north. Maybe because he was looking for the dogs and that's where they usually headed.

Or he had his own incomprehensible navigational logic.

I picked up my speed, outpaced Milo. Milo saw it and stiffened and that gave me another few seconds of advantage.

I used them to rush behind the man in brown.

He continued to plod, thick shoulders rounded, hands jammed in his coat pockets. I kept coming, trotting now.

He stopped, raised the back of the coat, and scratched his rear.

Still not hearing me.

Then a patch of particularly brittle grass caught on my pant leg and when I pulled away the *zzzip* was audible.

The man in the brown coat turned.

Saw me.

He didn't move.

I waved flamboyantly, as if meeting an old friend by chance.

The man in brown gaped. His flabby face quivered like uncooked haggis.

I moved in on him, waving, grinning. 'Hey, Grant! Long time!'

His jowls tightened. Widening his stance, he planted his legs, flailed the air randomly.

Pudding-faced, snub-featured, unlined by contemplation, problematic abstraction, or any of the mean little demands imposed by sanity.

Terrified.

This was the bogeyman, the nightmare apparition, the cruel messenger in the dark who'd wreaked so much chaos and misery.

Now he was too scared to budge, remained frozen in his too-heavy shearling, fleece collar unraveling, brown suede greasy, mangy as the dogs, a misshapen tent of a garment that drooped over a white shirt and filthy jeans.

I got within arm's reach. 'Grant, my name is Alex.'

Windmilling air with both hands, he stumbled back.

'I'm not out to hurt you, Grant.'

His mouth opened. Formed an O. No sound came out. Then a squeak. The same sound mice made, mired in sticky traps, as my father's boot rose above them.

Turning his back on me, he ran.

Straight into the arms of a big man with a gun.

Milo used his free hand to spin Huggler so that he was facing me again, twisted Huggler's left arm behind his thick torso, got a handcuff around it. He'd linked two sets of cuffs together, standard procedure for a broad suspect.

Huggler sniffed. Began crying.

His right arm remained at his side. Milo, one hand on his weapon, struggled to bend the uncooperative limb.

'Behind your back, Grant.'

Huggler's body sagged, as if ready to comply, but the arm stayed rigid.

I stepped forward.

Milo warned me back with a head shake, repeated the command.

Tears flowed down Huggler's cheeks. His right arm was steel.

Milo holstered the Glock, clamped both hands on Huggler's left wrist, twisted viciously.

Huggler's left arm finally relented, twisting back and up. Milo tried to affix the second cuff but Huggler's width and the bulk of the coat brought him a couple of inches short of the goal.

He pushed Huggler's right hand toward its mate.

Huggler cried out in pain.

'It's okay, Grant,' said Milo, lying the way detectives do.

Huggler said, 'Really?' in a soft, high, boyish voice.

'Just a little more, son, here we go.'

Huggler's right hand was a millimeter from capture when his shoulders shook like those of a rhino rudely awakened. The movement caught Milo off guard, caused his foot to catch.

For a second, his concentration shifted to maintaining his balance.

All at once, Huggler was facing him, had gripped the sides of Milo's head with huge, soft, hairless hands.

Expressionless, he began twisting. Clockwise.

Milo's optimal move might've been a quick grab of his gun but when vise-grip hands take hold of your head and try to rotate it and instincts tell you it won't take much to sever your spine and drain your brain of life-maintaining, thought-engendering nectar, you go for those hands.

Anything to stop the process.

Milo's fingers dug into the tops of Huggler's hands, straining, clawing, drawing blood.

Huggler remained impassive, kept twisting.

Patient, dry-eyed.

Comfort of the familiar.

Well-practiced routine with predictable results: one way, then the other, feel the body grow limp.

Lay it down gently. Sit and wait.

Explore.

Milo strained to free himself. His eyes bugged. His face was scarlet.

His struggle had twisted his body just enough to put the Glock out of my visual range.

Could I get hold of it fast enough, find a safe way to shoot . . .

My own instincts kicked in and I threw myself behind Huggler, kicked him hard behind the knee.

It's a blow that can reduce strong men to blithering cripples.

Huggler stood there, impassive, managed to move Milo's head a fraction of an inch. Enough to make Milo gasp.

I kicked Huggler's other knee. Like butting an oak stump.

Hooking my hands over the fleece collar, I got them around his massive neck, tried to compress his carotids.

His flesh was sweat-slick. I failed to get purchase.

He moved Milo's neck another tiny fraction of the fatal arc.

I found his Adam's apple, lowered my thumbs to the front of his neck where he'd been incised years ago and robbed of a healthy gland.

I squeezed.

He screamed. His hands flew to the side.

He fell back, tottered, clutching his neck.

I punched him beneath his rib cage, got one foot behind his left heel and hooked him forward as I shoved his chest backward with all the strength I could muster.

Still clutching his neck, he fell back, spine thudding hard on dirt.

He lay there. Helpless.

Synchrony.

Milo, panting, green eyes aflame with fear that wasn't fading quickly enough, fumbled for his Glock, two-handing the weapon, aiming it at Huggler's prone bulk.

His hands were shaking too hard for one to suffice.

Huggler saw the gun. His hands left his neck. His throat was rosy, swollen.

He coughed.

Smiled.

Sat up and lunged.

Milo fired into his left shoe.

Huggler looked down. A small, almost delicate mouth dropped open.

The toe of one grubby sneaker began seeping red.

Huggler's cuffed left hand jangled as he shuddered. He watched the blood stream from the spot where his big toe had once been.

Entranced.

Mystery of the body.

Milo rolled him over roughly, yanked Huggler's right hand hard enough to dislocate, finally got both limbs cuffed.

Huggler lay on his belly. The surrounding earth turned purple as his foot continued to bleed.

No spurt, venous seepage.

Huggler said something. The dirt muffled his words and he turned his head to the side.

Milo sucked in air. He touched the side of his face, grimaced.

Not looking at me.

He walked several steps away.

Another gull soared overhead. Or maybe the same bird, curious.

Grant Huggler said, 'Wow.'

I said, 'Wow, what?'

'My foot. Can I see it, please?'

42

PETRA'S PIZZA had just arrived when Milo called her. She left it behind, arrived nine minutes later. Taking care of business during the drive: calling for an ambulance, making contact with Camarillo PD, and using charm and calm and just enough facts to keep the locals from screaming.

She studied Huggler sitting on the dirt, cuffed, ankles bound, wounded foot wrapped in one of the clean rags Milo keeps in the trunk.

All those years with bodies, it pays to have something for the gore.

Huggler's neck had swelled and was starting to purple. He coughed a lot but was breathing okay. The finger marks on Milo's face had faded to ambiguous splotches. Petra knew something was up and I watched her eyes dance as her brain tried to figure it out.

She said nothing, too smart to ask.

Huggler didn't react to her arrival. Hadn't reacted to much of anything.

Now he looked at Milo. 'Um? Mister?'

Plaintive.

Please, sir, may I have more gruel?

'What?'

Huggler glanced at the bloody rag. 'Could you take this off?'

'Too tight?'

'Um . . .'

'What's the problem?'

'I want to see.'

'See what?'

'The inside.'

'Of what?'

Huggler pouted. 'Me.'

Milo said, 'Sorry, you need to keep it wrapped.'

Apologizing to the man who'd nearly sheared his spine.

Huggler said, 'Um, okay.' His face settled back into smooth, serene immobility.

I thought about his victims.

The broad, pale disk that had been the final image searing so many people's retinas before the lights went out for good.

Petra was good at maintaining composure but Huggler's request had startled her and she frowned and turned her back on all of us and looked up at the gorgeous sky. Pulling some gum from her purse, she chewed hard. Extended an arm in my direction and offered me a stick.

I took it. When I beared down to masticate, my entire face exploded in pain.

Every muscle and nerve on full-fire, it had been a while since they'd relaxed.

Milo looked at his watch, then at Huggler's shoe. The rag had bloodied some more but Huggler's color was decent, no sign of shock.

'Feel okay?'

Huggler nodded. 'Your hands are strong.'

'Had to be to deal with you, Grant.'

'It's always worked before,' said Huggler, puzzled. 'Oh, well.'

Camarillo EMTs strapped him onto a full-restraint gurney. The local detective was a white-haired man named Ramos who told the driver to wait as he approached Milo. He slid from distrust to professional curiosity to camaraderie as Milo explained the situation.

'Guess you did us a favor. How many victims we talking about?'

'At least six, probably more.'

'A situation,' said Ramos. 'Been doing this thirty years, never had anything like it.'

'You don't have to have it now,' said Milo. 'Unless you've got some masochistic urge to complicate your life.'

'You want to handle all of it.'

'We started it, we're ready to finish. Paperwork alone's gonna be a full-time job.'

Ramos grinned and pulled out a hard-pack of Winstons. Milo accepted the offer of a cigarette and the two of them smoked.

'You're making a point,' said Ramos. 'So what, we patch him up and ship him back to you in a Brink's truck?'

'A cage would be better.' Milo touched the right side of his face. We still hadn't made eye contact and I'd stayed a few inches behind him so as not to push the issue.

Ramos said, 'I'll check with my boss but he's a lazy type, can't see there being any problem.'

'Whatever works,' said Milo. 'The legal eagles are gonna be on this, our people will call your people.'

'We'll do lunch,' said Ramos. 'Half a dozen bodies, huh? I'm figuring I should send someone in the ambulance with the asshole. Just be careful.' He glanced at the ambulance. 'First impression, he looks like a nerd. The kid who never got chose for baseball.'

'Part of his charm.'

'He's charming, huh?'

'Not in the least.'

Ramos chuckled. 'Now I got a new worst thing. Before this, it was a case I picked up thirty-nine months ago. Woman shot her kid in the head because he was mouthing off. Just picked up a gun and drilled him, I'm talking a twelve-year-old. She looked like a schoolteacher.' He glanced at the ambulance. 'This is a whole different thing. You're doing me a favor.'

He waved a paramedic over.

Ramos said, 'I'm coming with you.' Beckoning a tall, husky cop. 'Officer Baakeland, too.'

'Tight fit,' said the EMT.

'We'll survive,' said Ramos. 'That's the point. Hey, who's that?'

'Animal Control,' said Milo.

Ramos looked over at the still-sleeping dogs. 'Oh, yeah, for them. Too bad they can't talk.'

Gaining access to the tunnel proved tricky. With no evidence any crime had been committed on the premises, John Nguyen said a warrant was probably required.

Milo said, 'Probably?'

'Gray area. With something like this you err on the side of caution.'

'John—'

'Your only alternative is to contact whoever owns the property and get consent.'

'That's a development firm.'

'Then that's who you contact.'

Sea Line Development was joint-headquartered in Newport Beach and Coral Gables, Florida. No one answered at either office, same for an 888 'emergency' number. Milo left a message, walked over to the mouth of the tunnel opening, squatted and stuck his head in, and got back on his feet. 'Too dark, can't see a thing.'

I said, 'They removed the hatch but there's got to be an inner door not too far down.'

He phoned Nguyen again. 'Can't reach the owners. Got a recommendation for a judge?'

'The usual suspects.'

No answers at four usually cooperative jurists. A fifth said, 'Camarillo? Get someone local.'

'Anyone in particular?'

'What?' said the judge. 'I look like a referral agency?'

Milo took out Rudy Borchard's card, punched the number. Cursed viciously and clicked off. 'No one answers their own damn phones anymore. Next week robots are scheduled to wipe our asses.'

Talking in my presence but not to me.

Petra said, 'It'll work out.'

'Easy for you to say, you're cute and thin.'

He trudged to the car, got back in. When I slipped into the passenger seat he pretended to sleep. His phone rang and he waited a while to answer.

'Yes, Maria . . . yes, that's true. Yes, I've talked to them and it's all ours . . . why? Because it is . . . whatever, Maria.'

He ended the conversation. The phone rang again. He turned it off. Went back to fake-sleep.

I got out of the car.

Petra came over, stuck her head in, sniffed. 'Smells like a kennel.'

Milo opened his eyes. 'Next time I'll use a better deodorant.'

She said, 'Speaking of scent, that dirt clearing looks awfully clean. What do you think about bringing in a cadaver pooch?'

'Soon as we get the damn warrant.'

She turned to me. 'This feels weird. A huge one gets closed and we end up sitting around.'

'Let's do something, then – put up some tape.'

'Around the hole or the entire clearing?'

'How much tape do you have?'

'Not enough.'

Milo's phone played Mendelssohn. He said, 'Damn pencil-pushers,' and switched to conference. 'What now?'

A deep male voice said, 'Pardon?'

'Who's this?'

'My name is Norm Pettigrew and I'm returning Lieutenant Sturgis's call.'

'Sturgis here. You're with Sea Line?'

'Vice president and coordinator of operations. What can I do for you?'

Milo told him.

Pettigrew said, 'Incredible. We had no idea anyone was squatting. Or that there was even a tunnel. We thought we had all of those sealed.'

'Looks like the grass was cleared to gain access.'

'How would anyone know to do that, Lieutenant? And why?'

301

'Good question,' said Milo, lying easily.

Pettigrew said, 'Well, by all means go down there, do whatever you need to do.'

'Thank you, sir.'

'Obviously, Lieutenant, we'd prefer if Sea Line wasn't linked to any of this.'

'I'll do my best, sir.'

'Let me be more specific,' said Pettigrew. 'Any encumbrances that can be avoided would be highly appreciated. Have you ever been to Laguna Beach?'

'A while back, sir.'

'We've got a project there. High-end condos with ocean views. A couple of the demos are fully furnished and livable and suitable for short-term usage. In your case, being a devoted public servant capable of providing security, I'm sure we can reach an agreement. You and the missus for a weekend. If you enjoy yourselves, two weekends. We've got a great Italian restaurant about to open.'

'Sounds great.'

'Sea Shore Villas,' said Pettigrew. 'That's the name of the project. Call me personally, I'll set it up.'

'Thank you, sir. And thanks for permission to search.'

'Oh, sure. I mean it, about Laguna. Come and enjoy the ocean on us.'

The line went dead.

Petra said, 'Last thing anyone offered me was a hit of crank if I didn't bust him.'

'You like the beach?'

'You don't?'

'Too damn peaceful . . . okay, kids, let's spelunk.'

43

INCHES BELOW the hole was a steel ladder that descended ten feet and planted us on a square of concrete with barely enough space for the three of us to stand. A bulb in a wire cage was screwed into the ceiling. The tunnel continued to the left, a cement-lined tube barely taller than Milo. A circular steel hatch like the one Borchard had showed us blocked further exploration. This one responded to the slightest tug before hissing open.

We passed through another twenty feet of vacant passage. No obvious ventilation but the tunnel was cool, dry, surprisingly pleasant. No smell of death, not much odor at all but for occasional wisps of mold and raw rock and, as we kept going, burgeoning human perspiration.

Milo and Petra both had their flashlights in hand but didn't need to turn them on; caged bulbs were set every five steps, bathing the tunnel in hard yellow light from hospital days, old wires forgotten, but still active. The floor was free of debris, swept clean like the clearing. Another circular hatch appeared, left wide open.

A room appeared to the right, fifteen or so square feet.

An old porcelain sign lettered in Gothic was bolted into the stone wall. *Hospital Storage, Non-Perishables Only. Stack Neatly.*

On the floor were two futons, rolled up precisely. Between them sat twin dressers still stickered with IKEA labels. The chest on the left bore a battery-op digital clock, two pairs of cheap reading glasses, a tube of lubricant, a box of tissues, three hardcover books: *Introduction to Psychology, Abnormal Psychology, Consultations in Forensic Psychology.*

Three drawers contained a modest assortment of men's clothing, size S. Laundry tickets were pinned to several items. A cedar freshener had been placed in each compartment.

The stand on the right was piled high with softcover books, four stacks, at least twenty per pile. Crosswords, anagrams, sudoku, sum doku, word search, brain-teasers, kakuro, anacrostics. Drawers below contained sweats, T-shirts, boxers, and tube socks, size XL.

An adjoining room, smaller, colder, contained two chemical porta-toilets, one clean, the other reeking. Gallon water bottles were lined up against a wall. A card table was piled with folded white towels. Bulk rolls of toilet paper still in cellophane sat nearby. Off to the side, two cardboard cartons of cookies, bread, cereal, beef jerky, canned spaghetti and chili shared space with three bags of generic dry dog food.

'Keeping house,' said Petra. 'Cozy.'

I noticed something behind the tallest stack of provisions, pointed it out.

Milo drew out a brown cardboard pizza delivery box. Pristine, unopened, printed with the image of a portly, gleeful mustachioed chef.

Lotta taste.

Ooh la la.

Three identical cartons were pinioned against the wall by cans and cases.

We returned to the tunnel, passed through a third hatch. The passageway ended at a final room. A Gothic sign said *No Further Entry*.

Petra tapped the rear stone wall to which the message had been bolted. 'Kind of redundant.'

Milo said, 'Some sign contractor probably greased palms.'

'My Lieutenant,' she said, though he wasn't, 'sage but so cynical.'

Milo stepped into the final room, approached the sole piece of furniture. Bare-topped desk, stickered like the end tables.

Muttering, 'Doing what they could for the Swedish economy,' he slid the top drawer open.

Inside was paper. A detective's treasure.

Check stubs documented a variety of welfare and disabilities payments from the State of California, Santa Barbara and Ventura Counties, mailed regularly to a Malibu post office box near Carbon Beach and cashed promptly at a nearby Bank of America. Totals varied from twelve hundred to nearly twice that amount.

The recipient: *Lewisohn Clark*.

Petra said, 'Some moniker. Sounds like the millionaire on Gilligan.'

'Say it out loud,' I said.

She did. 'Oh.'

Milo said, 'Lewis and Clark.'

I said, 'Master explorers.'

A separate collection of stubs revealed monthly payments of $3,800.14 sent to the same P.O.B. A recent letter from the state pension board announced that an automatic cost-of-living increase would add just under a hundred eighty bucks to next month's installment.

The recipient: *Sven Galley*.

Milo checked his pad. 'Harrie used his own damn Social Security number.'

Petra said, 'Guess not everyone's curious.'

She inspected a stub. 'Svengali.' Her jawline sharpened. 'I'm glad he's dead.'

A dark green simulated alligator box beneath the receipts told a new story.

Faded Polaroids of women, young, trussed, terrified. The same terrible sequence for each: rope around neck, fear-frozen eyes, lifeless eyes, gaping mouth.

Underneath the photos were articles printed off the Internet. Missing girls, eight of them, the cases arranged chronologically.

The first victim, a college student at UC Santa Cruz, had vanished ten years ago during a Carmel vacation. The most recent, a sixteen-year-old runaway from New Hampshire, had been last seen five months ago, hitchhiking on Ocean Avenue not far from the Santa Monica Pier.

It didn't take long to match the photos.

Milo opened the bottom drawer.

Another case, this one larger and covered in soiled gray shagreen, sat atop yet more paper. The press of a button-latch revealed an array of surgical tools resting in green velvet, each instrument snuggled in form-fitted compartments. Tiny gold lettering on the inside of the lid spelled out *Chiron, Tutlingen*.

The paper beneath the case was blank. Milo removed a sheet anyway. On the underside, centered perfectly, was the inevitable message.

?

Milo said, 'Not anymore, asshole. Let's get out of here.'

Petra said, 'Good idea, I need a breather, too.'

'It's not that, kid.' He brandished his cell phone. 'Not getting reception.'

As we made our way out, I let Petra pass in front of me, advanced closer to Milo, and stared until he made eye contact.

He nodded. Moved on.

By the time the black Lab and the springer spaniel arrived, darkness had settled over the field and field lamps faciliated by Detective Arthur Ramos had been propped.

The handler, a civilian from Oxnard named Judy Kantor who also bred and showed both breeds, said, 'They love the dark, less distraction. What's the area?'

Milo said, 'That clearance.'

'That's it?' said Kantor. 'No trees or brush or water? Piece of cake, there's something down there, they'll find it.' She clapped her hands. 'C'mon Hansel, c'mon Gretel, do your sniffy thing.'

Judy Kantor led the dogs around the perimeter, then she let them explore. Within moments, each animal was sitting. Ten feet apart. Judy Kantor marked the spots, signaled for them to resume.

Two more tells. This time, the dogs stayed seated.

She said, 'That's it, Lieutenant.'

Milo said, 'We suspect as many as eight victims.'

'If there was another grave nearby, they'd tell you,' she said. 'Unless it's super-deep – hey, maybe you've got stacked bodies.'

Milo thanked her, she gave the dogs treats, the three of them departed with obvious joy.

No stacking.

A quartet of intact skeletons, interred barely three feet below the surface.

Petra said, 'They're all pretty petite. Don't need to be an anthropologist to know they're girls.'

44

IT DID take an anthropologist to make sense of the bones. Moe Reed's girlfriend, Dr Liz Wilkinson, had the report on Milo's desk nine days later. The skeletons were consistent with the four most recent victims depicted in James Harrie's photo stash. Dental records for two victims solidified the I.Ds and the remaining two girls were differentiated using femur length.

Wilkinson opined that two of the victims had probably given birth, a fact that didn't emerge during interviews with their parents.

No reason to bring that up. Milo helped facilitate delivery of the bones and has attended every funeral.

A wider, deeper excavation of the field has produced no other bodies, no evidence of any kind.

The burial sites of Dr Louis Wainright and Nurse Joanne Morton remain unknown.

The eyes left behind in 'Bern Shacker's' Beverly Hills office were too degraded by formaldehyde for DNA analysis. Dr Clarice Jernigan has opined that they may not belong to any victim, could very well be anatomy specimens sold commercially to optometrists and ophthalmologists.

She's a tough-minded expert pathologist with a wealth of experience.

Then again, everyone engages in wishful thinking.

The pizza boxes found in the tunnel match those used by only one restaurant between Santa Barbara and Malibu, a stand in Oxnard just off Highway 1, catering to the motor trade. No one working there is aware of any pilferage. A teenage girl on-site during weekend evenings is almost certain a pleasant man resembling James Harrie was an occasional customer.

An A-student taking a full load of advanced placement courses, she's nearly as confident about his order.

Same thing each time: small plain cheese pie, large pepperoni and mushrooms.

Grant Huggler awaits trial at Starkweather State Hospital for the Criminally Insane. He is a model patient and has defied easy diagnosis. His public defender and deputy D.A. John Nguyen have separately indicated their intention to call me as an expert witness should the case go to trial. I've communicated my reluctance to both of them. They haven't pushed. But they're lawyers, haven't backed off, either.

I can live with the uncertainty.

Milo has never mentioned what happened in the field. He has asked me — twice, because he's been more absentminded than usual — if I think Huggler will ever make it into a courtroom or remain stashed in his isolation room.

'Or even shipped off to another loony bin. Maybe Kansas, huh? We owe them.'

Both times I told him I wasn't feeling like a gambling man.

I've been a little edgy, though I think I've been handling it pretty well with Robin and Blanche, saying and doing the right things, playacting a normal life.

For the most part, the dreams have stopped. I do think about the eyes, the four girls whose bodies haven't been found. Louis Wainright, Joanne Morton.

Belle Quigg was offered Louie but she demurred, telling Milo it was all she could do to make it through each day.

Louie and Ned were adopted by a family from Ojai, a Mormon clan with twelve kids and a long, honorable history of caring for old, ill castaway pets. I hear that both dogs have fattened up and once in a while, Ned's got the energy to play.

I've turned down several patient referrals, have increased my running time, spend more time listening to music, everything from Steve Vai to Bach's Brandenburg Concerto No. 6.

Every day I go into my office, close the door, pretend to work. Mostly I sit at my desk thinking, then trying not to.

I've contemplated recapturing my self-hypnosis chops. Or learning some new form of meditation that might succeed at emptying my head.

I think about meeting the parents of the four girls whose bodies haven't been found. Saying something to Dr Louis Wainright's two adult kids.

No one has inquired about Wainright's nurse, Joanne Morton, and that bothers me more than it should.

I wonder about what created Grant Huggler. James Harrie.

At this point, I'm not sure I want answers.